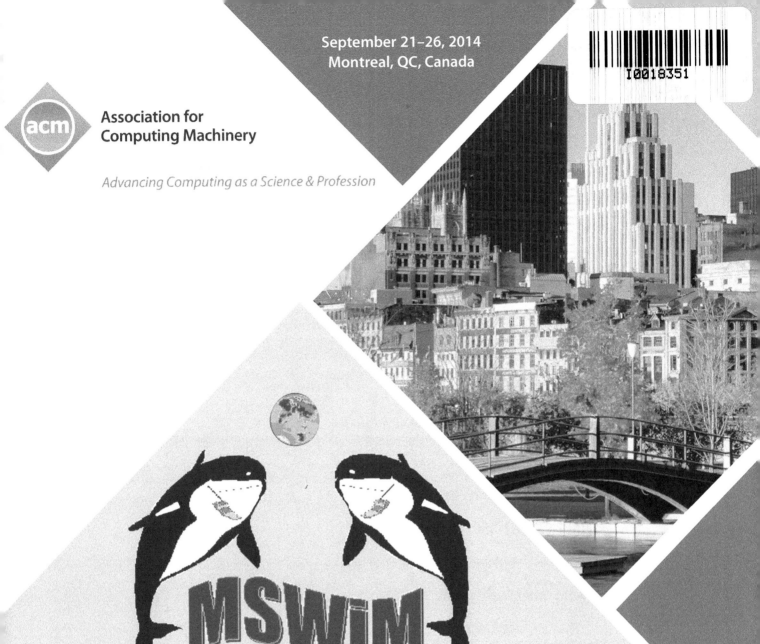

September 21–26, 2014
Montreal, QC, Canada

Association for Computing Machinery

Advancing Computing as a Science & Profession

MSWiM'14

Proceedings of the 17th ACM International Conference on

Modeling, Analysis and Simulation of Wireless and Mobile Systems

Sponsored by:
ACM SIGSIM

Association for Computing Machinery

Advancing Computing as a Science & Profession

The Association for Computing Machinery
2 Penn Plaza, Suite 701
New York, New York 10121-0701

Notice to Past Authors of ACM-Published Articles

ISBN: 978-1-4503-3030-5

Additional copies may be ordered prepaid from:

ACM Order Department
PO Box 30777
New York, NY 10087-0777, USA

Phone: 1-800-342-6626 (USA and Canada)
+1-212-626-0500 (Global)
Fax: +1-212-944-1318
E-mail: acmhelp@acm.org
Hours of Operation: 8:30 am – 4:30 pm ET

ACM Order Number: 617141

Printed in the USA

Chairs' Welcome Message

The technical program of the 17th ACM International Conference on Modeling, Analysis and Simulation of Wireless and Mobile Systems (MSWiM), held in 2014 in Montreal, Canada continues to build upon the high standards set by previous editions of the conference.

In 2014, the call for papers attracted 146 registered papers in all areas of mobile and wireless systems of which 128 were accepted into the review process. The submitted papers came from 39 countries. Members of the Technical Program Committee are affiliated to universities and industry in 17 countries spread over five continents, reflecting the truly international profile of MSWiM. The five most commonly listed topics for submissions to MSWiM'14 were:

- Wireless network algorithms and protocols
- Performance evaluation and modeling
- Wireless mesh networks, mobile ad hoc networks, VANET
- Sensor and actuator networks
- Analytical models

The submissions included a large number of papers of very high quality making the selection process difficult and competitive. In the end, we selected 32 regular papers, which corresponds to an acceptance rate of 25%. An additional 10 short papers were recommended for the program owing to their quality and contribution.

Among the 32 regular papers, the three shortlisted as candidates for the best paper award are:

- "Impact of Node Mobility on Single-Hop Cluster Overlap in Vehicular Ad Hoc Networks," Khadige Abboud and Weihua Zhuang
- "Dirichlet's Principle on Multiclass Multihop Wireless Networks: Minimum Cost Routing Subject to Stability," Reza Banirazi, Edmond Jonckheere, and Bhaskar Krishnamachari
- "Wireless Networking Testbed and Emulator (WiNeTestEr)," Joseph D. Beshay, Yongjiu Du, Pengda Huang, Niranjan Mahabaleshwar, Brooks McMillin, Ehsan Nourbakhsh, Kiruba S. Subramani, Tianzuo Xi, Bhaskar Banerjee, Joseph D. Camp, Jinghong Chen, Ping Gui, Ravi Prakash, and Dinesh Rajan

The winner among these three papers will be announced at the conference banquet, and will be reported in the proceedings of MSWiM 2015. At this point, we take the opportunity to congratulate the winners of the best paper award for MSWiM 2013:

- "Understanding the Benefits of Open Access in Femtocell Networks: Stochastic Geometric Analysis in the Uplink," authored by Wei Bao and Ben Liang.

Our thanks go to Professor Azzedine Boukerche and the Advisory Board for their vision in guiding MSWiM from workshop to symposium and finally to conference status over the past 15 years. Our thanks also go to Professor Ian Akyidiz and Professor Dharma Agrawal for sharing their experience and vision into the future in the keynote speeches. A special thank you goes to the Technical Program Committee members as well as the additional reviewers for their hard work and contributions in reviewing any judging all the submitted papers.

Finally, we would like to take this opportunity to welcome you to the conference. We hope you find the technical sessions to be intellectually stimulating and rewarding.

Ravi Prakash
General Co-Chair
University of Texas
USA

Azzedine Boukerche
General Co-Chair
University of Ottawa,
Canada

Cheng Li
TPC Co-Chair
Memorial University
Canada

Falko Dressler
TPC Co-Chair
University of Paderborn
Germany

Table of Contents

Session: LTE and Cellular Networks (I)

Keynote Speaker

Session: Optimization and Performance Evaluation

Session: LTE and Multihop Wireless Networks (II)

Session: Delay Tolerant and Opportunistic Networks

Session: Wireless Sensor Networks (II)

Session: Network Coding and Data Forwarding

Session: Tracking, Positioning, and Scheduling

Session: Mobility, Caching, and Compression

Session: Algorithms, Scheduling, and Optimization

Demonstrations

Author Index

MSWiM 2014 Conference Organization

General Co-Chairs: Ravi Prakash *(University of Texas at Dallas, USA)*
Azzedine Boukerche *(University of Ottawa, Canada)*

Program Co-Chairs: Cheng Li *(Memorial University of Newfoundland, Canada)*
Falko Dressler *(University of Paderborn, Germany)*

Poster Chair: Richard Pazzi *(University of Ontario Institute of Technology, Canada)*

Demo/Tools Chair: Laura Marie Feeney *(Swedish Institute of Computer Science, Sweden)*

Publicity Chair: Mirela A. M. Notare *(Sao Jose Municipal University, Brazil)*

Tutorials Co-Chairs: Weixiao Meng *(Harbin Institute of Technology, China)*
Luiz Perrone *(Bucknell University, USA)*

Publicity Chair: Mirela A. M. Notare *(Sao Jose Municipal University, Brazil)*

Local Arrangements Chairs: Abdelhamid Mammeri *(University of Ottawa, Canada)*
Dhrubajyoti Goswami *(Concordia University, Canada)*

Steering Committee Chair: Azzedine Boukerche *(University of Ottawa, Canada)*

Steering Committee: Sajal K. Das *(University of Texas at Arlington, USA)*
Lorenzo Donatiello *(Università di Bologna, Bologna, Italy)*
Jason Yi-Bing Lin *(National Chiao-Tung University, Taiwan)*
William C.Y. Lee *(AirTouch Inc., USA)*
Simon Taylor *(Brunel University, UK)*

Program Committee: Antonio A.F. Loureiro *(Federal University of Minas Gerais, Brazil)*
Abdallah Shami *(The University of Western Ontario, Canada)*
Adam Wolisz *(Technische Universität Berlin, Germany)*
Amy Murphy *(Fondazione Bruno Kessler – IRST, Italy)*
Andrea Passarella *(IIT-CNR, Italy)*
Andreas Willig *(University of Canterbury, New Zealand)*
Andrei Gurtov *(Aalto University, Finland)*
Angel Cuevas *(Universidad Carlos III de Madrid, Spain)*
Anna Förster *(University of Applied Sciences of Southern Switzerland)*
Bjorn Landfeldt *(Lund University, Sweden)*

Program Committee: Brahim Bensaou *(The Hong Kong University of Science and Technology, Hong Kong)*

Carla-Fabiana Chiasserini *(Politecnico di Torino, Italy)*

Carlos Bernardos *(Universidad Carlos III de Madrid, Spain)*

Chi Chung Cheung *(The Hong Kong Polytechnic University, Hong Kong)*

Christoph Sommer *(University of Paderborn, Germany)*

Damla Turgut *(University of Central Florida, USA)*

David Eckhoff *(University of Erlangen, Germany)*

Dirk Staehle *(Docomo Euro-Labs, Germany)*

Ehab Elmallah *(University of Alberta, Canada)*

Emmanouel Varvarigos *(University of Patras & Computer Technology Institute, Greece)*

Enzo Mingozzi *(University of Pisa, Italy)*

Falko Dressler *(University of Paderborn, Germany)*

Francesco Lo Presti *(Universita' di Roma Tor Vergata, Italy)*

Guillaume Jourjon *(NICTA, Australia)*

Holger Karl *(University of Paderborn, Germany)*

Hongyi Wu *(University of Louisiana at Lafayette, USA)*

Isabel Wagner *(University of Hull, UK)*

Isabelle Guérin Lassous *(Université Claude Bernard Lyon 1 - LIP, France)*

Jalel Ben-Othman *(University of Paris 13, France)*

James Gross *(Royal Institute of Technology (KTH), Sweden)*

Javier Gozalvez *(Universidad Miguel Hernandez de Elche, Spain)*

Jerzy Konorski *(Gdansk University of Technology, Poland)*

JJ Garcia-Luna-Aceves *(University of California at Santa Cruz, USA)*

Juan-Carlos Cano *(Universidad Politecnica de Valencia, Spain)*

Klaus Wehrle *(RWTH Aachen University, Germany)*

Laura Marie Feeney *(Swedish Institute of Computer Science, Sweden)*

Lavy Libman *(University of New South Wales, Australia)*

Lorenzo Donatiello *(Università di Bologna, Italy)*

Luciano Bononi *(University of Bologna, Italy)*

Marcelo Dias de Amorim *(UPMC Sorbonne Universités, France)*

Marco Di Felice *(University of Bologna, Italy)*

Marius Portmann *(University of Queensland, Australia)*

Martina Zitterbart *(Karlsruhe Institute of Technology, Germany)*

Matthias Wählisch *(Freie Universität Berlin, Germany)*

Merkourios Karaliopoulos *(National and Kapodistrian University of Athens, Greece)*

Mineo Takai *(University of California, Los Angeles, USA)*

Mónica Aguilar Igartua *(Universitat Politècnica de Catalunya, Spain)*

Nils Aschenbruck *(University of Osnabrück, Germany)*

Ozgur Akan *(Koc University, Turkey)*

Program Committee
(continued):   Raffaele Bruno *(IIT-CNR, Italy)*

Ravi Prakash *(University of Texas at Dallas, USA)*

Renato Lo Cigno *(University of Trento, Italy)*

Roberto Beraldi *("Sapienza" Università di Roma, Italy)*

Shengming Jiang *(Shanghai Maritime University, P.R. China)*

Sotiris Nikoletseas *(University of Patras and Computer Technology Institute, Greece)*

Stefan Fischer *(University of Lübeck, Germany)*

Stephan Eidenbenz *(Los Alamos National Laboratory, USA)*

Tahiry Razafindralambo *(Inria Lille - Nord Europe, France)*

Terence D. Todd *(McMaster University, Canada)*

Torsten Braun *(University of Bern, Switzerland)*

Victor Leung *(The University of British Columbia, Canada)*

Vincenzo Mancuso *(IMDEA Networks Institute, Spain)*

Violet Syrotiuk *(Arizona State University, USA)*

Yacine Ghamri-Doudane *(University of la Rochelle, France)*

Zygmunt Haas *(Cornell University, USA)*

Sponsor:

xi

MSWiM 2014 Additional Reviewers

Abdallah Shami	JJ Garcia-Luna-Aceves
Adam Wolisz	Juan-Carlos Cano
Amy Murphy	Klaus Wehrle
Andrea Passarella	Laura Marie Feeney
Andreas Willig	Lavy Libman
Andrei Gurtov	Lorenzo Donatiello
Angel Cuevas	Luciano Bononi
Anna Förster	Marcelo Dias de Amorim
Antonio A.F. Loureiro	Marco Di Felice
Azzedine Boukerche	Martina Zitterbart
Bjorn Landfeldt	Matthias Wählisch
Brahim Bensaou	Merkourios Karaliopoulos
Carla-Fabiana Chiasserini	Mineo Takai
Carlos Bernardos	Mónica Aguilar Igartua
Cheng Li	Nils Aschenbruck
Chi Chung Cheung	Ozgur Akan
Christoph Sommer	Raffaele Bruno
Damla Turgut	Ravi Prakash
David Eckhoff	Renato Lo Cigno
Ehab Elmallah	Roberto Beraldi
Emmanouel Varvarigos	Robson De Grande
Enzo Mingozzi	Shengming Jiang
Falko Dressler	Sotiris Nikoletseas
Francesco Lo Presti	Stefan Fischer
Guillaume Jourjon	Stephan Eidenbenz
Holger Karl	Tahiry Razafindralambo
Hongyi Wu	Terence D. Todd
Isabel Wagner	Torsten Braun
Isabelle Guérin Lassous	Victor Leung
Jalel Ben-Othman	Vincenzo Mancuso
James Gross	Violet Syrotiuk
Javier Gozalvez	Yacine Ghamri-Doudane
Jerzy Konorski	Zygmunt Haas

Wireless Sensor Networks in Challenged Environments such as Underwater and Underground

Ian F. Akyildiz
Broadband Wireless Networking Lab
School of Electrical and Computer Engineering
Georgia Institute of Technology
Atlanta, GA 30332, USA
http://www.ece.gatech.edu/research/labs/bwn

ABSTRACT

Oceanographic data collection, pollution monitoring, offshore exploration, disaster prevention, assisted navigation and tactical surveillance are typical applications for wireless underwater sensor networks. In this talk wireless underwater acoustic communication channel is explored, novel medium access control and routing protocols will be presented. On the other hand, sensor applications in soil media and tunnels have unique communication problems. In particular, the wireless channel pecularities in the underground make communication problems interesting which will be discussed in this talk. Electromagnetic and Magnetic Induction communication paradigms are explored. Future research challenges will be highlighted in both areas.

Categories and Subject Descriptors

C.2.1 [COMPUTER-COMMUNICATION NETWORKS]: Network Architecture and Design---Wireless communication; C.2.3 [COMPUTER-COMMUNICATION NETWORKS]: Network Operations---Network management.

Keywords

Networking; Aquatic Networks; Wireless communications

Bio

I. F. AKYILDIZ received his BS, MS, and PhD degrees in Computer Engineering from the University of Erlangen-Nuernberg, Germany, in 1978, 1981 and 1984, respectively. Currently, he is the Ken Byers Chair Professor with the School of Electrical and Computer Engineering, Georgia Institute of Technology, Director of the Broadband Wireless Networking Laboratory and Chair of the Telecommunications Group. He is an Honorary Professor with School of Electrical Engineering at the Universitat Politecnica de Catalunya, and Director of N3Cat (NaNoNetworking Center in Catalunya) in Barcelona, Spain,

MSWiM'14, September 21–26, 2014, Montreal, QC, Canada.
ACM 978-1-4503-3030-5/14/09.
http://dx.doi.org/10.1145/2641798.2653460

since June 2008. Dr. Akyildiz is also the Finnish Distinguished Professor with Tampere University of Technology, Tampere, Finland since January 2013.

He is the Editor-in-Chief of Computer Networks (Elsevier) Journal since 2000, the founding Editor-in-Chiefs of the Ad Hoc Networks Journal (2003), Physical Communication (PHYCOM) Journal (2008), and Nano Communication Networks (NANOCOMNET) Journal (2010) all published by Elsevier.

Dr. Akyildiz is an IEEE FELLOW (1996) and an ACM FELLOW (1997). He received the 1997 IEEE Leonard G. Abraham Prize award and the 2003 Best Tutorial Paper Award and the Best Paper Awards at IEEE ICC, June 2009 and IEEE Globecom 2010 conferences (all IEEE Communications Society).

He received the "Don Federico Santa Maria Medal" for his services to the Universidad of Federico Santa Maria in Chile in 1986. He served as a National Lecturer for ACM from 1989 until 1998 and received the ACM Outstanding Distinguished Lecturer Award for 1994. Dr. Akyildiz received the 2002 IEEE Harry M. Goode Memorial award (IEEE Computer Society) and the 2003 ACM SIGMOBILE Outstanding Contribution Award for his "pioneering contributions in the area of mobility and resource management for wireless communication networks".

Dr. Akyildiz received the 2004 Georgia Tech Faculty Research Author Award for his "outstanding record of publications of papers between 1999-2003". He also received the 2005 Distinguished Faculty Achievement Award from School of ECE, Georgia Tech, and the Georgia Tech Outstanding Doctoral Thesis Advisor Award for his 20+ years service and dedication to Georgia Tech and producing outstanding PhD students. He also received the 2009 ECE Distinguished Mentor Award by the Georgia Tech School of Electrical and Computer Engineering Faculty Honors Committee.

Dr. Akyildiz received the 2010 IEEE Communications Society Ad Hoc and Sensor Networks Technical Committee (AHSN TC) Technical Recognition Award with the citation: "For pioneering contributions to wireless sensor networks and wireless mesh networks", in December 2010. He received the 2011 IEEE Computer Society W. Wallace McDowell Award for pioneering contributions to wireless sensor network architectures and communication protocols and the 2011 TUBITAK (Turkish

National Science Foundation) Exclusive Award for outstanding contributions to the advancement of scholarship/research at international level.

He is the author of two textbooks on "Wireless Sensor Networks" and on "Wireless Mesh Networks" published by John Wiley & Sons in 2010 and 2007, respectively. Due to Google scholar, his papers received over 62+K citations and his h-index is 82 as of July 2014.

His current research interests are in Next Generation Cellular Systems, Nanonetworks, Cognitive Radio Networks and Wireless Sensor Networks.

NOTE:

This talk is based on the papers:

[1] I.F. Akyildiz, D. Pompili, and T. Melodia, "Underwater Acoustic Sensor Networks: Research Challenges," Ad Hoc Networks (Elsevier) Journal, March 2005.

[2] I.F. Akyildiz, Z. Su, and M.C. Vuran, "Signal Propagation Techniques for Wireless Underground Communication Networks," Physical Communication (Elsevier) Journal, September 2009.

DrySim: Simulation-Aided Deployment-Specific Tailoring of Mote-Class WSN Software

Moritz Strübe, Florian Lukas
FAU, University Erlangen-Nuremberg, Germany
{struebe, lukas}@cs.fau.de

Bijun Li, Rüdiger Kapitza
IBR, TU Braunschweig, Germany
{bli, rrkapitz}@ibr.cs.tu-bs.de

ABSTRACT

Despite intensive research in the field of mote-class Wireless Sensor Networks in recent years, real-life deployments are still challenging and systems are prone to failures. This can typically be attributed to fragile hardware or misbehaving software. Issues caused by software, often induced by the inherent constraints of resources, can be countered using simulations. However the simulation results often do not reflect those of the specific deployment.

We suggest analyzing the actual environment conditions of a deployed network and map them to a simulator. Then, based on simulations, software and parameters can be tailored to the specific deployment.

We developed two tool chains, REALSIM and DRYRUN, and compared results from simulation runs to those acquired from two different testbeds using Tmote Sky nodes. This was done in two campaigns, each altering 2 configuration parameters from the hardware to the application layer. The presented data is based on over 1100 experiments, respectively over 270 h, on real hardware and almost 7000 simulations. The close relation of simulation and real measurements shows that our DRYSIM approach is feasible.

Categories and Subject Descriptors

C.2.1 [**Computer-Communication Networks**]: Network Architecture and Design—*Wireless Communication*; I.6.0 [**Simulation and Modeling**]: General

Keywords

Wireless Sensor Networks; Simulation; Testbed; Deployment

1. INTRODUCTION

Despite more than one decade of intensive research in the field of mote-class Wireless Sensor Networks (WSNs), real-life deployments are still considered difficult and systems are fragile in many ways. In fact there is a substantial record of failed experiments [2,4]. The reasons are multifold, ranging from fragile hardware to faulty and misconfigured software. These issues are aggravated, and to a certain extent caused, by the serious resource constraints of the nodes.

Although the typical mote evolved only slightly in terms of memory and computing power during the last decade, the software running on these nodes had a great leap of its own technology. For example, providing an IPv6-based web-server is not out of the ordinary. WSN Operating Systems (OS) like Contiki [10] or TinyOS [20] provide a huge set of libraries, protocols and services. These OS target highly specialized deployments and therefore support many configuration options to tune the system to the specific needs.

Estimating the exact impact of changing a certain configuration parameter or choosing a different network protocol is difficult, even for a domain expert. Often the impact can only be determined by testing the different versions in the target environment. This is especially the case as the results are influenced by the network topology, the quality of the connections and the interactions between different software modules. If a specific configuration performs well in a certain environment (testbed), there is no guarantee that it will also perform well in another environment (real deployment).

A way of getting sound results is to test different configurations in the final environment. Alternatively one can choose a configuration that performs well in similar environments (testbed) and hope that it performs as expected in the final environment, too. While the first solution is suitable for a specific deployment, the second will work only if a generic solution is required (e.g. house automation). Both have in common that running the required amount of experiments is very laborious. The possible configurations quickly multiply up to huge numbers, and experiments must be repeated multiple times to get sound results. Not only changing environmental conditions, but also subtle effects like boot-up order, random offsets, packet loss and clock skew may have a significant impact on the outcome. For a real *wireless* deployment running a sufficient number of experiments is often not feasible.

Unlike the typical WSN mote, the average computer has developed tremendously. This provides us with the ability to simulate resource-constrained sensor nodes faster and more accurately than ever. If the simulator resembles a concrete network, it enables us to run a huge number of experiments and find a suitable setup for that specific deployment. To support this, we developed two tool chains, REALSIM to map a deployment to the simulator and DRYRUN to support setting up experiments to test combinations of multiple different configuration options. Both are publicly available [8].

Protocol	Boolean	Numeric
ConitikiMAC	9	19
IP	8	8
UDP	1	1
TCP	2	8
ARP	0	2
6LoWPAN	2	2
RPL	2	11
	24	51

Table 1: Configuration options per network protocol

The paper is structured as follows: In the *problem statement* we go into detail why it is necessary to run many experiments in the target environment to get a good setup and why this is not feasible (Section 2). An *overview* of our idea of simulating the target environment to gain a suitable setup is given in Section 3. This is followed by the *implementation details* (Section 4). We then discuss *related work* (Section 5). Our approach is *evaluated* by comparing results acquired from the simulation to those from the testbed (Section 6). In *discussion* we look at the current limits and opportunities of our approach (Section 7), before we end with a *conclusion* (Section 8).

2. PROBLEM STATEMENT

Modern WSN operating systems like Contiki and TinyOS usually provide a huge amount of possible configuration options. They are supposed to provide maximum flexibility and to allow tailoring the system to the requirements (e.g., bandwidth, power, memory, network size, network topology, network protocol, timeliness, and many others). In this context configuration does not only include adjustments of parameters but also selecting alternative code paths or modules (e.g. MAC-Protocol). Although most configuration options are within the network layer, they can be found in all layers of the system. As a result, one has to be an expert on all layers of a system to get optimal results. Based on the failed deployments in the past [4] this is a challenge even for an experienced WSN-system developer, let alone an application developer.

For example Contiki's IPv6 over Low Power Wireless Personal Area Network (6LoWPAN) stack consists of 7 protocols, providing a total of 75 configuration options (Table 1). This does not include flags that adjust the code due to other features like debugging, tracing and encryption, but only the protocol specific options.

Interactions.

The situation of having many configuration options is aggravated by the fact that different options closely interact with each other. These interactions are not only within a certain layer but often also cross-layer: Increasing the sampling frequency of a sensing application is likely to also require adjustments at the network layer. This can include having to change to a network protocol that is better suitable for more traffic. Not always obvious to see, these dependencies between the configuration options make it inherently complicated to adjust them.

Network Portability.

It is not only necessary to adjust the network stack to the application but also to the underlying network. A big network usually needs a different configuration (e.g. bandwidth, size of the routing table) than a small one. In addition to the size of the network, the topology and link attributes have a big impact on the performance of a network. Consequently, experiences gained in one environment can only be transferred to another environment with great care.

Running Trials.

The most reliable way to find a good configuration is running trials. In a testbed, flashing different firmware versions and collecting data can normally be done using a reliable, wired connection. It is still time-consuming, as testing 25 different configurations for 20 min each will take over 8 h. If repeating them four times to get more robust results, this already takes more than a day. As we show in our evaluation, a detailed analysis that is supposed to uncover interactions requires testing a lot more configurations and they must be repeated more often.

When testing in a real, *wireless* deployment, Over The Air (OTA) programming is required. To the additional overhead of reliably distributing different firmware to all nodes, the risk of bringing the network into an indeterminate state or even bricking a node is added. The additional overhead and possible manual interactions make this approach unfeasible.

3. OVERVIEW

We aim at a generic approach that allows tailoring the software system to a specific deployment. As discussed before, achieving this for complex software requires a rather large testing campaign that cannot be executed on the target deployment. We therefore propose *trace-based* simulation for *deployment-specific* testing of WSN software. It can be structured in five consecutive steps:

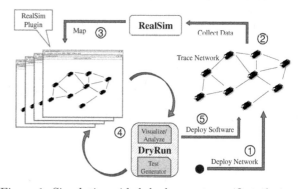

Figure 1: Simulation-aided deployment-specific tailoring of WSN software at a glance

1. Of course our approach does not eliminate thorough testing before deploying a WSN, but it does target the phase during or right after a deployment; therefore deploying the WSN is the first step.
2. After that the connectivity between the deployed nodes is profiled to obtain the network topology.
3. The acquired data are used to configure a simulator in a way that it resembles the tested network.
4. Running multiple Monte Carlo simulations in parallel allows testing a huge configuration space within a short time.
5. After evaluating the simulation, a suitable configuration can be chosen and programmed to the nodes.

Simulation ④.

The selection of the simulator is crucial for our approach, as its accuracy has a direct impact on the results. One of our goals is to show the effects of tuning certain parameters while taking the whole software system into account. Using a WSN simulator that is able to emulate the mote's hardware, it is possible to run the same binary code as on the real nodes. It is therefore ignorant of the implementation and is not dependent on a certain OS or library. Further on it allows uncovering hardware specific issues like unaligned reads or problems caused by the tool chain. These are not necessarily triggered when compiling for a different target.

Due to the simplicity of the RISC-based micro controllers used in mote-class WSNs, these simulators are also very timing accurate. Therefore the side effects caused by concurrency or by using algorithms that perform badly on a specific platform and then miss timing constraints, can be observed as well.

Based on these considerations we chose the Cooja Simulator [24]. While the network models are rather simple compared to some sophisticated network simulators like NS2 or OMNeT++, it integrates MSPSim [12], which supports emulating the Sky mote we used in our testbed, including its CC2420 radio hardware. By setting the seed of Java's Pseudo Random Number Generator (PRNG), Cooja supports reproducible Monte Carlo Simulations. In our setup the PRNG is used to determine start-up offsets and whether a packet is received based on the Packet Reception Ratio (PRR).

Data Acquisition ②.

There are multiple ways of acquiring connectivity data [6, 18, 22, 28]. Most of these have a rather sophisticated underlying protocol, often triggering measurements. For REALSIM, of which we already presented an early version [26], we decided to choose a simple approach that does not rely on any synchronization between nodes.

Each node sends beacons with increasing IDs. When a node receives such a beacon it obtains the Received Signal Strength Indication (RSSI) and Link Quality Index (LQI) from the radio chip and derives the PRR from the ascending order of the ID packed into the beacon. While a node is not receiving data, it regularly samples the RSSI of the background noise.

Mapping data ③.

As Cooja provides a Direct Graph Radio Medium (DGRM), it is the perfect target for our data. It allows us to set PRR, RSSI and LQI for each directed connection. Additionally we extended Cooja to support setting the background noise for each node.

Using the REALSIM tool chain it is possible to extract a certain time frame and load it into the simulation. The REALSIM plugin then replays the sample by adjusting the DGRM.

Testing Configurations ④.

While REALSIM is responsible for making the simulation more realistic, DRYRUN supports running large campaigns, testing many configurations. To create a campaign DRYRUN provides a test generator. As input, the test generator takes a script that describes how to set up the test environment and which configuration options to test. For each experiment a shell-script is generated, which initiates an isolated test environment (e.g. copy files), executes the experiment and collects the results. Setting up separate environments is necessary to be able to run the experiments in parallel or even distribute them to multiple machines without side effects.

The experiment scripts collect only the raw logs. The *dataextractor* extracts the relevant information, brings it in correlation with the input parameters of each experiment and saves them in a format that can be processed using tools like R. As the area of interest depends on the specific research question and due to the volume of the data there are currently no tools to further automatically analyze the data.

4. IMPLEMENTATION DETAILS

Challenges.

Developing a tool like REALSIM is not as trivial as it seems, even if major parts of the infrastructure are already provided by Cooja, MSPSim and Contiki. For REALSIM to work, all components of a huge software stack have to work together seamlessly. If the results are not as expected, this might be because the model is not accurate enough, or there is a bug somewhere in the tool surveying the network, the OS it is built upon, the processing tools, MSPSim, Cooja, the REALSIM plugin, the experiment setup tools or the scripts evaluating the results; maybe our hypotheses that it is possible to simulate real networks was wrong.

To demonstrate this we will discuss the way of a packet's RSSI-value from acquisition to simulation. The radio hardware averages the signal strength over the first 8 symbol periods. It then calculates RSSI value that corresponds to the signal strength in dBm with an offset as *signed byte*. In Contiki it is handled as *unsigned word*, which must be casted back, before pre-processing the data in the node. After passing through the serial and being processed, the REALSIM plugin sets the DGRM configuration in dBm. The averaging over the 8 symbols is done by Contiki's MSPSim adaption layer, before it is passed to MSPSim and written to the virtual register of the CC2420 emulator.

Data Acquisition ②.

To allow a random distribution, as well as a constant beacon rate, we randomly distribute the points of time to send a beacon over a certain time frame/episode (e.g. 6 beacons within 80 s). For each received packet we extract the RSSI and LQI provided by the radio chip. Based on the ID we detect whether a new episode started and calculate the PRR and average RSSI and LQI for that neighbor node and episode. It is possible to either send the aggregated data to a sink using the network, or print it directly to the serial.

We sample the background noise at a rate of 300 ± 50 ms, unless the radio chip indicates that it is currently sending or receiving. At the end of the local episode, the average RSSI value is calculated.

For some nodes in our testbed we were able to observe a background noise ranging from a RSSI value of -52 to -15. This roughly maps to -97 to -60 dBm. Considering that a delta of 37 dBm represents a factor of over 5000, averaging the RSSI value instead of the corresponding energy levels gave quite accurate simulation results. It is also much simpler and requires fewer resources.

```
1  implicit val exp = new Experiment
2
3  val files = new GetFile("src/*")
4  exp.addstep(files)
5
6  val mk = new Make
7  mk.addConf("CCA_THRESH",-54, -20, 2)
8  mk.addConf("TEST_RATE", 5, 30, 5)
9  exp.addstep(mk)
10
11 val cooja = new Cooja("test1.csc")
12 cooja.addRandRange(0, 9)
13 exp.addstep(cooja)
```

Listing 1: Example experiment setup

Mapping Data ③.

The data acquired by the nodes is printed to the serial and then saved together with a time stamp in a log file. From the log a certain time span can be selected, which is then converted to simple format supporting commands (e.g. setedge, rmedge) and a time when they are to be executed. At the beginning of a simulation REALSIM loads this data and executes the commands at the given simulation-time.

Experiment Generator ④.

The main part of the DRYRUN toolkit is the experiment generator. The generator uses the Scala runtime compiler to script the setup. Listing 1 shows a simplified setup. First a new Experiment object is created (l. 1). Then all the files from the src directory are copied to the build environment (l. 3). Explicitly adding it to the experiment ensures the correct order (l. 4). Lines 6 to 9 configure the experiment to be built using Make with CCA_THRESH ranging from −54 to −20 in steps of 2, and TEST_RATE from 5 to 30 in steps of 5. Finally Cooja is run with test1.csc as configuration file using 10 different seeds for Cooja's PRNG.

The listing will create a campaign of 850 experiments. Each experiment consists of a folder containing the configuration of the experiment and a shell-script. The shell-script sets up the environment in the temporary directory, runs the experiment and copies the resulting logs back to the experiment-folder. As the scripts are self-sufficient they can be executed in parallel or distributed over multiple machines. Additional functions include creating symbolic links, checking out files from git and retrieving additional information from the experiment environment. It is also possible to select a certain length of a network trace using different start offsets.

For our evaluation we used the same infrastructure to generate the experiments run on the testbed. Instead of running the simulation we flashed the firmware and collected the serial output.

5. RELATED WORK

Similar approaches have been published before. For example Marchiori et al. traced their testbed and developed their own simulator called WsnSimPy to replay these traces [22]. There are also quite some other works that tried to reproduce testbed results based on generic network simulators like NS2 or OMNeT++ [14, 17, 23] or the WSN Simulator Castalia [3, 19, 25]. As opposed to our approach, all of them only focus on simulating the network layer. It is therefore possible to quickly make a conceptual evaluation of a network protocol, but effects caused by the concrete implementation, OS, libraries used, timing and hardware are neglected.

In their position paper Greg et al. give an overview of different approaches for realistic simulations [13]. As opposed to us they suggest improving trace-based simulation in OMNeT++/MiXiM and TOSSIM. Both simulators do not emulate the target nodes but are directly interfaced. As TOSSIM is implemented as target platform for TinyOS, it is at least possible to see effects caused by the actual implementation and OS, but not the platform itself.

Using a very simple setup, Gama et al. show that the code running on the node does influence the results [1]. Instead of emulating the node, they add delays to the different processing layers (Hardware, Media Access Control (MAC), Application, etc.) to improve their simulation results. Though this approach provides a better performance than emulating each instruction, it has the drawback of inaccuracy and side-effects caused by concurrency, which cannot be detected.

Besides our generic approach of testing the whole system, there are also approaches that target certain layers. pTunes [28], for example, continuously optimizes the MAC layer. While these approaches probably yield better results for supported use-cases, they must be specifically adjusted to the code in use. Our solution, in contrast, is able to test any compile time parameter, independent of the code it addresses.

In [16] He et al. use simulation to predict the PRR for the connections in an office environment before the deployment. Considering the strong fluctuations and the effects we monitored when changing the position of a node, we do not think it possible to get reliable results without actual measurements. Their approach seems promising to gain a good initial setup, though.

The WiseML-plugin [21] for Cooja also supports adjusting the DGRM and is very similar to our REALSIM plugin. The WiseML format itself is more generic and supports detailed descriptions of the environment and nodes. This includes, for example, positions and sensor data. Although the plugin does support setting the temperature read by a node, it can only set the PRR, but not LQI and RSSI. As we show in our evaluation the RSSI has a significant impact on sophisticated network protocols like ContikiMAC.

6. EVALUATION

To verify our approach, we did not evaluate the approach itself, but evaluated the crucial point: Does the network that is mapped to the simulator resemble the traced, real network? For this we chose four different configuration parameters and compare the simulation results to two testbeds. The parameters were not selected by the expected novelty of the results, but because they are often used for system tuning. With our experiments we want to show that the simulation is able to yield results that are similar to those of the testbed, and that these results differ between testbeds. Therefore the results in general are probably not surprising for a domain expert.

As code base we used Contiki's UDP server/client example, where each client regularly sends data to the sink. We extended the code to allow querying the Energest [11] statistics at the end of an experiment. Energest, is part of Contiki and accounts the time of the system being in a certain state. For example, the time of the CPU being in low power mode or the radio being turned on. Multiplied with the energy input of the system being in that specific state, the energy consumption can be estimated.

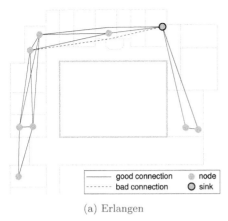

(a) Erlangen

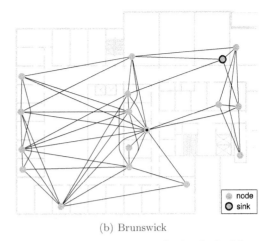

(b) Brunswick

Figure 2: The testbed in Brunswick is larger and closer meshed. The solid lines represent good, the dashed line a flaky connection. The sink is marked with a black border.

In our evaluation we tested the following parameters:

CCA Threshold The Clear Channel Assessment (CCA) threshold is a hardware configuration parameter of the `CC2420` radio chip. Based on its value the hardware decides whether the channel is clear to send data. The current CCA status can also be queried via a hardware pin; a feature used by the ContikiMAC protocol.

RDC/MAC Contiki distinguishes between the MAC and Radio Duty Cycling (RDC) layer. Currently Contiki supports four different RDC options: ContikiMAC [9], CX-MAC, an adjusted version of the X-MAC protocol [5], SICSLoWMAC that puts packets into 802.15.4 frames and nullrdc which passes the data on to the MAC layer. Choosing an RDC does not only change a simple parameter, but also includes different code into the binary.

CCR The Channel Check Rate (CCR) is the rate at which the RDC layer wakes up and checks for other nodes to send data. A low CCR lets the receiver wake up less frequently while the sender must potentially send more packets until the receiver wakes up to receive the packet.

Packet Rate In our test application we altered the packet rate, at which the "user"-program sends data to the sink.

At the end of each experiment we collected energy and network statistics for each node – over 50 parameters in total. When investigating why the specific configuration behaves the way it does, these can be very helpful. As we want to compare simulation and testbed, rather than understand the behavior of a specific protocol, we chose two metrics that are important for WSN deployments: The time spent with the radio turned on (rx and tx) and the number of packets that arrive at the sink. The CC2420 radio chip is one of the biggest energy consumers and uses about the same amount of energy for sending and receiving when in the default settings.

To aggregate the data, we took the mean of all nodes except the sink. We excluded the sink because it distorts the two metrics we chose: It does not send any packets and, in the example we derived our experiments from, the radio is always on.

As discussed we try to circumvent the limitations of running multiple experiments on a real deployment. Yet, to get a sound ground truth for our evaluation we had to do exactly that. Consequently all our experiments were run in a testbed

and we used the serial as convenient method of gathering data.

When running experiments on real hardware, it is not unlikely that the results show artifacts caused by random effects like packet loss or changes of the environment. We tried to mitigate this by running each experiment several times and executing them in a random order. In this way each configuration had the same chance of being executed at daytime or at night, when conditions were typically more stable. We tried to reconstruct this behavior for our simulations by not only using a different PRNG-seed for each repeated simulation, but also a different snippet from our trace. For each configuration we used the same seeds and snippets. Thus the simulation yielded the same results for different configurations, if the change had no impact on the behavior of the node. This effect can be seen if Figure 3a where the best result for SICSLowMAC at the Brunswick-testbed does not change for a CCA threshold above −39.

6.1 Testbeds

Our two testbeds are located in an office environment at the universities in Erlangen and Brunswick, Germany. Both testbeds are managed using Wisebed [7]. Due to network delays and the Wisebed infrastructure, it is not possible to accurately control the node bootup order. To minimize the effects of nodes booting in a system-inherent order, we randomly delayed the reset command of each node at the beginning of an experiment.

Erlangen.

The network in Erlangen (Figure 2a) consists of 9 Sky nodes that were placed as far apart as possible while still providing a stable connection. The room in the middle is a lecture hall with stronger walls, blocking the connectivity. Solid lines typically have a PRR of 100 % while the dashed line has around 10 %. The short ranged connections have a RSSI value of about −40 dB while the long range connections are at around (-85 ± 5) dB. This sink is marked with a black border.

Brunswick.

The testbed in Brunswick is also located in an office environment and consists of 17 Sky nodes. Figure 2b shows

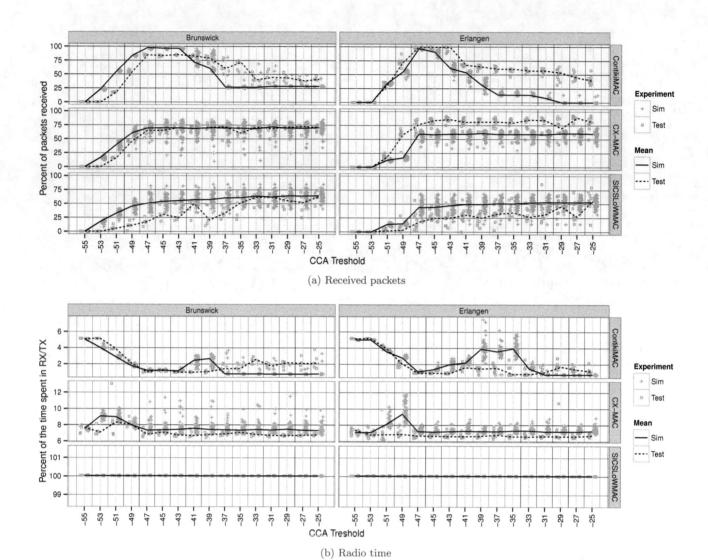

(a) Received packets

(b) Radio time

Figure 3: Impact of the CCA threshold on different RDC layers in simulation and test bed. Each dot represents the mean of the nodes of one run. The line connects the median of all runs with the same configuration.

the good connections between the nodes. In comparison to Erlangen the network is meshed much closer. We chose a sink (dark border) outside the central mesh to increase the number of packets that must be routed. The figure also shows that, especially in an office environment, the distance is not necessarily related to the connectivity. In the center there is a node marked with black dot, which has extraordinary connectivity in all directions, while the node right next to it, to the lower left, is only connected to two nodes. Similarly the node to the top right of the sink has better connectivity than the sink itself.

6.2 CCA vs RDC

In this campaign we investigate the impact of changing the hardware-configurable CCA as well as the RDC network layer. We tested the three available RDC layers (ContikiMAC, CX-MAC and SICSLoWMAC) and configured the CCA threshold from −55 to 25 in steps of 2. The runtime of an experiment was 20 min. We simulated each configuration 50 times, which resulted in a total of 2400 simulation runs for each location. In Erlangen each configuration ran 10 and in Brunswick 5

times. Unfortunately this also means that the jitter had a stronger impact. In Erlangen it took over a week to run the campaign and in Brunswick almost 4 days, flashing each node 480 and 240 times, respectively .

Figure 3 shows the results of the experiment. Every point shows the mean of all nodes except the sink. The results from the simulation are shown as cross and are placed to the right, while the results from the testbed are represented as square and placed to the left of the corresponding discrete value. The median of the experiments are connected with a line that is solid for the simulation and dashed for the testbeds.

The results show that although there are deviations, there is a clear similarity between simulation and testbed. Part of deviation can be accounted to the insufficient noise model.

The impact of this flaw in the radio model can be seen in the average number of packets received from each node (Figure 3a). If the measured noise is higher than the CCA threshold, the hardware does not send any data. Therefore no packets are sent if the CCA threshold is too low. This can be seen for all three protocols. While this matches quite well in

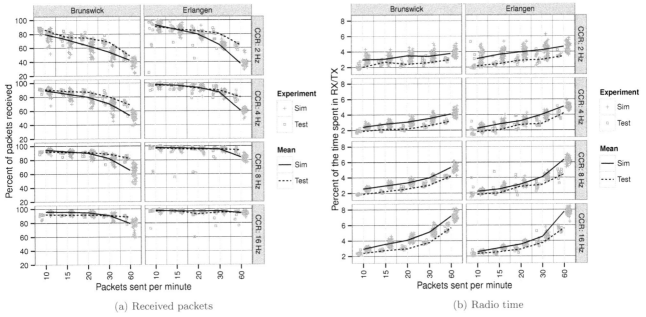

| (a) Received packets | (b) Radio time |

Figure 4: If the number of packets being sent is too high or the CCR too low, the networks starts losing packets. Each dot represents the mean of the nodes of one run. The line connects the median of all runs with the same configuration.

Erlangen, there is an offset of about two between simulation and testbed in Brunswick. In Brunswick, measured peaks of the background noise were not as high as in Erlangen and therefore the average value was lower. This allowed the simulated hardware to send packets at a lower CCA threshold.

The strong variation of the background noise in Erlangen is also accountable for the strong drop of the simulated ContikiMAC for higher CCA thresholds in Erlangen. ContikiMAC also uses the CCA threshold to test whether any other node is sending data. If the measured noise level is below the threshold, the radio is turned off right away, not being turned on long enough to receive a packet. In the noisy environment in Erlangen, the radio was kept on due to the noise and then received a packet by chance. Half of the nodes had a direct connection to the sink, which did not do any radio duty cycling. It was therefore sufficient to receive a single packet from the sink, to get the routing information and send data to the sink for the rest of the experiment. In Brunswick there was no such drop in the simulation because the nodes were placed closer together and therefore their signal was strong enough to keep the receiving radio on. If we extend our campaign to higher CCA thresholds we can probably see this effect in Brunswick as well. This cannot be seen for CX-MAC and SICSLowMAC, which only evaluate the CCA threshold when sending packets.

We did not investigate why CX-MAC outperforms the simulation in Erlangen and SICSLowMAC performs so much worse in the testbed. Nonetheless there are some effects of SICSLowMAC that can be seen in both the simulation and the testbed. For example, in Brunswick the results are better than in Erlangen. For CX-MAC we do see a slight positive trend towards higher CCA thresholds. A similar trend was also observed on the testbed.

As the SICSLowMAC has no duty cycling the radio is turned on all the time (Figure 3b). Besides the offset of the CCA threshold by two in Brunswick, which we already dis-

cussed, one can see that especially in Erlangen the simulated radio on time is significantly higher around a CCA threshold of about 37. This again is caused by the non-existing fluctuation of the radio signals in the simulation. In the simulation the signal strength is only adjusted every episode ($\approx 80\,\text{s}$ in our setup). Thus, if the signal strength oscillates around the CCA threshold, the sending node must wait at least until the next episode to be able to successfully send its packets. In the testbed the next change, and therefore the chance to receive the packet, typically is in the next RDC and thus within less than a second.

6.3 Application vs. MAC

To show the interactions of application, MAC and testbed we varied the rate at which the packets are sent to the sink. To avoid the effects already discussed, we chose to use ContikiMAC with a CCA threshold of −45, which performed well in both testbeds and the simulation. As second parameter we chose the CCR value. It tells ContikiMAC how often per second to check the channel for other nodes sending data. If it is too high, a lot of energy is spent checking for radio traffic, while if it is too low, the bandwidth is reduced and packets might be dropped.

For the CCR the lowest value supported is 2 Hz and the default is 8 Hz. We therefore chose 2, 4, 8 and 16 Hz. For the packets we chose a rate of 10, 15, 20, 30 and 60 min^{-1}. Based on the high number of packets we reduced the time of the experiment to 5 min. Each configuration was simulated 50 and tested 10 times on both testbeds.

The results are presented in Figure 4. We prepared the data the same way as in the previous trial: We calculated the average number of packets received and the average radio time for each experiment and plotted a cross for the simulation and a square for the testbed results. We then connected the median of the experiments with a line – solid for the simulation and dashed for the testbed.

Figure 4a shows the percentage of sent packets that were received. Even in a perfect environment, chances are high that not all packets arrive at the sink, as some are likely to be on their way when the experiment is ended. As expected, the much larger testbed in Brunswick goes into an overload situation much earlier than Erlangen. As the radio model drops all packets in case of a collision, the testbed outperforms the simulation in the overload situation. Considering the jitter of the measurements the results are quite close, though and the point clouds almost always overlap.

In terms of radio on time (Figure 4b), the testbed always outperforms the simulation, not only in an overload situation. We also account this to the radio model, as packets need to be re-transmitted more often. Even though, there is a clear correlation between simulation and testbed, and the dot clouds typically overlap.

7. DISCUSSION

Our evaluation shows that it is possible to get quite realistic results, even with a very simple radio model and simplified assumptions when tracing the network. To the best of our knowledge it was also the most comprehensive comparison between testbed and simulation using such a holistic approach. Actually, due to the many trials preceding the presented numbers, we found multiple bugs in all layers of the system. One of them, located in the implementation of the radio hardware, ignored the configured CCA threshold. Before we started varying the threshold in our experiments, it caused the simulations to yield unexplainable discrepancies to our real world experiments and was quite hard to find. Although we are certainly not the first to suggest verifying simulators using testbeds, with our tools this can now be accomplished by running a sufficient number of experiments with reasonable efforts.

We see multiple leverage points to improve our results. One is a more dynamic model for the background noise and the signal strength. This will likely have a significant influence on protocols like ContikiMAC, which heavily rely on the RSSI. To allow tracing networks outside a testbed, such a model must also be suitable to aggregate the data on the nodes themselves, though.

Further on, the signal strength is currently only evaluated by the radio hardware, but not the radio model. Therefore weak signals can interfere with strong ones. In this context Halkes et al. had very promising results with a Signal-to-Noise Ratio (SNR)-based model [15].

Yet another problem we faced while comparing the simulations with the testbed was the amount of data we collected. The numbers presented show only 2 of the over 50 different attributes we collected. With simulators the amount of data that can be collected suddenly becomes unlimited. They allow monitoring state that is too complex or changes too often to be printed to the serial [27]. While this provides great opportunities, it also requires the support of specialized tools to handle the data.

The amount of data that can be collected, as well as the huge number of different configurations when combining multiple parameters requires further tooling support. Once our simulation results are accurate enough, it is possible to use machine learning and evolutionary algorithms to find better configurations.

As soon as the number of experiments is only limited by the available processing power, many other things to investigate come to mind. For example, it is possible to test each node with an individual configuration. This might allow leaf-nodes to save more energy. It is also possible to derive scenarios from the traces, for example to test whether failing nodes can be tolerated. Yet another possibility is to enrich the simulation with an energy model and try to increase the network lifetime opposed to node lifetime.

Currently we are only targeting the pre-deployment stage. Extracting the required information from the packets sent over the network anyway would make this approach even more powerful. It would allow running simulations on an updated model of the network, without having to flash a special firmware. It is then possible to detect potential issues caused by the changed environment, or just test the next firmware version to be deployed.

8. CONCLUSION

To gain a reliable, robust and long-living mote-class WSN network, it is often not sufficient to use the default configuration, but the system must be tailored to the specific used case and deployment. This is likely to become a tedious task, even for a domain expert. We therefore presented our DRYSIM-approach of first mapping a deployment to the simulator and then tailoring the system based on simulations. By parallelizing the simulations it is possible to systematically test a huge number of different configurations.

To verify our approach we created a set of tools called REALSIM that we used to trace testbeds and map them into the Cooja WSN simulator. We chose the Cooja simulator because it allows us to emulate binary code and to execute it in simulation time. To allow testing different parameters by instrumenting Cooja and REALSIM we developed a second set of tools, DRYRUN, which simplify setting up campaigns to test different configurations.

In the evaluation we made a comprehensive comparison between the testbed and the simulation. Although there is plenty of room for improvements, it shows that our DRYSIM-approach is feasible and can support finding a suitable configuration for a specific deployment using simulation.

9. ACKNOWLEDGMENTS

This work was partly supported by the Bavarian Ministry of State for Economics, Traffic and Technology under the (EU EFRE funds) grant no. 0704/883 25 and the German Research Foundation (DFG) under grants no. FOR 1508.

10. REFERENCES

[1] Modelling the impact of software components on wireless sensor network performance. pages 1 – 6.

[2] G. Barrenetxea, F. Ingelrest, G. Schaefer, and M. Vetterli. The Hitchhiker's Guide to Successful Wireless Sensor Network Deployments. In Proc. of the 6th ACM conf. on Embedded network sensor systems (SenSys 2008), pages 43–56, 2008.

[3] L. Bergamini, C. Crociani, A. Vitaletti, and M. Nati. Validation of WSN simulators through a comparison with a real testbed. In Proc. of the 7th ACM workshop on Performance evaluation of wireless ad hoc, sensor, and ubiquitous networks (PE-WASUN 2010), pages 103–104, 2010.

[4] J. Beutel, K. Römer, M. Ringwald, and M. Woehrle. Deployment Techniques for Sensor Networks. In Sensor

Networks, Signals and Communication Technology, chapter Deployment, pages 219–248. Springer, 2009.

[5] M. Buettner, G. V. Yee, E. Anderson, and R. Han. X-MAC: a short preamble MAC protocol for duty-cycled wireless sensor networks. In Proc. of the 4th int. conf. on Embedded networked sensor systems (SenSys 2006), page 307, 2006.

[6] M. Chini, M. Ceriotti, R. Marfievici, A. L. Murphy, and G. P. Picco. Demo: TRIDENT, untethered observation of physical communication made to share. In Proc. of the 9th ACM Conf. on Embedded Networked Sensor Systems (SenSys 2011), SenSys '11, pages 409–410, 2011.

[7] G. Coulson, B. Porter, I. Chatzigiannakis, C. Koninis, S. Fischer, D. Pfisterer, D. Bimschas, T. Braun, P. Hurni, M. Anwander, G. Wagenknecht, S. P. Fekete, A. Kröller, and T. Baumgartner. Flexible experimentation in wireless sensor networks. Communications of the ACM, (1):82–90, 2012.

[8] DryRun and RealSim authors. Dryrun and realsim git repositories. https://github.com/cmorty/{dryrun|realsim}.

[9] A. Dunkels. The contikimac radio duty cycling protocol. Technical report, Swedish Institute of Computer Science, 2011.

[10] A. Dunkels, B. Grönvall, and T. Voigt. Contiki - a Lightweight and Flexible Operating System for Tiny Networked Sensors. In Proc. of the 1st IEEE Workshop on Embedded Networked Sensors (Emnets-I 2004), 2004.

[11] A. Dunkels, F. Osterlind, N. Tsiftes, and Z. He. Software-based on-line energy estimation for sensor nodes. In Proc. of the 4th workshop on Embedded networked sensors (EmNets 2007), pages 28–32, 2007.

[12] J. Eriksson, A. Dunkels, N. Finne, F. Österlind, and T. Voigt. Poster Abstract: MSPsim – an Extensible Simulator for MSP430-equipped Sensor Boards. In European Conf. on Wireless Sensor Networks (EWSN 2007), Poster/Demo session), pages 1–2, 2007.

[13] K. Garg, A. Förster, D. Puccinelli, and S. Giordano. Towards Realistic and Credible Wireless Sensor Network Evaluation. In Proc. of the 3rd Int. ICST Ad Hoc Networks (ADHOCNETS 2011), pages 49–64, 2011.

[14] C. Guo, M. Jacobsson, and R. V. Prasad. A Case Study of Networked Sensors by Simulations and Experiments. In Proc. of the 11th Int. Conf. on Thermal, Mechanical Multi-Physics Simulation, and Experiments in Microelectronics and Microsystems (EuroSimE 2010), pages 1–5, 2010.

[15] G. P. Halkes and K. G. Langendoen. Experimental evaluation of simulation abstractions for wireless sensor network MAC protocols. EURASIP Journal on Wireless Communications and Networking, pages 24:1—-24:2, 2010.

[16] D. He, G. Mujica, J. Portilla, and T. Riesgo. Simulation tool and case study for planning wireless sensor network. In Proc. of the 38th Annual Conf. on IEEE Industrial Electronics Society (IECON 2012), pages 6024 –6028, 2012.

[17] P. Hurni and T. Braun. Calibrating Wireless Sensor Network Simulation Models with Real-World

Experiments. In Proc. of the 8th Int. IFIP-TC 6 Networking Conf., LNCS, pages 1–13, 2009.

[18] A. Kamthe, M. A. Carreira-Perpiñán, and A. E. Cerpa. M&M: Multi-level Markov Model for Wireless Link Simulations. In Proc. of the 7th ACM Conf. on Embedded Networked Sensor Systems (SenSys 2009), SenSys '09, pages 57–70, 2009.

[19] E. Kolega, V. Vescoukis, and D. Voutos. Assessment of network simulators for real world WSNs in forest environments. In Proc. of the 2011 IEEE Int. Conf. on Networking, Sensing and Control (ICNSC 2011), pages 427 –432, 2011.

[20] P. Levis, S. Madden, J. Polastre, R. Szewczyk, K. Whitehouse, A. Woo, D. Gay, J. Hill, M. Welsh, E. Brewer, and D. Culler. TinyOS: An Operating System for Sensor Networks. In Ambient Intelligence, pages 115–148. Springer, 2005.

[21] Q. Li, F. Österlind, T. Voigt, S. Fischer, and D. Pfisterer. Making wireless sensor network simulators cooperate. In Proc. of the 7th ACM workshop on Performance evaluation of wireless ad hoc, sensor, and ubiquitous networks (PE-WASUN 2010), pages 95–98, 2010.

[22] A. Marchiori, L. Guo, J. Thomas, and Q. Han. Realistic performance analysis of WSN protocols through trace based simulation. In Proc. of the 7th ACM workshop on Performance evaluation of wireless ad hoc, sensor, and ubiquitous networks (PE-WASUN 2010), pages 87–94, 2010.

[23] G. Möstl, R. Hagelauer, G. Müller, and A. Springer. A Network and System Level Approach towards an Accurate Simulation of WSNs. In Computer Aided Systems Theory (EUROCAST 2011), LNCS, pages 17–24. Springer, 2012.

[24] F. Österlind, A. Dunkels, J. Eriksson, N. Finne, and T. Voigt. Cross-level Simulation in COOJA. In European Conf. on Wireless Sensor Networks (EWSN 2007), Poster/Demo session, 2007.

[25] H. N. Pham, D. Pediaditakis, and A. Boulis. From Simulation to Real Deployments in WSN and Back. In IEEE Int. Symposium on a World of Wireless, Mobile and Multimedia Networks (WoWMoM 2007), pages 1–6, 2007.

[26] M. Strübe, S. Böhm, R. Kapitza, and F. Dressler. RealSim: Real-time Mapping of Real World Sensor Deployments into Simulation Scenarios. In Proc. of the 6th ACM int. workshop on Wireless network testbeds, experimental evaluation and characterization (WiNTECH 2011), pages 95–96, 2011.

[27] M. Strübe, F. Lukas, and R. Kapitza. Demo Abstract: CoojaTrace, Extensive Profiling for WSNs. In Poster and Demo Proc. of the 9th European Conf. on Wireless Sensor Networks (EWSN 2012), pages 64–65, 2012.

[28] M. Zimmerling, F. Ferrari, L. Mottola, T. Voigt, and L. Thiele. pTunes: runtime parameter adaptation for low-power MAC protocols. In Proc. of the 11th int. conf. on Information Processing in Sensor Networks (IPSN 2012), pages 173–184, 2012.

Connectivity Analysis of Indoor Wireless Sensor Networks using Realistic Propagation Models

Gagan Goel
ECE Department
University of Toronto
Toronto, Ontario, Canada
ggoel@ece.utoronto.ca

Scott H. Melvin
ECE Department
University of Toronto
Toronto, Ontario, Canada
smelvin@ece.utoronto.ca

Yves Lostanlen
SIRADEL North America
Toronto, Ontario, Canada
yves.lostanlen@ieee.org

Dimitrios Hatzinakos
ECE Department
University of Toronto
Toronto, Ontario, Canada
dimitris@ece.utoronto.ca

ABSTRACT

Wireless Sensor Networks are increasingly employed as un-obtrusive and infrastructureless networks in both indoor and outdoor environments. In order to reach their full potential, a number of key issues, such as localization and topology control, need to be addressed. However, the performance of these protocols is significantly impacted by the assumptions made about the underlying physical layer. Realistic radio propagation models, used as the physical layer models, provide a more accurate evaluation of protocols when performing network simulations. This paper therefore analyzes the performance of a number of propagation models in a real indoor environment. Specifically, the Unit Disk, Log-normal Shadowing, Volcano Indoor Multi-Wall and WIN-NER II Stochastic channel models are investigated. Field measurements are performed in an office building to empirically determine the channel parameters and evaluate the models based on various error metrics. A network connectivity analysis is also performed using Monte Carlo simulations to demonstrate the impact the choice of the physical layer model has on the network backbone construction. This paper shows that the Volcano Indoor Multi-Wall and WIN-NER II Stochastic channel models provide better estimate of the actual path losses in an indoor environment. It also shows that the errors introduced can cause connectivity algorithms to significantly under-estimate (sometimes up to a 14 times under-estimation) the power requirements necessary to guarantee a connected network.

Categories and Subject Descriptors

C.2.1 [**Computer-Communication Networks**]: Network Architecture and Design—*Network communications; Wireless communication*

General Terms

Performance; Measurement.

Keywords

Channel Measurements; Indoor Propagation; Performance Evaluation; Propagation and Channel Modelling.

1. INTRODUCTION

Propagation of a radio frequency (RF) signal is highly influenced by the characteristics of the environment in which it operates. In complex indoor and outdoor environments, an RF signal is affected by various physical processes such as multi-path fading, shadowing/signal blockage and diffraction. As a result, the existence of a wireless link between a pair of nodes is a random phenomenon. A radio propagation model attempts to quantify the behavior of an actual wireless channel.

Now, consider the problem of constructing an energy-efficient, fully connected network backbone by means of a topology control algorithm [16]. A connected network is a fundamental requirement for performing various sensor network operations such as the communication of a sensed phenomenon between a source and a destination node. However, this task requires the generation of a communication graph consisting of a set of vertices (nodes) and a set of edges (links) connecting the vertices. Determination of these edges relies on very precise information about the path losses between the vertices. An edge between two vertices is possible only if the path loss between them is below the threshold set for a reliable communication. Accurate radio propagation modelling is therefore of primary concern in areas where the performance of a network protocol is highly influenced by the underlying physical layer.

The authors of [22] show that the major shortcoming of network protocols is unrealistic modelling of the physical layer. By means of experiments in an outdoor, open parking lot, they demonstrate the negative impact of radio irregularity on several Wireless Sensor Network (WSN) protocols. An experiment based investigation of the channel characteristics is performed in [18] using IEEE 802.15.4-compliant sensor nodes in a harsh factory setting. It is observed that the received signal strength shows spatial variation due to the complicated layout of the machine shop. It is further emphasized in [14] that multi-path fading and shadowing phenomenon should be accounted for in wireless channel modelling.

Recent theoretical advances have also been made in the coverage, capacity and connectivity analysis of wireless networks for different radio propagation models. These propagation models are generally referred to as connection models in the stochastic geometry and random graph theory literature [5]. In [9], an overview of various network parameters characterized for Unit Disk, Log-normal shadowing and the more generic Random connection models is given. An analytical framework for the analysis of network capacity and node isolation probability is proposed in [11] in the presence of channel randomness. The authors show that an increase in the standard deviation of the Log-normal shadowing model increases the connectivity of a wireless network. This result on the improvement of network connectivity in a shadow fading environment has also been validated in [2].

Concerning the previous work on indoor channel modelling for wireless sensor networks, it is shown in [20] that the small scale variations in the propagation channel between two sensor nodes follows a Rician distribution. Our work is complementary in the sense that it considers channel models based solely on large scale variations of the propagation channel. This facilitates the analysis of such sensor network properties as connectivity, one of the fundamental requirements for all network operations.

The authors of [3] devise a radio coverage tool for wireless sensor networks, again for indoor environments, and conclude that channel models that take into account wall attenuations can more accurately model an indoor wireless channel. However, their model is based on the received signal strength indication between a pair of nodes, which is specific to a particular sensor radio technology and is only an approximation to the actual received power levels. Further parameterization, based on empirical data, of the Log-normal model used for performance evaluation is not performed. Packet Reception Rate is used as a metric for indoor channel modelling in [10] which takes into account non-isotropic antenna radiation patterns and site-specific information to model signal attenuation. However, only a deterministic path loss model for a comparative analysis against the proposed scheme is considered.

In this paper, we analyze the performance of different path loss models for a given propagation scenario. Channel measurements have been performed in an indoor environment at 2.45 GHz. The measurement data is then used for the parameterization and calibration of the path loss models and further for their performance evaluation using different error metrics. Specifically, this work evaluates the Unit Disk and Log-normal Shadowing models along with two propagation models specific to an indoor office setup, the Volcano Indoor Multi-Wall and WINNER II Stochastic channel models. Channel parameters, i.e. the path loss exponent and the shadow fading standard deviation, are empirically determined and further characterized for different propagation conditions from part of the measurement data. It is further shown, by means of an application case study, how the characterization of the large-scale signal variations in a propagation environment affect the wireless sensor network connectivity analysis. Several spatial realizations of the sensor network are performed numerically to observe the average network behaviour under all path loss models, facilitating sensor network planning and dimensioning phases.

The rest of this paper is organized as follows: Details of the measurement campaign are provided in Section 2. Path loss models investigated in this work are explained in Section 3. In Section 4, channel parameters from the measurement data are analyzed along with the comparative analysis of the path loss models. We also present in this section, a case study on network connectivity analysis under different wireless channel conditions. Finally, conclusions are drawn in Section 5.

2. EXPERIMENTAL SETUP

2.1 Measurement Equipment

The block diagram of the radio equipment used for the path loss measurements is shown in Fig. 1. It consists of a single Transmitter (Tx) - Receiver (Rx) pair that operate in the unlicensed Industrial, Scientific and Medical (ISM) frequency band. At the transmitter side, an Agilent E5061B Network Analyzer with a frequency range of 5 Hz to 3 GHz was used as a signal generator. At the receiver side, an Agilent E4402B Spectrum Analyzer with a frequency range of 9 kHz to 3 GHz was used. An unmodulated, single tone Continuous Wave (CW) carrier at 2.45 GHz was broadcast by the transmitter. The IEEE 802.15.4 standard specifies the 2.45 GHz unlicensed frequency band for worldwide usage of Low Rate Wireless Personal Area Networks (LR-WPAN). Two identical, vertically polarized, monopole antennas were attached to the input and output of the Agilent equipment. These antennas are similar to those used worldwide for Wireless Local Area Network (WLAN) and WSN operations.

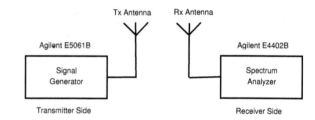

Figure 1: Radio Equipment Block Diagram

The equipment was mounted on moveable carts so as to easily perform measurements at multiple locations. The height of both the transmitting and receiving antennas was set to 1.5 m above the floor. Since the antennas are mounted vertically, their radiation pattern are toroidal in shape and uniform in the horizontal plane. Additionally, all measurements were made on the same floor, so the radiation patterns were essentially omnidirectional in the horizontal plane of interest.

2.2 Measurement Site and Procedure

Measurements were performed on the 4th floor of the Bahen Centre for Information Technology building at the University of Toronto's St. George Campus. This indoor environment offers a range of propagation scenarios such as room-to-room, corridor-to-corridor and room-to-corridor. The target measurement site is therefore typical of a complex indoor environment that can result in high radio channel randomness.

Overall, the propagation scenarios can be categorized as either Line-of-Sight (LOS) or Non Line-of-Sight (NLOS). A detailed description of the building layout and construction is important for propagation models that use such information for path loss calculations. One of the propagation models used in this study, the Volcano Indoor Multi-Wall Model [17], performs propagation predictions based on a digital building model of the measurement site. A section of the Bahen building floor plan [19] is shown in Fig. 2 detailing all of the measurement points used in this experimental study, which are highlighted with numeric and alphanumeric dots. Materials through which an RF signal can undergo partition losses within this building include: wooden doors, drywall walls, thin concrete walls, thick concrete walls, glass walls, windows and elevators.

A total of 142 path loss measurements were recorded using 55 locations inside the building, with each measurement resulting from a different transmitter-receiver location. As can be seen from Fig. 2, the majority of the experiments were performed with the transmitter (receiver) placed in one of the corridors and the receiver (transmitter) placed either in a corridor or in one of the rooms. A complete list of the Tx-Rx locations resulting in 142 path loss measurements can be found in Table 1.

Table 1: Transmitter-Receiver Pairs Used

Tx Location	Rx Locations
F9	F10×2, F11
F12	42
13	(F1-F8)×2, 1-12, 14-17, 19-28
18	1-17, 19-36, 37×2, 38-43
31	14-17, 19-28
35	1-17, 19-33, 37-43

System losses in the link budget were considered before beginning the measurement campaign. During radio hardware calibration, it was observed that the antennas had a non-zero gain (due to feed-line variations/impedence mismatching) which were balanced by the transceiver losses, within a reasonable degree of accuracy. Undesirable effects such as fast fading were removed at the receiving terminal by averaging out 500 received power samples at every measurement location. The transmission power of the signal generator was set to 0 dBm as it is quite representative of the power levels used for WSN operations. A frequency span of 100 kHz was used at the receiver, which consisted of 1000 points, resulting in a sweep time of 275 ms.

3. PATH LOSS MODELS

3.1 Unit Disk Model

Based on a simple extension to the Frii's Transmission Equation [1], a Unit Disk model or the Log-distance model (also referred to as the Gilbert's Random Disk Graph model in the Random Graph theoretic sense [5]), is a more general but still a basic radio propagation model in which the received power follows an inverse law of the distance raised to some constant α. It is of the form:

$$P_r = P_t G_t G_r \left(\frac{\lambda}{4\pi d}\right)^\alpha \qquad (1)$$

where α, P_r, P_t, G_r, G_t, λ and d are respectively the path loss exponent, received power, transmitted power, Rx antenna gain, Tx antenna gain, wavelength of transmitted signal and the distance between the Tx and the Rx antennas. Equation 1 reduces to the Frii's equation when $\alpha = 2$. Generally, α is determined empirically from field measurements. Equation 1 can be written in terms of the *average* path loss at a distance d (in dB) as:

$$PL(d) = PL_{fr}(d_o) + 10\,\alpha\,log_{10}\left(\frac{d}{d_o}\right) \qquad (2)$$

where $PL_{fr}(d_o)$ is the free space path loss at a reference distance d_o from the transmitter. Hence, a Unit Disk model adds both an analytical and an experimental basis to the determination of large-scale path loss. Typical values of α range from $1.6 - 1.8$ for Indoor LOS, $4 - 6$ for Indoor NLOS, and $3 - 5$ for Dense Urban environments [15]. Path loss, however, is still uniform in different directions at the same distance from the transmitter, i.e. it is isotropic. This simple path loss model does not capture the radio channel randomness in scenarios as complex as those shown in Fig. 2. However, it serves as a reasonable choice for a comparative analysis of the radio propagation models.

3.2 Log-normal Shadowing Model

By considering a probabilistic distribution of path losses, the Log-normal Shadowing propagation model provides a reasonable trade-off between the complexity and accuracy of a propagation model. It is an extension of the Unit Disk model. The path loss at a given distance from the transmitter follows a Log-normal probability density function (PDF) with a mean given by the deterministic Unit Disk model of Eq. 2 [15]:

$$PL(d) = PL_{fr}(d_o) + 10\,\alpha\,log_{10}\left(\frac{d}{d_o}\right) + \chi_{sf} \qquad (3)$$

where χ_{sf} is a random variable that accounts for shadowing due to obstacles. The PDF of χ_{sf} ($f_{\chi_{sf}}(x)$) in dB is:

$$f_{\chi_{sf}}(x) = \frac{1}{\sqrt{2\pi}\sigma_{sf}} \exp\left(\frac{-x^2}{2\sigma_{sf}^2}\right) \qquad (4)$$

where σ_{sf} is the shadow fading standard deviation. In the next section, we statistically determine σ_{sf} and α from part of the measurement data that is used for parameterization of the path loss models. Log-normal shadowing models are actively used for network level research. The authors of [2] consider the impact of shadow fading at the physical layer for the analysis of network connectivity.

3.3 Volcano Indoor Multi-Wall Model

The Volcano Indoor Multi-Wall propagation model is based on the Cost231 Multi-Walls Multi-Floors propagation model [4] which was designed to take into account the indoor building structure when calculating the path losses. Since the channel measurements were performed on a single floor of the building, we currently do not take into consideration the floor-to-floor propagation scenario supported by the Cost231 model. The formula for the Cost231 model (without multi-floor specific components) is:

$$PL(d) = L_{FSL} + L_c + \sum_{i=1}^{I} k_{wi}\,L_{wi} \qquad (5)$$

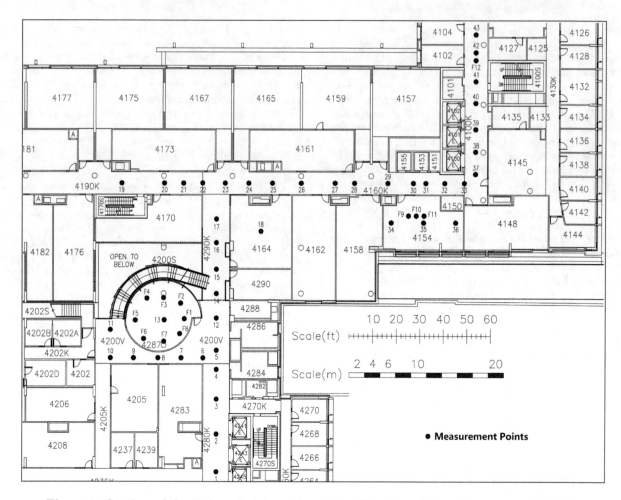

Figure 2: Section of the Bahen Building Floor Plan Showing all the Measurement Points

where L_{FSL} is the path loss calculated using Eq. 2 and L_c is an adjustable constant loss which is determined from measurement data. To account for the walls in the building, I represents the number of wall materials that exist in the building, k_{wi} is the number of the walls made from the ith material that exist along the transmission path between the transmitter and receiver, and L_{wi} is the loss associated with the signal passing through a wall made of the ith material. Determination of various parameters in Eq. 5 is done through the calibration of the Volcano model using the tuning portion of the measurement data. More details about this process are given in Section 4.1. Since the propagation environment under consideration (shown in Fig. 2) does not result in significant multipath reflections due to the inherent building construction (see Section 2.2), the 3D ray tracing capabilities of the Volcano model are not employed. However, the ray tracing has been shown to conform well with actual measurements performed in an environment rich in metallic structures [6].

3.4 WINNER II Stochastic Channel Model

It is a geometry based stochastic channel model in which channel parameters are determined stochastically based on statistical distributions extracted from field measurements. A wide variety of propagation scenarios can be modelled with its generic approach to radio channel parameteriza-tion, such as: Indoor Office, Indoor-to-Outdoor, Outdoor-to-Indoor, Urban Macro/Microcell and Rural Macrocell to name a few. Statistical distributions are defined for temporal and spatial parameters which include delay spread, angle spread and shadow fading. Channel realizations for indoor and outdoor environments can be generated by using a different set of channel parameters that are specific to a particular scenario. Path loss at a distance d from the transmitter is modelled with the following general equation [7]:

$$PL(d) = A \, log_{10}(d) + B + C \, log_{10}\left(\frac{f_c}{5.0}\right) + X \quad (6)$$

where A is a fitting parameter that includes the path loss exponent, B is the y-intercept on the scatter plot of Path Loss versus Distance on a Log-Log scale, C is a path loss frequency dependence parameter, f_c is system frequency in GHz, and X is an environment specific term that accounts for wall attenuations in NLOS scenarios. Based on extensive measurement campaigns and literature survey performed as part of the WINNER II project [7], parameters of Eq. 6 are quantified for LOS and NLOS Indoor Office environment:

$$PL'_{LOS}(d) = 18.7 \, log_{10}(d) + 46.8 + 20 \, log_{10}\left(\frac{f_c}{5.0}\right) \quad (7a)$$

$$PL_{LOS}(d) = PL'_{LOS}(d) + \chi_{LOS,sf} \quad (7b)$$

where $\chi_{LOS,sf}$ is the shadow fading parameter with $\sigma_{LOS,sf} = 3$. For the NLOS scenario:

$$PL'_{NLOS}(d) = 36.8\,log_{10}(d) + 43.8 + 20\,log_{10}\left(\frac{f_c}{5.0}\right) + X \tag{8a}$$

$$PL_{NLOS}(d) = PL'_{NLOS}(d) + \chi_{NLOS,sf} \tag{8b}$$

where $\chi_{NLOS,sf}$ has a $\sigma_{NLOS,sf} = 4$. The wall attenuation factor is $X = 5(n_w - 1)$ (assuming the majority of the rooms are composed of light walls). Here $n_w = \lfloor \frac{d}{10} \rfloor$ is the number of walls between a transmitter and a receiver, d meters apart. Equations 7b and 8b are valid for $d > 3$ m. For $1 < d < 3$ m, free space path loss is assumed with $\alpha = 2$. The probability of a LOS connection between a transmitter and a receiver is a function of the distance d (in meters) between them:

$$p_{LOS} = \begin{cases} 1 & \text{if } d \leq 2.5 \text{ m} \\ 1 - 0.9(1 - (1.24 - 0.61log_{10}(d))^3)^{\frac{1}{3}} & \text{if } d > 2.5 \text{ m} \end{cases} \tag{9}$$

Finally, using Eqs. 7b, 8b and 9, a weighted path loss is computed, considering the possibilities of both LOS and NLOS conditions at an arbitrary distance from the transmitter in a given propagation scenario:

$$PL(d) = p_{LOS}\,PL_{LOS}(d) + (1 - p_{LOS})\,PL_{NLOS}(d) \tag{10}$$

The WINNER II channel model can be applied to wireless systems operating in the 2 to 6 GHz frequency range with upto 100 MHz of RF bandwidth.

4. RESULTS

4.1 Parameter Estimation

As mentioned in Section 2.2, 142 channel measurements were performed at the measurement sites. The data was categorized into a tuning set and a performance evaluation set with 71 measurements each. The tuning set was used for the parameterization of the Unit Disk and Log-normal models, and also for the calibration of the Volcano Indoor Multi-Wall model. Channel parameters of the WINNER II model are not subject to tuning as they have already been extracted from extensive measurement campaigns and literature surveys on channel modelling [7].

For the Unit Disk and Log-normal models, this step involves fitting a linear regression curve on the tuning data to obtain an estimation of the path loss exponent. This estimation is then used for the computation of the standard deviation of the given sample size. Equation 2 is of the form: $\hat{y} = mx + c$. Here, $\hat{y}$ is the estimated path loss, $c = PL_{fr}(d_o)$, $m = \alpha$ and $x = 10\,log_{10}\left(\frac{d}{d_o}\right)$. A minimum mean square estimation (MMSE) of m is of the form: $\min\{E\{(y - \hat{y})^2\}\}$, where y is the path loss from the tuning data. Considering c to be a constant (free space loss at a reference distance of 1 m), m can be written as [8]:

$$m = \frac{E\{xy\} - cE\{x\}}{E\{x^2\}} \tag{11}$$

Finally, the unbiased estimation of the standard deviation for a sample size of n (the size of the tuning set) is:

$$\sigma = \sqrt{\frac{1}{(n-1)} \sum_{i=1}^{n} (y_i - \hat{y}_i)^2} \tag{12}$$

Figure 3 shows the results of this estimation on the tuning data. We classify the propagation scenarios on two basis: (1) Based on the distance between a transmitter and a receiver. (2) Based on LOS/NLOS conditions between them. As can be seen, the path loss exponent increases with increasing distances from the transmitter. Here, $\alpha = 2.19$ for $d \leq 10$ m as compared to 3.30 for $d > 25$ m. This is expected due to the inherent characteristics of a complex indoor environment. A higher d implies a higher probability of a NLOS scenario, which is known to have a higher path loss exponent. This is also evident from Fig. 3. The NLOS measurements have an $\alpha = 3.21$ which is higher then the α value for LOS measurements which was 1.77. Similar trends are also observed for the standard deviation estimations. Overall, considering the data as a whole, a path loss exponent of 2.92 and a standard deviation of 10.27 are obtained.

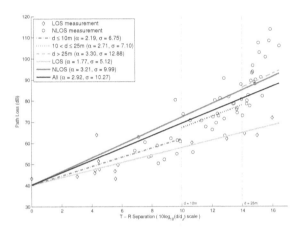

Figure 3: Scatter plots showing measurement points on a Log-Log scale along with the linear regression estimation curves for different propagation classes.

Referring to Fig. 3, the number of tuning measurement points belonging to the respective propagation classes are: 23 for $d \leq 10$ m, 25 for 10 m $< d \leq 25$ m, 23 for $d > 25$ m, and 15 for LOS measurements versus 56 for NLOS measurements. Based on this observation, weighted and average path loss exponents and standard deviations are calculated as shown in Table 2. The α for the LOS/NLOS (Weighted) case is close to that for All measurements. The α for Distance (Weighted) and Distance (Average) cases is the same. The σ for Distance (Average) is in between the σ for the Distance (Weighted) and the LOS/NLOS (Weighted) cases. The α and σ for the LOS/NLOS (Average) case are unreasonable as the NLOS measurements significantly outnumber the LOS measurements. We therefore use the highlighted channel parameter values for a comparative analysis of the path loss models.

Turning now to the Volcano Indoor Multi-Wall model, tuning is performed by first determining the types and number of walls encountered along the path between each Tx-Rx pair in the tuning data set. These values are then used to create a series of linear equations which are used to solve for the unknown parameters. A least square approach is taken to solve the system of linear equations. After calibration with the tuning set, L_c in Eq. 5 was -0.89 and $L_{FSL} = 40.225 + 19.055log_{10}(d)$ (both in dB), noting that $d_o = 1$ m and the frequency used was 2.45 GHz. Addition-

Table 2: Channel Parameters for Different Scenarios

	α	σ
All	**2.92**	**10.27**
Distance (Average)	**2.73**	**8.91**
Distance (Weighted)	2.73	8.86
LOS/NLOS (Average)	2.49	7.55
LOS/NLOS (Weighted)	2.90	8.96

ally a number of loss values (in dB) were derived for the various building wall materials.

4.2 Performance Evaluation

Based on the parameters found in Section 4.1, seven path loss models were evaluated. The models were the standard Free Space model with $\alpha = 2$, the Unit Disk model with $\alpha = 2.73$ and 2.92, the Log-normal model with the same α's as the Unit Disk model with their respective σ values of 8.91 and 10.27, the Volcano Indoor Multi-Wall model, and the WINNER II Stochastic channel model. These models were then used to estimate the path losses for the 71 performance evaluation measurements. Figure 4 shows the results of the 7 models along with the actual measured path losses for all the measurements. Measurements were assigned a Measurement Number sequentially in order of increasing distance between the transmitter and receiver. This was done as some measurements were at the same distance and others had distances very close to one another. Plotting based on distance would have caused overlap and congested the graph, not allowing the trends to be seen.

From Fig. 4a it can be observed that the Free Space model performs well at shorter distances (lower measurement numbers), but at longer distances (higher measurement numbers), it generates path losses that are much less than the actual values. Both Unit Disk models consistently produce higher path losses at shorter distances but perform much better at the longest distances. Figure 4b shows that the Log-normal models generally result in higher values of path loss until the largest distances are reached. Although, due to the randomness introduced by shadow fading, they occasionally predict results close to the observed values. The Volcano and WINNER II models are fairly consistent in their path loss computations within a reasonable error margin for all distances. Note that there are a couple outliers in the Volcano predictions at the highest distances (highest measurement numbers). This is primarily due to the fact that the building model used was an approximation to the actual building layout and some of the minor variances in wall thickness and materials were not accounted for.

The results of Fig. 4 can be explained by examining Fig. 3 and noting the following. At shorter distances, the propagation will be highly LOS and thus α will be close to 2 and there will be limited obstacles in the transmission path. At larger values of distance, α increases and the propagation paths are predominantly NLOS. To summarize the variations in performance of the models in an empirical way, Table 3 provides a summary of the Mean Error, μ_ϵ, and the Standard Deviation of the Error, σ_ϵ, in dB, between the actual and the computed path losses for the 7 models. Additionally, the Root Mean Square Error (RMSE) is also shown.

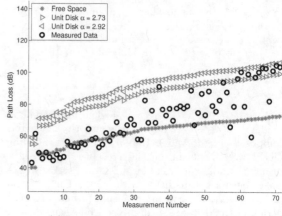

(a) Free Space and Unit Disk Models

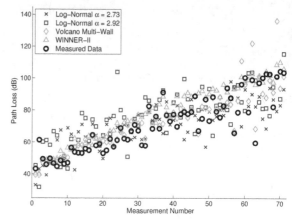

(b) Log-normal, Volcano and Winner-II Models

Figure 4: Predicted Path Losses and Actual Path Losses for All Measurement Points

Table 3: Error Performance Metrics of the Path Loss Models

Models / Error Metric	μ_ϵ (dB)	σ_ϵ (dB)	RMSE (dB)
Free Space ($\alpha = 2$)	-8.60	11.58	14.36
Unit Disk ($\alpha = 2.73$)	14.30	10.21	17.52
Unit Disk ($\alpha = 2.92$)	20.26	9.96	22.54
Log-normal ($\alpha = 2.73$, $\sigma = 8.91$)	**-0.71**	13.02	12.95
Log-normal ($\alpha = 2.92$, $\sigma = 10.27$)	5.25	15.22	16.00
Volcano Indoor Multi-Wall	1.65	**8.00**	**8.12**
WINNER II Stochastic	6.77	8.65	10.94

As can be observed, the Log-normal model using $\alpha = 2.73$ and $\sigma = 8.91$ has the lowest μ_ϵ but has one of the highest σ_ϵ thus offsetting the benefit of a low μ_ϵ. The Volcano Indoor Multi-Wall model has the lowest σ_ϵ and RMSE values of all the models. The WINNER II Stochastic model has the next best values of σ_ϵ and RMSE although it has a much higher μ_ϵ then the Volcano Indoor Multi-Wall model. From these observations, the Volcano Indoor Multi-Wall and WINNER II Stochastic models provide the best estimation of the actual path losses in the Bahen building. The performance of the Volcano Indoor Multi-Wall model could be even further improved by using an even more accurate building model of the Bahen building.

For example, if one were to remove the three outliers in the predicted values from Volcano (namely measurements 59, 62 and 69), the values of μ_ϵ, σ_ϵ and RMSE would be reduced to 0.86, 6.52 and 6.53 respectively. However, if such precise behavior of the propagation environment is not required, the WINNER II model can be a good alternative as it does not require model tuning or detailed building information.

4.3 Application Scenario: Network Connectivity Analysis

An immediate application of the characterization of a radio propagation environment is in the network planning and dimensioning phases, performed before the actual network deployment. In the context of wireless ad hoc and sensor networks, a fully connected network is a fundamental requirement for all network operations. Further, maintaining k-connectivity $(k > 1)$ is equally important from a fault-tolerance or network resilience perspective. A network is k-connected if there are at least k node-disjoint paths between all pairs of nodes in the network. Wireless engineers therefore seek to determine the minimum network parameters that ensure such connectivity requirements.

By means of Monte Carlo simulations [12] performed using OPNET modeler [13], we qualitatively analyze the average network behavior in terms of probability of 2-connectivity for a range of transmission power levels. Sensor nodes are distributed in the deployment region shown in Fig. 2 following a Poisson Point Process (PPP) [5]. On average, 14 nodes are deployed in 691 m^2 of the deployment region, i.e. we consider a node density of 0.02 nodes/m^2. 250 spatial realizations are performed to ensure 95% confidence in the obtained probabilities, with a 0.1 absolute error tolerance. Receiver sensitivity of the nodes was set to -80.0 dBm, i.e. a link between a pair of nodes is possible only if the received power at both terminals is ≥ -80 dBm. For commercially available IEEE 802.15.4 based radios, this received power threshold is in the range of -95 dBm to -80 dBm. The sensor network is homogeneous in the sense that all nodes transmit at the same (minimum) power setting that ensures 2-connectivity for a given spatial realization. Figure 5 shows one such realization of a PPP for Volcano-based path losses between the nodes. As can be seen, the connectivity of the network is 2 as the removal of nodes "7" and "15" disconnects the network.

Based on Table 3, the Free Space, Log-normal with $\alpha = 2.73$, $\sigma = 8.91$, Volcano and WINNER II models are considered for the connectivity analysis. Figure 6 shows the results of the simulations for these path loss models. Under different radio channel models, the power levels ensuring a fixed probability of network 2-connectivity are different. For a 90% probability of the network to be 2-connected, and considering Volcano-based connectivity probabilities as a benchmark, a 13.96 times increase in the power level based on free space path loss is required to more realistically model the minimum transmission power level for this simplistic path loss model (by first computing the mW equivalents of the dBm values of power levels for different path loss models for a 0.9 probability of network 2-connectivity).

A 3 times increase for the Log-normal model and a 0.4 times decrease in the power level for WINNER II model is

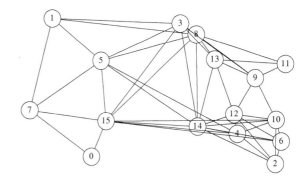

Figure 5: One spatial realization of a PPP resulting in 16 nodes in the network with -8 dBm homogeneous transmit power levels

required. Such scaling factors can facilitate quantification of power levels under asymptotic conditions [21] and therefore bridge the gap between theoretical characterization of network parameters based on purely deterministic path loss models and those observed under actual channel conditions. On the other hand, from a topology control perspective, significant power savings can be achieved by allowing the sensor nodes, under free space channel model, to transmit at -15 dBm power setting, as opposed to the maximum power level of 0 dBm, since both levels ensure almost same probabilities of 2-connectivity.

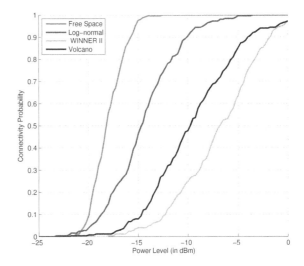

Figure 6: Probability of Network 2-Connectivity for All Path Loss Models

5. CONCLUSIONS

It is observed that the radio propagation models that make simplistic assumptions about the actual channel conditions do not accurately capture the radio channel randomness that is inherent in complex propagation environments. More accurate modelling of a radio channel is therefore necessary, both for the theoretical characterization of various network parameters as well as for the analysis and design of practical WSN protocols such as topology control and indoor localization. In this work, we first characterize the channel parameters for different propagation scenarios based on field measurements performed in an indoor office environment. Path loss exponents and standard deviations increase with increasing distances from the transmitter. Further, these parameters are lower for LOS scenarios as compared to NLOS scenarios. Based on the characterized channel parameters, we then take the measurement data as a benchmark for performance evaluation to investigate the degree of accuracy of the path loss models. Volcano Indoor Multi-Wall and WINNER II Stochastic channel models provided the best estimation of the actual path losses with root mean square error of 8.12 dB and 10.94 dB respectively. Usage of these two models will depend on the required accuracy of the path loss estimations as well as on the availability of detailed information of the indoor environment. A network connectivity analysis was also preformed to demonstrate the impact the choice of the physical layer model has on the network backbone construction. From the 2-connected network example used, it could be seen that the more simplistic channel models greatly underestimated the transmit power required to provide the same probability of network 2-connectivity. The analysis also shows that significant power savings can be achieved by allowing sensor nodes to operate at lower transmission power levels, without compromising network connectivity. This has direct implication on the problem of constructing an energy-efficient communication backbone for wireless sensor networks.

6. ACKNOWLEDGMENTS

This work has been supported by an Ontario Research Fund - Research Excellence (ORF-RE) grant.

7. REFERENCES

[1] C. A. Balanis. *Antenna Theory: Analysis and Design.* Wiley-Interscience, 3 edition, Apr. 2005.

[2] C. Bettstetter and C. Hartmann. Connectivity of wireless multihop networks in a shadow fading environment. *Wirel. Netw.*, 11(5):571–579, Sept. 2005.

[3] O. Chipara, G. Hackmann, C. Lu, et al. Practical modeling and prediction of radio coverage of indoor sensor networks. In *Proceedings of the 9th ACM/IEEE International Conference on Information Processing in Sensor Networks*, IPSN '10, pages 339–349, New York, NY, USA, 2010. ACM.

[4] E. Damosso, L. Correia, and European Commission. DGX III "Telecommunications, Information Market, and Exploitation of Research.". *COST Action 231: Digital Mobile Radio Towards Future Generation Systems: Final Report.* EUR (series). European Commission, 1999.

[5] M. Haenggi, J. G. Andrews, F. Baccelli, et al. Stochastic geometry and random graphs for the analysis and design of wireless networks. *IEEE J. Sel. Areas Commun.*, 27(7):1029–1046, Sept. 2009.

[6] H. Kdouh, H. Farhat, T. Tenoux, et al. Double directional characterisation of radio wave propagation through metallic watertight doors on board ships. *Electronics Letters*, 48(6):307–309, March 2012.

[7] P. Kyösti, J. Meinilä, L. Hentilä, et al. WINNER II channel models. Technical report, EC FP6, September 2007.

[8] A. Leon-Garcia. *Probability, Statistics, and Random Processes For Electrical Engineering.* Prentice Hall, 3 edition, Jan. 2008.

[9] G. Mao. Research on wireless multi-hop networks: Current state and challenges. In *2012 International Conference on Computing, Networking and Communications (ICNC)*, pages 593–598, Jan 2012.

[10] R. McNally, M. Barnes, and D. K. Arvind. A pragmatic approach to wireless channel simulation in built environments. In *2011 IEEE Workshop on Principles of Advanced and Distributed Simulation (PADS)*, pages 1–8, June 2011.

[11] D. Miorandi, E. Altman, and G. Alfano. The impact of channel randomness on coverage and connectivity of ad hoc and sensor networks. *IEEE Trans. Wireless Commun.*, 7(3):1062–1072, March 2008.

[12] F. N. Najm. Statistical estimation of the signal probability in VLSI circuits. Technical Report UILU-ENG-93-2211, DAC-37, University of Illinios at Urbana-Champaign, Coordinated Science Lab, April 1993.

[13] OPNET Technologies. OPNET modeler. http://www.opnet.com/solutions/network_rd/modeler.html, 2012.

[14] D. Puccinelli and M. Haenggi. Multipath fading in wireless sensor networks: Measurements and interpretation. In *Proceedings of the 2006 International Conference on Wireless Communications and Mobile Computing*, IWCMC '06, pages 1039–1044, New York, NY, USA, 2006. ACM.

[15] T. S. Rappaport. *Wireless Communications: Principles and Practice.* Prentice Hall, 2 edition, Jan. 2002.

[16] P. Santi. *Topology Control in Wireless Ad Hoc and Sensor Networks.* John Wiley and Sons, Ltd, 2005.

[17] SIRADEL. SIRADEL Volcano Propagation Models Website. http://www.siradel.com/1/volcano-software.aspx, 2014.

[18] L. Tang, K.-C. Wang, Y. Huang, and F. Gu. Channel characterization and link quality assessment of IEEE 802.15.4-compliant radio for factory environments. *IEEE Trans. Ind. Informat.*, 3(2):99–110, May 2007.

[19] University of Toronto. University of Toronto Space Inventory / Building Plans Website. http://osm.utoronto.ca/inv.html, 2014.

[20] S. Wyne, A. Singh, F. Tufvesson, and A. Molisch. A statistical model for indoor office wireless sensor channels. *IEEE Trans. Wireless Commun.*, 8(8):4154–4164, August 2009.

[21] H. Zhang and J. C. Hou. Asymptotic critical total power for k-connectivity of wireless networks. *IEEE/ACM Trans. Netw.*, 16(2):347–358, Apr. 2008.

[22] G. Zhou, T. He, S. Krishnamurthy, and J. A. Stankovic. Models and solutions for radio irregularity in wireless sensor networks. *ACM Trans. Sen. Netw.*, 2(2):221–262, May 2006.

TR-MAC: An Energy-Efficient MAC Protocol Exploiting Transmitted Reference Modulation for Wireless Sensor Networks

Sarwar Morshed
University of Twente
The Netherlands
s.morshed@utwente.nl

Geert Heijenk
University of Twente
The Netherlands
geert.heijenk@utwente.nl

ABSTRACT

The medium access control (MAC) protocol determines the energy consumption of a wireless sensor node by specifying the listening, transmitting or sleeping time. Therefore MAC protocols play an important role in minimizing the overall energy consumption in a typical wireless sensor network (WSN). Using transmitted reference (TR) modulation in the underlying physical layer opens up new possibilities and challenges to be investigated in the upper MAC layer. Hence this paper presents a new energy-efficient MAC protocol, called TR-MAC, to exploit all the benefits provided by the TR modulation in the physical layer while minimizing the drawbacks. TR-MAC enables both transmitter-driven and receiver-driven communication in the WSN, allows a pair of nodes to use individual frequency offsets for multiple access, and is capable of achieving fast synchronization in the receiver to reduce energy consumption. In short, TR-MAC is an energy-driven MAC layer communication protocol for asynchronous low data rate applications that enables nodes to adapt their duty cycle based on the available energy in the node.

Categories and Subject Descriptors

C.2.1 [**Computer-communication Networks**]: : Network Architecture and Design-Wireless communication

Keywords

WSN; TR modulation; energy-efficiency; energy-driven; MAC protocol; TR-MAC

1. INTRODUCTION

The Medium Access Control (MAC) protocol in wireless sensor networks is responsible for creating a network infrastructure with addressing and providing a channel access mechanism for network nodes to effectively communicate

MSWiM'14, September 21–26, 2014, Montreal, QC, Canada.
Copyright is held by the owner/author(s). Publication rights licensed to ACM.
ACM 978-1-4503-3030-5/14/09 ...$15.00.
http://dx.doi.org/10.1145/2641798.2641804.

in a shared wireless communication medium. The physical layer underneath the MAC layer deals with the modulation of the data signal to the reference signal and controls the channel access mechanism of the shared communication medium for multiple nodes. Transmitted Reference (TR) modulation [11] is a novel modulation technique in the physical layer that transmits the reference signal together with the modulated signal. Minimizing energy consumption in WSNs is always a big challenge in the MAC layer and this problem maximizes for a modulation technique like TR modulation that takes more energy burden in the transmitter side. Interestingly, TR modulation provides many lucrative advantages for the receiver and all together offers many opportunities to be exploited in the upper MAC layer.

The transmitter using TR modulation sends both the modulated and unmodulated signal with a known frequency offset [14], as presented in Figure 1. Thereby transmitter consumes more power than a traditional modulation technique but this approach enables the receiver some possibilities to reduce the power consumption in the network. Firstly, the receiver can restore the original signal quickly by correlating the received signal with a delayed version of itself using the same frequency offset since all multi-path components contain identically distorted pulses with consistent mutual delay. Secondly, the receiver can achieve faster synchronization consuming less energy without using rake receiver technique, channel state information or power-hungry stable oscillators. Thirdly, multiple frequency offsets can be used as link identifiers for implicit addressing and provide more flexibility to communicate simultaneously. Therefore, TR modulation can be a potential candidate for asynchronous low data rate communication in wireless sensor networks offering additional flexibility to the MAC layer.

In this paper we investigate the possibilities to optimally exploit the characteristics of TR modulation at the MAC layer for WSNs by extending a new energy-efficient MAC layer protocol called TR-MAC. The presented results show that TR-MAC protocol gives better energy consumption than two other reference MAC layer protocols. Also TR-MAC becomes energy-efficient by successfully minimizing the four major sources of energy wastage [26], namely collision, idle listening, overhearing, and control packet overhead.

The contributions of this paper are as follows: (1) we extend a new MAC protocol, TR-MAC, to exploit all the advantages provided by the TR modulation technique while minimizing its drawbacks; (2) we complete the mathematical

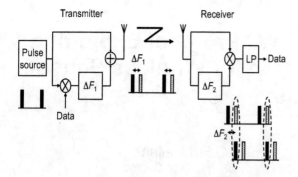

Figure 1: Transmitted Reference modulation

model of TR-MAC, introduced in [15], from the perspective of energy consumption for a single pair of nodes encompassing all possible states and also derived the analytical model of two similar reference MAC protocols; and (3) we evaluate the energy consumption and show that TR-MAC in combination with TR modulation works favorably over similar reference protocols.

This paper is organized as follows: Section 2 presents the related work, Section 3 presents the TR-MAC protocol design, Section 4 describes the mathematical modeling of TR-MAC and two other reference protocols and Section 5 analyzes and evaluates the results. Finally, Section 6 provides our conclusions and proposes future work.

2. RELATED WORK

MAC protocols in WSNs have been key focus of much research [3], specially in the context of energy-efficiency [5]. The MAC protocols for WSNs in the literature can be classified mainly into five categories: reservation-based scheduled protocols [23], protocols with common active period [26][22], asynchronous preamble sampling protocols [17][8], hybrid protocols [18] and MAC protocols with wake-up radios [19]. Several MAC protocols are also standardized like IEEE 802.15.4 [1]. Since TR modulation has a power penalty at the transmitter side, energy efficient MAC protocols essentially became our research interest. After extensive analysis the authors of [5] claimed that asynchronous preamble sampling protocols are the most energy efficient category of MAC layer protocols. Therefore we focus on preamble sampling protocols in our research.

The asynchronous preamble sampling MAC protocols enable a node in a sensor network to sleep most of its time minimizing its duty cycle, only requiring short wake ups to sample the channel for activity. Thus each node of the network can asynchronously choose its sleeping and listening time independent of all other nodes in the network. To enable successful communication the transmitter has to precede the data packet with a preamble packet of duration at least two consecutive channel sampling times of the receiver, known as sampling or check interval. During its sampling time the receiver continues listening if it detects any activity in the channel; otherwise returns back to sleep. Thus preamble sampling protocols are very suitable for low data rate asynchronous applications since this strategy enables the nodes to be energy efficient without any network-wide synchronization and management.

The preamble sampling protocols try to reduce the preamble duration mainly in three ways: protocols with packetization, schedule learning by piggybacking synchronization information, and adaptive duty cycles [5]. The protocols with packetization enables the transmitter to replace the long preamble by short preamble packet bursts with destination address. As a result, the target receiver successfully receives the data if it receives a single preamble packet, whereas a non-target receiver goes back to sleep after receiving a single preamble packet. Alternatively, the transmitter can send a preamble packet, listen for acknowledgement from the receiver and can continue to repeat this cycle to shorten its preamble length by an acknowledgement from the intended receiver when it wakes up and receives the preamble. However, preamble length adaptation for future transmissions and acknowledgement after successful data transmission are missing in these kind of protocols. X-MAC [4], SpeckMAC-B [24], ContikiMAC [7] are the most common packetized MAC protocols.

Alternatively, some preamble sampling MAC protocols learn the schedule of the next wake up time of another node using piggybacking synchronization information, hence reduce the preamble length using receiver-driven approaches. WiseMAC [8], CSMA-MPS [13], TrawMAC [27], SyncWUF [20] are examples of this category. However, receiver-driven protocols are unsuitable for broadcast traffic because one transmitter might have to adapt its preamble multiple times for its multiple neighbors. Furthermore, these protocols have to transmit the longest possible length of preamble for the first time communication.

Finally, some preamble sampling protocols adapt their duty cycle based on requests from the neighborhood, e.g., BEAM [2], traffic load, e.g., MaxMAC [16], or topology information, e.g., EA-ALPL [12]. However, these duty cycle adaptive protocols do not adapt their network operation based on energy availability on individual nodes and target only specific application scenarios.

MAC protocols with sleep and wake up schedules often need to manage clock drift and maintain timing synchronization to align transmitter and receiver wake up time. Regular communication ensures global timing synchronization within the network, however, low duty cycle WSNs allow nodes to have long sleeping period with less communication [25]. Thus the clocks in the transmitter and receiver may drift apart in long absence of communication and that depends mostly on the time since last communication. Many methods are proposed to maintain synchronization, for example using frequent resynchronization by transmitting more packets [10], using guard times [21], and using packets arrival time for reference broadcast synchronization [9]. However, these approaches consume a significant amount of energy.

3. TR-MAC PROTOCOL DESIGN

We propose a new energy-efficient protocol, TR-MAC, that will exploit the opportunities provided by TR modulation and at the same time will mitigate the transmit power penalty of TR modulation. The TR-MAC transmitter packetizes the preamble since transmitting is costly with TR modulation due to the fact of transmitting both the modulated and reference signal. The transmitter using TR modulation in the early state transmits a small preamble, then listens for a potential acknowledgement from the receiver

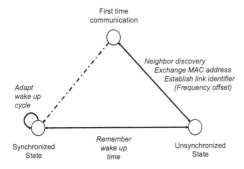

Figure 2: TR-MAC: Three states

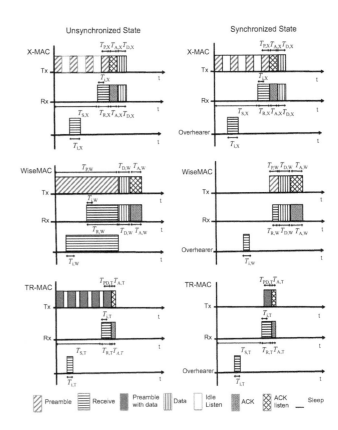

Figure 3: TR-MAC with two reference protocols

and continue this cycle until it receives and acknowledgement from the receiver. As a result the transmitter has the opportunity to shorten its preamble length from the maximum duration of two consecutive sampling intervals of the receiver, hence minimizing the energy at the transmitter.

TR-MAC saves energy on the receiving side by sleeping most of the time, only waking up to detect any activity in the channel to shorten its idle listening. Furthermore, TR-MAC receiver can detect very small preamble since TR modulation has fast synchronization capability. TR-MAC takes this advantage and appends small data packets ranging from very few bytes with the preamble, thus efficiently reducing the control packet overhead. Therefore preamble-listen cycles will be referred to as data-listen cycles from now on in this paper. The transmitter will indicate the receiver to continue listening using a single bit if larger data packets follow the initial small ones, as in WiseMAC [8]. Also the TR-MAC protocol solves the critical multiple access issue using individual frequency offsets for a pair of nodes, a key advantage offered by the underlying TR modulation. Thus collision can be avoided as future communication will take place in different virtual channels using frequency offsets, hence reduces the expense of costly retransmissions.

The newly proposed TR-MAC protocol has three states to have better capability to adapt to the situation, namely (1) first time communication; (2) unsynchronized state; and (3) synchronized state, as shown in Figure 2. In the beginning of operation, a node knows nothing about the system and its neighbors, this state is referred as first time communication state. In this state, a node transmits data-listen cycles in the default frequency offset if it has data to transmit. Other nodes in the system sleep most of the time and listens to the default frequency offset periodically for any data transmission, like other preamble sampling protocols. If the intended receiver receives a single data packet, then it responds with an acknowledgement indicating a successful transmission. In this state, one pair of nodes discover each other, exchange the full MAC address, and establish a link identifier by agreeing upon the frequency offset to be used for future communications, thus proceed to the next unsynchronized state.

In unsynchronized state the transmitter transmits data-listen cycles at the previously agreed upon frequency offset until it receives an acknowledgement from the receiver as shown in Figure 3. The receiver can derive the link identifier from the frequency offset and preamble part of the data packet. Potential overhearers can return to sleep just after detecting the preamble part of the data packet and decoding the link identifier. The acknowledgement packet sent from the receiver contains the receiver's next desired wake up time indicating whether its future check interval will be a default one, or a half or double of the previous one. The transmitter will transmit the same time back to the receiver if it agrees with the proposed time, meaning that the transmitter will follow the receiver. We refer this approach of communication as receiver-driven for this time instance. However, the transmitter proposes a new time if it does not agree with the previously proposed time. The receiver transmits the same time back in next acknowledgement if it agrees with the transmitter. We refer this approach as transmitter-driven communication as the receiver now follows the transmitter. Thus the nodes themselves decide whether future communication will be transmitter-driven or receiver-driven, hence providing enormous flexibilities to exploit in the upper layers. In addition, one node having less energy can request other node to follow its lead. A request to follow is considered urgent if the node sends the same time twice without agreeing with other node's proposal. Afterwards the protocol advances to its final synchronized state.

In synchronized state, the transmitter and receiver pair wake up to communicate in the previously agreed time instance in a known frequency offset. Thus the transmitter can optimally minimize the data-listen cycle length to as minimum as possible and the receiver can minimize its listening duration, as shown in Figure 3. Consequently the nodes can communicate in a very energy-efficient manner in this state. However, at low data rates the energy consumption between a pair of nodes sometimes may be more than expected because of the potential clock drifts between the pair of nodes and the last time of communication. We also provide an optimization technique in the synchronized state for TR-MAC to minimize the effect of clock drift that will be explained later in Section 4. But there might be situations when operating in synchronized state would be costly from energy perspective, then a pair of nodes can roll back to the unsynchronized state to minimize energy consumption.

Two similar MAC protocols, X-MAC [4] and WiseMAC [8] are also presented in Figure 3 with their behavior in corresponding states as TR-MAC. The X-MAC protocol always work in the same way where the transmitter sends packetized preamble and listen cycles waiting for the acknowledgement from the receiver. X-MAC has high control packet overhead since it does not adapt its preamble-listen duration, thus it does not have synchronized state. Also X-MAC does not send any acknowledgement after successful data packet transmission.

Alternatively, WiseMAC protocol has unsynchronized and synchronized states where the transmitter adapts the preamble length in the later state depending on remembering the receiver's next periodic wake up time. In synchronized state WiseMAC efficiently manages clock drifts and minimizes collision using small preambles. However, the potential receiver and the overhearers has to listen the complete preamble for the first time communication before receiving any data, which is costly for per packet overhead in low traffic condition. Furthermore, WiseMAC have to use long preambles for broadcasting instead of short ones and does not adapt duty cycles depending on the changing traffic pattern. The receiver-driven approach of WiseMAC makes a potential receiver collision-prone if many transmitter follows its next wake up and start transmitting at the same time, then WiseMAC has to add a medium reservation preamble in front of the wake up preamble [8].

The possibility of communication using transmitter-driven or receiver-driven technique provides some interesting opportunities to realize energy-efficient multi-hop communications at the network level. For instance, TR-MAC can offer an energy-efficient broadcasting approach by creating a ripple effect, where the transmitter instructs its first hop neighbors to follow its lead and those in turn instruct their respective neighbors to follow them: thus saving energy, increasing throughput and decreasing delay for broadcasting. Alternatively, a receiving node can instruct many transmitters to follow its duty cycle Furthermore, TR-MAC enables the nodes in the system to adapt their duty cycles based on available energy on the nodes, or traffic load or any other application requirement like increasing throughput or decreasing latency. For example, one node with less energy may request to sleep more to increase overall network lifetime, thus effectively shifting the energy burden to other nodes with more energy. As a result the newly proposed TR-MAC protocol is not only an energy-efficient protocol, rather effectively an energy-driven protocol.

4. TR-MAC PROTOCOL MODELING

We present mathematical modeling of TR-MAC for the total system with overhearers for both unsynchronized and synchronized states in terms of energy consumption per second. Moreover, we also present similar analytical models for X-MAC and WiseMAC for the previously mentioned scenarios to compare them with TR-MAC. The comparison results and analysis are presented in Section 5. We use comma separated subscript T, X and W to denote a symbol specific for TR-MAC, X-MAC and WiseMAC respectively. If the subscript is omitted, the symbol applies to multiple or all three MAC protocols.

A. Unsynchronized state:

Lets consider there are n nodes where one node will transmit, one node will listen and at most $(n-2)$ other nodes can be overhearing the communication. Also all the n nodes will have periodic listening. Therefore the general equation to compute energy consumption per second in unsynchronized state for all three protocols for the total system is given by

$$E_{\text{unsync}} = \lambda(E_{\text{Tx}}^{\text{unsync}} + E_{\text{Rx}}^{\text{unsync}} + (n-2)E_{\text{OH}}) + nE_{\text{PL}} \quad (1)$$

where E_{unsync} represents energy consumption of the total system, λ being the packet arrival rate, $E_{\text{Tx}}^{\text{unsync}}$ is energy to transmit a packet, $E_{\text{Rx}}^{\text{unsync}}$ is energy to receive a packet, E_{OH} is energy spent by the overhearers to receive the preamble and E_{PL} is energy for periodic listening. We model the energy to receive a packet by extending the periodic listen duration. The overhearers receive one iteration of the preamble and data part only, then sleep without sending any acknowledgement. The energy consumption in unsynchronized state for transmitting a packet, for receiving a packet, for periodic listening, and for overhearing are represented by Eq. 2, Eq. 3, Eq. 4 and Eq. 5 respectively

$$E_{\text{Tx,T}}^{\text{unsync}} = (\frac{1}{2}\frac{(T_{\text{S,T}} + T_{\text{P,T}})^2}{(T_{\text{i,T}} + T_{\text{S,T}})(T_{\text{PD,T}} + T_{\text{A,T}})} + 1) \\ * (P_{\text{Tx,T}}T_{\text{PD,T}} + P_{\text{Rx}}T_{\text{A,T}}), \quad (2)$$

$$E_{\text{Rx,T}}^{\text{unsync}} = P_{\text{Rx}}(\overline{T}_{\text{R,T}} - T_{\text{i,T}}) + P_{\text{Tx,T}}T_{\text{A,T}}, \quad (3)$$

$$E_{\text{PL}} = \frac{P_{\text{Rx}}T_{\text{i}} + P_{\text{S}}T_{\text{S}}}{T_{\text{S}} + T_{\text{i}}}, \quad (4)$$

$$E_{\text{OH}} = P_{\text{Rx}}(\overline{T}_{\text{R,T}} - T_{\text{i,T}}). \quad (5)$$

Here the TR-MAC data packet, $T_{\text{PD,T}}$, consists of 8 bits of preamble, $T_{\text{P,T}}$, 16 bits of header, T_{H}, followed by 32 bits of data, T_{Data}, thus having 56 bits. Also the sleeping time and power are represented by T_{S} and P_{S} respectively. Furthermore, $\overline{T}_{\text{R,T}}$ represents the expected extending listening duration. The check interval, T_{W}, here includes the sleeping time between two consecutive sampling intervals and one periodic listen cycle. The symbols and values are given in Table 1. The energy consumption and time for the transmitter-receiver turnarounds and vice-versa are much smaller compared to other values, thus are omitted from our modeling.

Table 1: System parameters

Sym.	Description	TR-MAC	X-MAC	WiseMAC
T_{P}	Preamble	8 bits	65 bits	T_{W}
T_{H}	Header	16 bits	16 bits	16 bits
T_{Data}	Data	32 bits	32 bits	32 bits
T_{D}	Data+header	48 bits	48 bits	48 bits
T_{A}	Ack.	24 bits	65 bits	80 bits
T_{i}	Periodic listen	40 bits	195 bits	8 bits
P_{Tx}	Tx power	2 mW	1 mW	1 mW
P_{Rx}	Rx power	1 mW	1 mW	1 mW

These equations for unsynchronized state are explained in [15] and are valid for at most one packet arrival per check interval duration.

B. Synchronized state:

In the synchronized state, a transmitter and receiver pair wake up at a previously agreed upon time to listen to a particular frequency offset. Even though the two communicating nodes try to wake up at a particular previously agreed upon time, yet there can be timing mismatch in waking up with respect to each other because of the respective clocks in those two nodes being drifted from the ideal depending upon the time since last communication. The total energy of the system in the synchronized state is calculated for a particular link without any overhearers and periodic listening since nodes are now synchronized and follow each others wake up time. Hence the total energy per second in synchronized state is given by

$$E_{\text{sync}} = \lambda(E[E_{\text{Tx,T}}^{\text{sync}}] + E[E_{\text{Rx,T}}^{\text{sync}}]) + nE_{PL} \qquad (6)$$

where $E_{\text{Tx,T}}^{\text{sync}}$ represents the expected energy to transmit a packet given by equation 7 and $E_{\text{Rx,T}}^{\text{sync}}$ represents the expected energy to receive a packet given by equation 8 respectively

$$E[E_{\text{Tx,T}}^{\text{sync}}] = \int_{d=d_{min}}^{d=d_{max}} P(D=d)\, E_{\text{Tx,T}}^{\text{sync}}|(D=d)\, \mathrm{d}d, \qquad (7)$$

$$E[E_{\text{Rx,T}}^{\text{sync}}] = \int_{d=d_{min}}^{d=d_{max}} P(D=d)\, E_{\text{Rx,T}}^{\text{sync}}|(D=d)\, \mathrm{d}d. \qquad (8)$$

The probability part of the previous two equations is derived from the possible clock difference between the transmitter and receiver's clock, represented by the random variable D with individual realization d. And the energy part calculates the amount of energy needed to transmit or receive a packet for individual clock difference. The equations to calculate the energy will be given in later part.

The main reason for difference between clocks of transmitter and receiver is clock drift. We assume that the clock drift of both transmitter C_T and receiver C_R are uniformly distributed, i.e.,

$$P(C_T = c) = P(C_R = c) = \begin{cases} \frac{1}{2\theta l}, & -\theta l \le c \le \theta l \\ 0, & otherwise \end{cases} \qquad (9)$$

where θ represents the frequency tolerance of the clock, l represents the time since last communication and c represents the individual realizations of C_T and C_R. For example, the receiver might be θl early or θl late compared to the transmitter based on the clock drift, hence the term $2\theta l$. In contrast, the transmitter can also be θl early or θl late with respect to the receiver. We are interested in the difference of the two clocks $C_T - C_R$, that is, how much the sender and receiver clocks are apart from each other. The difference between two uniformly distributed clock drifts results in a convolution between them that further produces a triangular distribution that will eventually determine the probability of the transmitter and receiver being awake to communicate and is given by

$$P(D = d) = \begin{cases} \frac{2\theta l + d}{(2\theta l)^2}, & -2\theta l \le d \le 0 \\ \frac{2\theta l - d}{(2\theta l)^2}, & 0 < d \le 2\theta l \\ 0, & otherwise \end{cases} \qquad (10)$$

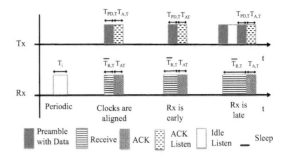

Figure 4: TR-MAC synchronized state

In the synchronized state, the transmitter has to transmit at least one data-listen cycle and may be more depending on the precise wake-up time of the receiver. Receiving an acknowledgement from the receiver marks a successful communication. The energy to transmit a packet in the synchronized state can be calculated by

$$E_{\text{Tx,T}}^{\text{sync}} = P_{\text{Tx,T}}T_{\text{PD,T}} + P_{\text{Rx,T}}T_{\text{A,T}} + N \\ *(P_{\text{Tx,T}}T_{\text{PD,T}} + P_{\text{Rx,T}}T_{\text{A,T}}) \qquad (11)$$

where $P_{\text{Tx,T}}$ and $P_{\text{Rx,T}}$ represents the power to transmit and receive a packet respectively, $T_{\text{PD,T}}$ represents the duration of preamble-data referred as only data in this paper and $T_{\text{A,T}}$ represents the acknowledgement duration and N represents the number of extra data-listen iterations. Figure 4 represents different scenarios that might take place in the synchronized state. The transmitter does not need to transmit any extra data-listen iterations if it is earlier than the receiver, meaning that N is zero. However, if the transmitter is late, then it has to transmit more than one data-listen iteration based on the positive value of N, thus spends much energy in this scenario. The positive fractional value of N is rounded to the next integer value since transmitter has to transmit one more data-listen cycle. The N is calculated depending on the specific clock drift and is given by

$$N = \left\lceil \frac{\max(d, 0)}{T_{\text{PD,T}} + T_{\text{A,T}}} \right\rceil. \qquad (12)$$

The receiver in the synchronized state spends energy to receive the data, later transmits an acknowledgement after successful reception. The receiver has to listen more than the ideal duration if it wakes up either early or late with respect to the transmitter. If the receiver is early, then it has to listen continuously till it receives a data packet. Alternatively if the receiver is late, then it has to listen continuously more than one iteration of data-listen cycles before transmitting an acknowledgement, thus the transmitter has to transmit more iterations of data-listen cycles. Therefore energy spent by the receiver to receive a preamble with data is given by

$$E_{\text{Rx,T}}^{\text{sync}} = P_{\text{Rx,T}}T_{\text{PD,T}} + P_{\text{Tx,T}}T_{\text{A,T}} + P_{\text{Rx,T}} \\ *(N(T_{\text{PD,T}} + T_{\text{A,T}}) - d). \qquad (13)$$

We also derived analytical modeling for the two reference protocols we consider, namely X-MAC and WiseMAC. X-MAC does not have a synchronized state, but wiseMAC has a synchronized form in the protocol since the receiver node include the next waking up time in the acknowledgement so that the transmitter node can follow that time to transmit the data in future. Hence we modeled WiseMAC for synchronous link considering similar equations mentioned for TR-MAC in Eq. 7 and 8. Here the probability part of the equation and the resulting triangular distribution mentioned in Eq. 10 will remain same, only the energy part will differ. Thus we model the energy part of WiseMAC.

Since the WiseMAC transmitter knows the receiver's next wake up time, it can transmit a preamble of duration $T_{PS,W} = min(4\theta l, T_W)$ where T_W is the periodic check interval. This value of the preamble is enough for the possible clock drifts of the transmitter and receiver, and the maximum value of T_W ensures that the next periodic channel sampling will receive the preamble. The energy for WiseMAC transmitter is given by

$$E_{Tx,W}^{sync} = P_{Tx,W}T_{PS,W} + P_{Tx,W}T_{D,W} + P_{Rx,W}T_{A,W}, \quad (14)$$

where $P_{Tx,W}$ and $P_{Rx,W}$ represents the power to transmit and receive a packet respectively, $T_{D,W}$ represents the data packet duration and $T_{A,W}$ represents the acknowledgement duration. The WiseMAC receiver spends energy to detect the preamble, to receive the data packet and to transmit the acknowledgement back to the transmitter. The energy for WiseMAC receiver is given by

$$E_{Rx,W}^{sync} = P_{Rx,W}T_{P,W} + P_{Rx,W}T_{D,W} + P_{Tx,W}T_{A,W}, \quad (15)$$

where preamble receiving duration, $T_{P,W}$, is considered to have the same value as the minimum duration to detect communication of TR-MAC protocol, $T_{P,T}$.

5. PERFORMANCE EVALUATION

We evaluate the analytical models of TR-MAC, X-MAC and WiseMAC for unsynchronized and synchronized states in Matlab to compare their respective energy consumption per second. For unsynchronized links, the total energy consumption includes the energy to transmit or receive a packet and for periodic listening. The interesting parameters used for analyzing the protocols are check interval duration, T_W, and packet arrival rate, λ. The symbols and corresponding values are given in Section 4 and Table 1. The transceiver power level is considered 1 mW [6], however, the transmitter using TR-MAC uses twice power than other MAC protocols. We considered a data rate of 25 kbps and correspondingly derived the duration of different parts of the packet.

The energy consumption of the overall system is presented in Figure 5 for all three protocols in unsynchronized state for varying check intervals with packet arrival rate of $\lambda = 0.1$ packets/s. We observe TR-MAC performs better than X-MAC but worse than WiseMAC for small check interval whereas the behavior reverses for larger check intervals. Thus we calculate the optimum check interval that minimizes the energy consumption for various packet arrival rate.

The optimized check interval values for a range of packet arrival rates for all three protocols is illustrated in Figure 6 in logarithmic scale for all three protocols. As observed, WiseMAC can consume less energy by making the check interval really small as it can have very short periodic listen only to detect a preamble in the medium. Contrary to that, TR-MAC and X-MAC have longer periodic listen duration in order to spread over the listen part of the data-listen cycles, hence consumes less energy for longer check intervals.

Afterwards we calculate the overall energy consumption in unsynchronized state using the optimized check interval calculated for each packet arrival rate for 12 nodes in the system; where one node transmits, one node listens and

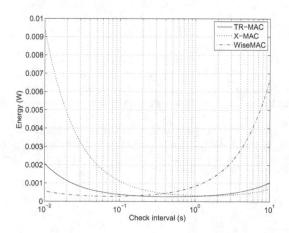

Figure 5: Unsynchronized state: Energy consumption for packet arrival rate=0.1 packets/s

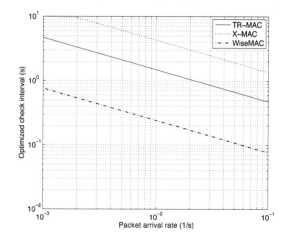

Figure 6: Unsynchronized state: Optimized check interval for packet arrival rate

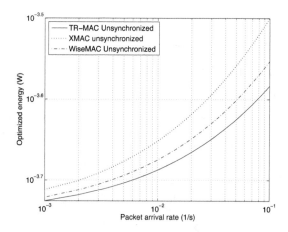

Figure 7: Unsynchronized state: Energy consumption calculated for optimized check interval

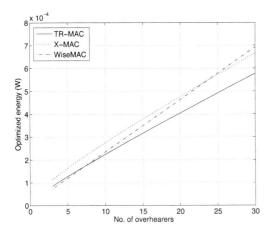

Figure 8: Unsynchronized state: Energy with over-hearers for packet arrival rate=0.1 packets/s

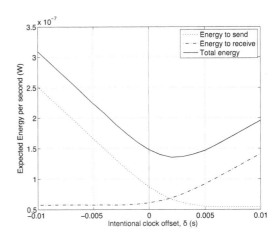

Figure 10: TR-MAC Synchronized state: Energy consumption for intentional clock offset

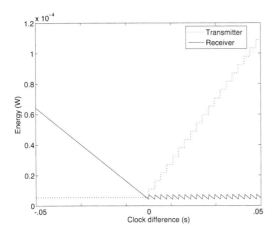

Figure 9: TR-MAC Synchronized state: Energy consumption when clocks are aligned

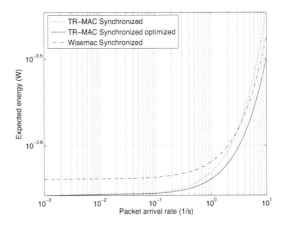

Figure 11: Synchronized state: Energy consumption for packet arrival rate

other 10 nodes are potential overhearers. Figure 7 represents the results and interestingly TR-MAC has better energy consumption than both of WiseMAC and X-MAC in the unsynchronized state even though TR-MAC transmitter has a two times power penalty over other protocols. The reason is TR-MAC overhearers can go back to sleep after receiving the preamble part of data-listen cycles if the same frequency offset is used or the overhearers do not listen to the transmission if a different frequency offset is used. However, WiseMAC overhearers have to listen till the end of the preamble in order to listen to the data packet, that essentially give a rise to the overall energy consumption of the system. Figure 8 represents the comparison of energy consumption for three protocols for different number of over-hearers in the system.

The TR-MAC protocol in synchronized state effectively minimizes its preamble in transmitter side as either the transmitter or the receiver follows each others next wake up time. The energy consumption in the synchronized state depends on the relative wake up time of the transmitter and receiver clocks as presented in Section 4 Figure 4. The individual energy consumption of transmitter and receiver depending

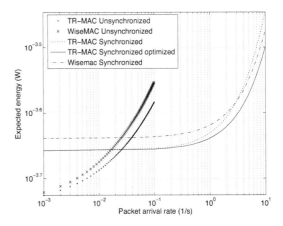

Figure 12: Unsynchronized and synchronized state comparison

27

on their relative wake up time difference can be observed in Figure 9. If the clocks are aligned, then minimum energy is spent by both the transmitter and receiver. The receiver waking up earlier than the transmitter will be costly in terms of energy consumption. However, the receiver being later than the transmitter will cause the transmitter to transmit more iterations of data-listen cycles, which is more costly than the receiver being early.

The fact that at system level, the receiver being late is more costly than the receiver being early led us to experiment with an intentional clock offset, δ. As a result, the expected energy to transmit or receive in Section 4 Eq. 7 and 8 will change their form. However, this clock offset will only affect the probability part of the triangular distribution in Eq. 10, not the energy part. The triangular distribution with a negative intentional clock difference of $P(D = D - \delta)$ is represented by

$$
P(D = d) = \begin{cases} \frac{2\theta l + (d+\delta)}{(2\theta l)^2}, & (-2\theta l - \delta) \le d \le (0 - \delta) \\ \frac{2\theta l - (d+\delta)}{(2\theta l)^2}, & (0 - \delta) < d \le (2\theta l - \delta) \\ 0, & otherwise \end{cases}
$$

(16)

This is illustrated in Figure 10 where the energy consumption to transmit or receive in synchronized state of TR-MAC is evaluated for random clock drifts and an offset, δ. The clock drift of both transmitter and receiver are assumed to be uniformly distributed between -30 ppm to 30 ppm. Furthermore, a clock offset, δ, is assumed where a positive offset represents the receiver being early on average, and a negative clock drift represents the transmitter being early on average. Interestingly, the total energy consumption does not reach its minimum value when the clock offset is zero, rather at a point with some positive clock difference, that is when the receiver is little early. Therefore waking the receiver little bit earlier than the transmitter results in minimum energy consumption.

In order to exploit this phenomenon the optimized clock offset is computed by finding the minimum total energy for various packet inter-arrival time. Afterwards the energy consumption in synchronized state is computed by varying the packet arrival rate with the ideal scenario with no clock offset and optimized clock offsets for minimum energy consumption. We modeled WiseMAC protocol for synchronized state, but omitted the X-MAC protocol since it does not have any synchronized state. Figure 11 illustrates the comparison where the optimized TR-MAC protocol outperforms the WiseMAC protocol in the synchronized state.

Finally, we combine the overall energy consumption of the system for both unsynchronized and synchronized state with respect to packet arrival rate as illustrated in Figure 12. The TR-MAC protocol will switch between its two available states based on the minimum energy consumption. We see from Figure 12 that TR-MAC outperforms the WiseMAC protocol in the both unsynchronized and synchronized state. The results are presented in logarithmic scale, thus a small difference in this result has more gain in the order of magnitude.

6. CONCLUSIONS AND FUTURE WORK

The TR-MAC with TR modulation underneath is an energy efficient MAC protocol suitable for short-range, low data rate applications that utilizes the advantages of TR modulation and at the same time minimizing its drawbacks. We analytically modeled TR-MAC and compared the unsynchronized and synchronized states of TR-MAC with X-MAC and WiseMAC. It turns out that TR-MAC has a very low energy consumption for both unsynchronized and synchronized states for a system of a realistic number of nodes. TR-MAC periodic listening is not affected by overhearing transmission for other receivers, as in the case of WiseMAC. Furthermore, similar to X-MAC but contrary to WiseMAC, TR-MAC needs very little energy to receive a packet. Finally, transmitting a packet is more costly than in X-MAC, especially due to the characteristics of TR modulation, but this can be compensated by choosing a shorter check interval. Also TR-MAC successfully mitigates the energy wastage by idle listening, overhearing, control packet overhead and collisions. Overall, TR-MAC is very promising for energy-efficient communications in noisy environments where only a limited amount of data is transmitted between a single pair of nodes.

As our future work, we will extend TR-MAC for network level multi-hop communication and evaluate for traffic adaptivity and scalability. We also expect to have better performance for TR-MAC in different scenario with related protocols that use data instead of preamble or use different frequency channels. Finally, energy harvesting will be incorporated in future by letting transmitters and receivers adapt their duty cycle based on locally available energy.

7. ACKNOWLEDGEMENT

This research is supported by the Dutch Technology Foundation STW, which is part of the Netherlands Organization for Scientific Research (NWO), and partly funded by the Ministry of Economic Affairs in the context of STW project 11317 - Walnut: Hard to Crack - Wireless Ad-hoc Links using robust Noise-based Ultra-wide band Transmission.

8. REFERENCES

[1] IEEE Standard for Local and metropolitan area networks - Part 15.4: Low-Rate Wireless Personal Area Networks (LR-WPANs), 2011.

[2] M. Anwander, G. Wagenknecht, T. Braun, and K. Dolfus. BEAM: A burst-aware energy-efficient adaptive MAC protocol for wireless sensor networks. In *Seventh International Conference on Networked Sensing Systems (INSS)*, pages 195 –202, June 2010.

[3] A. Bachir, M. Dohler, T. Watteyne, and K. K. Leung. MAC essentials for wireless sensor networks. *IEEE Communications Surveys and Tutorials*, 12(2):222–248, 2010.

[4] M. Buettner, G. V. Yee, E. Anderson, and R. Han. X-MAC: A short preamble MAC protocol for duty-cycled wireless sensor networks. In *Proceedings of the 4th International Conference on Embedded Networked Sensor Systems*, SenSys '06, pages 307–320, New York, NY, USA, 2006. ACM.

[5] C. Cano, B. Bellalta, A. Sfairopoulou, and M. Oliver. Low energy operation in WSNs: A survey of preamble sampling MAC protocols. *Comput. Netw.*, 55(15):3351–3363, Oct. 2011.

[6] F. Chen, Y. Li, D. Liu, W. Rhee, J. Kim, D. Kim, and Z. Wang. A 1mW 1Mb/s 7.75-to-8.25GHz chirp-UWB transceiver with low peak-power transmission and fast

synchronization capability. In *IEEE International Solid-State Circuits Conference Digest of Technical Papers (ISSCC)*,, pages 162–163, Feb 2014.

[7] A. Dunkels. The ContikiMAC Radio Duty Cycling Protocol. Technical Report T2011:13, Swedish Institute of Computer Science, Dec. 2011.

[8] A. El-Hoiydi and J.-D. Decotignie. WiseMAC: An ultra low power MAC protocol for multi-hop wireless sensor networks. In *ALGOSENSORS*, volume 3121 of *Lecture Notes in Computer Science*, pages 18–31. Springer, 2004.

[9] J. Elson, L. Girod, and D. Estrin. Fine-grained network time synchronization using reference broadcasts. In *Proceedings of the Fifth Symposium on Operating Systems Design and Implementation (OSDI)*, pages 147–163, Boston, MA, USA, December 2002.

[10] S. Ganeriwal, R. Kumar, and M. B. Srivastava. Timing-sync protocol for sensor networks. In *SenSys*, pages 138–149. ACM, 2003.

[11] R. Hoctor and H. Tomlinson. Delay-hopped transmitted-reference RF communications. In *IEEE Conference on Ultra Wideband Systems and Technologies*, pages 265–269, 2002.

[12] R. Jurdak, P. Baldi, and C. V. Lopes. Energy aware low power listening for sensor networks. In *Second International Workshop on Networked Sensing Systems (INSS05)*, 2005.

[13] S. Mahlknecht and M. Bock. CSMA-MPS: a minimum preamble sampling MAC protocol for low power wireless sensor networks. In *Factory Communication Systems, 2004. Proceedings. 2004 IEEE International Workshop on*, pages 73–80, 2004.

[14] A. Meijerink, S. Cotton, M. Bentum, and W. Scanlon. Noise-based frequency offset modulation in wideband frequency-selective fading channels. In *16th Annual Symposium of the IEEE/CVT*, Louvain-la-Neuve, Belgium, 2009. IEEE/SCVT.

[15] S. Morshed and G. J. Heijenk. TR-MAC: an energy-efficient MAC protocol for wireless sensor networks exploiting noise-based transmitted reference modulation. In *2nd Joint ERCIM eMobility and MobiSense Workshop, St. Petersburg, Russia*, pages 58–71, Bern, Switzerland, June 2013.

[16] Philipp Hurni and Torsten Braun. MaxMAC: a maximally traffic-adaptive MAC protocol for wireless sensor networks. 2010.

[17] J. Polastre, J. Hill, and D. E. Culler. Versatile low power media access for wireless sensor networks. In *SynSys*, pages 95–107, 2004.

[18] I. Rhee, A. Warrier, M. Aia, J. Min, and M. L. Sichitiu. Z-MAC: a hybrid mac for wireless sensor networks. *IEEE/ACM Trans. Netw.*, 16(3):511–524, 2008.

[19] C. Schurgers, V. Tsiatsis, S. Ganeriwal, and M. B. Srivastava. Optimizing sensor networks in the energy-latency-density design space. *IEEE Trans. Mob. Comput.*, 1(1):70–80, 2002.

[20] X. Shi and G. Stromberg. SyncWUF: An ultra low-power MAC protocol for wireless sensor networks. *IEEE Trans. Mob. Comput.*, 6(1):115–125, 2007.

[21] N. F. Timmons and W. G. Scanlon. Improving the ultra-low-power performance of ieee 802.15.6 by adaptive synchronisation. *IET Wireless Sensor Systems*, 1(3):161–170, 2011.

[22] T. van Dam and K. Langendoen. An adaptive energy-efficient MAC protocol for wireless sensor networks. In *SenSys*, pages 171–180. ACM, 2003.

[23] L. van Hoesel and P. Havinga. A lightweight medium access protocol (LMAC) for wireless sensor networks: Reducing preamble transmissions and transceiver state switches. In *1st International Workshop on Networked Sensing Systems, INSS 2004*, pages 205–208, Tokio, Japan, 2004. Society of Instrument and Control Engineers (SICE).

[24] K.-J. Wong and D. K. Arvind. SpeckMAC: Low-power decentralised MAC protocols for low data rate transmissions in specknets. In *Proceedings of the 2nd International Workshop on Multi-hop Ad Hoc Networks: From Theory to Reality*, REALMAN '06, pages 71–78, New York, NY, USA, 2006. ACM.

[25] Y. Wu, S. Fahmy, and N. B. Shroff. Optimal sleep/wake scheduling for time-synchronized sensor networks with QoS guarantees. *IEEE/ACM Trans. Netw.*, 17(5):1508–1521, 2009.

[26] W. Ye, J. Heidemann, and D. Estrin. An energy-efficient mac protocol for wireless sensor networks. In *INFOCOM 2002. Twenty-First Annual Joint Conference of the IEEE Computer and Communications Societies. Proceedings. IEEE*, volume 3, pages 1567–1576 vol.3, 2002.

[27] X. Zhang, J. Ansari, and P. Mähönen. Traffic aware medium access control protocol for wireless sensor networks. In *MOBIWAC*, pages 140–148. ACM, 2009.

Dirichlet's Principle on Multiclass Multihop Wireless Networks: Minimum Cost Routing Subject to Stability

Reza Banirazi, Edmond Jonckheere, Bhaskar Krishnamachari

Department of Electrical Engineering, University of Southern California, Los Angeles, CA 90089

E-mail: {banirazi, jonckhee, bkrishna} @usc.edu

ABSTRACT

Minimum cost routing is considered on multiclass multihop wireless networks influenced by stochastic arrivals, inter-channel interference, and time-varying topology. Endowing each air link with a cost factor, possibly time-varying and different for different classes, we define the Dirichlet routing cost as the square of the link packet transmissions weighted by the link cost-factors. Our recently-proposed Heat-Diffusion (HD) routing protocol [3] is extended to minimize this cost, while ensuring queue stability for all stabilizable traffic demands, and without requiring any information about network topology or packet arrivals. This is the first time in literature that such a multiclass routing penalty can be minimized at network layer subject to queue stability. Further, when all links are of unit cost factor, our protocol here reduces to the one in our recent paper [4], leading to minimum average network delay among all routing protocols that act based only on current queue congestion and current channel states. Our approach is based on mapping a communication network into an electrical network by showing that the fluid limit of wireless network under our routing protocol follows Ohm's law on a nonlinear resistive network.

Categories and Subject Descriptors

C.2.2 [**Computer Communication Networks**]: Network Protocols—*Routing protocols*; C.2.1 [**Computer Communication Networks**]: Network Architecture and Design—*Wireless communication, Packet-switching networks, Network communications, Distributed networks*

General Terms

Algorithms, Design, Performance, Theory

Keywords

Routing cost, network delay, throughput, queue stability, resource allocation, stochastic processing network, nonlinear resistive network, backpressure, heat diffusion

Permission to make digital or hard copies of all or part of this work for personal or classroom use is granted without fee provided that copies are not made or distributed for profit or commercial advantage and that copies bear this notice and the full citation on the first page. Copyrights for components of this work owned by others than ACM must be honored. Abstracting with credit is permitted. To copy otherwise, or republish, to post on servers or to redistribute to lists, requires prior specific permission and/or a fee. Request permissions from permissions@acm.org.

MSWiM'14, September 21–26, 2014, Montreal, QC, Canada.
Copyright 2014 ACM 978-1-4503-3030-5/14/09 ...$15.00.
DOI: http://dx.doi.org/10.1145/2641798.2641808.

1. INTRODUCTION

Consider a time-slotted wireless network in which new packets of the same size may randomly arrive to different nodes, destined for any other node, potentially several hops away. Due to environmental factors and user mobility, the topology of the network may randomly change in time. Due to inter-channel interference, not all wireless channels can transmit at the same time. The network is described by a *simple, directed* connectivity graph with set of nodes $\mathcal{V}$ and directed edges $\mathcal{E}$. Packets of the same destination form a *class* (regardless of their sources), where $\mathcal{K} \subseteq \mathcal{V}$ represents the set of all possible classes in the network. Given a wireless link $ij \in \mathcal{E}$ and a class $d \in \mathcal{K}$, the link *actual-transmission* $f_{ij}^{(d)}(n)$ counts the number of d-class packets (or d-packets in short) transmitted over the link at times-lot n. For each class d, every link ij is also endowed with a link *cost-factor* $\rho_{ij}^{(d)}(n) \geqslant 1$ that represents the cost of transmitting one d-packet over the link at slot n. The aim of this paper is to find a configuration of time-slotted actual-transmissions $f_{ij}^{(d)}(n)$ that solve the optimization problem

$$\text{Minimize: } \limsup_{\tau \to \infty} \frac{1}{\tau} \sum_{n=0}^{\tau-1} \mathbb{E}\Big\{ \sum_{ij \in \mathcal{E}} \sum_{d \in \mathcal{K}} \rho_{ij}^{(d)}(n) \big(f_{ij}^{(d)}(n) \big)^2 \Big\} \quad (1)$$

Subject to: Queue stability for all stabilizable arrivals

assuming that each nonzero packet arrival has a nonzero mean, and with $\mathbb{E}$ denoting expectation. We refer to the *quadratic* cost function of problem (1) as *Dirichlet routing cost* due to its connection with Dirichlet's principle in heat calculus [11], which shall be explained in this paper.

Note that the problem (1) needs to be solved at *network and link layer,* which totally disconnects it from cross-layer optimization techniques [14, 19, 10, 22]. The aim in the latter is to control flow at transport layer so as to keep the arrival rates within the network capacity region. The network-layer routing policy, on the other hand, has no control on arrivals. Instead, the basic assumption here is queue stabilizability, meaning that the arrival rates lie within the network capacity region. Then, an important quality factor of a protocol, called *throughput optimality,* is to stably support the entire capacity region. It should be obvious that minimum cost routing at network and link layer has no contradiction with flow control at transport layer in order to lay the arrival rates within the network capacity region.

Discussion on the Dirichlet routing cost. We remark that the quadratic form of cost function in (1), i.e. using the square of the number of d-packet transmissions on a link, is decreed by the Dirichlet principle, upon which our proof of optimality is founded. This is analogous to the concept of power loss in a resistor, defined by the square of the electrical current weighted by the resistance. One may be more interested in defining a minimization target without the square, consisting of a sum of costs multiplied by the number of packets suffering those costs. Then we can no longer claim that our protocol strictly minimizes such a linear routing cost, by exactly the same way that the power dissipation on a resistive network would no longer be minimized if it were defined linear in electrical current.

When the link cost-factors are correlated with a sort of resource consumption such as energy (resp., quality defect such as end-to-end delay), the constrained optimization problem (1) is closely related to minimizing average network resources (resp., average quality defects) subject to throughput optimality. The minimization target can represent different routing penalties that gives a wide-reaching impact to the minimization problem (1). Below are some examples that can be brought into this abstract model.

• *Link quality factor turned as a cost factor:* The quality of wireless communication depends on hardware and environmental factors. Different state-of-the-art link-quality metrics have been introduced such as Expected Transmission Count (ETX), Packet Reception Rate (PRR), Required Number of Packet Transmissions (RNP), etc. (See [1] for a review.) Most link quality measures can easily be merged with problem (1) as a link cost-factor.

• *Routing distance minimization:* The cost factor of each link ij for a class d can be assigned proportional to the hop-count or geographic distance between the receiving node j and the destination node d. Then, due to the close correlation between routing distance and packet latency, problem (1) may be interpreted as average delay minimization subject to throughput optimality.

• *Energy usage minimization:* Link capacity is a function of transmission power and channel condition. Assuming that power allocation happens independently of queue congestion, each link may receive a cost factor proportional to the ratio of allocated power to the link capacity.

• *Relaying cost minimization:* Nodes in ad-hoc networks, which belong to different users, may act in their own interests rather than forwarding traffic for others. Several protocols have addressed this non-cooperative behavior, based mostly on game theory and with no cost optimization or throughput optimality results (see [24] and references therein). Assume that every node declares a relaying cost for transferring one packet. Then in our framework, each incoming link to a node may receive a cost factor proportional to the node relaying cost.

Related works. It is shown in [17] that a stationary randomized algorithm can solve the constrained optimization problem (1). While such an algorithm exists in theory, it is intractable in practice as it requires a full knowledge of arrival statistics and channel state probabilities. Moreover, assuming all the statistics and probabilities could be accurately estimated, the algorithm would still need to solve a dynamic programming problem for each topology state, where the number of states grows exponentially with the number of wireless channels.

Thus far, the V-parameter Back-Pressure (BP) has been the only feasible approach to decreasing — not minimizing — a routing penalty at network layer [17]. It parametrizes the original BP [23] by a constant $V \geqslant 0$ to trade queue congestion for routing cost. It is proved that the average routing cost can come within $O(1/V)$ of its minimum, but at the expense of an increase in average network delay of $O(V)$ relative to that of the original BP. Specifically, while the algorithm can decrease a routing cost, it is not able to achieve the minimum cost subject to network stability. We remark, however, that the V-parameter approach holds for more general cost functions, and is not restricted to the particular structure of the Dirichlet routing cost in (1).

Adding distance information to link weights, [20] enhances BP to give priority to shorter paths. It does not minimize the average routing distance and uses the shortest path information in a heuristic manner. Energy-delay tradeoff for sensor networks was considered in [26]. Asymptotic energy usage as network size grows to infinity was studied in [13]. The V-parameter BP was used in [16] to reduce average energy usage for a multihop wireless network. A better energy-delay tradeoff was introduced in [18] for the special case of wireless downlinks. The work in [15] used ETX metric with V-parameter BP to decrease average packet transmissions. The authors in [25] restricted BP to the number of hop-counts on each flow, assuming that each node knows a-priori its hop distance from all others. Using greedy embedding, [21] modified BP by giving priority to the links with a shorter hyperbolic distance to the final destination.

Our chain of papers. In [2] we introduced a very infant idea of packet routing inspired by adiabatic heat process. That idea was vastly revised and developed in [3] to provide the best delay-cost tradeoff on a uniclass network through changing a control parameter $0 \leqslant \beta \leqslant 1$. In [4], we generalized the results of [3] for $\beta = 0$ to multiclass networks. This paper extends the results of [3] on the Dirichlet routing cost in two directions: First, rather than taking a free-capacity directed graph as in [3], here we formalize Dirichlet's principle on a capacity-constrained directed graph as the genuine representation of a communication network. This relaxes the main restriction in [3] that under a natural heat propagation, the flow on each wireless link needed to remain spontaneously lower than the link expected time average capacity (see Theorem 5 and Remark 2 in [3]). Second, here we consider multiclass networks that together with limited edge capacities make the Dirichlet principle far more sophisticated.

Contribution. First, we extend our recently-proposed Heat-Diffusion (HD) policy [3] to solve the *multiclass* routing cost problem (1) without requiring any information about network topology or packet arrivals. To this nontrivial extension, we fully develop a novel concept of multiclass electric conduction on a nonlinear resistive network with capacity-constrained directed edges.

Second, when all links are of unit cost factor, our protocol here reduces to the one developed in our recent paper [4], and so minimizes average network delay within the class of all routing policies that base their decision only on current queue congestion and current channel states in the network.

Third, the long-term average dynamics (fluid limits) of the wireless network under our protocol comply with Ohm's law. This opens a way to take advantage of classical tools from circuit theory in the analysis and optimization of the rate-level behavior of stochastic packet networks.

Fourth, our protocol enjoys the same algorithmic structure, complexity, and overhead signaling as BP. Thus all advanced improvements to BP (see [17] and references therein) can easily be leveraged to further enhance our protocol too.

Notation. For $\mathcal{S}$ as a set, $|\mathcal{S}|$ denotes its cardinality. A superscript $\top$ denotes the transpose operation. For $\boldsymbol{v}$ as a vector, $\|\boldsymbol{v}\| := (\boldsymbol{v}^\top \boldsymbol{v})^{1/2}$ denotes its norm. For $\boldsymbol{v}$ as a block vector, $\mathrm{diag}(\boldsymbol{v})$ denotes its block diagonal matrix expansion. We denote the zero vector with $\boldsymbol{0}$, the vector of all ones of size m with $\boldsymbol{1}_m$, and the identity matrix of size m with $\boldsymbol{I}_m$. Between vectors or matrices, the entrywise (Schur) product is denoted with $\odot$ and the tensor product with $\otimes$. For two vectors $\boldsymbol{u}$ and $\boldsymbol{v}$, the operators $\min\{\boldsymbol{u}, \boldsymbol{v}\}$ and $\max\{\boldsymbol{u}, \boldsymbol{v}\}$, also curly inequalities $\preccurlyeq$ and $\succcurlyeq$, act entrywise. For x as a real number, $\lfloor x \rfloor$ maps x to the largest preceding integer, and $\lceil x \rceil$ to the smallest following integer. The indicator function $\mathbb{I}_X$ takes the value 1 if the statement X is true, and 0 otherwise. For a vector $\boldsymbol{v}$, we define $\boldsymbol{v}^+ := \max\{\boldsymbol{0}, \boldsymbol{v}\}$. On a graph, or a network for that matter, for a value x corresponding to a directed edge ℓ from node i to node j, we use the notation x_ℓ and x_{ij} interchangeably.

Note. The page limit prevents us to include the proofs, which are all available in the full length paper [5].

2. PRELIMINARIES

To direct packets from their source toward their destination, a routing protocol makes a *routing decision* at every timeslot that consists of activating a set of links, selecting which class(es) to be served by each activated link, and assigning number of packets to be sent on each activated link. We assume that packets are not sent to *trapping nodes*, i.e. if a node accepts d-packets, there must exist at least one possible route from that node to the node d. Though this assumption is not necessary for any of our analytical results, it ensures that a dynamic routing, with no routing path constraint, will not mistakenly send a packet to a trapping node that prevents it from ever reaching its destination.

2.1 Stability and Throughput Optimality

A discrete-time stochastic process $x(n)$ is called stable if

$$\overline{x} := \limsup_{\tau \to \infty} 1/\tau \sum_{n=0}^{\tau-1} \mathbb{E}\{x(n)\} < \infty. \qquad (2)$$

The definition of stability and the overbar notation are extended entrywise to vectors and matrices. A network is *stable* if all its queues are stable. An arrival rate matrix is *stabilizable* if there exists a routing policy that stabilizes the network. For a routing policy, *stability region* is the set of all arrival rate matrices that it can stably support. Network *capacity region* is the union of the stability regions of all possible routing policies (probably unfeasible). A routing policy is *throughput-optimal* if its stability region coincides with the network capacity region; thus it secures network stability for all stabilizable arrival rates.

2.2 Inter-Channel Interference

Contrary to wireline networks where links are independent resources, two wireless links cannot simultaneously transmit if they have interference. An interference model specifies these restrictions on simultaneous transmissions. Given an interference model, we define a *maximal schedule* as a set of channels such that no two channels interfere with each other, and no more channel can be added to it without violating the constraints of interference model. We describe a maximal schedule with a *scheduling vector* $\boldsymbol{\pi} \in \{0,1\}^{|\mathcal{E}|}$ where π_{ij} takes the value 1 if the channel ij is included in the maximal schedule, and 0 otherwise. Given a connectivity graph $(\mathcal{V}, \mathcal{E})$, we also define the *scheduling set* Π as the collection of all *maximal* scheduling vectors.

The scheduling set varies according to interference model. The results of this paper remain valid for the family of all interference models under which a node is not allowed to transmit to more than one neighbor at the same time. Thus, in a most general case, a node may receive packets from several neighbors while sending packets over one of its outgoing links. Interference constraints used with all well-known network and link layer protocols, including general K-hop interference models, fall in this family.

2.3 Time-Varying Topology

Network topology may vary in time due to node mobility and/or surrounding conditions, e.g. obstacle effect, node mobility, and/or channel fading. We assume that the sets $\mathcal{V}$ and $\mathcal{E}$ change far slower than channel states; thus we take them fixed during the time of interest. Then, a temporarily unavailable channel is characterized by a zero link capacity. Persistent variations, due to e.g. non-local mobility, can be caught in a long scale regime that updates connectivity graph $(\mathcal{V}, \mathcal{E})$. We also assume that channel states remain fixed during a timeslot, while they may change across slots according to some (unknown) probability laws.

Let a stochastic process $\boldsymbol{S}(n) = \big(S_1(n), \cdots, S_{|\mathcal{E}|}(n)\big)$ represent channel states at slot n, describing all uncontrollable conditions that affect channel capacities, and possibly link cost-factors. Assume that $\boldsymbol{S}(n)$ evolves according to an ergodic stationary process and takes values in a finite (but arbitrarily large) set $\mathcal{S}$. For example, an irreducible Markov chain or any i.i.d. sequence of stochastic matrices are both ergodic and stationary. Then due to Birkhoff's ergodic theorem, each state $\boldsymbol{S} \in \mathcal{S}$ is of probability

$$S := \mathbb{P}\big\{\boldsymbol{S}(n) = \boldsymbol{S}\big\} = \limsup_{\tau \to \infty} 1/\tau \sum_{n=0}^{\tau-1} \mathbb{I}_{\boldsymbol{S}(n) = \boldsymbol{S}}$$

where $\sum_{\boldsymbol{S} \in \mathcal{S}} S = 1$. Though our proposed routing protocol does not require the state probabilities S, the existence of S is important to establish the network capacity region, and also for the theoretical analysis of our protocol.

2.4 State Model of Multiclass Network

Let $q_i^{(d)}(n)$ represent the integer number of d-classes in the node i at slot n. It is assumed that a packet leaves the network as soon as reaching its destination; thus the backlog of d-classes at the destination node d is zero for all $d \in \mathcal{K}$. Then the state variables of the queuing system are represented by the hyper-vector

$$\boldsymbol{q}_\circ(n) := \big[\boldsymbol{q}_\circ^{(1)}(n), \ldots, \boldsymbol{q}_\circ^{(|\mathcal{K}|)}(n)\big]^\top \in \mathbb{R}^{(|\mathcal{V}|-1)|\mathcal{K}|}$$

$$\boldsymbol{q}_\circ^{(d)}(n) := \big[q_1^{(d)}(n), \ldots, q_{d-1}^{(d)}(n), q_{d+1}^{(d)}(n), \ldots, q_{|\mathcal{V}|}^{(d)}(n)\big]$$

where $q_d^{(d)}(n) \equiv 0$ is dropped from the set of states.

Notation. A subscript $\circ$ denotes a reduced array by discarding the entries related to the destination node d.

Let a stochastic process $a_i^{(d)}(n)$ be the number of exogenous d-classes arriving into the node i at slot n. Discarding $a_d^{(d)}(n) \equiv 0$, the hyper-vector of node arrivals is

$$\boldsymbol{a}_\circ(n) := \big[\boldsymbol{a}_\circ^{(1)}(n), \ldots, \boldsymbol{a}_\circ^{(|\mathcal{K}|)}(n)\big]^\top \in \mathbb{R}^{(|\mathcal{V}|-1)|\mathcal{K}|}$$

$$\boldsymbol{a}_\circ^{(d)}(n) := \big[a_1^{(d)}(n), \ldots, a_{d-1}^{(d)}(n), a_{d+1}^{(d)}(n), \ldots, a_{|\mathcal{V}|}^{(d)}(n)\big].$$

For a link $ij \in \mathcal{E}$, the *capacity* $\mu_{ij}(n)$, which is frequently called link *transmission rate* in literature, counts the maximum number of packets the link can transmit at slot n. The link *actual-transmission* $f_{ij}^{(d)}(n)$, on the other hand, counts the number of d-packets *genuinely* sent over the link at slot n, which is determined by a routing protocol. We form the hyper-vector of link actual-transmissions as

$$\boldsymbol{f}(n) := \big[\,\boldsymbol{f}^{(1)}(n),\dots,\boldsymbol{f}^{(|\mathcal{K}|)}(n)\,\big]^{\top} \in \mathbb{R}^{|\mathcal{E}||\mathcal{K}|}$$
$$\boldsymbol{f}^{(d)}(n) := \big[\,f_1^{(d)}(n),\dots,f_{|\mathcal{E}|}^{(d)}(n)\,\big].$$

Given a directed graph $(\mathcal{V},\mathcal{E})$, let $\boldsymbol{B}$ denote the *node-edge* incidence matrix in which $B_{i\ell}$ — the entry related to node i and edge j — takes the value 1 if node i is the tail of directed edge ℓ, -1 if i is the head, and 0 otherwise. For a class d, let $\boldsymbol{B}_\circ^{(d)}$ denote a reduction of $\boldsymbol{B}$ that discards the row related to the destination node d. Extending this structure to a multiclass framework, we get

$$\boldsymbol{B}_\circ := \mathrm{diag}\big(\,\big[\,\boldsymbol{B}_\circ^{(1)},\dots,\boldsymbol{B}_\circ^{(|\mathcal{K}|)}\,\big]\,\big) \in \mathbb{R}^{(|\mathcal{V}|-1)|\mathcal{K}| \times |\mathcal{E}||\mathcal{K}|}.$$

One can then verify that $\boldsymbol{B}_\circ \boldsymbol{f}(n)$ is a hyper-vector in which the entry corresponding to node i and class d is

$$(\boldsymbol{B}_\circ \boldsymbol{f})_i^{(d)}(n) = \sum_{b\in\mathrm{out}(i)} f_{ib}^{(d)}(n) - \sum_{a\in\mathrm{in}(i)} f_{ai}^{(d)}(n)$$

where $\mathrm{in}(i)$ and $\mathrm{out}(i)$ respectively denote the set of incoming and outgoing neighbors of node i.

Using these ingredients, the $\boldsymbol{f}$-controlled, state dynamics of a multiclass queuing network is captured by

$$\boldsymbol{q}_\circ(n+1) = \boldsymbol{q}_\circ(n) + \boldsymbol{a}_\circ(n) - \boldsymbol{B}_\circ \boldsymbol{f}(n). \tag{3}$$

Notice that despite traditional notation in literature, we do not need any $(\cdot)^+$ operation in (3) due to the difference between link capacity and link actual-transmission.

2.5 V-Parameter Back-Pressure Algorithm

In the original BP [23], at every timeslot, each link receives a weight as the product of its capacity and the queue differential of its optimal class — the class with maximum queue differential. Then a set of non-interfering links with maximum cumulative weight are scheduled for the forwarding. To incorporate a cost function into the algorithm, the V-parameter BP [17] penalizes each link with its related cost via a user-assigned parameter $V \in [0,\infty)$ that determines the worthiness of reducing the cost at the expense of increasing the network delay, while $V = 0$ recovers the original BP.

To reduce the Dirichlet routing cost, defined in (1), as the cost function, at every timeslot n, the V-parameter BP observes queue backlogs $q_i^{(d)}(n)$, and estimates channel capacities $\mu_{ij}(n)$ and link cost factors $\rho_{ij}^{(d)}(n)$, to make a network-layer packet transmission decision as follows.

Weighing: On each directed link ij and for each class d find $q_{ij}^{(d)}(n) := q_i^{(d)}(n) - q_j^{(d)}(n)$ and select the optimal class

$$d_{ij}^*(n) := \arg\max_{d\in\mathcal{K}} q_{ij}^{(d)}(n). \tag{4}$$

Then give a weight to the link as

$$w_{ij}(n) := \mu_{ij}(n)\big(q_{ij}^{(d^*)}(n) - V\rho_{ij}^{(d)}(n)\,\mu_{ij}(n)\big)^+. \tag{5}$$

Scheduling: Find the scheduling vector such that

$$\boldsymbol{\pi}(n) = \arg\max_{\boldsymbol{\pi}\in\Pi} \sum_{ij\in\mathcal{E}} \pi_{ij} w_{ij}(n) \tag{6}$$

where ties are broken randomly.

Forwarding: On each activated link ij with $w_{ij}(n) > 0$ transmit from the class $d_{ij}^*(n)$ at full capacity $\mu_{ij}(n)$.

3. DIRICHLET'S PRINCIPLE

The idea of solving problem (1) has its root in *dissipative power minimization* that naturally occurs in the process of electrical conduction over a conducting medium and is mathematically codified by Dirichlet's Principle. As the first step to adopt this idea for a multiclass wireless network, this section envisions a so-called multiclass nonlinear resistive network, and generalizes the concept of Dirichlet's principle and dissipative power minimization on it. Inspired by this, Sec. 4 proposes a multiclass routing protocol that solves problem (1), proved by showing that under this protocol, the long-term average flow of packets on the wireless network takes the form of electric currents on its corresponding resistive network.

Consider $\mathcal{M}$ as a conducting medium manifold with boundary $\partial\mathcal{M}$. Let $A(\boldsymbol{z})$ be a current *source* density relative to a volume form $\mathrm{d}V$ defined on $\mathcal{M}$, and $Q(\boldsymbol{z})$ be the induced voltage potential on $\mathcal{M}$, while being prescribed on the boundary. Let vector function $\boldsymbol{F}(\boldsymbol{z})$ be the electrical current field at the point $\boldsymbol{z}\in\mathcal{M}$. In the steady-state equilibrated conduction, the principle of charge conservation asserts that the current entering into any bounded region $\mathcal{M}'\subset\mathcal{M}$ must be equal to the current leaving out the region,

$$\int_{\partial\mathcal{M}'} \big\langle \boldsymbol{F}(\boldsymbol{z}), \aleph(\boldsymbol{z}) \big\rangle\,\mathrm{dS} = \int_{\mathcal{M}'} A(\boldsymbol{z})\,\mathrm{dV}$$

where dS is the measure of the boundary and $\langle\cdot,\cdot\rangle$ denotes the inner product. Applying the Divergence theorem leads to $\int_{\mathcal{M}'} \mathrm{div}\boldsymbol{F}(\boldsymbol{z})\,\mathrm{dV} = \int_{\mathcal{M}'} A(\boldsymbol{z})\,\mathrm{dV}$. As $\mathcal{M}'$ is arbitrary and can be chosen infinitesimally small, the latter leads to

$$\mathrm{div}\boldsymbol{F}(\boldsymbol{z}) = A(\boldsymbol{z}). \tag{7}$$

By Ohm's law, on the other hand, current between two points is proportional to the gradient of voltage across the points scaled by the *conductivity* of the material,

$$\boldsymbol{F}(\boldsymbol{z}) = -\sigma(\boldsymbol{z})\,\nabla Q(\boldsymbol{z}). \tag{8}$$

where the conductivity $\sigma(\boldsymbol{z})$ is in general a positive definite symmetric matrix. Substituting (8) into (7), we get

$$\mathrm{div}\big(\sigma(\boldsymbol{z})\,\nabla Q(\boldsymbol{z})\big) + A(\boldsymbol{z}) = 0 \tag{9}$$

which is the classical Poisson equation in coordinate-free format. Dirichlet's principle states that Poisson's equation (9) has a unique solution that minimizes the Dirichlet energy

$$E\big(Q(\boldsymbol{z})\big) := \int_{\mathcal{M}} \Big(\frac{1}{2}\sigma\|\nabla Q(\boldsymbol{z})\|^2 - Q(\boldsymbol{z})A(\boldsymbol{z})\Big)\,\mathrm{dV}$$

among all twice differentiable functions $Q(\boldsymbol{z})$ that respect the prescribed voltage potential on the boundary $\partial\mathcal{M}$ [11].

3.1 Prelude: Linear Resistive Networks

Rather than a smooth conductor manifold $\mathcal{M}$, consider now a resistive network $(\mathcal{V},\mathcal{E})$ in which two neighboring nodes are connected via a linear lumped resistor. Exogenous current is injected into (resp., drawn from) the network via positive (resp., negative) current sources attached to different nodes. Assume that voltage is fixed to ground at a single *reference* node, also referred to as *sink*, which is somewhat analogous to a collapse of the boundary $\partial\mathcal{M}$ to a point on the continuous domain. One may visualize the reference as the node that collects the net current injected into the network, i.e. algebraic sum of current sources, and drains it back into the sources, so that building a *closed* system.

To solve circuit problems, it is essential to assign an *arbitrary* algebraic-topological orientation to each edge with the understanding that the particular choice of orientation has no impact on the solutions. Accordingly, every edge variable is signed, while a negative quantity is interpreted to be on the opposite direction of the edge orientation. Using the notion of arbitrary orientation for edges, the node-edge incident matrix $\boldsymbol{B}$, previously defined on a directed graph, can be defined in the same way on the undirected graph here.

Let $\boldsymbol{q}$ represent the vector of node voltages, $\boldsymbol{f}$ the vector of edge currents, $\boldsymbol{\sigma}$ the vector of edge conductances, and $\boldsymbol{a}$ the vector of node current sources. With d being the reference node, we assume $a_d \equiv 0$ and define the reduced arrays $\boldsymbol{q}_\circ$, $\boldsymbol{a}_\circ$ and $\boldsymbol{B}_\circ$ through discarding the entries related to the node d. Then the principle of charge conservation in (7) becomes Kirchhoff's Current Law (KCL) on the electrical network,

$$\boldsymbol{B}_\circ \boldsymbol{f} = \boldsymbol{a}_\circ \tag{10}$$

asserting that at each non-grounded node, the algebraic sum of currents is zero. Observe that each entry of the vector $\boldsymbol{B}_\circ \boldsymbol{f}$ reads the net current leaving the node through the resistive edges. Ohm's law in (8), on the other hand, becomes

$$\boldsymbol{f} = \mathrm{diag}(\boldsymbol{\sigma})\, \boldsymbol{B}_\circ^\top \boldsymbol{q}_\circ. \tag{11}$$

Substituting (11) into (10), we get

$$-\boldsymbol{L}_\circ \boldsymbol{q}_\circ + \boldsymbol{a}_\circ = \boldsymbol{0} \quad \text{with} \quad \boldsymbol{L}_\circ := \boldsymbol{B}_\circ \mathrm{diag}(\boldsymbol{\sigma}) \boldsymbol{B}_\circ^\top \tag{12}$$

as the graph combinatorial analogous of the classical Poisson equation. The matrix $\boldsymbol{L}_\circ$, called the *Dirichlet Laplacian*, is *symmetric positive definite* for a connected network.

Like the classical case, (12) has a unique solution that minimizes the combinatorial Dirichlet energy

$$E(\boldsymbol{q}_\circ) := \frac{1}{2}\, \boldsymbol{q}_\circ^\top \boldsymbol{L}_\circ \boldsymbol{q}_\circ - \boldsymbol{q}_\circ^\top \boldsymbol{a}_\circ. \tag{13}$$

The proof is much simpler in the combinatorial case than the smooth case. In fact, since $\boldsymbol{L}_\circ$ is positive definite, $E(\boldsymbol{q}_\circ)$ is convex and thus has a minimum at its critical point, which readily leads to the combinatorial Poisson equation (12).

An important implication of Dirichlet's principle is the minimization of *power dissipation* on a linear resistive network. For a vector of currents $\boldsymbol{f}$ subject to KCL (10), dissipative energy is defined as $E_R(\boldsymbol{f}) := \boldsymbol{f}^\top \mathrm{diag}(\boldsymbol{\sigma})^{-1} \boldsymbol{f}$. Let $\boldsymbol{f}^\star$ be the configuration of currents that minimize $E_R(\boldsymbol{f})$, and $\boldsymbol{q}^\star$ the configuration of voltages that minimize $E(\boldsymbol{q}_\circ)$ in (13). Then it is not difficult to shown that the $\boldsymbol{f}^\star$ and $\boldsymbol{q}^\star$ must be related to each other by Ohm's law (11).

3.2 Capacitated Directed Networks

Instead of an undirected network with free-capacity edges, consider now a network under both edge directionality and edge capacity constraints. The electrical network is of the same configuration as that in the linear resistive network with the exception that here, rather than using a linear resistor, we connect two neighboring nodes by a nonlinear resistor in series with an ideal diode. The nonlinear resistor limits the current to the edge capacity, while the diode allows the current only along the edge direction. For an edge ij with capacity μ_{ij}, the nonlinear resistor is described by

$$r_{ij} = \begin{cases} 1/\sigma_{ij} & \text{if } |q_{ij}| \leqslant \mu_{ij}/\sigma_{ij} \\ |q_{ij}|/\mu_{ij} & \text{if } |q_{ij}| > \mu_{ij}/\sigma_{ij} \end{cases}$$

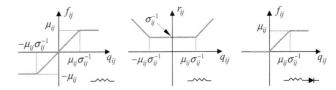

Figure 1: The nonlinear resistive edge with an ideal diode: (left) The current-voltage curve of the nonlinear resistor. (middle) The resistive-voltage curve of the nonlinear resistor. (right) The current-voltage curve of the resistor and diode together.

where σ_{ij} is the conductance in linear regime when the current is below the edge capacity (see Fig. 1).

On any electrical network, the KCL in (10) remains unchanged. However, on our nonlinear resistive network, Ohm's law (11) must be modified to allow the current in only one direction, and to limit it within the edge capacity. Let the arbitrarily-chosen algebraic-topological edge orientations concur with the edge directions. Then, with $\boldsymbol{\mu}$ being the vector of edge capacities, the modified Ohm law becomes

$$\boldsymbol{f} = \min\big\{\mathrm{diag}(\boldsymbol{\sigma})\big(\boldsymbol{B}_\circ^\top \boldsymbol{q}_\circ\big)^+,\, \boldsymbol{\mu}\big\}. \tag{14}$$

Plugging (14) in (10) leads to the analogous of Poisson's equation on a capacity-constrained directed network as

$$-\vec{\boldsymbol{L}}_\circ(\boldsymbol{q}_\circ) + \boldsymbol{a}_\circ = \boldsymbol{0}$$
$$\vec{\boldsymbol{L}}_\circ(\boldsymbol{q}_\circ) := \boldsymbol{B}_\circ \min\big\{\mathrm{diag}(\boldsymbol{\sigma})\big(\boldsymbol{B}_\circ^\top \boldsymbol{q}_\circ\big)^+,\, \boldsymbol{\mu}\big\}. \tag{15}$$

We call $\vec{\boldsymbol{L}}_\circ(\cdot)$ as *nonlinear Dirichlet Laplacian* operator.

Contrary to the standard Laplacian $\boldsymbol{L}_\circ$ on a linear resistive network, $\vec{\boldsymbol{L}}_\circ$ is an operand-dependent operator that retains neither linearity nor symmetry. Thus the easy way of proving Dirichlet's principle on free-capacity undirected networks ceases to exist here, as we can no longer claim that $\vec{\boldsymbol{L}}_\circ(\boldsymbol{q}_\circ)$ is the directional derivative of $\frac{1}{2}\,\boldsymbol{q}_\circ^\top \vec{\boldsymbol{L}}_\circ(\boldsymbol{q}_\circ)$ along $\boldsymbol{q}_\circ$. Nonetheless, the next theorem extends the concept of Dirichlet's principle, and from there the merit of minimizing dissipative energy, to capacity-constrained directed networks.

THEOREM 1. *Consider a capacitated directed network under a feasible vector of current sources $\boldsymbol{a}_\circ$, i.e. there exists at least one configuration of currents $\boldsymbol{f}$ that satisfy KCL at nodes. Then the nonlinear Poisson equation (15) has a unique solution that minimizes the Dirichlet-like energy*

$$\vec{E}(\boldsymbol{q}_\circ) := \frac{1}{2}\, \boldsymbol{q}_\circ^\top \vec{\boldsymbol{L}}_\circ(\boldsymbol{q}_\circ) - \boldsymbol{q}_\circ^\top \boldsymbol{a}_\circ. \tag{16}$$

Further, minimizing $\vec{E}(\boldsymbol{q}_\circ)$ is equivalent to solving

$$\begin{aligned} \text{Minimize:} \quad & \vec{E}_R(\boldsymbol{f}) := \boldsymbol{f}^\top \mathrm{diag}(\boldsymbol{\sigma})^{-1} \boldsymbol{f} \\ \text{Subject to:} \quad & 1)\ \ \boldsymbol{0} \preccurlyeq \boldsymbol{f} \preccurlyeq \boldsymbol{\mu} \\ & 2)\ \ \boldsymbol{B}_\circ \boldsymbol{f} = \boldsymbol{a}_\circ \end{aligned} \tag{17}$$

which formulates the minimization of dissipative energy subject to directionality and capacity of edges and KCL at nodes.

3.3 Multiclass Networks

In a traditional electrical network, the total net charge generated by all current sources is absorbed by one single grounded node — the sink. A more complex scenario, however, may be envisioned in parallel with multiclass problems in data networking. Specifically, consider a setting in which different types of charges are generated by current sources, where each type of charge is absorbed by a specific node as the sink of that charge. Using a similar terminology, let us refer to each type of charge as a *class*.

In the absence of edge capacity constraints, each class has its own independent conduction, so that the multiclass network can be viewed as the collection of fully decoupled uniclass networks with no mutual interaction. When the edges are of limited capacities, however, the conduction of different classes no longer happens independently, because the way of allocating edge capacities to each class has a direct impact on the conduction of that class, while the sum of allocated capacities on each edge is bounded. For example, allocating the total capacity of one edge to only one class means eliminating that edge for all other classes.

Consider now a multiclass electrical network $(\mathcal{V}, \mathcal{E}, \mathcal{K})$ subject to both edge directionality and edge capacity constraints. Let $0 \leqslant \theta_{ij}^{(d)} \leqslant 1$ represent the portion of total capacity of the edge ij devoted to the class d, i.e.,

$$\mu_{ij}^{(d)} = \theta_{ij}^{(d)} \mu_{ij} \text{ with } \sum_{d \in \mathcal{K}} \theta_{ij}^{(d)} \leqslant 1. \tag{18}$$

We accordingly form $\boldsymbol{\theta}^{(d)} \in \mathbb{R}^{|\mathcal{E}|}$ as the vector of edge capacity factors for the class d. Endowing edges with the possibility of having different conductivities for different classes, also let $\boldsymbol{\sigma}^{(d)} \in \mathbb{R}^{|\mathcal{E}|}$ be the vector of d-conductivity on edges. If one can figure out the vector $\boldsymbol{\theta}^{(d)}$ for each class d, then the conduction of each class will readily comply with the uniclass equations (14)–(15). For a compact formulation, let us form the *hyper-vectors* $\boldsymbol{q}_\circ$, $\boldsymbol{a}_\circ$, and $\boldsymbol{f}$ conformably structured as their counterparts defined in Sec. 2.4, and also $\boldsymbol{\sigma}$ and $\boldsymbol{\theta}$ in a similar way. Then the steady-state electric conduction on a multiclass capacitated directed network is described by

$$\boldsymbol{B}_\circ \boldsymbol{f} = \boldsymbol{a}_\circ. \tag{19}$$

$$\boldsymbol{f} = \min\left\{ \operatorname{diag}(\boldsymbol{\sigma})\left(\boldsymbol{B}_\circ^\top \boldsymbol{q}_\circ\right)^+, \boldsymbol{\theta} \odot (\mathbf{1}_{|\mathcal{K}|} \otimes \boldsymbol{\mu}) \right\} \tag{20}$$

$$-\vec{\boldsymbol{L}}_\circ(\boldsymbol{q}_\circ) + \boldsymbol{a}_\circ = \boldsymbol{0} \tag{21}$$

$$\vec{\boldsymbol{L}}_\circ(\boldsymbol{q}_\circ) := \boldsymbol{B}_\circ \min\left\{ \operatorname{diag}(\boldsymbol{\sigma})\left(\boldsymbol{B}_\circ^\top \boldsymbol{q}_\circ\right)^+, \boldsymbol{\theta} \odot (\mathbf{1}_{|\mathcal{K}|} \otimes \boldsymbol{\mu}) \right\}.$$

The term $(\mathbf{1}_{|\mathcal{K}|} \otimes \boldsymbol{\mu})$ extends $\boldsymbol{\mu} \in \mathbb{R}^{|\mathcal{E}|}$ to be of size $|\mathcal{E}||\mathcal{K}|$ and so can be used in a multiclass fashion, where its entrywise product with $\boldsymbol{\theta}$ shapes (18) in a hyper-vector form.

To answer the crucial question of how to allocate edge capacities to different classes, we first introduce a key property of the uniclass Ohm law in the following theorem:

THEOREM 2. *On a uniclass resistive network with capacity-free undirected edges (resp., capacity-constrained directed edges), the electrical current assigned by the linear Ohm law (11) (resp., by the nonlinear Ohm law (14)) uniquely minimizes the functional $\|\operatorname{diag}(\boldsymbol{\sigma})\boldsymbol{B}_\circ^\top \boldsymbol{q}_\circ - \boldsymbol{f}\|$ among all admissible network flows which respect KCL at nodes.*

Extending this result to a multiclass resistive network, the vector of multiclass currents $\boldsymbol{f}$ must minimize the multiclass functional $\|\operatorname{diag}(\boldsymbol{\sigma})\boldsymbol{B}_\circ^\top \boldsymbol{q}_\circ - \boldsymbol{f}\|$. In the absence of edge capacity constraints, this is readily concluded from Th. 2 together with the flow independency among different classes. Under limited edge capacities, however, the configuration of $\boldsymbol{f}$ depends on the configuration of edge capacity factors $\boldsymbol{\theta}$; thus the minimizing $\boldsymbol{f}$ determines $\boldsymbol{\theta}$,

$$\boldsymbol{\theta} = \arg\min_{\boldsymbol{\theta}} \|\operatorname{diag}(\boldsymbol{\sigma})\boldsymbol{B}_\circ^\top \boldsymbol{q}_\circ - \boldsymbol{f}\|$$
$$\text{subject to: } \sum_{d \in \mathcal{K}} \boldsymbol{\theta}^{(d)} \preccurlyeq \mathbf{1}_{|\mathcal{E}|}. \tag{22}$$

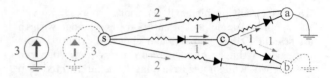

Figure 2: Node s injects two classes of electrical currents with intensity 3, one destined for node a and the other for node b. All nonlinear resistors have the conductance $\sigma_{ij}=1$ and the capacity $\mu_{ij}=5$.

It is worth noting that while the optimal $\boldsymbol{f}$ which solves (22) is unique, the related $\boldsymbol{\theta}$ is not necessarily unique, i.e. different $\boldsymbol{\theta}$ may lead to the same optimal $\boldsymbol{f}$. In Fig 2, for example, it is easily confirmed that to solve (22), two units of current destined for node a (resp., node b) should be sent via edge sa (resp., edge sb) and one unit via edges sc and ca (resp., edges sc and cb). Thus any division of edge capacities between the two classes is admissible as far as providing for class a (resp., class b) the capacity of at least two on edge sa (resp., edge sb) and the capacity of at least one on edges sc and ca (resp., edges sc and cb).

The upshot of this section is the next theorem that extends the concept of Dirichlet's principle, and from there the merit of minimizing dissipative energy, to multiclass conduction on capacity-constrained directed networks.

THEOREM 3. *Consider a multiclass capacitated directed network under a feasible vector of current sources $\boldsymbol{a}_\circ$, i.e. there exists at least one configuration of multiclass currents $\boldsymbol{f}$ that satisfy the multiclass KCL at nodes. Then the nonlinear Poisson equation (21) has a unique solution that minimizes the multiclass Dirichlet-like energy*

$$\vec{E}(\boldsymbol{q}_\circ) := \frac{1}{2}\, \boldsymbol{q}_\circ^\top\, \vec{\boldsymbol{L}}_\circ(\boldsymbol{q}_\circ) - \boldsymbol{q}_\circ^\top \boldsymbol{a}_\circ. \tag{23}$$

Further, minimizing $\vec{E}(\boldsymbol{q}_\circ)$ under the edge capacity allocation (22) is equivalent to solving

$$\text{Minimize: } \quad \vec{E}_R(\boldsymbol{f}) := \boldsymbol{f}^\top \operatorname{diag}(\boldsymbol{\sigma})^{-1} \boldsymbol{f}$$
$$\text{Subject to: } \quad 1)\ \ \mathbf{0} \preccurlyeq \sum_{d \in \mathcal{K}} \boldsymbol{f}^{(d)} \preccurlyeq \boldsymbol{\mu} \tag{24}$$
$$2)\ \ \boldsymbol{B}_\circ \boldsymbol{f} = \boldsymbol{a}_\circ$$

which formulates the minimization of dissipative energy subject to the network constraints and the multiclass KCL.

4. DIRICHLET-BASED ROUTING

On a multiclass data network, BP-based schemes transmit packets from only one class over each activated link at each timeslot. First, when the number of packets from individual classes is not enough to fill up the link capacities, network resources are squandered in this way. In other words, the larger capacity of network would be utilized, and so the average network delay would decrease, if the capacity of each activated link were properly stuffed with packets from different classes. Second, even if an individual class with the largest queue differential has enough packets to fill up a link, still, as we showed in [4], blindly stuffing the link with only that class would merely deplete the network resources with even negative impact on delay performance.

Our multiclass routing protocol is an answer to the question of how a dynamic routing policy, with no routing path constraint, can effectively utilize the maximum timeslot network resources. Our solution is inspired by the multiclass electric conduction developed in the previous section, telling us that a dissipative energy minimizing policy is supposed to send different classes on each activated link. Further, the optimal capacity allocation (22) suggests that a class d should receive a piece of capacity of edge ij proportional to $\sigma_{ij}^{(d)} q_{ij}^{(d)}$, i.e. its queue differential scaled by its related link profit-factor — reciprocal of the link cost-factor.

Our protocol has the same algorithmic structure, complexity, and overhead as BP that provides a convenient way of unifying it with the previous works on BP. Every timeslot n, it observes queue backlogs $q_i(n)$, and estimates channel capacities $\mu_{ij}(n)$ and link cost factors $\rho_{ij}^{(d)}(n)$, to make a network-layer packet transmission decision as follows.

Weighing: On every directed link ij and for each class d find $q_{ij}^{(d)}(n) := q_i^{(d)}(n) - q_j^{(d)}(n)$ and create a set

$$\mathcal{K}_{ij}(n) \subseteq \mathcal{K} \text{ such that } q_{ij}^{(d)}(n) > 0, \ \forall d \in \mathcal{K}_{ij}(n).$$

Fix $\widehat{f_{ij}^{(d)}}(n) = 0$ for each $d \notin \mathcal{K}_{ij}(n)$, and first find $\widehat{f_{ij}^{(d)}}(n)$ for every $d \in \mathcal{K}_{ij}(n)$ by solving the optimization problem

$$\text{Minimize: } \sum_{d \in \mathcal{K}_{ij}(n)} \left(\rho_{ij}^{(d)}(n)^{-1} q_{ij}^{(d)}(n) - \widehat{f_{ij}^{(d)}}(n) \right)^2$$

$$\text{Subject to: } \begin{cases} \sum_{d \in \mathcal{K}_{ij}(n)} \widehat{f_{ij}^{(d)}}(n) \leqslant \mu_{ij}(n) \\ 0 \leqslant \widehat{f_{ij}^{(d)}}(n) \leqslant q_{ij}^{(d)}(n), \ \forall d \in \mathcal{K}_{ij}(n) \end{cases} \quad (25)$$

where $\widehat{f_{ij}^{(d)}}(n)$ denotes the number of d-packets the link would transmit if activated — a predicted value that may not be realized. Then give a weight to each class $d \in \mathcal{K}_{ij}(n)$ as

$$w_{ij}^{(d)}(n) := 2 \rho_{ij}^{(d)}(n)^{-1} q_{ij}^{(d)}(n) \widehat{f_{ij}^{(d)}}(n) - \left(\widehat{f_{ij}^{(d)}}(n) \right)^2 \quad (26)$$

and aggregate them to determine the final link weight as

$$w_{ij}(n) := \sum_{d \in \mathcal{K}_{ij}(n)} w_{ij}^{(d)}(n). \quad (27)$$

Scheduling: Find the scheduling vector, in the same way as BP, using the max-weight scheduling (6).
Forwarding: On each activated link ij, transmit $\widehat{f_{ij}^{(d)}}(n)$ number of packets from the class d.

Discriminating link transmission predictions $\widehat{f_{ij}^{(d)}}(n)$, link actual transmissions $f_{ij}^{(d)}(n)$, and link capacities $\mu_{ij}(n)$ from each other is crucial to understand the algorithm. Another point is that like BP, our algorithm also rests on a centralized scheduling whose complexity can be prohibitive in practice. Fortunately, much progress has been made to ease this difficulty by designing decentralized schedulers with an arbitrary tradeoff between complexity and vicinity to the centralized performance (see [12, 8] and references therein).

Problem (25) is a standard least-norm optimization with variable bounds that can be solved in fast polynomial time at each node, i.e. in a fully decentralized manner. A related algorithm is developed as follows.

To simplify the notation, let us drop the overhat symbol and the time variable (n). First observe that

$$\text{if } \sum_{d \in \mathcal{K}_{ij}} q_{ij}^{(d)}/\rho_{ij}^{(d)} \leqslant \mu_{ij} \text{ then } f_{ij}^{(d)} = q_{ij}^{(d)}/\rho_{ij}^{(d)}$$

for each $d \in \mathcal{K}_{ij}$, and the problem is solved. Thus assume

$$\sum_{d \in \mathcal{K}_{ij}} q_{ij}^{(d)}/\rho_{ij}^{(d)} > \mu_{ij}.$$

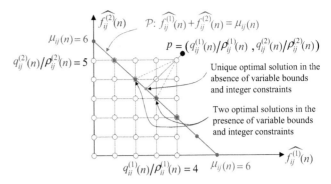

Figure 3: Geometry of solving (25) for a two-class case when $q_{ij}^{(1)}(n)/\rho_{ij}^{(1)}(n) + q_{ij}^{(2)}(n)/\rho_{ij}^{(2)}(n) > \mu_{ij}(n)$.

This converts the first constraint from inequality into equality, viz. $\sum_{d \in \mathcal{K}_{ij}} f_{ij}^{(d)} = \mu_{ij}$. Then a basic Lagrange argument shows that in the absence of lower variable bounds and integer constraints, the problem has a unique solution

$$f_{ij}^{(d)} = q_{ij}^{(d)}/\rho_{ij}^{(d)} + \left(\mu_{ij} - \sum_{d \in \mathcal{K}_{ij}} q_{ij}^{(d)}/\rho_{ij}^{(d)} \right)/|\mathcal{K}_{ij}|, \ \forall d \in \mathcal{K}_{ij}.$$

By geometry, the latter reads the projection of the point $p := \left(q_{ij}^{(1)}/\rho_{ij}^{(1)}, \cdots, q_{ij}^{(|\mathcal{K}_{ij}|)}/\rho_{ij}^{(|\mathcal{K}_{ij}|)} \right)$ onto the hyperplane

$$\mathcal{P}: \ \sum_{d \in \mathcal{K}_{ij}} f_{ij}^{(d)} = \mu_{ij}.$$

Under integer constraints, $\mathcal{P}$ becomes an integer lattice and the optimal solution(s) will be the vertex(es) of this lattice with the shortest Euclidean distance to the point p. Note that the solution to the integer problem is not necessarily unique. Subjecting the solution to the lower variable bounds, it must also meet $f_{ij}^{(d)} \geqslant 0$, $\forall d \in \mathcal{K}_{ij}$. A graphical demonstration of this procedure is illustrated in Fig. 3 for a two-class case. The following algorithm formulates this procedure to solve (25) when $\sum_{d \in \mathcal{K}_{ij}} q_{ij}^{(d)}/\rho_{ij}^{(d)} > \mu_{ij}$.

S1: Let $h = \left(\sum_{d \in \mathcal{K}_{ij}(n)} \rho_{ij}^{(d)}(n)^{-1} q_{ij}^{(d)}(n) - \mu_{ij}(n) \right)/|\mathcal{K}_{ij}(n)|$
and for $\forall d \in \mathcal{K}_{ij}(n)$ take $\widehat{f_{ij}^{(d)}}(n) = \rho_{ij}^{(d)}(n)^{-1} q_{ij}^{(d)}(n) - h$.

S2: Find $d_1 = \arg\min_{d \in \mathcal{K}_{ij}(n)} \widehat{f_{ij}^{(d)}}(n)$ and if $\widehat{f_{ij}^{(d_1)}}(n) < 0$, then remove d_1 from $\mathcal{K}_{ij}(n)$ and go back to S1.

S3: Let $r = \mu_{ij}(n) - \sum_{d \in \mathcal{K}_{ij}(n)} \lfloor \widehat{f_{ij}^{(d)}}(n) \rfloor$. For r randomly chosen classes in $\mathcal{K}_{ij}(n)$ assign $\widehat{f_{ij}^{(d)}}(n) = \lceil \widehat{f_{ij}^{(d)}}(n) \rceil$ and for other classes in $\mathcal{K}_{ij}(n)$ assign $\widehat{f_{ij}^{(d)}}(n) = \lfloor \widehat{f_{ij}^{(d)}}(n) \rfloor$.

Observe that S1 finds the optimal solution in the absence of variable bounds and integer constraints, S2 ensures that the solution meets the variable lower bounds, and S3 determines an integer solution by finding a vertex on the integer lattice $\mathcal{P}$ with the shortest distance to the initial solution obtained by S1-S2. The term "r randomly chosen classes" in S3 comes due to the fact that the integer problem may have more than one solution. Indeed, when the initial solution of S1-S2 is integer, it will be the solution to the integer problem too, and so unique. Otherwise, there potentially exist several vertices on the integer lattice with equal distance from the non-integer initial solution and shorter than the distance of all other vertices. This is best shown in Fig. 3.

We remark that on a uniclass network, link transmission predictions and link weights are simplified to

$$\widehat{f_{ij}}(n) := \min\{\rho_{ij}(n)^{-1} q_{ij}(n)^+, \mu_{ij}(n)\}$$

$$w_{ij}(n) := 2\,\rho_{ij}(n)^{-1} q_{ij}(n) \widehat{f_{ij}}(n) - \big(\widehat{f_{ij}}(n)\big)^2.$$

This recovers our Pareto-optimal Heat-Diffusion (HD) policy with $\beta = 1$, proposed for uniclass networks in [3].

5. PERFORMANCE ANALYSIS

In Sec. 3, we developed multiclass nonlinear electric conduction on resistive networks with capacity-constrained directed edges. In Sec. 4, on the other hand, we developed a routing protocol for multiclass interfering wireless networks. The former describes a deterministic continuous-time process, while the latter leads to a stochastic time-slotted process. This section shows how these two seemingly different problems are rigorously correlated with each other. It specifically shows that in a long-term average basis, packet flow on a wireless network governed by our protocol complies with electrical conduction on a suitably-defined resistive network, where the pivot is the notion of fluid limit. We also show the throughput optimality of our routing protocol and its delay minimization performance under uniform link cost-factors.

5.1 Throughput Optimality

Throughput optimality, as defined in Sec. 2.1, is an important quality factor of our routing protocol.

THEOREM 4. *Consider a multiclass wireless network with arrivals and channel states being i.i.d. random variables over timeslots and over nodes and links, and subject to an interference model that prohibits transmission to more than one neighbor at a timeslot. Then our routing protocol of Sec. 4 is throughput-optimal in the sense that it secures network stability for any stabilizable vector of arrivals $\boldsymbol{a}_\circ(n)$.*

5.2 Minimum Cost Routing

Fluid limit of a stochastic process is the limit dynamics obtained by *scaling* in time and amplitude. Let $\boldsymbol{X}(\omega, t)$ be a realization of a continuous-time stochastic process $\boldsymbol{X}$ along an arbitrary sample path ω, and define the scaled process $\boldsymbol{X}^r(\omega, t) := \boldsymbol{X}(\omega, rt)/r$ for any $r > 0$. Then a deterministic function $\tilde{\boldsymbol{X}}(t)$ is called *fluid limit* if there exist a sequence r and a sample path ω such that $\lim_{r \to \infty} \boldsymbol{X}^r(\omega, t) \to \tilde{\boldsymbol{X}}(t)$ uniformly on compact sets. The existence of fluid limit is guaranteed under very mild condition. Practically important, it is further shown that every fluid limit — a scaled trajectory — converges to a set of fully deterministic equations called *fluid model*, which provides an easy way to analyze the *rate-level* behavior of the original stochastic process. For the details, refer to [9, 7, 6] and references therein.

THEOREM 5. *Consider a multiclass wireless network under a stabilizable vector of arrivals $\boldsymbol{a}_\circ(n)$, and subject to an interference model that prohibits transmission to more than one neighbor at a timeslot. Suppose that the traffic is governed by our routing protocol of Sec. 4. Then the network fluid model is described by the conduction equations (19)–(22) where in those equations, $\boldsymbol{a}_\circ$ is replaced by the expected time average packet arrivals, $\boldsymbol{\mu}$ by the expected time average link capacities, and $\boldsymbol{\sigma}$ by the inverse of the expected time average link cost-factors from the wireless network, with the expected time average being defined in (2).*

Notice that fluid theorem is defined for continuous-time stochastic networks, while the wireless network is a time-slotted process. To resolve this issue, we derive a first-order continuous-time approximation of the wireless network dynamics using its cumulative processes [6]. Another point to remark is on the natural way that fluid theorem takes care of channel interference — the constraint that certain links may not be allowed to transmit at the same time. In fact, every constraint of wireless network and every action of a routing policy — our proposed protocol here — is considered in the derivation of network fluid model [6], which does not initially look like the conduction equations. Then Th. 5 is proved by showing that the dynamics of fluid model under our protocol asymptotically converge to (19)–(22).

Theorem 5 together with Th. 3 lead to the main goal of this paper on the minimization of routing cost.

COROLLARY 1. *Consider a multiclass wireless network under a stabilizable vector of arrivals $\boldsymbol{a}_\circ(n)$, and subject to an interference model that prohibits transmission to more than one neighbor at a timeslot. Then our routing protocol of Sec. 4 solves the minimum cost routing problem (1).*

To our knowledge, this is the first time that a feasible network-layer routing policy asserts the strict minimization of a general routing penalty subject to network stability. Note that in the V-parameter BP [17], the $[O(V), O(1/V)]$ delay-cost tradeoff prevents minimizing the average routing cost subject to network stability, i.e. delay grows to infinity as routing cost is pushed towards its minimum.

5.3 Average Network Delay Minimization

THEOREM 6. *Consider a multiclass wireless network with arrivals and channel states being i.i.d. random variables over timeslots and over nodes and links, and subject to an interference model that prohibits transmission to more than one neighbor at a timeslot. Suppose that all wireless links are of unit cost factor. Consider a class of network-layer routing policies that act based only on current queue congestion and current channel states. Within this class, our routing protocol of Sec. 4 minimizes the average network delay by solving the optimization problem*

$$Minimize: \quad \limsup_{\tau \to \infty} \frac{1}{\tau} \sum_{n=0}^{\tau-1} \mathbb{E}\Big\{ \sum_{i \in \mathcal{V}} \sum_{d \in \mathcal{K}} q_i^{(d)}(n) \Big\} \quad (28)$$

$$Subject\ to: \quad 0 \leqslant \sum_{d \in \mathcal{K}} f_{ij}^{(d)}(n) \leqslant \mu_{ij}(n), \; \forall ij \in \mathcal{E}.$$

Note that by Little's Theorem, for a given packet arrival rate, the expected time average total queue congestion in (28) is proportional to long-term average end-to-end network delay. Hence, solving (28) indeed ensures minimizing average network delay. In the light of Th. 5, this result should not be very surprising, as when all the links are of equal cost factors, the minimization of the Dirichlet routing cost becomes in fact equivalent to the minimization of average total routing path on the network, which is closely related to the average network delay.

6. SIMULATION RESULTS

We consider a wireless network with 50 nodes randomly distributed on a surface. Links are placed between every two nodes whose proximity distance is less than a threshold, and

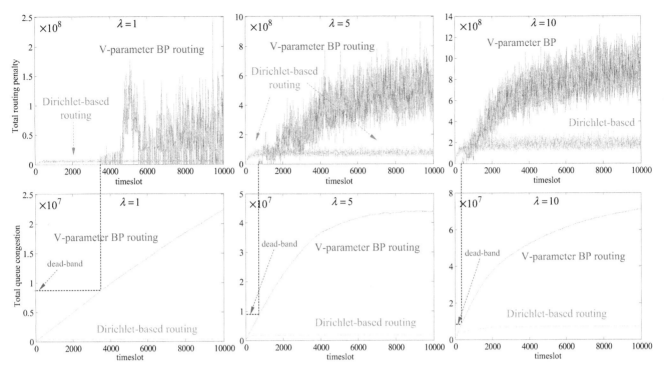

Figure 4: Comparing timeslot performance of our protocol and V-parameter BP with $V = 0.8$ for exogenous arrival rates $\lambda = 1, 5, 10$: (top) Total routing penalty. (bottom) Total number of packets in the network.

extra links are added to make the network connected. Links are considered as two-way wireless channels, i.e. for any directed link $ij \in \mathcal{E}$ there exists $ji \in \mathcal{E}$ with the same capacity and cost factor. The network runs under 1-hop interference model, i.e. links with common node cannot transmit at the same time. Assume that every node sends packets to every other node, forming a multiclass multihop wireless network. Different classes are generated at each node following Poisson's random variables with parameter λ, where all of them are i.i.d. over timeslots and over nodes and links.

Each link gets a random cost factor $\rho_{ij} \in [1, 10]$ for all classes at the beginning that remains constant during the simulation. At every timeslot, the capacity of each link follows a Gaussian distribution with the mean of m_{ij} packets and the variance of 150 packets. To assign m_{ij} to different links, we adopt Shannon capacity with power transmission P_{ij}, noise intensity N_{ij}, and a bandwidth of 1500, viz. $m_{ij} = 1500 \log_2(1 + P_{ij}/N_{ij})$. Each node can expend 30 units of transmission power per timeslot, which under 1-hop interference model leads to $P_{ij} = 30$ for each activated link. At the beginning, a noise intensity $N_{ij} \in [1, 5]$ is randomly assigned to each link and is kept fixed during the simulation.

The top panels in Fig. 4 display the timeslot evolution of total routing penalty $R(n) := \sum_{ij \in \mathcal{E}} \sum_{d \in \mathcal{K}} \rho_{ij} \left(f_{ij}^{(d)}(n) \right)^2$ for three arrival rates corresponding to the Poisson parameters $\lambda = 1, 5, 10$ packets per timeslot, comparing the performance of our routing protocol and V-parameter BP with $V = 0.8$. Note that the Dirichlet routing cost, as defined in (1), is the expected time average of $R(n)$. The bottom panels display the timeslot evolution of the total number of packets in the network for the same Poisson parameters.

Long-term average performance of the two routing policies are compared in Fig. 5 as a function of the arrival rate λ growing from 1 to 10 in unit steps. The average is taken

on the last 40000 slots, when the system runs for 50000 slots starting from zero initial condition. For $\lambda = 1$, average total number of packets under our protocol is only 312K packets, compared with 29400K packets under the V-parameter BP; likewise, the Dirichlet routing cost under our protocol is only 5100K units, compared with 91000K units under the V-parameter BP. This enormous difference in performance gets even larger by the growth of arrival rates λ.

Besides the long-term average performance in both queue congestion and routing cost, the top panels of Fig. 4 clearly show much smaller steady-state oscillations, and much faster transient-time response in the network under our routing protocol. Further, while our protocol shows an immediate act to the traffic rate, the V-parameter BP waits until the network reaches a minimum total queue congestion, called *dead-band* here, which is bigger than 8000K packets for $V = 0.8$ and grows even larger with the increase of V.

7. CONCLUSION

We developed a network-layer routing protocol for multiclass multihop wireless networks that minimizes a general quadratic routing penalty subject to throughput optimality. The protocol acts dynamically with no prescribed routing path information, and requires no knowledge of arrival statistics and topology probabilities, which make it useful on time-varying mobile and ad-hoc networks. We proposed a new methodology to study the long-term average behavior of packet routing in wireless networks with interference by mapping the communication network into a nonlinear resistive network in an effort to leverage classical methods in electrical circuits. This allowed us to formulate the least cost routing as a Dirichlet problem — with understood mathematical properties — subject to network constraints.

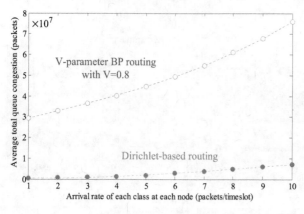 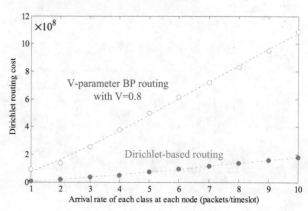

Figure 5: Expected time average total number of packets in the network against the exogenous arrival rates changing from $\lambda = 1$ to $\lambda = 10$. Dashed lines display third degree polynomial interpolation.

8. ACKNOWLEDGMENTS

This work has been supported in part by the NSF grants CNS-1017881 and CNS-1049541.

9. REFERENCES

[1] N. Baccour, A. Koubaa, L. Mottola, M. Zuniga, Y. Habib, C. Boano, and M. Alves. Radio link quality estimation in wireless sensor networks: a survey. *ACM Tr. Senor Networks*, 34:1–33, 2012.

[2] R. Banirazi, E. Jonckheere, and B. Krishnamachari. Heat diffusion algorithm for resource allocation and routing in multihop wireless networks. In *GLOBECOM*, 2012.

[3] R. Banirazi, E. Jonckheere, and B. Krishnamachari. Heat-Diffusion: Pareto optimal dynamic routing for time-varying wireless networks. In *INFOCOM*, 2014.

[4] R. Banirazi, E. Jonckheere, and B. Krishnamachari. Minimum delay in class of throughput-optimal control policies on wireless networks. In *ACC*, 2014.

[5] R. Banirazi, E. Jonckheere, and B. Krishnamachari. Dirichlet's principle on multiclass multihop wireless networks: minimum cost routing subject to stability. Available at http://eudoxus2.usc.edu, USC, 2014.

[6] R. Banirazi, E. Jonckheere, and B. Krishnamachari. Wireless network thermodynamics: interfering stochastic multiclass diffusion on limited capacity. Available at http://eudoxus2.usc.edu, USC, 2014.

[7] M. Bramson. Stability of queueing networks. *Probability Surveys*, 5:169–345, 2008.

[8] L. Bui, S. Sanghavi, and R. Srikant. Distributed link scheduling with constant overhead. *IEEE/ACM Tr. Networking*, 17:1467–1480, 2009.

[9] J. Dai. Stability of fluid and stochastic processing networks. *MaPhySto Misc. Pub.*, no. 9, 1999.

[10] A. Eryilmaz and R. Srikant. Fair resource allocation wireless networks using queue-length-based scheduling and congestion control. In *INFOCOM*, 2005.

[11] L. Evans. *Partial Differential Equations*. American Mathematical Society, 1998.

[12] L. Jiang and J. Walrand. Approaching throughput optimality in distributed csma scheduling algorithms with collisions. *IEEE/ACM Tr. Networking*, 19:816–829, 2011.

[13] L. Lin, N. Shroff, and R. Srikant. Asymptotically optimal power-aware routing for multihop wireless networks with renewable energy sources. In *INFOCOM*, 2005.

[14] X. Lin and N. Shroff. Joint rate control and scheduling in multihop wireless networks. In *CDC*, 2004.

[15] S. Moeller, A. Sridharan, B. Krishnamachari, and O. Gnawali. Routing without routes: the backpressure collection protocol. In *IPSN*, 2010.

[16] M. Neely. Energy optimal control for time varying wireless networks. In *INFOCOM*, 2005.

[17] M. Neely. *Stochastic Network Optimization with Application to Communication and Queuing Systems*. Morgan & Claypool, 2010.

[18] M. Neely. Optimal energy and delay tradeoffs for multiuser wireless downlinks. *IEEE Tr. Information Theory*, 53:3095–3113, 2007.

[19] M. Neely, E. Modiano, and C. Li. Fairness and optimal stochastic control for heterogeneous networks. In *INFOCOM*, 2005.

[20] M. Neely, E. Modiano, and C. Rohrs. Dynamic power allocation and routing for time varying wireless networks. In *INFOCOM*, 2003.

[21] E. Stai, J. Baras, and S. Papavassiliou. Throughput-delay tradeoff in wireless multi-hop networks via greedy hyperbolic embedding. In *MTNS*, 2012.

[22] A. Stolyar. Maximizing queueing network utility subject to stability: greedy primal-dual algorithm. *Queueing Systems*, 50:401–457, 2005.

[23] L. Tassiulas and A. Ephremides. Stability of constrained queueing systems and scheduling policies for maximum throughput in multihop radio networks. *IEEE Tr. Automatic Control*, 37:1936–1949, 1992.

[24] F. Wu, S. Zhong, and C. Qiaoi. Globally optimal channel assignment for non-cooperative wireless networks. In *INFOCOM*, 2008.

[25] L. Ying, S. Shakkottai, A. Reddy, and S. Liu. On combining shortest-path and back-pressure routing over multi-hop wireless networks. *IEEE/ACM Tr. Networking*, 19:841–854, 2011.

[26] Y. Yu, B. Krishnamachari, and V. Prasanna. Energy-latency tradeoffs for data gathering in wireless sensor networks. In *INFOCOM*, 2004.

Energy-Efficient Multi-Hop Broadcasting in Low Power and Lossy Networks

Chi-Anh La
Grenoble Institute of
Technology, Grenoble
Informatics Laboratory
Grenoble, France
Chi-Anh.La@imag.fr

Liviu-Octavian Varga
STMicroelectronics,
Crolles, France
liviu-
octavian.varga@st.com

Martin Heusse and
Andrzej Duda
Grenoble Institute of
Technology, Grenoble
Informatics Laboratory
Grenoble, France
{Heusse, Duda}@imag.fr

ABSTRACT

In this paper, we investigate schemes for energy-efficient multi-hop broadcasting in large-scale dense Wireless Sensor Networks. We begin with an initial simplified study of the schemes for relay selection. Our first finding is that MPR-based (Multipoint Relay) mechanisms work poorly in a dense network while the recently proposed *Multicast Protocol for Low power and Lossy Networks (MPL)* protocol based on Trickle performs better. However, Trickle requires to overhear packet retransmissions in the vicinity, while sensor nodes try to avoid overhearing by periodically waking up and going to sleep to save energy.

We propose *Beacon-based Forwarding Tree (BFT)*, a new scheme that achieves similar performance to MPL, although it fits better the case of nodes with low radio duty cycling MACs of the type of beacon-enabled IEEE 802.15.4. Our scheme also guarantees network coverage and its optimized version results in the shortest path distance to the broadcast source at a cost of lesser load mitigation. We compare and discuss the measured performance of MPL on top of Contiki-MAC and BFT over beacon-enabled 802.15.4 on a Contiki testbed. The experimental results of the comparisons show that BFT may achieve very good performance for a range of broadcast intensity, it has a predictable power consumption, a remarkable low power consumption for leaf nodes, and low loss rates. On the other hand, MPL over ContikiMAC can obtain very low duty cycles for low broadcast traffic.

Categories and Subject Descriptors

C.2.1 [**Computer-Communication Networks**]: Network Architecture and Design—*Network topology, Wireless communication*; C.2.2 [**Computer-Communication Networks**]: Network Protocols—*Routing protocols*

Keywords

Wireless Sensor Networks; beacon-enabled 802.15.4; IPv6; multicast; multi-hop broadcast

1. INTRODUCTION

In this paper, we consider the problem of energy-efficient multi-hop broadcasting in Wireless Sensor Networks (WSNs). We are interested in particular in networks called by IETF *Low power and Lossy Networks (LLNs)* that extend Internet connectivity to sensor nodes. Such networks mainly support the *many-to-one* type of data traffic (called also *convergecast* from sensor nodes to the sink) and *one-to-one* communications (sink to a node, node-to-node). A *multi-hop broadcast* or *one-to-all* mode of communication in which a node can send a packet to all other nodes in the network via multi-hop routes is also useful for many application purposes, for instance for code updates [1] or data dissemination [2, 3]. Multi-hop broadcasting is also a basic functionality used by routing protocols to spread routing updates or to look for routes [4, 5, 6, 7, 8]. This kind of traffic involves all nodes in the network so its performance is critical for overall energy efficiency. We consider large-scale and dense WSNs, because in this type of networks all problems are exacerbated, especially those related to network performance and energy consumption.

Packet forwarding in the process of multi-hop broadcasting needs to take into account *duty cycling* (nodes sleeping almost all the time to save energy) and node ability to perform a local broadcast—send a frame to all neighbors in the radio range. Many existing MAC access methods for wireless sensor networks propose different schemes to achieve low duty cycles that currently may go to less than 1%. In the context of LLNs that we want to consider in this paper, we are particularly interested in two MAC layers: Contiki-MAC [9] available in the Contiki uIPv6 stack [10] and the standard beacon-enabled IEEE 802.15.4 [11]. ContikiMAC follows the preamble sampling approach of CSMA-MPS [12] aka X-MAC [13] and optimizes further communications with the *phase-lock*—the sender learns the wake-up phase of the receiver so it can send subsequent frames right at the instant the receiver wakes up. However, ContikiMAC suffers from energy-expensive local broadcasts: a node has to send a broadcast frame several times so that its neighbors that may wake up at different instants will eventually receive the frame.

The IEEE 802.15.4 [11] *beacon-enabled* mode defines super-frames with beacons for synchronizing a node with its coordinator. Nodes associated with a coordinator contend for channel access according to a slotted CSMA/CA scheme during the *active period* at the beginning of the super-frame. An associated node can go to sleep just after its transmission (or after the beacon when the node does not have any data to send), which enables low duty cycles. The beacon-enabled mode offers inexpensive local broadcasts from the coordinator to its associated nodes, but the nodes cannot send local broadcasts to their coordinator and they need to use unicast frames.

Classical Flooding (CF) is the simplest way of implementing multi-hop broadcast: when a node receives a broadcast packet for the first time, it forwards the packet to its neighbors (duplicates are detected and dropped). Flooding is inefficient, because of a broadcast storm generated by concomitant packet retransmissions [14]. Thus, the main design problem related to multi-hop broadcasting is the choice of the forwarding nodes that relay a packet. As the energy consumption is proportional to the number of relayed packets (more precisely, to the time the sender and the receiver are awake for all packet transmissions during broadcast), we aim at minimizing this number. We also need to reduce the number of relays, but in a way that guarantees that all nodes receive the broadcast (all nodes need to be *covered* by the relays). Another aspect of the relay selection is to choose the relays that have the links with their neighbors of sufficient quality. At the same time, the number of relays should not be too low to guarantee a sufficiently high delivery rate in presence of links that may drop packets. Reducing the number of relaying nodes and their neighbors that compete for the radio channel also results in lower collision rate, which is an important consideration especially in dense networks.

Constructing the optimal core of relays for multi-hop broadcasting consists of building a *minimum Connected Dominating Set (CDS)* defined as the minimum set of relays that guarantees network connectivity. However, finding a minimum CDS is known as a NP-hard problem [15] to which several authors proposed distributed approximate solutions. Adjih et al. proposed *Multipoint Relays (MPRs)* selected based on the information gathered from the two-hop neighborhood to construct CDS [16]. MPRs are also used in OLSR (Optimized Link State Routing Protocol) [17], the standard routing protocol for ad hoc networks. The MANET IETF group also studied other approaches for relay selection [18].

Recently, the IETF ROLL working group standardized RPL, the routing protocol for LLNs [7]. It also proposed *Multicast Protocol for Low power and Lossy Networks (MPL)*, a forwarding mechanism for LLN networks [19]. By using the *Trickle* algorithm [1], MPL only requires each node to keep the information on MPL seeds, nodes that initiate multicasts in the considered domain and the last sequence number used by each seed. Nodes also need to buffer multicast packets that may require forwarding. The Trickle algorithm allows MPL to be density-aware, so that the communication rate scales logarithmically with density. MPL based on Trickle fits well the operational principle of ContikiMAC—Trickle governs the interval after which a node forwards a packet that may become long if the network is stable, thus leading to a low duty cycle. Moreover, the operation of Trickle requires overhearing, which is supported by ContikiMAC.

In the case of beacon-enabled 802.15.4, Trickle becomes irrelevant, because the wake up periods of nodes are governed by the beacon interval and not by the Trickle adaptation. In this paper, we propose a method called Beacon-based Forwarding Tree (BFT) for selecting forwarding relays in a beacon-enabled 802.15.4 network. We consider that for convergecast many-to-one communications, the network will construct a Collection Tree (CT) that will coincide with the underlying IEEE 802.15.4 Beacon-based Forwarding Tree built for connectivity at the MAC layer. BFT defines two beacon intervals: a short one and a long one. During the construction of the tree, a node starts with the long beacon interval and if a leaf node associates with it, the node becomes a coordinator and begins to use the short beacon interval, which increases the probability that other nodes will associate with it (they will receive the beacon before the beacons from other nodes that use the long interval). The resulting BFT tree will have a small number of coordinators (relays), but each coordinator will have a large number of associated nodes.

We start the paper with an initial simplified study of the schemes for relay selection. The study adopts simplified Unit Disk assumptions to analyze the primary properties of the relay core in dense wireless sensor networks. The study shows that MPL/ContikiMAC and BFT/802.15.4 result in the best performance. We then compare these two schemes in an experimental setup by measuring their implementations on an operational testbed. The comparison shows that:

- MPL/ContikiMAC can obtain very low duty cycles for low broadcast traffic,

- BFT/802.15.4 supports better an increased traffic intensity,

- BFT/802.15.4 also presents the advantage of asymmetric duty cycles: leaf nodes may obtain duty cycles much lower than other nodes and lower duty cycles than MPL/ContikiMAC, which is suitable for nodes with energy harvesting.

2. BEACON-BASED FORWARDING TREE (BFT)

Before comparing the schemes for relay selection, we define BFT in detail, the proposed method for beacon-enabled 802.15.4 networks. We aim at designing a mechanism to construct a forwarding tree that will also serve as a Collection Tree for convergecast. For convenience, we use the IEEE 802.15.4 cluster tree terminology: *coordinators* are relays for their *associated nodes*. An associated node can be at the same time a coordinator for other nodes (except the sink that is only a coordinator).

A coordinator defines a super-frame to synchronize the communication of its associated nodes. The super-frame is divided into an active period for communication with associated nodes and an inactive one during which the coordinator may go to sleep. Periodically, each Beacon Interval (BI), a coordinator sends a beacon frame to announce the start of its active period.

In BFT, each node may become a coordinator in the following distributed way. A node uses two beacon intervals BI_{min} and BI_{max} for sending beacons. As soon as a node

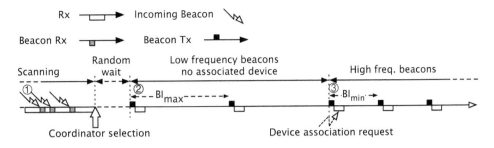

Figure 1: Principle of BFT: a node first scans for beacons from neighbors (1) and then choose a coordinator. It then sends beacons to enable other nodes to join the network: at first, it sends beacons at a small rate (2) and switches to a higher rate if it becomes a coordinator for at least one node (3).

associates with a coordinator, it randomly selects instant t at which it starts to send a beacon with the interval BI_{max}. If it receives an association request from a node, it becomes a coordinator (and a relay for broadcasts) and accelerates the beacon interval to BI_{min}. This change will make it more likely that other nodes wanting to join the network will receive its beacon and send association requests (cf. Figure 1). The change will also increase the duty cycle of the node. Similarly to the Guha-Khuller algorithm to build a CDS [20] described in detail later, or CORD [3] core node selection, the node with a larger number of neighbors is more likely to receive first an association request and become a relay. A node that remains with BI_{max} will not participate in forwarding broadcast packets. Moreover, such a node will have a much lower duty cycle, so it will consume less energy—only for its own sensing operations and for exchanging frames with its coordinator.

The aim of this scheme is to bias coordinator (and thus relay) selection towards selecting the nodes that are already relays (they send beacons at a fast rate). The probability that a newly arriving node receives first a beacon transmitted by an already active relay in presence of D nodes sending beacons with a slow rate is:

$$P[\text{Choose already active}] = \frac{BI_{max}}{BI_{max} + D \times BI_{min}}.$$

The probability is greater for greater ratio $\frac{BI_{max}}{BI_{min}}$, which results in more nodes joining an already active relay so the number of relays does not increase. Nevertheless, there is a tradeoff: a large value of BI_{max} gives us a lower number of relays throughout the network, but results in a long latency of association for a node that would be covered by a limited number of coordinators.

As a result of this scheme of operation, BFM creates a forwarding tree with a small number of relays. It guarantees the coverage of all nodes in the network, since they all associate with a coordinator as long as the network is not partitioned. To find minimal hop paths, nodes may include the distance from the broadcast source in beacons (typically, this information can be included in the payload of 802.15.4 beacon frames). To optimize the distance to the broadcast source, nodes should overhear all nearby coordinators and collect the distance information in beacons for scanning duration SP. SP can vary from 0 (no path optimization) to BI_{max} (the variant that we call an Optimized Beacon-based Forwarding Tree—Opt-BFT in the comparisons below). The

scanning procedure can be repeated later on to allow nodes to reselect the optimal paths in case of a topology change.

3. FORWARDING RELAY SELECTION SCHEMES

Much research has already addressed the problem of selecting forwarding relays in wireless networks. In this section, we present a brief description of the existing schemes together with the discussion of their advantages and drawbacks.

3.1 MPR-Based Mechanisms

The OLSR routing protocol for MANETs defined a mechanism based on MPRs to build a forwarding backbone for disseminating topology control messages. Each node constructs an MPR set by exchanging the information on the two-hop neighborhood in HELLO messages. An MPR set of a node is the minimum set of its one-hop neighbors that provides reachability to all of its two-hop neighbors. The selecting node informs its MPRs through a flag in HELLO messages [21]. Several variants of the MPR selection mechanism exist:

- *S-MPR (Source-specific MPR)*. Each node keeps track of its MPR selector and solely forwards a broadcast packet coming from its selector (downstream broadcast only). This technique avoids forwarding any packet from any direction, thus reducing flooding.

- *NS-MPR (Non-Source-specific MPR)*. It is similar to S-MPR, but it does not require the previous hop information when forwarding a broadcast packet. NS-MPR uses all MPRs to forward a packet from any host.

- *CDS-MPR (Connected Dominating Set MPR)*. It reduces the number of forwarding nodes to a less redundant subset than NS-MPR. After selecting the set of MPRs, a node using CDS-MPR forwards broadcast packets if and only if: i) its identifier is higher than all identifiers of its one-hop neighbors or ii) it has been selected as an MPR by the node that has the highest identifier in its one-hop neighborhood.

The CDS-MPR mechanism efficiently reduces the number of forwarders, since it coordinates nodes that use the same node as a forwarder. However, it does not guarantee minimal hop count paths [22]. If the goal of the selection mechanism is to provide an efficient flooding mitigation, CDS-MPR is the best MPR-based mechanism to achieve this goal.

3.2 MPL

In a WSN composed of resource-constrained devices, MPR-based mechanisms require the two-hop topology information and the cost of maintaining such information grows polynomially with network density. MPL avoids the need for constructing or maintaining a multicast or broadcast forwarding overlay. It uses the Trickle algorithm [23]: on receiving packet m, node i selects a random interval $I \in [I_{\min}, I_{\max}]$ and computes random waiting time $t \in [\frac{I}{2}, I]$ during which it counts the number of times k it receives forwarded packet m. After time t, node i suppresses forwarding of m if $k > K$ or forwards m otherwise. K controls the transmission redundancy throughout the network. MPL is simple to implement and requires only a limited memory to keep track of on-going broadcast dissemination processes. Basically, it needs to store the on-going broadcast packets and the associated counters k that count redundant retransmissions. The forwarder set in MPL is created on-demand and may change randomly with every packet, hence it is more dynamic compared to MPR-based mechanisms.

Nevertheless, MPL suffers from several drawbacks. Similarly to CDS-MPR, MPL does not guarantee minimal hop count paths. In a low duty cycle WSN with a MAC layer based on preamble sampling such as ContikiMAC, sending a local broadcast to all neighbors requires repeating the transmission during the whole duty cycle that may last for a long time compared to the packet duration, which consumes a large amount of energy. Packet repetitions increase the load on the channel and the latency whereas collisions increase the overhead and make it challenging to count the actual number of forwarded broadcast packets. Furthermore, the choice of the redundancy limit K in MPL may impact the broadcast delivery coverage, which is not guaranteed to include all destinations anyway. In fact, even when there is no packet loss, broadcast reachability can be affected by canceled retransmissions when K is reached even though some nodes have not received the packet.

3.3 RPL Preferred Parent (RPL-PP)

IETF standardized RPL, a Routing Protocol for Low-power and Lossy Networks [7]. RPL builds a DODAG (Destination Oriented Directed Acyclic Graph) rooted at the sink node to support multipoint-to-point traffic towards the sink. A node, upon joining the DODAG sends DIO (DODAG Information Object) messages to announce its rank R in the DODAG (its distance to the root). Each node uses the information in DIOs to identify a set of parents and to choose a preferred parent that provides the best rank. Nodes also send DAO (DODAG Destination Advertisement Object) messages to construct downward routes (from the sink to every node) for point-to-multipoint traffic.

A network running RPL can use the Preferred Parent Set as the relay set to forward multicast or broadcast packets [24]. Since every node should send DIOs and each node has its preferred parent, so all nodes are covered by the relay set. Note that the nodes in the set forward downward broadcast packets as well as unicasts. Furthermore, each node can always switch to a better rank parent, which results in the best (or shortest) path.

3.4 Centralized Connected Dominating Set (C-CDS)

Guha *et al.* proposed a simple centralized solution to build a CDS [20]. By default, all nodes are colored in white. The algorithm initially selects the node with the highest node degree, marks it in black (relay node) and its neighbors are colored in gray (they are now covered). Then, the algorithm iteratively selects the gray node with the greatest number of white neighbors, marks it black, and its neighbors become gray. The algorithm terminates when there are no more white nodes. Black nodes form a CDS with a size of at most $2(1 + H(\Delta))$ of the optimal solution, where H is the harmonic function and Δ is the maximum degree. Although this algorithm is centralized, so it stands out from other presented mechanisms, we use it as a reference for our evaluation.

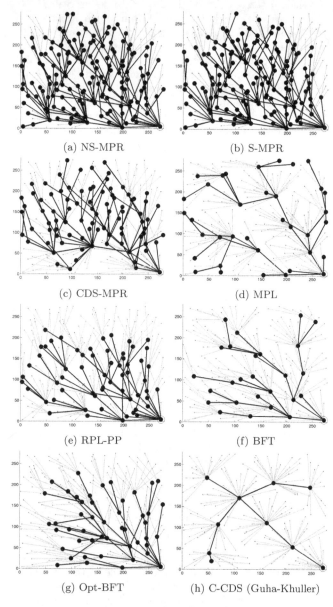

(a) NS-MPR (b) S-MPR

(c) CDS-MPR (d) MPL

(e) RPL-PP (f) BFT

(g) Opt-BFT (h) C-CDS (Guha-Khuller)

Figure 2: Forwarding relays for 200 nodes with average node degree of 40. Big black dots represent the relays. The broadcast source is at the right bottom corner.

4. PRELIMINARY ANALYSIS OF THE CONSIDERED SCHEMES

We have implemented all presented mechanisms: three MPR-based algorithms, MPL, RPL-PP, C-CDS, and the proposed BFT scheme in a simulator, a Matlab program that allows modeling the relay selection schemes with Unit Disk graph assumptions. For MPR-based mechanisms, nodes compute their MPR set using a greedy heuristic [17] that gave the best results in our experiments. For MPL, we set $I_{min} = 1$, $I_{max} = 20$, and $K = 3$, the time unit being the simulator time tick in this case, as only relative values matter in the simulation. To build BFT without path optimization, we use $BI_{min} = 1$, $BI_{max} = 20$, and $SP = 0$. For Opt-BFT, the scheme with path optimization, we select scanning duration $SP = BI_{max}$ to obtain the distance to the broadcast source of all nearby coordinators before selecting the relay.

We have run simulations for a varying number of nodes uniformly placed on variable size square areas. We set the radio range r to 80m (unless otherwise specified) resulting in an average node degree of 40 on the areas of side lengths from 280m to 640m with 200 to 1000 nodes. The broadcast source is randomly selected in each simulation run and we average the results from at least 5 simulations runs. To make the results comparable, we use the same set of broadcast sources for all evaluated schemes.

Figure 2 shows the set of relays selected by different schemes in a 200 node topology (the figure illustrates the cases in which the broadcast source is at the bottom right corner). Given the C-CDS computed by the Guha-Khuller algorithm as a reference, we find that BFT and MPL result in a reasonable relay set size, while MPR-based mechanisms cannot reduce the number of relays in this high-density network topology.

In the simulation, all MPR schemes suffer from the fact that relay selection is solely based on the local information within a 2-hop distance without breaking reachability to any node in the network over the shortest path. Unfortunately, in the considered dense topologies, each node needs to designate many MPRs to cover all of its 2-hop neighbors, so that many nodes end up being an MPR of one or more neighbors. The nodes at the edge of the considered area are less likely to become part of the relay set, as they have simply less neighbors to which they give access. Relay selection under MPL is interestingly biased in an opposite way: the nodes at the edge are more likely to become relays as they naturally have less opportunity to receive broadcast packets multiple times. Finally, BFT excludes the nodes at the edges, because they do not give access to any other node. BFT builds a sparse tree, because existing relays have more opportunity to propose association to other nodes.

4.1 Reduction of the Number of Relays

We have evaluated flooding mitigation by computing the number of relays generated by each scheme (cf. Figure 3). The figure gives a quantitative evaluation of what we can see in the forwarding overlays shown in Figure 2. We can observe that in a dense network, NS-MPR and S-MPR end up with over 90% of nodes becoming MPRs due to the lack of

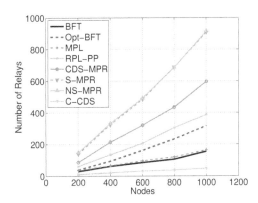

Figure 3: Number of relays with [200...1000] nodes. Average node degree of 40.

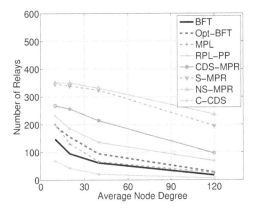

Figure 4: Number of relays with 400 nodes for varying average node degree [10...120].

coordination in the selection of MPRs among nodes. CDS-MPR also results in around 60% of MPR nodes, which shows that MPR-based mechanisms are not suitable for dense network topologies. In contrast, MPL and BFT perform better with only 18% of nodes selected as relays. For Opt-BFT, the results show that to optimize paths, we need to have more relays, but this number stays fairly low at around 30% of nodes compared to 90% in S-MPR.

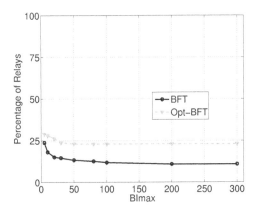

Figure 5: Number of relays with 400 nodes for varying BI_{max}.

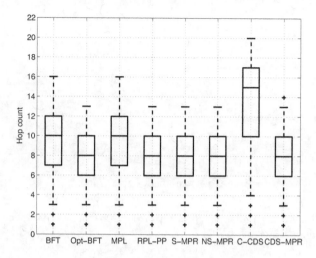

Figure 6: Distance from the broadcast source to nodes in the network with 1000 nodes and average node degree of 40.

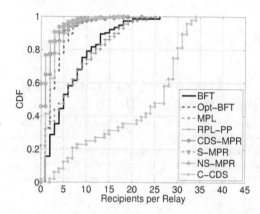

Figure 7: Effective broadcast recipients per relay in the network with 1000 nodes and average node degree of 40.

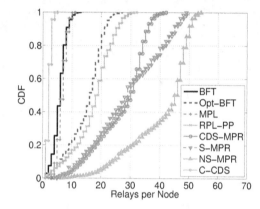

Figure 8: Broadcast redundancy: the number of relays per node with 1000 nodes and average node degree of 40.

To assess the impact of network density on the relay set size, we have simulated a network with 400 nodes and variable radio range r that generates a varying average node degree from 10 to 120. Figure 4 shows that in a highly dense network (average node degree of 120), S-MPR performs better than NS-MPR. Nevertheless, all MPR-based mechanisms result in a high number of relays. MPL and BFT give similar results with MPL having a slightly higher number of relays compared to BFT when the node degree is low (10–20). The Trickle redundancy factor K, which does not change with node density, is the main cause for this increased footprint. Opt-BFT also results in a lower number of relays compared to RPL-PP.

Figure 5 shows the number of relays in function of BI_{max} for BFT. Actually, long BI_{max} up to 200 can reduce the relay set size to 12% (twice as much as the C-CDS solution that results in 5%). For Opt-BFT, this number goes down to 24%.

4.2 Path Length

We have computed the distance in hops from the broadcast source to nodes. Figure 6 represents the hop distance in boxplot with 25th, 50th, and 75th percentile. The figure shows that MPR-based schemes have shorter paths compared to MPL and BFT. However, the difference is not large: the longest distance for MPL and BFT is 16 while it is 13 for MPR-based schemes. We can also observe that Opt-BFT results in shorter paths than MPL thanks to the distance information included in the beacon messages used for selecting coordinators. RPL-PP and Opt-BFT lead to the same distances as S-MPR and NS-MPR that guarantee the shortest hop paths [25], but they achieve this result with more relays than for the unoptimized BFT.

To evaluate the efficiency of multi-hop broadcast forwarding, we define an *effective broadcast recipient* of a relay: it is the first node in the relay vicinity that forwards a broadcast packet. If a relay has no effective recipients, it relays the packet for nothing. Conversely, a relay with many effective recipients plays a central role in packet dissemination. Figure 7 presents the CDF of the number of effective broadcast recipients per relay. We can observe that MPR-based schemes have a high number of relays with no effective recip-

ients. MPL performs better, but it still has more than 20% of relays without effective recipients. We can also observe how MPL, compared to BFT, leads to the use of more relays located at the edge of the simulation area, (the nodes having a degree lower than the average and consequently less effective recipients). These nodes have more probability to forward a broadcast since they receive less redundant broadcasts, hence the number of retransmissions cannot reach the redundancy limit K. BFT is more efficient with every relay having at least a recipient, which is achieved at the cost of the association request exchange, since a node becomes a relay only if it has at least one associated node.

4.3 Broadcast Redundancy

Wireless transmissions in WSNs are usually subject to losses, so achieving a high packet delivery rate may require some redundant transmissions. Redundancy is in fact the number of relays a given node may receive each packet from. Figure 8 shows a CDF of this number. MPR-based schemes lead to the highest redundancy (up to 30-45 on the average) while a C-CDS node has a low number of relays with an average of 2. BFT and MPL result in much lower redundancy with every node having 5-7 relays in the communication range. RPL-PP presents more redundancy than Opt-BFT due to a higher number of relays.

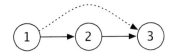

Figure 9: Simple topology—a chain of 3 sensors. Under ContikiMAC, some frames are directly received by Node 3 from Node 1. Under 802.15.4, Node 2 is associated with Node 1 and Node 3 with Node 2.

5. IMPLEMENTATION OF MPL AND BFT

We have implemented MPL and BFT under Contiki OS [10]. BFT uses our implementation of the IEEE 802.15.4 beacon-enabled mode. To include the information about the distance to the broadcast source in BFT, we have developed a routing layer on top of the 802.15.4 MAC. It allows a joining node to pick its neighbor closest to the sink as a coordinator. The implementation has been developed and optimized for sensor motes manufactured by STMicroelectronics (STM) containing a 32 bit microcontroller (STM32L1), a specific 802.15.4/802.15.4e radio transceiver, a PMU and several MEMs. we set the beacon-enabled 802.15.4 parameters to BO=5, SO=1, so the beacon interval is 0.5s and we use the intervals of 8s between beacons (BO=9) to achieve the slow beacon sending rate.

We compare BFT with MPL running on top of ContikiMAC configured with a channel check interval of 62.5 ms, whereas the broadcast transmission duration is 125ms. The parameters allow sending approximately the same amount of unicast traffic: 7 frames every 500ms in beacon-enabled 802.15.4 *vs.* 1 frame every 62.5ms with ContikiMAC.

We consider a simple topology formed by a chain of 3 nodes (cf. Figure 9) with the distance between Nodes 1-2 and 2-3 of 2 meters. We set the power of transmission to -23 dBm, which creates a two-hop network (even though from time to time, with ContikiMAC, some packets are directly received from Node 1 by Node 3). Although this configuration may include hidden nodes, we have observed that it is not harmful, because the modulations of the 802.15.4 radio standard are extremely robust[1].

Node 1 is the broadcast traffic source, Node 2 relays traffic, and Node 3 has no associated nor downstream devices. With one coordinator, one intermediate coordinator associated with Node 1 and a simple device, the difference between the behaviors of nodes is much more marked in BFT/802.15.4 compared to MPL/ContikiMAC in which all three nodes will relay packets as the redundancy limit cannot be reached. The setup is basic, but it already allows us to capture many properties of the two considered approaches. Besides, since we have already seen in Section 4 that the number of relays is similar under BFT and MPL, we focus here on assessing the energy consumption by BFT and MPL along with their associated MAC layers.

We first look at the time passed in transmission by the nodes in Figure 10. The general trends match the expected behavior: ContikiMAC is energy expensive under notable broadcast traffic. Conversely, beacon-enabled transmissions are strongly dominated by the energy consumption due to beacon transmissions, so the presence of traffic has much

---

[1]Nodes can differentiate two signals that arrive at the same time as long as they have at least a couple of dB of the received power ratio [26, 27].

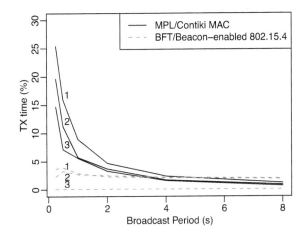

Figure 10: Proportion of time the radio is transmitting for a chain of 3 sensors.

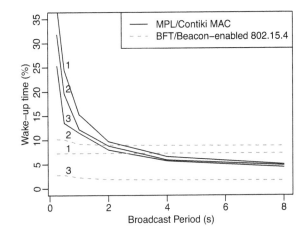

Figure 11: Proportion of time the radio is up for a chain of 3 sensors.

less impact. One important feature of BFT is apparent here: Node 3 that uses a slow beacon rate (it does not have any associated node), spends very little time in transmission mode.

As the energy consumption during idle listening is also significant, we evaluate the fraction of the time the radio is on for reception or transmission (cf. Figure 11). For ContikiMAC, it is the sum of packet transmission, reception, and periodic channel checks. For beacon-enabled 802.15.4, it includes the beacon transmission and the following CAP period for a coordinator (we do not define any GTS slots) as well as only the beacon reception for an idle leaf node. The performance difference between the relaying node and Node 3 under BFT is even more noticeable than for transmissions. We can observe that Node 2 is more active than Node 1, because it needs to receive the beacon from Node 1 and also act as a coordinator on behalf of Node 3.

Loss rate that we can observe in Figure 12 may be in part due to our implementation of ContikiMAC that fails to receive ≈10% of the packets, so that losses accumulate at Node 3, which explains the difference between the transmissions times observed between 3 nodes in the previous figures. For a broadcast transmission period of 0.5s, many packets are lost at Node 2 due to a failed Clear Channel As-

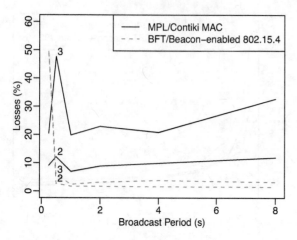

Figure 12: Percentage of lost frames at Node 2 and 3 with respect to the number of frames sent by Node 1.

sessment (CCA) before the transmission starts. Note that broadcast periods of less than 1s are well below the typical traffic MPL/ContikiMAC was engineered for and we have tuned I_{min} and I_{max} accordingly: $I_{min} = 1$ for periods less than 1s or 2, otherwise; I_{max} is equal to 2, 4, and 7, respectively, for periods of 0.25s, 0.5s, and 1s or more.

In BFT, losses for the 0.25s period are also due to the limitation of our implementation as nodes store only one packet for later transmission and they can only send one packet after each beacon.

5.1 BFT on a 16 Node Testbed

We have also run BFT on a testbed of 16 nodes. One node is the edge router, 4 nodes are Full Function Devices (FFD) that can act as relays if needed, whereas the remaining 11 nodes are (Reduced Function Devices) RFD that can only associate as leaf nodes.

Without BFT, when 4 FFDs send beacons at a nominal rate (BO=4), all 4 nodes have associated nodes and thus become relays 9 out of 10 times. With BFT, only one FFD sends beacons at a nominal rate (BO=4) and other FFDs use a larger BO=9 (32-fold increase of BI), which results in a single FFD becoming the relay.

5.2 Lessons Learned and Discussion

To limit the loss rate to 10% for ContikiMAC, we had to use long strobe times of two channel check intervals (125ms), which is twice the minimum value and increases the observed transmission durations.

In ContikiMAC, we have also frequently observed undue reception attempts after a periodic channel check that may be caused by some ISM band traffic (although we use channel 26 with no 802.11 activity) or simply noise at the receiver. An undue carrier sense is energy expensive, because typically the radio then stays up for several microseconds trying to synchronize with a frame preamble, which increases the radio wake-up time by a few percent [28]. The observed losses due to failed CCAs underline the importance of properly setting the MPL Trickle timers, which is even more important as the network density increases. We had not expected such artifacts—they are rarely mentioned if ever in the literature. Note that there is no such increase of the wake-up time due to the noise in beacon-enabled 802.15.4,

since nodes wake up precisely on time to receive beacons and coordinators wait for receptions during the active period.

We emphasize that for BFT, the presented measurements include sending the messages for building the Collection Tree, whereas in MPL/ContikiMAC, routing would need to be added, which necessarily incurs broadcasts. In fact, approximately half of the transmission time observed for BFT is due to the routing information message included in beacons. Similarly, the wake-up time of 802.15.4 could be further lowered either by using GTS or increasing BO, although the tradeoff with latency needs to be considered.

To conclude, BFT results in a predictable power consumption, a remarkable low power consumption for leaf nodes, and low loss rates. Conversely, MPL/ContikiMAC has the advantage of being stateless, but we need to take into account the additional overhead of a routing protocol. The power consumption under MPL/ContikiMAC strongly depends on the offered broadcast load—MPL can obtain very low duty cycles for low broadcast traffic.

6. RELATED WORK

Estrin et al. discussed the scalability problem of WSNs [29, 30]. The authors proposed to use a data-centric approach called Directed Diffusion for more efficient communication. Our approach, however, is designed for generic IP networks and does not consider application-specific data. Some researchers proposed to use additional geographical data to reduce the number of multicasts in WSNs [31, 32, 33]. However, the complexity of dealing with the geographical information can be an issue for most resource-constrained sensors. Several research papers focused on the construction of the optimal multicast tree with duty cycle aware and intermittent links [34, 35]. As part of the optimization process, these solutions require a lot of information exchanges. Multicast subscription mechanisms were proposed using forwarding information included in packets [36], or stored at relays using a Bloom filter to limit information storage [37]. These approaches allow any nodes to be a multicast source, but they require multi-hop message exchanges and underlying routing information. Macker et al. [22] evaluated MPR-based multicast mechanisms in MANETs, but they focused on the performance in function of node mobility. Clausen et al. [24] compared different RPL and MPR-based multicast mechanisms. Recently, Oikonomou et al. [38] proposed SMRF (Stateless Multicast RPL Forwarding) for RPL-based WSNs. The two last papers studied multicast mechanisms based on the existing DODAG structure of RPL that involves all routing nodes and do not significantly reduce the set of relays.

All the previous studies evaluated the performance of multicast mechanisms in networks with a few nodes, thus they did not reveal the problem of flooding mitigation in dense networks. The Trickle algorithm [1] used in MPL [19] is the first mechanism to address the multicast redundancy reduction in WSNs, but it does not provide options to optimize the path length and does not guarantee the reachability even if the redundancy factor is set to a high value. Mitton et al. proposed a density-aware cluster formation for broadcast in wireless networks [39]. This solution can reduce the number of relays to as low as 30%, but it does not provide path optimization. To the best of our knowledge, the present paper is the first study of the schemes for multicast relay reduction in large-scale and dense WSNs. We have identified MPL as a well performing scheme over preamble sampling MACs and we have proposed BFT as a scheme that takes advantage of beacon-enabled 802.15.4 to obtain very good properties. Moreover, BFT enables path optimization as an option. BFT is strongly related to beacon-enabled 802.15.4, but it is not only limited to MAC layers with association/disassociation procedures like in beacon-enabled IEEE 802.15.4.

7. CONCLUSION

The paper presents an evaluation of existing relay selection schemes for multi-hop broadcasting in large-scale and dense WSNs. Our main finding is that in this kind of networks, MPR-based schemes perform poorly and the Trickle based MPL results in better performance than other proposed schemes while requiring less complete topology information than MPR-based mechanisms. We have proposed Beacon-based Forwarding Tree (BFT), a new scheme that achieves similar performance to MPL, but fits better the case of nodes with low radio duty cycling MACs like beacon-enabled 802.15.4. Our scheme also guarantees broadcast reachability and it can be set to use the shortest paths to the broadcast source.

We have implemented MPL and BFT under Contiki OS. We have compared the performance of MPL on top of ContikiMAC and BFT over beacon-enabled 802.15.4 on an operational testbed. The experimental results show that BFT achieves very good performance for sustained broadcast traffic, it has a predictable power consumption, a remarkable low power consumption for leaf nodes, and low loss rates. MPL on ContikiMAC can obtain very low duty cycles for low broadcast traffic. We have finally discussed the pros and cons of MPL compared to BFT, each of them running on a matching duty cycling scheme on real hardware, to illustrate the problems at stake when it comes to consider operational protocol stacks.

8. ACKNOWLEDGEMENTS

This work was partially supported by the French National Research Agency (ANR) project project IRIS under contract ANR-11-INFR-016 and the European Commission FP7 project CALIPSO under contract 288879. The work reflects only the authors views; the European Community is not liable for any use that may be made of the information contained herein.

9. REFERENCES

[1] P. Levis, N. Patel, D. Culler, and S Shenker. Trickle: A Self Regulating Algorithm for Code Propagation and Maintenance in Wireless Sensor Networks. In *Proceedings of USENIX NSDI*, 2004.

[2] J. W. Hui and D. Culler. The Dynamic Behavior of a Data Dissemination Protocol for Network Programming at Scale. In *Proceedings of SenSys*, 2004.

[3] L. Huang and S. Setia. CORD: Energy-Efficient Reliable Bulk Data Dissemination in Sensor Networks. In *Proceedings of INFOCOM*. IEEE, 2008.

[4] C. Intanagonwiwat, R. Govindan, and D. Estrin. Directed Diffusion: a Scalable and Robust Communication Paradigm for Sensor Networks. In *Proc. of MOBICOM*, pages 56–67, 2000.

[5] C. Intanagonwiwat, R. Govindan, D. Estrin, J. Heidemann, and F. Silva. Directed Diffusion for Wireless Sensor Networking. *IEEE/ACM Trans. Netw.*, 11(1):2–16, 2003.

[6] A. Bachir, D. Barthel, M. Heusse, and A. Duda. O(1)-Reception Routing for Sensor Networks. *Computer Communications*, 30(13):2603–2614, September 2007.

[7] T. Winter *et al.* RPL: IPv6 Routing Protocol for Low power and Lossy Networks. RFC 6550, IETF, March 2012.

[8] T. Clausen and et al. The Lightweight On-Demand Ad Hoc Distance-Vector Routing Protocol—Next Generation (LOADng). Draft draft-clausen-lln-loadng-10, IETF, October 2013.

[9] A. Dunkels. The ContikiMAC Radio Duty Cycling Protocol. Technical Report SICS Technical Report T2011/13, December 2011.

[10] The Contiki OS. http://www.contiki-os.org/.

[11] IEEE Standard for Information technology Part 15.4: Wireless Medium Access Control (MAC) and Physical Layer (PHY) Specifications for Low-Rate Wireless Personal Area Networks (WPANs), 2006.

[12] S. Mahlknecht and M. Boeck. CSMA-MPS: a Minimum Preamble Sampling MAC Protocol for Low Power Wireless Sensor Networks. *Proceedings of IEEE Workshop on Factory Communication Systems*, Vienna, Austria, September 2004.

[13] M. Buettner et al. X-MAC: a Short Preamble MAC Protocol for Duty-Cycled Wireless Networks. *Proceedings of ACM SenSys*, Boulder, CO, November 2006.

[14] S. Ni, Y. Tseng, Y. Chen, and J. Sheu. The Broadcast Storm Problem in Mobile Ad hoc Networks. In *Proceedings of ACM MobiCom*, 1999.

[15] M. Garey and D. Johnson. Computers and Intractability: A Guide to the Theory of NP-Completeness. *Freeman, San Francisco*, 1978.

[16] C. Adjih, P. Jacquet, and L. Viennot. Computing Connected Dominated Sets with Multipoint Relays. In *Ad Hoc & Sensor Wireless Networks, Vol. 1*, 2005.

[17] T. Clausen and P. Jacquet. Optimized Link State Routing Protocol (OLSR). RFC 3626, IETF, October 2003.

[18] J. Macker. Simplified Multicast Forwarding. RFC 6621, IETF, May 2012.

[19] J. Hui and R. Kelsey. Multicast Protocol for Low power and Lossy Networks (MPL). Work in Progress draft-ietf-roll-trickle-mcast-02, IETF, October 2012.

[20] S. Guha and S. Khuller. Approximation Algorithms for Connected Dominating Sets. *Algorithmica*, 20(4):374–387, 1998.

[21] T. Clausen, C. Dearlove, and J. Dean. Mobile Ad Hoc Network (MANET) Neighborhood Discovery Protocol (NHDP). RFC 6130, IETF, April 2011.

[22] J. Macker *et al.* Evaluation of Distributed Cover Set Algorithms in Mobile Ad Hoc Network for Simplified Multicast Forwarding. *ACM SIGMOBILE Mob. Comput. Commun. Rev.*, July 2007.

[23] P. Levis, T. Clausen, J. Hui, O. Gnawali, and J. Ko. The Trickle Algorithm. RFC 6206, IETF, March 2011.

[24] T. Clausen and U. Herberg. Comparative Study of RPL-Enabled Optimized Broadcast in Wireless Sensor Networks. In *Proceedings of ISSNIP*, 2010.

[25] P. Jacquet, V. Laouiti, P. Minet, and L. Viennot. Performance of Multipoint Relaying in Ad Hoc Mobile Routing Protocols. In *Proceedings of Networking*, 2002.

[26] Ghalem Boudour, Martin Heusse, and Andrzej Duda. Improving Performance and Fairness in IEEE 802.15.4 Networks with Capture Effect. In *Proceedings of the IEEE ICC 2013 (International Conference on Communications)*, Budapest, Hungary, June 2013. IEEE.

[27] Ghalem Boudour, Martin Heusse, and Andrzej Duda. An Enhanced Capture Scheme for IEEE 802.15.4 Wireless Sensor Networks. In *Proceedings of the IEEE ICC 2013 (International Conference on Communications)*, Budapest, Hungary, June 2013. IEEE.

[28] M. Sha, G. Hackmann, and C. Lu. Energy-Efficient Low Power Listening for Wireless Sensor Networks in Noisy Environments. In *Proceedings of SenSys*, pages 277–288, Philadelphia, PA, USA, 2013. ACM.

[29] D. Estrin *et al.* Next Century Challenges: Scalable Coordination in Sensor Networks. In *Proceedings of ACM MobiCom*, 1999.

[30] C. Intanagonwiwat *et al.* Directed Diffusion: a Scalable and Robust Communication Paradigm for Sensor Networks. In *Proceedings of ACM MobiCom*, 2000.

[31] C. H. Feng *et al.* Stateless Multicast Protocol for Ad Hoc Networks. *IEEE Transactions on Mobile Computing*, 11(2), Feb. 2012.

[32] Juan A. Sanchez, Pedro M. Ruiz, and I. Stojmenovic. Energy-Efficient Geographic Multicast Routing for Sensor and Actuator Networks. *Computer Communications*, 30(13), 2007.

[33] Q. Huang, C. Lu, and G. C. Roman. Spatiotemporal Multicast in Sensor Networks. In *Proceedings of ACM SenSys*, 2003.

[34] Lu Su *et al.* oCast: Optimal Multicast Routing Protocol for Wireless Sensor Networks. In *Proceedings of IEEE ICNP*, 2009.

[35] K. Han, Y. Liu, and J. Luo. Duty-Cycle-Aware Minimum-Energy Multicasting in Wireless Sensor Networks. *IEEE/ACM Transactions on Networking*, 2012.

[36] A. Okura, T. Ihara, and A. Miura. BAM: Branch Aggregation Multicast for Wireless Sensor Networks. In *Proceedings of the IEEE MASS*, 2005.

[37] A. Marchiori and Qi Han. PIM-WSN: Efficient Multicast for IPv6 Wireless Sensor Networks. In *Proceedings of the IEEE WoWMoM*, 2011.

[38] G. Oikonomou and I. Phillips. Stateless Multicast Forwarding with RPL in 6LoWPAN Sensor Networks. In *Proceedings of the IEEE PerSeNS*, 2012.

[39] N. Mitton and E. Fleury. Efficient Broadcasting in Self-Organizing Multi-hop Wireless Networks. In *Proceedings of ADHOC-NOW*, 2005.

Wireless Networking Testbed and Emulator (WiNeTestEr)*

Kiruba S. Subramani,
Joseph D. Beshay,
Niranjan Mahabaleshwar,
Ehsan Nourbakhsh,
Brooks McMillin,
Bhaskar Banerjee,
Ravi Prakash
The University of Texas at Dallas
Richardson, Texas, USA
{kiruba.subramani, joseph.beshay,
niranjan.mahabaleshwar, ehsaan,
brooks.mcmillin, bhaskar.banerjee,
ravip} @utdallas.edu

Yongjiu Du, Pengda Huang,
Tianzuo Xi, Yang You,
Joseph D. Camp,
Ping Gui, Dinesh Rajan
Southern Methodist University
Dallas, Texas, USA
{ydu, phuang, txi,yyou, camp,
pgui, rajand} @smu.edu

Jinghong Chen
The University of Arizona
Tucson, Arizona, USA
{jhchen}@email.arizona.edu

ABSTRACT

Repeatability, isolation and accuracy are the most desired factors while testing wireless devices. However, they cannot be guaranteed by traditional drive tests. Channel emulators play a major role in filling these gaps in testing. In this paper we present an efficient channel emulator which is better than existing commercial products in terms of cost, remote access, support for complex network topologies and scalability. We present the hardware and software architecture of our channel emulator and describe the experiments we conducted to evaluate its performance against a commercial channel emulator.

Keywords

Wireless; RF; Channel Emulation; Testbed

1. INTRODUCTION

The ability to conduct repeatable experiments is crucial to the development of wireless devices and protocols. Most of the time, researchers make simplifying assumptions about the nature of their test environment and the experiment control procedures. However these assumptions do not always hold good [1] making it harder to isolate device/protocol performance from environmental effects.

The current wireless networking testbeds use a wide range of approaches, varying from fully software-simulated testbeds like ns-3 [2] to real hardware running in Faraday cages. How-

ever, the two extremes have their respective limitations. Simulators are easy to implement but they are limited by the models provided in software. Different simulators might yield different results due to the assumptions and simulation techniques used [3]. On the other hand using hardware in Faraday cages is not always affordable and it does not allow flexibility to test complicated scenarios involving mobility or signal reflections. The balance between the two extremes is provided by channel emulators.

The simplest form of channel emulation is achieved by using shielded RF cables between the transceivers and a programmable attenuator in the signal chain. An example of an emulator based on this design was ASSERT [4], developed by our group. By increasing (or decreasing) the attenuation we simulated the transceivers moving apart (or moving closer). The rate at which attenuation was varied corresponded to the relative speed of the transceivers. This scenario covered the fading effect of wireless channels.

However, wireless transmissions are not only affected by fading but also by multiple reflections of the same signal from obstacles in the surrounding environment (multi-path effects). Devices with multiple antennas (MIMO) exploit these signal reflections to achieve better throughput. Accurate emulation of multi-path effects requires creating multiple copies of the transmitted signal with different time delays (phases). This cannot be achieved by attenuators. Instead it is done by digitizing the signal and manipulating it using digital signal processing (DSP). The resulting digital signal is converted back to analog.

Commercial solutions exist for emulating environments with multi-path effects [5] [6]. However they are prohibitively expensive and are limited to simulating environments with 2 pairs of devices or less. Commercial channel emulators are thus impractical for researchers who are usually cost-constrained and interested in experiments that involve the interaction (and interference) between multiple devices with a higher degree of connectivity. As a result, researchers sought to develop their own channel emulators that could achieve multipath effects for multiple devices while maintaining relatively low cost. An example is the work in [7] which uses a single field programmable gate array (FPGA)

*This work is supported in part by the National Science Foundation MRI program under grant numbers 1040422 and 1040429.

to simulate a 90Mhz-wide environment for up to 15 devices operating in the 2.4 GHz ISM band. The design in [7] cannot scale due to the FPGA resource constraints.

In this paper, we present our Wireless Networking Testbed and Emulator (WiNeTestEr) which is designed to simulate 100-Mhz-wide environments with multipath in the 2.4 GHz ISM band. The main features of WiNeTestEr are:

- scalability: the system uses a distributed channel emulation algorithm running on multiple FPGAs so it can potentially scale to hundreds of nodes,

- remote access: a device control protocol allows the system to run experiments without onsite-operator intervention,

- concurrent experiments: the modular design allows for multiple independent experiments to be run by different users at the same time,

- multi technology support: experiments can be performed on different technology devices operating in their native frequencies (Bluetooth, WiFi, Zigbee, etc.). The design is flexible to allow adding more frequency bands in the future with minimal changes.

- full duplex channels: the channel between two devices is full duplex with support for non-reciprocal channel conditions i.e. the signal can experience a certain environment in one direction and a different one in the other.

WiNeTestEr's design is loosely based upon ASSERT [4]. ASSERT performs channel emulation in the 900 MHz ISM band using attenuation. Attenuators are used to control the transmitted signal strength to emulate the required channel conditions (deep fade, slow fade) but it cannot emulate multi-path effects. WiNeTestEr was developed to bridge this gap.

2. SYSTEM DESIGN

WiNeTestEr consists of two distinct networks; the control network and the RF network as shown in Figure 1. The control network is where the experiment control takes place. It consists of the Control PC and Wireless Open-Access Research Platform (WARP) v2.2 boards [8] connected by an Ethernet network. The RF network is where the channel emulation happens. It consists of a set of units under test (UUTs) interconnected across RF and combiner boards. All the connections in the RF network use shielded coaxial cables. The RF board has one input and three outputs, and is responsible for converting the input signal from analog to digital and passing it to the FPGA on the WARP board on which the RF board is mounted. The FPGA applies the desired channel conditions for each output. The RF board converts each signal back to analog to be output on the equivalent port. The combiner board is a passive board that is responsible for combining up to four signals into one to be sent to a UUT.

A unidirectional link from UUT A to UUT B is realized through seven steps as shown in Figure 1:

1. UUT A's output is connected to UUT A's RF board through a wideband duplexer (circulator).

2. RF board digitizes the signal and passes it to its WARP board's FPGA.

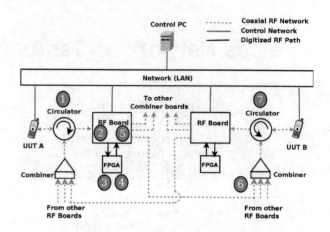

Figure 1: A simple topology of two UUTs connected over a single bidirectional link.

3. FPGA makes copies of the signal for each of the three outputs.

4. FPGA processes the digital signal based on the channel conditions set by the control PC for each output.

5. RF board converts the signals back to analog and outputs each of them on its port.

6. The equivalent RF board output is connected to UUT B's combiner board through a coaxial cable.

7. Combiner board passes the combined signal of all of its inputs to UUT B through the circulator.

Using the unidirectional link as a building block, it is possible to build any higher degree topology involving any number of UUTs. For example, a simple bidirectional link can be formed from two unidirectional links as shown in Figure 1. More details on topology formation are discussed in the implementation section.

An experiment is run by specifying the channel condition that should be applied to each link in the topology for a certain period of time. The Control PC orchestrates the experiment by applying the channel conditions to each RF board output and signaling the UUTs to start executing. Once the experiment expires, the Control PC collects the results from UUTs and resets the channel conditions.

In WiNeTestEr, the hardware and software modules go hand in hand in carrying out the experiments scheduled by the user. We introduce the hardware and software architecture of our system in sections 2.1 and 2.2 respectively.

2.1 Hardware architecture

Our solution is based on development boards by WARP Project [8]. The WARP development board version 2.2 has a Xilinx Virtex 4 FPGA, 2 PowerPC cores, external memory slots, a RAM slot and other peripheral connectivity solutions to interface with external boards and controlling devices. Each WARP board can house two RF boards which can be connected to two different input UUTs. Figure 2 shows the overall architecture of a WARP board with two RF boards mounted.

Channel emulation can be accurately performed in the digital domain. The signal transmitted by the UUT is downconverted to baseband and digitized. Once the digitized

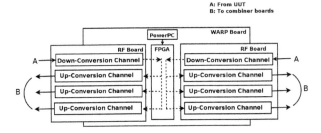

Figure 2: Architecture of a WARP board with two attached RF boards.

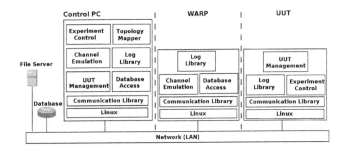

Figure 3: Software architecture.

signal is modified to reflect the desired channel emulation, it is converted back to analog and then up-converted. Channel emulation is done on the FPGA as instructed by a PowerPC processor.

The RF board consists of two signal chains, namely down-conversion and up-conversion. Each component on the board can be broadly classified as being part of one of the two chains. The down-conversion chain consists of digital step attenuator (DSA), quadrature demodulator, variable gain amplifier (VGA) and Analog to Digital Converter (ADC). The up-conversion chain consists of Digital to Analog Converter (DAC), VGA and quadrature modulator. Clock circuit present on each board helps in synchronizing data conversion operations. The clock circuit also provides reference input to Phase Locked Loop (PLL) which is used in generating Local Oscillator (LO) signal for down-conversion and up-conversion operations. As shown in Figure 2, the FPGA creates three identical copies of the original signal transmitted by the UUT. These signals can be independently modified as instructed by the PowerPC processor to emulate the desired environment. Each signal corresponds to an output port that will eventually be connected to a UUT via the combiner board.

2.2 Software architecture

The heart of WiNeTestEr's software architecture is the Control PC. It serves as the proxy between the user and other system components. The Control PC maintains a database of the experiment information as well as the hardware resources available in the system (WARP boards, RF boards, UUTs and cable connections). Users run a GUI application on their local machines and connect to the Control PC to retrieve the current system status, design their experiments and submit them for execution. To set the environment conditions, the Control PC sends the link parameters to the Power PC processors of the WARP boards to which the experiment's RF boards are connected.

The WARP board forwards the link parameters to the FPGA which applies them to the digitized signal received from the RF board. The FPGA could have directly read the link parameters from the Ethernet interface of the WARP board. However based on prior experiences from ASSERT, we decided to run embedded Linux on the WARP board (PowerPC processor) to provide a more advanced interface that can do more than receiving and parsing link parameters. Running Linux also allowed us to use high level libraries for log collection and experiment monitoring.

We designed a *UUT Management* protocol to be able to orchestrate experiments without human intervention. The

UUT management protocol allows the Control PC to transfer execution images to UUTs to be used for experiments. The protocol also provides the interface to start, monitor, stop and collect experiment results from the UUTs. For the default setup, UUTs are Beagle Bone Black boards [9] which have ARM processors running Linux. Each board has a WiFi dongle (IEEE 802.11 b/g). Execution images are compressed archives containing ARM binaries and configuration files provided by the user. The UUT management protocol is used to transfer the specific archive to each UUT and control the experiment execution. This protocol however is an optional component of our system. Users who want to test their devices without exposing their binaries/configuration files may choose to use their own management protocol and only use WiNeTestEr for simulating the environment. They also have the option to implement the experiment control subset of the protocol without the image transfer. Our design is flexible to support multiple heterogeneous UUTs to exist and be one of multiple experiments running concurrently.

The software components running on the Control PC, WARP board, UUTs are shown in Figure 3. The following section outlines the purpose of each component and the main design decisions involved.

3. IMPLEMENTATION

3.1 RF Board

The RF board is responsible for frequency translation of the signal which allows channel emulation to be carried out on the FPGA based on environment conditions provided by the PowerPC processor. The architecture of the RF board is shown in Figure 4. RF interface to the board is provided by means of SMA jacks and coaxial cables. The use of coaxial cables minimizes interference among signals thereby increasing the robustness and repeatability of experiments. The RF board supports input signal power in the range of -25 dBm to +26 dBm and an output power of -20 dBm to -110 dBm. To achieve this target specification, a maximum attenuation of 136 dB is required from the design. This value is divided among multiple components on the board such as DSA, VGA and FPGA.

DSA performs the first stage of attenuation on the input signal. Owing to high signal strength of the input, there is a very high chance of it saturating the quadrature demodulator. Placing a DSA at the start of the chain helps restrain signal strength to reasonable values. Modern wireless standards use complex modulation schemes such as QPSK or QAM to achieve higher speed and lower error rate. To support these standards, broadband quadrature modulator and demodulator with good performance specifications have been used in the up-conversion and down-conversion circuitry. For best-case performance of quadrature modulator, signal properties of In-phase (I) and Quadrature (Q) components need to be perfectly matched. In other words, a mismatch between these two components in terms of DC offset, gain and phase results in LO leakage and sideband issues thereby degrading the quality of output signal. Baseband VGAs are used to offset amplitude mismatches of I/Q signals. To obtain very low value of sideband signal, both gain and phase need to be carefully adjusted in the FPGA. Also, in down-conversion chain, VGA helps to amplify or attenuate the baseband signal to meet the dynamic range requirements of ADC. In WiNeTestEr, since the baseband signal has a bandwidth of 100 MHz, a sampling clock of 200 MHz is needed for the data converters to avoid aliasing. The clock circuit consists of a voltage controlled crystal oscillator (VCXO) as the clock source with clock distribution/divider IC's providing identical clocks to data converter chips (ADC and DAC).

Resolution of data converter ICs has significant impact on the performance of the system. During down-conversion, the demodulator outputs I/Q signals, requiring separate ADC to digitize each signal. Two 12-bit ADCs were used in the design to satisfy the signal to noise ratio (SNR) requirement of the receiver. Up-conversion, on the other hand, handles a wide range of output signal strength. Also, each RF board houses 3 up-conversion chains, with each chain having its own I/Q signals. Hence a dual 16-bit DAC was used on each chain to convert the signal back to analog domain.

Figure 5 shows the RF front end that was designed for WiNeTestEr. A single ended signal from the circulator is connected to the first SMA jack marking the input to the board. The other three SMA jacks correspond to the output from each up-conversion chain. The RF board supports three different power sources namely external adapter, WARP FPGA board and screw terminal. Selected source is regulated using low-dropout regulators (LDO) to generate 5V, 3.3V and 1.8V analog and digital supplies. Utmost care has been taken to reduce supply noise with the help of global

Figure 5: RF Board for WiNeTestEr.

and local decoupling capacitors and ferrite beads. Careful floor planning, layer management and termination techniques have been followed to obtain the best performance from the board.

3.2 WARP Board

We selected WARP v2.2 boards to house our RF boards due to the large number of pins available on 4 daughtercard slots. Each daughtercard slot has 124 pins which are routed to the dedicated I/O on the FPGA. With 4 such slots, we have 496 pins which are sufficient for communication between the FPGA and two RF boards. Xilinx Virtex 4 FPGA in WARP also has two PowerPC cores operating at 300 Mhz, one of which we used to run Linux. The Control PC communicates with the Linux via the Ethernet port on the WARP board.

Another notable feature in the WARP board is the System ACE chip. This chip connected to the CompactFlash slot on the board can program the FPGA and load Linux to the PowerPC processor using a single image file which has both the FPGA image and the Linux kernel. The System ACE chip reads these files from a FAT16 formatted CompactFlash card.

3.3 Combiner Board

The Combiner board is responsible for combining RF signals from different boards to implement multi-user interference. As shown in Figure 6, the combiner board contains four commercial low-noise amplifiers (LNA), four RF switches, and a custom designed 4-to-1 active combiner chip. The combiner chip uses active method to realize wideband RF signal combining and has a small chip area (1 mm × 1 mm, pads limited). The LNA is used to improve noise figure and sensitivity of the combiner board. When the input signal level is high, RF switches are used to bypass the LNA to improve the linearity of the combiner board.

3.4 Channel Emulation

The baseband channel emulation has been implemented on the FPGA and its architecture is shown in Figure 7. Each

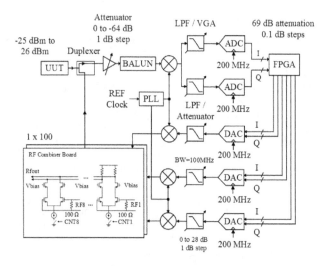

Figure 4: RF board architecture.

tap has a delay unit(r_x) controlled by a user-defined value, followed by scaling based on fading parameters $(\rho_x(t)\phi_x(t))$ where $x \in (0,6)$. The resulting signals from each tap are added together to emulate a multi-tap fading channel.

In WiNeTestEr, summation of sinusoids (SOS) method [10], [11] has been used to generate fading channel. This method of channel generation for emulation has been widely investigated in the past [12], [13], [14]. However, existing fading channel emulators demand large memory source to generate channels, which degrades the scalability. In this project, a novel structure to implement SOS based channel generation has been proposed [15]. With this structure, the generation of one Rayleigh channel consumes only 1 unit memory source ($\sim$ RAMB16) of the available 376 in the FPGA. Besides reducing memory requirements, this work has also optimized word length selection and channel data update rate. Intuitively, larger bit width generates higher channel accuracy at the cost of hardware resources. Similar tradeoff exists between channel data generation rate and accuracy over time domain. In this project, optimization on the two terms (bit width and update rate) are performed [15], aiming at minimizing hardware resources at a certain channel accuracy level. With the reduction of memory consumption and optimization on the two terms, scalability is drastically improved on WiNeTestEr.

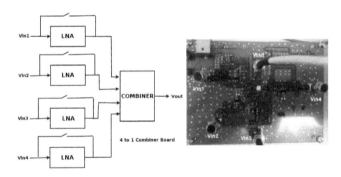

Figure 6: (Left) Architecture of the combiner board. (Right) Fabricated combiner board.

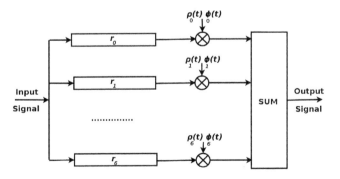

Figure 7: Multi-tap fading generator.

3.5 Software

WiNeTestEr is a distributed system with the Control PC, WARP boards and the UUTs being its components. The software slices running on each of these components are shown in Figure 3. We select the most significant slices and describe them in more details in the following paragraphs.

The different components of the system use a common *Communication Library* to exchange messages. We wrote it in both Java and C++. We used the Boost thread and system libraries [16] to maintain cross-architecture and cross-platform compatibility in C++. The library uses User Datagram Protocol (UDP) to provide services to send and receive messages in both blocking and non-blocking modes. Reliability is provided using optional acknowledgments and retransmissions on top of UDP. Communicating entities are identified by a unique ID, port and sub-system ID. Each module using the communication library creates an instance of it with its identity and a separate thread handles all communication responsibilities.

Logging is one of the integral part of our system. It is used for both debugging and collecting results and statistics of the experiment. We have implemented a log library which is used by all other software modules to log system events. Log messages are output to standard output/error streams and a log file. The log library allows software modules to log events and stamp them with the identity of the software module, time and severity of events.

Experiment Control is the main coordinator of all the software modules. It is present in the Control PC and coordinates all activities from the time an experiment is created until it is completed. When the user creates an experiment topology using the GUI, experiment control interacts with Topology Mapper and determines the the availability of the desired number of sites and the interconnections between them necessary to correctly emulate the network topology specified by the user. Once the experiment is flagged feasible, the Topology Mapper transfers the experiment parameters (channel conditions) from the GUI to the Channel Emulation module running on the PowerPC core which later forwards it to the FPGA. If the user has a UUT image, Experiment Control transfers the image to the UUT by interacting with the UUT Management module. The UUT management module controls the start and end of the experiment. It is also responsible for collecting experiment logs from the UUT and transferring them to the Control PC. Experiment Control makes these logs available to the user through the GUI.

A *GUI* application has been developed for the end user to run experiments. This is a standalone application which authenticates the user and allows them to create, start and abort experiments. It is also used to load any UUT images and collect the experiment logs. The user can create the experiment topology using the GUI, selecting different UUTs and specifying all the communication constraints among the UUTs. This application communicates only with the Experiment Control module in the Control PC. A screenshot of the GUI is shown in Figure 8. As shown in the figure, the user can create different types of UUTs, communication links between them and specify experiment parameters. This UUT topology can be saved on disk which can be used when the experiment needs to be repeated. The GUI can also be used to view properties of the testbed like physical topology of the UUTs, available/allocated UUTs for experiments etc.

A *MySQL database* stores all information about the testbed, completed and ongoing experiments. It stores information about the physical topology and the different UUTs in the testbed. When the testbed is first assembled, information about the different RF links and UUTs are manually entered into the database. When users want to use their own UUTs, information has to be manually entered into the database. All RF links are directed and are represented by the tuple *<UUT A, WARP board Number, Port Number, UUT B>* which captures the unidirectional connection from UUT A to UUT B through a RF board's output port. An RF link is considered available if and only if UUT A, UUT B and the WARP board on which the RF board is mounted are all up and running. Each of these components periodically send *Keep Alive* messages updating the database. Topology Mapper uses the requirements from an experiment and the information in the database to check the feasibility of the experiment. If it is feasible, it allocates RF links and UUTs to the experiment. Apart from this, the database has information about all authorized users of the system. When users first start the GUI, they are authenticated against the information in this database. *Data Access* is a library which wraps all the internals of database access and provides application specific primitives for the other software modules to access the database.

Topology of an experiment is restricted by the physical topology of the testbed and the presence of other concurrent experiments. The problem of mapping a set of links required by the user to the available physical connections in the testbed is an instance of Directed Subgraph Isomorphism. *Topology Mapper* uses an approximation algorithm to find a subgraph of the physical connections in the testbed that satisfies the user requirements. If such a subgraph is found, its links are exclusively allocated to the user experiment for the required duration. As explained above, the information about the available links and whether they are being used by other experiments or not, is retrieved from the database.

As the name suggests *UUT Management* controls the actions of the UUT. It accepts the execution image which consists of a user image and a start-up script having all the parameters, environment variables necessary for the execution of the user application. When the user uploads an execution image through the GUI, it is stored in the file server which is later fetched by the UUT Management using Trivial File Transfer Protocol (TFTP). It accepts commands to start, stop, abort an experiment from the user through the Experiment Control. It also informs the user about any premature termination of the user image. Once the experiment is terminated, it transfers the experiment logs back to the user. UUT Management communicates with the Experiment Control in the Control PC using the *Communication Library*.

Channel Emulation is responsible for transferring the experiment parameters from the user to the FPGA to get the desired channel conditions. Channel Emulation slice on the ControlPC reads the parameters from the user and writes it to the database. The Control PC sends the experiment ID to the channel emulation slice running on WARP boards allocated to this experiment by the Topology Mapper. Channel Emulation slice on the WARP board reads the emulation parameters from the database, converts them to the format required by the FPGA and writes them to a designated memory location.

4. EXPERIMENTAL VALIDATION

In this section we compare WiNeTestEr's channel emulation performance with a commercial channel emulator, Azimuth ACE MX MIMO [5]. It is one of the state-of-the-art channel emulators used by industry and academia to test complex wireless protocols. We chose not to perform any over-the-air experiments due to the difficulty in controlling the multi-path parameters. Even a seemingly simple environment like an open-air football field will have several taps (paths taken by different signal reflections).

We used two Ubiquiti SR-71 Cardbus WiFi adapters (Atheros AR9160 chipset) as UUTs. The cards were connected to two laptops running Linux 3.2 which includes the ath9k driver. Both cards were set to join an adhoc network operating on channel 14 (center frequency 2484 MHz) as per the IEEE 802.11 PHY/MAC standard for the 2.4 GHz ISM band. The basic rate of the adhoc network was fixed to 36 Mbps to avoid the results being affected by the driver's auto-rate algorithm. We could have picked another value for the fixed rate. However, we found 36 Mbps to provide a good balance between sensitivity to different channel conditions and the ability to gracefully degrade in performance as the channel worsens.

An experiment starts by the cards joining the adhoc network. Once the cards associate, we use Iperf [17] to send UDP packets carrying a 1470 byte payload from one machine to the other for 4 minutes while recording the average throughput achieved every second. At the end of the experiment, Iperf reports the number of packets lost during the session.

We defined four environments (channel conditions) each with a different number of taps. Table 1 shows the emulation parameters for Environment 1. It represent the basic case of having a single copy of the signal propagating through the channel. Environments 2, 3 and 4 use the top 2, 3 and 4 taps (respectively) of the ITU Vehicular - A Channel Model [18] shown in Table 2. The model uses a Doppler value of 184 Hz which results in the signal fading in a way roughly equivalent to that experienced by a vehicle traveling at 80 km/hr.

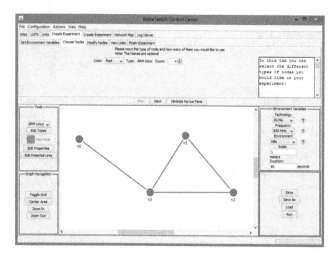

Figure 8: A screenshot of the GUI showing a topology of four UUTs.

Doppler	1 Hz		
	Tap_Delay(ns)	Tap_Gain(db)	K-Factor(db)
Tap 1	0	0	-99

Table 1: Environment 1 channel parameters.

Doppler	184 Hz		
	Tap_Delay(ns)	Tap_Gain(db)	K-Factor(db)
Tap 1	0	0	-99
Tap 2	310	-1.0	-99
Tap 3	710	-9.0	-99
Tap 4	1090	-10.0	-99
Tap 5	1730	-15.0	-99
Tap 6	2510	-20.0	-99

Table 2: ITU Vehicular A Channel Model.

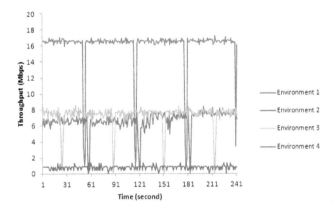

Figure 9: Throughput vs. Time plot for the experiments through WiNeTestEr.

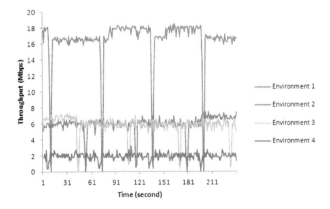

Figure 10: Throughput vs. Time plot for the experiments through Azimuth.

For each environment, we ran the experiment through both WiNeTestEr and Azimuth and recorded the throughput results. Figures 9 and 10 show the results obtained from WiNeTestEr and Azimuth, respectively.

4.1 Results Analysis

The results show a dip in the throughput roughly every minute. This happens with both WiNeTestEr and Azimuth. To isolate the issue, we ran the experiment over-the-air in an indoor interference-free environment. The cards experienced the same dips in throughput. While it would be interesting to dig deeper into this observation and find the root cause, it is out of the scope of this paper. We attribute these dips in throughput to the hardware or the driver of the adapters.

Both WiNeTestEr and Azimuth results share a trend of decreasing throughput with the increase of the number of taps. This matches the expectations we have for different environments especially environments 2,3 and 4 which emulate high mobility.

The results however are not identical. Despite sharing the same trend, WiNeTestEr and Azimuth achieve different throughput for the same channel parameters. We attribute this to the different level of control we have over the low level multi-path parameters in Azimuth compared to WiNeTestEr. Each tap in the multi-path parameters consists of a set of components. Unlike WiNeTestEr, Azimuth does not provide an interface to specify the value of each of these components. WiNeTestEr allows for repeating experiments under identical multi-path parameters even in terms of individual tap components. It is worth noting that specifying these components is optional and WiNeTestEr provides a set of default components for unfamiliar users.

5. CONCLUSION AND FUTURE WORK

Winetester is a scalable and cost-effective channel emulator that allows researchers to perform accurate, repeatable and complex experiments (topology, multipath effects). The distributed design of the system is evident in both the hardware and the software architecture. The hardware consists of UUTs, RF boards and combiner boards, interconnected to form the base topology. The software consists of a central Control PC that communicates with embedded Linux running on WARP boards and the FPGA that manipulates the signal using DSP. The paper discussed the different design and implementation aspects of each of the components.

Experimental results show that performance of WiNeTestEr is comparable to commercially available solutions. Being remotely accessible makes it an efficient alternative for researchers in academia and the industry alike.

WiNeTestEr is currently limited to operating in the 2400-2500 MHz band due to the RF board design. We intend to address this in the future revision of the RF board to be able to emulate environments in the range of 700 MHz to 6 GHz. Old RF boards will be swapped with the new ones without requiring any modification to the rest of the system. This will allow testing a wider range of devices and technologies (GSM, CDMA, LTE, 5 GHz Wifi, etc.).

6. ACKNOWLEDGMENT

We thank Krypton for their input in the design of RF and Combiner boards. We also thank Amba Kalur for her support during the initial phases of the RF board design.

7. REFERENCES

[1] Ryan Burchfield, Ehsan Nourbakhsh, Jeff Dix, Kunal Sahu, S Venkatesan, and Ravi Prakash. RF in the jungle: Effect of environment assumptions on wireless

experiment repeatability. In *IEEE International Conference on Communications*, pages 1–6. IEEE, 2009.

[2] NS-3. Network Simulator 3. http://www.nsnam.org/.

[3] David Cavin, Yoav Sasson, and André Schiper. On the accuracy of MANET simulators. In *Proceedings of the second ACM international workshop on Principles of mobile computing*, pages 38–43. ACM, 2002.

[4] Ehsan Nourbakhsh, Jeff Dix, Paul Johnson, Ryan Burchfield, S Venkatesan, Neeraj Mittal, and Ravi Prakash. ASSERT: A wireless networking testbed. In *Testbeds and Research Infrastructures. Development of Networks and Communities*, pages 209–218. Springer, 2011.

[5] Azimuth. ACE MX MIMO Channel Emulator for Broadband Wireless. http://www.azimuthsystems.com/products/ace-channel-emulators/ace-mx/, fetched April 2014.

[6] octoScope. octoBox MPE (Multi Path Emulator) Wireless Testbed. http://www.octoscope.com/English/Products/octoBox_MPE/octoBox_MPE.html, fetched April 2014.

[7] Kevin C. Borries, Glenn Judd, Daniel D. Stancil, and Peter Steenkiste. FPGA-based channel simulator for a wireless network emulator. In *69th Vehicular Technology Conference, VTC*, pages 1–5. IEEE, 2009.

[8] WARP Project. http://warpproject.org.

[9] Beagle Board. Beagle Bone Black. http://beagleboard.org.

[10] R.H. Clarke. A statistical theory of mobile-radio perception. *Bell Syst. Tech. J.*, 47:957 –1000, 1968.

[11] W.C. Jake. *Microwave Mobile Communication*. Wiley-IEEE Press, Piscataway, NJ, 1974.

[12] A. Alimohammad and B.F. Cockburn. Modeling and hardware implementation aspects of fading channel simulators. *IEEE Tran. on Vehicular Technology*, 57(4):2055 –2069, Jul 2008.

[13] Chengshan Xiao et al. Novel sum-of-sinusoids simulation models for rayleigh and rician fading channels. *Wireless Communications, IEEE Tran. on*, 5(12):3667 –3679, Dec 2006.

[14] Jianguo Xing et al. FPGA-accelerated real-time volume rendering for 3d medical image. In *3rd Int. Conf. on Biomedical Engineering and Informatics (BMEI)*, volume 1, pages 273 –276, Oct 2010.

[15] Pengda Huang, M.J. Tonnemacher, Yongjiu Du, D. Rajan, and J. Camp. Towards scalable network emulation: Channel accuracy versus implementation resources. In *Proceedings of IEEE INFOCOM*, pages 1959–1967, April 2013.

[16] Boost C++ Libraries. http://www.boost.org.

[17] Iperf. http://iperf.fr/.

[18] WP2.1 SUIT Project Deliverable. Fixed and Mobile Channel Models Identifications, July 2006.

Exact Analysis on Network Capacity of Airborne MANETs with Digital Beamforming Antennas

Jun Li
Communications Research
Centre Canada
Ottawa, ON K2H 8S2 Canada
jun.li@crc.gc.ca

Chi Zhang
School of Mathematics and
Statistics, Carleton University
Ottawa, ON K1S 5B6 Canada
zhangchi88@gmail.com

Yifeng Zhou
Communications Research
Centre Canada
Ottawa, ON K2H 8S2 Canada
yifeng.zhou@crc.gc.ca

Simon Perras
Communications Research
Centre Canada
Ottawa, ON K2H 8S2 Canada
simon.perras@crc.gc.ca

Yiqiang Q. Zhao
School of Mathematics and
Statistics, Carleton University
Ottawa, ON K1S 5B6 Canada
zhao@math.carleton.ca

ABSTRACT

Recently, the use of digital beamforming (DBF) antennas has been drawing lots of interest in airborne platforms for resolving the network partition problem in airborne mobile ad hoc networks (MANETs). In this paper, properties of the network capacity of an airborne MANET with DBF antennas are investigated. This paper considers an ad hoc network consisting of a number of uniformly distributed airborne platforms in a bounded area. These platforms are either directly or indirectly connected with each other through DBF antennas, and form an airborne MANET. We first formulate a digital beamforming antenna system model, referred to as the omni-direction plus sector (OPS) model, and then carry out an exact analysis for the network capacity. The OPS model characterizes the radiation pattern of a DBF antenna. Under the condition that a Hamiltonian path exists in the network, an explicit expression is derived for the network capacity. We show that, for fixed values of the OPS model, the network capacity increases as the network size increases until it reaches an optimal value. If the network size continues to increase, the network capacity will decrease until it reaches zero. Explicit expressions for the optimal network size and the maximum network capacity are also obtained. Finally, numerical results are presented. It is shown that both the optimal network size and the maximum network capacity increase as the antenna beamwidth decreases. They increase slowly when the beamwidth is large (e.g., $90° < \theta < 180°$), but as the antenna beam becomes narrower (e.g., $15° < \theta < 30°$), they increase faster.

MSWiM'14, September 21–26, 2014, Montreal, QC, Canada.
Copyright 2014 ACM 978-1-4503-3030-5/14/09 ...$15.00.
http://dx.doi.org/10.1145/2641798.2641821.

Categories and Subject Descriptors

C.2 [**Computer-Communication Networks**]: Miscellaneous; C.4 [**Performance of Systems**]: Modeling techniques, Performance attributes

General Terms

Theory

Keywords

Capacity analysis, Mobile ad hoc networks, Digital beamforming

1. INTRODUCTION

A wireless ad hoc network consists of a collection of wireless nodes that are connected either directly or indirectly via wireless links, and operates without the requirement for a pre-existing network infrastructure. In a wireless ad hoc network, multi-hop packet transmission is often required due to the limited transmission range of a radio transceiver. That is, a packet will travel more than one hop to reach its destination node. In an airborne mobile ad hoc network (MANET), since a pair of air platforms are typically tens of kilometers away from each other, omni-directional antennas may not be able to provide the required communication range for connectivity between air platforms. The lack of an appropriate communication range of omni-directional antennas may result in network partition (or disconnection) and more frequent changes in the network topology. The former will lead to communication losses while the latter will lead to increased signalling overhead. One solution to this problem is to use directional antennas, digital beamforming (DBF) antennas in particular, to increase the single-hop communication range in airborne MANETs. In fact, it is feasible for an airborne platform to be equipped with a DBF antenna system, which is typically more complex than an omni-directional [1].

A digital beamforming antenna adaptively controls the radiation pattern by using antenna array control algorithms, and in addition to an improved communication range, it provides many other advantages over omni-directional antennas for MANET applications [2, 14]. First of all, DBF antennas significantly mitigate interference to neighboring transmissions/receptions, which results in increase of radio frequency efficiency by allowing multiple simultaneous transmissions/receptions in one network neighborhood area [8]. Secondly, by radiating energy towards the intended direction, a DBF antenna increases the received signal power at the receiver, thus improving the signal-to-noise ratio (SNR). This results in an improvement of the link quality and the data transmission rate [6]. The above two advantages lead to an increased capacity of an airborne MANET. Finally, beamforming antennas reduce the risk of traffic jamming and eavesdropping, and thus are more beneficial to improve security of data communications in airborne networks [7].

In the literature, several studies have been conducted on the overall capacity of wireless ad hoc networks with digital beamforming antennas. In [10, 11] the authors introduced a sender-based interference model and investigated the capacity gains when directional transmission and/or reception were considered. They showed that the overall network capacity increases as the antenna beamwidth θ decreases, and derived a capacity improvement factor given by $4\pi^2/\theta^2$ when directional antennas are used for transmission and reception. The network capacity of multi-channel wireless ad hoc networks with multiple directional antennas (MC-MDA) was investigated in [4]. In the study, an upper bound of the MC-MDA capacity was derived, which depends on the ratio of the number of channels to the number of directional antennas. In [12], the authors carried out capacity analysis for a hybrid wireless network, which integrates a traditional cellular network and a wireless ad hoc network with directional antennas, under the L-maximum-hop resource allocation strategy. In [13], network capacity improvement was analyzed for a wireless sensor network with beamforming antennas and a unique data sink.

In addition to the above studies reporting asymptotic results of the network capacity in terms of the network size being large enough, studies have been conducted on closed-form or bound results for the capacity of wireless ad hoc networks with beamforming antennas. In [3], the authors studied the network-layer throughput performance for a MANET with digital beamforming antennas and derived a closed-form result for achievable per-node throughput. In [9], upper bound expressions of the network capacity were obtained for wireless ad hoc networks with directional antennas. These asymptotic and closed-form results provide limited use in practice. To the best of our knowledge, however, there have been no studies reporting exact analysis on the capacity of wireless ad hoc networks with beamforming antennas.

This paper investigates the properties of the capacity of airborne MANETs with DBF antennas with exact analysis. This work considers a mobile ad hoc network consisting of airborne platforms that are uniformly deployed in a bounded region. Each platform is equipped with a digital beamforming antenna for transferring data. A digital beamforming antenna system model, referred to as the omni-direction plus sector (OPS) model, is proposed to characterize the radiation pattern of the beamforming antenna. Under the condition that a Hamiltonian path exists in the airborne MANET, a maximum number of transmitter-receiver pairs, which can conduct simultaneous data transmissions, are constructed. By defining the network capacity as the total amount of information that can be correctly received during a unit time by the receiver of each transmitter-receiver pair, an ex-

plicit result for the network capacity is derived. It is shown that, for fixed values of the OPS model, the network capacity converges to zero as the network size approaches infinity. Moreover, an explicit expression of an optimal network size, at which the capacity of the network is maximized, is obtained. Numerical results are presented to show the performance trend of the network capacity with respect to the network size and the antenna beamwidth. It is also shown that, for a fixed beamwidth, the network capacity increases as the network size increases until the optimal value of the network size is reached, and then decreases as the network size grows further. Both the optimal network size and the corresponding maximum network capacity increase as the antenna beamwidth decreases. The gains are small with large beamwidth antennas (e.g., $90° < \theta < 180°$), but gains increase as the antenna beam becomes narrower (e.g., $15° < \theta < 30°$).

The rest of the paper is organized as follows. A digital beamforming antenna system model and an airborne MANET are described in Section 2. Analysis of the network capacity is carried out in Section 3. Numerical results are presented and discussed in Section 4. Concluding remarks are given in Section 5.

2. ANTENNA AND NETWORK MODEL

This section proposes a digital beamforming antenna system model and describes an airborne mobile ad hoc network model for analysis of the network capacity.

2.1 DBF Antenna System Model

Our DBF antenna system model or the OPS model is governed by a three-tuple vector (θ, G_m, G_s), where θ is the beamwidth of the antenna, G_m is the antenna gain in the main lobe, and G_s is the antenna gain in the side lobe. In this model, the antenna radiation pattern is shown in Figure 1, where R represents the maximum distance between a transmitter and a receiver when directional transmission and directional reception are used by the pair, and r represents the range covered by the side lobe of the transmitter. For a DBF antenna, the transmission energy is concentrated and radiated towards the main lobe direction, while the side-lobes are modeled as omni-directional with much lower level. Therefore $G_m >> G_s$, which indicates that G_m is significantly larger than G_s.

R is determined by assuming that the antenna efficiency is constant (set to "1"), and a transmitter and a receiver have the same antenna gain G_m in the main lobe. Let P_t be the transmitted power, λ be the radio signal wavelength, and σ be the receiving power threshold. Using the free-space propagation model, the ranges are determined as follows:

$$R = \frac{\lambda G_m}{4\pi}\sqrt{\frac{P_t}{\sigma}}; \qquad r = \frac{\lambda G_s}{4\pi}\sqrt{\frac{P_t}{\sigma}}. \qquad (1)$$

The circular area centered by a node with radius r is called the constrained area of the node, meaning that transmission ($A \rightarrow B$ in Figure 2) and reception ($C \leftarrow D$ in Figure 2) within this area cannot take place at the same time. Otherwise, data collisions occur at node C, while the transmission session between A and B is not affected. Due to the assumption that $G_m >> G_s$, in this study it entails that the constrained area of a node is sufficiently small so that no node exists in the area.

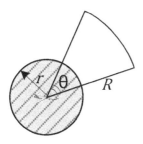

Figure 1: DBF Antenna System Model.

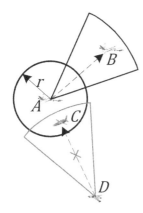

Figure 2: Constrained Area of Node A.

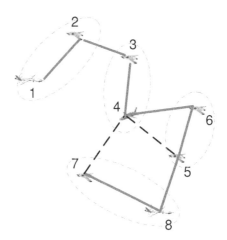

Figure 3: Hamiltonian Path in a Connect Graph.

2.2 Airborne Mobile Ad Hoc Network Model

A positive even number N of airborne platforms are sequentially identified by $1, 2, \cdots, N$, and uniformly distributed in a two-dimensional bounded region of area Λ. Each platform is equipped with a digital beamforming antenna system as described in Section 2.1 and operates on a same radio frequency band for data communications. Using the digital beamforming antenna system, a pair of platforms can communicate with each other if the Euclidean distance between them is no more than the range R computed from (1), in which case the two platforms are said to be connected. Given a range R, it is assumed that N is large enough so that the network is connected.

Based on the network topology described above, a bidirectional graph $G = (\mathcal{V}, \mathcal{E})$ is constructed, where the vertex set $\mathcal{V} = \{1, 2, \cdots, N\}$ represents a set of N network platforms, and the edge set $\mathcal{E}$ consists of communication links over which two platforms can communicate with each other. That is, an edge $\mu\nu \in \mathcal{E}$ if and only if the the Euclidean distance between μ and ν is less than or equal to R. It is assumed that a Hamiltonian path exists in G. A Hamiltonian path in the graph is defined as a path that visits every vertex exactly once [5]. Starting at one end of the Hamiltonian path, the vertices are reordered by sequentially grouping two vertices along the Hamiltonian path. Each pair of vertices are used to compose a subset of $\mathcal{V}$. As an example, the red solid line segments identified in the connected graph shown in Figure 3 build a Hamiltonian path $(1, 2, 3, 4, 6, 5, 8, 7)$. The vertex set is then partitioned into four subsets: $\{1, 2\}$, $\{3, 4\}$, $\{6, 5\}$, and $\{8, 7\}$.

According to the above argument, the vertex set of the graph, in which a Hamiltonian path exists, can be partitioned into $N/2$ subsets, each of which consists of exactly two connected vertices. This fact is elaborated in the following lemma, which we will use to construct transmitter-receiver pairs for network capacity analysis in the next section.

LEMMA 1. *Exactly $N/2$ distinct transmitter-receiver pairs can be constructed from an airborne mobile ad hoc network if a Hamiltonian path exists in its corresponding graph described above.*

3. ANALYSIS OF NETWORK CAPACITY

To analyze the capacity, a heavy traffic condition is assumed. That is, each network platform has infinite supply of data to transmit. In addition, a transmitter performs data transmission at a fixed rate Γ bits per second (bps). If there is no collision occurring at the intended receiver, all transmitted data are correctly received by the receiver at a fixed rate Γ *bps*. It is known by each platform pair which platform is the transmitter and which is the receiver before data transmission starts. Then there is a possibility that both platforms in a pair are transmitters or receivers, and there is an equal probability for a platform to be a transmitter or a receiver.

3.1 Throughput for an Individual Transmitter-Receiver Pair

This section analyzes the transmission throughput of an arbitrary transmitter-receiver pair denoted by (n_t, n_r), where n_t and n_r are the transmitting node and receiving node, respectively.

S_r is set as the receiving sector of n_r. The area of S_r is $\pi R^2 (\frac{\theta}{2\pi}) = \frac{\theta R^2}{2}$, and thus the probability that a platform is located in S_r is $\frac{\theta R^2}{2\Lambda}$. X is defined as the number of platforms (except n_t and n_r) that are located in S_r. Then X is a Binomial random variable with parameters $\frac{\theta R^2}{2\Lambda}$ and $\hat{N} = N - 2$. That is, for $x = 0, 1, \cdots, \hat{N}$,

$$\mathbb{P}[X = x] = \binom{\hat{N}}{x} \left(\frac{\theta R^2}{2\Lambda}\right)^x \left(1 - \frac{\theta R^2}{2\Lambda}\right)^{\hat{N} - x}. \quad (2)$$

Given that a node has an equal probability of being a transmitter or a receiver and $x = 0, 1, \cdots, \hat{N}$, Y is defined as the number of transmitting nodes in S_r. Then the following conditional probability is derived.

$$\mathbb{P}[Y = y | X = x] = \binom{x}{y} \left(\frac{1}{2}\right)^x, \quad y = 0, 1, \cdots, x. \quad (3)$$

Next, by denoting Z the number of nodes transmitting data towards the direction of n_r, the following conditional probability is obtained for $z = 0, 1, \cdots, y$.

$$\mathbb{P}[Z = z | X = x, Y = y] = \binom{y}{z} \left(\frac{\theta}{2\pi}\right)^z \left(1 - \frac{\theta}{2\pi}\right)^{y-z}. \quad (4)$$

The event that a successful reception at n_r is equivalent to the event that no platform in S_r except n_t transmits towards the direction of n_r, which is also equivalent to $\{Z = 0\}$. Therefore, the probability p_s that a successful reception at n_r is given by,

$$
\begin{aligned}
p_s =& \mathbb{P}[Z = 0] \\
=& \sum_{x=0}^{\hat{N}} \sum_{y=0}^{x} \mathbb{P}[X = x, Y = y, Z = 0] \\
=& \sum_{x=0}^{\hat{N}} \sum_{y=0}^{x} \mathbb{P}[Z = 0 | X = x, Y = y]\mathbb{P}[Y = y | X = x] \times \\
& \qquad\qquad\qquad\qquad\qquad\qquad \mathbb{P}[X = x] \\
=& \sum_{x=0}^{\hat{N}} \sum_{y=0}^{x} \left(1 - \frac{\theta}{2\pi}\right)^y \binom{x}{y} \left(\frac{1}{2}\right)^x \binom{\hat{N}}{x} \left(\frac{\theta R^2}{2\Lambda}\right)^x \times \\
& \qquad\qquad\qquad\qquad\qquad\qquad \left(1 - \frac{\theta R^2}{2\Lambda}\right)^{\hat{N}-x} \\
=& \sum_{x=0}^{\hat{N}} \binom{\hat{N}}{x} \left(\frac{1}{2}\right)^x \left(\frac{\theta R^2}{2\Lambda}\right)^x \left(1 - \frac{\theta R^2}{2\Lambda}\right)^{\hat{N}-x} \times \\
& \qquad\qquad\qquad\qquad \left\{\sum_{y=0}^{x} \binom{x}{y} \left(1 - \frac{\theta}{2\pi}\right)^y\right\} \\
=& \sum_{x=0}^{\hat{N}} \binom{\hat{N}}{x} \left(\frac{1}{2}\right)^x \left(\frac{\theta R^2}{2\Lambda}\right)^x \left(1 - \frac{\theta R^2}{2\Lambda}\right)^{\hat{N}-x} \left(2 - \frac{\theta}{2\pi}\right)^x \\
=& \sum_{x=0}^{\hat{N}} \binom{\hat{N}}{x} \left[\left(1 - \frac{\theta}{4\pi}\right)\left(\frac{\theta R^2}{2\Lambda}\right)\right]^x \left(1 - \frac{\theta R^2}{2\Lambda}\right)^{\hat{N}-x} \\
=& \left[\left(1 - \frac{\theta}{4\pi}\right)\left(\frac{\theta R^2}{2\Lambda}\right) + \left(1 - \frac{\theta R^2}{2\Lambda}\right)\right]^{\hat{N}} \\
=& \left(1 - \frac{(\theta R)^2}{8\pi\Lambda}\right)^{\hat{N}}. \quad (5)
\end{aligned}
$$

Then the throughput of the individual transmitter-receiver pair (n_t, n_r) is given by Γp_s.

3.2 Network Capacity and Its Optimization

According to Lemma 1, there are $N/2$ node pairs in the whole network that conduct data transmission simultaneously. Therefore, the capacity of the airborne mobile ad hoc network is given by,

$$C = \left(\frac{N}{2}\right)\Gamma p_s = \frac{\Gamma N}{2}\left(1 - \frac{(\theta R)^2}{8\pi\Lambda}\right)^{N-2}. \quad (6)$$

From (6), it is shown that for fixed parameters except the antenna beamwidth, the network capacity increases as the antenna beamwidth decreases. This fact is very intuitive. In addition, when other parameters are fixed, the network capacity is not monotone as the network size N varies. This is because the first factor in (6) is increasing with N while the second factor is decreasing as N grows. To determine an optimal value of the network size for which the network capacity is maximized, N is considered to be a positive real variable, and thus the network capacity C is continuous and differentiable at $N > 2$. It is easy to obtain,

$$C \to \begin{cases} \Gamma, & \text{as } N \to 2, \\ 0, & \text{as } N \to \infty. \end{cases} \quad (7)$$

By computing the derivative, the following equation needs to be solved.

$$\frac{\partial \ln(C)}{\partial N} = \frac{1}{N} + \ln\left(1 - \frac{(\theta R)^2}{8\pi\Lambda}\right) = 0, \quad (8)$$

which gives,

$$n_{opt} = \frac{-1}{\ln\left(1 - \frac{(\theta R)^2}{8\pi\Lambda}\right)}. \quad (9)$$

$[x]^*$ is denoted as the nearest even number to $x \in R^+$. Then the optimal network size for maximum network capacity is given by,

$$N_{opt} = [n_{opt}]^* = \left[\frac{-1}{\ln\left(1 - \frac{(\theta R)^2}{8\pi\Lambda}\right)}\right]^*, \quad (10)$$

and the maximum capacity is given by,

$$C_{max} = \frac{\lambda N_{opt}}{2}\left(1 - \frac{(\theta R)^2}{8\pi\Lambda}\right)^{N_{opt}-2}. \quad (11)$$

4. NUMERICAL RESULTS

In this section, numerical results of the network capacity are presented and the optimal values of the network size are analyzed. In the rest of this section, a bounded region is considered, where the airborne platforms are distributed, as a square of area $\Lambda = 30 \times 30\ km^2$. For an individual pair of transmitter and receiver, when directional transmission and reception are used, the maximum transmission distance and the transmission data rate are fixed to be $10\ km$ and $2\ Mbps$, respectively. That is, $R = 10\ km$, and $\Gamma = 2\ Mbps$.

Figure 4 plots network capacity results as the network size varies. It is observed that, with a fixed beamwidth and increasing values of the network size, the network capacity increases at first up to a peak value, and after the maximum capacity it decreases. With different values of the beamwidth, the network size values such that the network capacity is maximized are different. The narrower the beam, the larger the optimal value of the network size, and the greater the maximized network capacity.

In Figure 5, optimal values of the network size are plotted as the beamwidth varies from π to $\pi/12$. It is observed that the optimal network size value N_{opt} increases when

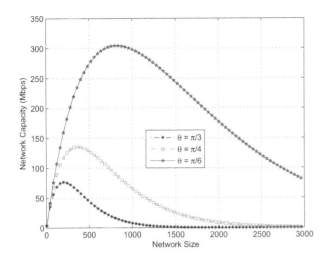

Figure 4: Overall Network Capacity versus Network Size.

crease when the beamwidth is decreased by 30 degrees from $\pi/3$ to $\pi/6$ or by 15 degrees from $\pi/6$ to $\pi/12$.

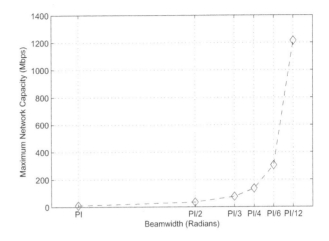

Figure 6: Maximum Overall Network Capacity versus Antenna Beamwidth.

beamwidth θ decreases. Moreover, a slow growth in the optimal network size is associated with a large beamwidth. Then the growth rate becomes larger as the beamwidth becomes smaller. For instance, the optimal network size value will have approximately three times increase when the beamwidth is decreased by 30 degrees from $\pi/3$ to $\pi/6$ or by 15 degrees from $\pi/6$ to $\pi/12$. This indicates that the number of transmitter-receiver pairs, at which the network capacity is maximized, is increasing faster and faster as the beam becomes narrower and narrower.

5. CONCLUSION

In this paper, a digital beamforming antenna system model was proposed to characterize the radiation pattern of a beamforming antenna, and exact analysis was conducted for the network capacity of an airborne mobile ad hoc network with digital beamforming antennas. Under the assumption that the maximum number of transmitter-receiver pairs are conducting simultaneous data transmissions, explicit results were obtained for the network capacity and the optimal network size at which the capacity of the network can be maximized. Numerical results showed that, for a fixed beamwidth, the network capacity increases with the network size until a peak value, and then decreases as the network size grows. The network capacity converges to zero when the network size goes to infinity. Both the optimal network size and the maximum network capacity increase as the antenna beamwidth decreases. Their increasing rate is small when the beamwidth is large (e.g., $90° < \theta < 180°$), but becomes faster as the antenna beam becomes narrower (e.g., $15° < \theta < 30°$).

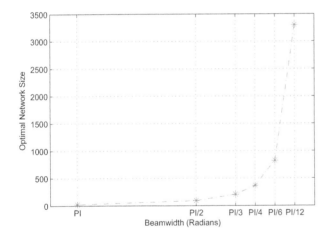

Figure 5: Optimal Network Size versus Antenna Beamwidth.

The maximum network capacity results are plotted in Figure 6 where the beamwidth values range from π to $\pi/12$. Similar to the trend of the optimal network size observed in Figure 5, Figure 6 shows that the maximum network capacity increases as the beamwidth decreases. In addition, the maximum network capacity increases faster and faster as the beamwidth becomes smaller and smaller. For instance, the maximum value of network capacity is of three-times in-

6. ACKNOWLEDGMENTS

The work reported herein was supported by Department of National Defence Canada.

7. REFERENCES

[1] A.I. Alshbatat, and L. Dong. Performance analysis of mobile ad hoc unmanned aerial vehicle communication networks with directional antennas. *International Journal of Aerospace Engineering*, vol. 2010, article ID 874586, December 2010.

[2] S. Bandyopadhyay, S. Roy, and T. Ueda. *Enhancing the performance of ad hoc wireless networks with smart antennas, first edition*. Auerbach Publications, Taylor & Francis Group, Boca Raton, FL., USA, May 2006.

[3] Y. Chen, J. Liu, X. Jiang, and O. Takahashi. Throughput analysis in mobile ad hoc networks with

directional antennas. *Ad Hoc Networks*, 11(3): 1122–1135, May 2013.

[4] H. Dai, K. Ng, R. Wong, and M. Wu. On the capacity of multi-channel wireless networks using directional antennas. In *Proceedings of the 27th IEEE Conference on Computer Communications (InfoCom 2008)*, pages 1301–1309, Phoenix, AZ, USA, April 2008.

[5] J.L. Gross and J. Yellen, *Graph theory and its applications, 2nd edition*. CRC Press, Taylor & Francis Group, Boca Raton, FL., USA, September 2005.

[6] P. Li, C. Zhang, and Y. Fang. Asymptotic connectivity in wireless ad hoc networks using directional antennas. *IEEE/ACM Transactions on Networking*, 17(4): 1106–1117, August 2009.

[7] G. Noubir. On connectivity in ad hoc network under jamming using directional antennas and mobility. In *Proceedings of the Second International Conference on Wired/Wireless Internet Communications (WWIC 2004)*, pages 186–200, Frankfurt, Germany, February 2004.

[8] R. Ramanathan, J. Redi, C. Santivanez, D. Wiggins, and S. Polit. Ad hoc networking with directional antennas: A complete system solution. *IEEE Journal on Selected Areas in Communications*, 23(3): 496–506, March 2005.

[9] A. Spyropoulos and C.S. Raghavendra. Capacity Bounds for Ad-Hoc Networks Using Directional Antennas. In *Proceedings of IEEE International Conference on Communications (ICC)*, pages 348–352, Anchorage, Alaska, May 2003.

[10] S. Yi, Y. Pei, and S. Kalyanaraman. On the capacity improvement of ad hoc wireless networks using directional antennas. In *Proceedings of the 4th ACM international symposium on Mobile ad hoc networking & computing (MobiHoc'2003)*, pages 108–116, Annapolis, MD, USA, June 2003.

[11] S. Yi, Y. Pei, S. Kalyanaraman, and B. Azimi-Sadjadi. How is the capacity of ad hoc networks improved with directional antennas?" *Wireless Networks*, 13(5): 635–648, October 2007.

[12] G. Zhang, Y. Xu, X. Wang, and M. Guizani. Capacity of hybrid wireless networks with directional antenna and delay constraint. *IEEE Transactions on Communications*, 58(7): 2097–2106, July 2010.

[13] J. Zhang, X. Jia, and Y. Zhou. Analysis of capacity improvement by directional antennas in wireless sensor networks. *ACM Transactions on Sensor Networks*, 9(1), article 3, November 2012.

[14] Y. Zhang, X. Li, and M.G. Amin. Mobile ad hoc networks exploiting multi-beam antennas. In *Handbook on Advancements in Smart Antenna Technologies for Wireless Networks (ed. C. Sun, J. Cheng, and T. Ohira)*, pages 398–424, July 2008.

Impact of Node Mobility on Single-Hop Cluster Overlap in Vehicular Ad Hoc Networks

Khadige Abboud
Department of Electrical and Computer
Engineering,
University of Waterloo
Waterloo, Ontario, Canada, N2L 3G1
khabboud@uwaterloo.ca

Weihua Zhuang
Department of Electrical and Computer
Engineering,
University of Waterloo
Waterloo, Ontario, Canada, N2L 3G1
wzhuang@uwaterloo.ca

ABSTRACT

Node clustering is a potential approach to improve the scalability of networking protocols in vehicular ad hoc networks (VANETs). High relative vehicle mobility and frequent topology changes inflict new challenges on maintaining stable clusters. As a result, cluster stability is a crucial measure of the efficiency of clustering algorithms for VANETs. This paper presents stochastic analysis of the vehicle mobility impact on single-hop cluster stability in terms of the overlapping state between neighboring clusters. A stochastic mobility model is adopted to capture the time variations of inter-vehicle distances (distance headways). Firstly, we propose a discrete-time lumped Markov chain to model the time variation of the distance between two neighboring cluster heads. Secondly, first passage time analysis is used to derive probability distributions of the time to the first change in cluster-overlapping state and the inter-cluster overlapping time as measures of cluster stability. Finally, numerical results are presented to evaluate the proposed model, which demonstrate a close agreement between analytical and simulation results.

Categories and Subject Descriptors

C.2.1 [**Computer-Communication Networks**]: Network Architecture and Design—*Wireless communication*; G.3 [**Mathematics of Computing**]: Probability and Statistics—*Markov processes*

General Terms

Theory

Keywords

cluster overlapping; vehicle mobility; cluster stability

MSWiM'14, September 21–26, 2014, Montreal, QC, Canada.
Copyright 2014 ACM 978-1-4503-3030-5/14/09:.$15.00.
http://dx.doi.org/10.1145/2641798.2641832.

1. INTRODUCTION

A vehicular ad hoc network (VANET) is a promising addition to our future intelligent transportation systems, which is provisioned to support various safety and infotainment applications [3]. Urban roads and highways are highly susceptible to a large number of vehicles and traffic jams. Therefore, the networking protocols for VANETs should be scalable to support such large sized networks. Node clustering is a network management strategy in which nearby nodes are grouped into a set called cluster. In each cluster, a node, called a cluster head (CH), is elected to manage the cluster. The remaining nodes are called cluster members (CMs), each belonging to one or multiple clusters. Node clustering, just as in traditional ad hoc networks, is a potential approach to improve the scalability of networking protocols such as for routing and medium access control in VANETs. For medium access control protocols, the CH can act as a central coordinator that manages the access of its CMs to the wireless channel(s) [14]. For routing protocols, CHs can be made responsible for the discovery and maintenance of routing paths, thus limiting the number of control-message overhead in these processes [8]. Despite the potential benefits of node clustering, forming and maintaining the clusters require explicit exchange of control messages. In VANETs, vehicles move with high and variable speeds causing frequent changes in the network topology, which can significantly increase the cluster maintenance cost. Therefore, forming stable clusters that last for a long time is a major issue in clustering of VANETs.

In a highly dynamic VANET, vehicles approach and move apart from one another, resulting in changes in cluster structure. The temporal changes in cluster structure are either internal or external [13]. An internal change in the cluster structure is concerned with a change inside the cluster such as when vehicles join or leave the cluster. Frequent changes in the internal cluster structure consume the network radio resources and cause service disruption for the cluster-based network protocols. On the other hand, an external change in the cluster structure is concerned with cluster's relationship with the other clusters in the network. One metric that evaluates the external relationship of a cluster, with other clusters, is the overlapping range among clusters. The time variations of the distance between neighboring CHs, due to vehicle mobility, can cause the coverage ranges of the clusters to overlap. When the overlapping range between the two clusters increases, it may cause the merging of the two clusters into a single cluster [14, 7, 12]. Frequent splitting and merging of clusters increase the control overhead and drain the channel resources [15, 6, 11]. As a result, both internal and external changes in cluster structure are indicators of cluster stability [13]. In this paper, we focus on the external change in the cluster structure as a measure of cluster stability. In general, a non-overlapping clustered structure produces a less number of clusters and lowers the design complexity of the network protocols that run on the clusters. For example, two clusters may utilize the same channel resources at the same time if they are non neighboring clusters [18] [17]. On the other hand, a highly overlapping clustered structure may cause complexity in the channel assignment, lead to broadcast storm, and form long hierarchical routes. Additional channel resources ought to be used to prevent inter-cluster interference due to overlapping. For example, assigning different time frames for neighboring clusters [4] and assigning different transmission codes to CMs located in a possibly overlapping region [19]. Although researchers have favored forming non-overlapping (or reduced overlapping) clustering algorithms [6] [15] [12] [19], encountering overlapping clusters during the network runtime is inevitable, especially in a highly mobile network. Overlapping clusters have received significant attention since the work by Palla et al. [10]. It is shown that real networks are better characterized by well-defined statistics of overlapping and nested clusters rather than disjoint partitions. Whether the objective clustering is overlapping or non-overlapping, characterizing the overlapping state between neighboring clusters and its change over time becomes crucial in the presence of node mobility. Despite the importance of cluster stability as a measure of clustering algorithm efficiency in VANETs, characterizing cluster stability, in the literature, has taken the form of simulations [7, 16, 11] or case studies [5].

In this paper, we present a stochastic analysis for the change in the overlapping state between neighboring clusters as a measure of cluster stability. We adopt a stochastic vehicle mobility model that describes the time variations of inter-vehicle distances and accounts for the realistic dependency of these variations at consecutive time steps. Firstly, the distance between two neighboring CHs, separated by a number of vehicles on the highway, is modeled as a discrete-time Markov chain with a reduced dimensionality. Secondly, using first passage time analysis, we derive the probability distributions of the time interval before the first change in the overlapping state and the inter-overlapping time period between two neighboring CHs. Finally, we conduct MATLAB simulations and demonstrate that the analytical results of our model match well with the simulation results.

2. SYSTEM MODEL

Consider a VANET on a multi-lane highway with no on or off ramps. We focus on a single lane with lane changes implicitly captured in the adopted mobility model. We choose a single lane from a multi-lane highway instead of a single-lane highway, in order to be more realistic in a highway scenario. Assume that the highway is in a steady traffic flow condition defined by a time-invariant intermediate vehicle density. All the vehicles have the same transmission range, denoted by R. Any two nodes at a distance less than R from each other are one hop neighbours. Time is partitioned with a constant step size. Let X_i be the distance headway between node i and node $i + 1$. The distance headway is the distance between two identical points on two consecu-

tive vehicles on the same lane. Define $X_i = \{X_i(m), m = 0, 1, 2 \dots \}$ to be a discrete-time stochastic process of the ith distance headway, where $X_i(m)$ is a random variable representing the distance headway of node i at the mth time step, $i = 0, 1, 2, \dots, m = 0, 1, 2, \dots$. Furthermore, assume that X_i's are independent with identical statistical behaviors for all $i \geq 0$. For notation simplicity, we omit the index i when referring to an arbitrary distance headway.

2.1 Node Clusters

We assume that CHs are selected according to some clustering scheme so that the network nodes are grouped into possibly-overlapping, single-hop clusters. The range of each cluster extends one hop on both sides of the CH. At the end of the cluster formation, the vehicles are distributed on the highway according to a stationary probability distribution of the distance headways. Let N_c be the number of nodes between two neighbouring CHs. The overlapping range between two neighbouring clusters is the common distance covered by the transmission range of both CHs. Define the overlapping state between two neighbouring clusters to be i) overlapping, when the distance between the two CHs is less than $2R$; or ii) non-overlapping, when the distance between the two CHs is greater than or equal to $2R$. In our analysis, the 0th time step refers to the time when the cluster formation has just finished. We assume that the clusters are initially overlapping and the CHs remain the same over a time interval of interest.

2.2 Node Mobility

The vehicles move according to the microscopic mobility model proposed in [1]. In this model, a distance headway, X, changes according to a discrete-time finite-state Markov chain. The Markov chain has $N_{\max}$ states corresponding to $N_{\max}$ ranges of a distance headway. Let $X_i(m) \in s_i$ denote the event that the ith distance headway is in state s_i at the mth time step, where $s_i \in [0, N_{\max} - 1]$ and $i, m \geq 0$. The distance headway transits from one state to another according to a tri-diagonal state-dependent transition matrix, denoted by M. Within a time step, a distance headway in state j can transit to the next state, the previous state, or remain in the same state with probabilities p_j, q_j, or r_j, $0 \leq j \leq N_{\max} - 1$, respectively, where $q_0 = p_{N_{\max}-1} = 0$ and $r_j = 1 - p_j - q_i$.

3. TIME VARIATIONS OF CLUSTER OVERLAPPING STATE

The distance between two neighboring CHs is equal to the sum of the distance headways between the two nodes. Label the $(N_c + 2)$ nodes with IDs $0, 1, \dots, N_c + 1$ where the following CH has ID 0, and the leading CH has ID $(N_c + 1)$. For notation simplicity, let $\mathbb{X}_c = (X_i)_{i=0}^{N_c}$ be the sequence of distance headways between the two CHs as illustrated in Figure 1, where $\mathbb{X}_c(m) = (X_i(m))_{i=0}^{N_c}$, and $\{\mathbb{X}_c(m) \in (s_0, s_1, \dots, s_{N_c})\} \equiv \{X_i(m) \in s_i, \forall i \in [0, N_c]\}$. Consider initially overlapping clusters, i.e., $\sum_{i=0}^{N_c} X_i(0) < 2R$. Two neighboring CHs remain overlapping until $\sum_{i=0}^{N_c} X_i(m) \geq 2R$ at some time step m. The sequence of $(N_c + 1)$ independent and identically distributed (i.i.d.) distance

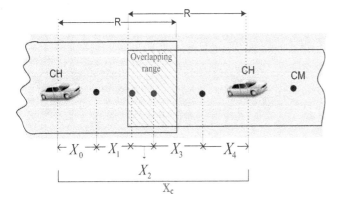

Figure 1: Two neighboring CHs separated by $N_c = 4$ nodes and $\mathbb{X}_c = (X_0, X_1, X_2, X_3, X_4)$.

headways, where each headway, X_i, is a birth and death Markov chain as described in Subsection 2.2, is an $(N_c + 1)$-dimensional Markov chain. For clarity, the term *state* refers to a state in the original Markov chain, X, the term *super state* refers to a state in the $(N_c + 1)$-dimensional Markov chain, and the term *lumped state* refers to a set of super states (to be discussed later in this section). Additionally, parentheses ( ) are used for a sequence, while curly brackets { } are used for a set. A super state in the (N_c+1)-dimensional Markov chain is a sequence of size $N_c + 1$, in which the ith element represents the state (in the 1-dimensional Markov chain) that the ith distance headway belongs to. That is, a super state, $(s_0, s_1, \ldots, s_{N_c})$, means that the distance headway X_i is in state $s_i \in [0, N_{\max} - 1]$. The sum of (N_c+1) distance headways representing the distance between the two CHs can be calculated from the (N_c+1)-dimensional Markov chain. The state space size of the $(N_c + 1)$-dimensional Markov chain is equal to $N_{\max}^{(N_c+1)}$, making it subject to the state-space explosion problem when N_c is large. However, since we are interested in the sum of the $(N_c + 1)$ distance headways, the state space can be reduced according to the following theorem.

THEOREM 3.1. *Let X be a discrete-time, birth-death, irreducible Markov chain with N_{max} finite states, and let the set $\mathbb{X} = (X_i)_{i=0}^{N-1}$ represent a system of N independent copies of chain X. The N-dimensional Markov chain that represents the system, $\mathbb{X}$, is lumpable with respect to the state space partition $\Omega = \{\Omega_0, \Omega_1 \ldots, \Omega_{N_{lump}}\}$, such that (s.t.) any two super states in subset Ω_i are permutations of the same set of states $\forall i \in [0, N_{lump} - 1]$, where $N_{lump} = \frac{(N_{max}+N-1)!}{N!(N_{max}-1)!}$ is the state space size of the lumped Markov chain.*

The proof of Theorem 3.1 is given in Appendix A.1. Since a lumped state, $\Omega_i = \{(s_0, s_1, \ldots, s_{N-1})\}, 0 \le i \le N_{lump} - 1$, contains all super states that are permutations of the same set of states, we can write the lumped state as a set of those states $\Omega_i = \{s_0, s_1, \ldots, s_{N-1}\}$. Since the $(N_c + 1)$-dimensional Markov chain is irreducible, the lumped Markov chain is also irreducible [2]. The stationary distribution of the lumped Markov chain can be derived from the stationary distribution of the 1-dimensional Markov chain according to the following Corollary.

COROLLARY 3.2. *Consider a system of N independent copies of a finite, discrete-time, birth-death, irreducible Markov*

chain, X, with stationary distribution $(\pi_i)_{i=0}^{N_{max}-1}$. The stationary distribution of the lumped Markov chain of Theorem 3.1, representing the system $\mathbb{X} = (X_i)_{i=0}^{N-1}$, follows a multinomial distribution with parameters $(\pi_i)_{i=0}^{N_{max}-1}$.

The proof of Corollary 3.2 is given in Appendix A.2.

3.1 Time to the first cluster-overlapping state change

Consider two overlapping clusters as described at the beginning of this section. At any time instant, the overlapping range between two neighbouring clusters is equal to $2R - \sum_{i=0}^{N_c} X_i(m), \forall m \ge 0$. Therefore, according to Theorem 3.1, the time variation of the overlapping range between the two clusters can be described by a lumped Markov chain with lumped states $\Omega_0, \Omega_1, \ldots, \Omega_{N_{lump}-1}$ which represents the system $\mathbb{X}_c = (X_i)_{i=0}^{N_c}$. Furthermore, divide the lumped states into two sets, Ω_{OV} and Ω_{NOV}. A lumped state $\Omega_i = \{s_0, s_1, \ldots, s_{N_c}\}$ belongs to Ω_{OV} and to Ω_{NOV} if $\sum_{i=0}^{N_c} s_i < 2N_R$ and $\sum_{i=0}^{N_c} s_i \ge 2N_R$, respectively, where N_R is the integer number of the states that cover distance headways within R in the distance headway's 1-dimensional Markov chain. Let the system of the distance headways between the two CHs be initially in the super state I_c i.e., $\mathbb{X}_c(0) \in I_c$, s.t. $I_c \in \Omega_k \in \Omega_{OV}, 0 \le k \le N_{lump} - 1$. Let the time period until the clusters are no longer overlapping given that the distance headways between them are initially in states I_c be $T_{ov}(I_c)$. Then, this time period is equal to the first passage time for the system, $\mathbb{X}_c$, to transit from the lumped state Ω_k to any lumped state $\Omega_{k'}$, s.t. $\Omega_{k'} \in \Omega_{NOV}$. That is, $T_{ov}(I_c) = \min \left\{ m > 0; \mathbb{X}_c(m) \in (k_0, k_1, \ldots, k_{N_c}), \quad \sum_{i=0}^{N_c} k_i \ge 2N_R \mid \mathbb{X}_c(0) \in I_c \right\}$. Let M_{N_c} be the transition probability matrix of the lumped Markov chain describing $\mathbb{X}_c$. One way to find the first passage time is to force the lumped states in Ω_{NOV} to become absorbing, i.e., set the probability of returning to the same lump state, Ω_i, within one time step to one $\forall \Omega_i \in \Omega_{NOV}$. Furthermore, let all the lumped states in Ω_{NOV} be merged into one single absorbing state and let it be the last $(\tilde{N}_{lump} - 1)^{\text{th}}$ state, where $\tilde{N}_{lump}$ is the number of states in the new absorbing lumped Markov chain. The transition probability matrix of the new absorbing lumped Markov chain, $\tilde{M}_{N_c}$, is derived from M_{N_c} as follows: $\tilde{M}_{N_c}(\Omega_i, \Omega_j) = M_{N_c}(\Omega_i, \Omega_j) \, \forall i, j, \, s.t. \Omega_i, \Omega_j \in \Omega_{OV}, \tilde{M}_{N_c}(\Omega_i, \Omega_{N'_{lump}-1}) = \sum_j M_{N_c}(\Omega_i, \Omega_j) \, \forall i, j, \, s.t. \Omega_i \in \Omega_{OV}$ and $\Omega_j \in \Omega_{NOV}$. The cumulative distribution function (cdf) of the time interval (from the instant that the clusters are initially formed, given that the distance headways are in super state $I_c \in \Omega_k$, till the time instant that the overlapping state changes) is given by

$$
\begin{aligned}
F_{T_{ov}(I_c)}(m) \quad &= \tilde{M}_{N_c}(\Omega_k, \Omega_{\tilde{N}_{lump}-1}) \\
&+ \sum_{\substack{j \\ \Omega_j \in \Omega_{OV}}} \tilde{M}_{N_c}(\Omega_k, \Omega_j) F_{T_{ov}(\Omega_j)}(m - 1), \\
&\qquad m \ge 1. \qquad (1)
\end{aligned}
$$

The size of the state space of the lumped Markov chain can still get large with an increased number of nodes between the two CHs, since $N_{\text{lump}} = \frac{(N_{\max}+N_c)!}{(N_c+1)!(N_{\max}-1)!}$. However, the state space of the absorbing lumped Markov chain, needed to

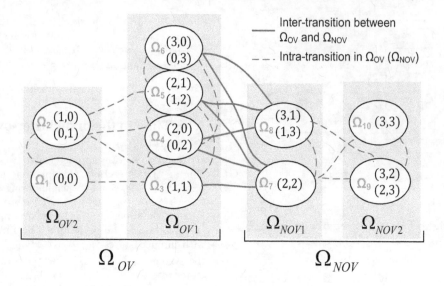

Figure 2: An illustration of a lumped markov chain for $N = 2, N_{\text{th}} = 4, N_{\text{max}} = 3$. A line between two lumped states represents a non-zero two-way transition probability in a single time step between the linked states. There exist non-zero transition probabilities between subsets of Ω_{OV1} and Ω_{NOV1}.

compute the time period until the overlapping state changes between the two neighboring CHs, is bounded according to the following Corollary.

COROLLARY 3.3. *Consider a system of N independent copies of an irreducible Markov chain according in Theorem 3.1, and let the event of interest be that the sum of the states of the N chains be larger than a deterministic threshold N_{th}. The absorbing lumped Markov chain, required to obtain the first occurrence time of the event of interest, has a state space that is bounded by a deterministic function of N_{th}, when $N > N_{th}$.*

The proof of Corollary 3.3 is given in Appendix A.3. In this subsection, we focus on the time interval from the instant that two partially overlapping neighboring clusters are formed till the time instant that they no longer overlap. Given an initial super state of the two neighboring clusters at the end of the cluster formation stage, consider the following: *i)* a proactive re-clustering procedure in which re-clustering is triggered after a fixed period of time, say τ seconds from the cluster formation; and *ii)* a reactive re-clustering procedure in which re-clustering is triggered when the cluster-overlapping state changes. In *i)*, the probability that the overlapping state changes between the two overlapping neighboring clusters before re-clustering is triggered is equal to $F_{T_{ov}(I_c)}(\tau)$. In *ii)*, the re-clustering period is equal to $T_{ov}(I_c)$ with the cdf calculated by (1). Up until now, we have considered a pair of neighboring clusters in a specific super state when they are initially formed. In reality, the initial state of a pair of neighboring clusters is a random variable. For a given N_c, since the distance headways are stationary when the clusters are formed, the probability that two overlapping neighboring clusters are initially in lumped state Ω_i is given by $\frac{\mho_i}{\sum\limits_{\Omega_j \in \Omega_{OV}}^{j} \mho_j}$ where $\mho_i$ is calculated by (9).

Using the law of total probability, the cdf of the time for a change in overlapping state to occur between two initially overlapping clusters is given by

$$F_{T_{ov}}(m) = \frac{\sum\limits_{\Omega_j \in \Omega_{OV}}^{j} \mho_j F_{T_{ov}(\Omega_j)}(m)}{\sum\limits_{\Omega_i \in \Omega_{OV}}^{i} \mho_i}, \quad m = 1, 2, \ldots. \quad (2)$$

3.2 Inter-cluster overlapping time period

In the preceding subsection, we have analysed the time interval during which two neighboring clusters remain overlapping since the clusters are formed. Suppose two neighboring clusters are overlapping in cluster formation and the overlapping state changes at time $T_{ov}(< \tau)$, the cluster overlapping state may change again before re-clustering is triggered. The second overlapping period is not equal to T_{ov}, since the initial state is not the same as that when the clusters are initially formed. We refer to this period as inter-cluster overlapping period, denoted by T_{Iov}.

To derive the distribution of T_{Iov}, the same approach used to find the distribution of T_{ov} can be used. Notice that the absorbing lumped Markov chain is the same as that used to calculate the distribution of T_{ov}. The only difference is the distribution of the initial state, I_c. One way to find the distribution of I_c at the time when the second overlapping state occurs is as follows:

- Make the lumped states in the set Ω_{NOV} absorbing, without combining them into one absorbing state. The corresponding transition probability matrix, M'_{N_c}, is equal to M_{N_c} with $M'_{N_c}(\Omega_j, \Omega_i) = 0$ and $M'_{N_c}(\Omega_j, \Omega_j) = 1 \; \forall i, j, \; s.t. \Omega_j \in \Omega_{NOV}$;

- Calculate the absorbing probability ψ_j for each absorbing lumped state $\Omega_j \in \Omega_{NOV}$ by

$$\psi_j = \sum\limits_{\Omega_i \in \Omega_{OV}}^{i} \frac{\mho_i}{\sum\limits_{\Omega_k \in \Omega_{OV}}^{k} \mho_k} \lim_{m \to \infty} M'^{(m)}_{N_c}(\Omega_i, \Omega_j) \quad (3)$$

where $M'^{(m)}_{N_c}(\Omega_i, \Omega_j)$ denotes the $(\Omega_i, \Omega_j)^{\text{th}}$ entry of the mth power of matrix M'_{N_c};

- Form another absorbing Markov chain by making the lumped states in set Ω_{OV} absorbing, without combining them into one absorbing state. The corresponding transition probability matrix, M''_{N_c}, is equal to M_{N_c} with $M''_{N_c}(\Omega_i, \Omega_j) = 0$ and $M''_{N_c}(\Omega_i, \Omega_i) = 1 \ \forall i, j$, $s.t. \Omega_i \in \Omega_{OV}$;

- Calculate the absorbing probability ϕ_i for each absorbing lumped state $\Omega_i \in \Omega_{OV}$ by

$$\phi_i = \sum_{\substack{j \\ \Omega_j \in \Omega_{NOV}}} \psi_j \lim_{m \to \infty} M''^{(m)}_{N_c}(\Omega_j, \Omega_i). \quad (4)$$

The probability that the distance headways between the two neighboring clusters are in state $\Omega_i \in \Omega_{OV}$ at the time when the second overlapping state occurs is equal to ϕ_i. Therefore, the cdf of the inter-cluster overlapping period is given by

$$F_{T_{Iov}}(m) = \sum_{\substack{i \\ \Omega_i \in \Omega_{OV}}} \phi_i F_{T_{ov}(\Omega_i)}(m), m = 1, 2, \dots \quad (5)$$

where $F_{T_{ov}(\Omega_i)}(m)$ is given by (1). However, using this approach, we lose the advantage of having a single absorbing state and, therefore, a bounded state space (according to Corollary 3.3). We propose to approximate the distribution of the system initial state at the time when the second overlapping state occurs, ϕ_i, as follows

$$\phi_i \approx \frac{\mho_i \tilde{M}_{N_c}(\Omega_i, \Omega_{\tilde{N}_{lump}-1})}{\sum_{\substack{i \\ \Omega_i \in \Omega_{OV}}} \mho_i \tilde{M}_{N_c}(\Omega_i, \Omega_{\tilde{N}_{lump}-1})}. \quad (6)$$

The approximated ϕ_i for lumped state $\Omega_i(\in \Omega_{OV})$ is equal to its stationary probability weighted with the absorption probability within one time step. Notice that this weight eliminates all the lumped states $\Omega_i \in \Omega_{OV}$ that are not directly accessible from states in Ω_{NOV}. Figure 2 illustrates an example for a lumped Markov chain, where the directly accessible lumped states are those connected by solid lines, i.e. Ω_{OV1} and Ω_{NOV1}. When the overlapping state of two neighboring clusters changes from non-overlapping to overlapping, the only possible states to be reached first are those in Ω_{OV1}.

4. NUMERICAL RESULTS AND DISCUSSION

This section presents numerical results for the analysis of the cluster overlapping state change time, T_{ov} and the inter-cluster overlapping period, T_{Iov}. We consider a VANET with an intermediate vehicle density of 26 vehicles per kilometer [9] and transmission range of R equal to 160 meters. For N_c's value, we simulate a simple weighted clustering algorithm, where CHs are chosen with the minimum average relative speed to its one-hop neighbors, such that each vehicle belongs to a cluster and no two CHs are one-hop neighbors (i.e., similar to the use of mobility information for clustering in [15, 12]). The distance headways of vehicles on the highway follow a gamma distribution and vehicles' speed is normally distributed with mean 100 kilometer per hour

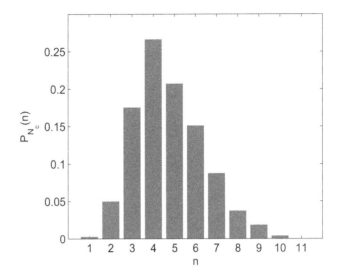

Figure 3: The pmf of the number of nodes between two neighboring CHs, N_c, calculated from simulating a simple weighted clustering of vehicles.

and standard deviation of 10 kilometer per hour [9]. Figure 3 plots the probability distribution of N_c for the resulting clusters from the simulation of the considered clustering algorithm. We set $N_c = 5$, which is the average value from the cluster formation results. Initially, we set I_c to the state with highest probability of occurrence at the cluster formation stage. The Markov-chain distance headway model has the following parameters: $N_{\max} = 9$, each state covers 20 meters range of distance headways, the time step is equal to 2 seconds, and the transition probabilities are tuned according to the intermediate density results in [1]. Based on these parameters, we generate time series of distance headway data according to the microscopic mobility model, using MATLAB. Each simulation consists of 20,000 iterations.

Figure 4 compares the distribution of the state of the system $\mathbb{X}_c$, when the second overlapping state occurs, calculated using the exact derivation (4) and the proposed approximation (6). The values on the x-axis represent arbitrary IDs given to the lumped states $\Omega_i \in \Omega_{OV}$. The results from the proposed approximation shows close agreement with the exact and the simulation results. Figure 5 plots the probability mass function (pmf) of the time interval for the first change in cluster overlapping state, for (a) a given initial state of $\mathbb{X}_c$ and (b) when averaging over random initial states, respectively. The theoretical results for the pmfs of the inter-cluster overlapping period is calculated from the cdf (5). The calculated pmf of T_{Iov} in Figure 5(a) is based on the approximation given in Figure 4. The distribution of $T_{ov}(I_c)$ changes with I_c belonging to different lumped states. The distribution of T_{ov} describes the average first overlapping period for a randomly picked cluster in the network. Note that the average inter-cluster overlapping period is less than the average first-overlapping period. When the second overlapping state occurs between neighbouring clusters, the clusters state is closer to non-overlapping than that when the clusters are initially formed, on aver-

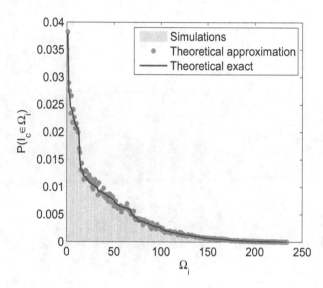

Figure 4: The pmf of the system $\mathbb{X}_c$ being in lumped state $\Omega_i \in \Omega_{OV}$ at the instant when the second overlapping cluster state occurs.

age. That is, the clusters state can only be in the accessible lumped states (Ω_{OV1} in Figure 2).

Figure 6 and Figure 7 plot the pmfs of T_{ov} and T_{Iov} for $N_c = 7$ and $N_c = 2$, respectively. The average time for the first change in the overlapping state and the average inter-cluster overlapping time reduce as the number of nodes between the two CHs increases. This reflects the cumulative behavior of multiple mobility factors. This is only true under the same vehicle traffic flow condition and therefore the same mobility behavior. The impact of vehicle traffic flow condition on the time variation of the cluster overlapping state needs further investigation.

The probability distributions of T_{ov} and T_{Iov}, derived in this paper, provide indicators for the stability of a cluster in terms of its relation with neighbouring clusters. This can be used to enhance network protocol design for VANETs. For example, the derived probability distributions can be used to update the transmission codes assigned to different clusters so that the hidden terminal problem caused by cluster overlapping is avoided with a certain desired probability threshold [19]. Additionally, the distribution of the inter-cluster overlapping period can be utilized to dynamically choose the value of the time threshold used to avoid frequent merging and splitting of neighbouring clusters in VANETs [14, 7, 12].

5. CONCLUSION

This paper presents a stochastic analysis of single-hop cluster stability in a highway VANET with focus on a single lane. The time period for the first change in cluster-overlapping state and the inter-cluster overlapping time period are proposed as measures of external cluster stability. A stochastic mobility model that describes the time variations of individual distance headways is adopted in the analysis. The system of distance headways that govern the change in the overlapping state between neighboring clusters is modeled by a discrete-time lumped Markov chain. The first pas-

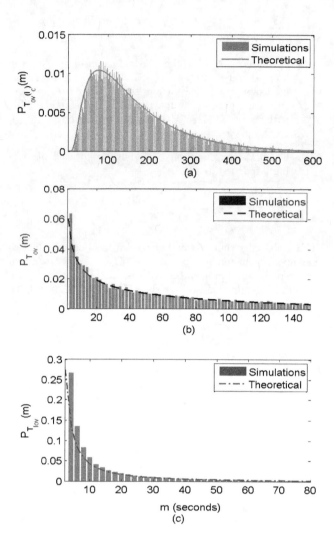

Figure 5: The pmfs of (a) the time to the first change in the overlapping state, $T_{ov}(I_c)$, for $I_c = \{0, 1, 1, 1, 1, 2\}$ when the clusters are initially formed; (b) the time to the first change in cluster overlapping state T_{ov}; and (c) the inter-cluster overlapping time, T_{Iov}.

sage time analysis is employed to derive the distributions of the proposed cluster stability metrics. The analysis are carried out for a given initial system state, random stationary initial state, and random inter-initial state. The analysis provides insights about the time periods during which a cluster is likely to remain unchanged in terms of its overlapping state with neighboring clusters. The probability distributions derived for the proposed cluster stability metrics can be utilized in the design of efficient clustering algorithms for VANETs.

APPENDIX
A.1 Proof of Theorem 3.1

PROOF. Let $M_N = \{M_N(S_i, S_j)\}$, $0 \le S_i, S_j \le N_{\max}^N - 1$ be the transition matrix of the N-dimensional Markov chain that represents the system of N independent copies of the

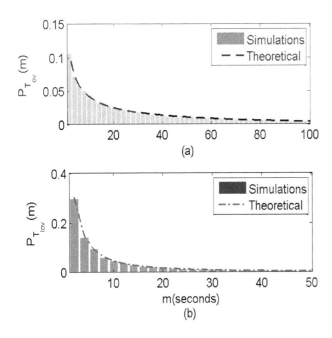

Figure 6: The pmfs of (a) the time to the first change in cluster overlapping state T_{ov}, and (b) the inter-cluster overlapping time, T_{Iov} for $Nc = 7$.

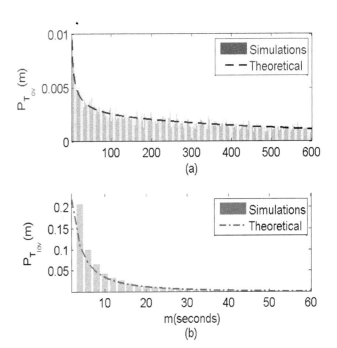

Figure 7: The pmfs of (a) the time to the first change in cluster overlapping state T_{ov}, and (b) the inter-cluster overlapping time, T_{Iov} for $Nc = 2$.

$1-$ dimensional Markov chain, X, with transition matrix $M = \{M(u_i, u_j)\}$, $0 \leq u_i, u_j \leq N_{\max} - 1$. A discrete-time Markov chain with stochastic transition matrix M_N is lumpable with respect to the partition Ω if and only if, for any subsets Ω_i and Ω_j in the partition, and for any super states S_1 and S_2 in subset Ω_i [2],

$$\sum_{S \in \Omega_j} M_N(S_1, S) = \sum_{S \in \Omega_j} M_N(S_2, S). \qquad (7)$$

Consider the left hand side (LHS) of (7). Since X is a birth-death process, the super state $S_1 = (u_0, u_1, \ldots, u_{N-1})$, $0 \leq u_i \leq N_{\max} - 1$, can transit to any super state in set $\mathbf{A} = \{(u'_0, u'_1, \ldots, u'_{N-1})\}$, where state $u'_i \in \{u_i - 1, u_i, u_i + 1\}$, i.e., $|\mathbf{A}| \leq 3^{N_{\max}}$. Let subsets $\mathbf{A_i} = \mathbf{A} \cap \mathbf{\Omega_i}$ and $\mathbf{A_j} = \mathbf{A} \cap \mathbf{\Omega_j}$. Since $M_N(S_1, S) = 0 \ \forall S \notin \mathbf{A}$, the LHS of (7) reduces to $\sum_{S \in \mathbf{A_j}} M_N(S_1, S)$.

Similarly, for the right hand side (RHS) of (7), the super state $S_2 = (v_0, v_1, \ldots, v_{N-1})$, $0 \leq v_i \leq N_{\max} - 1$, can transit to any super state in set $\mathbf{B} = \{(v'_0, v'_1, \ldots, v'_{N-1})\}$, where state $v'_i \in \{v_i - 1, v_i, v_i + 1\}$, i.e., $|\mathbf{B}| \leq 3^{N_{\max}}$. Let subsets $\mathbf{B_i} = \mathbf{B} \cap \mathbf{\Omega_i}$ and $\mathbf{B_j} = \mathbf{B} \cap \mathbf{\Omega_j}$. Since $M_N(S_2, S) = 0 \ \forall S \notin \mathbf{B}$, the RHS of (7) reduces to $\sum_{S \in \mathbf{B_j}} M_N(S_2, S)$.

Consider two sequences, S_i and S_j, that are permutations of each other, and define $\varrho(S_i, O_{ij}) = S_j$ to be the permutation operator on sequence S_i under index order O_{ij} that gives S_j, i.e., $S_j = (S_i(O_{ij}(k)))|_{k=1}^{|S_j|}$. For example, if $S_i = (1, 0, 2)$ and $S_j = (0, 2, 1)$, then $O_{ij} = (2, 3, 1)$.

Let $S'_1 = (u'_0, u'_1, \ldots, u'_{N-1})$ be a super state in subset $\mathbf{A_j}$, therefore, $M_N(S_1, S'_1) = \prod_{n=0}^{N-1} M(u_i, u'_i)$. Since $S_1, S_2 \in \Omega_i$, there exists an index order O_{12}, s.t. $\varrho(S_1, O_{12}) = S_2$. Additionally, $\exists S'_2 = (v'_0, v'_1, \ldots, v'_{N-1})$ s.t. $S'_2 = \varrho(S'_1, O_{12})$.

Note that $S'_2 \in \mathbf{B_2}$. As a result, $M_N(S_2, S'_2) = \prod_{n=0}^{N-1} M(v_i, v'_i) = \prod_{n=0}^{N-1} M(u_{O_{12}(n)}, u'_{O_{12}(n)})$. Since the product operation is commutative, we have $M_N(S_2, S'_2) = M_N(S_1, S'_1)$. In general, $\forall S_1, S_2 \in \Omega_i$ s.t. $\varrho(S_1, O_{12}) = S_2$ and $\forall S'_1 \in \mathbf{A_j}$, $\exists S'_2 \in \mathbf{B_j}$ s.t. $S'_2 = \varrho(S'_1, O_{12})$ and $M_N(S_2, S'_2) = M_N(S_1, S'_1)$. Hence, $\sum_{S \in \mathbf{A_j}} M_N(S_1, S) = \sum_{S \in \mathbf{B_j}} M_N(S_2, S)$, which ends the proof. $\square$

A.2 Proof of Corollary 3.2

PROOF. Consider the tri-diagonal probability transition matrix of the Markov chain, X, as described in Subsection 2.2. The stationary distribution of the chain, X, is given by

$$\pi_i = \prod_{k=0}^{i-1} \left(\frac{p_k}{q_{k+1}} \right) \pi_0, \quad 1 \leq i \leq N_{\max} - 1 \qquad (8)$$

where $\pi_0 = \left[1 + \sum_{i=1}^{N_{\max}-1} \prod_{k=0}^{i-1} \left(\frac{p_k}{q_{k+1}} \right) \right]^{-1}$. Consider the ith lumped state $\Omega_i = \{s_0, s_1, \ldots, s_N\}$. Let N_D be the number of distinct states in $\{s_0, s_1, \ldots, s_{N-1}\}$ in which $(u_1, u_2, \ldots u_{N_D})$ and $(n_{u_1}, n_{u_2}, \ldots, n_{N_D})$ are the sequences of distinct states and their corresponding frequencies, respectively, where $0 \leq u_i \leq N_{\max} - 1$ and $\sum_{i=1}^{N_D} n_{u_i} = N$. Note that the size of the lumped state is equal to the number of super states that are permutations of each other, i.e., $1 \leq |\Omega_i| \leq N!$, $0 \leq i \leq N_{\text{lump}} - 1$. Therefore, the lumped states result from all possible outcomes of choosing N states from $N_{\max}$ different states independently, where choosing state s_i has the probability π_i, $0 \leq s_i \leq N_{\max} - 1$. This is a generalization of the Bernoulli trial problem. Hence, the stationary distribution for the lumped state Ω_i is given by

$$\upsilon_i = \frac{N!}{\prod_{k=1}^{N_D} n_{u_k}!} \prod_{k=1}^{N_D} \pi_{u_k}^{n_{u_k}}. \qquad (9)$$

That is, the stationary distribution of the lumped Markov chain is multi-nomial, which ends the proof. $\square$

A.3 Proof of Corollary 3.3

PROOF. Let the lumped state $\Omega_j = \{s_0, s_1, \ldots, s_{N-1}\}$ be a lumped state such that if the system enters this state, the event of interest occurs. Then, $\{s_0, s_1, \ldots, s_N\}$ is an N-restricted integer partition of an integer that is greater than or equal to N_{th}. In combinatorics, an integer partition of a positive integer n is a set of positive integers whose sum equals n. Each member of the set is called a *part*. An N-restricted integer partition of an integer n is an integer partition of n into exactly N parts. Therefore, $\forall \Omega_j = \{s_0, s_1, \ldots, s_{N-1}\} \in \Omega_{OV}$, $\{s_0, s_1, \ldots, s_{N-1}\}$ is an integer partition of an integer that is less than N_{th}. Since, an integer N_{th} can be partitioned into at most N_{th} parts (i.e. when all the parts equal to one) and the order of the N states in the lumped state is not important, the number of lumped states $\in \Omega_{OV}$ when $N > N_{th}$ is equal to that when $N = N_{th}$. Notice that Corollary.3.3 applies only on the lumped Markov chain and not the original N-dimensional one. This ends the proof. $\square$

6. ACKNOWLEDGMENTS

This work was supported by a research grant from the Natural Sciences and Engineering Research Council (NSERC) of Canada.

7. REFERENCES

[1] K. Abboud and W. Zhuang. Stochastic analysis of single-hop communication link in vehicular ad hoc networks. *IEEE Trans. Intelligent Transportation Systems*, to appear.

[2] P. Buchholz. Exact and ordinary lumpability in finite Markov chains. *J. applied probability*, 31(1):59–75, 1994.

[3] H. T. Cheng, H. Shan, and W. Zhuang. Infotainment and road safety service support in vehicular networking: From a communication perspective. *Mechanical Systems and Signal Processing*, 25(6):2020–2038, 2011.

[4] Y. Gunter, B. Wiegel, and H. Großmann. Cluster-based medium access scheme for VANETs. In *Proc. IEEE ITS*, pages 343–348, 2007.

[5] Y. Harikrishnan and J. He. Clustering algorithm based on minimal path loss ratio for vehicular communication. In *Proc. IEEE ICNC*, pages 745–749, 2013.

[6] B. Hassanabadi, C. Shea, L. Zhang, and S. Valaee. Clustering in vehicular ad hoc networks using affinity propagation. *Ad Hoc Networks*, 13:535–548, 2014.

[7] S. Kuklinski and G. Wolny. Density based clustering algorithm for VANETs. In *Proc. IEEE TridentCom*, pages 1–6, 2009.

[8] J. Luo, X. Gu, T. Zhao, and W. Yan. A mobile infrastructure based VANET routing protocol in the urban environment. In *Proc. IEEE CMC*, pages 432–437, 2010.

[9] A. May. *Traffic Flow Fundamentals*. Prentice Hall, 1990.

[10] G. Palla, I. Derényi, I. Farkas, and T. Vicsek. Uncovering the overlapping community structure of complex networks in nature and society. *Nature*, 435(7043):814–818, 2005.

[11] Z. Y. Rawashdeh and S. M. Mahmud. A novel algorithm to form stable clusters in vehicular ad hoc networks on highways. *EURASIP J. Wireless Communications and Networking*, 2012(1):1–13, 2012.

[12] E. Souza, I. Nikolaidis, and P. Gburzynski. A new aggregate local mobility (ALM) clustering algorithm for VANETs. In *Proc. IEEE ICC*, pages 1–5, 2010.

[13] M. Spiliopoulou, I. Ntoutsi, Y. Theodoridis, and R. Schult. MONIC: modeling and monitoring cluster transitions. In *Proc. ACM KDD*, pages 706–711, 2006.

[14] H. Su and X. Zhang. Clustering-based multichannel mac protocols for QoS provisionings over vehicular ad hoc networks. *IEEE Trans. Vehicular Technology*, 56(6):3309–3323, 2007.

[15] Z. Wang, L. Liu, M. Zhou, and N. Ansari. A position-based clustering technique for ad hoc intervehicle communication. *IEEE Trans. Systems, Man, and Cybernetics, Part C: Applications and Reviews*, 38(2):201–208, 2008.

[16] G. Wolny. Modified DMAC clustering algorithm for VANETs. In *Proc. IEEE ICSNC*, pages 268–273, 2008.

[17] J. Yu and P. H. Chong. 3hbac (3-hop between adjacent clusterheads): a novel non-overlapping clustering algorithm for mobile ad hoc networks. In *Proc. IEEE PACRIM*, pages 318–321, 2003.

[18] J. Y. Yu and P. H. J. Chong. A survey of clustering schemes for mobile ad hoc networks. *IEEE Communications Surveys and Tutorials*, 7(1-4):32–48, 2005.

[19] L. Zhang, B.-H. Soong, and W. Xiao. An integrated cluster-based multi-channel mac protocol for mobile ad hoc networks. *IEEE Trans. Wireless Communications*, 6(11):3964–3974, 2007.

Entropy as a New Metric for Denial of Service Attack Detection in Vehicular Ad-hoc Networks

Mohamed Nidhal MEJRI
L2TI- Université Paris13
Sorbonne Paris cité, France
mejri@univ-paris13.fr

Jalel BEN-OTHMAN
L2TI- Université Paris13
Sorbonne Paris cité, France
jalel.ben-othman@univ-paris13.fr

ABSTRACT

Vehicular Ad hoc Networks (VANETs) aim to enhance driving conditions and provide with drivers and road users a high level of safety. Thus, they are exposed to several kinds of attacks, especially Denial Of Service attacks family (DOS) which affect the availability of services of authentic users. In this paper, we define "Packets entropy" as a new metric to be used for VANETs denial of service attack detection. We propose also a new detection scheme for this effect. Using "Packets entropy", the proposed method is able to detect VANET DOS attacks by the supervision of traffic traces during short monitoring periods. It presents the advantage of rapidity, to be executed by any node of the VANET network and does not require any modification of the 802.11p MAC layer protocol used as a standard for VANETs. Simulations show the high efficiency of the newly defined metric and the related proposed detection method.

Categories and Subject Descriptors

C.2.0 [**COMPUTER-COMMUNICATION NETWORKS**]: General, Security and Protection; C.2.1 [**COMPUTER-COMMUNICATION NETWORKS**]: Network Architecture and Design, Network Communications

Keywords

Vehicular Ad hoc NETworks (VANETs); Denial Of Service (DOS); Attacks; Entropy; Greedy behavior; IEEE 802.11p.

1. INTRODUCTION

In recent years, Vehicular Ad hoc Networks (VANETs) have made impressive progress by providing emerging platforms for researchers and automakers. VANETs are ad-hoc networks which use Vehicle to Vehicle (V2V) communications between vehicles, and Vehicle to Infrastructure (V2I)

communications between vehicles and road infrastructure [10, 15]. Vehicles can be grouped on self-organized sets called WIBSS (Wave Independent Basic Service Set) [13], without a real need to fixed infrastructure. In addition to the safety applications, VANETs provide useful assistance and coordination to drivers in order to enhance driving conditions and avoid critical situations. They provide also some comfort applications for passengers such as internet connection and online gaming. Given their critical importance, VANETs are exposed to severe attacks, basically due to the vulnerability of the wireless medium and also to the weakness of the IEEE 802.11p MAC layer protocol [1], which can be used to attack the entire network and expose users' lives to danger.

Among VANET attacks, we distinguish especially the Denial of Service (DOS) which is a dangerous family of attacks that target services availability and can have bad consequences on the whole network functioning. The attacker, who can be an internal or an external node to the network [20], aims to lock available services to legitimate users. Thus, he increases his chances of access to these services. A successful DOS attack can be achieved e.g by a greedy behavior, jamming attack, black-hole attack etc. Since these attacks mislead the critical network services, a high-level security requirement is mandatory for the right deployment of such technology.

In addition to the wireless medium vulnerability which facilitates attacks, VANETs are also characterized by frequent disconnections, a rapid change of topology and a high mobility of nodes. These characteristics make the detection of DOS attacks more difficult. To avoid such attacks it is essential to ensure regular protocols enhancement to reduce prospective exploitation of any existing vulnerabilities. It is also important to design attacks detection tools to prevent and escape the serious consequences that may arise.

Denial Of Service attacks have been widely studied by researchers in the field of MANETs (Mobile Ad hoc NETworks) but not in the case of VANETs which still remains a vast subject not fully explored. In this paper we focus essentially on the greedy behavior as an example of DOS attack. Thus, we define a new metric called "Packets entropy", to be used for the distinction between network normal behavior and network behavior when it is under DOS attack. Based on the new defined metric, we proposed also a new detection method which is able to supervise traffic traces during short monitoring periods and warns in the case of attack detection.

MSWiM'14, September 21–26, 2014, Montreal, QC, Canada.
Copyright 2014 ACM 978-1-4503-3030-5/14/09$15.00.
http://dx.doi.org/10.1145/2641798.2641800.

The rest of the paper is organized as follows : Section II runs through some backgrounds, essential to introduce the proposed idea. Section III overviews the related work in the domain of DOS attacks detection in MANETs and VANETs. We describe in section IV our new defined metric and our proposed detection method which is based on. Some experimental results are given in section V and finally section VI concludes the paper and gives direction for future work.

2. BACKGROUND

Our proposed method is based on a new defined metric using entropy concept. This metric is used to distinguish between the behavior of a network in normal operation and the behavior of a network under DOS attack. In this paper we focus primarily on greedy behavior as an example of DOS attacks. To facilitate the understanding of the rest of the paper, we provide in the following a brief introduction of the Greedy behavior and the techniques that can be used to perform this attack in the case of VANET. We provide also the mathematical basis of the entropy notion which is an information measurement parameter that we tamed for detecting attacks.

2.1 VANET DOS attack: The greedy behavior

Greedy behavior is a well known DOS attack, it specially targets the MAC layer operation and tries to exploit the medium access method weakness. Generally, a greedy node aims to decrease its waiting time, therefore it can access more quickly the medium and penalizes the other existing honest nodes. A greedy node violates restrictions of the MAC layer access method, It always tries to connect to the support and maintains it for its proper use. Like most DOS attacks, greedy behavior has the disadvantage of being executed by any legitimate VANET node which complicates more the detection phase.

IEEE propose WAVE(Wireless Access in Vehicular Environments) as an architecture for VANETs. In this architecture IEEE defines a complementary set of protocols that allow WAVE vehicles to work together. The ITS standards fact sheet of IEEE gives the latest WAVE protocols list [12]. The IEEE Std 802.11p - 2010 [1] is used for the PHY and MAC layers. Std IEEE 802.11p is an enhancement of the well known IEEE 802.11 protocol to be more suitable for VANETs. It uses the CSMA/CA (Carrier Sense Multiple Access with Collision Avoidance) access method which present some weakness that can be used to perform a greedy behavior attack. Several techniques are possible to achieve a greedy behavior attack in a VANET environment, among them we quote: backoff parameters manipulation, scrambling RTS/CTS frames, manipulation and/or over-sizing NAV and DATA frames [18]. For more details on CSMA/CA access method refer to [2], [1], and [16].

Unlike MANETs (Mobile Ad hoc NETworks) and due to VANETs nodes high mobility and short connection duration, the manipulation of backoff parameters is the most used technique to achieve greedy attack [11]. The attacker can greatly reduce his waiting time and access to the support more rapidly than other nodes. In our simulation we have performed greedy attack using this method.

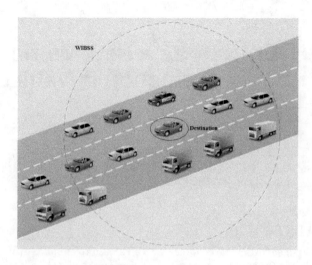

Figure 1: VANET decomposition according to information theory requirement.

2.2 The entropy

The entropy (also known as the Shannon entropy in the field of information theory) is a mathematical function that intuitively corresponds to the amount of information measured at a destination, and is present or is issued by an information source. The source of information can be a transmitter (such as a radio or network card), a text written in a given language, an electrical signal or any computer file (collection of bytes).

Thus, the entropy measures the uncertainty on the information sent by the source. The more data sent by the source are variable, the more entropy is high. That is to say, if a source is deemed to always send the same information, for example the word 'OK', then its entropy is zero. A source whose next transmitted information is unpredictable admits a maximum entropy. In the absence of specific constraints, the entropy is maximum for a source whose symbols are equiprobable. In particular, the more redundant the source is, the less it contains information.

Entropy is the primary metric in information theory, which is a theory to qualify and quantify the concept of content information on a data set. Mathematically and as defined in [19], the entropy of a source which emits n symbols, the source can be considered as a discrete random variable X having n symbols, each symbol x_i has a probability P_i to appear. Thus, the entropy H of the source X is defined as:

$$H(X) = E[\log_b P(X = x_i)] = \sum_{i=1}^{n} P_i \log_b \frac{1}{P_i} \quad (1)$$

where E denotes the mathematical expectation and log_b the logarithm to the base b. In general a base 2 logarithm is used and the entropy uses $bit/symbol$ as a unit. The symbols represent the possible realizations of the random variable X. In this case, the entropy $H(X)$ can be interpreted as the amount of information in bits that the source must provide to the receiver to determine the values of X unambiguously. Then, in base 2 equation (1) can be written as:

$$H(X) = -\sum_{i=1}^{n} P_i \log_2 P_i \quad (2)$$

In this paper, the system we design to be used for simulation is composed of several nodes (vehicles) which Form a WIBSS (Wave Independent Basic Service Set). In this architecture, any node can act as a receiver to which the other nodes send data. In this system, the symbols will be transmitted packets, each packet has a probability of occurrence. According to this decomposition shown in Fig.1, the receiving node (destination) can therefore measure the entropy of the system according to the formula given by the equation (2).

3. RELATED WORK

The Attack Detection in VANET networks, which is the object of this paper, is characterized by the fact that it is related to several research axes at the same time. Among these axis, we quote the vulnerabilities of the communication protocols, which facilitate the implementation of the attacks. We quote especially the vulnerabilities of MAC and physical layers protocols. The problem affects also attacks detection techniques in ad hoc networks, which are becoming more and more difficult in practice due to the high mobility and quick change of VANET topology and also the choice of appropriate metrics for the detection. To the best of our knowledge our proposed solution is the first to use the concept of entropy as a metrics to detect DOS attacks in VANETs, but it is important to look at other related works in the same research axis as our study.

In [18] Raya et al. proposed DOMINO which is a software component implementation of a greedy behavior detection scheme in infrastructured networks. DOMINO is designed for the IEEE 802.11 MAC layer protocol. It must be integrated with the AP (Access Point) software. DOMINO presented the advantage to detect and identify malicious nodes without any modification required for the MAC layer of the Access Point. Domino is also transparent to network users, but the presented solution cannot be suitable for mobile nodes not related to the infrastructure : Vehicle To Vehicle communications.

In [11] Hamieh et al. proposed the use of an additional software component to detect the denial of service greedy behavior attack in MANETs (Mobile Ad hoc Networks) using the mathematical concept of linear regression. The proposed solution did not require any modification of the MAC layer protocol and can be monitored by any network node. This kind of solution is classified as such DOMINO among the Monitoring-based solutions.

In [6] Buchegger and Le Boudec proposed a protocol called CONFIDANT for mobile ad hoc networks, based on selective altruism and utilitarianism. It aims to detect and isolate misbehaving nodes which refuse to cooperate with the other honest nodes of the network. CONFIDENT built routing decisions and trust relationships based on observation, experience, and reports on behavior of the other cooperate nodes. The proposed system can detect several types of attacks and thus honest nodes have the possibility to isolate misbehaved ones from the network. Decisions are based on a reputation system, nodes have reputation records for first-hand and trusted second-hand observations [7].

In [14, 8] Kyasanur respectively Cardenas and their co-authors present two newly MAC design based solutions both based on a modification of the backoff algorithm of the MAC layer. In general, for this category of solution, a new MAC layer is proposed to avoid backoff algorithm weakness against Denial of service attacks.

In [9] Cerasoli generalizes the use of Shannon's entropy for MANETs by the definition of two new metrics "Relative motion entropy" and "Energy entropy" respectively used for the characterizing of MANET node motion predictability and the efficient use of the energy by cluster-heads communicating to cluster members. The paper shows that "Energy entropy" is a very useful metric to use in spite of "Relative motion entropy" which lacks the features to be helpful for node motion prediction.

To the best of our knowledge there is no existing work for the detection of DOS attacks for Vehicular Ad hoc Networks and based on the Entropy as a metric of detection. Existing solutions are interested mainly in MANET and Wireless Mesh Networks (WMNs). In this paper we generalize the notion of "Shannon's entropy" by the definition of the "Packets entropy" as a new metric to be used to make decision and define efficiently the membership of vehicle to one of honest or attacker classes. The proposed solution has been tested in the case of greedy behavior and it was able to detect the violation of the proper use of the CSMA/CA protocol rules. The mathematical details of the design and the operating principle of the proposed detection method are given in the following section.

4. METHOD DESCRIPTION

4.1 New metric description

In the case of mobile wireless network working with a variant of the IEEE 802.11 protocol such as VANET network, we can divide the circulating packets between nodes into four main categories which are: DATA, ACK, RTS and CTS packets family. These packets may be transmitted by any network node. To model this choice, we define the random variable X where sent packets represent the possible realizations of this variable. Thus, mathematically we can write:

$$\sum_{i=1}^{n} P(X = x_i) = 1 \qquad (3)$$

In terms of packet categories, the equation (3) can be written as:

$$P(Data) + P(Ack) + P(RTS) + P(CTS) = 1 \qquad (4)$$

Where $P(Data)$, $P(Ack)$, $P(RTS)$ and $P(CTS)$ are the respective probabilities that the transmitted packet is of type Data, Ack, RTS and CTS respectively. It is assumed that any packet is in one of the mentioned types. For N nodes in the network, any kind of packet can be transmitted by any node. Thus, for Data packets type for example, we find packets that issue from node $n_1, n_2,... ,n_i$. It is the same for the other types of packets. For ease of notation, a packet is characterized by its issuer node n_i and its type {Data,

Ack, RTS, CTS}. Thus, we note e.g $Packet(n_i, Data)$, the packet issued from the node n_i and of type Data.

In a VANET the possible transmitted packets are in the following sets: $\{Packet(n_i, Data)\} \cup \{Packet(n_i, Ack)\} \cup \{Packet(n_i, RTS)\} \cup \{Packet(n_i, CTS)\}$, where $i \in N$.

In the following, we note:

- $P(n_i \setminus Data)$: the probability that the received packet is issued from the node i, knowing that is a Data packet.

- $P(n_i \setminus Ack)$: the probability that the received packet is issued from the node i, knowing that is an Ack packet.

- $P(n_i \setminus RTS)$: the probability that the received packet is issued from the node i, knowing that is an RTS packet.

- $P(n_i \setminus CTS)$: the probability that the received packet is issued from the node i, knowing that is a CTS packet.

Whatever the behavior of nodes in the network, we have always:

$$\sum_{i=1}^{N} P(n_i \setminus TYPE) = 1 \qquad (5)$$

However, for normal operation of a VANET, the event: "the transmitted packet comes from node i" has the same probability for all the nodes, they are called equipossible or to be "equally likely", then we can write:

$$P(n_i \setminus TYPE) = \frac{1}{N} \qquad (6)$$

where $TYPE \in \{Data, Ack, RTS, CTS\}$

4.2 Related detection method description

The detection idea that we propose in this study is based on the supervision of the entropy of a chosen type of transmitted packets in the network. To calculate this entropy we supervise and determine the packets emission probabilities for the chosen type of packets (e.g Data and Ack). Given that the probability of emission of packets changes, then the entropy change, and the distinction between a normal network and a network under attack can be performed by the calculation of the packets entropy in each case. In fact, a greedy node for example emits more data packets, since it occupies the support for much more time than other vehicles. Thus, the events: "the transmitted packet comes from node i" are never more equipossible.

Then for a greedy node n_G, using Data packets e.g and contrary to the equation (6), it is logical to have:

$$P(n_G \setminus Data) \gg \tfrac{1}{N}.$$

Based on what we have already explained, we defined our newly "Packets entropy" metric for the four types of packets exchanged in a VANET network based on IEEE 802.11p protocol. Thus, we define the four following packets entropy denoted H_{Data}, H_{Ack}, H_{RTS} and H_{CTS} respectively for Data, Ack, RTS and CTS entropy. Then we can write:

- $H_{Data}(X) = -\sum_{i=1}^{N} P(n_i \setminus Data) \log_2 P(n_i \setminus Data)$

- $H_{Ack}(X) = -\sum_{i=1}^{N} P(n_i \setminus Ack) \log_2 P(n_i \setminus Ack)$

- $H_{RTS}(X) = -\sum_{i=1}^{N} P(n_i \setminus RTS) \log_2 P(n_i \setminus RTS)$

- $H_{CTS}(X) = -\sum_{i=1}^{N} P(n_i \setminus CTS) \log_2 P(n_i \setminus CTS)$

To calculate $P(n_i \setminus TYPE)$, we know that mathematically and for two events A and B we have:

$$P(A \setminus B) = \frac{P(A \cap B)}{P(B)} \qquad (7)$$

where $TYPE \in \{Data, Ack, RTS, CTS\}$

Then $P(n_i \setminus TYPE)$ become:

$$P(n_i \setminus TYPE) = \frac{P(n_i \cap TYPE)}{P(TYPE)} \qquad (8)$$

Using the formula given by the equation (8), we are able to calculate the packets entropy metric for each chosen type among $\{Data, Ack, RTS, CTS\}$ set of packets types. Given that Data and Ack packets are the most exchanged in a VANET network and given that the RTS/CTS mechanism is enabled in the IEEE 802.11p protocol only for large packets, we performed our simulations with Data and Ack type packets. By the following described simulations we test in a realistic scenarios the effectiveness of our theoretical designed detection method.

5. PERFORMANCE EVALUATION

To evaluate the performance of our proposed DOS attack detection method, we used the ns-3 simulator [17], to simulate traffic and communications between vehicles (nodes) in a VANET based on IEEE 802.11p protocol. We have simulated two different scenarios using respectively 40, 70 and 100 vehicles. The two scenarios consist on testing respectively the behavior of a normal VANET network and a VANET under DOS attack (greedy behavior). To achieve the greedy attack we manipulate back-off parameters to minimize the waiting time of the greedy nodes. We suppose also that honest nodes are majority which is a realistic assumption. In each scenario we calculate the related Data and Ack packets entropy. For greater efficiency, and to approach realistic results, each use case was repeated 50 times with random initial conditions. According to the requirements of standards [4] and [5], The generated traffic was of type: WSMP (Wave Short Message Protocol). To simulate nodes mobility, we use a real city map with signs and traffic lights designed for this purpose under the mobility simulator SUMO [3]. Using SUMO, we generate a mobility traces file for each simulated scenario which can be used directly under ns-3. Each mobility file contains the coordinates and the speeds of all the nodes at each instant. This technique allows a real simulation environment and it is used instead of the predefined ns-3 mobility models especially designed for MANETs. We provided in Table 1 our used simulation parameters.

In our simulations, we chose a node to act as a listener (destination) for all the other transmitting nodes. All the

Table 1: Simulation parameters

Simulation parameters	
Transmission rate	OfdmRate6MbpsBW10MHz
Protocol	802.11p
Simulation time (s)	30
Packets size (bytes)	variable: 1000-1400
Access class	AC_VO
Speed (Km/h)	Variable: 30-60
Network size	500m x 500m
Node count	40 / 70 / 100
Routing protocol	OLSR
Mobility simulator	SUMO

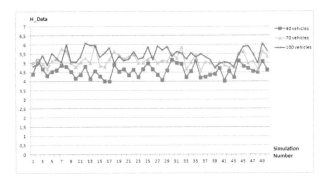

Figure 2: Data packet entropy of a VANET normal behavior.

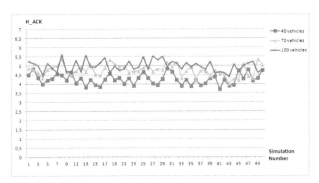

Figure 3: ACK packet entropy of a VANET normal behavior.

nodes are in the same WIBSS. Thus, the chosen node listen to the support and collect traffic traces for short periods. Using these short traffic traces, the destination node can calculate rapidly and easily the packets entropy H_{Data} or H_{Ack}.

5.1 Simulation of a normal network behavior

In a normal behavior of the network, and during the monitoring period, we can practically suppose that all the nodes have the same probabilities to send a Data packet. For example, in the case of $N = 40, 70$ and 100 vehicles, the theoretical H_{Data} can be respectively calculated as follows:

- $H_{Data} = -\sum_{i=1}^{40} \frac{1}{40} \log_2(\frac{1}{40}) = \log_2(400) \approx 5.32$

- $H_{Data} = -\sum_{i=1}^{70} \frac{1}{70} \log_2(\frac{1}{70}) = \log_2(70) \approx 6.13$

- $H_{Data} = -\sum_{i=1}^{100} \frac{1}{100} \log_2(\frac{1}{100}) = \log_2(100) \approx 6.64$

As shown in Figures 2 and 3, the measured H_{Data} and H_{Ack} are slightly lower than the theoretical results which is correct because the theoretical entropy measured in the case of equiprobable transmission between nodes, is the highest entropy that can be detected according to the information theory. We observe also that measured values for H_{Ack} are slightly smaller than H_{Ack} values because that no all the nodes can sent an acknowledgment packet due to the frequent disconnection and to the high mobility in the VANET.

5.2 Simulation of network under DOS attack: a greedy behavior

When the network is under DOS attack (e.g Greedy attack), we confirmed by simulations that one or two greedy nodes can consume alone about two third ($\frac{2}{3}$) of all transmitted data. The consumption of three or four greedy nodes can reach also three quarters ($\frac{3}{4}$) of all transmitted data. We suppose that the other nodes (honest nodes) have the same probabilities to send a Data packet. In the following part we present results for one and three greedy nodes because no significant variations have been seen between one and two or between three and four greedy nodes.The theoretical H_{Data} can be calculated respectively for $N = 40, 70$ and 100 vehicles as follows:

For one greedy node we have:

- $H_{Data} = -\frac{2}{3} \log_2(\frac{2}{3}) - \sum_{i=1}^{39} \frac{1}{3*39} \log_2(\frac{1}{3*39}) \approx 2.68$

- $H_{Data} = -\frac{2}{3} \log_2(\frac{2}{3}) - \sum_{i=1}^{69} \frac{1}{3*69} \log_2(\frac{1}{3*69}) \approx 2.95$

- $H_{Data} = -\frac{2}{3} \log_2(\frac{2}{3}) - \sum_{i=1}^{99} \frac{1}{3*99} \log_2(\frac{1}{3*99}) \approx 3.12$

For three greedy nodes we have:

- $H_{Data} = -\frac{3}{4} \log_2(\frac{1}{4}) - \sum_{i=1}^{37} \frac{1}{4*37} \log_2(\frac{1}{4*37}) \approx 3.30$

- $H_{Data} = -\frac{3}{4} \log_2(\frac{1}{4}) - \sum_{i=1}^{67} \frac{1}{4*67} \log_2(\frac{1}{4*67}) \approx 3.51$

- $H_{Data} = -\frac{3}{4} \log_2(\frac{1}{4}) - \sum_{i=1}^{97} \frac{1}{4*97} \log_2(\frac{1}{4*97}) \approx 3.63$

As it was observed in the case of a normal VANET, the measured H_{Data} and H_{Ack} for one and three greedy nodes shown in Figures 4, 5, 6 and 7 are slightly lower than the theoretical results for the same reasons previously detailed in the case of a normal network.

We discussed in the next section the obtained results for a normal behavior of a VANET and for a VANET under DOS greedy attack.

5.3 Discusion

By the simulations we carried out, the obtained results were significant. For each scenario, the practical results were close to the theoretical ones. The two observed metrics H_{Data} and H_{Ack} behaved in the same way. It has also been proved by the obtained results that the entropy is maximum for a source whose symbols are equipossible that mean: the more data sent by the source is variable, the more entropy is high. In fact, this is the case of a normal VANET where all the nodes have the same probability to transmit, contrary

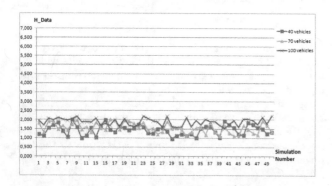

Figure 4: Data packet entropy of a VANET with one greedy node.

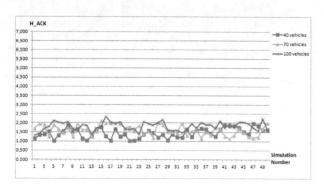

Figure 5: ACK packet entropy of a VANET with one greedy node.

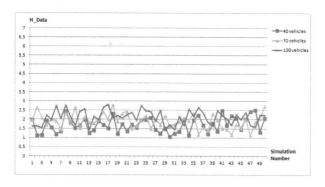

Figure 6: Data packet entropy of a VANET with three greedy nodes.

to a VANET under attack where some nodes (attackers) are completely different. Thus, it is normal to have a high packets entropy for a normal VANET behavior contrary to a VANET under attack. This difference allows our scheme to distinguish easily between a normal VANET and a VANET under attack by a simple fixed threshold. In our case for example, a H_{Data} lower than 3 indicate a very suspicious network behavior.

6. CONCLUSION

Nowadays, VANETs are growing rapidly and need to be highly secured especially among DOS attacks. In this paper, we defined "Packets entropy" as a new metric to be used for

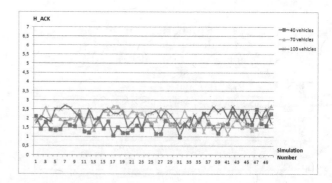

Figure 7: ACK packet entropy of a VANET with three greedy nodes.

VANET denial of service attacks detection. Based on this metric, we proposed also a new attack detection scheme. Using "Packets entropy", the proposed method is able to detect VANET greedy attacks using collected traffic traces during short monitoring periods. It presents the advantage of rapidity, to be executed by any node of the VANET network and does not require any modification of the 802.11p MAC layer protocol used as a standard for VANETs. Simulations show the high efficiency of the newly defined metric and the related proposed detection method. As a future work, we expect verify the efficiency of our defined metric for other DOS attack such as jamming.We expect also the design of a new reaction method against these attacks.

7. REFERENCES

[1] 802.11p-2010 - IEEE standard for information technology - local and metropolitan area networks - specific requirements - part 11: Wireless lan medium access control (MAC) and physical layer (PHY) specifications amendment 6: Wireless access in vehicular environments. 11 June 2010.

[2] 802.11-2007 - IEEE standard for information technology - telecommunications and information exchange between systems - local and metropolitan area networks - specific requirements - part 11: Wireless lan medium access control (MAC) and physical layer (PHY) specifications. IEEE STANDARD, 12 June 2007.

[3] Simulation of urban mobility, http:// sumo.sourceforge.net/. 2014.

[4] 1609.3-2010 - IEEE standard for wireless access in vehicular environments (wave)âĂŤnetworking services (revision of IEEE std 1609.3-2007). 30 December 2010.

[5] 1609.4-2010 - IEEE standard for wireless access in vehicular environments (wave)–multi-channel operation (revision of IEEE std 1609.4-2006). 7 February 2011.

[6] S. Buchegger and J.-Y. Le Boudec. Performance analysis of the confidant protocol. In *Proceedings of the 3rd ACM international symposium on Mobile ad hoc networking & computing*, pages 226–236. ACM, 2002.

[7] S. Buchegger, C. Tissieres, and J.-Y. Le Boudec. A test-bed for misbehavior detection in mobile ad-hoc networks-how much can watchdogs really do? In *Mobile Computing Systems and Applications, 2004.*

WMCSA 2004. Sixth IEEE Workshop on, pages 102–111. IEEE, 2004.

[8] A. A. Cardenas, S. Radosavac, and J. S. Baras. Detection and prevention of MAC layer misbehavior in ad hoc networks. In *Proceedings of the 2nd ACM workshop on Security of ad hoc and sensor networks*, pages 17–22. ACM, 2004.

[9] C. Cerasoli and J. Dimarogonas. The generalization of information entropy to manet metrics. In *Military Communications Conference, 2008. MILCOM 2008. IEEE*, pages 1–9. IEEE, 2008.

[10] A. Dhamgaye and N. Chavhan. Survey on security challenges in VANET. *International Journal of Computer Science*, 2, 2013.

[11] A. Hamieh, J. Ben-Othman, A. Gueroui, and F. Naït-Abdesselam. Detecting greedy behaviors by linear regression in wireless ad hoc networks. In *Communications, 2009. ICC'09. IEEE International Conference on*, pages 1–6. IEEE, 2009.

[12] ITS. Its standars fact sheets of IEEE, http://www.standards.its.dot.gov/factsheets/factsheet/80 seen february 25 2014. 2014.

[13] S. S. Kaushik. Review of different approaches for privacy scheme in VANETs. *International Journal*, 5, 2013.

[14] P. Kyasanur and N. H. Vaidya. Detection and handling of MAC layer misbehavior in wireless networks. In *DSN*, pages 173–182. Citeseer, 2003.

[15] M. N. Mejri, J. Ben-Othman, and M. Hamdi. Survey on VANET security challenges and possible cryptographic solutions. *Vehicular Communications*, 2014.

[16] L. Miao, K. Djouani, B. J. van Wyk, and Y. Hamam. Evaluation and enhancement of IEEE 802.11 p standard: A survey. *Mobile Computing*, 2012.

[17] NS-3. ns-3, http:// www.nsnam.org/. 2014.

[18] M. Raya, J.-P. Hubaux, and I. Aad. Domino: a system to detect greedy behavior in IEEE 802.11 hotspots. In *Proceedings of the 2nd international conference on Mobile systems, applications, and services*, pages 84–97. ACM, 2004.

[19] C. E. Shannon and W. Weaver. The mathematical theory of communication (urbana, il. *University of Illinois Press*, 19(7):1, 1949.

[20] S. Zeadally, R. Hunt, Y.-S. Chen, A. Irwin, and A. Hassan. Vehicular ad hoc networks (VANETs): status, results, and challenges. *Telecommunication Systems*, 50(4):217–241, 2012.

Socially Inspired Data Dissemination for Vehicular Ad Hoc Networks*

Felipe D. Cunha
DCC - UFMG
fdcunha@dcc.ufmg.br

Guilherme Maia
DCC - UFMG
jgmm@dcc.ufmg.br

Aline C. Viana
INRIA - Saclay
aline.viana@inria.fr

Raquel A. F. Mini
DCC - PUC Minas
raquelmini@pucminas.br

Leandro A. Villas
IC - Unicamp
leandro@ic.unicamp.br

Antonio A. F. Loureiro
DCC - UFMG
loureiro@dcc.ufmg.br

ABSTRACT

People have routines and their mobility patterns vary during the day, which have a direct impact on vehicular mobility. Therefore, protocols and applications designed for Vehicular Ad Hoc Networks need to adapt to these routines in order to provide better services. With this issue in mind, in this work, we propose a data dissemination solution for these networks that considers the daily road traffic variation of large cities and the relationship among vehicles. The focus of our approach is to select the best vehicles to rebroadcast data messages according to social metrics, in particular, the clustering coefficient and the node degree. Moreover, our solution is designed in such a way that it is completely independent of the perceived road traffic density. Simulation results show that, when compared to related protocols, our proposal provides better delivery guarantees, reduces the network overhead and possesses an acceptable delay.

Categories and Subject Descriptors

C.2.0 [**Computer-Communications Networks**]: General—*Data communications*; C.2.1 [**Computer-Communications Networks**]: Network Architecture and Design—*Wireless communication*

Keywords

VANETs; Broadcast Suppression; Intermittently Connected; Social Metrics

1. INTRODUCTION

Vehicular Ad Hoc Networks (VANETs) are a special type of Mobile Ad Hoc Networks in which vehicles have processing and wireless communication capabilities. Usually, these vehicles exchange information among themselves through multi-hop communication. In these networks, sending messages from a source to all vehicles located inside a geographic region will be very common. Such activity is known as data dissemination. Data dissemination solutions

---

*This work has been partially supported by INRIA, Fapemig and CNPq.

must consider two important challenges. The first one, known as the *broadcast storm problem*, happens when a group of vehicles close to one another starts to transmit data messages at the same time, leading to a high number of message collisions and severe contention at the link layer [7,9]. The second one, known as the *intermittently connected network problem*, happens in scenarios with low traffic densities, such as, daybreak, holidays and rural areas, in which the number of vehicles is not enough to disseminate data messages using direct multi-hop communication [6, 11].

A factor that contributes to the emergence of these problems is the driver's routine. Usually, people posses similar behavior, which increases the likelihood of going to the same places at the same time. Moreover, while moving around, drivers are susceptible to speed limits, traffic lights, obstacles, etc. Therefore, it is reasonable to assume that these factors combined lead to microscopic and macroscopic traffic density variations. We argue that, a better understanding of these routines and their impact on the overall traffic condition is fundamental in designing better communication protocols for VANETs.

There is a vast literature that investigates the social aspects inherent to VANETs [2–4]. In summary, they show that there are social properties encoded in these networks. With this in mind, in this work, we leverage these social aspects to design a *Socially Inspired Broadcast Data Dissemination* for VANETs. In our approach, we use two social metrics, *clustering coefficient* and *node degree*, to determine when vehicles should rebroadcast data messages in order to increase the delivery guarantee and reduce the overall network overhead, independently of the perceived road traffic condition. Simulation results show that, when compared to two related protocols – UV-CAST [11] and ABSM [6] – under a Manhattan grid scenario, our solution possesses a higher delivery ratio, decreases the total number of data messages transmitted and the number of collisions, and it also has an acceptable delay.

The remaining of this paper is organized as follows. Section 2 summarizes the recent related work. Section 3 presents our socially inspired proposal. Section 4 describes the simulation scenarios and discusses the results. Finally, Section 5 presents our final remarks and some future work.

2. RELATED WORK

Due to the peculiarities of VANETs, such as: vehicles move at very high speeds, frequent topology changes and short encounter times, the traditional solutions do not present good performance. Thus, many solutions especially designed for this network have been proposed [6,7,9,11]. For instance, Ros et al. [6] propose the ABSM, a data dissemination protocol for VANETs with varying road traffic conditions. The key idea of ABSM is to use the Minimum Connected Dominating Set (MCDS) concept. In summary, if only the vehicles in the MCDS rebroadcast a data message, then 100% coverage is guaranteed with a low overhead. However, determining the MCDS is a NP-hard problem. Therefore, the authors outline a distributed heuristic to determine whether a vehicle belongs to the MCDS or not. Vehicles in the MCDS are assigned a lower waiting delay to rebroadcast. To guarantee message delivery under intermittently connected VANETs, ABSM relies on periodic beacons as implicit acknowledgements. For that, vehicles insert the IDs of received data messages into beacons. When a vehicle receives a beacon from a neighbor and it does not acknowledge the receipt of a message, then the vehicle forwards the message to the neighbor.

Viriyasitavat et al. [11] propose UV-CAST for performing data dissemination under both dense and sparse VANETs. In UV-CAST, a vehicle can be in one of two states, broadcast suppression or store-carry-forward. When a vehicle receives a data message for the first time, it initially checks whether it is a border vehicle or not. Border vehicles are the ones that are at the edge of a connected component. UV-CAST assumes these vehicles have a higher probability of meeting new neighbors. If the vehicle verifies it is a border vehicle, then it stores the message and carries it around until an encounter with a new neighbor is made. Conversely, if the vehicle is not a border vehicle, it executes a broadcast suppression algorithm to rebroadcast the message.

3. PROPOSED SOLUTION

In this work, we choose to apply the clustering coefficient and node degree to design an efficient data dissemination solution for VANETs. We focus on these two metrics because they provide the possibility to be aware of vehicles density in a region and consequently, to adjust the dissemination in an efficient way. With the information extracted from those algorithms, our solution find network nodes that behaves as hub nodes (or start nodes): Nodes that have a lot of neighbors (i.e., have high degree) that do not see each other (i.e., have low cluster coefficient). These are very good candidates to guarantee the best performance in higher density regions and reach sparse regions with a low cost. This is possible because the metrics computation just use the beacons packets exchanged among the vehicles, in other words, packets that are already exchanged for others purposes in the network.

Data dissemination corresponds to the process in which a single source vehicle or roadside unit broadcasts data messages to all vehicles located inside a region of interest (ROI) through multi-hop communications, as illustrated in Figure 1. The ROI is defined by the application for which the messages must be disseminated. Moreover, in this work, we assume the ROI is defined as a circular region centered at the source. The main goal of our proposal is to guarantee message delivery to all vehicles inside the ROI independently of the road traffic condition. Therefore, the protocol must be able to operate under both dense (Figure 1(a)) and sparse (Figure 1(b)) VANETs, and for that, both the broadcast storm and intermittently connected network problems must be tackled.

We assume that vehicles store and carry each received data message for the whole period in which they are inside the ROI and the time-to-live for the message has not expired. Moreover, they are equipped with a Global Positioning System (GPS) or they can infer their positions through other means. Each vehicle periodically exchanges beacons with its neighbors. These beacons contain context information about the vehicle, for instance, the position and the number of neighbors (node degree). Furthermore, each beacon contains the IDs of the data messages which have being received and are being carried by the vehicle. Notice that, embedding the IDs of received data messages into beacons works as an implicit acknowledgement mechanism. Therefore, when a vehicle receives a

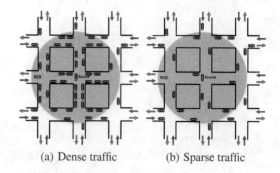

| (a) Dense traffic | (b) Sparse traffic |

Figure 1: Data dissemination to a group of vehicles under both dense and sparse traffic scenarios

beacon from a neighbor, it is able to verify whether it possesses any data message that has not been received by this neighbor and then, forward it accordingly.

Algorithms 1 and 2 show the main steps of our proposed data dissemination solution for both dense and sparse road traffic scenarios. Essentially, what these algorithms do is to determine which vehicles should rebroadcast a received data message and when they should perform it. By carefully coordinating these tasks, our proposal is able to avoid redundant retransmissions and increase the delivery probability to intended recipients. In the following two sections, we thoroughly describe each algorithm. Thereafter, we show how the clustering coefficient and node degree is used to calculate the waiting delay for a vehicle to rebroadcast.

3.1 Broadcast Suppression

Under dense road traffic conditions, when a vehicle receives a data message, it must carefully decide whether to rebroadcast it or not, and when to rebroadcast it in order to avoid redundant retransmissions and consequently, the broadcast storm problem. Algorithm 1 shows how a vehicle proceeds when it receives a data message m.

Algorithm 1: The broadcast suppression algorithm

---
1 **Event** *data message m received from neighbor s*
2 **if** *vehicle is outside the region of interest specified in m or the time-to-live of m expired* **then**
3   discard m;
4 **if** *m is not a duplicate* **then**
5   add message to the list of received messages;
6   insert m ID in subsequent beacons;
7      $t \leftarrow$ calculateWaitingDelay();
8   schedule *rebroadcast_timer* for m to fire up at $currentTime + t$;
9 **else**
10   **if** *rebroadcast_timer for m is scheduled* **then**
11   cancel *rebroadcast_timer* for m;
12 **Event** *scheduled rebroadcast_timer for m expires*
13 Rebroadcast m;

Initially, the vehicle verifies whether it has left the ROI or the time-to-live for the message m has expired. In such case, the vehicle discards m (lines 2–3). Otherwise, the vehicle checks whether m is a duplicate or not (Line 4). If it is not a duplicate, then the vehicle stores m in the list of received messages that are still valid. Furthermore, it will insert the ID of m into subsequent beacons, until the vehicle leaves the ROI or m expires (lines 5–6). The next and most important step is to calculate the waiting delay t to rebroadcast m (Line 7). In Algorithm 1, we omitted how this delay is calculated, because it will depend of the social metric employed, i.e., the clustering coefficient, node degree or both, as described in Section 3.3. For now, it is enough to know that such delay is a value in the interval $[0, T_{max}]$, where T_{max} is a configured parameter. After calculating the waiting delay, the vehicle uses it to schedule a rebroadcast for m (Line 8). Notice that, while the vehicle is scheduled to rebroadcast m, if it receives a duplicate, then it cancels the rebroadcast (lines 9–11), thus avoiding a possible redundant retransmission. However, when the waiting delay expires and the vehicle has not received any duplicate, then it rebroadcasts m (lines 12–13).

3.2 Store-carry-forward

On the other hand, when the road traffic is sparse and the network is partitioned, vehicles must hold received data messages and use their mobility capabilities to carry the messages to different parts of the ROI. Moreover, they must be able to determine whether a vehicle has already received a data message or not. For the former issue, vehicles rely on the store-carry-forward communication model. For the latter, beacons are used as an implicit acknowledgement mechanism. Algorithm 2 shows how our proposed solution delivers data messages even when the network is intermittently connected.

Algorithm 2: The store-carry-forward algorithm

---

1 **Event** *beacon b received from neighbor s*
2 **foreach** *message m in the list of received messages* **do**
3   **if** *m is not acknowledged in b* **then**
4         $t \leftarrow$ calculateWaitingDelay();
5   schedule *rebroadcast_timer* for m to fire up at *currentTime* $+ t$;

6 **Event** *data message m received from neighbor s*
7 **if** *m is a duplicate* **then**
8   **if** *rebroadcast_timer for m is scheduled* **then**
9   cancel *rebroadcast_timer* for m;

10 **Event** *scheduled rebroadcast_timer for m expires*
11 Rebroadcast m;

When a vehicle receives a beacon b from a neighbor s, it verifies whether there is a data message that has not been acknowledge by s in b (lines 1–3). For that, the vehicle looks into its list of received messages and compares their IDs with the IDs contained in b. If the vehicle finds any message m that has not been acknowledged, then it calculates a waiting delay t to rebroadcast m (Line 4). Once again, such delay will depend on the social metric employed, as described in Section 3.3. After calculating the waiting delay, the vehicle schedules to rebroadcast m with delay t (Line 5). As in the broadcast suppression algorithm, while the vehicle is scheduled to rebroadcast m, if it receives a duplicate, then it cancels the rebroadcast (lines 6–9), thus avoiding a possible redundant retransmission. However, when the waiting delay expires and the vehicle has not received any duplicate, then it rebroadcasts m (lines 10–11).

By using these two algorithms in conjunction, our proposed solution is able to tackle both the broadcast storm and the intermittently connected network problems. Moreover, it is worth noticing that a vehicle does not need to be aware of the current road traffic condition, i.e., whether the network is dense or sparse. In either case, the vehicle always tries to avoid redundant retransmissions and increase the message delivery capability to intended recipients.

3.3 Socially Inspired Dissemination

As outlined in the previous algorithms, calculating the waiting delay to rebroadcast a data message is the key step. Therefore, in this section, we show how the clustering coefficient and node degree can be used to turn our data dissemination solution into a socially-aware proposal. Initially, we show how to estimate the clustering coefficient using only one-hop neighbor information, and how to use it in the waiting delay computation. We then turn our attention to the node degree, which can be easily obtained through beacons. Finally, we also show how to calculate the waiting delay using a combination of both metrics.

3.3.1 Clustering Coefficient

The clustering coefficient for a vehicle v is the number of connections between neighbors of v divided by the total number of possible connections between neighbors of v. Therefore, to accurately calculate the clustering coefficient for vehicle v, it is necessary to know the two-hop neighborhood knowledge of v. Given that VANETs are extremely dynamic networks and obtaining such knowledge can be cumbersome, here we use position information to estimate the clustering coefficient, in particular, to determine whether two neighbors of a vehicle are connected or not. As already stated, each vehicle knows the position of each neighbor due to received beacons. Therefore, to verify whether two neighbors are connected or not, vehicle v must only check whether the distance between these two neighbors is below the estimated communication range. Thereafter, v is able to calculate its estimated clustering coefficient.

In possession of its own estimated clustering coefficient, a vehicle v is able to calculate its waiting delay to rebroadcast. According to an analysis of the estimated clustering coefficient with respect to the vehicle density (see Figure 2), for lower densities, the clustering coefficient is also low, but the variability is high. On the other hand, when the density is high, also is the value for the estimated clustering coefficient, but the variability is low. For our purposes, the greater the variability, the better. Otherwise, we risk assigning the same or similar waiting delay to all vehicles. Therefore, for this first proposal, we give a higher priority to rebroadcast for vehicles that have a low estimated clustering coefficient. In other words, the lower the estimated clustering coefficient, the lower the waiting delay. We calculate the waiting delay by the equation: $t_{cc} = T_{max} \times estimatedCC$, where the value for *estimatedCC* ranges in the interval $[0, 1]$.

3.3.2 Node Degree

When we look into the analysis of the node degree (see Figure 2), we can see that, when the vehicle density is low, the degree and its variability is also low. However, when the density increases, both the degree and its variability increase. Therefore, in the proposal based on the node degree, we use an opposite approach. That is, the higher the degree of a vehicle at a given neighborhood, the higher its priority to rebroadcast the message, i.e., the lower the waiting delay. Each vehicle will know its max neighbor degree due to the *degree* information in the received beacons. Equation 1 shows how the waiting delay is calculated using this approach. Here, *degree* is the degree of the vehicle that is calculating the waiting delay and *maxDegree* is the maximum between *degree* and the highest degree among all neighbors of the vehicle.

$$t_{degree} = T_{max} \times \left(1 - \left(\frac{degree}{maxDegree} \right) \right) \qquad (1)$$

3.3.3 Joint Solution

Here, we also propose a joint solution, i.e., one that uses both the estimated clustering coefficient and the node degree. The idea is that, assuming that a single metric may not be adequate for all traffic density scenarios, a combination of the two may produce better results. The waiting delay can be calculated using this joint approach, defined by the equation: $t = \alpha t_{cc} + \beta t_{degree}$. As can be observed, each metric contributes to a fraction of the total waiting delay, which is controlled by the factors α and β. In this work, to balance the equation delay, we assume that $\alpha = \beta = 0.5$.

4. PERFORMANCE EVALUATION

To evaluate the performance of our proposed approaches, we performed a series of simulations using the OMNeT++ 4.2.2. simulator [10]. We compare them to two well-known protocols - UV-CAST [11] and ABSM [6]. Moreover, in the presented results, the socially inspired protocols are identified as CC (clustering coefficient), Degree (node degree) and CC-Degree (joint solution). In the following sections, we describe the performance evaluation in detail. In particular, Section 4.1 shows the scenarios and the default parameters used in our analysis. Finally, simulation results and discussion are presented in Section 4.2.

4.1 Simulation Setup

Manhattan scenario: this is a scenario with ten evenly-spaced double-lane streets in an area of $1\,km^2$. Also, we consider signal attenuation effects caused by buildings. For that, we assume that each block has an 80m × 80m obstacle, which represents high-rise buildings. In order to quantify the traffic evolution in this scenario, we vary the vehicle density from 20 vehicles/km^2 to 500 vehicles/km^2. The road traffic simulation is performed by the Simulator of Urban MObility (SUMO 0.17.0) [1]. Moreover, we positioned the source vehicle at the center of the grid and it generates 100 messages of 2048 bytes to be disseminated to the whole network. The data rate is set to 1.5 Mbit/s.

To better understand the Manhattan grid scenario, Figure 2 shows the estimated cluster coefficient and the node degree for the considered vehicle densities. In particular, Figure 2-(a), we show the estimated cluster coefficient and its evolution. As we can see, the value for the estimated cluster coefficient under low densities is small, almost 40 %. Moreover, it has a higher variability. It happens because, for lower densities, there are few vehicles in transit. With the growth of the density, the estimated cluster coefficient increases. This is due to the fact that, under higher densities, the encounter probability is also higher, and the network will be more connected. Therefore, starting at 200 vehicles/km^2, the value for the estimated clustering coefficient has a constant behavior of about 75 %. This can be explained by the fact that even if the density of the network increases, connections among vehicles are constrained by physical restrictions, such as road shapes and obstacles. The Figure 2-(b) presents the node degree evolution. It is possible to observe how the node degree evolves over the density variation. As expected, with the increase of the density, the node degree also increases. For instance, at 100 vehicles/km^2, the average node degree is 5, representing that, on average, a vehicle has 5 neighbors.

Finally, to improve the quality of the following results and make them more realistic, we rely on the Veins 2.1 [8] network framework. It implements the standard IEEE 802.11p protocol stack for vehicle communication and an obstacle model for signal attenuation. Moreover, we set the bit rate at the MAC layer to 18 Mbit/s and the transmission power to 0.98 mW. With these parameters and a two-ray ground propagation model, it is possible to reach a communication range of 200 m. Beacons are sent every 1 s. For all scenarios, we simulate r replications in order to compute the confidence interval of 95%. According to the definitions presented in [5], the metrics evaluated are: *Delivery ratio*, *Total Messages Transmitted*, *Collisions* and *Delay*. The focus is to verify the coverage of

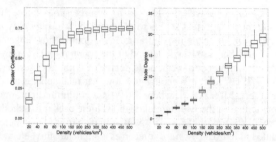

(a) Estimated cluster coefficient (b) Node degree evolution

Figure 2: Manhattan metrics evolution.

the protocol, the overhead induced by data messages and the latency for different network density conditions.

4.2 Results

Figure 3 shows the results for the Manhattan grid scenario. As we can note, overall, our socially inspired approaches present a better performance. When considering the delivery ratio (Figure 3-(a)), for lower densities, we can observe that CC, Degree, CC-Degree and ABSM deliver data messages to the same amount of vehicles. As the density increases, so does the delivery results for all protocols. However, for very high densities, the performance of ABSM and UV-CAST starts to deteriorate, while our proposals guarantee 100% delivery ratio. In summary, this result shows that the considered social metrics leads to the same delivery capability.

Figure 3-(b) shows the number of data messages transmitted. For lower densities, our proposals transmit more data messages when compared to ABSM and UV-CAST. As shown in the previous result, given that CC, Degree, CC-Degree and ABSM have the same delivery results for such lower densities, we can conclude that our proposals are not able to avoid redundant retransmissions when the network is sparse. Notice that, the broadcast storm problem is not much an issue in sparse networks. As the density increases, our solutions incur the lowest number of data messages transmitted. Among the three, the degree presents the best results, while the CC the worse. Recall from the results shown in Figure 2 that, at higher densities the variability for the degree is higher when compared to the one presented by the clustering coefficient. As already stated, the greater the variability, the greater the range of possible waiting delays, which leads to a better broadcast suppression approach. In a similar result, Figure 3-(c) shows the number of collisions for all protocols. Essentially, the behavior is almost the same for the number of messages transmitted. Our approaches perform better at higher densities. It is worth noticing that, at lower densities, among our solutions, the Degree leads to the highest number of collisions, while the CC leads to the lowest. This fact can also be explained by the variability results shown in Figure 2.

Figure 3-(d) shows the delay for all approaches. As expected, for lower densities, the delay for all protocols is very high due to the store-carry-forward performed by all protocols, i.e., vehicles need to store and carry messages around in order to deliver them. As the density increases, the delay for all protocols decreases. In particular, Degree has the lowest delay, while CC has the highest. According to the results shown in Figure 2, for higher densities, the clustering coefficient is also high. Therefore, the waiting delays chosen by vehicle will also be high, thus explaining the higher average delay. In the case of the Degree, for higher densities, the node degree is also high. However, contrary to the clustering coefficient, nodes with a high degree have a lower waiting delay, which explains the average delay to deliver data messages to intended recipients.

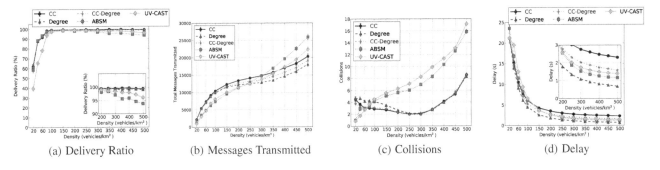

| (a) Delivery Ratio | (b) Messages Transmitted | (c) Collisions | (d) Delay |

Figure 3: Simulation results for the Manhattan street scenarios.

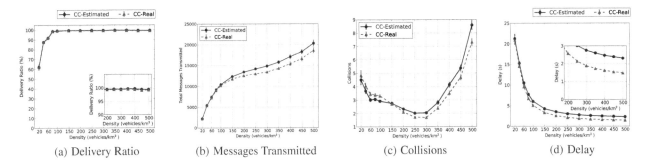

| (a) Delivery Ratio | (b) Messages Transmitted | (c) Collisions | (d) Delay |

Figure 4: Comparison for performance evaluation between cluster coefficient estimated and real for the Manhattan scenario.

Finally, aiming to analyze the difference between the estimated cluster coefficient and the real cluster coefficient, we present the results for these metrics in Figure 4 under the Manhattan grid scenario. Recall that, the estimated clustering coefficient is computed by considering the distance between vehicles and the estimated communication range. Therefore, signal attenuation caused by buildings has a direct impact on it. Conversely, the real clustering coefficient is calculated using the two-hop neighborhood knowledge of vehicles. As can be observed, overall, using the real clustering coefficient results on a better performance. However, the difference to the results of the estimated clustering coefficient are not significant, especially when we consider the extra cost to compute the real clustering coefficient.

5. CONCLUSION AND FUTURE WORK

This paper presented a new approach to perform data dissemination in vehicular ad hoc networks that take into account the social aspects of the network and the traffic evolution. Aiming to solve the broadcast storm and the intermittently connected network problems, our approach uses the information about the number of neighbors (node degree) and how these neighbors are connected (clustering coefficient) as a criterion to define which vehicles rebroadcast data messages during the dissemination process. We evaluated the performance of our approach, and we noted that in sparse scenarios our approach presents a performance a little worse when compared with related protocols. However, in high density scenarios, our approach presented substantial performance gains, especially regarding the delivery capability and the incurred overhead. As future work, we intend to investigate how other social metrics may be used to develop better data dissemination solutions and more efficient communication protocols.

6. REFERENCES

[1] M. Behrisch, L. Bieker, J. Erdmann, and D. Krajzewicz. SUMO - Simulation of Urban MObility: An Overview. In *Int. Conf. on Advances in System Simulation (SIMUL '11)*, pages 63–68, 2011.

[2] F. Cunha, A. Carneiro Viana, R. A. F. Mini, and A. A.F. Loureiro. Is it possible to find social properties in vehicular networks? In *IEEE Symposium on Comp.and Com.(ISCC '14)*, 2014.

[3] M. Fiore and J. Härri. The networking shape of vehicular mobility. In *ACM Int. Symposium on Mobile Ad Hoc Net. and Computing (MobiHoc '08)*, pages 261–272, 2008.

[4] D. Naboulsi and M. Fiore. On the Instantaneous Topology of a Large-scale Urban Vehicular Network: The Cologne Case. In *ACM Int.l Symposium on Mobile Ad Hoc Net. and Computing (MobiHoc '13)*, pages 167–176, 2013.

[5] S. Panichpapiboon and W. Pattara-Atikom. A review of information dissemination protocols for vehicular ad hoc networks. *Com. Surveys Tutorials, IEEE*, 14(3):784–798, Third 2012.

[6] F. Ros, P. Ruiz, and I. Stojmenovic. Acknowledgment-Based Broadcast Protocol for Reliable and Efficient Data Dissemination in Vehicular Ad Hoc Networks. *IEEE Transactions on Mobile Computing*, 11(1):33–46, 2012.

[7] R. S. Schwartz, R. R. R. Barbosa, N. Meratnia, G. Heijenk, and H. Scholten. A directional data dissemination protocol for vehicular environments. *Computer Com.*, 34(17):2057–2071, 2011.

[8] C. Sommer, R. German, and F. Dressler. Bidirectionally Coupled Network and Road Traffic Simulation for Improved IVC Analysis. *IEEE Transactions on Mobile Comp.*, 10(1):3–15, 2011.

[9] O. K. Tonguz, N. Wisitpongphan, and F. Bai. DV-CAST: a distributed vehicular broadcast protocol for vehicular ad hoc networks. *IEEE Wireless Com.*, 17(2):47–56, 2010.

[10] A. Varga and R. Hornig. An overview of the OMNeT++ simulation environment. In *International Conference on Simulation Tools and Techniques for Communications, Networks and Systems & Workshops (Simutools '08)*, pages 1–10, 2008.

[11] W. Viriyasitavat, O. Tonguz, and F. Bai. UV-CAST: an urban vehicular broadcast protocol. *IEEE Com. Mag.*, 49(11):116–124, 2011.

Semi-Static Interference Coordination in OFDMA/LTE Networks: Evaluation of Practical Aspects

Donald Parruca
Fahad Aizaz
Chair of Communication and
Distributed Systems
RWTH-Aachen University
Germany
parruca@umic.rwth-
aachen.de

Soamsiri Chantaraskul
The Sirindhorn International
Thai-German Graduate
School of Engineering (TGGS)
King Mongkut's University of
Technology North Bangkok
Thailand
soamsiri.c.ce@tggs-
bangkok.org

James Gross
School of Electrical
Engineering
KTH Royal Institute of
Technology
Sweden
james.gross@ee.kth.se

ABSTRACT

To minimize interference in LTE networks, several inter-cell interference coordination (ICIC) techniques have been introduced. Among them, semi-static ICIC offers a balanced trade-off between applicability and system performance. The power allocation per resource block and cell is adapted in the range of seconds according to the load in the system. An open issue in the literature is the question how fast the adaptation should be performed. This leads basically to a trade-off between system performance and feasible computation times of the associated power allocation problems. In this work, we close this open issue by studying the impact that different durations of update times of semi-static ICIC have on the system performance. We conduct our study on realistic scenarios considering also the mobility of mobile terminals. Secondly, we also consider the implementation aspects of a semi-static ICIC. We introduce a very efficient implementation on general purpose graphic processing units, harnessing the parallel computing capability of such devices. We show that the update periods have a significant impact on the performance of cell edge terminals. Additionally, we present a graphic processing unit (GPU) based implementation which speeds up existing implementations up to a factor of 92x.

Categories and Subject Descriptors

I [Computing Methodologies]: SIMULATION AND MODELING; I.6.4 [Model Validation and Analysis]: Methods—*performance measures*

General Terms

Algorithms, Measurement, Performance

Keywords

OFDMA; LTE; ICIC; Inter-Cell Interference Coordination; GPU; GA; Genetic Algorithm; 4G; Cellular Networks; Interference; Proportional Fair Scheduling

1. INTRODUCTION

Since the introduction of LTE systems there has been extensive research on mitigating inter-cell interference stemming from frequency reuse one. In inter-cell interference coordination (ICIC), power is allocated for specific parts of the frequency spectrum such that mobile stations in neighbouring cells experience low interference. A vast amount of ICIC schemes have been proposed taking quite different approaches. One way to group them is by the time dynamics. Static ICIC approaches [1] and [2], decide on a fixed parametrisation of frequency or power allocation. On the one hand the deployment efforts are low and taken during network planning phase. On the other hand, such schemes lack adaptation to the instantaneous load distribution in the cells leading to inefficient allocation of resources. In order to increase the efficiency, dynamic ICIC approaches have been introduced. Dynamic ICIC approaches adapt the power assignments to different frequency shares according to the current distribution of terminals and/or to the instantaneous channel gains.

Depending on the execution periodicity, dynamic schemes can further be distinguished into two categories. Highly dynamic schemes [3] and [4] adapt their coordination parameters in the range of a few milliseconds, e.g. 1-100 ms. In this category the negotiated parameters are combined with the local scheduler in order to adapt to the instantaneous channel gains. The nature of such a coordination approach requires exchange of overhead information between base stations, and if this is supposed to run at a high periodicity then the signalling overhead is very high. In addition to this, the short update periods leave little room for computing near-optimal allocations. As a consequence, the application of ICIC on short time scales in the range of milliseconds is unlikely to be feasible in practice.

A solution to the above problems has been originally proposed in [5] where semi-static ICIC is introduced. The power allocations are adapted over much longer time spans like seconds or longer. This is a form of soft frequency reuse (SFR)

[6], where the overall spectrum is reused by all base stations, but the transmission power in each resource block is restricted to a certain level. Although the idea of infrequent coordination intervals seems appealing, it also brings with it a wide set of challenges. Due to the long time span of the coordination period and the random evolution of fast fading and scheduling decisions, the overall system performance for a given power allocation becomes a random variable itself, turning the interference coordination problem into a stochastic optimization problem where the expected system performance is to be maximized. Optimization on expected systems performance turns out to be a highly non-linear optimization problem depending on the fading statistics of the signal-of-interest as well as all interfering signals. In addition, these statistics somehow translate into a throughput behaviour which is further influenced by the modulation and coding schemes as well as the dynamic resource scheduling at the individual base stations. So two fundamental problems are to be solved: (i) Modelling the expected system performance and (ii) Optimizing the power allocations accordingly. We have already addressed both these issues: In [7] we have addressed stochastic performance models for interference limited LTE systems. In [8] we have then fundamentally addressed the issue of solving the optimization problem. In our work we showed that - in principle - the resulting stochastic optimization problems could be solved near-optimal by the application of genetic algorithms (GA).

There still remains the question how frequent the semi-static ICIC approach should be executed. This depends mainly on two issues: How fast do the channel states change (in comparison to the underlying statistical model used for the computations). That is essentially a question of mobility. On the other hand, the question arises how fast the power allocations can be generated. Basically this is a trade-off because mobility-wise one would expect that the more frequent the power allocations are updated, the better the system should perform. However, there must be a limit to the computation times which sets a hard limit on the periodicity. The contribution of this paper is to address this trade-off. We deal with it by: (i) Firstly, evaluating how sensitive the system performance is when operating semi-static ICIC at different update periods (ii) Secondly, we introduce a highly efficient implementation of our proposed genetic algorithm in [8] for semi-static ICIC based on general purpose graphic processing units, taking advantage of their high degree of parallelism. Besides the programming aspects of our implementation we show in particular that the reuse of solutions from previous allocation phases results in a drastic speed-up of the execution run-time of the coordination scheme. This has a direct impact on the system, where with decreasing update times for the semi-static ICIC, an improvement in performance is noticed. In contrast, related works on semi-static ICIC [9] and [8] perform their evaluations on static drops of terminals and synthetic simulation models. In general, neither paper looks at the impact of the update period nor at the computation times of the stochastic optimization problem.

2. SYSTEM MODEL

We consider the downlink communication of an LTE cellular network. The multiple-access technique used is Orthogonal Frequency Division Multiple Access (OFDMA). The frequency spectrum with carrier frequency f_C and bandwidth B is equally split into N subsequent chunks called resource blocks, which are the minimal unit that can be used for data transmission over the air interface. Each resource block n is comprised of N_C orthogonal subcarriers which are used for the transmission of N_S sequential OFDM symbols. Time is organized in time slots of duration T_{TTI} where for each time slot t base stations take scheduling decisions, which we refer to in the following as fast resource assignments. In this process, packets from local queues at the base station are matched to resource blocks for transmission to mobile stations. In the following we assume proportional fair scheduling (PFS) for the fast resource assignment originally introduced in [10].

Each base station k transmits data packets to its set $J(k)$ of mobile stations through the air interface. Meanwhile, through a different interface (called X-2 in the LTE context), each base station communicates with K other neighbouring ones for inter-cell coordination purposes, forming a so called coordination cluster. Semi-static coordination is periodically performed for each base station involved in the cluster. A virtual master node, which we will refer to as *Central Entity* (CE), decides for every base station involved in the cluster on the power allocations per resource block $p_{k,n}(t)$. It is valid for the time duration T_C, being the total time needed to collect the pathloss values $\overline{h_{k,j}^2}$ at the CE, executing the semi-static ICIC algorithm and communicating the power masks $p_{k,n}(t)$ back to the corresponding base stations. It is much longer than the fast resource assignment interval ($T_{TTI} = 1$ ms). A schematic example of a cluster is shown in Figure 1. Network wide, mutually interfering base stations are grouped together forming independent inter-cell interference coordination clusters where their transmission powers are decided by the corresponding CE (which could be for example one of the base stations in the coordination cluster).

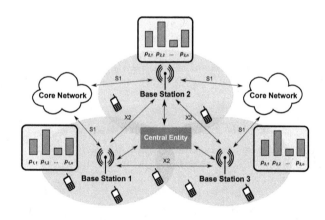

Figure 1: System model of semi-static ICIC for a cluster of three cooperating base stations.

Every TTI, each mobile terminal j feeds its instantaneous channel capacity $C(\gamma_j, n(t))$ back to its serving base station. It can be considered as a mapping of SINR to rate function where specific values can be found in [11]. The actual channel capacity directly depends on the instantaneous signal-to-interference-plus-noise ratio (SINR):

$$\gamma_{j,n}(t) = \frac{h_{0,j,n}^2(t) \cdot p_{0,n}(t)}{\sum_{k=1}^{K} h_{k,j,n}^2(t) \cdot p_{k,n}(t) + N_0}, \qquad (1)$$

where $h_{k,j,n}^2(t)$, $k = 0, \ldots, K$ are the instantaneous channel fading gains with corresponding means $\overline{h_{k,j}^2}$ (pathloss) of the serving ($k = 0$) and interfering base stations ($k > 0$). Furthermore, N_0 is the noise power.

For fast resource assignments according to PFS, the serving base station uses the instantaneous feedback to construct a priority metric $\hat{r}_j(t)$ based on the ratio of the instantaneous rate and the total scheduled data $\bar{r}_{j,n}$ over the last W time slots as the following:

$$\hat{r}_{j,n}(t) = \frac{C(\gamma_{j,n}(t))}{\bar{r}_{j,n}}. \qquad (2)$$

The mobile station j_n^* having the highest priority is then scheduled for transmission:

$$\forall k, n : j_n^*(t) = \arg \max_{j \in J(k)} \hat{r}_{j,n}(t). \qquad (3)$$

LTE operates with a unique modulation and coding scheme if multiple resource blocks are assigned to the same terminal. We assume in the following that this is utilized, i.e. no individual MCS selection per resource block is performed.

3. PROBLEM STATEMENT

ICIC is mainly in place to improve the cell-edge performance. Therefore, any optimization problem that improves this performance can be considered. In the following, we study a problem formulation where the CE decides on the power allocations $p_{k,n}(t)$ by solving the following max-min stochastic optimization problem:

$$\max \quad \rho \qquad (4)$$

$$\text{s.t.} \quad \sum_{n=1}^{N} \mathcal{R}_{j,n}(p_{k,n}(t)) > \rho \quad \forall k, \quad \forall j \in J(k),$$

$$\sum_{n=1}^{N} p_{k,n}(t) \leq P_{\max} \quad \forall k,$$

$$p_{k,n}(t) \leq p_{\max} \quad \forall k, n.$$

Above, $p_{k,n}(t)$ denotes the combination of transmission powers $p_{0,n}(t), \ldots, p_{K,n}(t)$ per resource block n and base station k in the cluster. Furthermore, the maximal allowed transmission power per resource block is $p_{\max}$ and the maximal one per base station $\sum_n p_{k,n}(t)$ is $P_{\max}$. The goal of the optimization problem is to maximize the expected rates of the terminals at the worst locations in the cluster area by an appropriate choice of the power allocations.

For the computation of the expected rates $\mathcal{R}_{j,n}(p_{k,n}(t))$ a stochastic model is needed taking into account the impact of the proportional fair scheduler on fading and interference limited wireless links. Considering the instantaneous SINR $\gamma_{j,n}(t)$ as a random variable $Z_{j,n}$, then from [7] the rate expectation $\mathcal{R}_{j,n}(p_{k,n}(t))$ for PFS based systems can be computed as:

$$\mathcal{R}_{j,n}(p_{k,n}(t)) = \frac{N_S \cdot N_C}{T_{TTI}} \qquad (5)$$

$$\cdot \int_0^\infty C(z) \prod_{\forall m \in J(k)/j} F_{Z_{m,n}}\left(\frac{\mathrm{E}[Z_{m,n}]}{\mathrm{E}[Z_{j,n}]} \cdot z\right) \cdot f_{Z_{j,n}}(z) \, dz,$$

where $F_{Z_{j,n}}(z)$, $f_{Z_{j,n}}(z)$ and $\mathrm{E}[Z_{j,n}]$ are respectively the SINR cumulative function (CDF), the SINR probability density function (PDF) and the SINR expectation. Assuming the instantaneous fading gains $h_{k,j,n}^2$, as exponentially distributed, from [12] and [13] we have the PDF and CDF of SINR for multiple interfering sources as:

$$F_{Z_{j,n}}(z) = 1 - \prod_{k=1}^{K} \frac{1}{1 + z \cdot \frac{\overline{h_{k,j}^2} p_{k,n}}{\overline{h_{0,j}^2} p_{0,n}}} \exp\left(-\frac{z N_0}{\overline{h_{0,j}^2} p_{0,n}}\right). \quad (6)$$

Then, taking the derivative of function $F_{Z_{j,n}}(z)$ with respect to variable z we obtain:

$$f_{Z_{j,n}}(z) = \left(\sum_{k=1}^{K} \frac{\overline{h_{k,j}^2} p_{k,n}}{\overline{h_{0,j}^2} p_{0,n} \left(1 + z \cdot \frac{\overline{h_{k,j}^2} p_{k,n}}{\overline{h_{0,j}^2} p_{0,n}}\right)^2} \right.$$

$$\cdot \prod_{q \neq k} \frac{1}{1 + z \cdot \frac{\overline{h_{q,j}^2} p_{q,n}}{\overline{h_{0,j}^2} p_{0,n}}} + \prod_{k=1}^{K} \frac{N_0}{\overline{h_{0,j}^2} p_{0,n} + z \cdot \overline{h_{k,j}^2} p_{k,n}} \right)$$

$$\cdot \exp\left(-\frac{z N_0}{\overline{h_{0,j}^2} p_{0,n}}\right). \qquad (7)$$

The rate model in Formula (5) is solved through numerical methods. Its accuracy and validity has been already evaluated with system level simulations in [12].

As it can be noticed optimization variable $p_{k,n}(t)$ has a non-linear relation to the rate expectation $\mathcal{R}_{j,n}(p_{k,n}(t))$. This makes it difficult to apply analytical methods in obtaining optimal power allocations. In our previous work [8], we showed, without considering algorithm computational runtimes and the mobility of terminals in the propagation environment, that such a problem can be solved near-optimally through genetic algorithms.

In contrast, in this work we are interested in characterizing the dependency of semi-static ICIC on the periodicity of executing the algorithm. On the one hand, we are interested in the overall system performance for different periodicities. On the other hand we are interested in characterizing the algorithm's run time for different system parametrizations. In the following we study how the system performance in realistic scenarios behaves for different values of the update period T_C. Secondly, we present an efficient semi-static ICIC implementation that can be executed in parallel on a GPU with low execution times. We aim to reduce the computational times of the ICIC algorithm presented here, such that they are significantly smaller than T_C. This approach still has to collect the pathloss from the base stations and then also signal the new power assignments back to the base stations requiring extra overhead time.

4. IMPLEMENTATION OF GA IN GPU

Genetic algorithms are stochastic search methods used to solve optimization problems based on natural selection principles. A candidate solution, which in our case are the quantized power allocations $p_{k,n}(t) \in \{0, p^l, 2 \cdot p^l, \ldots, L \cdot p^l\}$, where $p^l = p_{\max}/L$ are encoded as a two dimensional matrix $((K+1) \times N)$, which in GA lingo we refer to as chromosome and individual parts of it as genes. An initial population of chromosomes is repetitively altered by operations of evaluation, selection, crossover, mutation and validation. One iteration of the above operations is called a generation.

In each generation an intermediate population is generated when selection is applied. It initiates a tournament among randomly selected chromosomes where the fitness, decided in the evaluation process, is compared. The fittest chromosome is selected for crossover. Genes of randomly picked parent chromosomes from the intermediate population are swapped to form the next offspring. Afterwards, with a low probability, mutation is applied to the genes of the offspring. It alters the transmission power $p_{k,n}$ of a gene by adding or subtracting the value p^l. In this stage, it can happen that the chromosomes do not fulfill the power constraint of the given optimization problem. Therefore, during the validation process, a check is performed for the newly generated population. In case the allocated transmission power per cell is above the limit P_{max}, random genomes of the cell violating the constraint are picked up and their power is reduced. The process repeats itself until the constraint is met. Now, it is possible to evaluate the fitness of the chromosomes in the new population. It is the minimal expected rate among all terminals in the cluster for the given chromosome $p_{k,n}(t)$ which, is also the metric that we are optimizing: $\min_{\forall j} \left(\sum_n \mathcal{R}_{j,n}(p_{k,n}) \right)$. As it can be noticed, after each generation fitter candidate solutions are generated, bringing the evolution closer to the optimal solution (power combination).

We exploit the parallelism of GPUs for general purpose computation by using Compute Unified Device Architecture (CUDA) framework. CUDA framework provides a mapping between CUDA programming constructs and GPGPU hardware. CUDA uses a notion of *block* which maps to hardware streaming multi-processor. A number of blocks can be assigned to a multi-processor where they are time-shared internally by the CUDA programming environment. A defined number of *threads* can be configured for a block to run on streaming processors. Each thread executes a single instruction set called the *kernel*. The kernel code executes in batches of *warp* size of the device in a time-shared fashion, simultaneously over streaming processors. Each thread uses a number of private registers for its computation, whereas threads within a block share common limited memory called "shared memory". Threads and blocks are given a unique ID that can be accessed within the thread during its execution. These can be used by a thread to perform the kernel task on its part of the data resulting in a Single Instruction Multiple Data (SIMD) execution [14].

Our implementation of genetic algorithm on GPGPU exploits parallelism over several layers. We use multiple threads to evaluate a single chromosome in parallel and multiple blocks for different individuals simultaneously. This is realized by organizing the data in GPGPU memory in such a way that genes $(p_{k,n})$ of each individual can be accessed efficiently in a coherent manner by multiple threads handling it. This access pattern is known as coalesced access.

Each GA operation is implemented as a separate kernel function which executes one after another. The initialized population is retrieved from device memory. Each kernel operates on retrieved population in parallel and once all operators are executed, the new population is kept back in the global memory and thus a generation in GA life cycle is completed. We also take advantage of shared memory for keeping intermediate chromosomes during the process of se-

lection, crossover and mutation which reduces the number of access to the global memory and enhances the overall performance of computations. This process is shown in Figure 2.

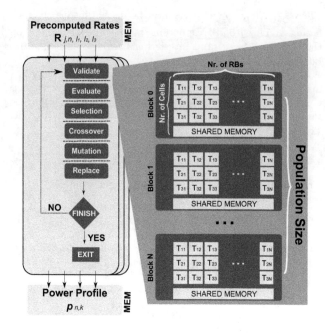

Figure 2: CUDA implementation of GA. Each thread $T_{k,n}$ manipulates the corresponding genes $p_{k,n}(t)$.

In literature related to GA implementations in GPU [15] and [16] the methodology applied by the authors for implementation of genetic algorithm on GPUs is similar. The basic idea exploited is to realize different phases of genetic algorithm as separate CUDA kernels and apply them on GPU for parallel execution. Despite all the similarities, the main difference that stands out in our approach is the evaluation of the fitness function. Based on the problem at hand, the fitness function needs to be evaluated for every generation on the fly for each of the candidate solutions. As specific power combinations for each resource block $p_{k,n}$ might need to be evaluated multiple times during the evaluation process, recomputation of user rates would add a significant overhead. In our case, we simplified the problem by pre-computing the user rates $\mathcal{R}_{j,n}(p_{(l_1,l_2,l_3),n})$ for every permutation of the set (l_1, l_2, l_3) that are required during fitness calculations.

A further very efficient way to reduce the execution time of GA is by minimizing the number of generations needed to reach a near-optimal solution. This is done by taking advantage of the spatial correlation of pathloss. It can be expected that the topology of terminals does not drastically change between subsequent runs. As a consequence, the best individuals of the GA will also be similar. Consequently, the less generations it will take to reach the optimum. We can take advantage of this feature by seeding 10% of the new population with the fittest solution of the previous allocation phase. The number of generations needed to reach the optimum is also directly connected to the mobility of the terminals. The slower the mobility is, the more similar are the optimal solutions, resulting in less generations to be computed. Carefully initializing the population also helps in quickly reaching a near optimal solution. We initialize the population with random and commonly used approaches of power allocations in static allocations, i.e. uniform and orthogonal power allocations.

In our previous work [8], the same optimization problem was solved using a serial implementation with GALib library on standard CPUs. The runtime achieved for solving the optimization problem (4) by the genetic algorithm was in the order of minutes, being too slow for practical deployments.

5. PERFORMANCE EVALUATION

In the first part of the evaluation we consider the dependency of the system performance with respect to different update periods T_C in realistic scenarios where mobility is present. The evaluation is further extended by analysing the performance of the proposed semi-static ICIC approach to different comparison schemes widely used in literature. Afterwards, we investigate the run times of the GA implementation for the GPU and evaluate its ability to deliver near-optimal solutions.

5.1 Comparison Schemes

We compared the performance of three different inter-cell interference coordination approaches for a cluster of three cooperating base stations.

- The first one is our proposed semi-static ICIC scheme periodically generating power profiles $p_{k,n}(t)$. Due to illustration reasons we name it as SFR. Four different periods of T_C : 0.1, 0.5, 1 and 2 seconds were simulated by re-using the genomes of previous solutions. According to the results of the next section (Section 5.3), we set the number of iterations to 1000 before terminating the genetic algorithm.

- The second scheme considered is fractional frequency reuse (FFR).In FFR, the frequency spectrum is split into two parts exclusively dedicated to cell center and cell edge terminals. Terminals in either group get resources exclusively assigned from the one or the other spectrum by the proportional fair scheduler. The spectrum dedicated for cell-centred users (RB index 1-10) is fully reused in the neighboring base stations. Meanwhile, for cell-edge terminals, a bunch of 5 resource blocks is orthogonally reused in the neighbouring cells. The categorization of terminals as centrally or edge located is periodically done every 100 ms. It is locally performed for every cell according to a greedy algorithm introduced in [12]. First, all users are assumed as centrally located then, the ones with the worst predicted rate are subsequently reallocated to the cell-edge spectrum. The process is repeated as long as the estimated minimal rate of the cell is increased. For estimation, the rate prediction model from Formula (5) is used. This FFR scheme is dynamic and has the same optimization goal as the SFR scheme proposed here making it a fair candidate for comparison.

- Finally, two static ICIC schemes are also considered. In the first one, the whole spectrum is re-used in the neighbouring cells. The difference to our proposed semi-static ICIC, is that here the power allocation is not changed from RB to RB but is the same for all resource blocks (equalling P_{max}/N) causing strong inter-

cell interference. We refer to this scheme as frequency reuse one (FR1). In the second, orthogonal frequency bands in the neighbouring cells are used, i.e. the frequency band is split into disjoint sets of frequency bands and each base station is operating on one of those bands. In our case a frequency reuse of 3 (FR3) scheme was used, resulting in a network where no interference at all is present.

5.2 Simulation Parameters

As simulation environment we chose the urban area of the city of Munich. From the German radio-monitoring agency [17] and [18] we obtained the geographical location and base station antenna orientation of a cellular network operator. From the vast amount of cells, we worked with a cluster of three sectors radiating inwards the simulation playground as shown in Figure 3a. The profile of $120°$ sectorized antennas and their corresponding orientation and position together with a 3D model of the city served as input for a ray-tracing algorithm [19] to generate a RF propagation map of the simulated area. As a result, we could associate to every pixel the corresponding path-loss with the neighbouring base stations. The corresponding long-term SINR of the simulation environment is shown in Figure 3a.

Through the ONE mobility simulator [20], the node movement across the streets was replicated. After initially dropping terminals in the environment (30 drops in total) mobile terminals started to move with a velocity of 30 kmph according to a map based random walk model [20]. The position of terminals was continuously traced and mapped to the corresponding pathloss $\overline{h_{k,j}^2}$ with the surrounding base stations.

The pathloss values $\overline{h_{k,j}^2}$ were fed into our OMNET++ based system level simulator, mimicking the radio access of an OFDMA/LTE system. Fast fading based on Jake's model was simulated and proportional fair scheduling on fully buf-fered traffic queues was performed. The simulated bandwidth was 5 MHz ($N = 25$ resource blocks) with carrier frequency of 1.8 GHz while the maximal transmit power P_{max} was set to 20 W. The total number of terminals considered was $J = 60$ and the noise power per resource block was assumed as $N_0 = -112$dBm. For every drop the downlink communication of 60 seconds duration was simulated.

5.3 System Performance Evaluation

We basically considered the average rate per terminal as performance metric. To capture the rate variability of the terminals at different positions, we evaluated the average rates by building the empirical cumulative distribution functions (ECDF) over all terminals rates observed during the simulation, which serves as primary performance metric. It tells us the likelihood that the minimal observed data rate X in the cluster is smaller than or equal to a number x. The 5% percentile on the rate ECDF is a common metric used in standardization to evaluate the cell-edge performance which we will use in the following as well. The corresponding curves are given in Figure 3b. Observing the lower part of Figure 3b (the 5-th % percentile) we notice that the semi-static approach proposed here delivered the best performance for the cell-edge terminals. For different update intervals (0.1 vs 2 s) there is a performance difference, with the shorter periodicity of 0.1 s offering slightly better results.

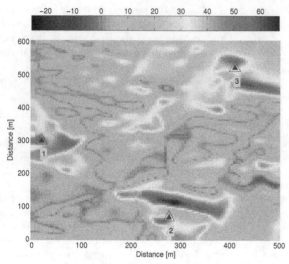

(a) SINR in dB of simulation playground.

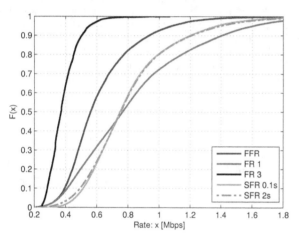

(b) General Rates ECDF Curves. The rate of all mobile terminals in the system is considered.

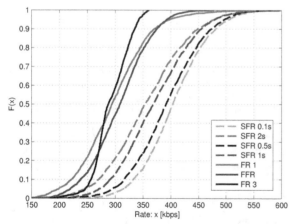

(c) Minimal Rates ECDF Curves. The rate of *only* cell-edge terminals in the system is considered.

Figure 3: Evaluation of different approaches for interference coordination by system level simulations.

The general rates ECDF metric gives information about the overall system performance. However, we are also interested to further highlight the performance of the optimization goal, namely the rate of cell-edge terminals for different update periods. In order to do so, we collect the minimal rates per simulation run and every second of simulation time. Based on these data the ECDF curves are computed, leading to Figure 3c. There, we can notice that the performance of cell-edge terminals is notably improved compared with the other comparison schemes and that shorter update periods result in a much better performance of cell-edge terminals. The quicker the update time is, the better the adaptation of power allocations to the topology of mobile terminals. With the time passing by, the position of mobile stations changes and so does also the pathloss with the neighboring base stations. This results in a mismatch between the predicted rates during the power mask optimization process and the actual rate obtained during network operation. The generated power allocations are not relevant to the topology of terminals with the time passing by resulting in a performance loss.

These observations bring us to the conclusion that significant gains can be harnessed in semi-static ICIC schemes for relatively low (smaller than 1 s) update periods. Therefore, efforts in minimizing the run-times of semi-static ICIC schemes are beneficial to the cell-edge terminals performance. It needs to be mentioned that the gain depends on the mobility of terminals and more investigations are required to consider also other mobilities, but were not performed in this paper due to space limitations. In the next section we evaluate the execution run-time of our proposed semi-static ICIC approach.

5.4 Evaluation of GAs Implementation

The run-time of our GA implementation for a fixed number of generations of 2000 and variable number of resource blocks and terminals is shown in Figure 4a. The measurements were performed on a NVIDIA Quadro 6000 GPU. We notice that, the execution runtime increases linearly with the number of RBs and terminals. This is due to the fact that we exploit parallelism (in GPU) in multiple dimensions. The increase in the number of terminals impacts runtime significantly as compared to the number of RBs. Although all the chromosomes in the population are operated in parallel, the evaluation of the genome is a search operation through all the users (i.e. finding the minimal rate). In total, for 60 mobile stations and 3 cells, it took only 0.38 s for the GA to execute[1]. Compared to our previous implementation running on a four-core machine with conventional CPUs (AMD Phenom(tm) II X4 945 processor and 8 GB RAM) the pre-computation implemented also in parallel took 64.20 seconds to complete and the optimization time of GA took 21.4 seconds. In total we notice a 92x improvement on the pre-computation and a 56x improvement on the GA optimization. This is already a significant improvement due to the GPU implementation discussed previously.

In the following, we investigate the number of generations needed from the GA to find the near-optimal solutions for the given search space. This is an important factor as the GAs execution run-time is linearly connected with the number of generations. For benchmarking purposes, we use a

---

[1]The pre-computation on the worst case it took 0.7 s and is subject to further optimization.

linearised version of the optimization problem (4) in finding the optimal solution. The linearised problem is given as follows:

$$\max \quad \rho$$

$$\text{s.t.} \quad \sum_{n=1}^{N} \sum_{l_1=0}^{L} \sum_{l_2=0}^{L} \sum_{l_3=0}^{L} \hat{\mathcal{R}}_{j,n,l_1,l_2,l_3} \cdot x_{n,l_1,l_2,l_3} > \rho \quad \forall j,$$

$$\sum_{n=1}^{N} \sum_{l_1=0}^{L} \sum_{l_2=0}^{L} \sum_{l_3=0}^{L} p(l_k) \cdot x_{n,l_1,l_2,l_3} \leq P_{\max} \quad \forall k,$$

$$\sum_{l_1=0}^{L} \sum_{l_2=0}^{L} \sum_{l_3=0}^{L} x_{n,l_1,l_2,l_3} = 1 \quad \forall n,$$

$$x_{n,l_1,l_2,l_3} \in \{0,1\}, \tag{8}$$

where x is the decision variable and rates $\hat{\mathcal{R}}_{j,n,l_1,l_2,l_3}$ are the precomputed input values to the optimization problem. Then, using an ILP solver we obtained the optimal solution to the ILP. The evaluation was performed for different mobilities of 3, 30 and 60 Kmph of mobile terminals and with different execution periods of 0.2, 0.5, 1 and 2 seconds. The GA was run for each period 30 times in order to gather statistical confidence.

The average number of generations needed for the GA to reach 97% of the optimum is shown in Figure 4b. The average number of generations to reach near-optimal solutions was between 200 and 800 generations, respectively lasting 37 ms and 130 ms. For the studied scenario, the 3 kmph run times are slightly higher than the 30 and 60 kmph ones. This is a scenario specific behaviour as, the path-loss of mobile stations moving with 3 kmph changes more slowly than scenarios with higher mobility. The search space (precomputed rate expectations) for the 30 consequent runs of the GA is more similar than for higher mobilities. Hence, the similarity in the number of generations for the 3 kmph mobility.

We repeat the GA evaluations by reusing the power profiles generated in the previous solutions. The motivation is that the topology of mobile stations does not change drastically in consequent GA runs. Therefore, optimal power profiles in consequent runs differ slightly, helping the GA to evolve quicker to a near-optimal solution. The corresponding results are presented in Figure 4c. Observing it, we notice a drastic speed-up for high frequency adaptation (200 ms) and low mobility (3 kmph). Less than 4 ms (10 generations) were needed instead of 86 ms (500 generations) to reach near-optimal values for low mobility scenarios of 3 Kmph, resulting in a 22x fold speed-up of the GPU implementation. Another trend to be noticed is also between the length of the period of optimization and the convergence to the optimum. The longer the coordination periods are the slower it takes for the GA to converge. The reason for that is that the topology of terminals differs more the longer the update periods are. The same can be said also for increasing mobility. The higher the mobility the more different will be the topology of terminals. Consequently, the number of generations to meet the optimum will also be larger.

For all mobility scenarios and update periods which we investigated so far, we could show that through an efficient implementation the run times can be reduced down to approximately 50 ms by using a GPU. That is a noticeable gain in computing time, taking into account that the previous CPU based implementation runs at 21.4 seconds.

6. CONCLUSIONS

Based on the evaluations performed in this work we observe that performance-wise smaller update periods of semi-static ICIC lead to better performance. However, the improvement by going from 0.5 seconds update period to 0.1 seconds is marginal. On the other hand, we show that by exploiting spatial correlation of path-loss and implementing the semi-static ICIC algorithm in GPU the computation time can be reduced from 20 seconds down to approximately 50 ms (and lower). Given these facts we conclude that practical implementations of near-optimal semi-static ICIC algorithms are possible and that GPU devices are an appropriate option to run such algorithms.

7. ACKNOWLEDGEMENTS

This work was partially supported by the DFG Cluster of Excellence on Ultra High-Speed Mobile Information and Communication (UMIC), German Research Foundation grant DFG EXC 89.

8. REFERENCES

[1] M. Liang, F. Liu, Z. Chen, Y. F. Wang, and D. C. Yang, "A novel frequency reuse scheme for ofdma based relay enhanced cellular networks," in *Proc. of the IEEE Vehicular Technology Conference, 2009.*, Apr., volume = 2009.

[2] D. Gonzalez Gonzalez, M. Garcia-Lozano, S. Ruiz Boque, and J. Olmos, "An analytical view of static intercell interference coordination techniques in ofdma networks," in *Proc. of IEEE Wireless Communications and Networking Conference Workshops*, pp. 300–305, Apr. 2012.

[3] S. Khalifa, H. Hamza, and K. Elsayed, "Inter-cell interference coordination for highly mobile users in lte-advanced systems," in *Proc. of the IEEE Vehicular Technology Conference*, pp. 1–5, Jun. 2013.

[4] S. Wang, Y. Zhang, and G. Bi, "A decentralized downlink dynamic icic method for multi-cell ofdma system," in *Proc. of International Conference on Wireless Communications and Signal Processing*, pp. 1–5, Nov. 2011.

[5] R1-060368, "Performance of inter-cell interference mitigation with semi-static frequency planning for eutra downlink." 3GPP TSG RAN WG1#44 Denver, USA, Feb. 2006.

[6] M. Bohge, J. Gross, and A. Wolisz, "Optimal power masking in soft frequency reuse based OFDMA networks," in *Proc. of the European Wireless Conference*, (Aalborg, Denmark), pp. 162–166, May 2009.

[7] D. Parruca, M. Grysla, S. Goertzen, and J. Gross, "Analytical Model of Proportional Fair Scheduling in Interference-limited OFDMA/LTE Networks," in *Proc. of IEEE Vehicular Technology Conference*, Sept. 2013.

[8] D. Parruca, M. Grysla, H. Zhou, F. Naghibi, M. Petrova, P. Mähönen, and J. Gross, "On semi-static interference coordination under proportional fair scheduling in lte systems," in *Proc. of the European Wireless Conference*, VDE VERLAG GmbH, 2013.

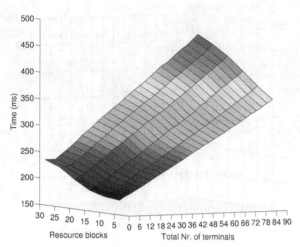

(a) Runtime of GA optimization for 2000 generations.

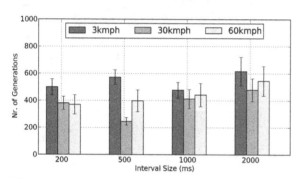

(b) Mean number of generations to reach 97% of ILP optimum for a random start of GA.

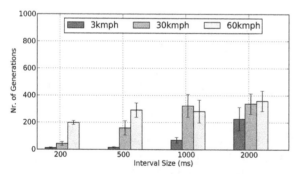

(c) Mean number of generations to reach 97% of ILP optimum for reuse simulations.

Figure 4: Implementation evaluation of the genetic algorithm.

[9] R. Madan, J. Borran, A. Sampath, N. Bhushan, A. Khandekar, and T. Ji, "Cell association and interference coordination in heterogeneous lte-a cellular networks," in *IEEE Trans. on Selected Areas in Communications*, vol. 28, pp. 1479–1489, Dec. 2010.

[10] A. Jalali, R. Padovani, and R. Pankaj, "Data throughput of CDMA-HDR a high efficiency-high data rate personal communication wireless system," in *Proc. of the IEEE Vehicular Technology Conference*, (Tokyo, Japan), May 2000.

[11] J. Ikuno, M. Wrulich, and M. Rupp, "System Level Simulation of LTE Networks," in *Proc. of the IEEE Vehicular Technology Conference*, (Taipei, Taiwan), May 2010.

[12] D. Parruca and J. Gross, "On the Interference As Noise Approximation in OFDMA/LTE Networks," in *Proc. of IEEE International Conference on Communicationsf*, June 2013.

[13] M. Haenggi and R. K. Ganti, *Interference in large wireless networks*. Now Publishers Inc, 2009.

[14] NVidia, "Parallel programming and computing platform." http://www.nvidia.com/object/cuda_home_new.html, May 2014.

[15] K. K. Rajvi Shah, P J Narayanan, "Gpu-accelerated genetic algorithms," in *Proc. of the Workshop on Parallel Architectures for Bio-inspired Algorithms*, pp. 27 – 34, 2010.

[16] J. Jaros, "Multi-gpu island-based genetic algorithm for solving the knapsack problem," in *Proc. of the IEEE Congress on Evolutionary Computation (CEC), 2012*, pp. 1–8, June 2012.

[17] R. Trautmann, "The radio monitoring service in Germany," in *Proc. of the 7th International Symposium on Electromagnetic Compatibility and Electromagnetic Ecology*, pp. 109–112, June 2007.

[18] E-Plus, "Network coverage." http://193.201.138.69/evinternet/, April 2014.

[19] AWE-Communications, "Winprop: Prediction of wave propagation." http://www.awe-communications.com/, April 2014.

[20] A. Keränen, J. Ott, and T. Kärkkäinen, "The ONE Simulator for DTN Protocol Evaluation," in *Proc. of the International Conference on Simulation Tools and Techniques*, (New York, NY, USA), ICST, 2009.

Handoff Rate Analysis in Heterogeneous Cellular Networks: a Stochastic Geometric Approach

Wei Bao and Ben Liang
Department of Electrical and Computer Engineering, University of Toronto
Toronto, Ontario, Canada
wbao@comm.utoronto.ca, liang@comm.utoronto.ca

ABSTRACT

Horizontal and vertical handoffs are important ramifications of user mobility in multi-tier heterogeneous cellular networks. They directly affect the signaling overhead and quality of calls in the system. However, they are difficult to analyze due to the irregularly shaped network topologies introduced by multiple tiers of cells. In this work, a stochastic geometric analysis framework on user mobility is proposed, to capture the spatial randomness and various scales of cell sizes in different tiers. We derive theoretical expressions for the rates of all handoff types experienced by an active user with arbitrary movement trajectory. Empirical study using real user mobility trace data and extensive simulation are conducted, demonstrating the correctness and usefulness of our analysis.

Categories and Subject Descriptors

C.2.1 [**Network Architecture and Design**]: Wireless communication

Keywords

Cellular networks; mobility; handoff; stochastic geometry; analytic geometry

1. INTRODUCTION

Traditional single-tier macro-cellular networks provide wide coverage for mobile user equipments (UEs), but they are insufficient to satisfy the exploding demand for high bandwidth access driven by modern mobile traffic, such as multimedia transmissions and cloud computing tasks. One effective means to increase network capacity is to provide more serving stations within a geographical area, i.e., installing a diverse set of small-cells such as femtocells [14] and WiFi hotspots [12], overlaying the macrocells, to form a multi-tier heterogeneous cellular network. Each small-cell is equipped with a shorter-range and lower-cost base station (BS) or access point (AP), to provide nearby UEs with

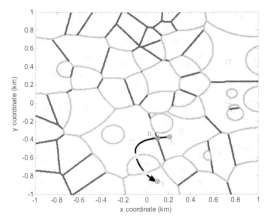

Figure 1: An example of a three-tier cellular network. Tier-1, 2, and 3 BSs are represented by squares, circles, and triangles respectively; blue curves show intra-tier cell boundaries; green curves show inter-tier cell boundaries. A UE starts a call at X and terminates it at Y. It experiences one horizontal handoff at B_1 and two vertical handoffs at B_2 and B_3.

higher-bandwidth network access with lower power usage, and to offload data traffic from macrocells. The commercial deployment of small-cells has attracted increasing attention in recent years. For example, AT&T Inc. now supplies a femtocell product [1], and it has also deployed WiFi APs in a number of metropolitan areas with dense population [2].

In the presence of multiple tiers of cells, however, mobile UEs may experience internetworking issues among different tiers. In particular, vertical handoffs (i.e., handoffs made between two BSs in different tiers) are introduced [41]. Compared with horizontal handoffs (i.e., handoffs made between two BSs in the same tier), vertical handoffs have a more complicated impact on both the UEs and the overall system. Additional risks are present during channel setup and tear down when a vertical handoff is made, such as (1) extra traffic latency; (2) additional network signaling; (3) more UE power consumption due to simultaneously active network interface to multiple tiers; and (4) higher risk in call drops or degraded quality of service (QoS) caused by the lack of radio resource after handoffs. Furthermore, vertical handoffs may be classified into inter-RAT (radio access technology) handoffs (e.g., handoffs made between LTE access and WiFi access) and intra-RAT handoffs, where the former could cause worse performance degradation on UEs [3].

The handoff rate is defined as the expected number of handoffs experienced by one UE per unit time, which directly affects the signaling overhead in the system and QoS of UEs. As a prerequisite to performance evaluation and system design in heterogeneous cellular networks, it is essential to quantify the rates of different handoff types. However, a study on handoff rates in heterogeneous cellular networks will inevitably be challenged by the irregularly shaped multi-tier network topologies introduced by the small-cell structure. An example topology with three tiers of BSs is shown in Fig. 1. First, BSs are spread irregularly, sometimes in an anywhere plug-and-play manner, leading to a high level of spatial randomness. Second, different tiers of cells are equipped with BSs communicating at different power levels, causing various scales of cell sizes. As a consequence, it is difficult to characterize the cell boundaries and to track boundary crossings made by UEs (i.e., handoffs) in the system. Few previous works have resolved the above challenges.

In this work, we contribute to user mobility modeling by providing new technical tools to quantify the rates of horizontal and vertical handoffs, under random multi-tier BSs, arbitrary user movement trajectory, and flexible user-BS association. A new stochastic geometric analysis framework on user mobility is proposed. In this framework, different tiers of BSs are modeled as Poisson point processes (PPPs) to capture their spatial randomness. To model flexible scaling of cell sizes in different tiers, we consider the biased user association scheme [10, 27, 32, 40], in which each tier of BSs is assigned an association bias value, and a UE is associated with a BS that provides the largest biased received power. Through stochastic and analytic geometric analysis, we derive exact expressions for the rates of all handoff types experienced by an active UE with arbitrary movement trajectory.

We confirm our theoretical analysis through an empirical study using the Yonsei Trace [17]. The trace provides a large data set, accumulating fine-grained mobility data from commercial mobile phones in an 8-month period. Numerical studies using the empirical trace data set, together with further simulation, demonstrate the correctness and usefulness of our analytical conclusions.

The rest of the paper is organized as follows. In Section 2, we discuss the relation between our work and prior works. In Section 3, we describe the system model. In Section 4, we present our contributions in handoff rates derivations. In Section 5, we present empirical study with the Yonsei Trace as well as simulation. Finally, conclusions are given in Section 6.

2. RELATED WORKS

2.1 Mobility Modeling Based on Queueing Systems

One common category of previous works employ queueing systems to model heterogeneous cellular networks. In this case, cells are modeled as queues, active users are modeled as units in the queues, and handoffs correspond to unit transfers among queues. Ghosh et al. [22] studied the single-cell scenario using an $M/G/\infty$ queue. Kirsal et al. [28] studied one WLAN cell overlaying one 3G cell, and a two-queue model is proposed accordingly. For multicell scenarios, queueing network models have been employed in [6, 9, 15, 19, 35]. However, none of these works explicitly

modeled the geometric patterns of cell shapes in heterogeneous networks.

2.2 Geometric Pattern Study

In order to characterize the geometric patterns of cellular network topologies, a second category of works model the shape of cells, mostly in non-random regular grids. Zonoozi and Dassanayake [45] modeled a one-tier cellular network as a hexagonal grid. Anpalagan and Katzela [4] studied a two-tier cellular network by modeling small-cells as hexagons, and each macrocell as a cluster of neighbouring small-cells. Shenoy and Hartpence [38] studied a two-tier network by modeling WLAN small-cells as squares, and macrocells as larger squares, each covering 5×5 WLAN cells. Hasib and Fapojuwo [24] studied a two-tier cellular network including one hexagonal macrocell and a predetermined N circular microcells. Lin et al. [31] conducted a pioneering study on the user mobility in one-tier macro cellular network considering randomly distributed BSs. Macrocells were modeled as a standard Poisson Voronoi. However, in [31], the authors did not consider multi-tier BSs with different scales of cell sizes. To the best of our knowledge, ours is the first work studying user mobility in *multi-tier* heterogeneous cellular networks that captures their *random* geometric patterns.

2.3 Real-world Trace Study

Another important category of related works employ empirical traces to investigate user mobility. Kotz et al. [25, 29] studied user mobility patterns on the Dartmouth campus. McNett and Voelker [34] characterized the mobility and access patterns of hand-held PDA users on the UCSD campus, and a campus waypoint model was proposed to characterize the trace. Halepovic and Williamson [23] studied mobility parameters such as the number of calls initiated per user, call inter-arrival time, and the number of cell sites visited per user, based on data traffic traces of a regional CDMA2000 cellular network. Rhee et al. [37] concluded that human walk patterns contain statistically similar features observed in Levy walks, based on a large daily GPS trace set accumulated in 5 different places in US and Korea. In [16], empirical study on spatial and temporal mobility patterns of the Yonsei Trace [17] was conducted, in order to predict users' future position precisely. Ficek and Kencl [21] proposed inter-call mobility model to locate users' position between calls based on the trace accumulated in a trip between San Jose and San Francisco. Baumann et al. [11] predicted user arrival and residence times in the system through extracting important parameters from the trace accumulated by Nokia Research.

These works based on real-world traces study are practically valuable for system evaluation and design. However, they are insufficient to provide in-depth analytical modeling of handoff and data rates. In our work, we use the Yonsei Trace [16, 17] to demonstrate the correctness and usefulness of our theoretical results.

2.4 Handoff and Association Decision Algorithms

Orthogonal to the scope of this work, there is a large body of previous works that study handoff timing algorithms, without considering the random geometric patterns of UEs and BSs. One type of handoff decision algorithms employ a threshold comparison of one or several specific metrics, (e.g., received signal strength, network loading, bandwidth, and so on) to derive handoff decisions [30, 33, 36, 44]. Another type uses dynamic programming (DP) [42] or artificial intelligence techniques (e.g., fuzzy logic [26]) to improve the effectiveness of handoff procedures.

3. SYSTEM MODEL

3.1 Multi-tier Cellular Network

We consider a heterogeneous cellular network with spatially randomly distributed K tiers of BSs. Let $\mathcal{K} = \{1, 2, \ldots, K\}$. In order to characterize the random spatial patterns of BSs, we use the conventional assumption that each tier of BSs independently form a homogeneous Poisson point process (PPP) in two-dimensional Euclidean space $\mathbb{R}^2$ [7, 8, 18, 27, 32, 39, 40]. Let Φ_k denote the PPP corresponding to tier-k BSs, and let λ_k be its intensity.

3.2 Biased User Association

Different tiers of BSs transmit at different power levels. Let P_k be the transmission power of tier-k BSs, which is a given parameter. If $P_t(\mathbf{x})$, for $P_t(\mathbf{x}) \in \{P_1, P_2, \ldots, P_K\}$, is the transmission power from a BS at $\mathbf{x}$ and $P_r(\mathbf{y})$ is the received power at $\mathbf{y}$, we have $P_r(\mathbf{y}) = \frac{P_t(\mathbf{x})}{\alpha|\mathbf{x}-\mathbf{y}|^\gamma}$, where $\alpha|\mathbf{x} - \mathbf{y}|^\gamma$ is the propagation loss function with $\gamma > 2$.

In order to capture various scales of different cell sizes, the biased user association is studied in this work [27, 32, 40]. Given that a UE is located at $\mathbf{y}$, it associates itself with the BS that provides the maximum *biased received power* as follows:

$$\mathcal{BS}(\mathbf{y}) = \arg \max_{\mathbf{x} \in \Phi_k, \forall k} B_k P_k |\mathbf{x} - \mathbf{y}|^{-\gamma}, \quad (1)$$

where $\mathcal{BS}(\mathbf{y})$ denotes the location of the BS chosen for the UE, $P_k|\mathbf{x} - \mathbf{y}|^{-\gamma}$ is the received power from a tier-k BS located at $\mathbf{x}$, and B_k is the association bias, indicating the received power preference of UEs toward tier-k BSs. B_k may be different in different tiers, mainly because (1) different radio access technologies may require different received power levels, and (2) some tiers could be assigned larger values of B_k, in order to offload data traffic from other tiers. As a consequence, the resultant cell splitting forms a generalized Dirichlet tessellation, or weighted Poisson Voronoi [5], an example of which is shown in Fig. 1. Let $\mathbf{T}^{(1)}$ denote the overall cell boundaries, and let $\mathbf{T}_{kj}^{(1)}$ denote the boundaries of tier-k cells and tier-j cells, which is also referred to as *type k-j cell boundaries* in this paper. Note that $\mathbf{T}_{kj}^{(1)}$ and $\mathbf{T}_{jk}^{(1)}$ are equivalent (type k-j cell boundaries and type j-k cell boundaries are equivalent).

Note that for $B_1, B_2, \ldots, B_K$, their effects remain the same if we multiply all of them by a same positive constant. For presentation convenience, we define $\beta_{kj} = \left(\frac{P_k B_k}{P_j B_j}\right)^{1/\gamma}$. Clearly, $\beta_{kj} = \frac{1}{\beta_{jk}}$.

Let A_k denote the probability that a UE associates itself with a tier-k BS. As derived in [27], we have

$$A_k = \frac{\lambda_k (P_k B_k)^{\frac{2}{\gamma}}}{\sum_{j=1}^K \lambda_j (P_j B_j)^{\frac{2}{\gamma}}}. \quad (2)$$

3.3 UE Trajectory and Handoff Rate

We aim to study the rates of all types of handoffs of some active UE moving in the network. Let $\mathcal{T}_0$ denote the tra-

jectory of the UE, which is of finite length. The number of handoffs the UE experiences is equal to the number of intersections of $\mathcal{T}_0$ and $\mathbf{T}^{(1)}$, which is denoted by $\mathcal{N}(\mathcal{T}_0, \mathbf{T}^{(1)})$. In this paper, a handoff made from a tier-k cell to a tier-j cell is called a *type k-j handoff*. The number of type k-j handoffs is denoted by $\mathcal{N}_{kj}(\mathcal{T}_0, \mathbf{T}_{kj}^{(1)})$.

If $j \neq k$, a type k-j (vertical) handoff is **not** equivalent to a type j-k handoff. When the UE crosses type k-j boundary, either a type k-j or a type j-k handoff is made, depending on the moving direction. Thus, the number of type k-j plus type j-k handoffs is equal to the number of intersections of $\mathcal{T}_0$ and $\mathbf{T}_{kj}^{(1)}$, which is denoted by $\mathcal{N}(\mathcal{T}_0, \mathbf{T}_{kj}^{(1)})$. In other words, we have $\mathcal{N}(\mathcal{T}_0, \mathbf{T}_{kj}^{(1)}) = \mathcal{N}_{kj}(\mathcal{T}_0, \mathbf{T}_{kj}^{(1)}) + \mathcal{N}_{jk}(\mathcal{T}_0, \mathbf{T}_{kj}^{(1)})$.

If $j = k$, $\mathcal{N}(\mathcal{T}_0, \mathbf{T}_{kk}^{(1)}) = \mathcal{N}_{kk}(\mathcal{T}_0, \mathbf{T}_{kk}^{(1)})$ indicates the number of type k-k (horizontal) handoffs.

In Section 4, we aim to study all types of handoff rates, which correspond to the expected numbers of handoffs experienced by the active UE per unit time.

4. HANDOFF RATE ANALYSIS IN MULTI-TIER CELLULAR NETWORKS

The proposed analysis of handoff rates consists of a progressive sequence of four components, which are described in the following subsections.

4.1 Length Intensity of Cell Boundaries

Handoffs occur at the intersections of the active UE's trajectory with cell boundaries. In order to track the number of intersections, we need to first study the length intensity of cell boundaries $\mathbf{T}^{(1)}$ (resp. $\mathbf{T}_{kj}^{(1)}$), which is defined as the expected length of $\mathbf{T}^{(1)}$ (resp. $\mathbf{T}_{kj}^{(1)}$) in a unit square. Higher length intensity of cell boundaries leads to greater opportunities for boundary crossing, and thus higher handoff rates.

The cell boundaries $\mathbf{T}^{(1)}$ is a fiber process [43] generated by $\Phi_1, \Phi_2, \ldots, \Phi_K$. $\mathbf{T}^{(1)}$ also corresponds to the set of points on $\mathbb{R}^2$, where a same biased power level is received from two nearby BSs, and this biased received power level is no less than those from any other BSs. Mathematically, we have

$$\mathbf{T}^{(1)} = \left\{ \mathbf{x} \,\middle|\, \forall k, j \in \mathcal{K}, \exists \mathbf{x}_1 \in \Phi_k, \mathbf{x}_2 \in \Phi_j, \mathbf{x}_1 \neq \mathbf{x}_2, \right.$$
$$\text{s.t. } P_r = \frac{P_k B_k}{|\mathbf{x}_1 - \mathbf{x}|^\gamma} = \frac{P_j B_j}{|\mathbf{x}_2 - \mathbf{x}|^\gamma}, \text{ and}$$
$$\left. \forall i \in \mathcal{K}, \mathbf{y} \in \Phi_i, P_r \geq \frac{P_i B_i}{|\mathbf{y} - \mathbf{x}|^\gamma} \right\}. \quad (3)$$

Similarly, $\mathbf{T}_{kj}^{(1)}$ can be expressed as

$$\mathbf{T}_{kj}^{(1)} = \left\{ \mathbf{x} \,\middle|\, \exists \mathbf{x}_1 \in \Phi_k, \mathbf{x}_2 \in \Phi_j, \mathbf{x}_1 \neq \mathbf{x}_2, \right.$$
$$\text{s.t. } P_r = \frac{P_k B_k}{|\mathbf{x}_1 - \mathbf{x}|^\gamma} = \frac{P_j B_j}{|\mathbf{x}_2 - \mathbf{x}|^\gamma}, \text{ and}$$
$$\left. \forall i \in \mathcal{K}, \mathbf{y} \in \Phi_i, P_r \geq \frac{P_i B_i}{|\mathbf{y} - \mathbf{x}|^\gamma} \right\}. \quad (4)$$

Note that $\bigcup_{k=1}^K \bigcup_{j=k}^K \mathbf{T}_{kj}^{(1)} = \mathbf{T}^{(1)}$.

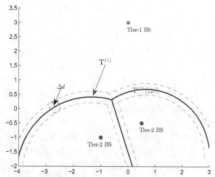

Figure 2: The blue bold curves show $\mathbf{T}^{(1)}$; and the region within red dashed curves shows $\mathbf{T}^{(2)}(\Delta d)$.

Let $\mu_1\big(\mathbf{T}^{(1)}\big)$ denote the length intensity of $\mathbf{T}^{(1)}$, which is the expected length of $\mathbf{T}^{(1)}$ in a unit square[1] [43]:

$$\mu_1\big(\mathbf{T}^{(1)}\big) = \mathbb{E}\left(\left|\mathbf{T}^{(1)}\bigcap [0,1)^2\right|_1\right), \tag{5}$$

where $|L|_1$ denotes the length of L (i.e., one-dimensional Lebesgue measure of L). Similarly, let $\mu_1\big(\mathbf{T}_{kj}^{(1)}\big)$ denote the length intensity of $\mathbf{T}_{kj}^{(1)}$:

$$\mu_1\big(\mathbf{T}_{kj}^{(1)}\big) = \mathbb{E}\left(\left|\mathbf{T}_{kj}^{(1)}\bigcap [0,1)^2\right|_1\right). \tag{6}$$

Note that we have $\mu_1\big(\mathbf{T}^{(1)}\big) = \sum_{k=1}^{K}\sum_{j=k}^{K}\mu_1\big(\mathbf{T}_{kj}^{(1)}\big)$.

4.2 Δd-Extended Cell Boundaries

It is difficult to directly quantify the one-dimensional measures $\mu_1\big(\mathbf{T}^{(1)}\big)$ and $\mu_1\big(\mathbf{T}_{kj}^{(1)}\big)$ on the two-dimensional plane. Instead, we first introduce the Δd-extended cell boundaries, which extends the one-dimensional measures to two-dimensional measures.

The Δd-extended cell boundaries of $\mathbf{T}^{(1)}$, denoted by $\mathbf{T}^{(2)}(\Delta d)$ is defined as

$$\mathbf{T}^{(2)}(\Delta d) = \left\{\mathbf{x}\,\middle|\,\exists \mathbf{y}\in\mathbf{T}^{(1)},\text{ s.t. } |\mathbf{x}-\mathbf{y}| < \Delta d\right\}. \tag{7}$$

In other words, $\mathbf{T}^{(2)}(\Delta d)$ is the Δd-neighbourhood of $\mathbf{T}^{(1)}$. A point is in $\mathbf{T}^{(2)}(\Delta d)$ iff its (shortest) distance to $\mathbf{T}^{(1)}$ is less than Δd, as shown in Fig. 2. Similarly, we define $\mathbf{T}_{kj}^{(2)}(\Delta d)$ as the Δd-extended cell boundaries of $\mathbf{T}_{kj}^{(1)}$ (i.e., Δd-neighbourhood of $\mathbf{T}_{kj}^{(1)}$):

$$\mathbf{T}_{kj}^{(2)}(\Delta d) = \left\{\mathbf{x}\,\middle|\,\exists \mathbf{y}\in\mathbf{T}_{kj}^{(1)},\text{ s.t. } |\mathbf{x}-\mathbf{y}| < \Delta d\right\}. \tag{8}$$

The area intensity of $\mathbf{T}^{(2)}(\Delta d)$ is defined as the expected area of $\mathbf{T}^{(2)}(\Delta d)$ in a unit square:

$$\mu_2\big(\mathbf{T}^{(2)}(\Delta d)\big) = \mathbb{E}\left(\left|\mathbf{T}^{(2)}(\Delta d)\bigcap [0,1)^2\right|\right), \tag{9}$$

where $|S|$ denotes the area of S (i.e., two-dimensional Lebesgue measure of S). Similarly, the area intensity of $\mathbf{T}_{kj}^{(2)}(\Delta d)$ is

$$\mu_2\big(\mathbf{T}_{kj}^{(2)}(\Delta d)\big) = \mathbb{E}\left(\left|\mathbf{T}_{kj}^{(2)}(\Delta d)\bigcap [0,1)^2\right|\right). \tag{10}$$

[1]Because $\Phi_1,\ldots,\Phi_K$ are stationary, $\mathbf{T}^{(1)}$ is also stationary, and thus the unit square could be arbitrarily picked on $\mathbb{R}^2$.

Because $\Phi_1,\Phi_2\ldots,\Phi_K$ are stationary and isotropic, $\mathbf{T}^{(2)}(\Delta d)$ and $\mathbf{T}_{kj}^{(2)}(\Delta d)$ are also stationary and isotropic. As a result, given a reference UE located at $\mathbf{0}$, the area intensity of $\mathbf{T}^{(2)}(\Delta d)$ (resp. $\mathbf{T}_{kj}^{(2)}(\Delta d)$) is equal to the probability that the reference UE at $\mathbf{0}$ is in $\mathbf{T}^{(2)}(\Delta d)$ (resp. $\mathbf{T}_{kj}^{(2)}(\Delta d)$).

$$\mu_2\big(\mathbf{T}^{(2)}(\Delta d)\big) = \mathbb{P}(\mathbf{0}\in\mathbf{T}^{(2)}(\Delta d)), \tag{11}$$

$$\mu_2\big(\mathbf{T}_{kj}^{(2)}(\Delta d)\big) = \mathbb{P}(\mathbf{0}\in\mathbf{T}_{kj}^{(2)}(\Delta d)). \tag{12}$$

We observe that the probabilities in (11) and (12) are analytically tractable, which will be presented in the next subsection.

4.3 Derivations of the Area Intensities

In this subsection, we present the derivations of $\mathbb{P}(\mathbf{0}\in\mathbf{T}^{(2)}(\Delta d))$ and $\mathbb{P}(\mathbf{0}\in\mathbf{T}_{kj}^{(2)}(\Delta d))$. First, we study the probability that the reference UE at $\mathbf{0}$ is in $\mathbf{T}_{kj}^{(2)}(\Delta d)$, given that it is associated to a tier-k BS at a distance of r_0 from it. By employing both analytic geometric and stochastic geometric tools, we derive the following theorem:

THEOREM 1. *Suppose the reference UE is located at $\mathbf{0}$, it is associated with a tier-k BS, and their distance is R. The conditional probability that $\mathbf{0}\in\mathbf{T}_{kj}^{(2)}(\Delta d)$ given $R = r_0$ is*

$$\mathbb{P}\left(\mathbf{0}\in\mathbf{T}_{kj}^{(2)}(\Delta d)\middle| R = r_0, \text{tier} = k\right) =$$
$$1 - \exp\left(-2\lambda_j\Delta dr_0\mathcal{F}(\beta_{kj}) + \mathcal{O}(\Delta d^2)\right), \tag{13}$$

where

$$\mathcal{F}(\beta) \triangleq \frac{1}{\beta^2}\int_0^\pi\sqrt{(\beta^2+1)-2\beta\cos(\theta)}\mathrm{d}\theta. \tag{14}$$

The proof is omitted due to the limited space.

Second, through stochastic geometric tools and deconditioning on R, we can derive the unconditioned probabilities that the reference UE at $\mathbf{0}$ is in $\mathbf{T}^{(2)}(\Delta d)$ and in $\mathbf{T}_{kj}^{(2)}(\Delta d)$:

THEOREM 2. *The area intensities of $\mathbf{T}^{(2)}(\Delta d)$ and $\mathbf{T}_{kj}^{(2)}(\Delta d)$ are:*
(a)

$$\mu_2\big(\mathbf{T}^{(2)}(\Delta d)\big) = \mathbb{P}(\mathbf{0}\in\mathbf{T}^{(2)}(\Delta d))$$
$$= \sum_{k=1}^{K}\frac{\lambda_k\left(\sum_{i=1}^{K}\lambda_i\Delta d\mathcal{F}(\beta_{ki})\right)}{\left(\sum_{i=1}^{K}\lambda_i\beta_{ik}^2\right)^{\frac{3}{2}}} + \mathcal{O}(\Delta d^2). \tag{15}$$

(b)

$$\mu_2\big(\mathbf{T}_{kj}^{(2)}(\Delta d)\big) = \mathbb{P}\left(\mathbf{0}\in\mathbf{T}_{kj}^{(2)}(\Delta d)\right)$$

$$= \begin{cases} \frac{\lambda_k\left(\lambda_j\Delta d\mathcal{F}(\beta_{kj})\right)}{\left(\sum_{i=1}^{K}\lambda_i\beta_{ik}^2\right)^{\frac{3}{2}}} + \frac{\lambda_j\left(\lambda_k\Delta d\mathcal{F}(\beta_{jk})\right)}{\left(\sum_{i=1}^{K}\lambda_i\beta_{ij}^2\right)^{\frac{3}{2}}} + \mathcal{O}(\Delta d^2) & \text{if } k\neq j, \\ \frac{\lambda_k^2\Delta d\mathcal{F}(1)}{\left(\sum_{i=1}^{K}\lambda_i\beta_{ik}^2\right)^{\frac{3}{2}}} + \mathcal{O}(\Delta d^2) & \text{if } k = j. \end{cases} \tag{16}$$

See Appendix for the proof.

4.4 From Area Intensities to Handoff Rates

In this subsection, we derive handoff rates from area intensities derived in Theorem 2. This involves two steps:

(1) from area intensities $\mu_2\big(\mathbf{T}^{(2)}(\Delta d)\big)$ and $\mu_2\big(\mathbf{T}_{kj}^{(2)}(\Delta d)\big)$ to length intensities $\mu_1\big(\mathbf{T}^{(1)}\big)$ and $\mu_1\big(\mathbf{T}_{kj}^{(1)}\big)$, and (2) from length intensities to handoff rates.

First, we derive the length intensity $\mu_1\big(\mathbf{T}^{(1)}\big)$ (resp. $\mu_1\big(\mathbf{T}_{kj}^{(1)}\big)$) from the area intensity $\mu_2\big(\mathbf{T}^{(2)}(\Delta d)\big)$ (resp. $\mu_2\big(\mathbf{T}_{kj}^{(2)}(\Delta d)\big)$) as follows

THEOREM 3. *The length intensities of* $\mathbf{T}^{(1)}$ *and* $\mathbf{T}_{kj}^{(1)}$ *can be computed as follows:*

(a)

$$\mu_1\big(\mathbf{T}^{(1)}\big) = \sum_{k=1}^{K} \frac{\lambda_k \left(\sum_{i=1}^{K} \lambda_i \mathcal{F}(\beta_{ki})\right)}{2\left(\sum_{i=1}^{K} \lambda_i \beta_{ik}^2\right)^{\frac{3}{2}}}. \tag{17}$$

(b)

$$\mu_1\big(\mathbf{T}_{kj}^{(1)}\big) = \begin{cases} \frac{\lambda_k \lambda_j \mathcal{F}(\beta_{kj})}{2\left(\sum_{i=1}^{K} \lambda_i \beta_{ik}^2\right)^{\frac{3}{2}}} + \frac{\lambda_j \lambda_k \mathcal{F}(\beta_{jk})}{2\left(\sum_{i=1}^{K} \lambda_i \beta_{ij}^2\right)^{\frac{3}{2}}} & \text{if } k \neq j, \\ \frac{\lambda_k^2 \mathcal{F}(1)}{2\left(\sum_{i=1}^{K} \lambda_i \beta_{ik}^2\right)^{\frac{3}{2}}} & \text{if } k = j. \end{cases} \tag{18}$$

PROOF. It follows Section 3.2 in [20] and [13] by taking $\Delta d \to 0$. $\square$

REMARK 1. *Note that, if we consider the single-tier case by taking $K = 1$, we have $\mathcal{F}(1) = 4$, and $\mu_1\big(\mathbf{T}^{(1)}\big) = \mu_1\big(\mathbf{T}_{11}^{(1)}\big) = 2\sqrt{\lambda_1}$. This matches the length intensity of a standard Poisson Voronoi. See Section 10.6 of [43].*

Second, we can derive the expected number of handoffs of an active UE as follows:

THEOREM 4. *Let $\mathcal{T}_0$ denote an arbitrary UE's trajectory on $\mathbb{R}^2$ with length $|\mathcal{T}_0|_1$. Then, the expected number of intersections of $\mathcal{T}_0$ and $\mathbf{T}^{(1)}$ (resp. $\mathbf{T}_{kj}^{(1)}$) are*

$$\mathbb{E}\left(\mathcal{N}(\mathcal{T}_0, \mathbf{T}^{(1)})\right) = \frac{2}{\pi} \mu_1\big(\mathbf{T}^{(1)}\big)|\mathcal{T}_0|_1, \tag{19}$$

$$\mathbb{E}\left(\mathcal{N}(\mathcal{T}_0, \mathbf{T}_{kj}^{(1)})\right) = \frac{2}{\pi} \mu_1\big(\mathbf{T}_{kj}^{(1)}\big)|\mathcal{T}_0|_1, \tag{20}$$

and the expected number of type k-j handoffs are

$$\mathbb{E}\left(\mathcal{N}_{kj}(\mathcal{T}_0, \mathbf{T}_{kj}^{(1)})\right) = \begin{cases} \frac{1}{2}\mathbb{E}\left(\mathcal{N}(\mathcal{T}_0, \mathbf{T}_{kj}^{(1)})\right) & \text{if } k \neq j, \\ \mathbb{E}\left(\mathcal{N}(\mathcal{T}_0, \mathbf{T}_{kj}^{(1)})\right) & \text{if } k = j. \end{cases} \tag{21}$$

PROOF. $\mathbf{T}^{(1)}$ and $\mathbf{T}_{kj}^{(1)}$ are stationary and isotropic fibre processes with length intensity $\mu_1\big(\mathbf{T}^{(1)}\big)$ and $\mu_1\big(\mathbf{T}_{kj}^{(1)}\big)$ respectively. The proof follows the conclusions in Section 9.3 of [43]. $\square$

Note that the expected number of type k-j handoffs is the same as the expected number of type j-k handoffs, both of which are equal to half of $\mathbb{E}\left(\mathcal{N}(\mathcal{T}_0, \mathbf{T}_{kj}^{(1)})\right)$.

Let v denote the instantaneous velocity of an active UE, $H(v)$ denote its overall handoff rate (i.e., sum handoff rate of all types), and $H_{kj}(v)$ denote its type k-j handoff rate. Then we have the following Corollary from Theorem 4:

COROLLARY 1.

$$H(v) = \frac{2}{\pi} \mu_1\big(\mathbf{T}^{(1)}\big) v, \tag{22}$$

$$H_{kj}(v) = \begin{cases} \frac{1}{\pi} \mu_1\big(\mathbf{T}_{kj}^{(1)}\big) v & \text{if } k \neq j, \\ \frac{2}{\pi} \mu_1\big(\mathbf{T}_{kj}^{(1)}\big) v & \text{if } k = j. \end{cases} \tag{23}$$

Note that the above handoff rates are instantaneous rates. Our analysis allows time-varying velocity for the UEs, in which case the handoff rates are also time varying.

5. EXPERIMENTAL STUDY

In this section, our analysis is validated via experimenting with real-world traces and simulations.

5.1 Yonsei Trace Data

We use the real-world Yonsei Trace [17] to validate our analytical results. The trace was accumulated from 12 commercial mobile phones during an 8-month period in 2011 in the city of Seoul. An application named SmartDC had been running on the commercial mobile phones equipped with GPS, GSM, and WiFi. For every 2 to 5 minutes, the application collected UE's location information (latitude and longitude), the MAC addresses of surrounding WiFi APs, and the cell IDs of nearby cellular BSs they could detect. Each AP has a unique MAC address and each BS has a unique cell ID. By analyzing the data set, we are able to determine which APs and BSs a UE could detect at the recorded coordinates and time instants. In the following, we regard cellular BSs as tier-1 BSs and APs as tier-2 BSs.

5.2 Data Processing

5.2.1 Location Approximations of APs and BSs

As the data set does not explicitly provide the latitudes and longitudes of APs and BSs, we apply the following approach to approximate their locations: for each AP (resp. BS), we list all the coordinates recorded by UEs when they are able to detect the AP (resp. BS). Then, we approximate the location of the AP (resp. BS), by taking the average of these recorded coordinates.

5.2.2 Reference Region

In order to avoid the edge effect, we define a reference region, in which most recorded coordinates are located. The UEs' trajectories are only accounted inside the reference region. By plotting the cumulative distribution function (cdf) of the latitude (resp. longitude) of all recorded coordinates, we observe a sharp step upward between $37.48^\circ N$ and $37.58^\circ N$ (resp. $126.9^\circ E$ and $127.1^\circ E$). As a consequence, we employ the rectangle defined by $37.48^\circ N$, and $37.58^\circ N$, $126.9^\circ E$, and $127.1^\circ E$ as the reference region.

5.2.3 UE Trajectory

In the trace data, the coordinates of a UE are recorded only once every few minutes. To recover its full trajectory, we regard it as moving in a straight line at a constant velocity between two consecutive recorded coordinates. Thus, interpolations can be made to determine the coordinate of the UE at any time. Note that only the trajectories inside the reference region are used.

5.2.4 Handoff Rates

Through the locations of BSs and APs, as well as the UE trajectories, we are able to derive all types of empirical handoff rates following the biased user association scheme discussed in Section 3.2. If we ignore all the APs, we can also derive the empirical handoff rates for one-tier case.

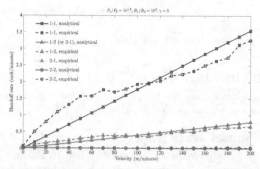

Figure 3: Two-tier case: comparison of analytical and empirical handoff rates.

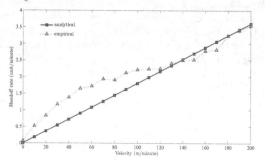

Figure 4: One-tier case: comparison of analytical and empirical handoff rates.

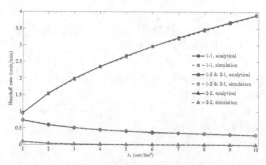

Figure 5: Two-tier case: handoff rates under different λ_1.

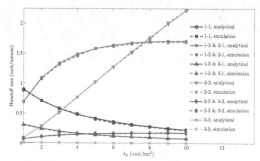

Figure 6: Three-tier case: handoff rates under different λ_2.

5.2.5 BS and AP Intensities

The AP (resp. BS) density is computed as the number of APs (resp. BSs) over the area of the reference region, which is 455.1 unit/km^2 (resp. 52.6 unit/km^2). This indicates an urban area with high population and BS densities.

5.3 Empirical Results

We compare the handoff rates derived from our analysis and those from our empirical study based on the Yonsei Trace. The empirical handoff rates are derived from the steps in Sections 5.2.1 - 5.2.4. For the analytical results, we use the BS and AP intensities shown in Section 5.2.5 as input parameters.

For the two-tier case, the comparison of analytical and empirical handoff rates is shown in Fig. 3. For the one-tier case (by eliminating all the APs), the comparison is shown in Fig. 4. Both figures illustrate the accuracy of our analysis. When the UE's velocity is low, empirical handoff rates are slightly greater than analytical handoff rates. This is because the locations of APs and BSs are not strictly homogeneous distributed (e.g., some APs and BSs are crowded along some streets, or at the center of the urban region). We also observe that UEs with lower velocity are more likely to be sampled in the region with higher AP and BS densities. As a consequence, the empirical handoff rates are higher than those expected by our analytical results.

Fig. 3 and Fig. 4 also show that type 1-1 horizontal handoff rates are almost the same in the one-tier and two-tier cases, but extra type 1-2 and type 2-1 vertical handoffs are introduced in the two-tier case. This agrees with our expectation that adding a second tier of APs brings more vertical handoffs. In addition, as a validation of (21), type 1-2 and type 2-1 handoff rates are almost the same in empirical results.

5.4 Simulation Study

In this subsection, we present simulation results to further demonstrate our analysis in more complex heterogeneous cellular networks.

5.4.1 Simulation Setup

The simulation procedure is as follows: in each round of simulation, two or three tiers of BSs are generated on a 10 km × 10 km square. Then, we randomly generate 5 waypoints $X_1, \ldots, X_5$ in the central 5 km × 5 km square (uniformly distributed). The five line segments $X_1X_2, X_2X_3, \ldots, X_4X_5$ construct the trajectory of an active UE. In this way, we derive the simulated handoff rates in this round of simulation. The above procedure is repeated 200 rounds to derive one simulated data point. Note that in this subsection, in order to avoid overlapping in figures, we only show the sum rate of type j-k and type k-j ($k \neq j$) handoffs for easier inspection; the individual handoff rates are half of the sum handoff rate.

5.4.2 Handoff Rates under Different BS Intensities

We study handoff rates under different BS intensities. Fig. 5 shows a two-tier case, with parameters as follows: $P_1 = 30$ dBm, $P_2 = 20$ dBm, and $B_1 = B_2 = 1$, $\lambda_2 = 1$ unit/km^2. Fig. 6 shows a three-tier case, with parameters as follows: $P_1 = 30$ dBm, $P_2 = 20$ dBm, $P_3 = 10$ dBm, $B_1 = B_2 = B_3 = 1$, and $\lambda_1 = \lambda_3 = 1$ unit/km^2. The parameter values $\gamma = 3$ and $v = 60$ km/h are used for both Fig. 5 and Fig. 6.

Fig. 5 illustrates that increasing λ_1 leads to higher type $1-1$ handoff rate but lower type $2-2$ handoff rate. Fig. 6 illustrates that increasing λ_2 leads to higher type $2-2$ handoff rate but lower type $1-1$ and $1-3$ & $3-1$ handoff rates. Both observations suggest that increasing the BS intensity

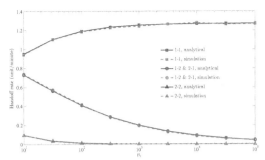

Figure 7: Two-tier case: handoff rates under different B_1.

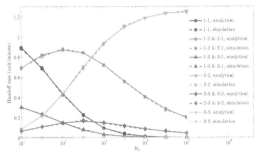

Figure 8: Three-tier case: handoff rates under different B_2.

of one tier causes higher horizontal handoff rate within this tier, but lower handoff rates outside this tier.

5.4.3 Handoff Rates under Different Association Bias Values

Next, we study handoff rates under different association bias values. Fig. 7 shows a two-tier case, with parameters as follows: $P_1 = 30$ dBm, $P_2 = 20$ dBm, $B_2 = 1$, and $\lambda_1 = \lambda_2 = 1$ unit/km^2. Fig. 8 shows a three-tier case, with parameters as follows: $P_1 = 30$ dBm, $P_2 = 20$ dBm, $P_3 = 10$ dBm, $B_1 = B_3 = 1$, $\lambda_1 = \lambda_2 = \lambda_3 = 1$ unit/km^2. The parameter values $\gamma = 3$ and $v = 60$ km/h are used for both Fig. 7 and Fig. 8. These figures suggest that, increasing the association bias value of one tier has a similar effect as increasing the BS intensity of this tier, leading to higher horizontal handoff rate within this tier, but lower handoff rates outside this tier.

6. CONCLUSIONS

In this work, we provide a theoretical framework to study user mobility in heterogeneous multi-tier cellular networks. Through establishing a stochastic geometric framework, we fully capture the irregularly shaped network topologies introduced by the small-cell structure. Theoretical expressions for the rates of all types of handoffs experienced by an active UE with arbitrary movement trajectory are derived. Empirical study on the Yonsei Trace and extensive simulation are conducted, validating the accuracy and usefulness of our analytical conclusions.

7. ACKNOWLEDGEMENTS

This work has been supported in part by grants from Bell Canada and the Natural Sciences and Engineering Research Council (NSERC) of Canada.

8. APPENDIX

Proof. (a) Let E_i denote the event that there is at least one tier-i BS located in $S_{ki}(\Delta d)$. Then

$$\mathbb{P}\left(\mathbf{0} \in \mathbf{T}^{(2)}(\Delta d) | R = r_0, \text{tier} = k\right)$$
$$= 1 - \mathbb{P}\left(\overline{E_1} \bigcap \overline{E_2} \bigcap \ldots \bigcap \overline{E_K} | R = r_0, \text{tier} = k\right)$$
$$= 1 - \exp\left(-\sum_{i=1}^{K} |S_{ki}(\Delta d)|\lambda_i\right)$$
$$= 1 - \exp\left(-\sum_{i=1}^{K} 2\lambda_i \Delta d r_0 \mathcal{F}(\beta_{ki}) + \mathcal{O}(\Delta d^2)\right)$$
$$= \sum_{i=1}^{K} 2\lambda_i \Delta d r_0 \mathcal{F}(\beta_{ki}) + \mathcal{O}(\Delta d^2). \quad (24)$$

Furthermore, according to the results in [27], the probability density function (pdf) of the distance between the reference UE and the reference BS is

$$f_k(r_0 | \text{tier} = k) = \frac{2\pi\lambda_k}{A_k} r_0 \exp\left(-\pi r_0^2 \sum_{i=1}^{K} \lambda_i \beta_{ik}^2\right). \quad (25)$$

Also, we have $\mathbb{P}(\text{tier} = k) = A_k$, thus

$$\mathbb{P}\left(\mathbf{0} \in \mathbf{T}^{(2)}(\Delta d)\right)$$
$$= \sum_{k=1}^{K} \int_0^\infty \mathbb{P}(\mathbf{0} \in \mathbf{T}^{(2)}(\Delta d) | R = r_0, \text{tier} = k)$$
$$\qquad \cdot f_k(r_0 | \text{tier} = k)\mathbb{P}(\text{tier} = k)dr_0$$
$$= \sum_{k=1}^{K} \int_0^\infty 2\pi\lambda_k r_0 \exp\left(-\pi r_0^2 \sum_{i=1}^{K} \lambda_i \beta_{ik}^2\right)$$
$$\qquad \cdot \left(\sum_{i=1}^{K} 2\lambda_i \Delta d r_0 \mathcal{F}(\beta_{ki}) + \mathcal{O}(\Delta d^2)\right)dr_0$$
$$= \sum_{k=1}^{K} \frac{\lambda_k \left(\sum_{i=1}^{K} \lambda_i \Delta d \mathcal{F}(\beta_{ki}) + \mathcal{O}(\Delta d^2)\right)}{\left(\sum_{i=1}^{K} \lambda_i \beta_{ik}^2\right)^{\frac{3}{2}}}, \quad (26)$$

which completes the proof of (a).

(b)
Similar to (26), if $k \neq j$ we have

$$\mathbb{P}\left(\mathbf{0} \in \mathbf{T}_{kj}^{(2)}(\Delta d)\right)$$
$$= \int_0^\infty \mathbb{P}(\mathbf{0} \in \mathbf{T}_{kj}^{(2)}(\Delta d) | R = r_0, \text{tier} = k)f_k(r_0 | \text{tier} = k)$$
$$\qquad \cdot \mathbb{P}(\text{tier} = k)dr_0$$
$$+ \int_0^\infty \mathbb{P}(\mathbf{0} \in \mathbf{T}_{kj}^{(2)}(\Delta d) | R = r_0, \text{tier} = j)f_j(r_0 | \text{tier} = j)$$
$$\qquad \cdot \mathbb{P}(\text{tier} = j)dr_0$$
$$= \frac{\lambda_k \left(\lambda_j \Delta d \mathcal{F}(\beta_{kj}) + \mathcal{O}(\Delta d^2)\right)}{\left(\sum_{i=1}^{K} \lambda_i \beta_{ik}^2\right)^{\frac{3}{2}}} + \frac{\lambda_j \left(\lambda_k \Delta d \mathcal{F}(\beta_{jk}) + \mathcal{O}(\Delta d^2)\right)}{\left(\sum_{i=1}^{K} \lambda_i \beta_{ij}^2\right)^{\frac{3}{2}}}. \quad (27)$$

Otherwise, if $k = j$ we have

$$\mathbb{P}\left(\mathbf{0} \in \mathbf{T}_{kk}^{(2)}(\Delta d)\right) = \frac{\lambda_k \left(\lambda_k \Delta d \mathcal{F}(1) + \mathcal{O}(\Delta d^2)\right)}{\left(\sum_{i=1}^{K} \lambda_i \beta_{ik}^2\right)^{\frac{3}{2}}}, \quad (28)$$

which completes the proof of (b). $\square$

9. REFERENCES

[1] AT&T 3G Microcell.
http://www.att.com/standalone/3gmicrocell.

[2] AT&T Wi-Fi hot spot locations.
https://www.att.com/maps/wifi.

[3] I. Akyildiz, J. Xie, and S. Mohanty. A survey of mobility management in next-generation all-IP-based wireless systems. *IEEE Wireless Communications*, 11(4):16–28, Aug. 2004.

[4] A. Anpalagan and I. Katzela. Overlaid cellular system design, with cell selection criteria for mobile wireless users. In *Proc. of IEEE Canadian Conference on Electrical and Computer Engineering*, Edmonton, Canada, May 1999.

[5] P. F. Ash and E. D. Bolker. Generalized Dirichlet tessellations. *Geometriae Dedicata*, 20(2):209–243, Apr. 1986.

[6] F. Ashtiani, J. Salehi, and M. Aref. Mobility modeling and analytical solution for spatial traffic distribution in wireless multimedia networks. *IEEE Journal on Selected Areas in Communications*, 21(10):1699 – 1709, Dec. 2003.

[7] F. Baccelli and B. Blaszczyszyn. Stochastic geometry and wireless networks, volume 1: Theory. *Foundations and Trends in Networking*, 3(3-4):249 – 449, 2009.

[8] F. Baccelli and B. Blaszczyszyn. Stochastic geometry and wireless networks, volume 2: Applications. *Foundations and Trends in Networking*, 4(1-2):1–312, 2009.

[9] W. Bao and B. Liang. Insensitivity of user distribution in multicell networks under general mobility and session patterns. *IEEE Trans. on Wireless Communications*, 12(12):6244–6254, Dec. 2013.

[10] W. Bao and B. Liang. Structured spectrum allocation and user association in heterogeneous cellular networks. In *Proc. of IEEE INFOCOM*, Toronto, Canada, Apr. 2014.

[11] P. Baumann, W. Kleiminger, and S. Santini. How long are you staying? predicting residence time from human mobility traces. In *Proc. of ACM MobiCom*, Miami, FL, Sep. 2013.

[12] M. Bennis, M. Simsek, A. Czylwik, W. Saad, S. Valentin, and M. Debbah. When cellular meets WiFi in wireless small cell networks. *IEEE Communications Magazine*, 51(6):44–50, Jun. 2013.

[13] A. Chambolle, S. Lisini, and L. Lussardi. A remark on the anisotropic outer Minkowski content. *Advances in Calculus of Variations*, 7(2):241–266, Apr. 2014.

[14] V. Chandrasekhar, J. Andrews, and A. Gatherer. Femtocell networks: a survey. *IEEE Communications Magazine*, 46(9):59–67, Sep. 2008.

[15] Y. Chen, J. Kurose, and D. Towsley. A mixed queueing network model of mobility in a campus wireless network. In *Proc. of IEEE INFOCOM*, Orlando, FL, Mar. 2012.

[16] Y. Chon, H. Shin, E. Talipov, and H. Cha. Evaluating mobility models for temporal prediction with high-granularity mobility data. In *Proc. of IEEE International Conference on Pervasive Computing and Communications (PerCom)*, Lugano, Switzerland, Mar. 2012.

[17] Y. Chon, E. Talipov, H. Shin, and H. Cha. Mobility data collected by Lifemap monitoring system at Yonsei University in Seoul. Downloaded from http://crawdad.cs.dartmouth.edu/yonsei/lifemap/, May 2012.

[18] H. Dhillon, R. Ganti, F. Baccelli, and J. G. Andrews. Modeling and analysis of K-tier downlink heterogeneous cellular networks. *IEEE Journal on Selected Areas in Communications*, 30(3):550–560, Apr. 2012.

[19] A. Farbod and B. Liang. Structured admission control policies in heterogeneous wireless networks with mesh underlay. In *Proc. of IEEE INFOCOM*, Rio de Janeiro, Brazil, Apr. 2009.

[20] H. Federer. *Geometric Measure Theory*. Springer, 1969.

[21] M. Ficek and L. Kencl. Inter-call mobility model: A spatio-temporal refinement of call data records using a Gaussian mixture model. In *Proc. of IEEE INFOCOM*, Orlando, FL, Mar. 2012.

[22] A. Ghosh, R. Jana, V. Ramaswami, J. Rowland, and N. Shankaranarayanan. Modeling and characterization of large-scale Wi-Fi traffic in public hot-spots. In *Proc. of IEEE INFOCOM*, Shanghai, China, Apr. 2011.

[23] E. Halepovic and C. Williamson. Characterizing and modeling user mobility in a cellular data network. In *Proc. of ACM PE-WASUN*, Montreal, Canada, Oct. 2005.

[24] A. Hasib and A. Fapojuwo. Mobility model for heterogeneous wireless networks and its application in common radio resource management. *IET Communications*, 2(9):1186–1195, Oct. 2008.

[25] T. Henderson, D. Kotz, and I. Abyzov. The changing usage of a mature campus-wide wireless network. In *Proc. of ACM MobiCom*, Philadelphia, PA, 2004.

[26] J. Hou and D. O'brien. Vertical handover-decision-making algorithm using fuzzy logic for the integrated radio-and-OW system. *IEEE Trans. on Wireless Communications*, 5(1):176–185, Jan. 2006.

[27] H.-S. Jo, Y. J. Sang, P. Xia, and J. G. Andrews. Heterogeneous cellular networks with flexible cell association: A comprehensive downlink SINR analysis. *IEEE Trans. on Wireless Communications*, 11(10):3484–3495, Oct. 2012.

[28] Y. Kirsal, E. Gemikonakli, E. Ever, G. Mapp, and O. Gemikonakli. An analytical approach for performance analysis of handoffs in the next generation integrated cellular networks and WLANs. In *Proc. of International Conference on Computer Communications and Networks*, Zurich, Switzerland, Aug. 2010.

[29] D. Kotz and K. Essien. Analysis of a campus-wide wireless network. In *Proc. of ACM MobiCom*, Atlanta, GA, Sep. 2002.

[30] C. W. Lee, L. M. Chen, M. C. Chen, and Y. S. Sun. A framework of handoffs in wireless overlay networks based on mobile IPv6. *IEEE Journal on Selected Areas in Communications*, 23(11):2118 – 2128, Nov. 2005.

[31] X. Lin, R. Ganti, P. Fleming, and J. Andrews. Towards understanding the fundamentals of mobility in cellular networks. *IEEE Trans. on Wireless Communications*, 12(4):1686–1698, Apr. 2013.

[32] Y. Lin and W. Yu. Optimizing user association and frequency reuse for heterogeneous network under stochastic model. In *Proc. of IEEE Globecom*, Atlanta, GA, Dec. 2013.

[33] M. Liu, Z. Li, X. Guo, and E. Dutkiewicz. Performance analysis and optimization of handoff algorithms in heterogeneous wireless networks. *IEEE Trans. on Mobile Computing*, 7(7):846–857, Jul. 2008.

[34] M. McNett and G. M. Voelker. Access and mobility of wireless pda users. *ACM SIGMOBILE Mobile Computing and Communications Review*, 9(2):40–55, Apr. 2005.

[35] G. Mohimani, F. Ashtiani, A. Javanmard, and M. Hamdi. Mobility modeling, spatial traffic distribution, and probability of connectivity for sparse and dense vehicular ad hoc networks. *IEEE Trans. on Vehicular Technology*, 58(4):1998 – 2007, May 2009.

[36] G. Pollini. Trends in handover design. *IEEE Communications Magazine*, 34(3):82–90, Mar. 1996.

[37] I. Rhee, M. Shin, S. Hong, K. Lee, S. J. Kim, and S. Chong. On the Levy-walk nature of human mobility. *IEEE/ACM Trans. on Networking*, 19(3):630–643, Jun. 2011.

[38] N. Shenoy and B. Hartpence. A mobility model for cost analysis in integrated cellular/WLANs. In *Proc. of International Conference on Computer Communications and Networks*, Chicago, IL, Oct. 2004.

[39] S. Singh and J. G. Andrews. Joint resource partitioning and offloading in heterogeneous cellular networks. *IEEE Trans. on Wireless Communications*, 13(2):888 – 901, Feb. 2014.

[40] S. Singh, H. Dhillon, and J. G. Andrews. Offloading in heterogeneous networks: Modeling, analysis, and design insights. *IEEE Trans. on Wireless Communications*, 12(5):2484–2497, May 2013.

[41] M. Stemm and R. H. Katz. Vertical handoffs in wireless overlay networks. *ACM/Springer Mobile Networks and Applications*, 3(4):335–350, Jan. 1998.

[42] E. Stevens-Navarro, Y. Lin, and V. Wong. An MDP-based vertical handoff decision algorithm for heterogeneous wireless networks. *IEEE Trans. on Vehicular Technology*, 57(2):1243–1254, Mar. 2008.

[43] D. Stoyan, W. Kendall, and J. Mecke. *Stochastic Geometry and Its Applications*. Wiley, second edition, 1995.

[44] A. H. Zahran, B. Liang, and A. Saleh. Signal threshold adaptation for vertical handoff in heterogeneous wireless networks. *ACM/Springer Mobile Networks and Applications*, 11(4):625–640, Aug. 2006.

[45] M. M. Zonoozi and P. Dassanayake. User mobility modeling and characterization of mobility patterns. *IEEE Journal on Selected Areas in Communications*, 15(7):1239–1252, Sep. 1997.

Mobile Device Video Caching to Improve Video QoE and Cellular Network Capacity

Hasti A. Pedersen and Sujit Dey
Dept. of Electrical and Computer Engineering,
University of California San Diego, La Jolla, CA
hasti@ucsd.edu, sdey@ucsd.edu

ABSTRACT

As the video resolution, storage, and rendering capabilities of mobile devices improve, consumers tend to watch more videos on their devices. To address this increasing demand, there is a need to improve the capacity of cellular networks while also improving video Quality of Experience (QoE). Ensuring video QoE via wireless links remains a challenge, not only due to the backhaul demand, but also due to the varying wireless channel conditions caused by fading, multiuser interference, and peak traffic loads. Here, we introduce a reactive Mobile Device Caching (rMDC) framework to improve video capacity (number of concurrent video viewing sessions) and QoE in the presence of the challenges explained above. Using rMDC, a mobile device caches videos reactively as it requests them, evicts the videos least likely to be requested according to its neighbors aggregate User Preference Profile (UPP), and sharing video contents using D2D communication. We use a discrete event statistical simulation framework to study the performance of rMDC. Our simulation results demonstrate the effectiveness of rMDC, along with UPP-based caching, in achieving higher capacity and better QoE compared to no mobile device caching.

Keywords

Mobile Device Caching; D2D Communication; Wireless Network Capacity; Video Quality of Experience.

1. INTRODUCTION

According to the Cisco Visual Networking Index (VNI) forecast report, mobile video traffic will grow at a compound annual growth rate of 69% between 2013 and 2018 [4]. Even when offloading video traffic through alternative methods, this forecasted growth in video traffic will put severe strain on mobile networks.

When Internet video is accessed by a mobile device, it must be fetched from the servers of a Content Delivery Network (CDN) and traverse through the mobile carrier Core Network (CN), Radio Access Network (RAN), and wireless channel to reach the mobile device. In [7] [6], the authors proposed video caching in the RAN along with User Preference Profile (UPP)-based caching policies, and showed that caching along with video aware backhaul scheduling can increase the capacity of the RAN backhaul while improving users' QoE. Subsequently, [6] and [8] showed that using Adaptive Bit Rate (ABR) aware RAN caching together with backhaul and wireless channel scheduling further improves end-to-end video capacity of the cellular networks beyond what can be achieved by either ABR or RAN caching individually, while preserving the advantages in terms of QoE obtained by each of them.

In this paper, we extend RAN caching to utilize the storage available on mobile devices as well as D2D links (like Wi-Fi Direct) to off-load the traffic from cellular links and thus further enhance end-to-end cellular video capacity and experienced QoE. Our proposed solution reactively caches videos on mobile devices as they are being requested, and opportunistically shares cache contents using D2D communication. Therefore there is no bandwidth penalty associated with preloading the caches, and our framework performs well even for video consumption in cellular networks where relatively few mobile devices are within D2D range.

Our proposed solution, reactive Mobile Device Caching (rMDC), efficiently utilizes the storage and multiple radio resources available at the mobile devices to reactively cache video contents and share them with neighbor devices over unlicensed bands. For this research, we mostly focus on legacy Wi-Fi and Wi-Fi Direct protocols. Thus, the proposed framework is cellular resource aware as the cellular resources that are consumed to cache a video could have been used for faster downloading of an already ongoing video request. The idea behind the rMDC caching framework is to address the inherent challenges and trade-offs associated with mobile caching to improve the video QoE for mobile devices, as well as capacity of the cellular network.

In summary, the proposed rMDC framework consists of the following two parts: (a) a reactive policy where mobile devices reactively cache video contents and share their cache contents with their neighbor devices through D2D links to off-load traffic from cellular networks; and (b) capability of downloading different parts of the video from multiple sources – e.g. portions of a video from different neighbor devices and the (e)NodeB to speed up downloads; we termed this capability Video Retrieval Process.

Fig. 1 illustrates possible download options for a mobile device in the rMDC framework. In this example a mobile device, UE_1, downloads parts of the video from its own cache,

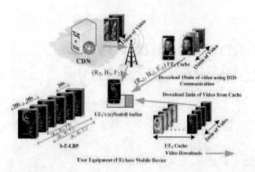

Figure 1: rMDC framework: Reactive Caching, Shared Caches and Possible Download Paths, and S-E-LBP.

acquiring parts of the video from the neighbor mobile device caches and the remaining parts (chunks) of the video from the (e)NodeB. Thus, depending on where the video source is available, the mobile device can obtain its contents from multiple sources.

The concept of data sharing has been widely implemented and adopted through Peer-2-Peer (P2P) protocols such as BitTorrent [5], Gnutella, PeerCast, PeerStreamer [1], and their client implementations. The historic motivation behind P2P protocols were to speed up downloads by working around data rate disparity between uplink and downlink due to the uneven provisioning in the wired networks. Using P2P, instead of one user transferring an entire file to the requesting user, multiple collaborating users that have the contents in their caches, transfer different parts (chunks) of the files to the requesting user. Thus, using multiple uplinks simultaneously improves the overall achieved rate in the P2P networks. The essence of retrieving video contents in rMDC framework is that of P2P protocols, in which a requesting video user receives different video chunks from different sources. However, more stringent scheduling of the users compared to P2P protocols is required due to: (1) cooperation range of devices with rMDC (Wi-Fi range) is smaller than that of P2P (any two users with connections to the Internet can share contents), and (2) P2P protocols do not aim to improve the capacity of the operators' network, and might negatively impact the cable providers' network throughput. On the contrary, rMDC aims to improve overall capacity and QoE.

Like in [7], we propose to use Leaky Bucket Parameters (LBP) associated with a requested video to select a transmission rate that, if met by the network, can ensure playback without stalling and guarantee a maximum initial delay. Here, we extend the LBPs to consider the additional flexibility of partial downloads from different sources of videos: the mobile device's own cache, cache of cooperative mobile devices, and (e)NodeB. We call the proposed LBP, Segmented E-LBP (S-E-LBP). As shown in Fig. 1, unlike LBP that is three tuples generated for the entire video, S-E-LBP is for parts of the videos, for instance, 30s into the video up to 120s. Using LBP instead of S-E-LBP is always an option but the parameters are more conservative.

In summary, the novelty and importance of the contributions of this paper are: (a) it is the first to propose a caching framework along with a video-retrieval approach to opportunistically use the storage and radio capacities of the mobile devices to improve capacity and QoE regardless of the application; and (b) it is the first paper to use S-E-LBP table

to ensure initial delay and improve probability of stalling by coordinating between downloads from different sources.

We have developed a simulation framework to demonstrate the effectiveness of the rMDC framework. The simulation results demonstrate significant increase in possible video capacity and video QoE using our approach, as opposed to no UE caching.

1.1 Related Work

The field of mobile caching and D2D communication is rich in contributions and is an active area of research both in academia [3] and industry [12]. The majority of the previous research on D2D communication focused on addressing the challenges of using cellular spectrum for both D2D communication and cellular links by methods of interference reduction or avoidance among cellular and D2D users [3] or methods of estimating Channel State Information (CSI) of D2D links for more efficient scheduling. However, today's mobile devices are equipped with multiple radio interfaces, (e.g., Wi-Fi, Bluetooth, NFC), and using this free spectrum as we propose in this paper can further improve the performance of cellular networks. The efforts in mobile device caching are mostly focused on improving application experience rather than the cellular networks. We believe none of the previous works address the problem that we address here: *Use mobile device cache and radio resources available to opportunistically assist (e)NodeB to improve cellular networks' video capacity and QoE during peak traffic load.*

Browser caching for webpages and their components has been done with size restrictions in mobile device operating systems such as Android and iOS. Recently, YouTube rolled out a feature that preloads videos from the "subscription" or "watch later" list into cache memory [2]. With this feature, users can play back videos from their cache later – as long as they maintain connection to the YouTube servers – and thus experience better video quality. Although this feature improves users' QoE, its effectiveness relies on users updating their "subscription" and "watch later" list. Furthermore, the download process is ignorant of the backhaul and wireless channel bandwidth availability.

Recently, [10] and [9] proposed a promising caching solution to improve the video capacity of cellular networks. However, the former approach uses Most Popular Videos ranking to distribute contents among mobile devices, which may not lead to optimal results as explained and shown in [7]. The latter requires presence of additional helper nodes (e.g., Femto cells) where videos are cached, which may be hard to satisfy throughout a network.

The remainder of this paper is organized as follows: In section 2, we first explain the objective of our work and then provide an overview of our solution: the rMDC framework. Subsequently, in section 3, we detail our proposed mobile device UPP-based proactive caching policies. In section 4, we introduce the video retrieval process and buffer management. Section 5 outlines our simulation framework, and provides experimental results. We conclude the paper in section 6.

2. OVERALL APPROACH

Fig. 2 shows an overview of the rMDC framework, including network and peer establishment as well as caching, and video retrieval steps. Once a mobile device becomes active in a cell, the neighbor establishment process commences.

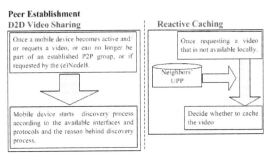

Peer Establishment

D2D Video Sharing	Reactive Caching
Once a mobile device becomes active and/ or requets a video, or can no longer be part of an established P2P group, or if requested by the (e)NodeB.	Once requesting a video that is not available locally.
	Neighbors' UPP
Mobile device starts discovery process according to the available interfaces and protocols and the reason behind discovery process.	Decide whether to cache the video

Figure 2: rMDC Network and Peer Establishment

In rMDC approach, a mobile device sends a request to the R-UPP cache agent at the (e)NodeB with a listing of its cache contents and location. Meanwhile, a mobile device may self-initiate a peer establishment process, or initiate the process upon a request from the cache agent at the (e)NodeB. A mobile device self-initiates the peer establishment process if (a) it does not belong to a D2D group and it becomes active in a cell or requests a video that is not available in its cache, or (b) it can no longer stay connected with an already established group. During the peer establishment process, a mobile device starts a discovery process to identify the cooperating mobile devices in its vicinity. For instance, following Wi-Fi direct protocol [11], a mobile device starts looking in social channels, envisioned in Wi-Fi direct protocol, for a group or it initiates a group itself. The cache agent running on the (e)NodeB tracks the mobile devices' peer associations and potential peers for future video sharing. Occasionally, (e)NodeB sends a group or peer change request to a mobile device if the alternative peer association facilitates downloads such as when, for instance, the requested video is available in a mobile device within the vicinity of the requesting mobile device, but not the group that the mobile device is currently associated with.

In the event of a new video request, a mobile device first searches its own cache and then neighbor caches, or caches within its Wi-Fi direct group in an attempt to retrieve the contents locally. If parts of the video are not available locally, the R-UPP cache agent at the (e)NodeB first tries to identify another device in the requesting mobile device's vicinity (but not within the same group) that has the content and initiate a group change request. Ultimately, if it does not find the missing content in any neighboring device, then the R-UPP cache agent schedules the remaining chunks either from the eNodeB cache, if it is a cache hit, or downloads them from the CDN, and schedules the video through the cellular link. Within the rMDC framework, when the mobile device downloads the requested video, it caches the video reactively according to the R-UPP mobile device caching policy described in section 3. Thus, after watching one or more videos, without adding any additional burden on the cellular link for downloading the requested video, a mobile device is capable of sharing those videos using D2D communication with other mobile devices within its Wi-Fi communication range.

In the rMDC framework, the buffer manager running at the mobile device is responsible for retrieving video chunks in time for the playback from different neighbor caches and/or the cellular links. We provide details of retrieval process and content coordination in section 4. Next, we describe our R-UPP caching policy that assists downloads of neighbor devices using D2D links.

R-UPP Mobile Device Caching Algorithm
R-UPP Cache agent running at the (e)NodeB
1. **For** each active mobile device in a cell site
2.   Calculate the aggregate UPP of the device itself and all the neighbor devices
3. **End**
R-UPP Mobile Device Caching Policy running at the (e)NodeB
1. **For** new Video Request V_j
2.   **If** chunks $V_j \in U_i$ cache
3.   transfer video chunks from cache to playback buffer, B_i
4.   **End**
5.   **If** any remaining chunks c_j of $V_j \notin B_i$ and c_j of $V_j \in$ Neighbor Device
6.   Download the chunks c_j from the neighbor device
7.   **End**
8.   **If** any chunks of $V_j \notin B_i$
9.   Schedule missing chunks of V_j through cellular links
10.   Calculate P_R for V and the cached videos and generate LLR subset
11. LLR_j: subset of LLR videos with least P_R that has to be evicted
from cache to fit V
12.   **If** $P_R(V_j) - \sum P_R(LLR_j) > 0$
13.   Cache = Cache + V_j - $\{LLR_j\}$
14.   **Else**
15.   Do not cache V_j
16. **End For, End If, End If**

Figure 3: P-UPP Mobile Device Caching Algorithm.

3. R-UPP MOBILE DEVICE CACHING

We first proposed the R-UPP caching algorithm in [7] to improve the cache hit ratio of relatively small sized caches at the (e)NodeBs of the cellular networks without the overhead of preloading the caches. The R-UPP caching policy reactively caches videos as they are being requested and evicts videos according to the average cell site UPP.

In this paper, we propose R-UPP mobile device caching policy to facilitate video content sharing locally through D2D links among neighboring devices, without the associated overhead of consuming cellular resources to cache videos just for the purpose of D2D communication. The approach of reactive caching is especially suitable within the setting presented in this paper, as existence of D2D links within the cellular network is opportunistic and therefore cannot be taken for granted.

Fig. 3 depicts the R-UPP mobile device caching algorithm. Whenever there's a change in a mobile device's neighbor list, the R-UPP cache agent running at the (e)NodeB calculates the aggregate neighbor UPP and communicates it to the mobile device (lines 1-3). R-UPP mobile device caching policy calculates the request probability of the videos in its cache using the following equation:

$$P_R(v_{Uj}) = \sum_{c=1}^{|VC|} p_{vc}^{(U)}(c) p_j(c) \qquad (1)$$

where $|VC|$ is the total number of video categories, $p_{vc}^{(U)}(c)$ is the probability that a device in neighbor group U requests a video belonging to category c, and $p_j(c)$ is the request probability for video j given category c. Like in [7], here, we assume, the category of each video is known.

Upon a video request, if the request is a cache hit in the mobile device's cache, U_i, the buffer manager transfers video chunks to the playback buffer (line 3). For any chunks of the video not found in the cache, the mobile device requests it locally using D2D communication (lines 5-6). If the requested chunk is not available locally (line 8), the mobile device fetches it from the (e)NodeB. If the UE cache is full, R-UPP caching policy calculates the request probability of the videos in its cache as well as the request probability of the requested video using eq. 1, forming a Least Likely Requested (LLR) subset (lines 10-11). R-UPP mobile device caching policy calculates the difference between request probability of the newly requested video, and that of the subset of LLR videos from the cache with the least P_R values that need to be evicted in order to free up space for the new video. Only if the difference in request probability is greater than zero, does R-UPP caching policy effectuate the cache update (lines 12-13). The above approach ensures that the cached videos maintain the highest probability of requests by the current neighbor devices.

4. VIDEO RETRIEVAL PROCESS

The rMDC framework aims to improve video capacity of cellular networks, as well as user's video QoE by reducing the stalling probability and initial delay. A mobile device with rMDC framework may potentially receive video chunks from many different sources: receiving parts of a video from its own cache, parts from neighbor devices, and parts from the cell site. Although these multiple download paths result in cellular capacity savings, as well as improved QoE, retrieving video chunks on time to ensure stall-free playback is important. Thus, as in [7], rMDC framework uses LBP to facilitate playback with bounded initial delay and without stalling.

LBPs consist of N 3-tupples (R, B, F) corresponding to N sets of transmission rates and resulting buffer size parameters for a given bit stream [7]. An LBP tuple guarantees that as long as the average transmission rate is maintained at R bits/second, the client has a buffer size of B bits, and the buffer is initially filled with F bits before video playback starts, the video session can proceed without any buffer underflow (stalling) or buffer overflow. As part of the rMDC framework, we introduce Segmented E-LBP (S-E-LBP) table. With S-E-LBP, a video is divided into segments for which individual LBP parameters are given. Fig. 1 shows example S-E-LBP for a video sequence, where (R1, B1, F1) are the LBP corresponding to the entire sequence of video, (R2, B2, F2) are the LBP parameters applicable to downloading from 30s into the video and to the end of the video, and (Rs2, Bs2, Fs2) are the LBP for the segments of the video that starts 30s within the video up to 240s in the video. Fig. 1 shows an example that demonstrates the S-E-LBP usage. In the example, UE_1 finds chunks corresponding to the first 2 minutes of the movie Avatar in its own cache, retrieves these chunks without delay, and subsequently starts the playback. Meanwhile, the mobile device achieves a cache hit in the neighbor mobile device (UE_2) and downloads additional chunks (corresponding to 15 minutes of video playback) from that device. When requesting the video from the neighboring device, UE_1 can select a rate that is associated with the initial delay of 2 minutes (because the mobile device already has in its cache the chunks corresponding to the first 2 minutes of that video). Thus, the network can potentially associate a lower transmission rate to this mobile device if sufficient capacity is not available. Finally, the remainder of the video is fetched through the cellular link with the initial delay of up to 2+15=17 minutes maximum; thus requiring a much lower transmission rate through the cellular link and helping increase its capacity.

Video buffer management and video playback algorithm
1.   If $V_j \in U_i$ cache
2.   Transfer video bits to playback buffer
3.   Identify the missing chunks of the video from the beginning
4.   **If** enough bits in video buffer
5.   Starts the playback right away
6.   **End If**
7.   Request remaining chunks from neighbor devices
8.   **If** any chunk is not found locally
9.   Request download from (e)NodeB according to S-E-LBP table to ensure stall free playback
10. **End If, End If**

Figure 4: Buffer Management and Playback Algorithm.

Fig. 4 shows the buffer management and playback algorithm. If any part of the video is available in the mobile device's cache, the buffer manager transfers the video chunks to the video playback buffer. Subsequently, it identifies the missing chunks from the beginning of the video and schedules download from the neighbor devices or (e)NodeB with transmission rates according to S-E-LBP.

5. SIMULATION RESULTS

In this section, we evaluate the impact of our proposed rMDC framework on the capacity and user video QoE using the MATLAB statistical simulation framework we developed earlier [6][8]. Like in [8], we assume a database of 20,000 videos following a Zipf popularity distribution with exponent value of -0.8. The video duration is exponentially distributed with mean of 8 minutes and truncated to a maximum of 30 minutes and a minimum of 2 minutes. We assume the video codec bit rate is uniformly distributed between 200kbps (QVGA quality) and 2Mbps (HD quality). The simulation assumes a pool of 5000 potential users and uses a Poisson arrival and departure model with average user active time of 45 minutes and inter-arrival time of 12 seconds. Video requests are generated independently per active user and follow a Poisson process with a mean inter-arrival time between requests. In terms of video QoE, we assume maximum acceptable initial delay of 10s for each user – i.e. playback should start no later than 10s after a video is requested. In terms of resources, we assume 1000Mbps for backhaul bandwidth (backhaul is not bottleneck) and the baseline wireless channel is modeled with parameters listed in table II of [8]. The results presented in this paper cover 5,000 video requests per simulation.

Next, we study the effectiveness of rMDC framework in improving capacity and video QoE. We also demonstrate the impact of cache size and D2D communication range on video capacity and QoE. Fig. 5(a) shows capacity for no mobile device caching with and without ABR, rMDC framework with cache size (C) ranging from 500Gbit to 5000Gbit and with D2D communication ranges (R) of 100m and 500m. Note that each point in this graph captures the case where the blocking probability is exactly 0.01, which is achieved by changing the user inter-arrival time such that the steady-state target blocking rate is achieved and noting the number of concurrent video requests sustained at that specific user inter-arrival time. Fig. 5(a) shows that significant improvement can be achieved in terms of capacity using rMDC framework. Furthermore, the figure shows that as the D2D range increases, the capacity increases. For instance, for cache size of 5000Gbit, increasing the D2D communication range from 100m to 500m results in 24% improvement in

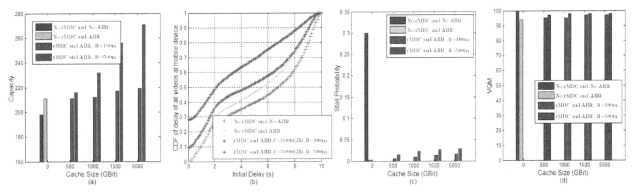

Figure 5: Performance of rMDC framework: (a) End-to-end capacity for rMDC with different D2D range and cache size; (b) CDF of initial delay of all videos at mobile device with rMDC mobile device caching framework; (c) Stalling probability for rMDC with different D2D range and cache size; (d) Average VQM for rMDC with different D2D range and cache size configuration.

terms of capacity. We also observe that as the D2D range increases the impact of cache size on capacity becomes more significant. For instance, for D2D range of 500m, increasing cache size from 500Gbit to 5000Gbit results in 25% capacity improvements while for D2D range of 100m, it results in 4% capacity improvement. Overall allowing for D2D with communication range of 500m and reactive cache size of 5000GBit results in 28% and 37% improvement in terms of capacity compared to not using rMDC framework with and without ABR respectively.

Next, we study the impact of rMDC framework on video QoE. Fig. 5(b) shows the CDF of initial delay when rMDC framework with cache size of 5000Gbit and D2D communication range of 100m and 500m are used. Fig. 5(b) shows that caching at the mobile device improves initial delay. For instance, using rMDC framework with cache size of 5000Gbit and D2D range of 500 improves the probability of achieving an initial delay of less than 1s by 26% compared to not using rMDC framework. Furthermore, Fig. 5(b) illustrates that increase in D2D communication range from 100m to 500m for cache size of 5000Gbit, results in 8% improvements in terms of experienced initial delay.

Fig. 5(c) and Fig. 5(d) show the probability of stalling and achieved average VQM for rMDC framework. Fig. 5(c) demonstrates that using ABR results in 136-fold reduction in the number of video requests that experience stalling. From the figures, we can infer that there can be significant improvement in terms of capacity and initial delay using our proposed rMDC mobile device caching approach, with only marginal degradation in stalling probability and almost similar VQM, compared to just using ABR without mobile device caching.

6. CONCLUSION AND FUTURE WORK

In this paper we proposed a novel video mobile device caching framework that uses storage and radio resources available at the mobile device along with our proposed user preference profile based reactive caching policy to improve capacity and QoE of the cellular networks.

Using simulation results, we showed that using the proposed reactive caching policy and the video retrieval policy can result in capacity and video QoE improvements.

7. REFERENCES

[1] http://en.wikipedia.org/wiki/p2ptv.
[2] www.youtube.com.
[3] A. Asadi and V. Mancuso. A survey on device-to-device communication in cellular networks. *submitted to IEEE Communications Surveys and Tutorials.*
[4] Cisco. Cisco visual networking index: Global mobile data traffic forecast update, 2013-2018. *Cisco White Paper.*
[5] B. Cohen. Incentives build robustness in bittorrent. *Proceedings of the 1st Workshop on Economics of Peer-to-Peer Systems*, 2003.
[6] H.Ahlehagh and S.Dey. Video aware scheduling and caching in the radio access network. *To appear in IEEE Transactions on Networking, VOL. 22, NO. 5. (IEEE Xplore).*
[7] H.Ahlehagh and S.Dey. Video caching in radio access network: Impact on delay and capacity. *Proceedings of the 2012 IEEE Wireless Communications and Networking Conference (WCNC 2012)*, 2012.
[8] H.Ahlehagh and S.Dey. Adaptive bit rate capable video caching and scheduling. *Proc. IEEE Wireless Communication and Networking Conference*, 2013.
[9] N. Golrezaei et al. Femtocaching: Wireless video content delivery through distributed caching helpers. *International Conference on Computer Communications (INFOCOM)*, 2012.
[10] N. Golrezaei et al. Wireless device-to-device communications with distributed caching. *IEEE International Symposium on Information Theory (ISIT)*, 2012.
[11] Wi-Fi Alliance Technical Committee P2P Task Group. Wi-fi peer-to-peer (p2p) technical specification. 2010.
[12] X. Wu et al. Flashlinq: A synchronous distributed scheduler for peer-to-peer ad hoc networks. *IEEE Allerton Conference on Communication, Control, and Computing, pp. 514-521*, 2010.

Towards Mobility-Aware Predictive Radio Access: Modeling, Simulation, and Evaluation in LTE Networks

Hatem Abou-zeid
Electrical and Computer
Engineering Dept.
Queen's University
Kingston, Canada
h.abouzeid@queensu.ca

Hossam S. Hassanein
School of Computing
Queen's University
Kingston, Canada
hossam@cs.queensu.ca

Ramy Atawia
Electrical and Computer
Engineering Dept.
Queen's University
Kingston, Canada
ramy.atawia@queensu.ca

ABSTRACT

Novel radio access techniques that leverage mobility predictions are receiving increasing interest in recent literature. The essence of these schemes is to lookahead at the future rates users will experience, and then devise *long-term* resource allocation strategies. For instance, a YouTube video user moving towards the cell edge can be prioritized to pre-buffer additional video content before poor coverage commences. While the *potential* of mobility-aware resource allocation has recently been demonstrated, several practical design aspects and evaluation approaches have not yet been addressed due to the complexity of the problem. Furthermore, since prior works have focused on *specific* applications there is also a strong need for a unified framework that can support different user and network requirements. For this purpose, we present a novel two-stage Predictive Radio Access Network (P-RAN) framework that can *efficiently* leverage both *future* data rate predictions in the order of tens of seconds, and *instantaneous* fast fading at the millisecond level. We also show how the framework can be implemented within the open source Network Simulator 3 (ns-3) LTE module, and apply it to optimize stored video delivery. A thorough set of performance tests are then conducted to assess the performance gains and investigate sensitivity to various prediction errors. Our results indicate that P-RANs can jointly improve both service quality and transmission efficiency. Additionally, we also observe that P-RAN performance can be further improved by modeling prediction uncertainty and developing *robust* allocation techniques.

Categories and Subject Descriptors

C.2.1 [**Computer-Communication Networks**]: Network Architecture and Design—*Wireless communication*; C.2.5 [**Computer-Communication Networks**]: Local and Wide-Area Networks—*Access Schemes*

1. INTRODUCTION

Advances in vehicular communications and telematics are driving an unprecedented growth of mobile traffic. Such developments will, however, introduce excessive congestion across wireless infrastructure, compelling operators to expand their networks. An alternative to expansion is to develop more efficient content delivery paradigms. In particular, alleviating Radio Access Network (RAN) congestion is paramount to it postpones costly investments in radio equipment installations and new spectrum. Novel approaches in RAN design are therefore receiving increasing interest to support future vehicular connectivity at sustainable costs.

Fortunately, the predictability of human mobility [14], particularly that of vehicles [12], offers unique opportunities to devise proactive RAN transmission schemes. Knowing the routes vehicles are going to traverse enables the network to anticipate the future rates users will experience, and forecast spatio-temporal demands. To accomplish this, mobility trajectories are coupled with Radio Environment Maps (REMs) [24, 27] that provide estimates of the supported data rates at different geographical locations. This form of *predictive* radio access that leverages mobility information has been a recent topic of investigation. For instance, contemporary works have demonstrated its significant potential to improve network throughput and fairness [3, 23], video streaming experience [6, 21], as well as energy efficiency [5,18]. However, due to the complexity of the problem that involves joint optimization over a time horizon, several practical aspects have not yet been addressed. Additionally, the effects of uncertainty in the predicted information such as user trajectories, and radio map accuracy remain mostly unexplored. A further requirement towards realizing the emerging Predictive Radio Access Networks (P-RANs) is the development of a unified framework that can accommodate different applications and network objectives. The design and practical evaluation of such a P-RAN is the focus of this paper. Our contribution towards this end is two-fold:

1. We develop a generic P-RAN that can efficiently leverage both *future* rate predictions and *instantaneous* opportunistic scheduling. This is accomplished by a two-stage approach that i) can be easily tailored for different requirements and network objectives, and ii) adapts to uncertainty in the predicted information through two levels of feedback. Implementation details using the open source Network Simulator 3 (ns-3) LTE module [26] are also provided.

2. We define (and conduct) comprehensive *sensitivity* tests that investigate the robustness of P-RANs to 1) REM errors, 2) localization errors, 3) exploiting fast-fading, and 4) varying prediction window sizes. These tests can provide a guideline to assess the practical viability of future P-RAN schemes.

The rest of this paper is organized as follows: Section 2 provides the necessary background and reviews related work, while the system overview is covered in Section 3. The proposed two-stage P-RAN framework is then presented in Section 4 along with the corresponding ns-3 LTE implementation details. This is followed with extensive performance analysis in Section 5 and concluding remarks in Section 6.

2. BACKGROUND AND RELATED WORK

2.1 Human Mobility Predictability

LTE networks support a wide range of location positioning methods with varying levels of granularity, and a dedicated LTE Positioning Protocol (LPP) is also devised to coordinate signaling between the User Equipment (UE) and the BS [11]. Concurrently, a plethora of navigation hardware and software is also available in today's smart phones enabling users to report their current location. Determining a mobile user's location is therefore readily possible.

Recent analyses on human mobility traces also indicate that people tend to follow particular routes regularly, thereby enabling high *predictability* [14]. Several promising research results have also been presented based on real data from both cellular networks and GPS traces. While some works focus on short-term mobility prediction (next cell) [28], others predict the full trajectory [7], [12]. Approaches used include data mining [28], Markov renewal processes [7], and learning routes between common destinations via string matching [19]. User behavior profiling [9] is also a promising approach which is gaining momentum in the Location Based Services (LBS) industry as well.

2.2 Radio Environment Maps

Network operators commonly conduct road drive tests to measure signal strengths and other performance metrics at different locations. These measurements are used to generate radio, or network performance maps [13]. Openly accessible radio maps are also available online where signal strength is crowdsourced from users [24]. In addition to experimental location-rate mapping, several analytical studies have modeled the geographical correlation of channel capacity. Phillips *et al.* [25] present a comprehensive survey of path loss modeling approaches for different environments. Sampling strategies and interpolation techniques that incorporate practical measurements into the derived models are also presented. The authors conclude that online learning strategies and data mining approaches using measurement-based models are likely to provide the most robust radio mapping frameworks as conducted in [22].

While radio maps have typically been used to estimate the *current* supportable data rates, they can also enable the prediction of *future* rates users will experience, provided their mobility trajectories are known. Practical measurements confirming this have been recently conducted [27], [16]. Yao *et al.* [27] analyze bandwidth traces collected from two independent cellular providers for routes running through differ-

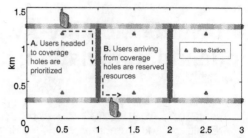

(a) User prioritization and resource reservation.

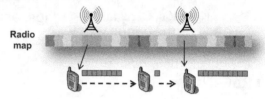

(b) Strategic prebuffering of video streams.

Figure 1: Mobility-aware predictive radio access.

ent radio conditions. Their findings confirm the correlation between rates and location, and indicate that bandwidth uncertainty can be reduced drastically when observations from past trips are also used. Han *et al.* [16] also conduct a similar measurement study, and consider user speed, time of day, and humidity to improve the prediction accuracy.

2.3 Predictive Radio Access Networks

The use of mobility predictions in cellular networks has been previously investigated with promising results in location management/paging [20,30], and handoff resource reservation [10, 29]. However, only limited work has considered *long-term* resource allocation based on radio maps. The approaches proposed in handoff management are mostly concerned with optimizing resource reservation for imminent handoffs, primarily voice calls. Today, mobile application usage is changing. This is driven by both higher connectivity speeds as well as larger screen sizes of pads, tablets, and more recently phablets. Trends of long, data-intensive sessions are anticipated to continue to grow with the emergence of telematics and infotainment systems in vehicles.

To cope with the increasing demand of vehicular content, a number of predictive resource allocation techniques have recently been proposed [3,5,21,23]. This emerging direction of P-RANs can be viewed as a cross-layer framework where future estimates of Physical layer (PHY) information are coupled with context information from the application layer to optimize long-term RAN functionality. Previous P-RAN literature can be classified into the following three categories.

Throughput and Fairness: Fig. 1(a) illustrates how P-RANs enable Base Stations (BSs) to prioritize users headed to low rate areas (marked in red) and plan resource reservations for users arriving from low rate areas. The potential increases in throughput and fairness of such schemes have been demonstrated in [3,8,23].

Video Delivery: Another practical application of P-RANs is for stored video delivery such as YouTube. As opposed to live streaming, stored videos can be strategically delivered in advance at the UE to prevent video stalling. This is illustrated in Fig. 1(b) where content is pre-buffered to a user known to be moving towards the cell edge, before poor coverage commences. Significant Quality of Service (QoS) gains have been reported in [6, 21], where the Resource Allocation (RA) problem is solved over a time horizon to optimize the video content delivered to each user, at each time slot, based on their mobility predictions.

Energy Efficiency: Rate predictions have also been proposed to develop energy efficient RAN transmission [4,5,18]. For instance, consider a video streaming user approaching the BS during low load. To save energy, only the minimum amount of content required for smooth streaming can be transmitted (i.e., without prebuffering) until the user reaches the cell center where a bulk of content can be efficiently transmitted in a short time.

This paper differs primarily from preceding works by 1) proposing a robust P-RAN framework that can be applied to any of the aforementioned applications, and integrated on top of traditional LTE schedulers, and 2) defining necessary sensitivity tests to assess practical P-RAN performance.

3. SYSTEM OVERVIEW

We consider a BS with an active user set $\mathcal{M}$, where an arbitrary user is denoted by $i \in \mathcal{M}$. Users enter from the left cell edge and move in a straight line towards the other edge. The wireless link is assumed to be the bottleneck, and the requested content is always available at the BS.

3.1 Radio Map and Mobility Information

The REM assumed to be typically available at the service provider would contain the average data rates at different network locations. In order to represent such a radio map, we use the Friis path loss propagation model as implemented in ns-3 [26]. The Signal to Interference plus Noise Ratio (SINR) at each x and y coordinate is then computed and the corresponding achievable rate is determined based on mappings in 3GPP standards for Long Term Evolution (LTE) [1].[1] Fast fading is modeled according to the vehicular power delay profile defined in 3GPP [2].

We first assume that user mobility information is known accurately for the upcoming T seconds, which we call the *prediction window*. Localization errors are then introduced to investigate the impact of uncertainty. By coupling a user trajectory with the REM is it possible to determine an estimate of the upcoming rates a user can receive.

3.2 Scheduling Time Scales

Scheduling in LTE is typically performed every Time Transmission Interval (TTI) by channel and/or queue-aware schedulers based on the users' Channel Quality Indicators (CQIs). However, the objective of P-RANs is to plan scheduling for multiple time instances jointly, optimized over a time window (of the order of tens of seconds). It is therefore not practical to design the long-term RA plan at the millisecond (TTI) level for two reasons: 1) a prediction window of only 60 seconds would generate $\approx 60,000$ TTIs requiring joint optimization, and 2) it is not practically possible to predict the average data rate at a TTI granularity. We therefore propose two time scales of operation as illustrated in Fig. 2. A prediction slot τ is defined as the duration over which the average user rate can be assumed to be con-

[1]While this model is used to represent a REM, the presented P-RAN framework can be directly applied with any REM.

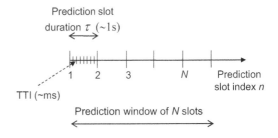

Figure 2: Relationship between the time intervals.

stant. A typical value of $\tau = 1\,\text{s}$, for user speeds up to $20\,\text{m/s}$, during which the average SINR will not vary significantly. As shown in Fig. 2, several prediction slots make up the *prediction window*, which is composed of $N = T/\tau$ slots. As time progresses the prediction window slides to include more information of the future user rates. Therefore, at time slot n, the set of considered prediction slots is denoted by $\mathcal{N}_n = \{n, n+1, \cdots, n+N-1\}$. We define the matrix of future user rates observed at time slot n by $\hat{\mathbf{r}} = (\hat{r}_{i,n'} : i \in \mathcal{M}, n' \in \mathcal{N}_n)$.

4. PREDICTIVE RADIO ACCESS FRAMEWORK FOR LTE

4.1 Architecture

The proposed predictive radio access framework is composed of two stages operating at different time scales but interacting dynamically as shown in Fig. 3.

Long-term RA: This upper level RA is responsible for the long-term allocation planning over a finite time horizon, based on user rate predictions. It is here that mobility information is leveraged to provide an additional level of RA diversity, and bulk transmissions are strategically planned. The output of this stage is an airtime allocation matrix $\mathbf{x} = (x_{i,n'} \in [0,1] : i \in \mathcal{M}, n' \in \mathcal{N}_n)$ which gives the fraction of time during each slot n' that the BS bandwidth is assigned to each user. The actual number of bits transmitted, at each slot, is the element-wise product $\mathbf{x} \odot \hat{\mathbf{r}}$ as illustrated by the bars in the sample allocation plan in Fig. 4.

Instantaneous Scheduling: A lower level opportunistic scheduler operating at the TTI level with instantaneous user CQI is used to implement the long-term RA plan. The primary objective is to exploit fast fading diversity and ensure that users receive their per slot data requirements as specified by the upper allocator.

Feedback: Two levels of feedback are incorporated in the P-RAN. First, the instantaneous scheduler monitors the cumulative number of bits transmitted *during* a prediction slot n, and only users that have not reached their target are considered for future TTIs. The second level of feedback occurs at the *end* of each slot n as shown in Fig. 3. Here, the actual rates $\bar{r}$ transmitted to each user are computed. This may differ from the originally planned allocation due to rate prediction errors, i.e. if $\hat{\mathbf{r}}$ is not accurate. This information is then fed back to the upper level RA to update the future allocation plan based on the actual data transmitted. Since practical systems will exhibit rate uncertainty, incorporating feedback is important to enable robustness to errors.

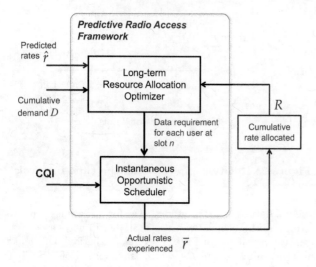

Figure 3: Predictive radio access framework.

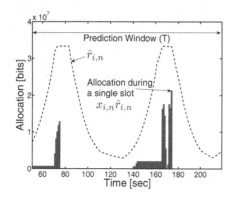

Figure 4: Sample predicted rate and long-term resource allocation plan for a user.

There are several advantages of this two stage architecture. First, by separating long-term RA from instantaneous scheduling, the framework can be integrated above existing traditional schedulers as detailed in the ns-3 LTE implementation in Section 4.4. And secondly, the predictive RA component can be designed to support different applications in a modular approach without affecting the underlying TTI level scheduler. Moreover, the rate of re-planning long-term RA can also be controlled to reduce overhead based on feedback. For instance a low variation between $\hat{\mathbf{r}}$ and $\bar{\mathbf{r}}$ indicates a stable operation an may require less frequent re-allocations. We now discuss each scheduling stage in detail.

4.2 Long-term Resource Allocation Planning

The objective of this stage is to make a long-term allocation plan at time slot n for the upcoming N slots. To do so, the upcoming user demand $d_{i,n}$ at a per slot level is first defined. For example, in video streaming $d_{i,n} \approx V\tau$ where V is the streaming bit rate and τ is the slot duration. Other applications may be similarly defined by a minimum per slot bit rate. To optimize RA over a time horizon it is useful to define the *cumulative* demand requested *by* slot n, which is denoted by $D_{i,n} = \sum_{n'=1}^{n} d_{i,n'}$. With these definitions, an application specific RA problem can be formulated

to determine the optimum airtime allocations $x_{i,n}$ based on the predicted user rate matrix $\mathbf{r}$, and the cumulative user demand $D_{i,n}$. Detailed examples of such formulations have been presented to improve throughput and fairness [3], enhance video streaming QoS [6], and minimize BS airtime [4]. In this paper, we focus on applying the proposed P-RAN framework to minimize BS airtime of stored video delivery.

Minimizing Transmission Time of Stored Videos: The essence of predictive video streaming in P-RAN is to *strategically* transmit content ahead of time at the UE, after which transmission can be momentarily suspended while the user consumes the buffer [4, 21]. If we consider a user requesting a stored video at slot $n = 1$, with a streaming rate of V [bit/s], then the cumulative content requested is $D_{i,n} = V\tau n$. To experience smooth streaming, the cumulative allocation made to a user i by slot n should be greater than or equal to $D_{i,n}, \forall n$. BS transmission time can be minimized by leveraging future user rate knowledge $\hat{\mathbf{r}}$ to make bulk transmissions at times of high channel conditions, while making the minimal transmissions that ensure smooth streaming at other times. This achieves lower airtime usage, resulting in lower power consumption or more resources for other services.

The optimization problem of minimizing BS airtime at time slot n over the prediction window, without causing any streaming discontinuities can be formulated as the following Linear Program (LP)[2]:

$$\underset{\mathbf{x}}{\text{minimize}} \quad \sum_{n'=n}^{n-1+N} \sum_{i=1}^{M} x_{i,n'} \qquad (1)$$

$$\text{subject to:} \quad \sum_{i=1}^{M} x_{i,n'} \leq 1, \qquad \forall n' \in \mathcal{N}_n,$$

$$R_{i,n-1} + \sum_{n''=n}^{n'} x_{i,n''}\hat{r}_{i,n''} - D_{i,n'} \geq 0, \quad \forall i, n',$$

$$x_{i,n'} \geq 0 \qquad \forall i \in \mathcal{M}, n' \in \mathcal{N}_n.$$

The objective in Eq. 1 minimizes the total BS airtime consumed over the prediction window. The first constraint expresses the resource limitation at each base station, while the second constraint captures the smooth video streaming requirement. The first term of this constraint denotes the cumulative rate allocated to a user in *previous* time slots, based on actual (i.e., not predicted) channel conditions, and is fed back to the optimizer as shown in Fig. 3, with $R_{i,0} = 0, \forall i$. This enables the long-term allocator to re-adjust the *future* allocation plan at every slot, and has not been considered in previous works [4, 21] which do not incorporate feedback or a sliding window. The second and third components of this constraint denote the cumulative allocation plan and cumulative demand $\forall n' \in \mathcal{N}_n$, respectively. Note that the advantage of defining resource allocation with the airtime fraction variable $x_{i,n}$ (as opposed to using discrete resource blocks) is that it enables a linear RA formulation without integer variables, thereby greatly simplifying the RA problem. Another important remark is that it is not necessary to formulate the long-term RA with a optimization problem; any algorithm that achieves similar objectives by exploiting

---

[2]A similar formulation has been considered in [4], but without the sliding window or the cumulative rate feedback R.

the predicted rates $\hat{\mathbf{r}}$ can be developed within the P-RAN framework and applied as the upper level allocator.

4.3 Instantaneous Opportunistic Scheduling

For each prediction slot n, scheduling is performed at the TTI level in the lower level scheduler. Here the reported user CQIs are used to opportunistically schedule users at peaks of their fast fading channel responses and avoid scheduling during deep fades. The target data requirement as determined by the upper level resource allocator is provided, and users are scheduled to meet this demand. Note that the number of bits $x_{i,n}\hat{r}_{i,n}$ required during slot n, and not the airtime fraction $x_{i,n}$ is used as this stage. The reason is that if the actual channel rate differs from the predicted rate $\hat{r}_{i,n}$, then the airtime calculated by the long-term RA will not be correct. By using the number of bits, the lower level scheduler provides a degree of robustness to prediction errors.

Let $r_{i,t}^{\mathrm{TTI}}$ denote the instantaneous rate supported by user i at TTI t, within prediction slot n. We can define several scheduling rules, such as

$$i^* = \arg \max_{\forall i \in \mathcal{M}_u} r_{i,t}^{\mathrm{TTI}}, \qquad (2)$$

where $\mathcal{M}_u$ is the set of users whose allocation requirement $x_{i,n}\hat{r}_{i,n}$ remains unsatisfied. In this rule, the scheduler will choose the user with the higher rate, which is much like a Maximum-Rate scheduler. However, once a user has met its target for slot n, it will be excluded from the set $\mathcal{M}_u$. We refer to this framework implementation as P-RAN:MaxRate. Alternatively, the following approach, dubbed P-RAN: RelativeRatio selects the user with the higher instantaneous rate *relative* to its predicted rate:

$$i^* = \arg \max_{\forall i \in \mathcal{M}_u} \frac{r_{i,t}^{\mathrm{TTI}}}{\hat{r}_{i,n}}. \qquad (3)$$

The intuition of this rule is to provide a more fair and distributed scheme that waits until users achieve their own *relative* peaks. Note that other more complex rules/scheduling algorithms can also be applied within the P-RAN framework to define the instantaneous lower level scheduler.

At the end of the prediction slot n, the actual rates transmitted $\tilde{r}_{i,n}$ are determined, and fed back to the upper level RA. The long-term RA is then re-run to account for the actual rates transmitted in the previous slot.

4.4 NS-3 LTE Implementation

We implemented the P-RAN framework within the LTE module in the open source Network Simulator (ns-3) LTE module [26]. Our extension involved modifying existing methods, and introducing a new method to implement the upper level predictive resource allocator. An optimization solver was also integrated in ns-3 to solve the BS airtime minimization problem for stored video transmission defined in Eq. 1. This framework may also be used to investigate a broader category of P-RAN formulations, objectives, and lower-level schedulers, with only minor modifications.

Simulation Environment: The definition of system nodes (i.e. UEs and eNB), the UE-eNB assignment and physical parameters such as transmit power and bandwidth are set through the existing *LteHelper* class. This class contains predefined methods that enable seamless integration between the different network entities.

Channel Model: The *TraceFadingLossModel* class implemented in the ns-3 LTE module is used to generate the desired channel model. This class imports MATLAB generated tracing files that model the fast fading and was modified to include a log-normal shadowing effect that is added to the average received power every prediction slot n.

Mobility Model: The *LteHelper* supports different types of random and fixed velocity models. The *WaypointMobilityModel* class which imports a user trajectory file was chosen in our simulation. This choice enables a direct specification of the x and y user coordinates at different time instances. Localization error effects are then simply implemented by adding a Gaussian random variable to the user coordinates.

Scheduler: The P-RAN framework illustrated in Fig. 3 is implemented by inheriting the existing *RrFfMacScheduler* class which implements a round-robin scheduler. The three main functions in Fig. 3 are executed by modifying two existing methods and introducing a new one as follows:

- *UpdateDlRlcBufferInfo*: This method exists in the *RrFfMacScheduler* class to decrement the allocated user's buffer data by one Transport Block (TB) size every TTI. The function was modified to implement the cumulative data computation used for feedback in Fig. 3. This is done by increasing the cumulative data of the current user by the amount decremented from the buffer.

- *DoPredictSchedul*: This method is introduced to implement the upper level long-term RA optimizer in Fig. 3. It has three main inputs: the long-term predicted rates matrix $\hat{\mathbf{r}}$, the users' demands matrix $\mathbf{D}$ and the cumulative received data $\mathbf{R}$ calculated by the aforementioned method. This method uses the C++ interface of the Gurobi Optimizer [15] to solve the predictive allocation plan over a time horizon according to the formulation in Eq. 1. This method is executed every prediction slot n or when a new user arrives.

- *DoSchedDlTiggerReq*: This method already exists in the inherited *RrFfMacScheduler* class and is triggered every TTI to implement the instantaneous lower-level opportunistic scheduler. It consists of two main functions: user scheduling and buffer update. In user scheduling, a *DoPredictSchedul* method is first called to obtain the data requirement for each user during each slot n. The scheduling metrics defined in Eq. 2 and Eq. 3 are then implemented to select the user that is scheduled during each TTI. After scheduling, the buffer update function is implemented by calling the aforementioned *UpdateDlRlcufferInfo* method to determine when users achieve their target rates as specified from the *DoPredictSchedul* method.

Other minor modifications related to the video application were also made in accordance with the system setup. Specifically, the eNB buffer size (*MaxTxBufferSize* in the *LteRlcUm* class) was increased to store the incoming video content before transmission. The BER variable in the *LteAmc* class was also modified to reflect the application requirements.

5. PERFORMANCE AND DISCUSSION

Simulation Setup: The LTE network setup follows the model parameters in Table 1. The total number of users $M = 6$ with an arrival rate 0.2/s, and a simulation time of 60 s. Average BS airtime and Video Degradation (VD) are used as network efficiency and QoS performance metrics, respectively. Video degradation is defined as the total

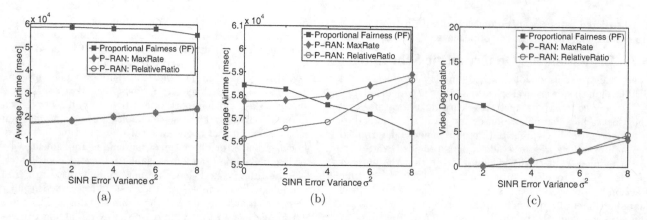

Figure 5: Sensitivity to SINR error variance (a) Average BS airtime (low load), (b) Average BS airtime (high load), and (c) Video degradation (high load).

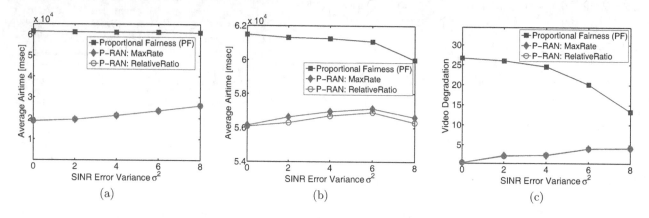

Figure 6: Sensitivity to SINR error variance without fast fading (a) Average BS airtime (low load), (b) Average BS airtime (high load), and (c) Video degradation (high load).

Table 1: Summary of Model Parameters

Parameter	Value
BS transmit power	43 dBm
BW	5 MHz
τ	1 s
BER	10^{-5}
Velocity	30 km/h
Packet size	8×10^3 [bits]
Packet rate (from core network to BS)	$10^3 s^{-1}$
Buffer size	10^9 [bits]

percentage of constraint violation, i.e. the second constraint in 1. To provide a performance reference of a non-predictive RA approach, we present the results of the popular Proportional Fair (PF) scheduler [17] as implemented in [26].

5.1 Numerical Results

Sensitivity to REM Uncertainty: Uncertainty in the REM will lead to errors in the predicted user rate $\hat{\mathbf{r}}$. For instance, in cases where the actual rate is less than anticipated, users may not receive their target rates. If content was not previously buffered, then video stalling may occur.

We model REM uncertainty as a log-normal random variable with a variance σ^2 overlaid on the predicted SINR. In Fig. 5(a) the streaming rate is $V = 0.5$ Mbit/s which we

refer to as the low load scenario. Here airtime is reduced by approximately 66 % with the P-RAN compared to traditional PF scheduling, while VD ≈ 0 for all schemes (which is not shown for space limitations). The reason is the network's ability to delay transmissions until users approach the cell center without violating streaming constraints. Interestingly, airtime increases only slightly while VD remains close to zero. This is due to the feedback in the lower-level scheduler that adjusts the planned user airtime to meet the data requirement at each slot n in the presence of errors.

Fig. 5(b) and Fig. 5(c) show the results for a higher load scenario where $V = 1.5$ Mbit/s, where airtime savings are not large but video degradation is reduced. Note that the airtime of the P-RAN: RelativeRatio scheme is slightly less than the P-RAN: MaxRate scheme. We can see that at a variance $\sigma^2 = 8$ the gains of P-RAN diminish due to the very high variations between the predicted and actual rates.

In Fig. 6(a)-(c) we conduct similar performance tests but this time without fast fading. The reason is that the fast fading model gives rather optimistic results at high velocities, since throughput peaks become frequent even when users are far from the cell center (we assume the reported instantaneous CQI is accurate). The results show similar trends, but the airtime and VD performance of PF is affected since it can no longer exploit high throughput spikes at the cell edge (which is generally not possible in practice).

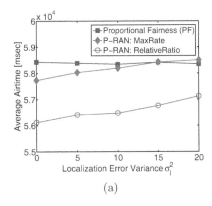
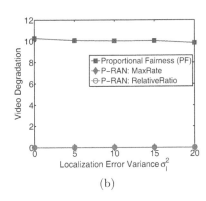

(a)

(b)

Figure 7: Sensitivity to localization error variance (a) Average BS airtime, and (b) Video degradation.

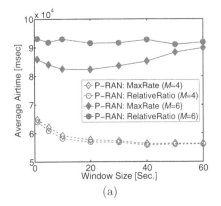
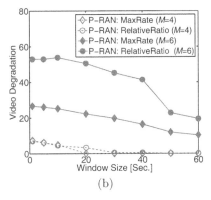
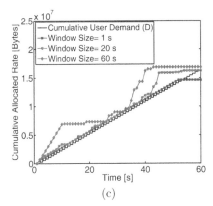

(a)

(b)

(c)

Figure 8: Effect of prediction window size (a) Average BS airtime, (b) Video degradation, and (c) Cumulative allocated rate for a sample user with P-RAN:MaxRate, $M = 6$.

On the other hand, the P-RAN framework does not rely on such peaks, and maintains its previous performance.

Sensitivity to Localization Uncertainty: Localization uncertainty is modeled as a zero mean Gaussian random variable with a variance σ_l^2 in both x and y dimensions (in meters). Fig. 7 shows the impact of localization errors with increasing variances. We observe that even at high variance the airtime increases slightly but the VD remains unaffected. The reason is that localization errors up to 50 m do not impact the received rates significantly due to the discrete Modulation and Coding Schemes (MCSs). This applies to the considered highway scenario where the REM follows a gradual increase and decrease with the distance from the BS. However, for more complex scenarios where strong shadowing or tunnels exist, the REM may vary significantly over a small geographical region. If this is the case, the localization errors will affect P-RAN performance more.

Effect of Prediction Window Size: In Fig. 8 we investigate the effect of varying the prediction window size for both $M = 4$ and $M = 6$ with $V = 2.25$ Mbit/s. During the defined window size perfect channel knowledge (i.e. with no errors or fast fading) is assumed to isolate the effects of smaller windows. The trends in Fig. 8(b) are expected, where a larger window leads to a gradual decrease in the VD. However, note that with only four users, a window of 30 s is sufficient to completely eliminate VD. Increasing the win-

dow size any further brings only a slight airtime reduction as shown in Fig. 8(a) for $M = 4$.

The case for $M = 6$ is more complex for increasing window sizes. While VD also decreases with increasing windows, the performance of P-RAN:RelativeRatio is considerably worse than P-RAN:MaxRate. The reason is that at this high load it is not possible to completely eliminate VD, and thus the problem in Eq. 1 is no longer feasible. In this case, a linear relaxation of constraints is made to find a solution that minimizes the error by which the constraint's boundary is violated. Here it is more spectrally efficient to schedule competing users based on their MaxRate as opposed to the RelativeRatio metric, which is equal to 1 for all the users in this case (since fast fading is not modeled as previously highlighted). The P-RAN:RelativeRatio therefore selects a user at random, leading to lower spectral efficiency. An interesting observation also appears in Fig. 8(a) where airtime decreases and then increases for P-RAN:MaxRate. The initial decrease in airtime results from a more efficient RA due to the larger window. However, increasing the window further enables the network to foresee that a higher load is anticipated in the future. This knowledge is used to trigger content prebuffering allocations to users that are in poor channel conditions. We depict this behavior in Fig. 8(c) which demonstrates how for a window size of 60 s content prebuffering is planned well in advance. While this consumes more airtime, the VD decreases as shown in Fig. 8(b). The conclusion is that varying the window size can have changing dynamics that are specific to the modeled application and metrics of interest, and should therefore be investigated thoroughly to avoid instability and undesired behaviors.

In summary, the preceding results demonstrated that significant gains are achievable even when only *trends* in the predicted information are available, i.e., in the presence of significant errors and limited lookahead time.

6. CONCLUSIONS

Exploiting mobility-awareness to devise predictive radio access schemes has been recently investigated with promising results [3,5,21,23]. This is driven by numerous human mobility studies and analyses of bandwidth traces demonstrating that a user's future channel states are highly reproducible [14,16,27]. While these studies indicate the significant potential of P-RANs, abstract implementations and ideal conditions were mostly considered.

In this paper, our goal was to introduce a more practical design and evaluation approach towards a unified P-RAN framework that can be easily adapted for different applications and network objectives, and integrated into traditional LTE schedulers. This was accomplished by a two-stage RA approach with feedback that can jointly leverage rate predictions and instantaneous opportunistic scheduling. We also implemented the framework within the Network Simulator ns-3 LTE module and demonstrated how a broad category of predictive schemes can be enabled through the framework. Extensive sensitivity tests indicated that even trends in predictive information provide considerable QoS and network efficiency gains. While these promising results validate the use of P-RANs, we foresee that robust prediction models and RA schemes are needed to fully exploit their potential.

7. REFERENCES

[1] 3GPP. LTE; evolved universal terrestrial radio access (E-UTRA); physical layer procedures. Technical Specification TS 36.213 v8.8.0, 2009.

[2] 3GPP. E-UTRA; base station (BS) radio transmission and reception (release 10). Technical Specification TS 36.104 V10.2.0, Dec. 2011.

[3] H. Abou-zeid, H. Hassanein, and S. Valentin. Optimal predictive resource allocation: Exploiting mobility patterns and radio maps. In *Proc. IEEE GLOBECOM*, pages 4714–4719, 2013.

[4] H. Abou-zeid and H. S. Hassanein. Predictive green wireless access: Exploiting mobility and application information. *IEEE Wireless Commun.*, 20(5):92–99, 2013.

[5] H. Abou-zeid, H. S. Hassanein, and S. Valentin. Energy-efficient adaptive video transmission: Exploiting rate predictions in wireless networks. *IEEE Trans. Veh. Technol.*, 63(5):2013 – 2026, 2014.

[6] H. Abou-zeid, H. S. Hassanein, and N. Zorba. Enhancing mobile video streaming by lookahead rate allocation in wireless networks. In *Proc. IEEE CCNC*, pages 768–773, 2014.

[7] H. Abu-Ghazaleh and A. S. Alfa. Application of mobility prediction in wireless networks using markov renewal theory. *IEEE Trans. Veh. Technol.*, 59(2):788–802, 2010.

[8] S. H. Ali, V. Krishnamurthy, and V. C. M. Leung. Optimal and approximate mobility-assisted opportunistic scheduling in cellular networks. *IEEE Trans. Mobile Comput.*, 6(6):633–648, 2007.

[9] M. A. Bayir, M. Demirbas, and N. Eagle. Mobility profiler: A framework for discovering mobility profiles of cell phone users. *Pervasive and Mobile Computing*, 6(4):435–454, 2010.

[10] M.-H. Chiu and M. A. Bassiouni. Predictive schemes for handoff prioritization in cellular networks based on mobile positioning. *IEEE J. Select. Areas Commun.*, 18(3):510–522, 2000.

[11] E. Dahlman, S. Parkvall, and J. Skold. *4G: LTE/LTE-Advanced for Mobile Broadband*. Academic Press, 2011.

[12] J. Froehlich and J. Krumm. Route prediction from trip observations. *Society of Automotive Engineers (SAE) World Congress*, pages 53–58, 2008.

[13] A. Galindo-Serrano, B. Sayrac, S. B. Jemaa, J. Riihijärvi, and P. Mähönen. Cellular coverage optimization: A radio environment map for minimization of drive tests. In *Cognitive Communication and Cooperative HetNet Coexistence*, pages 211–236. 2014.

[14] M. C. Gonzalez, C. A. Hidalgo, and A.-L. Barabasi. Understanding individual human mobility patterns. *Nature*, 453:779–782, 2008.

[15] Gurobi. Gurobi Optimization. http://www.gurobi.com/. Accessed Feb. 11th, 2014.

[16] D. Han, J. Han, Y. Im, M. Kwak, T. T. Kwon, and Y. Choi. MASERATI: Mobile adaptive streaming based on environmental and contextual information. In *Proc. ACM WiNTECH*, pages 33–40, 2013.

[17] F. Kelly. Charging and rate control for elastic traffic. *European Transactions on Telecommunications*, 8(1), 1997.

[18] P. Kolios, V. Friderikos, and K. Papadaki. Energy-aware mobile video transmission utilizing mobility. *IEEE Network*, 27(2):34–40, 2013.

[19] K. Laasonen. Route prediction from cellular data. In *Proc. Workshop on Context Awareness for Proactive Systems*, pages 147–158, 2005.

[20] B. Liang and Z. J. Haas. Predictive distance-based mobility management for multidimensional PCS networks. *IEEE/ACM Trans. on Netw.*, 11(5):718–732, 2003.

[21] Z. Lu and G. de Veciana. Optimizing stored video delivery for mobile networks: The value of knowing the future. In *Proc. IEEE INFOCOM*, pages 2806–2814, 2013.

[22] M. Malmirchegini and Y. Mostofi. On the spatial predictability of communication channels. *IEEE Trans. Wireless Commun.*, 11(3):964–978, 2012.

[23] R. Margolies, A. Sridharan, V. Aggarwal, R. Jana, N. K. Shankaranarayanan, V. A. Vaishampayan, and G. Zussman. Exploiting mobility in proportional fair cellular scheduling: Measurements and algorithms. In *Proc. IEEE Int. Conf. on Computer Commun. (INFOCOM)*, 2014, to appear.

[24] OpenSignal. The OpenSignal project homepage. http://opensignal.com/, 2013. Accessed Feb. 15th, 2013.

[25] C. Phillips, D. Sicker, and D. Grunwald. A survey of wireless path loss prediction and coverage mapping methods. *IEEE Commun. Surveys Tuts.*, 15(1):255–270, 2013.

[26] G. Piro, N. Baldo, and M. Miozzo. An LTE module for the ns-3 network simulator. In *Proc. Int. ICST Conf. on Simulation Tools and Techniques*, pages 415–422, 2011.

[27] J. Yao, S. S. Kanhere, and M. Hassan. An empirical study of bandwidth predictability in mobile computing. In *Proc. ACM WiNTECH*, pages 11–18, 2008.

[28] G. Yavaş, D. Katsaros, Ö. Ulusoy, and Y. Manolopoulos. A data mining approach for location prediction in mobile environments. *Data & Knowledge Engineering*, 54(2):121–146, 2005.

[29] F. Yu and V. Leung. Mobility-based predictive call admission control and bandwidth reservation in wireless cellular networks. *Computer Networks*, 38(5):577–589, 2002.

[30] H. Zang and J. C. Bolot. Mining call and mobility data to improve paging efficiency in cellular networks. In *Proc. ACM MOBICOM*, pages 123–134, 2007.

Magic of Wireless Sensor Networks

Dharma P. Agrawal
Center for Distributed and Mobile Computing
EECS Department
University of Cincinnati
Cincinnati, OH 452221-0030, USA
dpa@cs.uc.edu
www.cs.uc.edu/~dpa

ABSTRACT

Wireless Sensor Networks (WSNs) have been primarily introduced for defense application, with an objective of monitoring enemy's activities without any human intervention, using a large number of wireless sensor nodes (SNs) and a Base Station (BS) or a sink to collect information from all SNs. In recent years, advances in miniaturization, low-power circuit design, improved low cost, and small-size batteries have made it possible for monitoring physical parameters such as temperature, pressure, velocity, acceleration, stress and strain, fatigue, tilt, light intensity, sound, humidity, gas-sensors, biological, pollution, impurity level detection, nuclear radiation, civil structural sensors, blood pressure, sugar level, white cell count, and many others. The magic of WSNs is also expanded to Wireless Body Area Sensor Network (WBASN) as applied to human health. We introduce an interesting application of WBASN in the field of Sports Medicine by monitoring postural balance and stability of athletes in real time and providing valuable feedback to the coaches so as to minimize athletes' injury and maximize their playing potential. We also consider a fascinating application of continuous, non-invasive wireless home monitoring of patients with movement disorders and Parkinson's disease. We discuss an effective home based monitoring system that could monitor patients in their homes. Final comments are added to provide glimpse of what WSNs can do in numerous areas.

Categories and Subject Descriptors

C.2.1 [COMPUTER-COMMUNICATION NETWORKS]: Network Architecture and Design---Wireless communication; C.2.3 [COMPUTER-COMMUNICATION NETWORKS]: Network Operations---Network management.

Keywords

Networking; Wireless Sensor Networks; Wireless communications

MSWiM'14, September 21–26, 2014, Montreal, QC, Canada.
ACM 978-1-4503-3030-5/14/09.
http://dx.doi.org/10.1145/2641798.2660247

Bio

Dharma P. Agrawal is the Ohio Board of Regents Distinguished Professor and the founding director for the Center for Distributed and Mobile Computing in the Department of Electrical Engineering and Computing Systems. He has been a faculty member at the ECE Dept., Carnegie Mellon University (on sabbatical leave), N.C. State University, Raleigh and the Wayne State University. His current research interests include applications of sensor networks in monitoring Parkinson's disease patients and neurosis, applications of sensor networks in monitoring fitness of athletes' personnel wellness, applications of sensor networks in monitoring firefighters physical condition in action, efficient secured communication in Sensor networks, secured group communication in Vehicular Networks, use of Femto cells in LTE technology and interference issues, heterogeneous wireless networks, and resource allocation and security in mesh networks for 4G technology.

His recent contribution in the form of a co-authored introductory text book on Introduction to Wireless and Mobile Computing has been widely accepted throughout the world and fourth edition is in press. The book has been has been reprinted both in China and India and translated in to Korean and Chinese languages. His co-authored book on Ad hoc and Sensor Networks, 2nd edition, has been published in spring of 2011. A co-edited book entitled, Encyclopedia on Ad Hoc and Ubiquitous Computing, has been published by the World Scientific and co-authored books entitled Wireless Sensor Networks: Deployment Alternatives and Analytical Modeling, and Innovative Approaches to Spectrum Selection, Sensing, On-Demand Medium Access in Heterogeneous Multihop Networks, and Sharing in Cognitive Radio Networks have being published by Lambert Academic.

He is a founding Editorial Board Member, International Journal on Distributed Sensor Networks, International Journal of Ad Hoc and Ubiquitous Computing (IJAHUC), International Journal of Ad Hoc & Sensor Wireless Networks and the Journal of Information Assurance and Security (JIAS). He has served as an editor of the IEEE Computer magazine, and the IEEE Transactions on Computers, the Journal of Parallel and Distributed Systems and the International Journal of High Speed Computing. He has been the Program Chair and General Chair for numerous international conferences and meetings. He has received numerous certificates from the IEEE Computer Society. He was awarded a Third Millennium Medal, by the IEEE for his outstanding contributions. He has delivered keynote speech at 34 different international conferences. He has published over 657 papers, given 56 different tutorials and extensive training courses in various conferences in USA, and numerous institutions in

Taiwan, Korea, Jordan, UAE, Malaysia, and India in the areas of Ad hoc and Sensor Networks and Mesh Networks, including security issues. He has graduated 70 PhDs and 58 MS students.

He has been named as an ISI Highly Cited Researcher, is a Fellow of the IEEE, the ACM, the AAAS and the World Innovation Foundation, and a recent recipient of 2008 IEEE CS Harry Goode Award. Recently, in June 2011, he was selected as the best Mentor for Doctoral Students at the University of Cincinnati. Recently, he has been inducted as a charter fellow of the National Academy of Inventers. He has also been elected a Fellow of the IACSIT (International Association of Computer Science and Information Technology), 2013.

Multi-Channel Slotted Aloha Optimization for Machine-Type-Communication

Osama Arouk
IRISA, University of Rennes 1
Campus Beaulieu, 35042 Rennes, France
osama.arouk@irisa.fr

Adlen Ksentini
IRISA, University of Rennes 1
Campus Beaulieu, 35042 Rennes, France
adlen.ksentini@irisa.fr

ABSTRACT

Deploying a massive number of MTC (Machine - Type - Communication) devices in the current cellular mobile networks represents a great challenge as they may cause congestion and system overload for both RAN (Radio Access Network) and CN (Core Network) parts. To address this issue, we propose a novel algorithm, named Multi-Channel Slotted ALOHA-Optimal Estimation (MCSA-OE), which estimates the network status (the number of active devices), and thus better controlling the RAN access. Unlike most existing methods that consider only one channel, MCSA-OE uses the statistics of all the channels in order to estimate the number of arrivals (UE and MTC devices) in each RA (Random Access) slot. Simulation results demonstrate that MCSA-OE well tracks the number of arrivals as long as they are smaller than $\ln(R^R)$, where R is the number of channels. Moreover, we propose to use MCSA-OE estimation to dynamically adjust the $acb\_BarringFactor$ of the Access Class Barring (ACB) mechanism. Again, simulation results show that the behavior of our proposition merely tends to that of the best acknowledgment case, i.e. when the number of arrivals in each RA slot is well known.

Categories and Subject Descriptors

C.2.1 [**Computer-Communication Networks**]: Network Architecture and Design — *Wireless communication*

Keywords

3GPP; LTE; M2M; MTC; Congestion Control; Overload Control; Multi-Channel Slotted ALOHA; Optimal Estimation

1. INTRODUCTION

Machine - to - Machine (M2M), or Machine - Type - Communication (MTC), is an emerging type of communication that connects devices (things) to each other and to the Internet without a necessarily human intervention. It attracts

a great interest as it promises to provide revenue growth with the proliferation of M2M devices in a broad variety of applications, such as smart grid, health care, Intelligent Transport System (ITS), tracking/tracing, etc. M2M communications are different from the traditional Human - to - Human (H2H) communications, for which the current cellular mobile networks are designed, as they involve different markets, and have many characteristics that are unique for M2M. Some of these characteristics are time controlled, low/no mobility, and small data transmission. In addition, recent forecasts [9] predict that by 2020, 60 billion of M2M devices will be connected to the Internet. Therefore, a great pressure will be put on the underlying networks to support the raising traffic load from M2M. Particularly, if we focus on cellular networks, as the main target for deploying M2M devices due to their availability, supporting this enormous number of devices would be very challenging. Indeed, a very larg amount of signaling/data traffic generated by the M2M devices may cause congestion and overload in both RAN (Radio Access Network) and CN (Core Network) parts.

Many studies in the standardization groups (e.g. 3GPP (3rd Generation Partnership Project)) and the literature have been done to solve, or alleviate, the problem of congestion and system overload caused by M2M in the cellular mobile networks. Some of 3GPP solutions are: 1) separate RACH (Random Access Channel) resources; 2) dynamic allocation of RACH resources; 3) Access Class Barring (ACB) scheme [6]. Besides 3GPP propositions, several solutions exist in the literature, such as grouping MTC devices [17, 8], aggregating MTC traffic [17, 16], etc. However, it is well established that knowing, or at least estimating, the network status would efficiently help to treat the congestion and system overload issue. Many works have been proposed to estimate the network status, such as Q+-Algorithm [13], stable control procedure [11], and FASA (Fast Adaptive Slotted Aloha) [20]. FASA exploits the history of many consecutive slots in order to estimate the number of active devices. Through computer simulation, the authors have demonstrated the superiority of FASA compared to Q+-Algorithm whose throughput suffers due to the estimation's fluctuation [20]. Note that FASA has been proposed for one-channel system, and it is mentioned that it can be generalized to multi-channel system by borrowing the idea of [10]. However, the generalization of FASA to multi-channel can not be done directly, as demonstrated later. The authors in [11] have proposed the stable control procedure for stabilizing multi-channel slotted Aloha with MTC traffic load. In spite of its performance, as demonstrated by simulation for Poisson traffic load, this method does not work well under heavy traffic load, e.g. Beta distribution based traffic load [6], as proved later. Accordingly, in this paper a novel algorithm is proposed in order to better estimate the number of arrivals in each RA (Random Access) slot, and thus to better control the access to the network. The main idea of our proposition is to take the statistics of all the RACH channels, i.e. whether the channels are idle, success, or collided, and then exploit them to approximate the number of arrivals. The main advantage of our proposition is that it is independent of the traffic, and hence could work under any traffic model.

The remainder of this paper is organized as follows. In section 2, some background on the RACH (Random Access Channel) procedure and the congestion control are introduced. Section 3 presents the algorithm MCSA-OE in more details. The performance evaluation of MCSA-OE is introduced in section 4. Finally, the conclusion is presented in section 5

2. RELATED WORK

Before presenting solutions to alleviate system overload in the RAN part of LTE (Long Term Evolution) and LTE-A (LTE-Advanced) networks, we begin by giving some background on the main mechanism used at the RAN part, namely the RACH (Random Access Channel) procedure.

2.1 RACH procedure

Usually, each terminal in the idle state has to perform the RACH procedure in order to establish communication with the network. The signaling flow representing this procedure is illustrated in figure 1. Generally, there are two forms of the RACH procedure: Non-Contention-based and Contention-based RACH procedures. In the first one, the network informs the terminal when and which channel can be used. Therefore, no collision can occur as the channel will be used by only one terminal at a certain time. This type can be used, for example, for handover or Downlink (DL) data arrival. The Contention-based RACH procedure is used, for example, for the initial access in order to establish a radio link (moving from RRC_Idle to RRC_CONNECTED), or to restore the Uplink synchronization if Uplink or Downlink data arrives and the terminal is in the state RRC_ CONNECTED but not synchronized. The steps constituting the Contention-based RACH procedure are as follows:

1. Random Access Preamble Transmission (Msg1): in the first step, a randomly chosen preamble will be transmitted in the next available RA slot. This step allows the network to estimate the transmission timing of the terminal, allowing the terminal to adjust its uplink synchronization later.

2. Random Access Response (Msg2): After transmitting a preamble, the terminal monitors the PDCCH (Physical Downlink Control Channel) channel for the RAR (Random Access Response) message during the RAR window. The RAR message contains, among other things, TA (Timing Advance) command used to adjust the uplink synchronization, and TC-RNTI (Temporary Cell-Radio Network Temporary Identifier). TC-RNTI is the temporary ID of the terminal in the cell to which it is attached, and can be promoted to C-RNTI

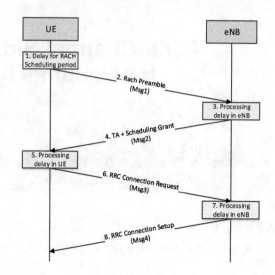

Figure 1: Signaling flow of Contention-based RACH procedure

if the terminal has not yet one. Msg2 also assigns uplink resources to be used by the terminal in the next step. For Non-Contention-based RACH procedure, the terminal supposes that the procedure has been successfully finished, while the others with Contention-based Procedure will continue to the next step.

3. RRC Connection Request (Msg3): after receiving the RAR message, the terminal adjusts its uplink synchronization and sends the message Msg3, using the uplink resources assigned in the second step, containing its ID and RRC Connection Request.

4. RRC Connection Setup (Msg4): this step is very important to solve the problem when more than one terminal uses the same preamble and the network successfully detects it. Indeed, these terminals have received the same Msg2, and therefore they share the same TC-RNTI. Each terminal receiving the downlink message (Msg4) compares the identity in the received message with that one transmitted in the third step. Only the terminal that observes a match between the two IDs will declare that the RACH procedure has been successfully finished. However, the others will restart the RACH procedure.

2.2 Congestion Control

As mentioned before, the existence of a huge number of MTC devices may cause congestion in the RAN part and the Core Network (CN) part. The RAN congestion control can be considered as the first defense line of the network against the congestion, and therefore the majority of the congestion's problem can be avoided if a well-designed RAN method can be introduced. A simple solution is to do backoff once the device has a collision, and then it retransmits after a backoff time [4]. However, using this method may work under low traffic load, but it is not practical under heavy traffic load [1]. Many RAN congestion control methods have been agreed by 3GPP [6]. These methods can be divided into Pull based mechanisms and push based mechanisms. In the pull based mechanisms, the network initiates the RACH procedure, and therefore all the process is centralized. This type of methods can be applied when the network is aware when the devices have data to be sent or the MTC server needs some information from the MTC devices. Thus, the CN can page the concerned MTC devices by sending a paging message to them [3, 8]. Although this kind of methods achieves good performances, as the control is totally held by the network, it is not always applicable as the behavior of MTC devices may not be known in advance like in the case of event driven applications, i.e. the MTC devices will be activated once an event has been detected. In the push based mechanisms, the MTC devices initiate the RACH procedure, and thus all the process is decentralized. Separating the RACH resources is an example of this type of mechanisms, where the RACH resources (preambles and frequency bands) are separated for MTC and UEs in order to alleviate the impact of MTC devices on the UEs. Dynamic allocation of RACH resources can be viewed as an improvement on the separation of RACH resources. However, it can be applied only when the network is able to predict the period when the traffic load will be high. Another method belonging to the second category is using the Access class Barring (ACB) principle. In this scheme, a separate Access Class is assigned to each class (e.g. based on QoS requirements) of MTC devices, allowing the network to control their access and the access of UEs too. When ACB mechanism is applied, the network broadcasts two parameters: (i) $acb\_BarringFactor$ that determines the probability that the device can access the network and (ii) $acb\_BarringTime$ that represents the associated backoff time before the next trial if the device is not allowed to access the PRACH (Physical RACH). When a MTC device is barred, the backoff time is calculated by the following equation [7]:

$$T\_Barring = (0.7 + 0.6 * rand()) * acb\_BarringTime \quad (1)$$

where $rand()$ is a random number uniformly distributed in the range $0 \leq rand() < 1$. ACB mechanism is an effective solution to alleviate the congestion [2]. Moreover, there are many methods proposed in the literature to improve the performance of ACB, such as [12, 14]. The authors in [12] have proposed a method to calculate the proper barring factor in order to control the CN congestion, but they did not take into consideration the RAN congestion. The proposed method in [14] works when the network includes small cells, where the ACB barring parameters are jointly decided by all the base stations (small cells and eNBs (Evolved Node B)). However, this method can be applied only in the overlapped regions between the cells (macro and micro cells). Usually, the best way to control the network is by knowing its status. The estimation of the network status is challenging when the network includes M2M devices, as a large number of devices can be simultaneously (or near simultaneously) activated. Methods of estimating the network status can be classified into additive and multiplicative schemes, wherein the estimation is updated in an additive or multiplicative manner, respectively. Pseudo Bayesian ALOHA (PB-ALHOA) [15] is an example on the additive class. However, the additive methods can not properly track the network status in the case of high traffic load [20]. On the other hand, multiplicative methods, such as Q+-Algorithm [13], are more efficient and can quickly track the network status. The authors in [20] have proposed an adaptive method, named FASA (Fast Adaptive Slotted ALOHA), in order to track the network status based on the statistics of access outcomes in the past.

The advantage of FASA is that it is more stable compared to Q+-Algorithm that suffers from the estimation's fluctuation [20]. However, FASA is designed for only one channel, and can not be directly generalized, as demonstrated in the next section. The work in [11] presents another way to estimate the network status. Whilst it well performs with Poisson traffic model, the stable control procedure [11] is not adequate for high traffic load, e.g. Beta traffic model, as demonstrated later.

2.2.1 Why can not FASA be directly generalized to multi - channel?

As stated before, FASA is detailed for one channel. In this section, we will prove that FASA cannot be directly generalized to multi-channel case. First, we briefly recall the equations used in FASA to estimate the number of arrivals, by focusing on the case where there is no arrivals, i.e. $Z_{t-1} = 0$,

$$K_t = \begin{cases} -\min\{K_{0,t-1}, k_m\} & \text{if } Z_{t-1} = 0 \\ 0 & \text{if } Z_{t-1} = 1 \\ -\min\{K_{c,t-1}, k_m\} & \text{if } Z_{t-1} = c \end{cases} \quad [20]$$

$$K_{t+1} = \begin{cases} -\min\{| K_t | +1, k_m\} & \text{if } K_t < 0, Z_t = 0 \\ -1 & \text{if } K_t \geq 0, Z_t = 0 \end{cases} \quad (17)[20]$$

$$\hat{N}_{t+1} = \max\{1, \hat{N}_t - 1 - h_0(v)| K_{t+1} |^v\} \text{ if } Z_t = 0 \quad (19)[20]$$

where Z_t is the access outcome at the time t and takes the values 0, 1, or c whether the slot is idle, success, or collided, respectively, k_m is the maximum number of consecutive slots, $K_{0,t-1}$ is the number of consecutive idle slots up to the slot $(t-1)$, v is a parameter, K_t is the number of consecutive slots, and $h_0(v)$ is a function of v that guarantees the right direction of the estimation. After many idle consecutive slots, the absolute value of K_t becomes large, and thus the absolute value of K_{t+1} also becomes large as K_t is negative. As a result, the term $h_0(v)| K_{t+1} |^v$ will be large, and therefore $\hat{N}_{t+1} = 1$ even if the channel is idle. Now, if we borrow the idea of [10] for extending FASA to multi-channel, the estimated number of devices is calculated by the equation (9) form [10], as follows:

$$\hat{U}_{t+1} = \sum_{r=1}^{R} \hat{U}_{r,t+1} \quad (9)[10]$$

where R is the number of channels, $\hat{U}_{r,t+1}$ is the estimated number of devices for the channel r ($\hat{U}_{r,t+1} = N_{t+1}$), and $\hat{U}_{t+1}$ is the estimated number of devices for R channels. As we see from the equation (19) from [20], $\hat{U}_{r,t+1}$ is equal to 1 when the channel is idle. If $R = 54$, for example, the estimated value $\hat{U}_{t+1}$ is equal to 54, though all the channels are idle. Figure 2 shows the performance of FASA for multi-channel system under heavy traffic load, where there are 30000 MTC devices and 1000 UEs with Beta and Poisson distribution based traffic loads, respectively. The simulation parameters are summarized in Table 1, while the parameters of FASA are $v = 1$ and $k_m = 16$. We observe from this figure that the estimated number of arrivals $\hat{U}(t)$ remains equal to R at the start of the time. By increasing the number of arrivals, the estimated value $\hat{U}(t)$ increases with large steps, moving away from the true value. Therefore, the extension of FASA from one channel to multi-channel can not be directly done. The same case can be found for the equation of Q+-algorithm used in [20].

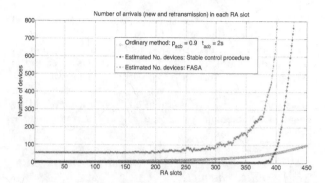

Figure 2: The behavior of stable control procedure and FASA for 30000 MTC devices following Beta distribution, $\alpha = 3$, $\beta = 4$, and 1000 UEs following Poisson distribution

2.2.2 Why is not the stable control procedure adequate for high traffic?

Now, we will focus on the work presented in [11], named stable control procedure, to prove its inefficiency for high traffic load. Indeed, although stable control procedure has been proposed for MTC with Poisson traffic load, we found that this method can not be adequate for high traffic load, e.g. Beta distribution based traffic load. This method uses the following model to estimate the number of arrivals in each RA slot:

$$Z(t+1) = \max\{1, Z(t) + \Delta Z(t)\} \qquad (2)[11]$$

$$\Delta Z(t) = \sum_{i=1}^{R} (aI(v_i(t) = 0) + bI(v_i(t) = 1) + cI(v_i(t) \geq 2))$$

where $Z(1) = 1$, $v_i(t)$ is the number of devices attempting to access the channel i at the time t, $I(.)$ is th indicator function, and $a = -1$, $b = -1$, and $c = \frac{2}{e-2}$. Let $R_I(t)$, $R_S(t)$, and $R_C(t)$ denote the number of channels, where $(v_i(t) = 0)$, $(v_i(t) = 1)$, and $(v_i(t) \geq 2)$, respectively, at the time t. So, the equation of $\Delta Z(t)$ can be written as:

$$\Delta Z(t) = aR_I(t) + bR_S(t) + cR_C(t)$$
$$= -R_I(t) - R_S(t) + \left(\frac{2}{e-2}\right) R_C(t) \qquad (2)$$

where $R_I(t) + R_S(t) + R_C(t) = R$. At the start of the time, there is a little traffic (when Beta distribution based traffic load is applied), and thus $R_I(t) + R_S(t) > \left(\frac{2}{e-2}\right) R_C(t)$. This means that $\Delta Z(t)$ will be negative, and therefore $Z(t+1) = 1$. When $\Delta Z(t)$ is equal to zero, we have,

$$-R_I(t) - R_S(t) + \left(\frac{2}{e-2}\right) R_C(t) = 0 \qquad (3)$$

but $R_I(t) + R_S(t) = R - R_C(t)$. By substituting in the equation 3, we find

$$R_C(t) = \left(\frac{e-2}{e}\right) R \qquad (4)$$

It is worth noting that the collision probability can be approximated by $\hat{P}_C(t) = \frac{R_C(t)}{R}$, and thus $\hat{P}_C(t) = \frac{e-2}{e} = 1 - 2e^{-1}$. We know that the collision probability can be

written as $P_C = 1 - P_I - P_S = 1 - e^{-\frac{M}{R}} - \frac{M}{R} e^{-\frac{M}{R}}$. Therefore, we find that this collision probability corresponds to the case when the number of arrivals $M(t)$ is equal to the number of channels R. Therefore, $\Delta Z(t)$ is equal to zero once $M(t) = R$, and at this point $Z(t+1)$ will start to become more than 1. This can be true when $R = 1$, i.e. for one channel, while it is not true for multi-channel, especially when $R = 54$ for LTE and LTE-A networks. Figure 2 proves this result, where the estimated number of devices $\hat{M}(t)$ remains 1 until $M(t)$ reaches the number of channels R that is equal to 54 for the considered parameters. By increasing the number of devices, the estimated value $\hat{M}(t)$ augments with large steps, moving away from the true value.

3. MULTI-CHANNEL SLOTTED ALOHA - OPTIMAL ESTIMATION (MCSA-OE):

The main objective of the proposed mechanism is to estimate the number of arrivals in each RA slot, and thus tries to optimize the network, i.e. maximizing the capacity of Multi-Channel Slotted ALOHA . The proposed mechanism, named MCSA-OE (Multi-Channel Slotted Aloha- Optimal Estimation), is composed of two parts: estimation and fitting. Firstly, the estimation of the idle probability and the incoming number of devices are done. Then, fitting these values is done in order to avoid the large fluctuations in the estimation. Note that the two steps are done at the same time. In the following, we give more details on each step.

3.1 Estimation and fitting of Idle probability

Let R denote the number of available preambles in each RA slot. After having transmitted by the terminals, we assume that the eNB (Evolved Node B) computes the number of successful, collided , and idle preambles. Let t be the time of the RA slot, where $t = 0, 1, 2, ...$ Generally, the number of preambles at any time can be written as:

$$N_S(t) + N_I(t) + N_C(t) = R \qquad (5)$$

where, $N_S(t)$ is the number of preambles that are successfully received by the eNB, $N_I(t)$ is the number of preambles that are idle, and $N_C(t)$ is the number of preambles that are used by more than one device, MTC or UE, at the time t. Dividing the equation (5) by R, we obtain:

$$\frac{N_S(t)}{R} + \frac{N_I(t)}{R} + \frac{N_C(t)}{R} = \hat{P}_S(t) + \hat{P}_I(t) + \hat{P}_C(t) = 1 \quad (6)$$

where $\hat{P}_S(t)$, $\hat{P}_I(t)$, and $\hat{P}_C(t)$ are the estimated success, idle, and collision probabilities, respectively, at the time t. For hereunder, we will be interested only by the estimated idle probability. It is worth noting that the idle probability $P_I(t)$ can be written as in [18]:

$$P_I(t) = \left(1 - \frac{1}{R}\right)^{M(t)} \simeq e^{-\frac{M(t)}{R}} \qquad (7)$$

where $M(t)$ is the number of arrivals at the time t. Therefore, $M(t)$ can be estimated from the equation (7) as follows:

$$\hat{M}(t) = R \ln\left(\frac{1}{\hat{P}_I(t)}\right) \qquad (8)$$

It is clear from the equation (8) that small changes in $\hat{P}_I(t)$ will be accompanied with large changes in the estimated number of devices $\hat{M}(t)$, hence fitting procedure is needed.

Algorithm 1 is used to fit the idle probability (it should be noted that ΔP_I and ΔM are used to avoid the large fluctuations in the estimation). Regarding the fitting, it is

---

Algorithm 1 Estimation and fitting of the idle probability $\hat{P}_I(t)$ with the estimation of the number of devices $\hat{M}(t)$

$\Delta P_I \leftarrow 1/R$
if $t \leq 2$ **then**
    $\hat{P}_{I_n}(t) \leftarrow \hat{P}_I(t)$
else

$$\hat{P}_{I_n}(t) \leftarrow (2*\hat{P}_{I_n}(t-1) + \hat{P}_{I_n}(t-2) - \hat{P}_{I_n}(t-3))/2 \quad (9)$$

end if
if $|\hat{P}_{I_n}(t) - \hat{P}_I(t)| \leq \Delta P_I$ **then**
    $\hat{P}_{I_n}(t) \leftarrow \hat{P}_I(t)$
    $\hat{M}(t) \leftarrow R*\ln(1/\hat{P}_{I_n}(t))$
else
    if $\hat{P}_{I_n}(t) - \hat{P}_I(t) > 0$ **then**
        $\alpha \leftarrow (\hat{P}_{I_n}(t) - \hat{P}_I(t)) - \Delta P_I$
        $\hat{P}_{I_n}(t) \leftarrow \hat{P}_I(t) - \alpha$
    else
        $\alpha \leftarrow -(\hat{P}_{I_n}(t) - \hat{P}_I(t)) - \Delta P_I$
        $\hat{P}_{I_n}(t) \leftarrow \hat{P}_I(t) + \alpha$
    end if
    $\hat{M}(t) \leftarrow R*\ln(1/\hat{P}_{I_n}(t))$
end if

---

inspired from the Infinite impulse response (IIR) filter [19], a well known digital filter. The IIR filter can be expressed as:

$$y[t] = \sum_{k_1=0}^{P} b_{k_1} x[t-k_1] - \sum_{k_2=1}^{Q} b_{k_2} y[t-k_2] \quad (10)$$

where, b_{k_1} and b_{k_2} are the feedforward and feedbackward filter coefficients, and P and Q are the feedforward and feedbackward filter orders, respectively. As seen from Algorithm 1, the following equation has been used to fit the idle probability

$$\hat{P}_{I_n}(t) = \hat{P}_I(t) - (\hat{P}_{I_n}(t-1) + 0.5\hat{P}_{I_n}(t-2)$$
$$- 0.5\hat{P}_{I_n}(t-3) - \hat{P}_I(t)) \mp \Delta P_I$$
$$= 2\hat{P}_I(t) - \hat{P}_{I_n}(t-1) - 0.5\hat{P}_{I_n}(t-2) +$$
$$0.5\hat{P}_{I_n}(t-3) \mp \Delta P_I \quad (11)$$

or

$$\hat{P}_{I_n}(t) = b_0 \hat{P}_I(t) - \sum_{k_2=1}^{3} b_{k_1} \hat{P}_{I_n}(t-k_1) \mp \Delta P_I \quad (12)$$

From the equations 10 and 12, we find that the model used for fitting is IIR filter with $P = 0$ and $Q = 3$, where the coefficients have been obtained empirically. In fact, as the estimation of the number of arrivals is instantaneous and depends on the statistics of the number of preambles that are idle, the estimated value should be limited to avoid the large fluctuations. Therefore, the changes of the estimated idle probability is limited by the smallest change, which is $\Delta P_I = 1/R$.

3.2 Fitting of the estimated number of devices

The second step of the mechanism is to fit the estimated number of devices $\hat{M}(t)$. This step is necessary when the number of devices is large. As mentioned before, the idle probability can be expressed as $P_I(t) = e^{-M(t)/R}$. Taking the variation of $P_I(t)$, we obtain

$$\frac{\Delta P_I(t)}{\Delta M(t)} = -\frac{1}{R} e^{-\frac{M(t)}{R}} \quad (13)$$

$$| \Delta M(t) | = R \Delta P_I(t) e^{\frac{M(t)}{R}} \quad (14)$$

where $\Delta P_I(t)$ is set to a fixed value, i.e. $\Delta P_I(t) = \Delta P_I$. The number of arrivals in the case when $P_I(t) = \Delta P_I$ is equal to:

$$\hat{M}(t) = R\ln\left(\frac{1}{\Delta P_I}\right) = R\ln(R) = \ln\left(R^R\right) \quad (15)$$

By substituting in the equation 14, we find:

$$| \Delta M(t) | = e^{\frac{1}{R}\ln\left(R^R\right)} = R \quad (16)$$

Therefore, the changes in the estimated number of arrivals will be limited to the value R. Algorithm 2 is proposed for fitting $\hat{M}(t)$, and is similar to that of $\hat{P}_I(t)$. Indeed, it follows the same IIR filter principle. The output of the algorithm is $\hat{P}_{I_F}(t)$ and $\hat{M}_F(t)$, which are the estimated values of $P_I(t)$ and $M(t)$, respectively.

Algorithm 2 Fitting of the estimated number of devices $\hat{M}(t)$ in each RA slot

---

$\Delta M(t) \leftarrow e^{\hat{M}(t)/R}$
if $\Delta M > R$ **then**
    $\Delta M \leftarrow R$
end if
if $t \leq 2$ **then**
    $\hat{M}_F(t) \leftarrow \hat{M}(t)$
else

$$\hat{M}_F(t) \leftarrow (2*\hat{M}_F(t-1) + \hat{M}_F(t-2) - \hat{M}_F(t-3))/2 \quad (17)$$

end if
if $|\hat{M}_F(t) - \hat{M}(t)| \leq \Delta M$ **then**
    $\hat{M}_F(t) \leftarrow \hat{M}(t)$
    $\hat{P}_{I_F}(t) \leftarrow e^{-\hat{M}_F(t)/R}$
else
    if $\hat{M}_F(t) - \hat{M}(t) > 0$ **then**
        $\alpha \leftarrow (\hat{M}_F(t) - \hat{M}(t)) - \Delta M$
        $\hat{M}_F(t) \leftarrow \hat{M}(t) - \alpha$
    else
        $\alpha \leftarrow -(\hat{M}_F(t) - \hat{M}(t)) - \Delta M$
        $\hat{M}_F(t) \leftarrow \hat{M}(t) + \alpha$
    end if
    $\hat{P}_{I_F}(t) \leftarrow e^{-\hat{M}_F(t)/R}$
end if

---

4. PERFORMANCE EVALUATION

4.1 System model

In this paper, we consider the traffic model 2 as proposed by the 3GPP group [6], i.e. the arrival of devices follows Beta distribution with $\alpha = 3$ and $\beta = 4$. We assume that there is one eNB, and there are 30000 MTC devices as well as 1000 UEs activated according to Beta and Poisson distributions, respectively, during $10s$ for the both. The ACB mechanism will be applied only on the MTC devices, while

Table 1: simulation parameters

Parameter	setting
Traffic model for MTC devices	Beta distribution (α=3, β=4)
Traffic model for UEs	Poisson distribution
Average number of MTC devices	30000
Average number of UEs	1000
Distribution period	10 s
Cell Bandwidth	5MHz
PRACH config index	6
The total number of preambles in a random access slot	54
Maximum number of RARs that can be carried in one response message	3
Size of random access response window in sub-frame unit	5
mac-ContentionResolutionTimer	48
Backoff Inicator	20 ms
HARQ retransmission probability for Msg3 and Msg4 (non-Adaptive HARQ)	10%
Maximum number of HARQ transmission for Msg3 and Msg4 (non-Adaptive HARQ)	5
acb_BarringFactor	0.9
Acb_BarringTime	2 s

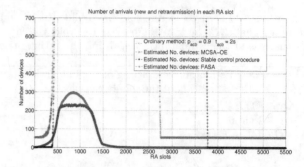

Figure 3: The number of devices in each RA slot with static ACB

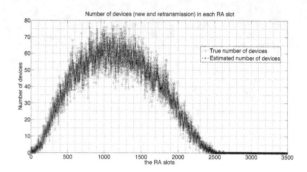

Figure 4: The performance of MCSA-OE for one experiment

the UEs directly pass to the RACH procedure. Regarding ACB parameters, $acb\_barringTime$ will be fixed to the value $2s$ for all the concerned methods, while $acb\_barringFactor$ is set to 0.9 only for the ordinary method, i.e. when applying the ACB mechanism with fixed parameters. Additionally, $acb\_barringFactor$ will be dynamically adjusted according to the number of arrivals for the best acknowledgment case (i.e. the number of arrivals in each RA slot is known) and for the proposed algorithm MCSA-OE. The best acknowledgment case is used as a benchmark in the comparison. We decided to use the aforementioned values for the ACB parameters to show how MCSA-OE behaves under such a worse case, where the number of cumulative arrivals (new and retransmission) for the ACB mechanism with the considered values reaches up to 300 arrivals.

4.2 Simulation Results

Computer simulation has been conducted on C++-based simulator in order to verify the proposed algorithm. The RACH parameters specified in Table 6.2.2.1.1 in [6] and the control-plane latency analysis determined in Table B.1.1.1-1 in [5] are used in the simulation. The parameters used in the simulation are summarized in Table 1. The evaluation of the algorithm will be done on two parts. The first part is for showing the performance of MCSA-OE when the $acb\_BarringFactor$ is fixed. In other words, MCSA-OE is applied in order to only estimate the number of arrivals. In the second part, MCSA-OE is used to dynamically adjust the $acb\_BarringFactor$ based on the estimated number of arrivals.

4.2.1 The performance with fixed ACB parameters:

In this case, we fix the $acb\_BarringFactor$ and see how the algorithm behaves. Figure 3 illustrates the number of devices in each RA slot. It is clear that the algorithm well works until certain value and then the estimated number of arrivals will fluctuate around this value, which represents the limitation of the algorithm. To explain this, we recall that $\Delta P_I = 1/R$. Thus, when the estimated idle probability $\hat{P}_I(t)$ reaches ΔP_I, the estimated number of devices reaches the limited value, which is $\hat{M}(t) = R\ln(1/\Delta P_I) = R\ln(R)$ or $\hat{M}(t) = \ln(R^R)$. For the considered parameters, we have $\hat{M}(t) = \ln(54^{54}) \simeq 215$, and hence $\hat{M}(t)$ fluctuates near

this value. Regarding the stable control procedure, it is demonstrated, again, that this method can not track the number of arrivals under heavy traffic load. Figure 3 also proves that FASA can not be directly generalized to multi-channel.

4.2.2 The performance with dynamic ACB:

In this case, we evaluate the algorithm with dynamic acb, i.e. $acb\_BarringFactor$ is adjusted according to the estimated number of arrivals and sent to the devices at the end of each RA slot. Figure 4 shows the true and the estimated number of devices in each RA slot for just one experiment. We see clearly that MCSA-OE well tracks the number of devices. The performance of MCSA-OE compared to the ordinary method (ACB mechanism with fixed parameters) and the best acknowledgment case is depicted in figure 5. We remark from this figure that the behavior of MCSA-OE merely tends to that of the best acknowledgment. This is clearly observed in figure 6, where MCSA-OE mostly reaches the maximum capacity. It is worth noting that the maximum capacity can be reached when the number of arrivals $M(t)$ is equal to the number of channels R, and thus the success probability is equal to $P_S(t) = (\frac{M(t)}{R} * e^{-\frac{M(t)}{R}}) = e^{-1} \simeq 0.37$. The success probability and the average access delay for the concerned methods is shown in Table 2. We remark that the performance of MCSA-OE is similar to that of the best acknowledgment case with a slightly augmentation in the access delay for MTC devices, but with a little difference regarding the UEs. These results validate the ones shown in figure 6, wherein the behavior of our algorithm is similar to the best acknowledgment case.

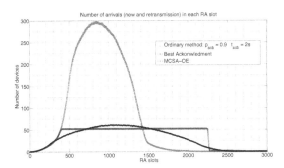

Figure 5: The number of devices in each RA slot with dynamic ACB

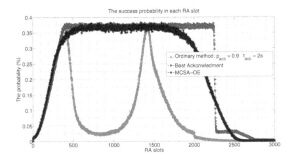

Figure 6: The success probability in each RA slot with dynamic ACB

Table 2: The success probability and the average access delay for the considered methods

	Success Probability(%)		Average Delay(ms)	
	MTC	UE	MTC	UE
Ordinary ACB	33.88	61.74	426.7	43.9
Best Acknowledgment	95.17	99.05	1844.91	52.66
MCSA-OE	94.72	98.43	1878.24	53.46

5. CONCLUSION

In this paper, the algorithm MCSA-OE is presented to estimate the number of arrivals in each RA slot, and thus to better control the congestion in the network. Our proposition has been tested on two parts; estimating the number of arrivals and adjusting the *acb_BrringFactor* of the ACB mechanism according to the estimated number of arrivals. Simulation results of the first part have proved that MCSA-OE well tracks the number of arrivals as long as they are smaller than $\ln(R^R)$. By dynamically adjusting the *acb_BarringFactor* of the ACB mechanism based on the estimated number of arrivals, MCSA-OE behavior tends to that of the best acknowledgment case, as proved by simulation. Therefore, our proposition achieves of best case regarding the success probability and the average access delay with high traffic load. Furthermore, MCSA-OE does not depends on the traffic model, and thus it may well work with any traffic model.

6. REFERENCES

[1] 3GPP R2-104662. MTC simulation results with specific solutions. ZTE, RAN2#71, August 2010.

[2] 3GPP R2-113197. Performance comparison of access class barring and MTC specific backoff schemes for MTC, May 2011.

[3] 3GPP R2-113198. Further analysis of group paging for MTC, May 2011.

[4] 3GPP TR 36.321. Medium Access Control (MAC) protocol specification, December 2012.

[5] 3GPP TR 36.912. Feasibility study for Further Advancements for E-UTRA (LTE-Advanced), September 2012.

[6] 3GPP TR 37.868 V11.0.0. Study on RAN improvement for Machine-type-Communications, September 2012.

[7] 3GPP TS 36.331 V11.5.0. Radio Resource Control (RRC); Protocol specification, 2013.

[8] O. Arouk, A. Ksentini, Y. Hadjadj-Aoul, and T. Taleb. On improving the group paging method for Machine-type-Communications. In *IEEE ICC 2014 - Ad-hoc and Sensor Networking Symposium (ICC'14 AHSN)*, pages 484–489, Sydney, Australia, June 2014.

[9] L. Changwei. Telco development trends and operator strategies. *WinWin Magazine*, (13):19–22, July 2012.

[10] S. Dongxu and V. O. K. Li. Stabilized multi-channel aloha for wireless ofdm networks. In *Global Telecommunications Conference, 2002. GLOBECOM '02. IEEE*, Month Published.

[11] O. Galinina, A. Turlikov, S. Andreev, and Y. Koucheryavy. Stabilizing multi-channel slotted aloha for machine-type communications. In *Information Theory Proceedings (ISIT), 2013 IEEE International Symposium on*, Month Published.

[12] A. Ksentini, Y. Hadjadj-Aoul, and T. Taleb. Cellular-based machine-to-machine: overload control. *Network, IEEE*, 26(6):54–60, 2012.

[13] D. Lee, K. Kim, and W. Lee. *Q+ -Algorithm: An Enhanced RFID Tag Collision Arbitration Algorithm*, volume 4611 of *Lecture Notes in Computer Science*, chapter 3, pages 23–32. Springer Berlin Heidelberg, 2007.

[14] S.-Y. Lien, T.-H. Liau, C.-Y. Kao, and K.-C. Chen. Cooperative Access Class Barring for Machine-to-Machine Communications. *Wireless Communications, IEEE Transactions on*, 11(1):27–32, 2012.

[15] R. L. Rivest. Network control by Bayesian broadcast. *Information Theory, IEEE Transactions on*, 33(3):323–328, 1987.

[16] T. Taleb and A. Ksentini. On alleviating MTC overload in EPS. *Ad Hoc Networks*, (0), 2013.

[17] T. Taleb and A. Kunz. Machine type communications in 3GPP networks: potential, challenges, and solutions. *Communications Magazine, IEEE*, 50(3):178–184, 2012.

[18] C.-H. Wei, C. Ray-Guang, and S.-L. Tsao. Modeling and estimation of one-shot random access for finite-user multichannel slotted aloha systems. *Communications Letters, IEEE*, 16(8):1196–1199, 2012.

[19] wikipedia. Infinite Impulse Response (IIR) Filter.

[20] H. Wu, C. Zhu, R. La, X. Liu, and Y. Zhang. FASA: Accelerated S-ALOHA Using Access History for Event-Driven M2M Communications. *Networking, IEEE/ACM Transactions on*, 21(6):1904–1917, 2013.

On Optimal Relay Placement for Improved Performance in Non-coverage Limited Scenarios

Mikhail Zolotukhin
Department of Mathematical
Information Technology
University of Jyväskylä
Finland
mikhail.m.zolotukhin@jyu.fi

Alexander Sayenko
3GPP standardization
Nokia Solutions and Networks
Espoo, Finland
alexander.sayenko@nsn.com

Timo Hämäläinen
Department of Mathematical
Information Technology
University of Jyväskylä
Finland
timo.t.hamalainen@jyu.fi

ABSTRACT

Low power nodes have been a hot topic in research, standardization, and industry communities, which is typically considered under an umbrella term called heterogeneous networking. In this paper we look at the problem of deploying optimally low power nodes in the context of relay networking, when an operator connects low power nodes (or small cells) via the wireless backhaul that uses the same spectrum and the same wireless access technology. We present an analytical model that can calculate optimal coordinates for low power nodes based on the input parameters, such as preferred number of nodes, their transmission power, parameters of the environment etc. The analytical calculations are complemented by extensive dynamic system level simulations, by means of which we analyze overall system performance for the obtained coordinates. We also show that even relatively marginal deviations from optimal coordinates can lead to worse system performance.

Categories and Subject Descriptors

C.2.1 [**Wireless Communication**]: Low power nodes and relay networking

Keywords

Wireless communication; relays; deployment; simulations

1. INTRODUCTION

Despite all the recent advances in wireless communications to improve achievable data rates, throughput demands from end customers have also been increasing thus putting a constant pressure on operators to seek for various solutions to meet new requirements. In the context of mechanisms, which are either already adopted in wireless technologies or which are being currently standardized, it bears mentioning trends such as multi-carrier deployments, higher order MIMO, coordinated multi-point/muti-flow technologies and also heterogeneous networking. Referring to that list,

it is crucial to mention that every solution has its disadvantages and benefits, whereupon disadvantages may play a decisive role in not deploying a particular mechanism or limiting it only to a specific case. As an example, multi-carrier deployments require huge operator investments to acquire new spectrum, higher order MIMO is also typically limited by amount of investments as an operator has to install more antennas at the base station sites, coordinated multi-point/multi-flow bring benefits only to the cell edge users and may require very tight coordination between the base station nodes. In that sense, heterogeneous networking starts to look very appealing for operators as this approach allows for improved performance by deploying more base stations within the existing spectrum instead of investing into more spectrum and/or deploying more complex macro sites. It is worth mentioning that even though heterogeneous networking is typically associated with *small cells*, it should be construed at a more general level that assumes that the network comprises base stations with different characteristics.

Referring specifically to small cells, there already have been large scale deployments, even for the HSPA technology, of compact base stations with transmission power less than 5W (as opposed to macro 10W or even 20W). However, one of the immediate challenges that an operator faces is how to connect such a base station to the wireless backhaul network. Wired connection is the most reliable and straightforward solution, but it limits immediately an area where such a base station can be deployed. An operator could resort for using the microwave wireless connection, which is a common solution for macro sites, but its cost and installation expenses become quite noticeable when compared to the cost of the low power base station. Furthermore, the microwave beam is typically just a few degrees and due to propagation properties of a high frequency range where it operates, it becomes not attractive as a wireless connection for the low power base stations or small cells.

At this point of time it bears mentioning that all the recent wireless technologies have an option for so-called relay networking. In one of the modes (see section 2 for more details) the relay node works exactly the same as base station or a small cell, but it uses the same wireless access technology to communicate with the super-ordinate base station. It provides quite an appealing option for an operator to deploy small cells and to connect them to the wireless backhaul through the relaying mechanisms. Furthermore, relaying can be used in the small cell initial deployment phase, so that the small cells can be switched later to the wired connection if such an opportunity arises. The only challenge with relays is that an operator should take a special care of deciding where to place (or not to place) the relay node. Of course, if an operator can identify clearly a hotspot with concentration of mobile users, then a choice for placing a low power node becomes almost trivial. Otherwise, if concentration patterns cannot be identified and/or mobile users tend to follow the uniform distribution, then this task becomes more challenging. The matter is that since a relay uses a portion of the wireless access network resources to communicate with the super-ordinate base station, that link might become a bottleneck or it might take too much resources thus leaving less space for exchanging data with mobile terminals. In addition, despite relatively low transmission power, low power nodes still cannot be placed too close because of mutual interference.

The problem of finding relay stations' optimal positions, which would ensure a high level of signal to interference/noise ratio (SINR) and as a result high data transmission rate, is investigated in many recent studies. For example, paper [5] considers a region which contains only one base station and proposes a method to deploy a fixed number of relay stations in such a way that the bandwidth requirement of mobile users are satisfied. The proposed scheme takes into account the IEEE 802.16j frame constraint and bandwidth requirement constraint, but it does not consider interference caused by base and relay stations; instead, it assumes that SINR depends only on the distance between the sender and the receiver. In study [15], the problem of determining optimal positions of macro base stations and relays in 802.16j network is formulated as an integer programming problem and solved with the help of branch and bound algorithm. Although the study takes into consideration user demand and cost information, it accounts neither for the size of relay and access zones nor increased interference caused by deployed relay stations. Study [16] aims to deploy relay stations in a way that allows for maximization of SINR for every user in the cell by formulating the problem as a non-convex integer programming problem and solving it with a genetic algorithm. However, this work does not take into consideration size of relay and access zones and the distribution of the bandwidth resource between mobile users.

In this research, we propose an algorithm to find optimal coordinates for the given number of relay stations in a region already covered by macro base stations; in other words we consider the non-coverage limited scenario. The algorithm aims to maximize downlink throughput for all mobile users in the considered region. The proposed solution takes into account interference caused by all the nodes, size of relay and access zones and the distribution of the bandwidth resource between mobile users. Numerical calculations and network performance simulations are carried out to show that calculated relay station positions allow to increase throughput of mobile users.

The rest of this paper is organized as follows. Section 2 provides a coarse overview of standardization solutions for relay networking already adopted in wireless standards, such as IEEE 802.16 WiMAX and 3GPP LTE. Section 3 delves into

a method for finding optimal coordinates for relays based on given parameters such path loss model, preferred number of relays, base station and relay transmission power etc. Section 4 provides exemplary optimal relay coordinates calculated for several scenarios, and presents dynamic system level simulations results for the aforementioned scenarios and coordinates. Finally, Section 5 summarizes the paper and outlines future research work.

2. STANDARDIZED RELAY SOLUTIONS

In this section, we provide a brief overview of standardized solutions for relaying networking, which one can found in wireless technologies such as IEEE 802.16 WiMAX and 3GPP LTE (3GPP HSPA does not have relays). IEEE 802.16 allows for a plethora of different relay options, technical description of which is given in [2] and a good overview is presented in [9]. From the viewpoint of the spectrum usage, relays can be either in-band or out-band. From the viewpoint of the downlink (DL) management signaling, they can be either transparent or non-transparent.

There is a strong motivation to consider the non-transparent in-band relays working in the distributed scheduling mode. Firstly, an in-band relay reuses the *existent* spectrum instead of requiring a new frequency band. Secondly, a non-transparent relay with the distributed scheduling mode works in exactly the same way as a base station or a low power node from the viewpoint of all the key internal radio resource management algorithms. In particular, it makes scheduler implementation simpler and allows for reusing an existent macro base station software at relays without implementing a complicated centralized scheduling, and also allows for faster scheduling as both macro and relay schedulers work as independent entities.

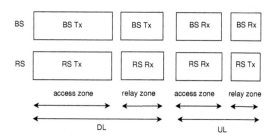

Figure 1: Non-transparent in-band relay frame structure (TDD).

For the sake of further clarity, Fig. 1 presents the frame structure of the non-transparent in-band relay working in the time division dumplexing (TDD) mode. The relay zone is a one where the base station (BS) and relay station (RS) exchange data. It must be noted that both BS and RS transmit simultaneously in the DL access zone to the associated mobile stations (MS) thus mutually interfering. A similar situation occurs in the uplink (UL) access link when MSs associated with RS and BS start to interfere with each other. The frequency division duplexing (FDD) frame structure is identical to the one described in Fig. 1 with the only different is that DL and UL sub-frames are not following each other on the same carrier, but rather reside on separate carriers with parallel and independent activity.

Even though Fig. 1 illustrates the frame structure of the IEEE 802.16 system, LTE relays works logically in exactly the same way [3, 4]. The only difference is that the LTE system allocates certain sub-frames for communication either between BS and RS (which corresponds to the relay zone in the IEEE 802.16 terminology), whereupon other sub-frames are for the communication with sub-ordinate mobile terminals (which corresponds to the access zone in the IEEE 802.16 terminology).

3. OPTIMAL RELAY PLACEMENT

In this section, we present an analytical model to find optimal coordinates for low power nodes connected to the wireless backhaul network through the same wireless access technology. We firstly describe details of the developed analytical model, which is formulated as optimization problem, and then describe the genetic algorithm to solve it.

3.1 Problem Formulation

Firstly, we focus on the deployment of a given number of RS nodes n^r. We consider an area that already contains n^b BS nodes, positions of which are $X^b = \{x_1^b, x_2^b, \ldots, x_{n^b}^b\}$. We assume that there are n^s MS nodes distributed uniforml in this region, whose positions are denoted as $X^s = \{x_1^s, x_2^s, \ldots, x_{n^s}^s\}$. Each MS is connected to a particular BS or RS node such that received signal power from that node is maximal among signals from other BSs and RSs.

The power of the signal P^{rv} received at the point x^{rv} from a source located at the point x^{tx} is calculated as follows:

$$P^{rv}(t^{tx}, t^{rv}, x^{tx}, x^{rv}) = \frac{P^{tx}(t^{tx})A(t^{tx}, x^{tx}, x^{rv})}{L(t^{rv}, x^{tx}, x^{rv})}, \quad (1)$$

where t^{tx} denotes the type of the transmitter: BS (b) or RS (r), t^{rv} is the type of the receiver: RS (r) or MS (s), P^{tx} is the transmitted signal power, L is path-loss on the distance between the transmitting station located at x^{tx} and receiver at the point x^{rv} and A is the antenna gain of the transmitting station.

The set of MSs X_{ti}^s served by the i-th node of type t^{tx} can be denoted as follows:

$X_{t^{tx}i}^s(X^r)$ is set of $x \in X^s$ such as:

$$\begin{cases} P^{rv}(t^{tx}, s, x_i^t, x) \geq P^{rv}(t^{tx}, s, x_l^t, x), \ l = 1, \ldots, n^t, \ l \neq i, \\ P^{rv}(t^{tx}, s, x_i^t, x) \geq P^{rv}(\bar{t}^{tx}, s, x_j^{\bar{t}^{tx}}, x), \ j = 1, \ldots, n^{\bar{t}^{tx}}, \end{cases} \quad (2)$$

where $\bar{t}^{tx}$ is type of node different than t^{tx}, i.e. if $t^{tx} = b$ then $\bar{t}^{tx} = r$, and if $t^{tx} = r$ then $\bar{t}^{tx} = b$.

The maximal available capacity C^s over the link between the i-th node of type t^{tx} and an MS located at $x \in X_{t^{tx}i}^s(X^r)$ is calculated based on the equation of Shannon channel capacity [13] as follows:

$$C^s(x, X^r) = Z_a B \log_2\left(1 + \frac{P^{rv}(t^{tx}, s, x_i^{t^{tx}}, x)}{N_0 + N(t^{tx}, s, x_i^{t^{tx}}, x)}\right), \quad (3)$$

where Z_a is the portion of the access zone in the downlink part of the frame, N_0 is thermal noise and N is the interfer-

ence caused by other transmitting base and relay stations:

$$N(t^{tx}, s, x_i^{t^{tx}}, x) = \sum_{\substack{l=1 \\ l \neq i}}^{n^{t^{tx}}} P^{rv}(t^{tx}, s, x_l^{t^{tx}}, x) +$$

$$+ \sum_{j=1}^{n^{\bar{t}^{tx}}} P^{rv}(\bar{t}^{tx}, s, x_j^{\bar{t}^{tx}}, x) \quad (4)$$

Each RS or BS node serves a number of MS nodes, whereupon MS individual throughput depends on the BS/RS scheduler. If we follow an approach that the scheduler allocates resources in a fair way, then achievable downlink throughput T^s for a MS at point $x \in X_{t^{tx}i}^s(X^r)$ can be calculated as follows:

$$T^s(x, X^r) = \alpha^s(x, X^r)C(x, X^r), \quad (5)$$

where $\alpha^s(x, X^r)$ is a portion of the bandwidth resources allocated by the scheduler. Following an approach presented in [10], this portion is inversely proportional to MS SINR at location x and also depends on SINR values of all the other MS nodes under the same BS or RS:

$$\alpha^s(x, X^r) = \frac{1}{C^s(x, X^r) \sum_{x \in X_{t^{tx}i}^s(X^r)} (C^s(x, X^r))^{-1}}, \quad (6)$$

Respectively, throughput of every MS from the set $X_{t^{tx}i}^s(X^r)$ is calculated as follows:

$$T^s(x, X^r) = \frac{Z_a B}{\sum_{x \in X_{t^{tx}i}^s(X^r)} (C^s(x, X^r))^{-1}}, \quad (7)$$

Similarly, we can describe the throughput of the link between the j-th RS and the $i(j)$-th BS to which this RS is logically connected to. The Shannon capacity value C^r is equal to

$$C^r(x_j^r, X^r) = Z_r B \log_2\left(1 + \frac{P^{rv}(b, r, x_{i(j)}^b, x_j^r)}{N_0 + \sum_{\substack{l=1 \\ l \neq i(j)}}^{n^b} P^{rv}(b, r, x_l^b, x_j^r)}\right), \quad (8)$$

where Z_r is the portion of the relay zone in the downlink part of the frame. The value of downlink throughput for the j-th RS at point x_j^r is calculated as follows:

$$T^r(x_j^r, X^r) = \frac{Z_r B}{\sum_{x_l^r : i(l)=i(j)} (C^r(x_j^r, X^r))^{-1}}, \quad (9)$$

Throughput T of a MS connected to the j-th RS depends not only on the SINR values of other MSs associated with that RS, but also on the throughput of the link between the j-th RS and the $i(j)$-th BS. Thus, throughput T of a MS located at coordinates x can be expressed as follows

$$T(x, X^r) = \begin{cases} T^s(x, X^r), & \text{if } x \in X_{bi}^s(X^r), \\ \min\left(T^s(x, X^r), \frac{T^r(x_j^r, X^r)}{|X_{rj}^s(X^r)|}\right), & \text{if } x \in X_{rj}^s(X^r). \end{cases} \quad (10)$$

To find optimal relay coordinates, we have to choose a certain performance metric that we will either maximize or minimize. As an example, in the coverage limited scenario a performance metric could be formulated as "obtain the minimum SINR level over the largest possible area so that as many MSs as possible can at least receive DL control channels". Since we consider non-coverage limited case, i.e. reception of the DL control channels is not an issue, one of the natural choices could be to maximize the mean throughput. However, catering for the mean throughput can lead to such coordinates that high throughput MSs will have even higher throughput at the expense of low throughput ones. Thus, we consider the target function that aims at maximizing the minimum throughput. As a result, the following optimization problem can be formulated:

$$\max_{X^r} \min_{x \in X^s} (T(x, X^r)),$$
$$\text{subject to } X^r \subset \Omega^r, \tag{11}$$

where Ω^r is the set of RS node coordinates. For the sake of simplicity, let us assume that this set is finite. Thus, the optimization problem (11) is an integer programming problem with non-convex objective function.

3.2 Genetic Algorithm

This optimization problem can be solved by applying a genetic algorithm (GA). GA is stochastic algorithm in which the principles of organic evolution are used as rules in optimization. Genetic algorithm is applied to an optimization problem when specialized techniques are not available or standard methods fail to give satisfactory answers [6, 8].

Genetic algorithm starts with an initial set of feasible solutions called population. After population size N_{ppl} is determined, the algorithm randomly picks sets of relay station positions X_k^r, where $k \in \{1, 2, \ldots, N_{ppl}\}$. Every relay station position in the k-th set satisfies the following conditions:

$$x_{kj}^r \in \Omega^r, \ \forall j \in \{1, 2, \ldots, n^r\}. \tag{12}$$

GA tends to an optimal solution, using processes similar to evolution: crossover and recombination. Recombination produces spontaneous random changes in various solutions of the current population. In this paper, two recombination operators are employed. In the first operator, each relay station position of every set is modified with probability which is defined beforehand. A new position is chosen randomly in such a way that the obtained solution has to satisfy conditions (12). This operator is used to maintain genetic diversity from one generation of a population to the next.

In the second operator, the best solution of the previous population X_{k*}^r is defined, and several modifications of this solution are added. These modifications are constructed in such a way, that they consist of relay station positions that are located in corresponding neighborhoods of relays in X_{k*}^r. The size of the neighborhood is defined beforehand, and all new positions are supposed to satisfy conditions (12). Thus, the operator alters slightly the best set of relay station positions, which potentially allows us to obtain even better solutions.

Crossover is a genetic operator that combines two solutions, or parents, to produce a new solution. The idea behind crossover is that the new solution may be better than any of the parents if it takes the best characteristics from each of the parents. In this research we use a single-point crossover. In this case, two parents are selected randomly from the current population. After that, a crossover point n_c^r is selected randomly so that $n_c^r \in \{1, \ldots, n^r\}$. A new solution is constructed by taking the coordinates of the first n_c^r relay stations from the first parent and the coordinates of the remaining $n^r - n_c^r$ relays from the second parent. The new solution has to satisfy conditions (12). Otherwise, a new set of parents is selected.

After crossover and recombination are performed, some solutions are selected for the next generation. In this paper we use the elitist selection method [14]. That means that we select N_{ppl} solutions, that maximize the objective function. Thus, we obtain the next generation, for which the processes of crossover, recombination and selection are applied again. The process of forming new generations continues till the maximal number of generations is reached.

4. NUMERICAL EXAMPLE & SIMULATIONS

In this section, we present a few numerical examples for optimal relays coordinates, complemented by extensive dynamic system simulations. The general methodology is that firstly we calculate optimal coordinates by means of the analytical model described in section 3, and then we substitute obtained coordinates to the dynamic system simulator where we have accurate modeling of physical, medium access, and application layers including the TCP protocol.

As a baseline scenario we choose the sub-urban area where an operator is interested in increasing the overall throughput by considering to deploy a certain number of RSs per a cell. The numerical example is conducted for the following scenarios: a) two RS nodes per cell with 5W transmission power; b) three RS nodes per cell with 5W transmission power; c) four RS nodes per cell with 2.5W transmission power. The choice for the number of RSs is motivated based on the cost analysis in [7] that states that it is better to have a few higher power RS nodes rather than a large number of very low-power ones. Furthermore, there is also a common assumption in the 3GPP simulation methodologies where a typical number of additional low power nodes per cell vary from one to four.

Table 1 presents the network parameters that we use in the analytical model. It is worth noting that RS uses an omni-directional antenna, has a lower transmission power and a smaller antenna height. The motivation is that a lower power requires a simpler and a less expensive amplifier chain. The omni-directional antenna simplifies the design and the installation efforts. Furthermore, an omni-directional antenna at the RS node allows for communicating efficiently to any MS around the RS node. The pathloss 802.16m SMa model for an access link and the 802.16j TypeD model for the relay link are taken from[1].

Most of the large scale simulations, conducted for instance in 3GPP, involve 19 sites with the 3-sector macro bases stations, thus resulting in 57 cells. Calculating optimal coor-

Table 1: Network parameters.

Parameter	Value
Inter-site distance	1500 m
Center frequency	2.5 GHz
Bandwidth	10 MHz
Reuse factor	1/3
BS / RS / MS Tx power	10 / 5 / 0.25 W
BS / RS / MS antenna pattern	3GPP / omni / omni
BS / RS / MS antenna gain	17 / 5 / 0 dBi
BS / RS / MS antenna height	32 / 7 / 1.5 m
access / relay link path loss	.16m SMa / .16j TypeD
Antenna technique	SISO
Thermal noise	-174 dBm/Hz

dinates for such a number of cells is an expensive computational task (even though it is has to be performed only once). Thus, in this paper we consider only three cells, which however belong to three different sites as depicted in Fig. 2. The point is that in frequency reuse 1/3 networks, these three macro base stations will have directional antennas facing each other, and thus it will account for dominating interfering nodes (as opposed to a case if we considered three cells belonging to the same site where directional antennas would point into opposite directions).

Table 2: Algorithm parameters.

Parameter	Value
Distance between MSs	10 m
Distance between candidates in Ω^r	10 m
Size of population	100
Probability in the first recombination operator	0.5
Size of the neighborhood in the second recombination operator	50 m
Maximal number of generations	100

To calculate optimal coordinates of RS nodes, we implement the algorithm presented in Section 3 in Matlab. Table 2 presents additional parameters that we applied while running the algorithm. In particular, to have as many points with SINR values as possible, we fill in the whole area with stations at distance of 10m.

Table 3 below presents calculated optimal RS coordinates for a case when an operator decides to deploy two, three, or four RS nodes per a cell. Since relays coordinates are the same in each cell with respect to the macro base station antenna direction, we express them in the polar system through the angle and the distance from the center of the hexagon area.

Table 3: Calculated RS coordinates.

Num. of RSs	Coordinates
2 RSs	{-29° 618} {29° 618}
3 RSs	{-30° 654m} {0° 279m} {30° 654m}
4 RSs	{+/-32° 678m} {+/-26° 427m}

Fig. 2 illustrates at the coarse level locations of the RS nodes as calculated by the analytical model (refer to Fig. 3 for exact coordinates of RS nodes and stations). As can be seen for a case of two RS nodes per cell, they are placed closer to the cell edge to the left and to the right of the macro BS antenna direction, which is due to the fact that it is an area with lower SINR values because of the macro BS antenna directional pattern. At the same time, it is worth noting that RS nodes are not placed too far from BS to avoid a situation when a link between BS and RS becomes

a bottleneck. When there are three RS nodes per cell, two side relays have almost the same locations, but are placed a bit farther from each other to avoid excessive interference with the third RS, while the latter is placed right in front of the macro BS antenna direction. In case of four RS nodes, two of them are placed even farther from each other when compared to previous scenarios, while two central RS nodes are placed closer to the cell center.

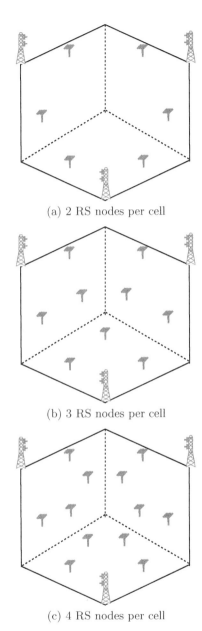

(a) 2 RS nodes per cell

(b) 3 RS nodes per cell

(c) 4 RS nodes per cell

Figure 2: RS node locations within the macro cell.

To test calculated coordinates in a more complex dynamic system level simulator, we use IEEE 802.16 as a reference wireless broadband system with a module described in [12], with additional enhancements such as full interference tracking model and hop-by-hop ARQ mode for relays (see below). Table 4 presents key parameters used in the simulation. As the application level traffic, we consider the DL full-buffer

TCP transmission over the best effort connections, where the IP level service data unit (SDU) size is 1000 bytes.

It is worth mentioning that depending on how many RSs we have per cell, two or three/four, the DL relay zone is set to 6 and 8 symbols accordingly. This is needed to ensure that the relay link does not become a bottleneck, especially when we have three RSs per cell. The UL zone size is fixed and has the constant size of 3 symbols.

Table 4: System parameters.

Parameter	Value
Duplexing mode	TDD
Frame duration	5 ms
CP length	1/8 symbol
TTG+RTG	296+168 PS
OFDM symbols	47
DL/UL symbols	30/15
DL/UL relay zone size	6...8 / 3 symbols
DL/UL subcarrier permut.	DL PUSC / UL PUSC
Channel report type / interval	CQICH / 10ms
Channel measurements DL/UL	preamble / data burst
Channel measurements filter	EWMA, $\alpha = 0.25$
Link adaptation model	target FEC BLER, 10^{-1}
DL MAP MCS	QPSK1/2 Rep6
Compressed MAPs	ON
Ranging transm. opport.	1
Ranging backoff start/end	0/15
Request transm. opport.	2
Request backoff start/end	1/15
CDMA codes	256
ranging+periodic ranging	64
bandwidth request	192
handover	–
PDU size	140 B
Fragmentation & Packing	ON
HARQ processes	16
HARQ retransmissions	4
HARQ advance timer	100 ms
ARQ block size	16 B
ARQ window	1024
ARQ block rearrangement	ON
ARQ deliver in order	ON
ARQ timers	
feedback interval	60 ms
retry	200 ms
block lifetime/Rx purge	500 ms

Unlike in previous simulations of relays environments [11], in this paper the ARQ mechanism works in the so-called hop-by-hop mode, whereupon each RS runs its own ARQ state machine. Even though ARQ mechanism can also work in the end-to-end mode thus logically bypassing RS nodes, it is less efficient especially when an RS serves MSs with low DL channel performance.[1]

To gather statistically reliable results, we run 20 different simulations, where each of them contains 16 MSs placed in random locations within each cell. In other words, 48 MSs

---

[1] Even though it is not the main topic of this article, it bears mentioning that relays *not* supporting hop-by-hop ARQ mode are simpler in implementation and ideally are better candidates for low cost low power nodes. At the same time, absence of intermediate ARQ state machine requires a relay node to support an additional flow control mechanism that would prevent super-ordinate BS from pushing more data than a relay can send. Otherwise, it may lead to expiry of ARQ timers and unnecessary re-transmissions or even ARQ resets. In that sense, it is better to invest development efforts into the intermediate ARQ state machine rather than an additional flow control mechanism.

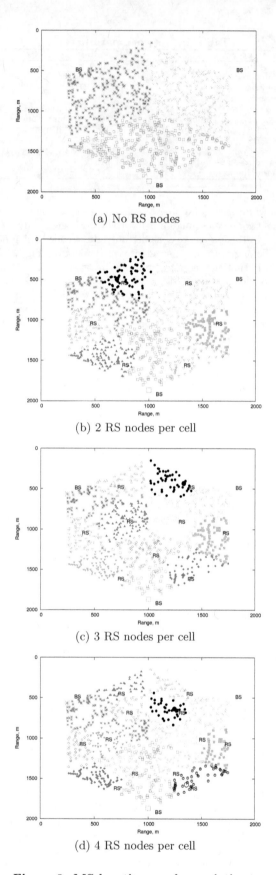

(a) No RS nodes

(b) 2 RS nodes per cell

(c) 3 RS nodes per cell

(d) 4 RS nodes per cell

Figure 3: MS locations and associations.

are injected into the simulation environment upon each run. Each simulation run lasts for 10 seconds, which is enough for the TCP protocol to stabilize.

Fig. 3 presents locations of *all* stations from all the simulation runs, and also indicates with which BS or RS each station has associated to exchanged data. As anticipated, RS nodes absorb quite a noticeable percentage of subscriber stations thus offloading macro BSs and improving performance of stations associated with them. It is also interesting to observe how stations get associated with either BS or RS depending on the latter transmission power and antenna patterns.

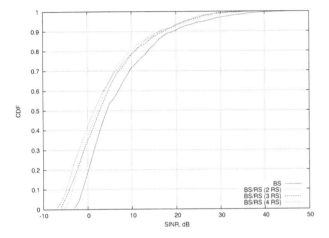

Figure 4: Mean downlink SINR

Fig. 4 show the ditsribution of the DL SINR values as measured at the mobile station side based on the DL preambles transmitted by BS and RS nodes. Since the actual SINR varies due to the fast fading, the figure shows the *mean* SINR averaged for each station over the whole simulation run, which implicitly filters out the fast fading component. As can be seen, deploying relays decreases the overall SINR by a few dBs because there are more transmitting nodes in the system, which in turn increase the overall interference level. In particular, the lowest SINR value of -3dB can decrease further down to -7dB with three/four RS nodes. However, despite the increased interference level, the overall system throughput improves as follows from Fig. 5. The matter is that there are more nodes that can independently schedule and send data, which in turn boosts achievable throughputs. As can be seen from Fig. 5, two RS nodes per cell improve the overall performance by approximately 39% when compared to the baseline case, and three RS nodes per cell improve the mean performance by 77%. As somewhat logically anticipated, four RS nodes with 2.5W have almost that same performance as two RS nodes with 5W. Nevertheless, it is worth noting that four RS nodes perform a bit better beause four different nodes can schedule independently transmissions to and from MSs.

Fig. 6 provides a better insight on the MS mean connection throughput when RS nodes are added to the simulation environment. The mean connection throughput is calculated as the total amount of data received by an MS divided by the simulation time. One of the first observations is that regard-

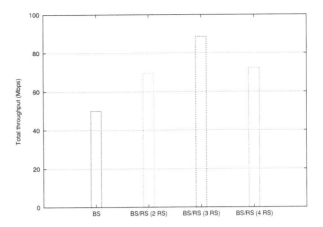

Figure 5: Mean total system throughput.

less of the number of RS nodes per cell, adding RS nodes may also impact negatively performance of certain MSs. As can be seen from the figure, there are 10-20% of MSs that experience somewhat lower throughput when compared to the baseline case. As mentioned a few times before, adding relays increase the overall interference level, especially with the full buffer traffic. Thus, unless MSs have interference canceling receivers, adding more interfering nodes will always cause some degradation to some users. As for the throughput gains, interestingly enough, adding three or four RS nodes to the simulation environment does not change noticeably performance of around 80%-tile MSs when compared to the gains already provided by two RS nodes. Performance improvement comes from 20% of high throughput MSs that contribute to the final gains when more RS nodes are deployed.

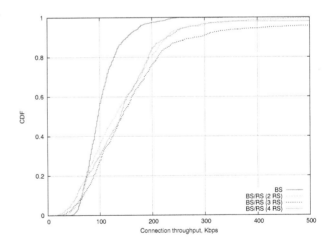

Figure 6: Mean connection throughput.

To illustrate what happens when RS coordinates are chosen in the non-optimal way, we conduct the simulation scenarios with coordinates as presented in Table 5. When compared to Table 3, we place RS nodes closer to each other and at a different distance from the macro base station. We intentionally do not change drastically coordinates to show that relatively marginal changes can be already become visible at the connection throughput level.

Table 5: Non-optimal RS coordinates.

Num. of RSs	Coordinates
2 RSs	{-23° 534m} {23° 534m}
3 RSs	{-23° 632m} {0° 346m} {23° 632m}
4 RSs	{+/-23° 618m} {+/-10° 346m}

For the sake of clarify, we present only the connection throughput CDF to show how it differs when compared to the optimal coordinates. As can be seen from Fig. 7, connection throughput has decreased for all the scenarios. In fact, the full picture is that for instance connection throughput 80%-tile remains almost the same. At the same time, one can observe performance degradation in a low throughput range: up to 40-50% of MSs now experience worse performance even when compared to the baseline scenario, which is especially the case for the scenario with four RS nodes. This is explained by the fact that if we put RS nodes closer to each other, as we did with the non-optimal coordinates, then their mutual interference start to diminish gains of close proximity with MSs.

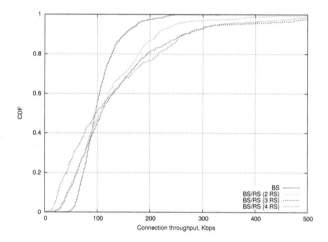

Figure 7: Mean connection throughput (non-optimal coordinates).

Comparing results presented in Fig. 6 and Fig. 7, one can see quite eloquently that even relatively marginal changes in RS coordinates can lead to quite noticeable changes in the resulting performance.

5. CONCLUSIONS & DISCUSSIONS

In this paper we have considered a problem of the optimal placement of low power relay nodes in the non-coverage limited scenario when an operator aims at improving the overall system performance. We developed an analytical model that allows for calculating optimal coordinates based on the provided parameters, such as distance between macro base stations, preferred number of low power nodes, their transmission power etc. Extensive dynamic system level simulations have confirmed that analytically calculated coordinates are indeed optimal, as moving low power nodes to different locations results in declined system performance.

It should be understood that obtained optimal parameters are optimal under the considerations we made, so changing the overall system load, path loss, introduction of shadowing or introduction of more advanced receivers may change the point that maximizes the target function. Nevertheless, from the viewpoint of the real life deployments, even if we specify accurately all the input parameters and obtain optimal coordinates, then it does not mean that an operator will have a possibility to deploy a low power node at calculated locations. In that sense, results of this research could be used as a guidance or a recommendation regarding where the lower power nodes should be, while their actual coordinates may be further constrained by other factors. In fact, simulation results from non-optimal coordinates presented in Table 5 also result in performance gains. So, deviating from the optimal point does not necessarily mean that the performance will become absolutely worse than in the baseline scenario.

Apart from tasks connected to real life deployments, obtained results can serve as input to various relay simulations and simulation methodologies. It is often the case that small cells simulations either do not have an agreed set of coordinates for low power nodes, or they are chosen semi-randomly. As showed in this paper, non-optimal coordinates can lead to worse performance, which in some simulations may be construed wrongly as a sign of a particular technology or a solution not meeting target requirements. Thus, by providing optimal coordinates for low power nodes the research community can construe better achievable gains.

Finally, it is worth noting that simulation results of two, three and four RS nodes per cell have showed that with uniform distribution of mobile stations, the majority of them benefit from introduction of two RS nodes, whereas introduction of more RS nodes has improved performance of approximately 20% of mobile stations. Furthermore, even though this paper does not aim at studying optimal number of low power nodes, it seems that two RS nodes with 5W might be more efficient than four RS nodes with lower transmission power. If we make an assumption that a low power node price does not heavily depend on its transmission power and operational expenses are proportional to the number of nodes, then an operator may consider deploying fewer nodes, but with a higher transmission power. A choice for deploying more low power nodes might be motivated only if mobile stations are not distributed uniformly and an operator can clearly identify so-called hotspot zones. So, in addition to calculating optimal coordinates of the given number of RS nodes, there is a broader challenge that can be formulated as an incremental gain from introduction of an additional low power node versus its initial and operational expenses versus the percentage of stations that will have better performance.

6. REFERENCES

[1] Multi-hop relay system evaluation methodology (channel model and performance metrics). IEEE 802.16 Broadband Wireless Access Working Group, Feb 2007.

[2] Air interface for broadband wireless access systems: Multihop relay specification. IEEE Standard 802.16j, Jun 2009.

[3] 3GPP TR 36.806. Relay architecture for E-UTRA (LTE-Advanced), Sep 2009.

[4] 3GPP TS 36.300 v12.0.0. Evolved universal terrestrial radio access (E-UTRA) and evolved universal terrestrial radio access network (E-UTRAN); overall description; stage 2, Mar 2014.

[5] C. Chang, C. Chang, M. Li, and C. Chang. A novel relay placement mechanism for capacity enhancement in IEEE 802.16j WiMAX networks. In *IEEE International Conference on Communications (ICC)*, pages 1–5, 2009.

[6] J. Herrmann. A genetic algorithm for minimax optimization problems. In *Proceedings of the Congress on Evolutionary Computation*, pages 1099–1103, 1999.

[7] E. Lang, S. Redana, and B. Raaf. Business impact of relay deployment for coverage extension in 3GPP LTE-Advanced. In *IEEE International Conference on Communication*, Jun 2009.

[8] H. Muhlenbein, M. Georges-Schleuter, and O. Kramer. Evolution algorithms in combinatorial optimization. *Parallel Computing*, 7(1):65–85, 1988.

[9] S. W. Peters and R. W. Heath. The future of WiMAX: multihop relaying with IEEE 802.16j. *IEEE Communications Magazine*, Jan 2009.

[10] A. Sayenko, O. Alanen, and T. Hämäläinen. Scheduling solution for the IEEE 802.16 base station. *Computer Networks*, 52:96–115, 2008.

[11] A. Sayenko, O. Alanen, and H. Martikainen. Analysis of the non-transparent in-band relays in the IEEE 802.16 multi-hop system. In *IEEE Wireless Communications and Networking Conference*, pages 1–6, Apr 2010.

[12] A. Sayenko, O. Alanen, H. Martikainen, V. Tykhomyrov, O. Puchko, V. Hytönen, and T. Hämäläinen. WINSE: WiMAX NS-2 Extension. *Special Issue of Simulation: Software Tools, Techniques and Architectures for Computer Simulation*, 87:24–44, Jan 2011.

[13] C. Shannon. Communication in the presence of noise. 37:10–21, 1949.

[14] R. Sharapov and A. Lapshin. Optimal feature selection for support vector machines. *Pattern Recognition and Image Analysis*, 16(3):392–397, 2006.

[15] Y. Yang, S. Murphy, and L. Murphy. Planning base station and relay station locations in IEEE 802.16j multi-hop relay networks. In *Consumer Communications and Networking Conference (CCNC)*, pages 922–926, 2008.

[16] M. Zolotukhin, V. Hytönen, T. Hämäläinen, and A. Garnaev. Optimal relays deployment for 802.16j networks. *Springer. Mobile Networks and Management. Lecture Notes of the Institute for Computer Sciences, Social Informatics and Telecommunications Engineering*, 97:31–45, 2012.

Performance of Simple Polling MAC With Wireless Re-charging in the Presence of Noise

Jelena Mišić
Ryerson University
Toronto, ON, Canada
jmisic@scs.ryerson.ca

Mohammad Shahnoor
Islam Khan
Ryerson University
Toronto, ON, Canada
m329khan@ryerson.ca

Vojislav B. Mišić
Ryerson University
Toronto, ON, Canada
vmisic@ryerson.ca

ABSTRACT

We consider a simple Medium Access Control (MAC) protocol that lends itself well for the operation of wireless sensor networks (WSN) with wireless RF recharging of sensor node energy source. Since individual nodes are equipped with a single antenna, data transmission must be temporarily interrupted when one or more nodes request energy recharging. We develop a probabilistic model of the energy depletion process within the proposed round-robin MAC operating with a 1-limited scheduling policy. We evaluate the impact of recharging period on the MAC operation under varying traffic load and varying bit error rate.

Keywords

wireless sensor networks; RF recharging; MAC protocol

1. INTRODUCTION

Sensor networks often need to operate unattended and without regular replacement or recharging of their batteries. To this end, periodic recharging of individual node batteries can be done through energy harvesting from the environment [3], which is by necessity only a best-effort approach since there is no guarantee that the harvested energy will suffice for node operation, or indeed that it will be available at all when needed.

A better solution is, then, to use RF pulses emitted by the network base station/sink or the network coordinator [10, 9]. In this case, recharging may occur in periodic intervals or on demand, when one or more sensor nodes report that their energy source is depleted beyond a predefined threshold. Such recharging is more reliable (provided that the coordinator's power source is reliable and, preferably, not dependent on recharging itself), and the energy increment obtained in this manner can be tailored to the needs of individual nodes; in fact, it mostly depends on the attenuation of the wireless signal between the coordinator and the nodes in the network. However, if network nodes are equipped with a single antenna (which is often done for simplicity and cost effectiveness) network operation is not possible during the recharging process regardless of the RF bands in which normal operation and recharging

MSWiM'14, September 21–26, 2014, Montreal, QC, Canada.
Copyright 2014 ACM 978-1-4503-3030-5/14/09 ...$15.00.
http://dx.doi.org/10.1145/2641798.2641831.

are performed. As the result, the interplay between normal operation and recharging must be investigated in detail.

Evaluation of MAC protocols with provisions for recharging has been done mostly for energy harvesting using solar batteries or fluorescent lamps which offer continuous energy replenishment. The MAC protocols investigated were typically variants of CSMA and polling based protocols [1]. ALOHA-like protocols with continuous energy harvesting have been proposed as well [2]. General treatment of energy replenishment which includes battery replacement or generic recharging was presented in [4]. A MAC protocol that explicitly requests energy replenishment through a subsequent RF pulse has been reported in [7]. We have also described and analyzed a MAC protocol in which recharging is done through a high power RF pulse but in a different band so that data transmission is never interrupted [6].

In this paper we focus on RF energy recharging performed by the coordinator in a network with round-robin 1-limited MAC protocol based on polling. We assume that nodes have a single antenna each and thus can't transmit data while recharging although the sensing process itself is active, which means that data are being collected in the node buffer at all times. We focus on the evaluation of battery depleting process and the impact of recharging pause on the operation of the node. The paper is organized as follows: Section 2 described basic operation of the MAC with RF recharging. Section 3 models the energy depletion process of the node and consequently derives probability distribution of the time period between successive recharging events. In Section 4 we model the total time between successive medium access by a node. Section 5 presents performance results for the proposed MAC. Finally, Section 6 concludes the paper and highlights some future research.

2. 1-LIMITED MAC FOR WSNS WITH RF RECHARGING

We consider a network of m nodes consisting of a coordinator node and regular network nodes, the layout of which is shown in Fig. 1. Network nodes contain sensing unit which generates data values that need to be delivered to the coordinator. We assume a round-robin polling MAC where the coordinator explicitly polls each node by sending a POLL packet with the MAC address of the node. In case the coordinator needs to send data to the node, the POLL packet can be replaced with a data packet, similar to Bluetooth [5]. The polled node replies with a data packet, if its queue is not empty, or with a short NULL packet, if it is, the latter meaning that it has received the POLL but has no data to deliver. Note that each node has to listen to the header of each POLL/data packet in order to check the ID of the polled node. In our analysis, we will refer to the time elapsed between two consecutive visits to a target network node as the polling cycle of the coordinator. Thus

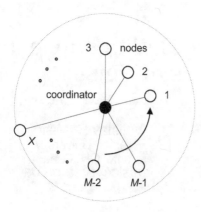

Figure 1: Logical layout of the network.

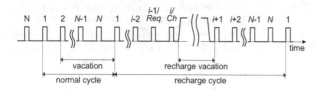

Figure 2: Polling cycle and recharging.

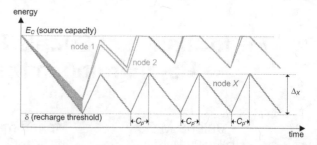

Figure 3: Periods of energy recharging and expenditure.

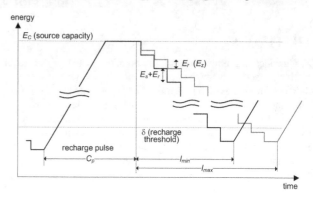

Figure 4: Details of energy expenditure period.

each node can transmit at most one data packet in any given polling cycle.

A node that detects that its remaining energy has dropped below a given threshold δ will request recharging by appending a suitable request into the header of the first data or NULL packet it sends to the coordinator. The coordinator will then append the information about a pending recharge pulse onto the header of the immediately following POLL or data packet, and begin the recharge pulse soon afterwards, as indicated in Figure 2. The recharge pulse lasts for the time period C_p with transmitted power of P_w. Since nodes are located at different distances from the coordinator, the amount of collected energy per node is proportional to the path loss Pl_i between the coordinator and the given node – in other words, a single recharge pulse will increase the energy of node i by $\Delta_i = P_w \cdot C_p \cdot Pl_i$. After recharge, normal network operation is resumed.

We assume that each packet (including its acknowledgment) has a length of L bits. Packets may be corrupted through noise and interference. If bit error rate is denoted with BER, the packet error rate will be $PER = 1 - (1 - BER)^L$. Transmission reliability is supported through an Automatic Repeat Request (ARQ) technique with up to n_r retries for packet. Namely, a packet sent by node i that has been correctly received by the coordinator is acknowledged in the header of the next POLL or data packet towards the same node; this event will occur in the next polling cycle.

In order to understand the impact of recharging on data transmission performance, we need to develop an analytical model of the recharging period coupled with the delay model at the node queue. For simplicity, we assume uniform traffic load over the nodes.

Initially, all nodes have equal amount of energy E_c equal to the energy capacity of the node's battery. In normal operation, node must use energy to sustain the sensing process, receive POLL and/or data packets, listen to the headers of other POLL packets, and transmit (or re-transmit) data and NULL packets of its own. Energy variation over time will depend on the traffic intensity of

the node, bit error rate, reliability threshold n_r and network size m; this is shown schematically in Fig. 3.

When the amount of energy at a node i falls to level δ, the node will request recharging. Note that the recharging request can be posted by any node. After recharging, the energy source of node i will amount to $\min(Ec, \delta + \Delta_i)$. As nodes have different path loss values, their energy will be replenished to different levels after recharging.

It is worth noting that energy expenditure will fluctuate from one polling cycle to the other due to random packet re-transmissions, as shown in Fig. 4. This occurs despite our assumptions of uniform traffic load, constant network size and constant reliability threshold.

However since bit error rate is uniform in the network, properties of the random battery draining process are uniform for all nodes; moreover, mean time to reach the energy threshold will be equal for all nodes. First recharge will be requested by the node which had the largest number of transmission cycles. However, the node furthest away from the coordinator will get the smallest amount of energy, and it will be this node, denoted with X in Fig. 1, that will generate recharge requests in the second, third, ... recharging cycles, while other nodes will not drain their batteries to the threshold. In fact, other nodes may well reach the full capacity of their batteries in subsequent recharge periods, as shown in Fig. 3.

3. MODEL OF THE RECHARGING PROCESS

Fig. 4 depicts the energy consumption process at the node which reached E_c in recharging. Due to random packet losses, the period between two successive recharge events is a random variable and we need to find its probability distribution. In the model that follows, we will use energy units listed in Table 1. Energy consumption per polling cycle can, then, be calculated by tracking the

Table 2: Description of energy consumption units at polling cycle level.

Energy expenditure	label
cycle with no data packet	$E_z = E_p + (m-2)E_a + E_{tn}$
cycle with first transmission attempt	$E_n = E_s + E_p + (m-2)E_a + E_{td}$
cycle with packet re-transmission	$E_r = E_p + (m-2)E_a + E_{td}$

Table 1: Basic energy consumption units.

Energy expenditure	label
sensing	E_s
listening to the POLL packet	E_p
listening to the header of POLL packet	E_a
data packet transmission	E_{td}
NULL packet transmission	E_{tn}

number of cycles after which the energy budget is spent at furthest node X. Therefore we need the joint probability distribution of time (i.e., the number of polling cycles) and consumed energy. Furthermore, since energy consumed by re-transmission is not an integer multiple of sensing energy, for the sake of analytical tractability we need to track sensing energy, NULL and data packet transmission energy separately at the level of single packet transmission. (This condition will be relaxed later when we compute the energy consumption over the recharging cycle.)

Basic quanta of energy expenditure within single polling cycle by the coordinator are given in Table 1. During a single polling cycle a node can have three kinds of energy expenditure; these are given in Table 2.

Energy expenditure E_z occurs when the node buffer is empty; this event occurs with the probability of $1 - \rho_b$, where ρ_b is effective utilization of the node (this parameter will be modeled and calculated later).

The other two units of energy expenditures, E_n and E_r, occur when the node buffer is not empty, i.e. with probability ρ_b. We note that energy expenditure for a new packet transmission differs from that needed for the re-transmission of existing packet, since in the former case energy must have been used sensing as well; therefore, $E_n = E_r + E_s$. Since sensing energy E_s is the smallest unit and it is constant with respect to the network size, we will track data transmission expenditures through E_s and E_s instead of E_n and E_r.

Probability generating function (PGF) for the energy consumption and number of polling cycles needed for correct transmission of single data packet is given as

$$Ep(w,z,y) = \frac{zwy(1-PER)\sum_{i=0}^{n_r}(yw)^i PER^i}{(1-PER)\sum_{i=0}^{n_r} PER^i} \qquad (1)$$

where variable z follows the consumption of sensing energy, w denotes consumption of single packet re-transmission energy, and y denotes the polling cycle of the network.

When we include scenarios in which the node buffer is empty and node transmits a NULL packet, we need another variable ξ to track energy consumption in NULL cycles. Thus the final PGF for the expenditure/duration of a single packet transmission becomes

$$Etot(w,z,\xi,y) = \rho_b Ep(w,z,y) + (1-\rho_b)\xi y \qquad (2)$$

Let us assume that, immediately after recharging, the farthest node X has the energy budget of $E_b = \delta + \Delta_X$ which exceeds the recharge threshold. By looking into the dynamics of data and NULL packet transmissions, we observe that the energy resource will be exhausted at a time between $l_{min} = \dfrac{E_b}{(n_r+1)E_r + E_s}$ and $l_{max} = \dfrac{E_b}{E_z}$ packet transmissions, depending on the traffic intensity, errors during transmission and allowed number of re-tries. The number of new packet transmissions between successive recharging events is at a minimum when the node always has a new data packet and it is re-transmitted n_r times; it is at the maximum value when the node buffer is always empty and only NULL packets are transmitted. Probabilities of both boundary events are small but nevertheless non-zero.

In the following step, we need to gather all possible numbers of new data and/or NULL packet transmissions in a joint probability distribution of total energy consumption and duration in polling cycles. The PGF for all possible numbers of packet transmissions when energy resource can be exhausted is

$$SEp(w,z,\xi,y) = \frac{\sum_{i=l_{min}}^{l_{max}} Etot(w,z,\xi,y)^i}{l_{max} - l_{min} + 1} \qquad (3)$$

Since we need to calculate the total energy expenditure, we need to combine energy quanta for sensing, re-transmission and NULL packet transmission. According to Tables 1 and 2, we can define the translation ratios between re-transmission and NULL packet transmission energy, respectively, with sensing energy as

$$rT = E_r/E_s \qquad (4)$$

$$zT = E_z/E_s \qquad (5)$$

We can use these ratios to map $w = z^{rT}$ and $\xi = z^{zT}$ in (3). However since the variable w is already present there and its exponent is typically high, it is possible to collect the coefficients, round the powers and combine them in a joint energy consumption variable u which is dimensionally equivalent to z. Algorithm 1 shows the aggregation of the energy variables w, ξ, z into a single energy variable u.

Note that this action could not have been done directly on (2) due to insufficient accuracy of rounding exponents of energy variable to integers. The resulting PGF is now $SEu(u,y)$ in which exponents of the variable u are integer multiples of E_s. Minimum and maximum degrees of $SEu(u,y)$ with respect to u are denoted as $mindeg$ and $maxdeg$, respectively.

3.1 Period of energy depletion

We recall that under uniform traffic, recharging will be initiated by the node X which is furthest away from the coordinator: i.e., node X requests an energy recharge when it reaches the threshold δ, and gets an energy increase of Δ_X in a single recharge. Let us express the energy budget in multiples of sensing energy quantum, $\Delta_X = E_{th}E_s$, so that it matches unit of variable u in PGF $SEu(u,y)$.

Algorithm 1: Transformation of PGF for energy and time.

Data: $SEp(w, z, \xi, y)$, translation ratios rT and zT

Result: PGF for total energy expenditure in E_s quanta and number of polling cycles between successive recharging events

1 Find minimal Se_l and maximal Se_h degree of variable w in $SEp(w, z, \xi, y)$;

2 **for** $i \leftarrow Se_l$ **to** Se_h **do**

3   Find coefficient wc[i] which multiplies w^i (polynomial on z, ξ and y) ;

4   Find minimal w_l and maximal w_h degree of variable ξ in wc[i];

5   **for** $k \leftarrow w_l$ **to** w_h **do**

6   Find coefficient xic[i,k] which multiplies ξ^k in wc[i] (polynomial on z and y) ;

7   Find minimal ξ_l and maximal ξ_h degree of variable ξ in $xic[i, k]$;

8   **for** $j \leftarrow \xi_l$ **to** ξ_h **do**

9   Find coefficient $zc[i, k, j]$ which multiplies z^k in xic[i,k] (polynomial on y); form aggregate integer energy consumption coefficient $cb[i, k, j] = \lceil i \cdot rT + k \cdot zT + j \rceil$;

10   form new element of new polynomial as $zc[i, k, j]u^{cb[i,k,j]}$

11   form third level sum mini[i,k] $\leftarrow \sum_{j=\xi_l}^{\xi_h} zc[i, k, j]u^{cb[i,k,j]}$;

12   form second level sum small[i] $\leftarrow \sum_{kk=w_l}^{w_h}$ mini[i, kk] ;

13 form new PGF as $SEu(u, y) \leftarrow \sum_{ii=Se_l}^{Se_h}$ small[ii] ;

We will denote coefficients of PGF $SEu(u, y)$ associated with the energy variable u and its power i, with

$$bc[i] = \text{coeff}(SEu(u, y), u, i) \qquad (6)$$

Note that $bc[i]$, which is polynomial in y, represents the conditional probability distribution of the number of polling cycles after which the energy iE_s has been consumed. The polynomial conditioned to the event that the energy resource is exceeded can be calculated as

$$Tr(y) = \sum_{i=E_{th}}^{maxdeg} bc[i] \qquad (7)$$

As the variable y carries the number of polling cycles, the polynomial $Tr(y)$ represents the conditional PGF for the number of polling cycles for which the energy budget of a node will be exceeded. To become a complete probability distribution of number of polling cycles when recharging request can occur, this polynomial has to be unconditioned, in which case it becomes

$$T(y) = \frac{Tr(y)}{Tr(1)} \qquad (8)$$

Mean number of polling cycles between two successive recharging requests is

$$\overline{T} = T'(1) \qquad (9)$$

Since the proposed MAC operates under 1-limited scheduling policy [8], there is at most a single packet transmission per polling cycle, and the rate or probability of recharge can be calculated as $P_r = \frac{1}{T}$.

4. UNAVAILABLE TIME OF THE MEDIUM

Time when the node can't access the medium consists of the time when other nodes in piconet are transmitting/receiving and when nodes are recharging their batteries. From queuing theoretic viewpoint, this time is called a vacation (of the servicing facility, i.e., the medium). In this section we will derive the probability distribution of this time.

MAC time is organized in basic slots, with POLL and NULL packets taking up one slot each. Packets arrive to a node according to a Poisson process with the arrival rate of λ. Downlink traffic consists of polling packets which have a constant size of one slot. Therefore, the PGFs for uplink and downlink data packets are $Gp(z)$ and $Gd(z) = z$, respectively, and the total mean packet time for a node is $Gp'(1) + Gd'(1)$. The offered load per node is $\rho = \lambda(Gp'(1) + Gd'(1))$. However, 1-limited scheduling and the use of transmission reliability will effectively increase the offered load. Presence of a vacation after each packet transmission increases the offered load to

$$\rho_1 = \rho + \lambda \overline{V} \qquad (10)$$

where $\overline{V}$ denotes the mean length of vacation period. Further, the use of transmission reliability effectively transforms the single packet transmission into a burst transmission with the PGF of

$$Gb(z) = \frac{(1 - PER)z \sum_{i=0}^{n_r} z^i PER^i}{(1 - PER) \sum_{i=0}^{n_r} PER^i} \qquad (11)$$

with the mean value of $\overline{Gb} = Gb'(1)$.

Therefore the total scaled uplink offered load becomes

$$\rho_b = (\rho + \lambda_u \overline{V})\overline{Gb} \qquad (12)$$

A polling MAC with 1-limited round-robin scheduling can be modeled as a M/G/1 gated limited system with vacations [8], in which case the vacation consists of two components:

1. The cyclical vacation is composed of packets transmitted / received by other nodes during polling cycle. This vacation is comprised of service times of $m - 2$ nodes, as it excludes the coordinator and the target node itself. The PGF of this vacation is

$$V_{cyc}(z) = (\rho_b Gp(z)z + (1 - \rho_b)z^2)^{(m-2)} \qquad (13)$$

2. The recharging vacation is nested in the cyclical one, with the PGF of

$$V_{rec}(z) = P_r z^{C_p} + (1 - P_r) \qquad (14)$$

The probability distribution (expressed as a PGF) for the total vacation experienced by a single node is

$$V(z) = V_{rec}(z)V_{cyc}(z) \qquad (15)$$

Mean value and standard deviation of total vacation can be found as

$$\overline{V} = V'(1) \qquad (16)$$

$$V_{stdev} = \sqrt{(V''(1) - (V'(1))^2 + V'(1))} \qquad (17)$$

Note that the offered load depends on mean vacation time while the cyclical vacation depends on the offered load; therefore equations (12) and (16) have to be solved together as a system.

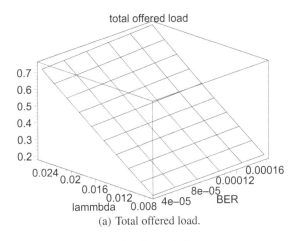

(a) Total offered load.

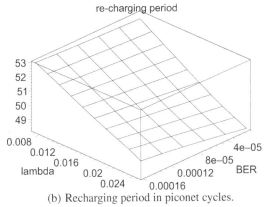

(b) Recharging period in piconet cycles.

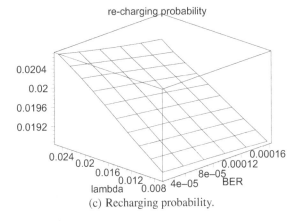

(c) Recharging probability.

Figure 5: Descriptors of load and recharging process.

5. PERFORMANCE RESULTS

We assume that piconet has $m = 5$ nodes. Bit error rate is varied between $BER = 10^{-5}$ and $BER = 1.6 * 10^{-4}$ and the maximum number of packet re-transmissions is $n_r = 3$. Uplink packet arrival rate is uniform for all nodes and is varied between 0.007 and 0.025 packets per node per unit slot. Downlink traffic consists of POLL packets only. Packet transmission time is constant and equal to one slot. Charging pulse is 1000 slots wide. Range of distances from the individual nodes to the coordinator is in range 1 to 10 meters, with path loss coefficient equal to 2 (i.e., we assume free space propagation).

In Fig. 5(a) we present total offered load defined in 12. We notice a small increase of offered load with the increase of BER, due to the major impact of recharging period and cyclical vacation. Figs. 5(b) and 5(c) show mean recharging period and recharging probability, respectively. Fig. 5(b) looks counter-intuitive at first, since one would expect that higher BER leads to a faster depletion of energy resource of the farthest node. However, cycles with re-transmission consume E_r of energy while cycles with new transmission consume $E_r + E_s$. Since the number of re-transmissions is smallest with lowest BER, first transmission will succeed in most cycles, and energy will be depleted faster with lower BER. T_{rec} decreases with the increase of packet arrival rate, as expected, since the proportion of new data packets to transmit, as opposed to NULL packets, is higher. Finally, recharging probability is reciprocal to the recharging period, which is why its behavior is just opposite from the recharging period.

Descriptors of vacation time are presented in Fig. 6. Mean vacation time grows with packet arrival rate since the recharging probability increases, and it decreases when BER increases since energy is consumed at a slower pace and recharging events are less frequent. Standard deviation of vacation time has a similar but less steep behavior with respect to the packet arrival rate since higher arrival rates decrease the proportion of NULL packets. It also increases more rapidly with the increase of BER due to increased variability in the transmission process. For that same reason the coefficient of variation $V_{stdev}/\overline{V}$ decreases with increase of packet arrival rate but increases with increase of BER. We note that the coefficient of variation is hyper-exponential.

Probability distribution of the number of polling cycles between two successive recharging points which was derived in (8) is evaluated under varying packet arrival rate and BER. Fig. 7 shows the distribution of the number of cycles when $BER = 10^{-5}$. Figs.7(a) and 7(b) show probability distribution of the number of cycles for lowest ($\lambda = 0.007$ per slot) and highest packet arrival rate ($\lambda = 0.025$) used in the experiment, while Fig. 7(c) shows the ensemble of cycle distributions for packet arrival rates between lowest and highest value in steps of $\Delta\lambda = 0.002$. We note that the probability distribution of the number of cycles is very narrow at low arrival rates: the recharging period is almost entirely contained within the range between 47 and 57 cycles. When packet arrival rate increases, more new packet are transmitted, and possibly re-transmitted, hence the lower bound of the distribution decreases while its upper bound remains essentially constant since it corresponds to re-transmissions and NULL packets.

In second experiment we have set BER to $BER = 1.6 * 10^{-4}$, while the packet arrival rate was varied in the same range and with the same increment as above; the resulting limiting distributions and ensemble are shown in Fig. 8. Comparing the results of the two experiments, we note that the left boundaries are almost the same for the two distributions, since they mostly depend on new packet arrivals. However, the right boundaries have shifted to the higher number of cycles (60 instead of 57) due to the increased number of packet re-transmissions which is the consequence of the higher BER value.

6. CONCLUSION AND FUTURE WORK

In this paper we have proposed and evaluated a simple MAC protocol which supports wireless recharging in wireless sensor networks. The performance of the MAC is mostly influenced by breaks in activity due to wireless recharging. We have developed a precise model of the duration of period between successive recharging points. We have evaluated it against varying packet arrival rate and bit error rate. recharging has large impact on the distribution of the

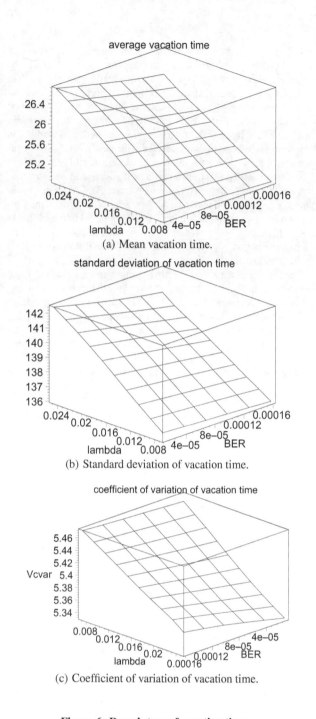

(a) Mean vacation time.

(b) Standard deviation of vacation time.

(c) Coefficient of variation of vacation time.

Figure 6: Descriptors of vacation time.

time between two successive packet transmissions and its duration has to be carefully selected in order to prevent large access delays in the network. In future work we will find optimal duration of recharging which render lowest packet waiting times.

7. REFERENCES

[1] Z. A. Eu, H.-P. Tan, and W. K. Seah. Design and performance analysis of MAC schemes for wireless sensor networks powered by ambient energy harvesting. *Ad Hoc Networks*, 9(3):300–323, May 2011.

[2] F. Iannello, O. Simeone, and U. Spagnolini. Medium access control protocols for wireless sensor networks with energy

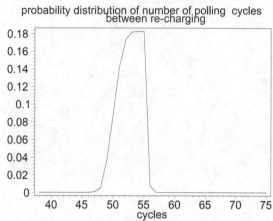

(a) Distribution of number of cycles when $\lambda = 0.007$

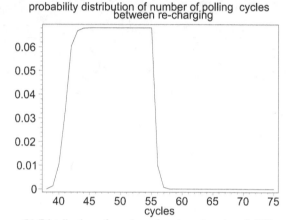

(b) Distribution of number of cycles when $\lambda = 0.025$

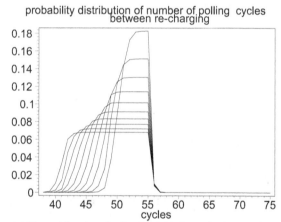

(c) Ensemble of cycle distributions for arrivals rates $\lambda = 0.007..0.025$

Figure 7: Probability distributions of number of polling cycles between two successive rechargings when $BER = 10^{-5}$.

harvesting. *IEEE Transactions on Communications*, 60(5):1381–1389, 2012.

[3] A. Kansal and M. B. Srivastava. An environmental energy harvesting framework for sensor networks. In *Int. Symp. Low*

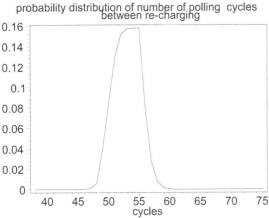

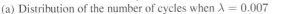

(a) Distribution of the number of cycles when $\lambda = 0.007$

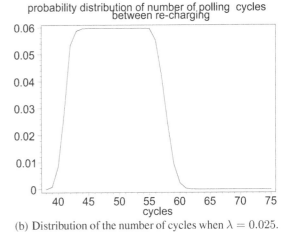

(b) Distribution of the number of cycles when $\lambda = 0.025$.

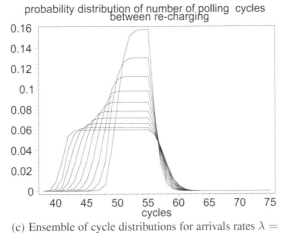

(c) Ensemble of cycle distributions for arrivals rates $\lambda = 0.007..0.025$

Figure 8: Probability distributions of the number of polling cycles between two successive rechargings when $BER = 1.6 * 10^{-4}$.

Power Electronics and Design (ISLPED 2003), pages 481–486, 2003.

[4] J. Lei, R. Yates, and L. Greenstein. A generic model for optimizing single-hop transmission policy of replenishable sensors. *IEEE Transactions on Wireless Communications*, 8(2):547–551, 2009.

[5] J. Mišić and V. B. Mišić. *Performance Modeling and Analysis of Bluetooth Networks: Network Formation, Polling, Scheduling, and Traffic Control*. CRC Press, Boca Raton, FL, July 2005.

[6] V. B. Mišić and J. Mišić. A polling MAC for wireless sensor networks with rf recharging of sensor nodes. In *27th Queen's Biennial Symposium on Communications*, Kingston, ON, Canada, 2014.

[7] P. Nintanavongsa, M. Y. Naderi, and K. R. Chowdhury. Medium access control protocol design for sensors powered by wireless energy transfer. In *IEEE INFOCOM*, pages 150–154, Apr. 2013.

[8] H. Takagi. *Queueing Analysis*, volume 1: Vacation and Priority Systems. North-Holland, Amsterdam, The Netherlands, 1991.

[9] L. Xie, Y. Shi, Y. T. Hou, and A. Lou. Wireless power transfer and applications to sensor networks. *IEEE Wireless Communications*, 20(4):140–145, 2013.

[10] L. Xie, Y. Shi, Y. T. Hou, and H. D. Sherali. Making sensor networks immortal: An energy-renewal approach with wireless power transfer. *IEEE/ACM Transactions on Networking*, 20(6):1748–1761, Dec. 2012.

Regret-based Learning for Medium Access in LTE Femtocell Networks *

Ying Wang, Jason Min Wang, Brahim Bensaou
Department of Computer Science and Engineering
The Hong Kong University of Science and Technology
ywangbf@cse.ust.hk, jasonwangm@cse.ust.hk, brahim@cse.ust.hk

ABSTRACT

With the increased density of LTE femtocell base station (FBSs) deployments, mutual interference between FBSs becomes a bottleneck to network performance. Inter-femtocell coordination has been invoked in the past to address this problem, however it is not practically possible as LTE FBSs do not possess the X2 interface to enable them to communicate with each other. In this paper, we opt for a fully distributed approach and introduce a self-learning MAC protocol for FBSs to allocate resources based on historical user feedback. In our approach, each FBS independently learns about the asymmetric contention level on its links, and transfers resources from highly-contended links to low-contention ones to avoid wasting resources. The learning process is modelled as a cluster-structural regret-based game and simulation results show that our algorithm outperforms alternative algorithms from the literature on a wide range of metrics.

Categories and Subject Descriptors

C.2.1 [**Network Architecture and Design**]: Wireless communication

Keywords

OFDMA; Femtocell; Distributed scheduling; Regret learning game

1. INTRODUCTION

Deploying femtocell base stations in LTE networks has become highly popular as it turns out to be an effective and economic way to improving data rates and network coverage. According to a recent small cell market status report from the Smallcell Forum [1], the number of femtocell base stations will grow from 2.5 million in 2012 to 59 million by 2016, a 24 fold increase.

Despite the benefits and popularity of femtocell networks, interference is still a critical issue as the density of the network increases. In general, an LTE network comprises two types of base stations: macrocell base stations (MBSs) and femtocell base stations (FBSs). As a result, there can be four major types of downlink interference and collisions: on one hand, macrocell to macrocell (m2m) interference, often called inter-macrocell interference; on the other hand macrocell-to-femtocell (m2f), femtocell-to-macrocell (f2m), and femtocell-to-femtocell (f2f) interferences known also as intra-macrocell interference. Inter-macrocell (m2m) interference can be mitigated by classic techniques such as frequency planning and fractional frequency reuse, thanks to the X2 interfaces readily available in all MBSs to provide fast and reliable inter-macrocell communication [11]. Intra-macrocell interference on the other hand poses greater challenges as the FBSs do not possess X2 interfaces. So in general, m2f and f2m interference can be solved by separating the frequency spectrum of an MBS and its FBSs into orthogonal bands. Unfortunately, for f2f interference, the random deployment of FBSs (for example in the customer premises), the lack of X2 interfaces to enable coordination, and the use of orthogonal frequency division multiple access (OFDMA) as link access technique may lead to a dramatic throughput degradation in the femtocell network due to excessive collisions. These three aspects, compel the use of some uncoordinated yet intelligent f2f interference management method that relies only on what the FBSs can learn from their past experienced transmission trials and failures. In this paper, we focus on designing such self-learning algorithm to enable efficient bandwidth sharing between FBSs in an LTE network.

A large body of work is dedicated to interference management and resource allocation in femtocell networks. In [12], a hashing-based distributed resource allocation algorithm is proposed for femtocell networks[1] that rely on OFDMA. In this work, the femtocells are taken as the units of randomized contention, instead of the individual links. In the same context a Q-learning algorithm was used in [3] to adjust FBS transmit power and reduce f2m interference. Unfortunately this model does not take into account the existence of f2f interference. An algorithm is proposed in [9] to maintain max-min fair user bandwidth in a two-tier femtocell network. The joint problem of subchannel allocation, power adjustment, and association was studied while assuming prior knowledge of the network conflict graph. In practice, constructing the conflict graph requires a huge overhead. Recently, minimizing f2f interference via effective resource management was studied in several works including [2, 13]. In these works, users in the same femtocell are assigned to different frequency regions to avoid interference with neighbouring femtocells. The model in [2] relies on the existence of a central controller that collects the necessary information and decides the allocations while the distributed model in [13] assumes instanta-

*This work is in part supported by a grant from the Hong Kong research grant council RGC-GRF 610411

---

[1]We use the distributed model proposed in [12] as our benchmark in the simulation.

neous inter-cell cooperation and even hardware modification, making both approaches impractical. Distributed allocation algorithms are developed in [8, 7] for self-organizing networks to maximize either bandwidth or energy efficiency, however such models assume again inter-cell coordination and the possibility of obtaining path-loss measurements for all the links in the network.

In summary, prior work cannot be invoked to solve the f2f interference problem. The challenges that need to be addressed are as follows: First, the FBSs lack X2 interfaces, therefore, fast and reliable coordination between FBSs is not possible. This makes the centralized and cooperative distributed approaches (e.g., [9, 2, 13]) inaccurate and even impractical. Second, most work relies dramatically on the knowledge of topology information, such as conflict graphs (e.g., [9]). In practice, it is difficult, if at all possible, to obtain the complete topology information, especially in networks with channel variations. Furthermore, constructing the conflict graph requires periodic user measurement and fast coordination. Third, the contention levels of the links in the network are asymmetric. Even in the same femtocell, one user may suffer from larger competition than others who enjoy a larger bandwidth. Therefore, resource allocation without considering link contention level (e.g., [12, 3]) is insufficient and may result in a waste of resources.

To take on these challenges, we design a self-learning MAC protocol for LTE femtocell networks where the FBSs learn by experience to distinguish the good subchannels from the bad ones when transmitting to their respective users. Specifically, we model the learning process as a regret-based learning game with cluster structure. Each FBS independently learns the channel quality on behalf of its links based on the historical feedback provided by its users. In our proposed approach, when allocating subchannels, the FBS favours links with lower contention levels, as in multi-tiered LTE networks, users that suffer from high contention on the FBS can always handoff to the MBS and still obtain reasonable bandwidth. In addition, to satisfy the objective of pure throughput maximization, our proposed model can also be applied to networks with heterogeneous link demands.

This paper's contributions can be summarized as follows:

• We propose a self-learning MAC protocol to address the interference management problem in LTE femtocell networks without coordination between femtocell base stations.

• Our proposed model exploits asymmetric link contention levels to maximize network resource utilization. In addition, our model takes into consideration heterogeneous link demands in the network.

• We demonstrate via extensive simulation experiments the considerable improvements that can be achieved by our algorithm compared to alternative approaches that adopt unreasonably max-min fairness.

The rest of the paper is organized as follows. A brief introduction to LTE resource allocation problem is given in Section 2. We present and discuss our system model in Section 3. We evaluate the performance of the proposed model in Section 4. Finally, we conclude our work in Section 5.

2. RESOURCE ALLOCATION IN LTE

In LTE MAC layer, OFDMA is used for efficient two-dimensional resource sharing among links. Here a link is defined as an active flow between a base station and one of its users. As shown in Figure 1, each LTE radio frame is divided into C subchannels[2] in the frequency domain and ten subframes in the time domain. The

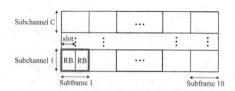

Figure 1: LTE Radio Frame Structure

basic element of radio resource is called a resource block (RB). An RB occupies one subchannel in the frequency domain and one slot in the time domain, with two consecutive slots forming a subframe (1ms). The minimum size of radio resource that can be allocated is one subframe length.

In LTE, downlink and uplink transmissions are separated in the frequency domain using frequency division duplexing (FDD) or in the time domain using time division duplexing (TDD). Our work focuses on downlink transmission. The resource allocation to links is scheduled by the base station. Before each transmission, using the physical downlink control channel (PDCCH), the base station indicates to its users the subchannels and subframes they are allocated. Base stations that operate in the dynamic scheduling mode, can schedule their transmission on the fly in each subframe. Hybrid automatic repeat request (HARQ) protocol is used to improve transmission reliability. In downlink HARQ transmission, users feedback ACK/NACK periodically to the base station. The ACK/NACK is in the unit of a transport block (TB), that is composed of all the RBs occupied by a link in one subframe. If a TB is decoded successfully at the user, then an ACK is sent back, otherwise a NACK is sent requesting for retransmission of this entire TB. The ACK/NACK is usually delayed by several subframes[3].

In LTE cellular networks, to different types of application requirements, quality of service (QoS) is defined in terms of a finite set of bearers. A bearer is simply an end-to-end flow between the user and the gateway with predefined traffic requirements and QoS requirements (e.g., bandwidth, loss, delay requirements, and so on). The part of a bearer that spans the wireless link between a base station and the user acts as a radio bearer. The QoS of radio bearers is provided by the air interface, which turns out to be one of the main QoS bottlenecks in LTE networks. In femtocell networks, the QoS of the air interface should not be decoupled from MAC resource scheduling, since it is constrained by the interference from neighbouring cells. Bearers of different applications may have different rate requirements. In the air interface, the rate requirement can be translated to the amount of resource demand in an OFDMA radio frame. For example, the resource demand of a link can be defined as the number of subchannels occupied by this link in one subframe. This is to ensure that the radio bearer will not violate the whole bearer's QoS requirement.

3. SYSTEM MODEL

Consider a LTE femtocell network composed of one MBS and collection of FBSs. Denote by $B = \{i|i = 1,..,K\}$ the set of FBSs and by M the MBS. The FBSs are distributed without any mutual information exchange. We assume there is no interference from other macrocells (i.e., no m2m interference), and the frequency spectrum is orthogonally split between the FBSs and the MBS as described previously to address the f2m and m2f interfer-

---

[2]C varies with different bandwidth, e.g., $C = 100$ in 200MHz bandwidth.

[3]For example, in the FDD mode, a user transmits ACK/NACK in subframe t for transmissions that took place in subframe $t - 4$.

ence. The spectrum allocated to the FBSs is divided into C sub-channels ($c = 1, ..., C$), and the overlap of transmissions from randomly deployed FBSs generates f2f interference. We also assume the PDCCH interference between the neighbouring FBSs is already mitigated by a scrambling mechanism [11]. Denote by L_i, $i \in B$, the set of links originating at FBS i. The set of all links in this networks is defined as $L = L_1 \cup, ..., L_K$. Links in the network, even those originating at the same femtocell, may face different levels of contention. Besides, the links may have various bandwidth demands matching different kinds of application requirements. If necessary, each link is attached with a demand d_l, expressed as a number of subchannels required in each subframe. Considering downlink traffic, our objective is to reduce f2f interference and improve network resource utilization while taking into consideration different link contention levels and bandwidth demands.

3.1 Regret-based Learning Game with Cluster Structure

We capture the competitions between links in a femtocell network by a regret-based learning game with cluster structure [5]. In this game, the links are defined as the players, and each group of players that attach to one FBS forms a cluster. Links from different femtocells do not cooperate, whereas links in the same femtocell cooperate since they are coordinated by their FBS (actually they are played by the FBS). Every player's goal is to maximize its own payoff in the game by choosing the proper strategies. The strategies consist in the choice of subchannels in each subframe. The players choose their strategies by adopting regret-based learning [6], where the probability of choosing a strategy k is proportional to the "regret for not having played k in the past". The calculation of the regret relies only on historical feedback from the users as well as on in-cluster cooperation.

3.1.1 Game Definition

An n-person repeated game G in strategic form is defined as $G = (L, (S_l)_{l \in L}, (\theta_l)_{l \in L})$, where L is a finite set of players; S_l is the strategy space of player $l \in L$; and $\theta_l : \prod_{l' \in L} S_{l'} \to \mathbb{R}$ is the payoff function of player l, mapping a strategy from L to a real number. Game G is played repeatedly over discrete time slots ($t = 1, 2, ...$). Denote the strategy of player l in slot t as $s_{l,t}$ ($s_{l,t} \in S_l$), and denote by $s_{L \setminus \{l\}, t}$ the strategies of all players in set L other than player l at time slot t. The payoff of player l in slot t denoted as $\theta_{l,t}$ is determined not only the strategy of l but also the strategies of other players. That is: $\theta_{l,t} = \theta_{l,t}(s_{1,t}, ..., s_{l,t}, ..., s_{|L|,t}) = \theta_{l,t}(s_{l,t}, s_{L \setminus \{l\}, t}), \forall l \in L, t = 1, 2, \cdots$.

3.1.2 Game Process

In each slot t, player l chooses strategy $s_{l,t}$ according to the probability distribution $p_{l,t}(k), k \in S_l$. The distribution $p_{l,t}(k)$ is calculated in each slot as follows:

$$p_{l,t}(k) = \frac{1}{|S_l|}, t = 1, \tag{1}$$

$$p_{l,t}(k) = \begin{cases} (1-\delta)\frac{1}{\mu}Q_{l,t-1}(j,k) + \delta\frac{1}{|S_l|}, k \neq j \\ 1 - \sum_{h \neq j, h \in S_l} p_{l,t}(h), k = j \end{cases}, t > 1 \tag{2}$$

That is, in the first slot ($t = 1$), the probability of choosing any strategy k is uniformly distributed as in (1)[4]. In slot t ($t > 1$), given the previously chosen strategy j in slot $t-1$, the probability $p_{l,t}(k)$ of choosing k given by (2) is expressed as a convex combination of

[4]We can also use any other initial strategy.

i) the regret of having used j instead of k ($j \neq k$) in the past (expressed by $Q_{l,t-1}(j,k)$) and ii) a random term ($1/|S_l|$) that ensures the progression of the game by allowing every possible strategy to have (for a fraction δ) an equal probability of being chosen. The probability of staying with the previous strategy j (i.e., choosing $k = j$), is simply the remaining probability $1 - \sum_{h \neq j, h \in S_l} p_{l,t}(h)$. Constant μ is a normalization constant to guarantee $p_{l,t}(\cdot)$ is a probability distribution[5] ($\sum_{k \in S_l} p_{l,t}(k) = 1, p_{l,t}(k) > 0$).

The regret $Q_{l,t}(j,k)$ is calculated based on the historical payoff $\theta_{l,t}$. In the cluster-structural regret-based learning game, the instantaneous payoff $\theta_{l,t}$ is divided into two parts, the internal payoff $\theta_{l,t}^I$ and the external payoff $\theta_{l,t}^E$.

$$\theta_{l,t} = \theta_{l,t}^I + \theta_{l,t}^E \tag{3}$$

The internal instantaneous payoff $\theta_{l,t}^I$ is received under the control of in-cluster competition. The external instantaneous payoff $\theta_{l,t}^E$ is received from competition with players from outside the cluster.

The regret $Q_{l,t}(j,k)$ is defined as the average payoff increase resulting from replacing strategy j in the past t slots with another strategy k. Since the payoff equals the sum of the internal and external payoff, the average payoff increase can be written as the sum of internal regret $Q_{l,t}^I(j,k)$ and external regret $Q_{l,t}^E(j,k)$:

$$Q_{l,t}(j,k) = [Q_{l,t}^I(j,k) + Q_{l,t}^E(j,k)]^+ \\ = \max\{Q_{l,t}^I(j,k) + Q_{l,t}^E(j,k), 0\} \tag{4}$$

The internal regret can be calculated as:

$$Q_{l,t}^I(j,k) = \frac{1}{t} \sum_{\substack{\tau = 1, ..., t: \\ s_{l,\tau} = j}} \left(\theta_{l,\tau}^I(k, s_{L_i \setminus l, \tau}) - \theta_{l,\tau}^I(s_{L_i, \tau}) \right), \tag{5}$$

where, $\theta_{l,t}^I(k, s_{L_i \setminus l, \tau})$ is the internal payoff that should be received in slot τ if we replace player l's strategy j by strategy k while maintaining the strategies of all other players in cluster L_i; and $\theta_{l,\tau}^I(s_{L_i, \tau})$ is the original internal payoff received by player l in slot τ. Since players in the same cluster are aware of each other's strategies at the end of each slot, the internal regret calculation is accurate.

Without coordination with players outside the cluster, the external regret cannot be calculated directly like the internal regret. Therefore, we propose to estimate the external regret based on historical received payoff as follows:

$$Q_{l,t}^E(j,k) = \frac{1}{t} \sum_{\substack{\tau = 1; \\ s_{l,\tau} = j}}^{t} \left(\theta_{l,\tau}^E(k, s_{L \setminus l, \tau}) - \theta_{l,\tau}^E(s_{L,\tau}) \right)$$

$$\approx \frac{1}{t} \sum_{\substack{\tau = 1; \\ s_{l,\tau} = k}}^{t} \frac{p_{l,\tau}(j)}{p_{l,\tau}(k)} \theta_{l,\tau}^E(s_{L,\tau}) - \frac{1}{t} \sum_{\substack{\tau = 1; \\ s_{l,\tau} = j}}^{t} \theta_{l,\tau}^E(s_{L,\tau}) \tag{6}$$

Since it is impossible to know the term $\theta_{l,\tau}^E(k, s_{L \setminus l, \tau})$, which is the external payoff to be received when replacing j with k in the past, without knowing the strategies of other clusters. We estimate it via the running average external payoff received by player l when choosing strategy k over the past t slots. The weight $\frac{p_{l,\tau}(j)}{p_{l,\tau}(k)}$ is used to equalize (or rescale) the estimated payoff when the frequency of playing k and the frequency of playing j in the past are not equal. $\theta_{l,\tau}^E(s_{L,\tau})$ is the external payoff received by player l in slot τ. Note that one player can calculate its received external payoff by

[5]In our experiments, parameter δ is set to 0.01, and constant μ is set as $2\theta_l^{max}(|S_l| - 1)$. θ_l^{max} is the maximum payoff of player l.

deducting the calculated internal payoff from the received payoff, according to Eq. (3).

The update equations for the internal and external regret can be rewritten as follows:

$$Q_{l,t}^I(j,k) = \frac{1}{t}\left(\theta_{l,t}^I(k, s_{L_i \setminus l,t}) - \theta_{l,\tau}^I(s_{L_i,t})\right) I_j(s_{l,t}) +$$
$$(1 - \frac{1}{t})Q_{l,t-1}^I(j,k), t = 1, 2, ..., \quad (7)$$

$$Q_{l,t}^E(j,k) = \frac{1}{t}\left(\frac{p_{l,t}(j)}{p_{l,t}(k)}\theta_{l,t}^E(s_{L,t})I_k(s_{l,t}) - \theta_{l,t}^E(s_{L,t})I_j(s_{l,t})\right) +$$
$$(1 - \frac{1}{t})Q_{l,t-1}^E(j,k), t = 1, 2, ..., \quad (8)$$

$$Q_{l,0}^I(j,k) = 0, \quad (9)$$

$$Q_{l,0}^E(j,k) = 0, \quad (10)$$

where $I_j(s_{l,t})$ and $I_k(s_{l,t})$ are indicator functions, for example:

$$I_j(s_{l,t}) = \begin{cases} 1, & s_{l,t} = j \\ 0, & s_{l,t} \neq j \end{cases} \quad (11)$$

A correlated equilibrium is achieved in such games if each player realizes that the best it can do is to choose a strategy by following the recommendation (the probability distribution $p_{l,t}(k)$, $\sum_{k \in S_l} p_{l,t}(k) = 1$), on the condition that all the other players do the same. A correlated ε-equilibrium has been proved to exist for game G in [5].

3.1.3 Cast into LTE Femtocell Networks

In this subsection, we explain how to cast the self-learning model into LTE femtocell networks. Specifically, we model the competition of links as game G, where each link l is a player in the game. Links of the same femtocell form a cluster. An OFDMA subframe is a slot in the game. The strategy $s_{l,t} \in S_l$ of link l is a set of subchannels to access. Exhaustively listing all subchannel access combinations to construct the strategy space would result in an exponential growth (2^C). Therefore, we examine two approximate definitions of the strategy space with polynomial space size: we call these the *Binary Branch* strategy space and the *Consecutive List* strategy space, and define them as follows:

In the *Binary Branch*, we use a binary branch tree, where each node represents one strategy. For convenience, the total number of subchannels C is assumed to be a power h of two, where h is the height of the binary tree. In layer i ($i = 1, 2, ..., h$) of the binary tree, the C subchannels are divided into $2^{(i-1)}$ nodes, and each node is an individual block occupying $2^{(h-i+1)}$ consecutive subchannels. In addition to these layers, the player can also choose to access none of the subchannels. In the *Consecutive List*, the strategy set is defined as the set of all possible blocks that occupy c consecutive subchannels ($c = 0, 1, ..C$).

The state space size of the *Binary Branch* is $2C$, and the state space size of the *Consecutive List* is $(C + 1)C/2$. Actually the *Consecutive List* strategy space contains all the strategies defined in the *Binary Branch*. Theoretically, the larger the strategy state space size, the higher the computational complexity, and the higher the probability of obtaining good strategies.

Next, we focus on the definition of payoff function in game G.

If the objective is pure network throughput maximization, the payoff $\theta_{l,t}$ can be defined as the total number of successful subchannels of player l in slot t. The payoff is obtained from the user ACK/NACK. If an ACK is received, the payoff is equal to the size of the TB, or the number of successful subchannels in the subframe. Otherwise the payoff is equal to zero, since the entire TB needs to be retransmitted.

If our objective is to satisfy heterogeneous link demands, the payoff can be defined (for example) as $\theta_{l,t}^{d_l}(x)$:

$$\theta_{l,t}^{d_l}(x) = \begin{cases} x, x \leq d_l \\ 2d_l - x, x > d_l \end{cases}, d_l > 0, \quad (12)$$

where d_l is the link demand, and x is the number of subchannels successfully received in slot t. When x is below the demand d_l, the payoff increases linearly with x; when x is above the demand, the payoff decreases linearly with the excess allocation (to avoid allocating unnecessarily more bandwidth than requested).

The internal payoff $\theta_{l,t}^I$ is defined as the number of subchannels allocated by the FBS in the internal subchannel allocation part (explain in the subsection 3.2). In our model, we assume the delay of ACK/NACK is negligibly small. It should be pointed out that our model still applies to networks with delayed ACK/NACK by simply postponing the regret update by several slots.

3.1.4 Regret-based Learning Algorithm

The process of each link in game G is described in Algorithm 1. The algorithm is executed by each link l iteratively on each subframe (slot) (Algorithm 1 only shows the steps for one slot t).

Algorithm 1 Regret-based Learning Algorithm at slot t

Pick a Strategy:
1: **if** $t = 1$ **then**
2:     Evaluate distribution $p_{l,t}(k), k \in S_l$ by (1)
3: **else**
4:     Evaluate distribution $p_{l,t}(k), k \in S_l$ by (2)
5: Determine strategy $s_{l,t}$ following distribution $p_{l,t}(k)$
Regret Update:
6: At the end of slot t, receive payoff $\theta_{l,t}$
7: Obtain strategies of players in the cluster $\{s_{l,t} | \forall l \in L_i\}$
8: Update the regret matrix $Q_{l,t}(j,k)$ by (4), (5), and (6).

At the beginning, the player chooses a strategy following probability distribution $p_{l,t}(k)$, calculated based on the regret in step 1-5. At the end of slot t, the player uses the received payoff and other players' strategies in slot t to update the regret matrix in steps 6-8. The updated regret will be used in the next slot. Playing as a central controller inside each femtocell, the FBS assumes the roles of each of its links and manages the calculations to determine the strategies of its links. Therefore, in practice, there is no strategy information exchange inside the cluster as all the link strategies are readily available inside the FBS scheduler.

The complexity of Algorithm 1 is related to the definition of the strategy space. For the *Binary Branch*, "picking a strategy" has a time complexity $O(C)$ in calculating probabilities of $2C$ strategies. In the "regret update", the two-dimensional regret matrix ($2C * 2C$) is updated. According to (7) and (8), the time required for updating one element in the regret matrix is $O(1)$. Therefore for the *Binary Branch*, the computational complexity of Algorithm 1 is $O(C^2)$, and the space complexity is also $O(C^2)$. Similarly, for the *Consecutive List*, both the computational complexity and the space complexity are $O(C^4)$.

Thanks to the in-cluster cooperation, the proposed game G with cluster structure has a more accurate estimation on the regret and a faster convergence speed to the ε-correlated equilibrium compared with pure non-cooperative regret-based learning games.

3.2 Internal Subchannel Allocation

Before each slot, the FBS provides each link with its strategy, or recommendation of subchannels to use, as learned in game G.

However, since the choice of strategies is probabilistic, there is still a possibility that the recommended strategies of the links within a femtocell conflict with each other. Obviously, since the FBS is in charge of all the downlink transmissions, it should avoid such internal collisions in allocating subchannels to its links. To this end, in each subframe, the FBS needs to solve a subchannel allocation problem to its links based on their recommended subchannels. We call such scheduling process, the internal subchannel allocation.

3.2.1 Subchannel Allocation Problem

We consider the subchannel allocation problem of link set $L_i, i \in B$ in subframe t. Define Ψ as the set of all possible couples of subchannel and link: $\Psi = \{(c,l)|s_{l,t}(c) = 1, c = 1, ..., C, l \in L_i\}$. It is possible to assign subchannel c to link l only if c is recommended in l's strategy $s_{l,t}$.

Let X be the set of all feasible solutions of the subchannel allocation problem, $X = \{x|x \subseteq \Psi\}$. A solution x is feasible if and only if x is a subset of Ψ, and each subchannel is assigned to at most one link in x. Partition set Ψ into C disjoint sets: $\Psi = \Psi_1 \cup, ..., \Psi_c \cup, ..., \Psi_C$, where set Ψ_c is the set of all possible couples containing subchannel c in Ψ. Hence solution x is feasible if constraints $|x \cap \Psi_c| \leq 1, \forall c = 1, ..., C$ are satisfied.

The objective of the subchannel allocation problem is to maximize the total utility of the number of subchannels allocated to each of the link by the FBS in solution x. The number of subchannels obtained by link l in allocation x is the internal payoff it received in game G. To ensure fairness in allocating subchannels to users of one femtocell, define $f(\cdot)$ as a concave utility function (with $f(0) = 0$) that embodies the diminishing return principle. The subchannel allocation problem can be formulated as:

$$\max \sum_{x \in X, l \in L_i} f\left(\theta_{l,t}^I(x)\right)$$
$$s.t. \quad |x \cap \Psi_c| \leq 1, \forall c = 1, ..., C, \tag{13}$$
$$\Psi_c = \{(l', c')|c' = c, (l', c') \in \Psi\}.$$

3.2.2 Greedy Subchannel Allocation Algorithm

Problem (13) is in essence a submodular welfare maximization problem, which is known to be NP-hard [4] (we establish the submodularity of utility $f(\cdot)$ in Lemma 2 in the next subsection). Since (13) is NP-hard, we use a greedy strategy shown in Algorithm 2 to provide a 1/2-approximate solution for the subchannel allocation problem.

Algorithm 2 Greedy Subchannel Allocation Algorithm

Require: $\{s_{l,t}, l \in L_i\}$
1: $\Psi = \{(c,l)|s_{l,t}(c) = 1, c = 1, ..., C, l \in L_i\}$
2: $x = \emptyset$
3: $F = 0$
4: **while** $\Psi \neq \emptyset$ **do**
5: $\quad (c^*, l^*) = \underset{\substack{(c,l) \in \Psi, \\ x' = x \cup \{(c,l)\}}}{\arg\max} \left(\sum_{l \in L_i} f\left(\theta_{l,t}^I(x')\right) - F \right)$
6: $\quad x = x \cup \{(c^*, l^*)\}$
7: $\quad F = \sum_{l \in L_i} f\left(\theta_{l,t}^I(x)\right)$
8: $\quad \Psi = \Psi - \{(c,l)|c = c^*, (c,l) \in \Psi\}$
9: **return** x

The algorithm is executed is a loop. In each iteration, the algorithm adds one allocation pair (c^*, l^*) that leads to the highest marginal value of the objective function of (13) to the current so-

lution x (in steps 5-6). The allocation pair (c^*, l^*) is chosen from candidate set Ψ, which contains the current eligible pairs to be chosen in order to ensure the feasibility of x. Then in step 7, the objective function value F in terms of current solution x is updated. Next, in step 8, the pairs containing the newly allocated subchannel c^* are deleted from the candidate pair set Ψ to maintain solution feasibility. Finally, solution x is returned when the candidate set Ψ is empty.

The complexity of Algorithm 2 is $O(C|L_i|)$. In each subframe, the FBS executes Algorithm 2 and allocates subchannels to its links according to the output solution x. Adopting Algorithm 2 in internal subchannel allocation results in a more efficient resource utilization and in turn helps accelerate the learning procedure in G.

3.2.3 Algorithm Approximation Analysis

In this subsection, we prove Algorithm 2 achieves an $\frac{1}{2}$ approximation factor for Problem (13).

PROPOSITION 1. *Algorithm 2 is an $\frac{1}{2}$-approximation algorithm.*

PROOF. Algorithm 2 is in the form of $\max_{e \in \psi} F(x \cup \{e\}) - F(x)$, where $F(x) = \sum_{l \in L_i} f\left(\theta_{l,t}^I(x)\right)$ is the maximization objective of Problem (13). In each iteration, Algorithm 2 tries to add the couple with the largest marginal value of F while maintaining the solution feasibility.

If an original problem is to maximize a submodular function over a partition matroid, then a greedy algorithm solving the problem in the above form has been proved to achieve an $\frac{1}{2}$ approximation factor in [10]. Therefore, to complete the proof, it is sufficient to demonstrate that problem (13) maximizes a submodular function over a partition matroid, which we establish in Lemmas 1 and 2. □

LEMMA 1. *The set X of all feasible solutions of problem (13) is a partition matroid.*

PROOF. X is a partition matroid only if the following four conditions hold:

1. $\emptyset \in X$,

2. If $x \in X$ and $y \subseteq x$, then $y \in X$,

3. If $x, y \in X$, and $|x| > |y|$, then there exists an element $e \in x \setminus y$, such that $y \cup \{e\} \in X$,

4. $|x \cap \Psi_c| \leq 1, x \in X, \forall c = 1, ..., C$.

Condition 1 and 2 are obviously true. Since it is required that a subchannel can be assigned to no more than one link, condition 4 holds too. For condition 3, since $|x| > |y|$, there should exist at least one pair $e = (c,l)$ such that c never appears in y. Thus $y \cup \{e\}$ is still a feasible solution. □

LEMMA 2. *$F(\cdot)$ is a submodular function on X.*

PROOF. Since $F(\cdot)$ is the sum of utility $f(\cdot)$ over all links, $F(\cdot)$ is a submodular function if $f(\cdot)$ is a submodular function.

Function $f(\cdot)$ is a submodular function if the following three conditions hold:

1. $f(\emptyset) = 0$,

2. $f(x \cup \{e\}) - f(x) \geq 0, x \cup \{e\} \in X, \forall x \in X, \forall e \in \Psi$,

3. $f(x \cup \{e\}) - f(x) \leq f(y \cup \{e\}) - f(y), x \cup \{e\}, y \cup \{e\} \in X, y \subseteq x, \forall x, y \in X, \forall e \in \Psi$.

149

If no subchannel is allocated, then $f(0) = 0$. Therefore condition 1 holds. For condition 2, if $x \cup \{e\}$ is feasible, then the subchannel c in pair $e = (c, l)$ never appears in x. Assuming subchannel c is assigned to link l when pair e is added. For links other than l, we have:

$$f(x \cup \{e\}) - f(x) = 0, \qquad (14)$$

and for link l, we have:

$$
\begin{aligned}
& f(x \cup \{e\}) - f(x) \\
= & f(n+1) - f(n) \geq 0 \qquad (15) \\
& (n = 0, 1, ..., C - 1)
\end{aligned}
$$

Since the utility function $f(\cdot)$ is a non-decreasing concave function, $f(n+1) - f(n) \geq 0$ is satisfied and condition 2 holds.

For condition 3, similarly for links other than l, for all $e = (c, l)$, we have:

$$(f(x \cup \{e\}) - f(x)) - (f(y \cup \{e\}) - f(y)) = 0, \qquad (16)$$

and for link l, the equation can be written as:

$$
\begin{aligned}
& (f(x \cup \{e\}) - f(x)) - (f(y \cup \{e\}) - f(y)) \\
= & (f(n+1) - f(n)) - (f(n'+1) - f(n')), \qquad (17) \\
& y \subseteq x \Rightarrow n' \leq n, n, n' = 0, 1, ..., C - 1,
\end{aligned}
$$

Since $y \subseteq x$, n is no smaller than n'. Then because $f(\cdot)$ is a non-decreasing concave function satisfying the diminishing return principle, the inequality $(f(n+1) - f(n)) - (f(n'+1) - f(n')) \leq 0$ holds. Condition 3 is satisfied. Both $f(\cdot)$ and $F(\cdot)$ are submodular functions. □

4. PERFORMANCE EVALUATION

4.1 Experimental Setup

We evaluate the performance of our regret-based learning algorithm with cluster structure, denoted as L*, by developing our simulation program written in Java. The simulation setup is as follows.

We focus on downlink transmissions. There are 10 subframes in each OFDMA frame. The total number of subchannels is set to 32. The transmission range of each FBS is set to 10 meters. A collision happens in one subchannel if more than one user (in the same contention range) access this subchannel simultaneously. One or more collisions in one TB (for one link) lead to the retransmission of the whole TB in the next subframe. If no collision happens, the TB is transmitted successfully. At the end of each subframe, each user notifies its FBS about the status of the last transmission via an ACK/NACK.

To investigate the benefits of in-cluster cooperation, we also study the pure regret-based learning algorithm without any information sharing between the cluster members [6], denoted as L, as a baseline. We compare the two strategy definitions (*Binary Branch* and *Consecutive List*) within these two algorithms, and denote them L-B, L-C, L*-B, and L*-C respectively. For comparison sake, we also study the performance of a hashing-based benchmark algorithm H proposed in [12], which is the closest to our work to the best of our knowledge. In the simulation, for both algorithms L and L*, parameter δ is fixed to 0.01. For L-B and L*-B, constant μ is set to 4096, and for L-C and L*-C, μ is set to 33792.

4.2 Maximizing Network Throughput

We design a fixed topology with three FBSs and nine links (or users, numbered n1 to n9), as shown in Figure 2(a). We assume that in this group of simulation experiments, there is no bandwidth

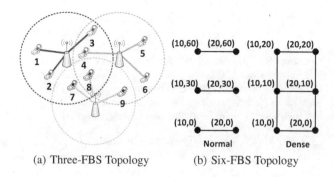

(a) Three-FBS Topology   (b) Six-FBS Topology

Figure 2: Topology

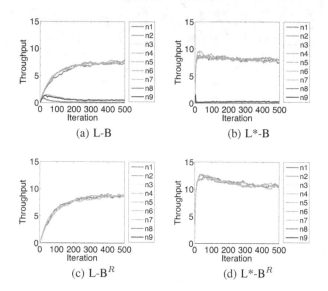

(a) L-B   (b) L*-B

(c) L-B^R (d) L*-B^R

Figure 3: Convergence Analysis

demand information attached with the links. The throughput (performance metric) is defined as the number of successful subchannels obtained by each user in each iteration (subframe), and each link greedily maximizes its own throughput in the learning game.

4.2.1 Convergence

We first investigate the convergence of the two learning algorithms with the Binary Branch strategy definition (L-B and L*-B). The sample paths are averaged over 1000 independent rounds of simulation with the same initial strategy (accessing zero subchannels). We can see from Figure 3(a) and 3(b) that algorithm L* converged much faster than L thanks to the in-cluster shared regret information. Algorithm L* converged in less than 150 iterations, i.e., 0.15 seconds (one iteration took 1 ms), while Algorithm L converged in about 500 iterations.

By checking the individual throughput obtained by each link in Figure 3(a) and 3(b), we observe that links n1, n2, n5, n6 grabbed the bandwidth resource successfully since they have low contention levels. However, links n3, n4, n7, n8, and n9, suffered from large interference, and achieved a very low throughput. We draw the attention of the reader here to the subtlety of this result: the low throughput of these nodes is not a consequence of repeated access attempts followed by failures like in other alternative approaches but rather the result of the regret-based learning. That is, the FBSs learned of this "hidden" contention information based their histor-

Table 1: Average Throughput Comparison

	L-B	L*-B	L*-B^R	L-C	L*-C	L*-C^R	H
1	7.67	7.96	10.94	3.03	8.54	8.78	1.77
2	7.62	8.21	10.74	2.86	8.52	8.98	1.77
3	0.12	0.06	0	0.46	0.08	0	1.77
4	0.11	0.05	0	0.49	0.08	0	1.78
5	7.55	7.99	10.71	3.01	8.25	9.40	1.78
6	7.75	8.10	10.90	3.17	8.52	9.09	1.79
7	0.45	0.34	0	0.83	0.39	0	0.91
8	0.10	0.05	0	0.49	0.07	0	0.91
9	0.48	0.31	0	0.85	0.40	0	0.91
T	31.84	33.07	43.30	15.20	34.85	36.25	13.39

[1] The table entries are accurate to two decimal places.

[2] T represents the total average throughput.

ical data, and as a result assigned more resources to the "better" links gradually and less to the bad ones. In other words there is no waste of bandwidth. Furthermore users who suffer from large contention are able to recognize themselves from their low throughput (thanks to the regret-based learning) and may trigger the handoff process to re-associate with the MBS on an orthogonal frequency spectrum from the FBSs. Such user re-association/handoff would further reduce the bandwidth waste on high-contention links due to the large interference and also improves the throughput for all the links. Figure 3(c) and 3(d) show the throughput of good links n1, n2, n5, and n6 after the re-association of the bad links with the MBS (L-B^R and L*-B^R). Compared to the previous figures, we can see the throughput of these users increased after re-association, while the convergence is similar to the previous cases.

4.2.2 Average Throughput Comparison

Table 1 summarizes the performance of all the algorithms in terms of average link throughput over 500 iterations (subframes), with each entry in the table being an average of 1000 simulation runs. Entries in the table set to 0 are for the nodes that are assumed to have re-associated with the MBS. We did not simulate the MBS in our experiments as it is beyond the scope of the paper, nevertheless, since the MBS possesses X2 interface and has plenty of resources, typically it will assign enough bandwidth to each of its users to guarantee their QoS. Since we are only interested in f2f interference mitigation we only focus on the throughput achieved through the femtocells.

Our algorithms L*-B and L*-C achieved much better average throughput compared to the benchmark algorithm H (around 3 fold) thanks to their strong feedback-based learning abilities. The benchmark H, being a randomized fair hashing algorithm, allocates bandwidth equally to all links in the same femtocell regardless of their contention levels. Furthermore, in algorithm H, the number of contenders of each FBS is inaccurate since it does not count for the hidden ones. As a result in H, the system capacity would have to be reduced greatly in order to take care of the high-contention links and achieve fairness at a dramatic cost in bandwidth. While such fairness would have been appropriate in say WLANs, in femtocell networks it is meaningless since nodes that suffer a bad channel can always fall back to the MBS, which we adopt in our approach. Algorithm L* (L*-B and L*-C) achieves higher total average throughput compared to algorithm L (L-B and L-C) thanks to the in-cluster cooperation. The total average throughput is improved after re-association (L*-B^R and L*-C^R).

Our algorithm L* under the *Binary Branch* and the *Consecutive List* strategy definition (L*-B and L*-C) showed similarly good performance while L*-B has lower computational complexity than

L*-C. Therefore we choose the *Binary Branch* strategy for our algorithm L* in the following simulation experiments.

4.3 Satisfaction Ratio in Networks with Heterogeneous Link Demands

4.3.1 Satisfaction Ratio

Next we investigate the benefit of our algorithm in larger networks with heterogeneous link demands. In such networks, since links only need what they request for, i.e., their demands, it would be desirable to evaluate the satisfaction of each link instead of its throughput. As some of the link demands cannot be fully satisfied, we propose to use a satisfaction ratio metric $R_{d_l}(x)$ for evaluation,

$$R_{d_l}(x) = \begin{cases} \frac{x}{d_l}, x \le d_l \\ 1, x > d_l \end{cases} , d_l > 0, \qquad (18)$$

where x is the number of successful subchannels in each subframe, and d_l is the link demand, i.e., the number of subchannels requested. The idea of satisfaction ratio is to capture the ratio between the obtained bandwidth and the demand. When the throughput exceeds the demand, the ratio is maximized at 1. Therefore, the satisfaction ratio $R_{d_l}(x)$ ranges from 0 to 1. Note that the payoff function in our algorithm is still as defined in (12).

4.3.2 Results

We compare the satisfaction ratio achieved by our algorithm L*-B (*Binary Branch*) and that of the benchmark algorithm H in two scenarios: Normal and Dense. In both scenarios, the network contains six FBSs, whose topologies are shown in the form of a conflict graph in Figure 2(b). An edge between two FBSs represents possible conflict between the two femtocells. In the Normal scenario, links from at most two FBSs may conflict with each other. While in the Dense scenario, links from at most four FBSs may conflict with each other. Each FBS has 3 or 4 users with probability 0.5 for each. User locations are generated randomly in the range of the FBS coverage. For each scenario, 1000 different user distributions were randomly generated and the simulation results of the 1000 tests are averaged.

There were two types of link demands in our simulation: 10 and 32. Each link was attached with only one kind of demand. Link demand 10 occupied about one third of the bandwidth while link demand 32 required the whole bandwidth. For each scenario, we examine three different ratios between the number of low-demand links and the number of high-demand links: high demand only (0:1), even low-high demand (1:1), and low demand only (1:0).

Figure 4 shows the total average satisfaction ratio comparison (averaged over 500 subframes and summed over all the links) for the three different ratios (low-demand links to high-demand links) in both Normal and Dense scenarios. As can be observed from the figure, our algorithm L* consistently achieved a higher total average network satisfaction ratio than the benchmark algorithm H. Overall, larger link demand and higher network density leads to lower total average satisfaction ratio. Specifically, in high demand only (0:1), our algorithm achieved twice the satisfaction ratio compared of the benchmark in both Normal and Dense scenarios. Our algorithm also improved the total average satisfaction ratio compared to the benchmark by 10% to 20% in the even demand scenario (1:1) and the low demand only scenario (1:0) respectively.

In addition to the total average satisfaction ratio, we also study the variation of the link satisfaction ratio to see whether links were satisfied fairly. Specifically, we plot the cumulative distribution function (CDF) for the link average satisfaction ratio (averaged over 500 subframes), which can show the satisfaction distribution

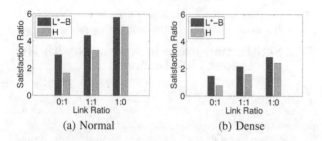

(a) Normal   (b) Dense

Figure 4: Total Average Satisfaction Ratio of Network with Heterogeneous Link Demands

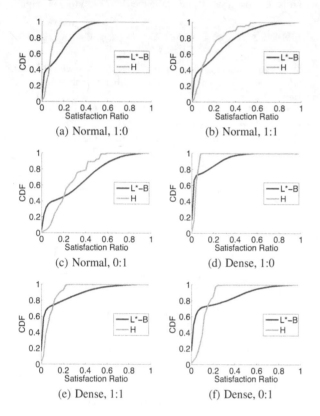

(a) Normal, 1:0   (b) Normal, 1:1

(c) Normal, 0:1   (d) Dense, 1:0

(e) Dense, 1:1   (f) Dense, 0:1

Figure 5: CDF of Satisfaction Ratio in Network with Heterogeneous Link Demands

over all links. The CDFs for high demand only (0:1), even demand (1:1), and low demand only (1:0) in the two scenarios Normal and Dense networks are shown in Figure 5. As an example, algorithm H achieved worse performance compared to our algorithm in Figure 5(a). The CDF of H reaches 1 at a satisfaction ratio of 0.2, meaning that all users got satisfaction ratios of no more than 0.2, while the CDF for our algorithm did not reach 1 until satisfaction ratio of 0.5. Since a CDF is always non-decreasing, the larger the area under the curve, the worse the performance.

5. CONCLUSION

In this paper we have studied the problem of improving resource utilization in LTE femtocell networks by reducing femtocell-to-

femtocell interference in a fully distributed approach. We have designed a femtocell base station MAC scheduling algorithm by adopting a regret-based learning game with cluster structure. Each femtocell base station learns the good channel access strategies on behalf of its links based on the historical feedback provided by its users. Simulation results highlight the considerable improvements achieved by our algorithms compared to other alternative approach that relies on a randomized hashing for different network scenarios. One of the subtle virtues of our algorithm is that it enables links that suffer from great interference to learn gradually about this interference without degrading the network throughput. As a result such nodes may choose to handoff to the macrocell base station to benefit themselves and the rest of the nodes in the network.

6. REFERENCES

[1] Informa Telecoms & Media, Small cell market status. Feb. 2013. Online: http://goo.gl/iGYrd9 (access on Apr, 2014).

[2] M. Y. Arslan, J. Yoon, K. Sundaresan, S. V. Krishnamurthy, and S. Banerjee. Fermi: a femtocell resource management system forinterference mitigation in ofdma networks. In *ACM MobiCom 2011*, pages 25–36.

[3] M. Bennis and D. Niyato. A q-learning based approach to interference avoidance in self-organized femtocell networks. In *IEEE GLOBECOM Workshops 2010*, pages 706–710.

[4] U. Feige and J. Vondrak. Approximation algorithms for allocation problems: Improving the factor of 1-1/e. In *IEEE FOCS 2006*, pages 667–676.

[5] O. N. Gharehshiran and V. Krishnamurthy. Learning correlated equilibria in noncooperative games with cluster structure. In *Game Theory for Networks*, pages 115–124. Springer, 2012.

[6] S. Hart and A. Mas-Colell. *A reinforcement procedure leading to correlated equilibrium*. Springer, 2001.

[7] I.-H. Hou and C. S. Chen. An energy-aware protocol for self-organizing heterogeneous lte systems. *IEEE JSAC 2013*, 31(5):937–946.

[8] I.-H. Hou and P. Gupta. Proportionally fair distributed resource allocation in multiband wireless systems. *IEEE/ACM TON 2013*.

[9] Z. Lu, T. Bansal, and P. Sinha. Achieving user-level fairness in open-access femtocell-based architecture. *IEEE TMC 2013*, 12(10):1943–1954.

[10] G. L. Nemhauser, L. A. Wolsey, and M. L. Fisher. An analysis of approximations for maximizing submodular set functions–I. *Mathematical Programming*, 14(1):265–294, 1978.

[11] S. Sesia, I. Toufik, and M. Baker. *LTE: The UMTS Long Term Evolution, From Theory to Practice*. Wiley, 2009.

[12] K. Sundaresan and S. Rangarajan. Efficient resource management in ofdma femto cells. In *ACM MobiHoc 2009*, pages 33–42.

[13] J. Yoon, M. Y. Arslan, K. Sundaresan, S. V. Krishnamurthy, and S. Banerjee. A distributed resource management framework for interference mitigation in ofdma femtocell networks. In *ACM MobiHoc 2012*, pages 25–36.

User Satisfaction Based Joint User Selection and Beamforming in TD-LTE-A Downlink

Xuanli Wu,Nannan Fu
Harbin Institute of Technology
Communication Research
Center
Harbin, China
xlwu2002@hit.edu.cn
betterfunan@126.com

Di Lin
University of Electronic
Science and Technology of
China
School of Information and
Software Engineering
di.lin2@mail.mcqill.ca

Wanjun Zhao
Harbin Institute of Technology
Communication Research
Center
Harbin, China
wjzhit@126.com

ABSTRACT

In TD-LTE-A downlink, user selection is a key technique when the number of users exceeds the amount could be supported by eNodeB at one Transmission Time Interval (TTI). In order to improve the fairness of different users and consider the difference of user traffic in the process of user selection, a Signal to Leakage and Noise-Ratio (SLNR) beamforming based joint user selection and beamforming algorithm is proposed in this paper. Since in TD-LTE-A systems, the traffic can be classified into two types: Guaranteed Bit Rate (GBR) traffic and Non-Guaranteed Bit Rate (Non-GBR) traffic, user satisfaction for GBR and Non-GBR traffic are defined at first, and then, based on the difference of traffic, a user satisfaction based joint user selection and beamforming algorithm is proposed. Simulation results show that compared with conventionally used joint user selection and beamforming algorithm, user satisfaction of GBR traffic can be increased by 300% due to the fact that GBR traffic always has higher priority than Non-GBR traffic. Moreover, user fairness can also be improved in terms of the variance of user satisfaction.

Categories and Subject Descriptors

H.4.3 [**Communications Applications**]: User selection, beamforming

Keywords

TD-LTE-A; user selection; user traffic; user fairness; Signal-to-Leakage-and-Noise-Ratio (SLNR)

1. INTRODUCTION

Over the past decade, wireless technologies have continuously evolved to accommodate high spectral efficiency through utilization of multi-user multiple-input multiple-output (MU-MIMO) techniques [1]. In LTE-A standard, MIMO techniques can be classified into 3 types: spatial multiplexing,

transmit diversity and beamforming [2]. Through different data stream transmission in dependent channels, spatial multiplexing increases transmission rate of users. And transmit diversity improves the reliability of transmission information in non-correlative channels. While beamforming enhances transmission performance by decreasing multi-users interference. Due to different requirements of signal transmission in different channel, the application scenarios of these three techniques are different. When SNR is high, spatial multiplexing can be used to improve transmission date rate through multiplexing technology. When Signal to Noise Ratio (SNR) is low, transmit diversity can be used to increase throughput of cell edge users and coverage area of eNodeB through improving the received SNR. And beamforming is used to improve users' peak transmission date rate through decreasing co-channel interferences (CCI). For improving users' peak transmission rate, beamforming technique in MU-MIMO has attracted more attention [3].

Considering reciprocity property between downlink and uplink channel in Time Division Duplexing (TDD) mode, downlink channel information can be easily obtained for beamforming. Therefore the downlink non-codebook based beamforming can be easily realized in TD-LTE-A downlink [4].Based on the acquired position of non-codebook beamforming matrix, non-codebook beamforming algorithms can be divided into two types: nonlinear beamforming and linear beamforming. The optimal beamforming algorithm, Dirty Paper Coding (DPC), which is nonlinear, can achieve optimal system sum capacity with extremely high complexity [5]. In order to reduce the complexity, linear algorithms are proposed to realize suboptimal system sum capacity, such as Zero Forcing (ZF), Minimum Mean Square Error (MMSE), Block Diagonalization (BD) and Signal to Leakage and Noise Ratio (SLNR) algorithm. Although ZF and BD algorithms can mitigate CCI among users completely, the number of transmitting antennas in eNodeB must be more than that in receiver end, and perfect channel estimation is also difficult to be realized [6]. SLNR beamforming algorithm is proposed to solve above problems [7]. By replacing SINR with SLNR, the calculation complexity of beamforming algorithm can be decreased. Therefore, compared with other beamforming algorithms, SLNR algorithm is a better choice with the tradeoff between realization complexity and system sum capacity. Hence, the proposed user selection algorithm in this paper is based on SLNR algorithm.

In TD-LTE-A system, in some cases, the number of users waiting for selection are more than those system could support in one Transmission Time Interval (TTI), and then eNodeB should select users to transmit information from waiting users group [8]. Through appropriate users selection, space diversity gain could be utilized completely. As we know, exhaustive search algorithm is an optimal algorithm for user selection, however, it requires high computational complexity. Hence, suboptimal user selection algorithms are proposed to decrease computational complexity, e.g. a user selection algorithm using correlation of channel matrices is presented in [9]. However, system throughput need to be improved further. As in [10], eNodeB selects users with approximate algorithm obtained through channel capacity and system throughput has been improved. Nonetheless, user fairness is neglected in [10]. To improve system throughput and guarantee user fairness, maximum weighted sum rate user selection combined with MMSE beamforming and semi-orthogonal user selection combined with ZF beamforming are proposed in [11] and [12], respectively. Although they take user fairness into consideration, the difference of user traffic is not considered. For measuring user services quality, user satisfaction is proposed through utility function in [13].

In order to maximize sum capacity with the consideration of traffic priority and user satisfaction, in this paper, we propose a user satisfaction based joint user selection and beamforming algorithm. User satisfaction indicators of GBR and Non-GBR traffic are given at first to show satisfaction of different users. Then user feeds back their satisfaction into transmitter to adjust user selection and beamforming matrix so that user fairness can be improved. Simulations results show that compared with conventional user selection algorithms, average user satisfaction and user satisfaction of GBR traffic can be increased respectively by 155% and 300% when SNR equals to 10dB. Moreover, user fairness in the proposed algorithm is improved in terms of the variance of user satisfaction. For lower variance of user satisfaction, the selection possibility of each user by eNodeB is the same, and hence, the lower variance, the better fairness.

The rest of this paper is organized as follows: in Section 2, the referenced user selection algorithm Maximum Minimum SLNR is given; and then the proposed user satisfaction based joint user selection and beamforming algorithm is explained in Section 3. Simulation results are obtained in Section 4 and conclusions are drawn in Section 5.

2. CONVENTIONAL USER SELECTION COMBINED WITH SLNR BEAMFORMING ALGORITHM

Conventional multi-user selection and beamforming in TD-LTE-A downlink is illustrated in Figure 1.

The total number of users waiting to be selected is K_{all} , and maximum number of users that system can support in one TTI is K. N_t is the number of transmitting antennas at the eNodeB and each user has the same number of antennas, N_r. The beamforming matrix of user k is

$$\mathbf{W}_k = [\mathbf{W}_1, \mathbf{W}_2, \ldots, \mathbf{W}_{m_k}] \in {}^{N_t \times m_k}, \qquad (1)$$

where, m_k represents the number of data stream for user k. The transmitted signals supported by TD-LTE-A system are

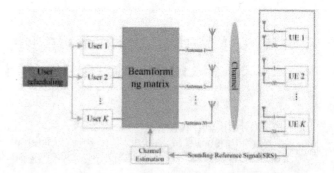

Figure 1: User selection and beamforming in TD-LTE-A system

$\mathbf{S} = [\mathbf{s}_1, \mathbf{s}_2, \ldots \mathbf{s}_K]$, where $\mathbf{s}_k \in {}^{m_k \times L}$ is transmitted signal of user k, and L is the number of transmitted symbols.

Our research mainly focuses on the joint user selection and beamforming. Hence, the power allocation of different users is not considered, and equal power allocation is used in this paper. Then the signal received by user k can be expressed as:

$$\mathbf{r}_k = \mathbf{H}_k \mathbf{W}_k \mathbf{s}_k + \sum_{i=1, i \neq k}^{K} \mathbf{H}_k \mathbf{W}_i \mathbf{s}_i + \mathbf{n}_k, \mathbf{r}_k \in {}^{N_t \times m_k} \qquad (2)$$

where, $\mathbf{H}_k \in {}^{N_r \times N_t}$ represents channel between user k and eNodeB, and $\mathbf{n}_k$ stands for additive white Gaussian noise with zero mean and variance σ^2.

From (2), interferences from other users could be found clearly and SLNR beamforming algorithm can significantly minimize the leakage interference to other users. Then the SLNR of user k can be written as:

$$
\begin{aligned}
J(\mathbf{W}_k) &= \frac{\|\mathbf{H}_k \mathbf{W}_k\|_F^2}{N_r \sigma^2 + \sum_{i=1, i \neq k}^{K} \|\mathbf{H}_i \mathbf{W}_k\|_F^2} \qquad (3) \\
&= \frac{tr\left(\mathbf{W}_k^H \mathbf{H}_k^H \mathbf{H}_k \mathbf{W}_k\right)}{tr\left(\mathbf{W}_k^H \left(\bar{\mathbf{H}}_k^H \bar{\mathbf{H}}_k + N_r \sigma^2 \mathbf{I}_{N_t}\right) \mathbf{W}_k\right)},
\end{aligned}
$$

where, $\bar{\mathbf{H}}_k = \left[\mathbf{H}_1^H, \cdots, \mathbf{H}_{k-1}^H, \mathbf{H}_{k+1}^H, \cdots, \mathbf{H}_K^H\right]^H$, $(\bullet)^H$ and $\|\bullet\|_F^2$ represents conjugate transpose and Frobenius norm of matrix, respectively. σ^2 refers to variance of white Gaussian noise and $\mathbf{I}_{N_t}$ is identity matrix with dimension of N_t. The purpose of SLNR beamforming algorithm is to maximize SLNR at the transmitter, therefore, the optimal beamforming matrix in SLNR beamforming can be expressed as:

$$
\begin{aligned}
\mathbf{W}_k^{opt} &= \arg\max_{\mathbf{W}_k} J(\mathbf{W}_k) \qquad (4) \\
&= \arg\max_{\mathbf{W}_k} \frac{tr\left(\mathbf{W}_k^H \mathbf{H}_k^H \mathbf{H}_k \mathbf{W}_k\right)}{tr\left(\mathbf{W}_k^H \left(\bar{\mathbf{H}}_k^H \bar{\mathbf{H}}_k + N_r \sigma^2 \mathbf{I}_{N_t}\right) \mathbf{W}_k\right)}.
\end{aligned}
$$

From (4), it can be seen that $\mathbf{W}_k$ is only determined by beamforming vectors of user k, and other users have no effect on the value of beamforming vectors. Hence, the optimal beamforming matrix can be obtained easily. We can obtain from [14] that if $\lambda_1 \geq \lambda_2 \geq \ldots \geq \lambda_{N_t}$ are generalized eigenvalues of matrix $\left\{\mathbf{H}_k^{\bar{H}} \mathbf{H}_k, (\bar{\mathbf{H}}_k^H \bar{\mathbf{H}}_k + N_r \sigma^2 \mathbf{I}_{N_t})\right\}$, and $\mathbf{T}_k$ is is the corresponding generalized eigenvector of generalized eigenvalues, then optimal beamforming matrix is

$$\mathbf{W}_k^{opt} = \alpha_k \mathbf{T}_k \left(:, 1 : m_k\right), \qquad (5)$$

where, α_k is the coefficient to adjust transmit power so that maximum transmit power constraint can be satisfied.

In TD-LTE-A system some cases, all users cannot admit system in one TTI, so user selcetion is pretty necessary. Ref. [15] proposed a suboptimal user selection algorithm combined with SLNR beamfoming called Maximum Minimum SLNR. The user selection policy is described as:

$$\max_{K_{all}}(\min_{k \in \Phi}(SEIG_k)) \quad s.t. \quad \sum_{i=1}^{K} \|\mathbf{W}_i\|_F^2 \le P, \qquad (6)$$

where, $\Phi = \{k\,|1,2,\cdots,K\}$ is the number of selected users in one TTI, $SEIG_k$ is generalized eigenvalue of user k. $\mathbf{W}_i$ is beamforming matrix of user i, and P is maximum transmit power constrain of eNodeB.

In this referenced paper, Maximum Minimum SLNR algorithm selects users through comparing generalized eigenvalues of users. The eigenvalue of first biggest users are selected for transmitting. Through (6), we can obtain the service probability of users with higher generalized eigenvalues is high. And these users can be allowed to admit system for obtaining better performance. While the users with lower generalized eigenvalue cannot obtain admission chance when user selection happens. At this time, the user fairness in [15] cannot be guaranteed. To increase user satisfaction and improve user fairness, user selection jointed with beamforming method is proposed in this paper by feedback of user satisfaction. And the detail description is introduced in Section 3.

3. PROPOSED USER SATISFACTION BASED JOINT USER SELECTION AND BEAMFORMING ALGORITHM

3.1 User Satisfaction of GBR and Non-GBR Traffic

In LTE-A system, there are 9 typical service traffic [16], which can be classified into two types: GBR traffic and Non-GBR traffic. In this paper, both of them are taken into account to represent different service priorities. In [17], the user satisfaction of GBR traffic and Non-GBR traffic are defined in (7) and (8), respectively.

$$sat_k^{GBR} = \qquad\qquad (7)$$
$$\begin{cases} 1 & \overline{r_k} \ge r_{k,tar}\, and\, \overline{d_k} \le d_{k,tar} \\ (\frac{\overline{r_k}-r_{k,\min}}{r_{k,tar}-r_{k,\min}})^{\varphi} & otherwise \\ 0 & \overline{r_k} < r_{k,\min}\ \overline{d_k} > d_{k,tar} \end{cases}$$

$$sat_k^{Non-GBR} = \qquad\qquad (8)$$
$$\begin{cases} 1 & \overline{r_k} \ge r_{k,tar}\, and\, \overline{d_k} \le d_{k,tar} \\ (\frac{\overline{r_k}}{r_{k,tar}})^{\Omega} & otherwise \\ 0 & \overline{d_k} > d_{k,tar} \end{cases}$$

where, $sat_k \in [0,1]$ represents satisfaction of user k. Higher value of user satisfaction represents better satisfaction of the user. $\overline{r_k}$, $r_{k,tar}$ and $r_{k,\min}$ is average transmission data rate, maximum target transmission rate and desired minimum transmission rate, respectively. $\overline{d_k}$ and $d_{k,tar}$ is average transmission delay and maximum target transmission delay, respectively. φ and Ω is reference index of GBR and Non-GBR traffic, respectively.

3.2 User Satisfaction Based Joint User Selection and Beamforming Algorithm

User satisfaction can not only be used to reflect the user satisfaction of transmission, but also to indicate the user fairness. Considering that user satisfaction is fed back to user selection algorithm, the user selection policy (6) can be optimized as:

$$\max_{K_{all}}(\min_{k \in \Phi}(SEIG_k^i / \overline{SAT_k^i})) \quad s.t. \quad \sum_{i=1}^{K} \|w_i\|_F^2 \le P, \qquad (9)$$

where, $\overline{SAT_k^i}$ is the average satisfaction of user k in i^{th} TTI and $SEIG_k^i$ is generalized eigenvalue of user k in i^{th} TTI. Due to selection policy (9), when average user satisfaction of user is higher in current TTI, its probability of being selected in next TTI would be smaller in terms of the quotient of generalized eigenvalue and average user satisfaction. While when the average user satisfaction of user is lower in current TTI, its probability of being selected in next TTI increases. Thus, the fairness between users is improved through adjusting the selected probability of different users. At the same time, system performance would also be guaranteed by selecting users with higher generalized eigenvalue in selection policy (9).

System sum capacity is used to evaluate the capacity performance of LTE-A system and it can be obtained through the Shannon formulation. The sum capacity can be expressed as:

$$C = B\log_2(1 + SNR). \qquad (10)$$

where, C is system sum capacity, B is system bandwidth.

The whole proposed algorithm is explained in Algorithm 1. The first step is initialization. In first TTI, eNodeB sets satisfaction initial value as 0.1. Because of higher priority of GBR traffic, the users transmitting GBR traffic are selected in the first place. Considering the limited amount users who can be served within one TTI, when the number of admitted users is high, not all users could be selected in one TTI. If the user number transmitting GBR traffic is larger than the user number supported by eNodeB in one TTI, eNodeB only selects users in the users transmitting GBR traffic through users' channel gain. The channel gain can be obtained through channel norm. It can be expressed as:

$$G_k = \|\mathbf{H}_k\|, k = 1, 2, ..., K_{all}, \qquad (11)$$

where, G_k is channel gain of user k and $\mathbf{H_k}$ is channel matrix of user k. And the first M users with biggest values of channel gain in the users transmitting GBR traffic are selected. If the user number transmitting GBR traffic is smaller than the user number supported by eNodeB in one TTI, eNodeB would select all the users transmitting GBR traffic first and continue to select users in the users transmitting Non-GBR traffic. The method of selecting the users transmitting Non-GBR traffic is the same as that of selecting the users transmitting GBR traffic. Hence, eNodeB could obtain the selection set $\Phi(1)$ in the first TTI. In the $(i-1)^{th}$ TTI, eNodeB obtains user satisfaction through the feedback of users. Average user satisfaction $\overline{SAT_k^i}$ of user k in the ith TTI can be obtained through the average of previous TTIs. It is expressed as:

$$\overline{SAT_k^i} = \{(i-1)\overline{SAT_k^{i-1}} + SAT_k^i\}/i, i = 1, 2, ..., \qquad (12)$$

where, $\overline{SAT_k^i}$ is average satisfaction of user k in i^{th} TTI, $\overline{SAT_k}^{i-1}$ is average satisfaction of user k in $(i-1)^{th}$ TTI. And SAT_k^i is satisfaction of user k in i^{th} TTI. If the user number transmitting GBR traffic is larger than the user number supported by eNodeB in one TTI, eNodeB only selects users in the users transmitting GBR traffic through comparing values of $SEIG_k/\overline{SAT_k^i}$. Where, $SEIG_k$ can be obtained through SLNR beamforming and $\overline{SAT_k^i}$ can be obtained through (12). If the user number transmitting GBR traffic is smaller than the user number supported by eNodeB in one TTI, eNodeB would select all the users transmitting GBR traffic first and continue to select users in the users transmitting Non-GBR traffic. Through ordering the values of $SEIG_k/\overline{SAT_k^i}$, the $M-m$ biggest users in the users transmitting Non-GBR traffic could be selected. Therefore, eNodeB could obtain the selection set $\Phi(i)$ in i^{th} TTI. After final selection set is ensured, the corresponding beamforming matrix can be obtained through (4) and (5).

Algorithm 1 User Satisfaction Based Joint User Selection and Beamforming Algorithm

---

Input: :

transmitted signals of each user, i.e., $\mathbf{S}_1, \mathbf{S}_2, ..., \mathbf{S}_{K_{all}}$

estimated channel matrix $\mathbf{H}_k \in \mathbb{C}^{N_r \times N_t}$

the user number transmitting GBR traffic m

supported user number in one TTI M

Output: :

selected users number in set $\Phi(i)$ in i^{th} TTI and corresponding beamforming matrix $\mathbf{W}_k^{opt}$

1: **Initialization**: set initial value of satisfaction as $\overline{SAT_k} = 0.1$ in first TTI.

2: **IF** $(m > M)$

3:     **Select** the M biggest users transmitting GBR traffic through (11) and **obtain** selection set $\Phi(1)$.

4: **ELSE**

5:     **Select** all the users transmitting GBR traffic and $M - m$ biggest users transmitting Non-GBR traffic through (11) and **obtain** selection set $\Phi(1)$.

6: **END IF**

7: **In** the ith TTI, the $\overline{SAT_k^i}$ of user k can be obtained through (12).

8: **IF** $(m > M)$

9:     **Select** the M biggest users transmitting GBR traffic through (9) and **obtain** selection set $\Phi(i)$.

10: **ELSE**

11:     **Select** all the users transmitting GBR traffic and $M - m$ biggest users transmitting Non-GBR traffic through (9). **Obtain** selection set $\Phi(i)$.

12: **END IF**

13: **Obtain** the last selection set $\Phi(i)$ in the ith TTI and the corresponding beamforming matrix $\mathbf{W}_k^{opt}$ through (4) and (5).

---

4. SIMULATION RESULTS AND ANALYSIS

In this Section, the proposed algorithm is compared with conventional user selection algorithms, such as Round Robin, maximum channel norm and MMSLNR algorithms in [16]. Simulation parameters are defined as: the number of antennas at eNodeB and UE is 8 and 1, respectively. System bandwidth is 1.4MHz. Without loss of generality, user 1-

Table 1: Simulation parameters

Parameter	Setting	Parameter	Setting
Bandwidth	1.4MHz	Stream per UE	1
CQI	4	UE Number	20
Cyclic Prefix	Normal	GBR UE	1-4
TTI	1ms	Non-GBR UE	5-20
N_t per eNodeB	8	Modulation	QPSK
N_r per UE	1	Channel	Rayleigh

Table 2: Parameters for GBR and Non-GBR

Traffic	$r_{k,tar}$ (Mbps)	$r_{k,min}$ (Mbps)	φ/Ω	$d_{k,tar}$ (ms)
GBR	1	0.512	2	100
Non-GBR	1	-	1	100

4 transmits GBR traffic and other users in system transmits Non-GBR traffic. The total user number in system is $K_{all} = 20$. The channel between eNodeB and UE is Rayleigh flat fading channel. Detailed simulation parameters are listed in Table I. Parameters of user satisfaction for GBR and Non-GBR are listed in Table II, where the reference index parameters of user satisfaction for GBR and Non-GBR traffic are set according to [17].

Figure 2 shows average user satisfaction for all users obtained with these four user selection algorithms. As can be seen from Figure 2, the user satisfaction of proposed algorithm reaches 0.46 when average SNR equals to 10dB. The proposed algorithm outperforms all other user selection algorithms. It is observed that the improvement of user satisfaction for the proposed algorithm is bigger than 155% compared with other algorithms due to the reason that user satisfaction is considered in the process of joint user selection and beamforming. eNodeB adjusts user selection jointed with beamforming policy through user satisfaction feedback. Figure 3 shows user satisfaction of GBR traffic under four user selection algorithms. For GBR users, it is obvious that the proposed algorithm has better performance, and compared with MMSLNR user selection algorithm more than 300% improvement can be obtained when SNR is 10dB. The reason is that the proposed algorithm modifies MMSLNR selection criteria through user satisfaction. Figure 4 is the average user satisfaction variance of GBR and Non-GBR traffic. And variance could be used to reflect user fairness. Due to the classification of traffic, the proposed algorithm improves user fairness significantly, especially for the transmitting GBR traffic users. Figure 5 shows sum capacity of different user selection algorithms. Compared with MMSLNR algorithm, sum capacity of the proposed user selection algorithm decreases only about 2bps/Hz, which is smaller than the declination of other user selection algorithms in Figure 5. Hence, the proposed algorithm can realize the tradeoff between sum capacity and user fairness.

5. CONCLUSIONS

In order to improve user satisfaction for user selection in TD-LTE-A downlink and guarantee user fairness as well, a

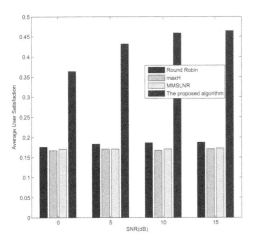

Figure 2: Average user satisfaction of different user selection algorithms

user satisfaction based joint user selection and beamforming algorithm is proposed in this paper. Considering user satisfaction of GBR and Non-GBR traffic in user data transmission, the average user satisfaction of proposed algorithm has 106%-147% promotion compared with Maximum Minimum SLNR algorithm. Especially for the users transmitting GBR traffic, an significant improvement of more than 300% can be obtained. The user satisfaction variance is lower than referenced MMSLNR algorithm for the users transmitting GBR traffic and Non-GBR traffic, respectively, which indicates that the proposed algorithm has a better user fairness compared with MMSLNR algorithm. Hence, the proposed algorithm can realize the tradeoff between sum capacity and user fairness.

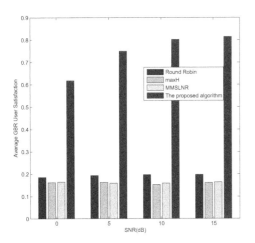

Figure 3: Average GBR user satisfaction of different user selection algorithms

6. ACKNOWLEDGMENTS

This work has been support in part by National Basic Research Program of China (973 Program, No.2013CB329003), National Nature Science Foundation, No.61301100, Next Generation Wireless Mobile Communication Network of China, No.2013ZX03001024-003, Heilongjiang Postdoctoral Science-Research Foundation under Grant No.LBH-Q12081.

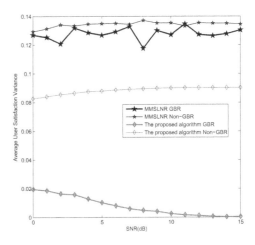

Figure 4: Variance of average user satisfaction

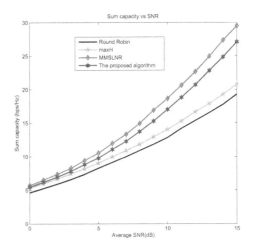

Figure 5: Sum capacity of different user selection algorithms

7. REFERENCES

[1] L. Liu, R. Chen, S. Geirhofer, K. Sayana, Z. Shi and Y. Zhou. 2012. Downlink MIMO in LTE-advanced: SU-MIMO vs. MU-MIMO. IEEE Communications Society, 140 - 147.

[2] J. Shen, S. Q. Suo, H. Y. Quan, X. W. Zhao, H. J. Hu and Y. H. Jiang. 2008. 3GPP Long Term Evolution:Principle and System Design. Pose Telecom Press. Beijing.

[3] S. H. Moon, C. Lee, S. R. Lee, I Lee. 2013. A Joint Adaptive Beamforming and User Scheduling Algorithm for Downlink Network MIMO Systems. IEEE ICC Wireless Communications Symposium, 5392-5397.

[4] B. Dai, W. Xu and C. Zhao. 2011. Multiuser Beamforming Optimization via Maximizing Modified SLNR with Quantized CSI Feedback. Wireless Communications, Networking and Mobile Computing (WiCOM), 1-5.

[5] M. Sharif, B. Hassibi. 2007. A comparison of time-sharing, DPC, and bemforming for MIMO broadcast channels with many users. IEEE Trans. Communication, vol. 55, no. 1.

[6] D. Debbarma, Q. Wang, S. H. Groot and A. Lo. 2013. A Throughput Fair SLNR Scheduling Algorithm for Hybird Fi-Wi Indoor Downlink MU-MIMO. IEEE 24th International Symposium on Personal, Indoor and Mobile Radio Communications, 902-906.

[7] C. C. Tian, W. Q. Yang, L. Fang, Z. J. Wang and Y. F. Wang. 2009. On the performance of Eigen based Beamforming in LTE-Advanced. PIMRC, 2070-2074.

[8] L. Bai, Y. Li, Q. F. Huang, X. Dong and Q. Yu. 2013. Spatial Signal Combining Theories and Key Technologies. Post Telecom Press, Beijing.

[9] T. Ji, C. Zhou, S. Zhou and Y. Yao. 2007. Low Complex User Selection Strategies for Multi-user MIMO Downlink Scenario. IEEE Wireless Communication and Networking Conference, 1532-1537.

[10] Z. B. Jie, Y. B. Tian, P. Y. Yan and Q. H. Liu. 2012. User selection algorithm for multi-user MIMO system.

Computer Engineering and Applications, vol. 48, no. 28, 107-111.

[11] M. Ahn, K. Lee, K. Lee and I. Lee. 2013. SLNR-based User Scheduling for MISO Downlink Cellular Systems. IEEE 77th Vehicular Technology Conference, 1-5.

[12] T. Yoo and A. Goldsmith. 2006. On the optimality of multiantenna broadcast scheduling using zero-forcing beamforming. IEEE J. Sel. AreasCommun., vol. 24, no. 3, 528-541.

[13] Z. Chen, K. Xu, F. Jiang and Y. Wang. 2008. Utility based scheduling algorithm for multiple services per user in MIMO OFDM system. IEEE International Conference on Communications, 110-114.

[14] P. Cheng, M. Tao, W. Zhang. 2010. A New SLNR-Based Linear Precoding for Downlink Multi-User Multi-Stream MIMO Systems. IEEE Communications Letters, vol. 14, no. 11, 1008-1010.

[15] X. L. Wu, M. X. Luo, L. K. Sun, N. N. Fu. 2013. Signal to Leakage and Noise Ratio Based Beamforming and User Scheduling for TD-LTE-A Systems. Advanced Materials Research, vol. 760-762, 551-555.

[16] 3GPP Technical Specification 23.203, Policy and charging control architecture http://www.3gpp.org/ftp/Specs/html-info/23203.htm.

[17] L. Qiu, J. Xu, B. Liu, X. W. Liang. 2011. Multi-user multi-cell MIMO communication technology. Post Telecom Press. Beijing.

Modeling of IEEE 802.11 Multi-hop Wireless Chains with Hidden Nodes

Thiago Abreu
Université Lyon 1 - LIP
France
thiago.wanderley@ens-lyon.fr

Bruno Baynat
Université Pierre et Marie
Curie - LIP6
France
bruno.baynat@lip6.fr

Thomas Begin
Université Lyon 1 - LIP
France
thomas.begin@ens-lyon.fr

Isabelle Guérin-Lassous
Université Lyon 1 - LIP
France
isabelle.guerin-lassous@ens-lyon.fr

Nghi Nguyen
Université Lyon 1 - LIP
France
huu.nguyen@ens-lyon.fr

ABSTRACT

In this paper, we follow up an existing modeling framework to analytically evaluate the performance of multi-hop flows along a wireless chain of four nodes. The proposed model accounts for a non-perfect physical layer, handles the hidden node problem, and is applicable under workload conditions ranging from flow(s) with low intensity to flow(s) causing the network to saturate. Its solution is easily and quickly obtained and delivers estimates for the expected throughput and for the datagram loss probability of the chain with a good accuracy.

1. INTRODUCTION

Most WLANs are based on the IEEE 802.11 standard, which implements a probabilistic media access control (MAC) layer. The IEEE 802.11 standard is generally appreciated for its ease of implementation and simple configuration. However, the performance evaluation of these WLANs are generally not straightforward because of their non-deterministic nature (due to the use of a probabilistic contention algorithm and to the dynamic behavior of the radio medium).

In the case of infrastructure mode, where nodes communicate through an access point, a large body of analytical models have been proposed in the literature [3, 6]. These models afford a quick means for researchers and practitioners to forecast many aspects of a WLAN behavior before its deployment, or to better set it up.

Multi-hop wireless networks are another type of WLANs where each node participates in routing by forwarding packets for other nodes. Typically, their decentralized nature makes them suitable for cases where there are no central nodes or for emergency situations like natural disasters. How-

ever, multi-hop wireless networks raise new issues with regards to the routing protocols and to the discovery and refinement of their performance.

This paper addresses the performance evaluation of a multi-hop wireless network based on IEEE 802.11, where packets need to hop several relay nodes before reaching their final destination. We refer to these networks as chains. There is only a handful of works specifically devoted to the analytical performance evaluation of such chains based on IEEE 802.11 [2, 4, 1]. Besides, it seems that none of them handles at the same time realistic assumptions regarding the behavior of the MAC protocol, the inter-dependencies in the distribution of the workload among the nodes (some nodes may be in saturation while others may be in starvation) and the hidden node problem, which are fundamental properties of a wireless chain with several nodes.

In a previous paper [1], we analyzed the behavior of the simplest chain which has only one relay node. Though a necessary milestone, its limited size allowed us to overlook the well-known but complex issue of hidden node problem. The contributions of this paper are twofold. First, we extend our modeling framework to evaluate the performance for a flow conveyed through larger chains in which the hidden node problem takes place. The solution to the model is based on a simple iterative scheme that is solved typically within less than a second. In general, the proposed model delivers good forecasts for the expected throughput and for the datagram losses as a function of the actual positions of the relay nodes and for various values of the flow rate. Second, our model affords a convenient means to quickly investigate the performance behavior of a chain under various conditions. Given the fast solution of our model, we explore many possible configurations for the relay nodes and for the levels of the flow rate in order to get a better understanding of multi-hop wireless networks and to highlight properties inherent to those networks.

2. SCENARIO DESCRIPTION

The scenario under consideration is depicted in Figure 1. It consists of a wireless multi-hop chain with 4 nodes, each equipped with a single IEEE 802.11 communication interface. The nodes communicate using the DCF mode of IEEE

MSWiM'14, September 21–26, 2014, Montreal, QC, Canada.
Copyright is held by the owner/author(s). Publication rights licensed to ACM.
ACM 978-1-4503-3030-5/14/09 ...$15.00.
http://dx.doi.org/10.1145/2641798.2641826.

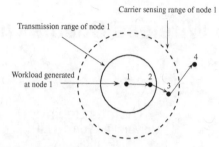

Figure 1: Multi-hop chain with 4 nodes

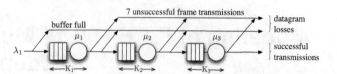

Figure 2: Global queueing model

802.11. In our scenario, we disabled the RTS/CTS mechanism since it is known to be inefficient in the case of a chain [7]. Every node can communicate only with its 1-hop neighbors, but its carrier sensing range covers its 2-hop neighbor nodes. Note that there are no restrictions to the nodes alignment and position, as long as they meet the aforementioned assumptions for the communication and for the carrier sensing ranges.

The physical layer used for the frame transmission is unreliable (non-perfect), and therefore, frames may be lost because of bits error or alteration. This is taken into account by the Bit Error Rate (BER), which gives the probability that a bit is misinterpreted at a receiver node due to the transmission process (which includes noise, distortion, attenuation, etc). In our study, the BER is affected by the propagation process and noise. In addition to BER, frames may also be lost when nearby nodes are transmitting simultaneously, which causes frame collisions. In a four-nodes chain, collisions are frequent since nodes 1 and 4 are exposed to the hidden node problem.

The four-nodes chain conveys packets (datagrams) from node 1 up to node 4 (see Figure 1). All datagrams are of same length and the datagrams generation at node 1 follows a Poisson process with a rate λ_1. This flow of datagrams constitutes the workload for the chain.

3. MODEL

In [1] we introduce the first parts of a general framework for performance evaluation of a multi-hop wireless chain. The analysis was restricted to a simple scenario with only three nodes. Here, we extend markedly our proposed framework by introducing one important missing feature in the previous analysis, i.e., the hidden node problem which takes place in larger chains. Unlike our previous study of [1] in which virtually no frames collisions can occur, larger chains are prone to frequent frames collisions. In this paper, we present a practical means to handle these collisions within our modeling framework. By doing so, we also demonstrate that our preliminary work is extendable to more general scenarios, with the ultimate objective being to derive a whole framework for the performance evaluation of any multi-hop wireless chain.

Following the framework developed in [1], our model is composed of two levels: a global queueing network model, and several local Markov chain models. Since only three nodes are effectively transmitting frames (node 4 only returns acknowledgments), the global queueing model associated with the chain is composed of three queues with fi-

nite buffer as illustrated in Figure 2. The customers of this queueing model are the datagrams of the chain and the buffer size of queue i is denoted by K_i. The service rate μ_i of queue i is, by definition, the inverse of the mean service time S_i of queue i, which corresponds to the average time node i needs to transmit a datagram that is ready to be sent over the radio channel. As developed in [1], S_i includes all successive frame (re)transmissions (corresponding to the considered datagram), as well as all IEEE 802.11 DCF protocol delays (DIFS, backoff, SIFS, timeout) and all freezing times due to another node transmission during the backoff of node i. This parameter will be estimated thanks to the local Markovian model associated with node i. The local Markov chain models are similar to those presented in [1].

Like in our previous model [1], a datagram can be lost either because of a buffer overflow or because of excessive retransmissions of the associated frames. But there is a fundamental difference between the global model presented here and the one previously developed in [1]: a frame loss can either be due to low quality of the channel or to collision over the shared medium. The frame loss probability p_{f_i} of node i must account for these two possibilities, whereas in [1] it was only related to the BER. If we denote by p_{BER_i} the probability that a given frame sent by node i is lost because of the BER, and by p_{coll_i} the probability that the frame sent by node i is lost because of a collision with another frame, and if we assume that these two events are independent but not disjoint (a frame can be both in error and in collision), the frame loss probability p_{f_i} of node i can be obtained as:

$$p_{f_i} = p_{coll_i} + p_{BER_i} - p_{coll_i}\, p_{BER_i} \qquad (1)$$

As for the BER probability, which was solely used in [1] for estimating the frame error probability, its derivation remains identical. However, the collision probability, which was virtually null in the case handled by [1], can not be neglected and, as will be seen later, is a very sensitive parameter that must be carefully estimated.

A frame collision may be the result of two different factors. First, a collision can result from the well known hidden problem of two nodes that are not in the carrier sensing range of each other. Second, because of the sensing mechanism of 802.11, a collision can also occur when two neighboring nodes finish their backoff countdown simultaneously. By assuming that these two possibilities result in disjoint events (which turns out to be exact in our scenario), we can decompose the frame collision probability of node i as the sum of the probability of both events:

$$p_{coll_i} = p_{hid_i} + p_{st_i} \qquad (2)$$

Let us first consider the hidden problem case and see how we can estimate the collision probability at node i due to frame collision with nodes that are hidden from node i, denoted as p_{hid_i}. In our scenario, since we assume a 2-hop carrier sensing range, the hidden problem can only take place

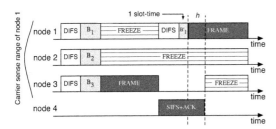

Figure 3: Collision between ACK from node 4 and frame from node 1

between node 1 and node 4, and more precisely, between a data frame sent by node 1 to node 2 and an acknowledgement ("ACK") sent back by node 4 to node 3. As an illustration, in Figure 3, node 3 senses the medium idle for the duration of its backoff and then starts the transmission of a frame, freezing the backoff countdowns of nodes 1 and 2. The associated acknowledgement ("ACK") sent by node 4 does not prevent node 1 from resuming its backoff countdown (event "B'_1"), since nodes 1 and 4 are hidden. If the remaining backoff of node 1 is short enough (it corresponds to 1 time-slot in the example), node 1 will transmit its frame and a collision will occur for both frame and ACK. Although the ACK from node 4 collides, we consider that a collision happens at node 3, since the retransmission mechanism will be performed by this node.

As can be seen on the figure, the duration of the collision is bounded by the maximum overlap h between the frame transmission of node 1 and the ACK transmission of node 4:

$$h = \text{SIFS} + \text{ACK} - \text{DIFS} - 1 \text{ time slot} \quad (3)$$

We subtract 1 time slot to it, since after a backoff freezing period, the remaining backoff has at least 1 time slot to decrement.

By considering that the nodes have always a frame to transmit, the collision probability p_{hid_i} of node i due to a hidden node j can be estimated in a first approximation as the ratio between the duration of a possible collision (h) and the time during which a collision may take place ($h + \overline{B}_j$) in between two transmissions of node i:

$$p_{hid_i} = \frac{h}{h + \overline{B}_j} \quad (4)$$

In this relation, $\overline{B}_j$ is the mean backoff duration of node j (see [1] for more details).

Relation (4) has however two limitations. First, by only considering the average duration of the backoff ($\overline{B}_j$), we do not take into account the high variability of the binary exponential backoff used in IEEE 802.11. For instance, if node 1 is in the first stage of its backoff, an ACK from node 4 will very likely collide with a frame of node 1. Conversely, when node 1 is in one of the last stages of its backoff, an ACK from node 4 will have a high chance to be transmitted successfully. Let us define $tb_j(k)$, the proportion of time during which hidden node j remains in backoff stage k. $tb_j(k)$ is the ratio between the average time effectively spent in the k-th backoff stage of node j ($p_{f_j}^{k-1} t_{k,j}$) and the average service time of node j (S_j):

$$tb_j(k) = \frac{p_{f_j}^{k-1} t_{k,j}}{S_j} \quad (5)$$

The collision probability p_{hid_i} can thus be rewritten as:

$$p_{hid_i} = \sum_{k=1}^{7} tb_j(k) \, \frac{h}{h + \overline{B}(k)} \quad (6)$$

where $\overline{B}(k)$ is the average backoff duration at stage k.

Second, relation (4) (or equivalently relation (6)) implicitly assumes that node j has a datagram to transit (otherwise no collision can occur with node i) and should actually be denoted as the conditional probability $p_{hid_i|\text{node } j \text{ is not idle}}$. From the law of Total Probabilities, we can obtain the unconditioned collision probability, by noting that the probability $p_{hid_i|\text{node } j \text{ is idle}}$ is null and by reminding that the probability that node j is not idle is nothing but node j utilization (denoted $\overline{U}_j$):

$$p_{hid_i} = p_{hid_i|\text{node } j \text{ is not idle}} \, \overline{U}_j \quad (7)$$

By combining previous relations, the collision probability due to hidden nodes can finally be expressed as:

$$p_{hid_i} = \sum_{k=1}^{7} tb_j(k) \, \frac{h}{h + \overline{B}(k)} \, \overline{U}_j \quad (8)$$

Let us now consider the possible simultaneous transmissions of two neighboring nodes. As explained above, two nodes in the carrier sensing range of each other are very likely to synchronize themselves (mainly when the load is high). And there is a non negligible probability that the backoff countdowns of these two nodes expire simultaneously and that the two nodes start their transmission exactly at the same time, resulting in frame collisions. Let p_{st_i} denote the probability that a frame of node i collides with a frame of any node that is in its carrier sensing range and that starts a transmission at the same time as node i. This probability can be estimated as follows:

$$p_{st_i} = 1 - \prod_{j \neq i} (1 - \tau_j \overline{U}_j) \quad (9)$$

where τ_j is the probability that a given node j in the carrier sensing range of node i starts its transmission at the same time as node i, provided node j has something to transmit. This is an approximation, assuming that three (or more) nodes have a very small chance to start their transmission all together. Now we simply estimate the missing conditional probability τ_j as the inverse of the average backoff duration of node j expressed in number of time slots:

$$\tau_j = \frac{1}{\overline{B}_j} \quad (10)$$

4. NUMERICAL RESULTS

In this section we address the accuracy concern of our proposed model. Throughout this section, we use the parameter values of IEEE 802.11b as reported in Table 1. The communication and carrier sensing ranges cover 399 and 700 meters, respectively. The received signal power at each node is computed using a transmission power of 31.6 mW, an antenna gain of 1 dBi and the two-ray ground reflection model. We derive the BER, which accounts for the non-perfect physical layer, based on a relation between the received signal power and the used modulation.

To evaluate the accuracy of our model, we compare its performance parameters obtained with an implementation

DIFS	$50\mu s$
SIFS	$10\mu s$
Time slot	$20\mu s$
Contention window size (min,max)	31, 1023
Frame retransmission limit	7
Physical rate	11 Mb/s

Table 1: IEEE 802.11b parameters

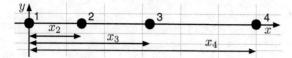

Figure 4: Topology used for the numerical results

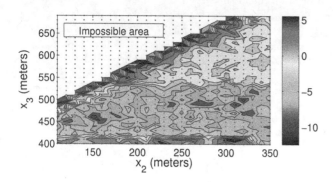

Figure 5: Percentage relative errors for the expected throughput for various positions of relay nodes (x_2 and x_3) with K_i=20 and λ_1=2 Mb/s

in MATLAB with those delivered by a discrete-event simulator (Network Simulator version 2.35 - ns-2.35 [5]) for a large set of possible chains with four nodes. Note that all simulation results have been performed by generating 100,000 packets at the source node. We define the percentage relative error of our model versus the actual values (delivered by ns-2.35) as the ratio $100\times$ *(approximate - actual) / actual*. To simplify the presentation of the results, the four nodes of the chain are scattered in a straight line as illustrated by Figure 4. Nodes 1 and 4 are steady while the positions of nodes 2 and 3 vary. We denote by x_i the distance between node i and node 1. Values of x_2 are within the interval [110, 350] meters, while x_3 belongs to the interval [400, 690] meters. x_4 is constantly set to 750 meters. Note that the positions of nodes 2 and 3 must obey certain rules so that 1-hop neighbors can communicate. This is the reason behind the white "impossible area" band in Figure 5. Aside from x_i, two additional parameters can be tuned in our scenario: the size of buffers K_i, and the workload rate λ_1. Datagrams have a size of 1500 bytes.

We focus on the ability of our model to provide fair predictions for the expected throughput of the 4-nodes chain. Figure 5 represents the relative error value on the chain throughput for our proposed model as a function of the distances of both relay nodes 2 and 3 to node 1.

In this example, the buffers are of length $K_i = 20$, and the workload is set to a high, but not excessive level, which corresponds to a datagrams arrivals rate at the source node (node 1) of $\lambda_1 = 2$ Mb/s. We choose this value of λ_1 because it leads to analytical difficulties as the buffer at node 1 is neither completely full nor empty. Note that this figure corresponds to hundreds of data points explored (both by the simulator and by the model), and the surfaces shown are obtained using an interpolation from sets of scattered data points. The relative error tends to be low as it stands below 10% for virtually all of the nearly 550 configurations we have performed to generate this figure. We observe that the relative error tends to attain its maximum value (near 10%) (in the top points of the figure) when the link between nodes 2 and 3 is at is maximum distance, causing very high values of BER and a frame loss probability exceeding 60%. By studying the overall distribution of relative errors in the throughput, we observe that the mean error is around 4%, in close to 90% of cases the error remains below 10% and it never exceeds 15% in all considered cases.

We have assessed the accuracy of our model on other performance parameters, e.g. the datagram loss probability, as well as on many different configurations. It is our conclusion that, in general, the accuracy of the model is good and that the results presented above reflect its typical behavior.

Acknowledgments

This work was funded by the French National Research Agency (ANR) under the projects ANR VERSO RESCUE (ANR-10-VERS-003) and ANR-JST PETAFLOW (ANR-09-BLAN-0376).

5. REFERENCES

[1] T. Abreu, B. Baynat, T. Begin, and I. Guérin-Lassous. Hierarchical Modeling of IEEE 802.11 Multi-hop Wireless Networks. In *Proceedings of ACM MSWiM*, pages 143–150. ACM, 2013.

[2] A. Aziz, M. Durvy, O. Dousse, and P. Thiran. Models of 802.11 multi-hop networks: Theoretical insights and experimental validation. In *IEEE COMSNETS*, 2011.

[3] G. Bianchi. Performance analysis of the IEEE 802.11 distributed coordination function. *IEEE JSAC*, 18(3), 2000.

[4] M. M. Hira, F. A. Tobagi, and K. Medepalli. Throughput analysis of a path in an IEEE 802.11 multihop wireless network. In *Proceedings of IEEE WCNC*, 2007.

[5] NS2. http://www.isi.edu/nsnam/ns/.

[6] I. Tinnirello, G. Bianchi, and Y. Xiao. Refinements on IEEE 802.11 distributed coordination function modeling approaches. *IEEE Transactions on Vehicular Technology*, 59(3), 2010.

[7] K. Xu, M. Gerla, and S. Bae. Effectiveness of RTS/CTS handshake in IEEE 802.11 based ad hoc networks. *Ad Hoc Networks*, 1, 2003.

Interference-Aware Mesh Multicast
for Wireless Multihop Networks

Daniel Lertpratchya   Douglas M. Blough   George F. Riley

d.lertpratchya@gatech.edu doug.blough@ece.gatech.edu riley@ece.gatech.edu

School of Electrical and Computer Engineering
Georgia Institute of Technology, Atlanta, Georgia 30332

ABSTRACT

In this paper, we consider the problem of building mesh-based multicast routing structures that account for the impact of interference in wireless multihop networks. Our analysis is based on the most accurate known interference model, namely the physical interference model. We first analyze interference-aware mesh structures that augment individual paths in a multicast tree. Based on this analysis, we propose two interference-aware multicast mesh routing structures, which extend an interference-aware Steiner multicast tree in two different ways to form interference-aware meshes. We evaluate the performances of our proposed interference-aware multicast mesh structures in wireless networks where wireless links are bursty and nodes can be faulty. Under these conditions, we show that our proposed algorithms provide up to 80% increase in goodput over existing tree-based multicast routing structures and up to 45% increase in goodput over existing mesh-based multicast routing structures.

Categories and Subject Descriptors

C.2.1 [**Computer-Communication Networks**]: Network Architecture and Design—*Wireless communication*

General Terms

Algorithms

Keywords

Multicast routing, Wireless interference

1. INTRODUCTION

In multicast, a single message is delivered to a group of destinations in a network. This problem has been studied for both wired and wireless networks. A survey of multicast protocols for ad hoc networks can be found in [3]. A major limitation of research in this area is that the vast majority of works ignore interference. The few works that do consider interference use inaccurate models.

MSWiM'14, September 21–26, 2014, Montreal, QC, Canada.
Copyright 2014 ACM 978-1-4503-3030-5/14/09 ...$15.00.
http://dx.doi.org/10.1145/2641798.2641836.

Multicast routing approaches can be classified into three main categories: structure-less (e.g. [6,9]), tree-based (e.g. [4,10]), and mesh-based (e.g. [1,7]). Tree structures provide simple and cost effective routing infrastructures at the cost of robustness since there exists exactly one path between the source and each destination.

One possible solution to improve robustness is to use a mesh as the underlying routing structure instead of a tree. A mesh is a connected graph where there is more than one path from a multicast source to each multicast destination. These extra paths can deliver multicast packets to the destinations if the transmissions on other paths have failed. However, most of the mesh-based multicast protocols are concerned only with the problem of building and maintaining a multicast mesh efficiently but they ignore interference.

A few studies have been done on theoretical aspects of multicast mesh structures [11, 12]. Zhao and others [11] proposed four heuristics to build a resilient multicast mesh structure. Two heuristics, NDT and RNDT, build a multicast mesh by merging two node-disjoint MNT multicast trees [8] to form a multicast mesh. The other two heuristics, SDM and MDM, build a multicast mesh by finding a pair of node-disjoint shortest paths from the source node to each multicast receiver, then merging all the node-disjoint paths to form a multicast mesh. The proposed heuristics, however, do not take interference into account.

In this paper, we propose two interference-aware mesh multicast algorithms. Interference-aware multicast meshes are built by extending the interference-aware multicast tree [4]. The first algorithm creates a mesh by creating two redundant paths for each overlay link on the overlay multicast tree. The second algorithm uses Delaunay triangulation to build a multicast overlay mesh. We evaluate the performances of our proposed multicast mesh structures through simulation where link failure and node failure may occur. Simulation results show that our proposed multicast mesh structures provide up to 80% increase in goodput over existing tree-based routing structures and up to 45% increase over existing mesh-based routing structures. These results also show that our proposed interference-aware mesh routing structures are robust to the burstiness of wireless links.

2. SYSTEM MODEL AND PROBLEM FORMULATION

We consider a communication graph G, where $V(G)$ is a set of all wireless nodes and $E(G)$ is a set of edges. An edge $(u, v) \in E(G)$ if and only if $d(u, v) \leq r_t$, where $d(u, v)$ is the Euclidean distance between nodes u and v and r_t is the maximum transmission range. We are given a multicast source $s \in V(G)$ and a set of multicast destinations $M \subset V(G)$. The problem is to find a communication graph H where H is a connected subgraph of G and $M \cup \{s\} \subset V(H)$. As previously shown, the benefit of considering interference when building a multicast tree can be achieved even without explicit transmission scheduling [4]. Our goal is to find H that achieves the highest multicast packet reception ratio (MPRR), which is defined as the average packet reception ratio over all multicast destinations.

We adopt the classical model for radio signal propagation, which is referred to as the log-distance propagation loss model. The radio signal strength at a distance d from the transmitter is given by $\frac{P_t}{d^\alpha}$, where P_t is the transmission power and α is the path loss coefficient. We assume that all nodes use the same transmission power and they are not equipped with interference cancellation capabilities. We consider the physical interference (PI) model [2]. In the PI model, interference from all concurrent transmitters in the network is factored into the signal-to-interference ratio (SIR) value at the receiver. The transmission will be correctly received if and only if the SIR value at the receiver exceeds the SIR threshold (SIR$_{\min}$).

To assist the analysis, we consider an ideal network where node density is infinite so we are able to pick nodes that satisfy the analysis when building multicast routing structures.

3. INTERFERENCE-AWARE MESH ROUTING STRUCTURES

In this section, we present algorithms to build interference-aware multicast mesh structures. The algorithms build a mesh by creating redundant paths on an interference-aware Steiner tree (IAST) [4] to form an interference-aware multicast mesh. The goal of the algorithms is to reduce the impact of interference among the paths in the mesh. before presenting algorithms to build interference-aware multicast meshes, we provide a quick review of the interference-aware Steiner tree (IAST).

3.1 Interference-aware Steiner Tree (IAST)

The high level idea of the interference-aware Steiner tree is as follows. Given nodes that must be connected in a multicast tree (the source node and all the destination nodes), the algorithm first identifies how these nodes should be connected in a tree. To accomplish this, the algorithm uses a Euclidean Steiner Tree approximation algorithm to build a Steiner tree, using $M \cup \{s\}$ as input. The Euclidean Steiner tree approximation algorithm returns a Steiner tree T where $V(T)$ is a set of nodes in the Steiner tree and $E(T)$ is a set of edges in the Steiner tree. The returned Steiner tree, also called an overlay tree, shows the "big picture" of connections between nodes in the tree. An edge between two nodes in the overlay tree suggests that the two nodes should be connected by a path in the multicast tree.

3.2 Overlay link extension algorithm

Our first tree extension algorithm is called the overlay link extension algorithm (OLE). Given an overlay tree T, the idea of our first multicast mesh algorithm is to create two redundant paths for each edge in the overlay tree. For each edge $(t_a, t_b) \in E(T)$, OLE creates two redundant paths between t_a and t_b. OLE places two shadow nodes u and v

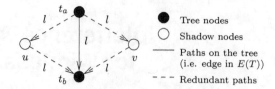

Figure 1: Overlay link extension algorithm.

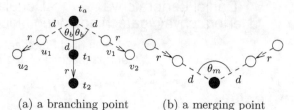

(a) a branching point   (b) a merging point

Figure 2: Two scenarios to be considered for OLE.

and creates two paths between t_a and t_b, one through each shadow node. Let $d(t_a, t_b) = l$, OLE places u and v such that $d(t_a, u) = d(t_a, v) = d(u, t_b) = d(v, t_b) = l$. The general idea of our first algorithm is illustrated in Figure 1.

By introducing two redundant paths between t_a and t_b, we have created one mesh branching point at t_a and one mesh merging point at t_b where the two redundant paths merge to t_b. Next, we determine optimal structures involving the branching point and the merging point in an ideal network.

3.2.1 Mesh branching nodes

Consider a mesh branching node t_a that branches into three nodes – one node on the overlay tree (t_1) and two nodes on the redundant paths (u_1 and v_1) as shown in Figure 2(a). Let $d = d(t_a, t_1) = d(t_a, u_1) = d(t_a, v_1)$ and $r = d(t_1, t_2) = d(u_1, u_2) = d(v_1, v_2)$. The transmission from t_a is done by broadcasting to all three children. Assuming that all three nodes successfully received the packet from t_a, the three nodes forward the packet to their next hops at the same time. Our goal is to find r such that the three transmissions will be successful. Among the three receivers, the node t_2 on the overlay tree experiences the largest interference. The total interference at t_2 is given by

$$\frac{2P_t}{(d^2 + dr + r^2)^{\alpha/2}}.$$

Combining the received signal strength and the interference, we set SIR to SIR$_{\min}$ and convert units to decibel, we get $r = b \cdot d$ where

$$b = \frac{1 + \sqrt{1 + 4(10^{\frac{10\log 2 + \text{SIR}_{\min}^{\text{dB}}}{5\alpha}} - 1)}}{2(10^{\frac{10\log 2 + \text{SIR}_{\min}^{\text{dB}}}{5\alpha}} - 1)}.$$

The result shows that the distance between the transmitting nodes and the receiving nodes is proportional to the distance between the transmitting node and the mesh branching node. The distance grows as the transmitting node gets farther away from the mesh branching node until the distance reaches the maximum transmission range.

3.2.2 Mesh merging nodes

Next, we consider a mesh merging node in Figure 2(b) where the redundant paths finally merge back to the node on the overlay tree. Since the length of the tree path is l and the length of the redundant path is $2l$, the transmissions on the tree path will have already arrived at the merging node when the two redundant paths converge. Applying similar analysis as the mesh branching nodes, we get $r = m \cdot d$ where

$$m = \frac{3 + \sqrt{12 \cdot 10^{\frac{\text{SIR}_{\min}^{\text{dB}}}{5\alpha}} - 3}}{2(10^{\frac{\text{SIR}_{\min}^{\text{dB}}}{5\alpha}} - 1)}.$$

Here, the distance between nodes must shorten as the nodes get closer to the merging node. However, the last transmissions to the merging node cannot take place at the same time. The transmissions to the merging node may need to be scheduled to avoid collision.

After the overlay mesh in an ideal network is formed, the algorithm builds a multicast mesh routing structure using the overlay mesh as a guideline. Since the real network is finite, it is not possible to find nodes that are exactly at the shadow nodes' locations. The algorithm first finds a node that is nearest to a shadow node location and assigns the selected node as the shadow node.

Next, the algorithm builds a mesh by connecting nodes with paths, using the analyses for the mesh branching nodes and mesh merging nodes to select nodes on the paths. Again, since the real network is finite, finding nodes that completely satisfy the analyses is not possible. To solve this problem, we use a scaling factor (f) [4]. Let the distance from the analysis in an ideal network be r_i, the algorithm uses the distance $r_i^* = f \cdot r_i$, where $0 < f \leq 1$, when selecting nodes on the path. The purpose of the scaling factor is to account for the imperfect choices of nodes in a finite network.

One advantage of the OLE algorithm is that the analyses can be used as guidelines to select nodes on the final multicast mesh. However, the OLE algorithm creates two redundant paths for all overlay links that can result in overlapping redundant paths.

3.3 Delaunay mesh extension algorithm

In this section, we propose our second algorithm to extend a multicast tree to form a mesh, called Delaunay mesh extension algorithm (DME). Our goal in designing the second algorithm is to take the *overall* tree structure into account when building a multicast mesh.

3.3.1 Basic Delaunay mesh extension

The idea of the Delaunay mesh extension algorithm is to use Delaunay triangulation on the set of overlay nodes in the overlay multicast tree to identify the positions of the mesh nodes (also called Delaunay nodes). Given a Delaunay triangulation, the algorithm identifies a center point of each triangle as a position of a potential mesh node. The algorithm creates redundant paths between a potential mesh node and each of its corresponding nodes in the Delaunay triangulation if the overlay node is not a Steiner node. We do not create a redundant path between the potential mesh node and a Steiner node since a Steiner node is not a source or a receiver in the multicast group and does not need to be protected by a redundant path.

One advantage of the DME algorithm is that the redundant paths will not overlap each other. However, one drawback of the DME algorithm is that the analysis cannot be applied directly like the overlay link extension since the lengths of the redundant paths are not identical. To solve this problem, we again use a scaling factor to scale down the maximum distance between two nodes when building a multicast mesh. The distance between two nodes is fixed to $r = f \cdot r_t$ where $0 < f \leq 1$. In other words, DME algorithm uses a fixed, shortened distance when building a multicast mesh instead of using different routing strategies for branching nodes and merging nodes.

Even though the DME algorithm does not create overlapping redundant paths, it is still possible for two Delaunay nodes to be located close together. To solve this problem, we propose a variation of the DME algorithm next.

3.3.2 Delaunay mesh extension with nodes merging

The goal of the Delaunay mesh extension with nodes merging algorithm (DME-merge) is to merge two Delaunay nodes that are located closer than a given distance into one node.

The algorithm takes the mesh structure from the DME algorithm and repeatedly combines two Delaunay nodes if they are separated by a distance smaller than the given `merging_distance` by placing a new Delaunay node at the midpoint of the two nodes. The new Delaunay node connects to all the overlay nodes that were connected to the two Delaunay nodes. The merging process continues until no two Delaunay nodes satisfy the merging condition.

For comparison, we show an example of the three proposed interference-aware multicast routing structures in Figure 3.

4. PERFORMANCE EVALUATION

We evaluate the performances of our interference-aware multicast mesh structures through simulations. We evaluate the multicast routing structures under two major causes of network disconnection: link burstiness and node failure. A stochastic bursty wireless link model [5] is used for links. To simulate node failure, nodes in the network randomly drop multicast packets.

4.1 Simulation parameters and assumptions

We use ns-3.15 simulator to evaluate all algorithms. We use a physical model of 802.11g at the data rate of 6 Mbps. All nodes use the transmission power of 40 mW and thermal noise is computed at 290K. All wireless links are modeled with ideal bursty link model [5], unless stated otherwise. In all simulations, 2000 nodes were uniformly distributed in a deployment area of 1000 m by 1000 m. All results reported are reported using multicast packet reception ratio (MPRR) and are averaged from 100 simulations.

4.2 Scaling factor and merging distance

We first evaluate the scaling factor since it is a significant parameter affecting both OLE and DME. In this simulation, one source node is randomly selected as a multicast source. The source node sends multicast packets at the rate of 10 packets per second. Scaling factor was varied from 0.3 to 1.0 for both OLE and DME. We did not use the scaling factor below 0.3 since the network became disconnected in some simulations. Simulation results are reported in Figure 4.

As seen from Figure 4, the choice of scaling factor affects the performance of OLE and DME algorithms. If the scaling factor is too small, the extra nodes included create more interference that can outweigh the gain of spatial reuse. If the scaling factor is too large, the links are prone to interference from other concurrent transmissions. The optimal scaling

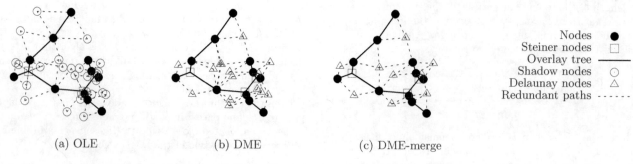

(a) OLE　　　　　　(b) DME　　　　　　(c) DME-merge

Figure 3: Examples of different interference-aware multicast routing structures.

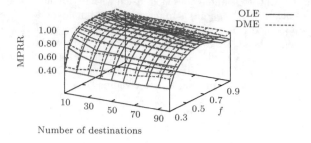

Figure 4: MPRR with varying scaling factors.

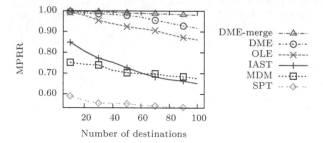

Figure 6: MPRR of different multicast routing structures.

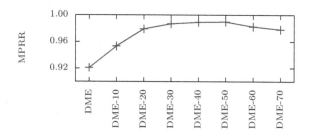

Figure 5: MPRR of DME-merge algorithm with different merging distance.

factor is also dependent on the number of multicast destinations in the network as the number of nodes in the multicast trees changes. Performances are quite stable across a fairly wide range of scaling factors for both OLE and DME, e.g. 0.5 to 0.7. Based on this analysis, we have set the scaling factor for both algorithms to 0.7.

Next, we evaluate the merging distance parameter of DME-merge algorithm. In this simulation, the merging distance of DME-merge was varied from 10 m to 70 m (DME-10 to DME-70). MPRR of DME-merge are reported in Figure 5.

Figure 5 confirms that the choice of merging distance affects the performance of DME-merge algorithm. When the merging distance is small, only a few Delaunay nodes are merged together, and the mesh structure of DME-merge is still similar to the mesh structure of DME. However, if the merging distance is large, DME-merge will aggressively merge Delaunay nodes. This aggressive merging can result in reduced performance. When DME-merge merges two Delaunay nodes, the resulting Delaunay node is responsible for all links of the original Delaunay nodes. Thus, the more that Delaunay nodes are merged, the more links the new Delaunay node must handle. In an extreme case, this can create a

Delaunay node that is connected to all other overlay nodes, while having only one incoming path to the Delaunay node.

Performance are quite stable across a fairly wide range of merging distances, e.g. 30 to 50. Based on these results, we have set the merging distance to 50 m.

4.3 Multicast routing with bursty wireless links

In this simulation, we evaluate the performances of different multicast routing structures when the wireless links exhibit bursty behavior. The number of multicast destinations was varied from 10 to 100. A single multicast source was randomly selected among the remaining nodes. The source node generates multicast packets at the rate of 10 packets per second for 600 seconds. We have implemented another mesh multicast routing structure called MDM for comparison [11]. Simulation results are reported in Figure 6.

As seen from Figure 6, the performances of different multicast routing structures vary. The shortest path tree has the lowest MPRR among all multicast routing structures. Since the shortest path tree does not consider interference when building a tree, it is more prone to interference than other structures. The tree structure is also vulnerable to even a single transmission failure as the tree will be disconnected.

The interference-aware Steiner tree provides improvement over the shortest path tree since IAST takes interference into account when building a tree. As a result, IAST is less prone to interference than the shortest path tree. Still, a single transmission failure will disconnect the multicast tree of IAST. MDM also provides improvement over the shortest path tree by including redundant paths to reach the destinations. However, since MDM does not take interference into account when building a mesh, it is still prone to transmission failure along the mesh.

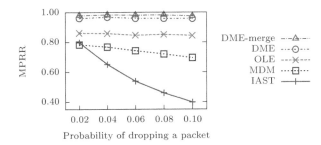

Figure 7: MPRR at varying faulty node probability.

OLE and DME algorithms have higher MPRR than other multicast routing structures, including our previously proposed interference-aware Steiner tree algorithm. The redundant paths allow the multicast packets to be delivered to the destinations even if some multicast packets were dropped on the way to the receivers. Moreover, the paths built by both OLE and DME algorithms are interference-aware, which makes the links less prone to transmission failure than other multicast mesh routing structures. Among our three mesh algorithms, Delaunay mesh extension with nodes merging provides the best MPRR.

4.4 Multicast routing with faulty nodes

In this set of simulations, we study another cause for disconnected graph – node failure. For simplicity, we assume that wireless links are not bursty in this study. To simulate a faulty node, each node randomly drops a multicast packet instead of forwarding the packet to the next node. The probability of dropping a multicast packet was varied from 0.02 to 0.10. The decision to drop the packet is made independently for each packet. The number of multicast destinations was kept constant at 50. MPRR of different multicast routing structures are reported in Figure 7.

As seen from Figure 7, the performances of most multicast routing structures drop as the failure probability increases. The performance drop is substantial for IAST since it relies on a tree as a multicast routing structure. A single faulty node along the tree will disconnect the subtree below the faulty node.

For MDM, the multicast packet reception ratio drops from about 0.80 to about 0.70. MDM relies on mesh structure, which makes it more robust when a few nodes are faulty. However, the number of redundant paths of MDM is not large enough to handle a large number of faulty nodes, which results in a drop in multicast packet reception ratio when the failure probability is high.

Our proposed mesh multicast routing structures can withstand a larger number of faulty nodes than MDM and IAST as can be seen by the almost constant multicast packet reception ratios even at a high fault probability. The extra paths included by OLE, DME, and DME-merge make them more robust to faulty nodes than other routing structures.

5. CONCLUSION

In this paper, we have proposed two algorithms to extend the interference-aware Steiner multicast tree to create an interference-aware multicast mesh. The main idea of both algorithms is to include a set of redundant paths that are connected back to the overlay tree to form an overlay mesh. The algorithms build the actual multicast mesh structure us-

ing the overlay mesh as a guideline. We have evaluated our proposed algorithms in three different settings and showed that our algorithms provide higher multicast packet reception ratios than other multicast routing structures that do not consider interference.

Acknowledgements

This research was supported in part by the National Science Foundation under Grants CNS-1017248 and CNS-1319455.

6. REFERENCES

[1] I. Er and W. Seah. Distributed Steiner-like multicast path setup for mesh-based multicast routing in ad hoc networks. In *IEEE Intl. Conf. Sensor Networks, Ubiquitous, and Trustworthy Computing, 2006.*, volume 2, pages 192–197, June 2006.

[2] P. Gupta and P. Kumar. The capacity of wireless networks. *IEEE Trans. Information Theory*, 46(2):388–404, Mar 2000.

[3] L. Junhai, Y. Danxia, X. Liu, and F. Mingyu. A survey of multicast routing protocols for mobile ad-hoc networks. *IEEE Communications Surveys Tutorials*, 11(1):78–91, First 2009.

[4] D. Lertpratchya, D. M. Blough, and G. F. Riley. Interference-aware multicast for wireless multihop networks. In *IEEE Wireless Communications and Networking Conference*, WCNC 2014, April 2014.

[5] D. Lertpratchya, G. F. Riley, and D. M. Blough. Simulating frame-level bursty links in wireless networks. In *Proc. 7th Intl. ICST Conf. Simulation Tools and Techniques*, SimuTools '14, March 2014.

[6] J.-S. Park, M. Gerla, D. Lun, Y. Yi, and M. Medard. Codecast: a network-coding-based ad hoc multicast protocol. *IEEE Wireless Communications*, 13(5):76–81, October 2006.

[7] S. Park and D. Park. Adaptive core multicast routing protocol. *Wireless Networks*, 10(1):53–60, 2004.

[8] P. Ruiz and A. Gomez-Skarmeta. Approximating optimal multicast trees in wireless multihop networks. In *Proc. 10th IEEE Symp. Computers and Communications*, pages 686–691, June 2005.

[9] J. Sanchez, P. Ruiz, and I. Stojmenovic. GMR: Geographic multicast routing for wireless sensor networks. In *3rd Annual IEEE Communications Society Conf. Sensor and Ad Hoc Communications and Networks*, volume 1, pages 20–29, Sept 2006.

[10] J. Yi and C. Poellabauer. Real-time multicast for wireless multihop networks. *Computers & Electrical Engineering*, 36(2):313 – 327, 2010. Wireless ad hoc, Sensor and Mesh Networks.

[11] X. Zhao, C. T. Chou, J. Guo, and S. Jha. Protecting multicast sessions in wireless mesh networks. In *Proc. 31st Annual IEEE Intl. Conf. Local Computer Networks*, LCN 2006, pages 467–474, Nov 2006.

[12] Y. Zheng, U. T. Nguyen, and H. L. Nguyen. Data overhead impact of multipath routing for multicast in wireless mesh networks. In *2012 Third FTRA Intl. Conf. Mobile, Ubiquitous, and Intelligent Computing (MUSIC)*, pages 154–157, June 2012.

Analysis of Social Structure and Routing in Human based Delay Tolerant Network

Suvadip Batabyal
School of Mobile Computing & Communication
Jadavpur University, Kolkata
mailto.sbatabyal@gmail.com

Parama Bhaumik
Department of Information Technology
Jadavpur University, Kolkata
parama@it.jusl.ac.in

ABSTRACT

Recent advances in mobile communication shows proliferation in networks formed by human carried devices known as the Pocket Switched Network (PSN). In this paper we analyze the nature of community formation since communication in such networks is highly dependent on the socializing behavior of humans. Using real world mobility traces we propose an online algorithm for the nodes to detect their community members based on the mobility parameters contact time (CT) and inter-contact time (ICT). We also derive an estimator for power-law index since CT and ICT follow power-law distribution. Based on the obtained information we propose a social based routing algorithm, named Community Aware Two-Hop routing, and compare it with generic Epidemic and Prophet routing and Bubble-Rap, a social based routing. Results show that the proposed routing protocol performs better than Bubble-Rap and achieve similar performance with respect to Epidemic and Prophet, but at a much lower cost.

Categories and Subject Descriptors

C.2.2 [**Network Protocols**]: Routing Protocols
; I.6.6 [**Simulation and Modeling**]: Simulation Output Analysis

General Terms

Algorithms, Experimentation, Measurement, Performance

Keywords

Pocket Switched Network, Delay Tolerant Network, Human Social Network, Social Network Analysis, Routing

1. INTRODUCTION

Human beings are social animals. They like to stay in groups and tend to form social communities. Researchers have long focused on the socializing behavior of humans and

studied this behavior to form a concrete idea regarding the nature of human mobility. In order to study this behavior, physicists, biologists and other group of researchers have collected mobility and network traces and tried to analyze and characterize the nature of mobility and community formation in humans. One of the main purposes of studying human mobility pattern is to use such information in developing wireless networks of wireless devices carried by common people. We can envision a future where communication can be made possible by individuals carrying hand-held devices (like PDAs, Palmtops, or other mobile devices) by forming dynamic networks. Such communication is possible when individuals carrying such devices meet, and are able to exchange messages with the help of wireless communication interface present in such devices. Therefore, a deeper insight to the socializing behavior of human social network is required which can aid in designing knowledge based or socially aware routing algorithms for such networks.

In this paper we study the socializing nature of humans for message dissemination in Pocket Switched Network. Pocket Switched Network (PSN [10]), is a type of Delay Tolerant Network (DTN [18]) that can employ frequent contact opportunities between individuals and communities to exchange information without network infrastructure. In such type of network, messages are propagated in a hop-by-hop basis and store-carry-forward manner from a given source to a destination. Here nodes must make use of brief contact periods to transfer messages from one node to another. Therefore, message transfer and performance of PSNs is largely dependent on the nature of node mobility, encounter events and community forming nature of individuals. Researchers have used tools from complex and social network analysis to design routing protocols in PSNs. Label [20], Bubble Rap [22], SimBet [6] are some of the well-known social based routing protocols which have been proposed for PSNs. But the main questions that arise is: how can the individual nodes identify or learn their communities and groups and more importantly how can such information be used to disseminate packets in such dynamic networks?

In general, communities or social linkages are represented as weighted or unweighted contact graphs [17], where presence of an edge between any two node represent the familiarity/acquaintance and absence of an edge represent stranger. Using tools from social network analysis, contact graphs can be used to extract information like average degree, network diameter, page rank, cluster co-efficient, modularity, spectral gap and spectral radius. For example, diameter of a social graph determines the path length (or hop length) between two farthest nodes in the graph and spectral gap determine how strongly a community is connected. However, contact graphs largely depend on node mobility and should be so constructed which is able to *truly* represent the underlying mobility and social graph. The two parameters which largely determine the nature of mobility is the contact time (CT) or contact duration and the inter-contact time (ICT) or contact frequency [13] and the nature of contact graph largely depend on these two parameters. Several researchers[12, 8] have done empirical studies on CTs and ICTs and showed that their CCDF follow a power-law distribution. Some of the notable works like [6, 15, 21] have used a threshold based algorithm to construct a contact graph based on the aggregated values of CT and ICT. That is, an edge is added between two nodes, say i, j, if the aggregated value of contact time ($CT_{aggr.}^{i,j} = \sum_{k=1}^{n} CT_k$) is greater than selected threshold value of contact time (CT_{thresh}) and if aggregated value of inter-contact time ($ICT_{aggr.}^{i,j} = \sum_{k=1}^{m} ICT_k$) is smaller than the selected threshold value of inter-contact time (ICT_{thresh}). That is the adjacency graph contains,

$$i, j \begin{cases} 1, & if \ CT_{aggr.}^{i,j} \geq CT_{thresh}, \ ICT_{aggr.}^{i,j} \leq ICT_{thresh} \\ 0, & otherwise \end{cases}$$

State-of-art algorithms for contact aggregation include time-window based aggregation [21] and graph density based aggregation [15]. However, an aggregated value may not be the correct criteria to form a contact graph since a large accidental contact time may greatly influence the overall contact time between two nodes but which may not be true for most of the time. It may lead to creation of false edges and hence may distort the graph properties. Secondly, most of the earlier works select a threshold based on intuition and does not take into consideration the distribution of CT and ICT. And most importantly, CT and ICT are not uniformly distributed; hence simple aggregation may fail to reflect the true underlying social graph.

Therefore, in order to select an appropriate threshold value (for CT and ICT) we first provide an estimator for power-law index, since these follow a power-law distribution. Then we provide an online algorithm for the individual nodes to detect/learn their community members in form of contact graphs. We then study the obtained contact graph and derive various node and graph information which will help in designing an effective opportunistic routing algorithm. Using the obtained information we propose a naïve routing algorithm known as the Community Aware Two-Hop routing, which implements a restricted two hop flooding using node's affiliation to a community. In this scheme, the first hop is utilized by using relays belonging to separate communities (inter-community transfer) and the second hop is used to deliver directly to the destination (intra-community transfer). We use two classes of mobility traces or social scenarios[1], that is, conference and campus area, to perform a comparative study of two different types of social structures. We compare the proposed routing algorithm with an existing social-based forwarding scheme called Bubble Rap,

and an encounter-history based scheme such as Prophet [9]. We also compare the proposed community aware two-hop routing with simple Epidemic [24] routing to prove its efficiency.

2. RELATED WORKS

Social based routing has been an active area of research in DTNs and PSNs for past few years. Social based routing takes help of Social Network Analysis (SNA) which focuses on studying relationships among social entities and forming the contact or social graph. Researchers use contact graphs which can be obtained by studying contact patterns between different individuals from mobility traces. However, contact graphs may widely differ and evolve over time. Moreover, performance of social based routing protocols depends heavily on the way contact graphs are constructed out of mobility traces. Hossmann *et al.* [15] specified a method to construct contact graph from mobility trace by selecting appropriate aggregation period for contact aggregation. Hui *et al.* [21] have earlier proposed a decentralized online community detection algorithm. But the algorithm suffers from high computation cost. They used SIMPLE, k-Clique and MODULARITY as a skeleton framework to determine communities from mobility traces. However, MODULARITY has a computation cost of $O(n^4)$ in the worst case where n is the size of the network and k-Clique has a computation cost of $O(n^2)$ [29]. Bulut *et al.* [3] introduced a method of detecting the quality of friendship by calculating the social pressure metric (SPM) from contact graphs. However, use of probability distribution of CT and ICT to construct the contact graph is still lacking.

Other than algorithms for constructing the contact graph, there have been several works on routing in PSNs, Bubble-Rap [22] being the most popular of all. Bubble-Rap a social based routing technique which uses the idea of global and local rank based on betweenness centrality to disseminate messages in PSNs. However, such a strategy may fail when the destination belongs to the community where all the members have low global centrality values. To mitigate this we propose an inter-community message spread based on the notion of unique encounter (section 4.2).

3. MOBILITY TRACES AND CONTACT GRAPH

This section provides the detailed algorithm for constructing the individual communities based on real-life mobility traces. That is, each node tries to learn its own set of community members based on CTs and ICTs with the node it encounters. In this paper we have used four mobility traces downloaded from CRAWDAD [5] repository. The first three that is, Cambridge, Infocom'05, Infocom'06 data sets have been gathered by the Haggle Project [19] over the period of two years and the fourth data set have been collected by the Reality Mining project [23] at Massachusetts Institute of Technology. Out of these four data sets, two of them (Cambridge and MIT Reality) have been collected from campus area and the other two (Infocom'05 and '06) from conference area. Some details about the datasets are shown in table 1.

The two classes of data sets help in performing an unbiased analysis of the community structure and performance of routing protocol. The first class of data set is from campus area where most of the nodes are well acquainted with each other and form perfect communities with large mem-

---

[1]Social scenario represent the group or population of individuals within a given area or location, about which one is interested. For example, group of students and staffs in an academic institution or set of individual visiting a shopping mall or conference.

Table 1: Summary of Mobility Traces

Name	#Nodes	Duration (days)	Granularity (seconds)	Device Type	Network Interface
Cambridge	36	11	120	iMote	Bluetooth
Infocom 2005	41	4	120	iMote	Bluetooth
Infocom 2006	78	4	120	iMote	Bluetooth
MIT Reality Mining	100	246	300	Cell phone	Bluetooth

bership. The other class is from conference scenario where most individuals are stranger to each other and community structures are difficult to identify. That is, it has many communities with small membership; sometimes even with single member. As mentioned before, the two most important characteristics of human mobility which influence opportunistic forwarding are contact duration and inter-contact time. The analysis of underlying probabilistic distribution of contact time (CT) and inter-contact time (ICT) of all the collected traces have helped researchers in developing theoretical foundations for opportunistic forwarding algorithms. [12, 8, 4] are some of the notable works which have deeply studied human mobility characteristics. Figure 1a and 1b depicts the ccdf (complimentary cumulative distribution function) of CT and ICT in log-linear scale, for the four above mentioned mobility traces. We can see that both CT and ICT follow power-law distribution with exponential cut-off. By methodical study of graph (as in [8]) we can see that for the Cambridge trace 50% of all CTs are greater than 120 seconds (2 minutes) and 50% of all ICTs are less than 1200 seconds (20 minutes). Similar observations can be obtained for other datasets. We can also calculate the actual power-law index by means of curve-fit.

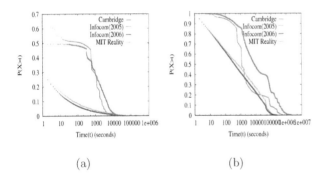

(a)   (b)

Figure 1: CCDF of contact time(a) and inter-contact time(b) for all the datasets in linear-log scale

To construct the contact graph and hence determine the community members, we can select the desired threshold by graphical or analytical method. Since, CT and ICT follow pareto distribution (80-20 rule), we can select all ICTs where $P(X > t) = 0.8$. From the graph we can see that for Cambridge dataset ICT_{thresh} can be approximated to 800 seconds; that is 80% of inter-contact times are greater than 800 seconds and we form an edge between two nodes only if ICT between two nodes is less than 800 seconds. However, graphical method is not applicable in a distributed environment. Hence, we must resort to analytical methods to determine the threshold values.

3.1 From Trace to Contact Graph

We now describe the online algorithm on how to construct a contact graph from mobility traces and how each node tries to learn about its own neighbors. Note that in this section we consider a known threshold value for CT and ICT and its estimation is provided in the next section. We call all nodes adjacent to a given node as its' "virtual or dummy neighbors", since they are not actually connected over a wired link, but are neighbors only because they encounter a given node more frequently compared to other nodes. In order to form the CCDF of CT and ICT, we have used ONE-1.4.1 [1], a discreet event simulator. ONE accepts space delimited trace file where each line is in form of 'time_instant event_type node1 node2 event'. For example, a sample trace file may look like fig. 2.

```
...
1200 CONN 2 12 up
1202 CONN 5 26 up
...

...
1350 CONN 2 12 down
1355 CONN 20 11 up
...
```

Figure 2: Sample trace file in ONE[1] format

Here "1200 CONN 2 12 UP" denotes that at time instant 1200, node id 2 and 12 are within communication range (i.e. their communication link is 'up') and can exchange packets. Similarly at time instant 1350 they move out of each other's range. We have used a small module of our own in order to convert the raw trace from the repository into ONE format. From the mobility trace we derive the node relationship based on the mobility parameters; that is contact duration/time (CT) and inter-contact time/contact frequency (ICT). Every time a node encounters another node, it records the contact duration and time difference between the two encounters. Each node keeps a track of CT and ICT with all the other nodes in form of a vector, each sorted in a non-decreasing order. For example the CT of node i looks similar to $i = [j = \{D_1, D_2, \ldots, D_k\}, l = \{D_1, D_2, \ldots, D_m\}, \ldots]$, where j, l are nodes encountered till time instant t and $D_1, D_2, \ldots$ are contact duration at each encounter event for a given node and $D_1 \leq D_2 \leq \cdots \leq D_k$. Note that we do not use an aggregated value for either CT or ICT since it may not reflect the true nature of underlying community structure. Instead, for each encountered node with respect to a given node, we selected a characteristic time (t) CT_t and ICT_t for CT and ICT respectively, which denotes that most of these values are greater than CT_t or less than ICT_t. We use the 80-20 rule of the power-law distribution for selecting CT_t and ICT_t. For example, w.r.t the vector of contact times (CT) for node i with node

$j, i = [j = \{D_1, D_2, \ldots, D_c, \ldots, D_k\}]$, we select D_c as the characteristic time where $c = |ICT_j^i| \times 0.8$. Therefore the CT/ICT vector for each node is now represented with respect to characteristic time (t) instead of a sequence of values. That is, $i = [j = \{D_j\}, k = \{D_k\}]$. This denotes that node i stays in contact with node j for duration of D_j and node k for duration of D_k with high probability.

Next we must select a threshold to construct the edges (weighted or unweighted) between two nodes based on the observed CT/ICT samples. As stated before, a contact graph depends on the selection of threshold values of CTs and ICTs and different threshold values can result in different contact graphs. Moreover, in order to give same priority to all the node relations, we must select an unbiased threshold values over all the contact times and inter-contact times. For example, if we take average of all the CTs, it may not reflect an unbiased value. Let us say that average of CTs between two nodes i and j is 10 minutes and other two nodes k and l is 50 minutes. Now we are left in a dilemma over which of them should be selected as the threshold value. Moreover, a node may not know the CT/ICT of the other nodes. Therefore, we must first estimate the power-law index and then calculate the threshold value based on the Pareto rule.

3.2 Estimator for Power Law Index

Several works have shown that CCDF of CTs and ICTs follow either power law distribution or have power-law head with exponential tail. Power law distribution is generally used to describe phenomenon where large events are rare, but small ones are quiet common. Power law can be represented as:

$$p(x) = \frac{\alpha - 1}{x_{min}} \left(\frac{x}{x_{min}}\right)^{-\alpha} \qquad (1)$$

where α is known as the *power-law index* or the *shape parameter*. The term $C = (\alpha - 1)x_{min}^{\alpha-1}$ is known as the normalization constant and (1) makes sense for $\alpha > 1$. It can be shown that, when $1 < \alpha < 2$, the first moment (the mean or average) is infinite, along with all higher moments. When $2 < \alpha < 3$, the first moment is finite, but the second (the variance) and higher moments are infinite.

In order to select the threshold value for CT and ICT a node must correctly estimate the power-law index based on random samples of CT or ICT. We use the method of log-likelihood function for parameter estimation such that,

$$L(x_1, x_2, \ldots, x_n; \theta) \triangleq \log f_x(x_1, x_2, \ldots, x_n; \theta)$$

where $x_1, x_2, \ldots, x_n$ denote n random variables representing observations $\mathbf{x_1} = x_1, \mathbf{x_2} = x_2, \ldots, \mathbf{x_n} = x_n$ and θ is the unknown parameter to be estimated.

Let us consider that a node records the ICTs, denoted by $x_1, x_2, \ldots, x_n$, with resepct to another node whenever it meets that node. Then $x_1, x_2, \ldots, x_n$ are i.i.d power-law random variable with unknown parameter α. Thus, $x_i > 0$ and

$$f_x(x_1, x_2, \ldots, x_n; \alpha) = \frac{n(\alpha - 1)}{x_{min}} \prod_{i=1}^{n} \left(\frac{x_i}{x_{min}}\right)^{-n\alpha}$$

This gives log-likelihood function to be

$$
\begin{aligned}
L(x_1, x_2, \ldots, x_n; \alpha) &= \log f_x(x_1, x_2, \ldots, x_n; \alpha) \\
&= \log n(\alpha - 1) - \log x_{min} \\
&\quad - n\alpha \sum_{i=1}^{n} \log \frac{x_i}{x_{min}}
\end{aligned}
$$

Differentiating L w.r.t α we get

$$\frac{\partial L}{\partial \alpha}\bigg|_{\alpha=\hat{\alpha}} = \frac{1}{\alpha - 1} - \left[n\sum_{i=1}^{n}\log \frac{x_i}{x_{min}}\right]\bigg|_{\alpha=\hat{\alpha}} = 0$$

$$Hence, \ \hat{\alpha} = 1 + \left[n\sum_{i=1}^{n} \log \frac{x_i}{x_{min}}\right]^{-1} \qquad (2)$$

Hence, power-law index can be determined by eqn. 2. For example, let us consider a sample of ICTs between node i and some nodes j, for $j = 1, 2, \ldots, N, and \ j \neq i$ for the Cambridge trace, such that $ICT_i = \{761, 1273, 5214, 5450, 7678, 16581, 52955, 57594\}$. Then $\hat{\alpha} = 1.02$ where $n = 8$ and $x_{min} = 600$. Figure 3 shows the values of $\hat{\alpha}$ estimated by each node for all the datasets. We can see the estimated value closely resembles the actual value estimated by method of graph-fitting. The actual value for power-law index is 1.26, 1.53, 1.48 and 1.14 for Cambridge, Infocom(2005), Infocom(2006) and MIT Reality respectively. We have used $x_{min} = 600$ for determining $\hat{\alpha}$ of ICT for all the cases. This is because [8] showed that ICT has power-law distribution between 10min (600sec) and 10 hour. We also calculated mean deviation of $\hat{\alpha}$ from the actual α and found that $\hat{\alpha}$ deviates from its actual value by 0.23, 0.11, 0.09, and 0.03 for Cambridge, Infocom(2005), Infocom(2006) and MIT Reality datasets respectively. The value ICT_{thresh} can now be calculated from eqn. 1 by substituting $\hat{\alpha}$ for α and assigning appropriate value to $p(x)$, say 0.8. The power-law index for contact time can be estimated similarly and hence an appropriate threshold value for CT (CT_{thresh}) can be calculated.

4. ROUTING IN PSN

4.1 Encounters and Unique Encounters

We can use the knowledge of node encounter history and unique encounters to make forwarding decisions in PSNs. It has been seen that a destination often belongs to the same community as the source node itself; or to a community with which the source is well acquainted (even though it may not belong to that community). This is because users with common interest tend to meet with each other more often than with other users [25]. If the destination belongs to some other community, the source node can use a relay from the same community as the destination to deliver the message. However, most of the time it is unknown exactly to which community the relay or the destination node belongs. Hence, the source node must encounter at least one *popular* relay node from each community to deliver the message with maximum probability. The community aware two-hop scheme uses this idea to deliver messages to the destination. To prove the viability of the scheme, we need to measure two important parameters viz. i) number of encounters, and ii) number of unique encounters.

Number of encounters of a node, within a given time period, determines how frequently it comes in contact with

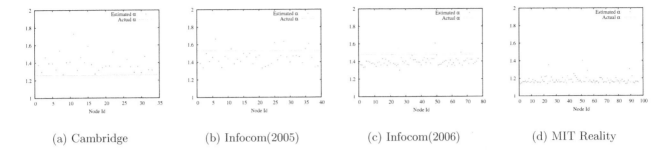

| (a) Cambridge | (b) Infocom(2005) | (c) Infocom(2006) | (d) MIT Reality |

Figure 3: Estimated values of α for all the dataset

other nodes in the network and how long it remains isolated. It should however be noted that a large encounter value is not sufficient to measure the popularity of a node because the node may repeatedly encounter only a small set of nodes or many nodes with insignificant contact times. As a result number of unique encounters is also required to correctly judge the importance of a node. Number of unique encounters for a given node is the number of unique nodes it encounters within a given time instant. A large set of unique ids along with large number of encounters determine the popularity of a node within the social scenario. Greater number of unique encounters will ensure that a source node meets at least one relay from each community which will help in delivering a message to the destination. Figure 4 shows the number of encounters and number of unique encounters for all the nodes for two data sets, that is Cambridge and Infocom (2006) data sets respectively. We can see that for Cambridge data set node ids 6, 16, 34, 25, and 4 (in order/rank-wise) are the popular nodes; similarly for Infocom '06 data set node ids 44, 59, 66, 8, and 20 are popular nodes. To prove the correlation between node popularity with respect to number of encounters and unique encounters, we first ranked the nodes in each data set based on number of encounters and unique encounters taken together. On the other hand we also ranked the nodes based on the number of messages relayed by each node. By comparing these two sets of rank, we found that nodes having higher rank relayed greater number of messages than nodes placed lower in ranking. The rank correlation coefficient between the two rankings is 0.8910 and 0.788, for Cambridge and Infocom'06 data sets respectively. That is nodes having greater number of encounters and unique encounters are in fact popular nodes and hence help in relaying large number of messages within a given network. There are other important characteristics with respect to community formation which can be observed in these data sets. These are:

- Nodes in a conference scenario encounter greater number of nodes outside their community compared to campus scenario. This is clearly reflected in the number of unique encounters (fig. 4b and 4d). Figure 4d shows that almost all the nodes have unique encounter value above 60; that is each node encounter atleast 60 nodes out of 78 nodes for Infocom 2006 trace. This is not true for campus scenario as there are many nodes (almost 50%) that have unique encounter value below 15.

- Students in a campus are mostly confined to their

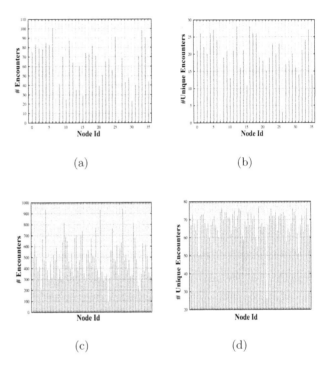

Figure 4: Histograms of encounters and unique encounters for Cambridge (a,b) and Infocom 2006 (c,d) datasets, respectively

own community and have smaller encounter probability outside their community compared to individuals in a conference scenario.

- Number of popular nodes (by proportion) is greater in a campus scenario compared to conference scenario. Hence, there are greater numbers of nodes which can act as popular relays or hubs in a campus scenario.

These observations lay the foundation for our next routing protocol, the community aware two-hop routing.

4.2 Community Aware Two-Hop Routing

From figure 4 we see that each node encounters many nodes even outside their own community with high probability, albeit less frequently and for brief contact duration.

We make use of this phenomenon to propose our next routing protocol, the community aware two-hop routing, where each node tries to muster the community to which a relay node belongs before replicating a message. Instead of restricting message replication only to its neighbors, messages should be uniformly distributed across all the communities of the network so as to facilitate better delivery chance. For this we propose the community aware two-hop routing algorithm where the central idea to "push" at least one message copy (of a given message) across all the communities instead of just replicating within its' (source) own community or virtual neighbors. Since we are often unaware of the community to which the destination node belongs, it is best to replicate at least one message copy for each community to ensure delivery with maximum probability.

In this, each node in the network is aware of the community to which it belongs, it addition to its virtual neighbors. The algorithm takes care that each community receives a copy of a given message, and for this a source node never replicates the same message to more than one node belonging to the same community (unless it is the destination itself). The algorithm associates two variables with each message viz., $number\_of\_hops$ and $list<communities>$. In this case the number of hops is restricted to two. The attribute $list<communities>$ keeps track of all the community ids to which the message has been passed on; that is each intermediate node must belong to separate communities since the source node never replicates a message to more than one intermediate node belonging to the same community. It is now the responsibility of the intermediate relay node to deliver the message to the destination, if they belong to the same community. The proposed idea is derived from the observation that a node often meets other nodes outside its own community and can be used to deliver messages to destinations not belonging to the same community as the source. Moreover, nodes having high betweenness centrality can act as inter-community agents for relaying messages to and from communities. The algorithm of the proposed community aware two-hop routing protocol is shown below.

Algorithm 4.1: COMMUNITYAWARETWOHOPROUTER($MessageM$)

---

for each $EncounteredNode\_i$
  do
  $\begin{cases}\end{cases}$ **if** ($EncounteredNode\_i = Destination$)
    then
    comment: transfer message M to the encountered node
    $EncounteredNode\_i.transferMessage(M)$
  else
    comment: get community of the encountered node
    $community \leftarrow EncounteredNode\_i.getCommunity()$
    comment: get number of hops of message M
    $hop \leftarrow M.getHops()$
    comment: get list of communities containing message M
    $list < communities > \leftarrow M.getCommunities()$
    if ($hop = 0$ && !$list.contains(community)$)
      then
    $hop \leftarrow hop + 1$
    $M.updateHops(hop)$
    $M.updateCommunities(community)$
    $EncounteredNode\_i.transferMessage(M)$

---

5. SIMULATION AND RESULTS

In order to evaluate the proposed routing strategy we have used ONE-1.4.1 [1], an agent-based discreet event-driven simulator and used the Cambridge and the Infocom'06 data sets as inputs to the simulator. The first data set will help evaluating protocols in campus scenario while the later in a conference scenario. We compare the proposed community aware two-hop routing with:

- Bubble Rap [22]: a social based forwarding algorithm,

- Prophet [9]: replication with encounter history based routing algorithm, and

- Epidemic[2] [24]: unrestricted replication/flood based routing algorithm

For all the cases we simulated the network for duration of 7 days. Each node is equipped with a Bluetooth interface with a maximum range of 10 meters and data speed of 256kBps. Messages were generated randomly by the nodes each with a size of 64 kB and variable ttl (time-to-live). The ttl was varied from 20 minutes to a maximum of 1 day. Each source node selected a message destination from uniform distribution, thus providing an equal chance of intra-community and inter-community communication. A small buffer size of 5MB (80 messages) was used so as consider the case of delivery under constraint buffer with drop tail buffer management policy. We measure the efficiency of all the protocols based on three major performance metrics viz., delivery ratio, overhead ratio or delivery cost, and delivery latency.

5.1 Effect on Delivery Ratio

Delivery ratio (or delivery probability) denotes the ratio of number of messages delivered to the number of messages created. Performance of replication based routing largely depends on the number of packets replicated within a given time interval. Moreover, the ttl value should be ideally greater than ICT_{thresh} to prevent packet drop due to ttl expiry before it is delivered. From figure 5a and 5d we see that Epidemic, Prophet and Community Aware Two-Hop algorithm perform better in conference scenario compared to campus scenario. This is because both number of encounters and unique encounters are significantly greater in conference scenario; as a result nodes are able to relay greater number of packets in conference scenario compared to campus area.

Bubble-Rap is forwarding based algorithm and performs poorly for low ttl values. Each node has to wait until it meets another node which has greater global rank (or centrality value) than itself. This often leads to packet drop due to ttl expiry especially when $ICT_{thresh} > ttl$.

Performance of community aware two-hop router depends on the number of unique encounters and is less dependent on the number of hubs present in the network. A source tries to push a message copy to each community; hence a large number of unique encounters help distribute messages uniformly across the network. Communities in campus scenario have higher modularity compared to conference scenario. That is, most nodes try to remain within their own community and

---

[2]We compare with epidemic routing, since it tries to deliver messages along all possible paths and thus serves as a *theoretical* upper bound for delivery ratio and overhead ratio and a lower bound for delivery latency.

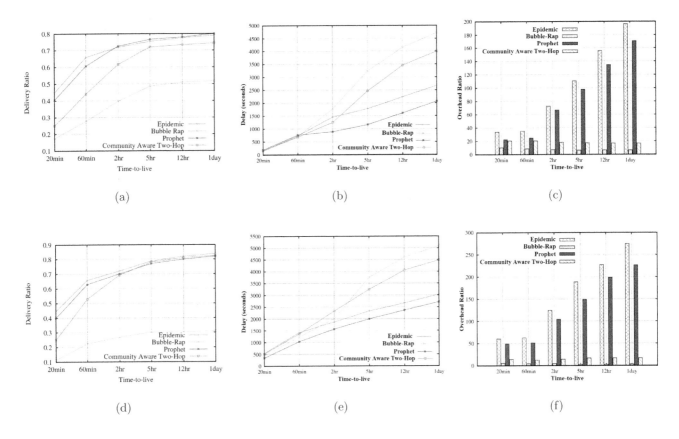

Figure 5: Simulation results for Cambridge (a,b,c) and Infocom 2006 (d,e,f) dataset

rarely encounter nodes from other communities. As a result inter-community communication is highly affected. We can see that two-hop routing is able to achieve almost same delivery ratio as the epidemic for higher ttl values and shows a significant improvement over Bubble-Rap.

5.2 Effect on Delivery Latency

Delivery latency or message delay denotes the total time required to deliver a message from source to destination. Although opportunistic networks are largely resistant to delay, still there has been sincere effort on the part of researchers in this field to minimize the delay. Epidemic routing serves as the theoretical lower bound on the delay, although several authors [14, 7] have shown that a practical lower value on delay can be achieved using different routing strategies and proper buffer management techniques [16]. Delay largely depends on the ICT, since rate of message spread is directly proportional to encounter rate between the nodes [11]. However, delay also depends on finding the shortest route to destination although such route is difficult to predetermine in these types of networks. The average path/hop-length is lower for campus scenario compared to conference scenario due to presence of greater number of hubs with high centrality values. Hence, all the routing protocols perform better with respect to delay in campus scenario (fig. 5b and 5e).

The Community Aware Two-Hop routing has lower delay by almost 16% and 12% for the two datasets, respectively, compared to Bubble-Rap. The proposed algorithm exploits greater number of paths against Bubble-Rap which must

wait until it encounters a node with greater global rank with leads to additional delay.

5.3 Effect on Overhead Ratio

Overhead ratio (or delivery cost) denotes the ratio of number of messages replicated/relayed to the number of messages delivered. It is also an indirect measure of energy consumed to deliver a single packet, energy consumption being directly proportional to cost. Uninformed and unrestricted replication based algorithm such as epidemic incurs maximum cost and serves as the upper bound for the cost required to deliver a packet for a given network with given node density. From fig. 5c and 5f we observe that that there is a steady increase in overhead ratio for both the Epidemic and Prophet routing. For Bubble-Rap the cost decreases and then attains a steady value after a certain point.

For epidemic and prophet routing, overhead ratio shows a constant increase with increase in ttl value, as the packet is replicated a number of times without significant increase in delivery ratio after a certain ttl value. It has been shown in [2] that for epidemic routing, $N/2$ message replicas are sufficient to deliver packet with maximum probability and any further replication is redundant and only leads additional overhead without a significant improvement in delivery ratio. The same phenomenon can be seen from figure 5a and 5d; delivery ratio attains steady value for both the epidemic and prophet routing after a certain ttl value. Hence, overhead ratio increases almost linearly for increase in ttl value.

Since Bubble-Rap follows a rank based forwarding algorithm, the overhead ratio steadily decreases as more number of messages gets delivered for same number of messages replicated. After a certain point it attains a constant value as delivery ratio also reaches a maximum value. It is to be noted that this value is also of order of half-a-day.

The overhead ratios for Community Aware Two-Hop router for both the traces remain almost constant and vary insignificantly with ttl value. For two-hop routing overhead ratio is depends on the number of communities (C) in the network. Hence the lower bound on overhead ratio for two-hop routing is $\Omega(C)$. It can be seen that cost is significantly low (by almost 90%) for higher ttl values compared to epidemic and prophet, and marginally high compared to Bubble-Rap.

6. CONCLUSION

The main aim of this paper is to develop a decentralized learning algorithm for community detection in PSNs, where each node can identify its group members with minimal knowledge exchange. For this we first develop an estimator for power-law index since mobility parameters like contact time and inter-contact time follow a power-law distribution. We also propose a novel community aware two-hop routing algorithm where each node can utilize their knowledge of community affiliation to disseminate messages in PSNs. We work using real-life mobility traces in two social scenarios viz., campus and conference scenario.

We found that community aware two-hop routing is able to achieve similar performance compared to epidemic, especially in conference scenario, but at much less cost. In future we intend to perform a comparative study of proposed online community detection algorithm with other existing algorithm and perform a detailed contact graph analysis using tools from complex and social network analysis.

7. REFERENCES

[1] T. Karkkainen A. Keranen and J. Ott. Simulating mobility and dtns with the one. *Journal of Communications*, 5(2):92–105, Feb. 2010.

[2] S. Batabyal and P. Bhaumik. Estimators for global information in mobile opportunistic network. In *IEEE Advanced Networks and Telecommunications Systems (ANTS'13)*, 2013.

[3] E. Bulut and B.K Szymanski. Friendship based routing in delay tolerant mobile social networks. In *GLOBECOM '10*, pages 1–5, 2010.

[4] Han Cai and Do Young Eun. Toward stochastic anatomy of intermeeting time distribution under general mobility models. In *MobiHoc '08*, pages 273–282, 2008.

[5] CRAWDAD: A community resource for archiving wireless data at Dartmouth. Available: http://crawdad.cs.dartmouth.edu/.

[6] E. M. Daly and M. Haahr. Social network analysis for routing in disconnected delay-tolerant manets. In *(MobiHoc '07)*, pages 32–40, 2007.

[7] A. Balasubramanian et al. Dtn routing as a resource allocation problem. In *ACM SIGCOMM '07*, pages 373–384, 2007.

[8] A. Chaintreau et al. Impact of human mobility on opportunistic forwarding algorithms. In *ACM MobiCom*, pages 183–194, 2007.

[9] A. Lindgren et al. Probabilistic routing in intermittently connected networks. 7(3):19–20, 2003.

[10] P. Hui et al. Pocket switched networks and the consequences of human mobility in conference environments. In *ACM SIGCOMM workshop on Delay-tolerant networking(WDTN '05)*, pages 244–251, 2000.

[11] R. Groenevelt et al. The message delay in mobile ad hoc networks. In *El-sevier Journal of Performance Evaluation (2005)*, 2005.

[12] T. Karagiannis et al. Power law and exponential decay of intercontact times between mobile devices. In *ACM MobiCom*, pages 183–194, 2007.

[13] T. Spyropoulos et al. Performance analysis of mobility-assisted routing. In *INFOCOM '06*, pages 49–60, 2006.

[14] T. Spyropoulos et al. Efficent routing in intermittently connected mobile networks: The multiple-copy case. *IEEE/ACM Transactions on Networking*, 16(1):77–90, 2008.

[15] T.Hossmann et al. Know thy neighbor: Towards optimal mapping of contacts to social graphs for dtn routing. In *IEEE INFOCOM*, pages 1–9, 2010.

[16] Y. Li et al. Adaptive optimal buffer management policies for realistic dtn. In *GLOBECOM '09*, pages 1–5, 2009.

[17] Y. Zhu et al. A survey of social-based routing in delay tolerant networks: Positive and negative social effects. *IEEE Communications Surveys & Tutorials*, 15(1):387–401, 2013.

[18] K. Fall. A delay tolerant networking architecture for cahllenged internet. In *ACM SIGCOMM*, pages 27–34, 2003.

[19] HAGGLE. www.haggleproject.org.

[20] P. Hui and J. Crowcroft. How small labels create big improvements. In *IEEE Pervasive Computing and Communications Workshops (PerCom '07)*, pages 65–70, 2007.

[21] P. Hui and E. Yoneki. Distributed community detection in delay tolerant networks. In *2nd ACM/IEEE international workshop on Mobility in the evolving internet architecture(MobiArch '07)*, page 7, 2007.

[22] J. Crowcroft P. Hui and E. Yonek. Bubble rap: Social-based forwarding in delay tolerant networks. In *ACM SIGCOMM workshop on Delay-tolerant networking(WDTN '05)*, pages 241–250, 2000.

[23] MIT Reality Mining Project. http://reality.media.mit.edu.

[24] A. Vahdat and D. Becker. Epidemic routing for partially connected ad hoc networks. *Tech. Rep. CS-2000-06, Department of Computer Science, Duke University, Durham, NC*, 2000.

[25] Y. Zhang and J. Zhao. Social network analysis on data diffusion in delay tolerant networks. In *MobiHoc '09*, pages 345–356, 2009.

Efficient Solutions for the Authenticated Fragmentation Problem in Delay- and Disruption-Tolerant Networks

Michael Noisternig
Secure Mobile Networking Lab
TU Darmstadt, Germany
michael.noisternig@seemoo.tu-darmstadt.de

Matthias Hollick
Secure Mobile Networking Lab
TU Darmstadt, Germany
matthias.hollick@seemoo.tu-darmstadt.de

ABSTRACT

Transmission opportunities in delay- and disruption-tolerant networks (DTNs) may be scarce and short-lived. In consequence, the fragmentation of larger messages at intermediate nodes is an important requirement to efficiently utilize any available connectivity. At the same time, bandwidth must be protected against any unauthorized transmission attempt, which implies that source authentication mechanisms are needed. However, naive solutions for supporting both message fragmentation and authentication are inefficient in terms of bandwidth or computational requirements. The problem has been clearly identified in the literature and various solutions have been suggested, but a systematic treatment of the problem has not been carried out so far.

In this work, we approach the problem of authenticated fragmentation by rephrasing it as a multicast authentication problem. We identify a number of computationally efficient multicast authentication protocols that are suitable for DTN scenarios and highlight known computational or bandwidth optimality results for two classes of solutions. We generalize the remaining protocols into a single third class and provide a theoretical analysis, which proves the bandwidth optimality of a protocol that has been independently suggested for the authenticated fragmentation problem. We extend the setting of the protocol by considering a network scenario where neighboring nodes can communicate reliably and show theoretically that in this scenario the amortized bandwidth overhead converges to the minimum possible. Finally, we review a number of approaches presented in the literature on the authenticated fragmentation problem and outline their inadequacies.

Categories and Subject Descriptors

C.2.0 [**Computer-Communication Networks**]: General—*Security and protection*; C.2.1 [**Computer-Communication Networks**]: Network Architecture and Design—*Wireless communication*

MSWiM'14, September 21–26, 2014, Montreal, QC, Canada.
Copyright 2014 ACM 978-1-4503-3030-5/14/09
http://dx.doi.org/10.1145/2641798.2641829.

Keywords

Authentication; bundle fragmentation; delay- and disruption-tolerant networking; security

1. INTRODUCTION

The current Internet has evolved into a largely fixed communication infrastructure that supports continuous end-to-end connectivity by utilizing reliable and fast links between nodes in the infrastructure. However, recent years have seen considerable interest in implementing end-to-end communication support in so-called "challenged networks", where nodes may not find an end-to-end path at any particular point in time due to node mobility coupled with frequent link disruptions and possibly large link transmission delays. This interest has its origin in the works for an interplanetary network for deep-space communication, which have been picked up by the IRTF and soon has led to the concept of delay-tolerant networking (DTN) [1]. While initial research had focused on scenarios with long-delay links and scheduled contacts, the IRTF quickly became to account for so-called disruption-tolerant networks, a re-interpretation of DTNs in terrestrial environments where link delays are more ordinary but disruptions are frequent and connectivity is often opportunistic. This re-interpretation is due to the DARPA, which considered mainly military applications. Whether the focus is on delay or disruptions, the unifying concept is that of a continuously changing network topology, a large end-to-end delay, and the frequent unavailability of an end-to-end path. This precludes interactivity between endpoints and necessitates store-and-forward (or "store-carry-forward") routing as a means for data delivery from a source to a destination.

The IRTF has foreseen the bundle protocol architecture as a universal solution for DTN scenarios [2]. It envisages a DTN as an overlay network, connecting otherwise separate networks through a system of intermediate DTN gateways with the help of a bundle protocol (BP). In the BP architecture, applications send data in the form of blocks or bundles, each of which may be separately processed by applications on the destination side. As bundles are potentially large while transmission opportunities may be scarce and short-lived, the BP supports the fragmentation of larger bundles into smaller fragment bundles to make efficient use of any available connectivity. Fragmentation may occur either proactively at the source and at DTN gateways before forwarding a bundle, or reactively in response to receiving an incomplete block at a gateway.

A separate IRTF bundle security protocol (BSP) specification addresses security concerns for DTNs [3]. In particular, a consequence of the limited connectivity in DTNs is that devices not admitted to the DTN must not be able to consume the little bandwidth available; neither should it be possible for compromised nodes to impersonate other nodes nor to manipulate their bundles without such forgery attempts quickly being detected. This implies that intermediate nodes must participate in the verification of bundles in the network before forwarding them towards their intended destinations. One approach supported by the BSP is the use of hop-by-hop authentication based on secret keys shared between neighboring nodes, but this does not allow the detection of bundles modified by compromised nodes. Alternatively, nodes may use digital signatures to protect their bundles such that intermediate nodes can verify the bundle data using the originator's public key. However, authentication is an issue when bundles get fragmented as a DTN node receiving only partial block data will not be able to verify the integrity or authenticity of the fragment. In particular, a receiver is faced with the question whether to cache the fragment and wait for the remaining bundle data to arrive, which may take a completely different path to the destination because of a continually changing network topology, or to forward a potentially forged fragment bundle. It is clear that more fine-grained authentication information must be made available to a receiver; however, the simple solution discussed so far in the IRTF of splitting a bundle into smaller fragment blocks and attaching a digital signature to each of them is computationally expensive.

Contributions. This paper focuses on the problem of efficient authenticated fragmentation in DTNs. The main contributions are as follows:

- We rephrase the problem of fragment authentication as a multicast authentication problem and survey the available literature on multicast authentication to identify shortcomings as well as suitable solutions for the problem of fragment authentication in DTNs.

- We generalize some of the identified solutions and show principal limits in their constructions. In particular, we derive lower bounds for the communication overhead of multicast authentication schemes that are based on one-way hash functions, use a single digital signature, and are fully loss-tolerant.

- Based on this analysis, we identify a generally applicable fragment authentication scheme that is computationally efficient and has the least bandwidth requirements possible.

Outline. The remainder of the paper is organized as follows: Section 2 provides background on the terminology used throughout the paper and describes the threat model assumed. Section 3 motivates the problem of efficient fragment authentication with some simple approaches. Section 4 reviews the available literature on multicast authentication in the context of DTNs. The search for efficient constructions and the identification of an optimal scheme is addressed in Section 5. Related literature on the problem of fragment authentication in DTNs is reviewed in Section 6, where we identify several issues with previously suggested approaches and provide answers to open questions that have been raised. The paper concludes in Section 7.

2. PRELIMINARIES

2.1 Terminology

We define a *(DTN) node* as any entity that may forward data to or receive data from another node in the DTN. Nodes send data in the form of *bundles*, which may consist of one or more fragments or *bundle fragments*. Any node may break a bundle into multiple *fragment bundles*, each of which constitutes a new but smaller bundle. The original producer of a bundle in an end-to-end communication is called a *source*, whereas the eventual consumer of a bundle is referred to as a *destination*. Any node forwarding bundle data to another node is called a *sender*, and a node accepting incoming bundle data is called a *receiver*. Neighboring nodes may be directly connected via *reliable* or *unreliable* links, and we expect a reliable link to additionally deliver all data in order—in the BP architecture, this may be accomplished by DTN gateways using a reliable transport protocol such as TCP, whereas in a network with native DTN functionality nodes may reliably exchange data using link-layer acknowledgments (e.g., based on IEEE 802.11).

2.2 Threat Model

We are concerned with active attackers that may compromise the integrity or authenticity of transmitted bundle data, drop individual bundles or fragment bundles, and carry out denial-of-service attacks based on forging invalid bundle data with the aim of consuming valuable network resources such as bandwidth or computational and memory resources of intermediate nodes. Attacks may be carried out by outsiders (that is, nodes not admitted to the network) and insiders (legitimate but possibly compromised nodes), and they may act independently or in collaboration. Though we allow any node to be an adversary, we consider sources in a communication scenario to be non-compromised (or otherwise attesting to the origin of transmitted bundle data becomes meaningless). Finally, as a standard assumption, we consider adversaries to be computationally bounded and cryptographic algorithms to be computationally secure.

3. SIMPLE APPROACHES

Ideally, a receiver may verify the integrity and authenticity of received bundle data at any point in time, including right after a link to a sender gets broken. However, this implies that for each forwarded byte a new authentication value should be sent, which would result in considerable bandwidth overhead; this is because each authentication value must be large enough to deter brute-force forgery attempts. The key approach is thus to split large bundles into comparably small bundle fragments such that the relative authentication overhead per fragment is small and the loss of data when a fragment could not be forwarded in its entirety and thus is dropped by a receiver is acceptable.

In the most basic approach, "sign-each", each fragment is separately protected with a digital signature, where either signatures are interspersed within the original bundle data or each fragment is sent as an individual authenticated fragment bundle. Modern signature schemes such as based on bilinear pairing offer relatively small signature sizes, but their computational requirements are large. Alternatively, instead of signing each fragment separately, a list of fragment hash values could be compiled, all of which are protected by a single digital signature. This scheme—let us call it a hash list—can considerably reduce the computational overhead for the original bundle, but it comes at the price that partial bundle data (i.e., single or multiple fragments) always needs to be accompanied with the complete authentication information, which may be significant if the number of fragments is large. Furthermore, if a receiver accepts fragments from multiple bundles the memory requirements for storing the authentication information may be considerable. More efficient solutions are thus desirable.

4. FRAGMENT AUTHENTICATION AS A MULTICAST AUTHENTICATION PROBLEM

The problem of fragment authentication can be stated as follows: how can a single sender securely and efficiently distribute a sequence of data pieces towards any number of receivers, each of which can efficiently verify the authenticity of received data but is being precluded from producing new data seemingly originating from the source? In other words, how can source authentication be implemented in a multicast or broadcast transmission without the use of a digital signature per data piece? This is precisely the problem studied under the terms "multicast (source) authentication" and "broadcast authentication" in the context of high-volume real-time multi-receiver data transmissions over the Internet in the past.

Academic literature offers a large number of approaches for addressing the multicast authentication problem in the Internet. Challal *et al.* have compiled an extensive survey on the topic [4], and distinguish between solutions providing non-repudiation and those that do not (see Figure 1). Dropping non-repudiation, a security requirement that is primarily meaningful at the application layer, is an important prerequisite to obtain highly efficient multicast source authentication protocols. As these protocols avoid the use of digital signatures, they introduce asymmetry in one of three following ways: using *information asymmetry*, using *time asymmetry*, or by combining both approaches. On the other hand, multicast authentication protocols supporting non-repudiation attempt to amortize the overhead of a digital signature over a group of data pieces (that is, packets[1]) or to reduce the online computational effort with the use of hash-based one-time signature schemes. Solutions have been assigned to one of three categories: *signature propagation* protocols, *signature dispersal* schemes, and *differed signing* approaches. Time asymmetry and signature propagation schemes have also been characterized as *graph-based* constructions by Miner and Staddon [5], who studied various design approaches, while somewhat more recently a number of new *erasure code-based* constructions have been presented in the literature [6, 7], all of which can be classified as signature dispersal schemes. Finally, we augment this list of protocols by considering *batch signatures*, which have been proposed with the aim of significantly reducing the com-

putational effort of multiple signature verifications at receivers [8]. The various solutions will be reviewed below in the context of fragment authentication in DTNs. For more details on the protocols discussed in Subsections 4.1 to 4.4 and further examples, the reader is referred to [4].

4.1 Protocols without Non-Repudiation

Information asymmetry is based on the idea of the sender maintaining a rather large set of secrets, each of which is used for computing authentication information for a packet (i.e., a data piece), while each legitimate receiver shares only a unique subset of these secrets with the sender. Receivers verify a message by recomputing the authentication information for the secrets in their subsets; since each entity is expected to have a different subset, a message for which all authenticators are determined to be correct is assumed to be authentic. The problem here is that sufficiently many entities pooling their secrets gain enough information to forge seemingly valid authenticators for other receivers. Canetti *et al.* have presented a solution that uses symmetric keys for the computation of MACs [9], and whose construction was shown to be asymptotically optimal for a conditionally secure approach that is based on pseudo-random functions [10]. Even though the protocol provides a flexible trade-off between resistance to collusions and authenticator size it is suitable in DTNs only if participants are predetermined and if users are either largely trusted or keys are stored in tamper-resistant memory.

In time-asymmetry protocols, a sender derives a sequence of symmetric keys based on iterated application of a one-way hash function on some initial seed value, and on using these keys in reverse order for the authentication of messages. Each key is used either once per packet or during a predefined time interval, after which the next key in the hash chain is selected. Previous keys are successively released into the network when the sender is confident that each receiver has received all messages authenticated with these prior keys. Practical protocols such as TESLA [11] assume a worst-case end-to-end transmission delay and require all devices in the network to be loosely time-synchronized. Time synchronization is a well-known problem in DTNs; more importantly, an upper bound on the transmission delay cannot be assumed when data is to be sent over opportunistic links. For the same reason, hybrid protocols, which attempt to avoid the approach's inherent receiver latency in message authentication by combining the time asymmetry with the information asymmetry approach, are impractical for DTNs. Last but not least, large delays in key disclosure enable an adversary to carry out denial-of-service (DoS) attacks by flooding a (nearby) receiver's storage with forged messages, each of which can be verified only after receiving the authentication keys for their time intervals.

4.2 Signature Propagation Protocols

The core concept of signature propagation protocols is that only a single or a few number of packets are protected by a digital signature. However, each of these signed packets contains some short authentication information about other packets, and those packets may authenticate yet other packets. As such, packets are linked together in a way that the source authentication and non-repudiation properties of the digital signature propagate throughout all the packets that are connected to the initial packets. The challenge in

---

[1]Packets in the original multicast authentication problem equate to fragments in the authenticated fragmentation problem. Throughout the rest of the paper, we will use *packets* whenever we discuss solutions for the general multicast authentication problem and refer to *fragments* when we examine a solution's application in the DTN bundle fragmentation setting.

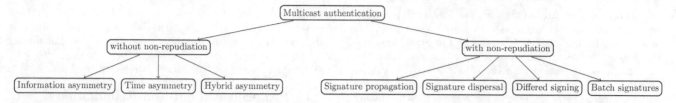

Figure 1: Classification of multicast authentication schemes based on [4] and augmented with batch signatures.

designing these schemes is how to assure connectivity when individual or multiple packets are lost during transmission.

Numerous solutions implement authentication information by means of one-way hash values. Packets are linked together in the form of directed acyclic graphs, and schemes offer different robustness levels depending on the graph structure. Offline chaining [12] creates a simple hash chain, where each packet includes a hash value of the next packet in the transmission queue. In more detail, let $(p_1, \ldots, p_n)$ denote a sequence of packet payloads. Then each p_i for $1 \le i < n$ is augmented in advance ("offline") with authentication information a_i of the form $a_i := h(p_{i+1}|a_{i+1})$, where h denotes a collision-resistant one-way hash function and $|$ a string concatenation operator. The first packet, p_1, is additionally signed with a conventional digital signature. This scheme requires little bandwidth overhead and is easy to implement, but the loss of a single packet has the adverse effect that no subsequent packets can be authenticated. Furthermore, in the context of DTNs, nodes cannot send the first couple of bundle fragments to one neighbor and then resume transmission with forwarding subsequent fragments to another neighbor as the chain to the first packet is broken. A simple tweak that we suggest here can somewhat lessen the problem of always starting anew: rather than retransmitting already forwarded fragments, fragment hash values can be sent, and authentication information can be computed as $a_i := h(h(p_{i+1})|a_{i+1})$. On reliable links, this loss-tolerant modification has, in average, both lower bandwidth and lower receiver storage requirements than the hash list approach.

Several proposed graph constructions offer protection against random or burst packet loss. EMSS [11] and the p-random authentication scheme [5] are both examples of random-loss constructions where hash links are created from a packet to several target packets such that multiple paths to one or more of the available signature packets exist. Target packets are selected randomly and the solutions thus provide probabilistic authentication guarantees. Such an approach is quite undesirable for fragment authentication as it means that the scarce bandwidth availability in the network may have been used to transmit bundle data that cannot be authenticated by a receiver. Deterministic burst-loss authentication schemes such as periodic chaining [13] and piggybacking [5] can provide strict authentication guarantees, but only under the assumption that no more than a predefined number of packet burst losses of a maximum length have occurred. In the context of fragment authentication this means that even fully received contiguous blocks of bundle fragments are unlikely to be authenticable since missing fragments in the front or at the back of the block must be interpreted as burst losses, which are likely to exceed the loss threshold.

Online signing [12] replaces the one-way hash values of offline chaining with public keys and signatures of a one-time signature scheme. As such, this solution does not require advance knowledge of transmitted data, making it applicable for real-time streaming applications. However, it is not tolerant to packet loss either, and both public keys and signatures of one-time signature schemes are known to be large. Assuming that bundle sources in DTNs wait for the entire application data unit to be received from an application before formatting it as a bundle, this scheme does not provide any benefits compared to the offline chaining approach.

A common problem of signature propagation schemes is that they assume packets to be delivered in order and, additionally, the signature(s) to be transmitted reliably. If reordering occurs, receivers must buffer incoming data until it can be verified. Furthermore, depending on the construction of the scheme, there may be backward hash links, which implies that receivers must buffer packets even if they arrive in order; examples are the EMSS and periodic chaining schemes mentioned above. In both cases, this creates an opportunity for adversaries to initiate DoS attacks by flooding a receiver with messages it cannot immediately verify.

4.3 Signature Dispersal Schemes

Signature dispersal schemes are based on the concept of computing authentication information over a group of packets and dispersing it among the packets in such a way that even if some packets are lost receivers can authenticate the remaining packets.

Tree chaining, first described in [14] for the purpose of multicast authentication, employs a binary (Merkle) or d-ary tree structure, where packet hashes represent the tree's leaves and the root is signed with a digital signature. Authentication information in a packet consists of a small number of hash values, each of which corresponds to a sibling on the path from the packet leaf to the root. The binary tree structure has more recently been suggested for implementing fragment authentication in DTNs [23]. Tree chaining has the advantage of being fully tolerant to packet or fragment loss at low computational requirements, but the per-packet bandwidth overhead of the hash values and the root signature may be considerable for slow links.

SAIDA [15] was an early suggestion for the use of an (n, k)-erasure code over a block of packet hash values and their signature such that the reception of k out of n packets suffices to recover the entire authentication information. The construction provides a flexible trade-off between bandwidth overhead and resilience to packet loss. However, this and other erasure-code-based schemes are highly vulnerable to DoS attacks since a single forged packet results in a failure of the decoding process. Two main solutions have been proposed to address this issue: a combination with a hash tree provides efficient detection of forgeries but it inherits the tree structure's bandwidth overhead; and polynomial reconstruction (list decoding) based on an error-correcting

Table 1: Inherent Limitations of Multicast Authentication Schemes in the Context of Authenticated Fragmentation in DTNs

	Vulnerable to collusions	Assumes bounded end-to-end delay	Fails at arbitrary fragment loss	Vulnerable to DoS attacks	High computational overhead	High bandwidth overhead
Information asymmetry	x					x
Time asymmetry		x		x		
Offline chaining			x			
Online signing			x			x
Loss-tolerant chaining			x	$(x)^a$		$(x)^a$
Hash tree						x
Code-based (simple)			x	x		
Code-based (w/ forgery detection)			x		$(x)^b$	x
Online/offline signatures					x	x
Batch signing (RSA-based)					$(x)^c$	x
Batch verification				x	$(x)^c$	

^{a}Chaining schemes that require receiver buffering for verification are vulnerable to DoS attacks. The bandwidth overhead is determined by the loss tolerance.

^{b}Decoding in schemes using polynomial reconstruction is very slow and drops further as the number of acceptable packet losses or forgeries is increased.

^{c}Despite RSA has moderate computational requirements for receivers, verifying each fragment in a block (batch) with a different public-key exponent may be costly. In contrast, batch verification schemes are generally efficient for receivers, but only in the case that no (or few) DoS attacks occur.

code can be used to identify invalid packets among the received data, but its computational requirements are largely precluding (see [6,7] for current solutions and detailed discussions). Moreover, schemes using polynomial reconstruction assume upper bounds on the number of packet losses and forgeries, and both the computational and bandwidth overhead increases as these bounds are raised. Yet, the principal drawback of code-based schemes in the DTN context is their requirement for receiving at least k fragments; this is because DTN nodes can neither guarantee to successfully forward at least k bundle fragments to receivers nor can they exploit connection opportunities as long as they have not received enough fragments themselves.

4.4 Differed Signing

The idea of differed signing, proposed in the form of online/offline digital signatures [16], is to take the computationally costly step of signing packet data with a traditional digital signature scheme "offline" by instead signing a large number of public keys associated with an efficient one-time (or k-time) signature scheme well in advance. Senders can then efficiently sign packets using one-time keys, but receivers need to verify both the one-time signature of a packet and the classical signature on the one-time public key delivered with the packet. In opportunistic communication scenarios, sources may find sufficient time to refill their pool of signed one-time public keys when no neighbors are available, but the tradeoff of reduced computational effort for bundle sources versus increased bandwidth overhead and processing requirements at receivers seems questionable. In particular, if bundle sources can also take the role of intermediate forwarding nodes any benefit of the solution becomes void.

4.5 Batch Signatures

Batch signature schemes exploit the homomorphic properties of number-theoretic digital signature systems to reduce the computationally expensive exponentiations in multiple signature generations or verifications to that of a single signature. Batch signatures have been first proposed by Fiat for the purpose of efficient RSA signature generation [17], and the described solution is easily applicable in DTNs for reducing the computational overhead at bundle sources. Later papers on batch signature schemes have fo-

cused instead on efficient signature verification. Nacacche et al. have described a system to improve batch verification of DSA signatures [18], and subsequent solutions for other signature schemes followed (see [8,20]). However, batch verification schemes suffer from the problem of bogus packets inserted by a malicious entity. Even though a number of efficient algorithms for the identification of forged messages have been proposed [19,20], it has been shown that when more than 38 percent (and conjectured that when more than one third) of the messages are forgeries the simple solution of individually verifying each message is more efficient [20]. Batch verification may thus be suitable when the probability of active attacks is low. It shall be noted that batch verification schemes as described cannot be combined with Fiat's batch signature generation scheme.

Batch signatures may also be considered an orthogonal solution to signature propagation and dispersal schemes, similar to what has been suggested in [8]. As each block of packets/fragments has its own signature, sources may more efficiently sign multiple blocks and receivers may more efficiently verify packet/fragment signatures from multiple blocks.

4.6 Summary

We identify four approaches to be suitable for the fragment authentication problem in DTNs, with various tradeoffs (see Table 1 for a short overview on the limitations of the various multicast authentication schemes): the information asymmetry technique, batch signatures, the modified offline chaining protocol, and the tree chaining (or hash tree) method. While an optimal solution for information asymmetry has been presented in the literature the approach is not universally applicable due to its vulnerability to collusions and the requirement for key predistribution. Batch signatures are a promising technique but batch verification is not applicable either when the chance of active attacks is large. Furthermore, bandwidth-efficient solutions that simultaneously reduce the computational requirements for both sources and receivers are missing. Modified offline chaining and the hash tree scheme are computationally efficient in that they require a single digital signature operation at both sources and receivers, but the bandwidth overhead may be large. With tradeoffs for the first two approaches

Figure 2: Graph structures of the hash-list (left), hash-tree (middle), and modified offline-chaining (right) fragment/multicast authentication schemes. Fragment/packet hashes are depicted as unfilled circles, additional authentication values as filled circles, and arrows represent the application of a one-way hash function.

studied in other works, the next section focuses on the latter two protocols as well as the simple hash list with the goal of identifying efficient constructions and lower bounds for the bandwidth overhead of fragment authentication schemes that are based on one-way hash functions and implement a single digital signature.

5. GENERALIZATION AND LOWER BOUNDS

Offline chaining and the hash-tree scheme have been discussed as conceptually different solutions in the literature, with the former being described as a graph-based signature propagation scheme and the latter as a signature dispersal protocol. However, it can be observed that the hash tree also implements a graph structure on the basis of a one-way hash function. Indeed, the two solutions as well as the hash list scheme can all be concisely described as directed acyclic graphs, and they represent three extremes in the solution space of one-way hash function-based graph constructions. The common approach in the three protocols is the reduction of a set of fragment/packet (hash) values $x_1, \ldots, x_n$ to a single hash value y, which is covered by a single digital signature, and the distribution of some authentication information a_i along with x_i such that a receiver can reconstruct y based on x_i and a_i. In more detail, a set of authentication functions $f_i : \{0,1\}^* \times \{0,1\}^{l \cdot \ell_i} \to \{0,1\}^l$ ($1 \le i \le n$) is defined, each of which takes as input an arbitrary-length fragment/packet value and an authentication vector consisting of $\ell_i \ge 1$ l-bit hash values, and which yields y of bit length l whenever the inputs are correct, that is, $f_i(x_i, a_i) = y$. Furthermore, each f_i is solely composed of a one-way hash function $h : \{0,1\}^* \to \{0,1\}^l$ and the concatenation operator $|$, which combines two bit strings into a single one. For example, in the hash list approach $a_i = (x_1, \ldots, x_{i-1}, x_{i+1}, \ldots, x_n)$ and $f_i(x, \alpha) := h(\alpha_1 | \ldots | \alpha_{i-1} | x | \alpha_i | \ldots | \alpha_{n-1})$, whereas in the hash tree method a_i is comprised of hash values associated with the vertices in the tree and f_1, for instance, may be of the form $f_1(x, \alpha) := h(h(\cdots h(h(x | \alpha_1) | \alpha_2) \cdots) | \alpha_{|\alpha|})$. As h is one-way, the computation of y with the functions f_i may be visualized as a rooted tree with y as a sink. Figure 2 shows the resultant graphs for the three authentication schemes discussed in this section, with offline chaining being represented in its modified form as described in Section 4.

As can be observed, the hash list scheme essentially depends on the transmission of the complete authentication information when delivering a fragment or packet; that is, the root signature and all but the current fragment/packet's hash values must be forwarded. The modified offline chaining approach at best requires the transmission of a single hash value (in addition to the signature), but in the

worst case (that is, for the transmission of the last fragment/packet) it is as inefficient as the hash-list solution. In contrast, the binary hash tree scheme requires the transmission of approximately $\log_2 n$ hash values in both the best and the worst case. The following questions thus arise: what are inherent lower bounds for the bandwidth overhead of graph-based authentication schemes that are suitable for the authenticated fragmentation problem, and more specifically, which graph-based structure(s) can provide the lowest average and worst-case overhead in terms of the authentication information that must be distributed per fragment/packet? The theorems below will provide answers to these questions.

THEOREM 1. *The worst-case per-packet bandwidth overhead of a fully loss-tolerant multicast authentication scheme that is based on an (unkeyed) one-way hash function and implements a single digital signature is at least $\lceil \log_2 n \rceil$ unsigned plus one signed hash value large, where n is the number of packets authenticated. A balanced binary hash tree matches the lower bound with equality.*

PROOF. We take a constructive approach towards minimizing the bandwidth overhead of a general graph structure. Consider first an arbitrary connected and acyclic digraph where each packet is represented by one or more vertices. Some of the vertices in the graph are jointly protected by a single digital signature, and for each packet vertex there must be a path to one of the signed vertices for the packet to be verifiable. Receivers verify a packet by recomputing the value of a signed vertex using the siblings on such path—we will call it a "valid path". We first exclude all vertices and edges that do not lie on any valid path since such vertices only contribute to bandwidth overhead when they are siblings to vertices on a valid path. Thus, all sources (i.e., vertices without inward edges) are packet vertices, and all packet vertices are sources (for the hash function would not be one-way otherwise). Now suppose that there is a signed vertex v that is not a sink (i.e., it has an outdegree greater than zero). Then, in a similar argument as before, all vertices and edges succeeding v on a valid path towards another signature vertex can be excluded when they do not lie on a valid path that does *not* include v. Thus, all signed vertices are sinks. Now let us suppose that a packet can be verified via different valid paths. Then there is a vertex v with two or more outward edges, one of them on a path $(v, u_1, \ldots, u_\ell = s)$ for some sink s and $\ell \ge 1$. If for all u_i the indegree is one, then $(u_1, \ldots, u_\ell)$ and the edge vu_1 can be removed from the graph, thus reducing the bandwidth overhead by eliminating one signed vertex. Otherwise, let k be the smallest index such that u_k has an indegree greater than one. Then we can remove $u_1, \ldots, u_{k-1}$ and all adjacent edges, which reduces the bandwidth overhead for all valid paths passing through u_k. Eliminations are repeated iteratively until every source has a single valid path towards a sink. In consequence, the number of sinks is also one; if it were greater, then, since the graph is connected, there would exist a source with more than one valid path towards a sink. The structure of the graph is thus a tree.

Now consider a vertex v with an indegree $d > 2$, where its children are denoted as $u_1, \ldots, u_d$. We can remove $u_2, \ldots, u_d$ from v and put them under a new vertex u', which in turn becomes a new child of v. Then the authentication overhead for all paths through one in $u_2, \ldots, u_d$ remains the same (u_1 has been replaced by u' as a sibling of $u_2, \ldots, u_d$), but the overhead for paths through u_1 has been decreased by $d - 2$ hash values (u' has been added whereas $u_2, \ldots, u_d$ have been removed as siblings of u_1). We can iteratively proceed and turn the tree into a binary tree. Some vertices may not have any siblings; as they do not contribute to bandwidth overhead, we can conceptually remove them and connect their edges to turn the tree into a *full* binary tree. It is well known that a balanced tree provides the lowest height among d-ary trees of a given degree d. In particular, the height of a balanced binary tree with n leaves is $\lceil \log_2 n \rceil$, which corresponds to the worst-case amount of unsigned hash values in the authentication information of a packet.

Finally, consider a graph that is not connected. Clearly, each connected component can be separately optimized in terms of its authentication overhead; we can thus assume a forest of k balanced binary trees for some $k > 1$. The k roots of the trees are covered by a digital signature, and the largest number of unsigned hash values in the authentication information of a packet corresponds to the largest height t among all the trees. If all the trees are of the same height t then the number of packets that can be supported is $k \cdot 2^t$. However, a single tree of height $t + \lceil \log_2 k \rceil$ can support $2^{\lceil \log_2 k \rceil} \cdot 2^t \geq k \cdot 2^t$ packets, at the cost of $t + \lceil \log_2 k \rceil$ unsigned and one signed hash value. For $k > 2$, the overhead of the $\lceil \log_2 k \rceil$ unsigned hash values falls below that of the additional $k - 1$ signed hash values in the forest structure, leaving both a single balanced binary hash tree and a forest of two equally balanced binary hash trees (where the levels of any two leaves differ by no more than 1) as graph structures with equal upper bounds on the number of hash values to be transmitted. However, only the single-tree structure requires a single hash value to be signed. This concludes the proof. $\square$

THEOREM 2. *The average per-packet bandwidth overhead of a fully loss-tolerant multicast authentication scheme that is based on an (unkeyed) one-way hash function and a single digital signature is at least $\lfloor \log_2 n \rfloor + (n - 2^{\lfloor \log_2 n \rfloor})/n \approx \log_2 n$ unsigned plus one signed hash value large, where n is the number of packets authenticated. A balanced binary hash tree matches the lower bound with equality.*

PROOF. The proof of Theorem 1 shows that any connected graph structure can be reduced to a binary tree without increasing the authentication overhead for any packet. Furthermore, an unconnected graph must have the form of a forest of binary trees. We now show that all trees are equally balanced. Suppose the level of some leaf x is greater by at least 2 than the level of another leaf y. Then we can remove x (by moving its sibling to the position of the parent) and add it to the path of y (by grouping x together with y under a new parent vertex). This increases the level of y by 1, but decreases the level of both x and its old sibling. As we continue this process, the average level of leaves attains a minimum when a forest of equally balanced binary trees is obtained. Now let t refer to the minimum level of a leaf in such a forest of k trees, and let $k \cdot 2^t \leq n < k \cdot 2^{t+1}$ denote the number of leaves. Then the average bandwidth overhead amounts to $z := t + (n - k \cdot 2^t)/n$ unsigned and k signed hash values. In comparison, the average per-packet overhead of a single balanced tree with a minimum leaf level of $t + \lceil \log_2 k \rceil$ and the same number of leaves is $t + \lceil \log_2 k \rceil + (n - 2^{t+\lceil \log_2 k \rceil})/n = z + \lceil \log_2 k \rceil - 2^t(2^{\lceil \log_2 k \rceil} - k)/n \leq z + \lceil \log_2 k \rceil$ unsigned and one signed hash values. The total number of hash values in the authentication information is thus lowest for both a balanced binary hash tree and a forest of two equally balanced binary hash trees, but only the former requires a single hash value to be signed. This concludes the proof. $\square$

Theorem 2 shows that the bandwidth overhead for independently transmitting all n packets covered by a graph-based authentication scheme is at least about $n \log_2 n$ unsigned hash values and n copies of a signed hash value. However, receivers may cache any received authentication information for future use. In particular, receivers in DTNs are expected to retain authentication information as long as a connection to the neighboring sender is available and further bundle data is still incoming. The question then is, how much authentication information does a sender need to forward to a receiver when transmitting (reliably and in order) a contiguous subsequence of m packets (fragments) out of the packet (fragment) sequence $(p_1, \ldots, p_n)$?

Let us denote a contiguous subsequence of m packet (or fragment) hash values as $(x_k, \ldots, x_{k+m-1})$ for some $1 \leq k \leq n - m + 1$. It is clear that a lower bound for the total number of hash values to be distributed as authentication information is m if we want to verify each packet as it arrives (this considers that links may break anytime and allows receivers to forward any received data in an authenticated manner). We can provide a simple explicit construction that exceeds the bound by a single hash value by letting $v_1 := h(x_k | \ldots | x_{k+m-1})$ and $v_2 := h(x_1 | \ldots | x_{k-1} | x_{k+m} | \ldots | x_n)$, and distributing as authentication information along with the first packet the hash values $x_{k+1}, \ldots, x_{k+m-1}, v_2$, and the signed root $h(v_1 | v_2)$. However, that construction is dependent on the values k and m. A hash chain can provide a near-optimal solution for arbitrary m, but requires $k = 1$. A consequence of Theorem 1 is that no graph can exist that is optimal for every possible contiguous subsequence of packets. This is because there is at least one packet that when transmitted alone requires $\lceil \log_2 n \rceil + 1$ or more hash values for authentication. However, Theorem 4 shows that the per-packet overhead of a balanced binary hash tree quickly amortizes as m grows. Specifically, by Theorem 3 the overhead of transmitting all n packets is just n hash values, which is optimal.

THEOREM 3. *Let a sender deliver reliably and in order all n packets authenticated by a balanced binary hash tree structure to a receiver caching authentication information. Then the total bandwidth overhead is exactly $n - 1$ unsigned plus one signed hash value.*

PROOF. An unsigned vertex v is part of a packet's authentication information if and only if the packet leaf is within the subtree rooted by v's sibling. As packets are delivered consecutively from the start, a receiver can reconstruct v based on previously received packets if and only if v is a left-hand child of its parent. Thus, the total authentication information a sender must forward consists of all $m-1$ right-hand siblings in the tree plus the signed hash value of the root. □

THEOREM 4. *Let a sender deliver reliably and in order m contiguous packets out of a sequence of n packets authenticated by a balanced binary hash tree to a caching receiver. Then the worst-case total bandwidth overhead amounts to $m + 2\lceil \log_2 n\rceil - 1$ unsigned plus one signed hash value.*

PROOF. The sequence of packet hash values can be partitioned into a unique sequence of sets of packet hash values $(S_1, \ldots, S_\ell)$ such that each S_i is covered by a balanced binary subtree T_i with $|S_i|$ leaves and where each T_i is rooted at some level $d_i \geq 0$ with the following property: there exists $1 \leq k \leq \ell$ such that $d_{i\,(i<k)} > d_{i+1}$, $d_{i\,(i>k+1)} > d_{i-1}$, and $d_{k\,(k<\ell)} \leq d_{k+1}$. The authentication information for T_1 in the overall hash tree consists of $d_1 \leq \lceil \log_2 n\rceil$ hashes for the authentication of T_1's root plus $|S_1|$ hash values as per Theorem 3, thereby concluding the proof for $\ell = 1$. Now assume $\ell > 1$. Each $T_{i\atop 1<i\leq k}$ has the path from its root to the hash tree's root covered by the authentication information for T_1, and therefore the authentication information for $\bigcup_{1 \leq i \leq k} S_i$ consists of $\sum_{1 \leq i \leq k} |S_i| + d_1 - (k-1)$ hash values. Similarly, $\bigcup_{k+1 \leq i \leq \ell} S_i$ is authenticated by $\sum_{k+1 \leq i \leq \ell} |S_i| + d_\ell - (\ell - k - 1)$ hash values. However, some of the d_ℓ hash values may be recoverable from the authentication information for T_1. The total authentication information for all m packets therefore consists of at most $\sum_{1 \leq i \leq \ell} |S_i| + d_1 + d_\ell - \ell + 2 \leq m + 2\lceil \log_2 n\rceil$ hash values (one of which is signed). □

We note that a caching receiver does not need to rebuild the entire hash tree as it suffices to maintain a single authentication path, which can be continually updated with the authentication information and hash values of subsequent packets or fragments. Furthermore, just as a sender can save on the communication overhead a caching receiver can reduce its computational efforts by considering cached non-leaf hash values as roots of smaller subtrees. Finally, a sender can reconstruct all authentication values in a sequence of fragments based on knowledge of an authentication path for the first and the last fragment, only.

Theorems 1 to 4 show that a balanced binary hash tree provides an optimal solution among all graph-based constructions that rely on a single digital signature and are suitable for DTNs. In addition to being bandwidth-efficient when used over reliable links, the solution also has low computational and memory requirements (see Table 2), and it is generally applicable. The results refine the basic binary hash tree overhead evaluations presented in [23] and address an open issue stated therein, namely whether there is a more space-efficient (and computationally efficient) approach for authenticating fragments than the binary hash tree structure.

6. RELATED WORK

Little literature is available on the subject of efficient authentication of bundle fragments in DTNs. While the IRTF

Table 2: Comparison of the Simple "Sign-Each" Approach with Various Graph-based Constructions Applicable in DTNs

	Avg. overhead of reliably forwarding m out of n fragments		
	Bandwidth	Verifications	Storage
Sign-each	m signatures		
Hash list	n hashes + 1 signature	m hashes + 1 signature	$n - m$ hashes + 1 signature
Hash chain (modified)	$(m+n)/2$ h. + 1 signature	$(3m+n)/2$ hashes + 1 signature	$(n-m)/2 + 1$ h. + 1 signature
Hash tree	$< m + 2\lceil \log_2 n\rceil$ hashes + 1 signature		$\leq 2\lceil \log_2 n\rceil$ hashes + 1 signature

research group on delay-tolerant networking has been recurrently discussing the issue on their mailing list, to the best of our knowledge, only three research papers [23–25] are concerned with identifying efficient solutions for the problem. Below, we review all solutions that have been proposed.

Sign-each. The IRTF research group has only considered the basic "sign-each" method, referring to it as the "toilet-paper" approach [21, 22]. Fragmentation is carried out conceptually such that each bundle is accompanied with a list of authentication values, one per fragment. This approach allows some moderate bandwidth savings due to the transmission of only a single bundle header but it does not address the core problem, which is the transmission of a digital signature for each fragment.

Hash tree. In a technical report [23], Asokan *et al.* have suggested the use of a binary hash tree as a more efficient approach for fragment authentication. This is precisely the solution that our work has shown to be optimal. In contrast, the report provides neither a detailed theoretical nor practical analysis. Furthermore, even though the report points out that receivers may cache hash tree root signatures for reduced bandwidth consumption, it does not consider the caching of hash values.

Bloom filter. The use of a Bloom filter has been proposed as a space-efficient probabilistic data structure for the carriage of fragment hash values [24]. However, albeit the paper considers the presence of an active adversary, the chosen error probability of the Bloom filter does not reflect this. In particular, the error probability is specified at a level that is appropriate for accidental errors but not for an adversary that may compute a matching Bloom filter entry by brute force. Adjusting the error probability properly reveals that the solution is $(\ln 2)^{-1} \approx 1.44$ times more costly in terms of bandwidth requirements than the hash list scheme. The authors have also mentioned various multicast authentication protocols in their related-work section but they did not further investigate this research field to correctly identify shortcomings and benefits of available solutions for the fragment authentication problem.

Function definitions. So far, to the best of our knowledge, only a single paper has been entirely devoted to the problem of authenticated bundle fragmentation in DTNs [25]. In this paper, Partridge highlights some general issues that arise from fragmentation and discusses suitable forwarding strategies for verified and unverified fragment data before suggesting a few simple variants of the toilet-paper method. Unfortunately, none of these suggestions provide clear benefits. On the last variant, the author proposes to encode authentication information in the form of a concise representation of a dynamically selected function (out of a set of functions) that maps each fragment to a known result such as a fragment sequence number. Specifically, minimal perfect hash functions are suggested for the encoding, and the author raises as an open issue whether "space-efficient" one-way minimal perfect hash functions exist. Indeed, such functions can be constructed (in the simplest case, using a one-way permutation, which requires no encoding at all) but the range of the hash functions is necessarily large for the functions to be one-way. This is an issue as a receiver may not easily identify valid fragments as described in the paper. On the other hand, modifying perfect hash functions with a small range such that they map forged fragments to some "invalid" hash value does not help either, as in this case a single hash function can no longer be perfect for multiple inputs—a simple combinatorial argument then yields that the hash function has a minimum representation size of $\log_2 \binom{2^l}{n} \geq nl - n\log_2 n$ bits if the order of the fragments is ignored (where l denotes the output bit length of a cryptographic hash function and n is the number of fragments in the bundle), or exactly nl bits otherwise, which is precisely the amount of space required for the hash list approach. Augmenting inputs to a perfect hash function with some per-fragment initialization vector, as suggested in the paper, is also no solution as in the best case the space saved in the encoding of the hash function is made up for by the space required to carry the initialization vectors. Finally, for the same combinatorial arguments presented above there can also be no efficient representation of a pseudo-random generator that yields the sequence of fragment hash values, as proposed towards the end of the paper.

7. CONCLUSION

By rephrasing the problem of efficient bundle fragment authentication in DTNs as a multicast authentication problem, we have identified a number of computationally efficient protocols that are suitable for DTNs. Among these protocols, graph-based schemes are the only class that offers generally applicable solutions for the authenticated fragmentation problem. We have shown that a balanced binary hash tree requires the least bandwidth overhead among all graph-based constructions that rely on one-way hash functions and a single digital signature, and that are fully loss-tolerant such as to be applicable in DTNs. Even though the bandwidth overhead for a single fragment is still large compared to popular discrete logarithm-based digital signatures, the overhead quickly amortizes as a sender delivers more bundle fragments to a receiver caching authentication information. Furthermore, the hash tree has low storage requirements at such receivers. Our work presented, to the best of our knowledge, the first systematic treatment of the authenticated fragmentation problem and the first detailed theoretical analysis of graph-based schemes that are suitable for the fragment authentication problem, and identified the hash tree as an optimal scheme, thereby addressing an open issue stated in related work.

8. REFERENCES

[1] S. Farrell, V. Cahill, D. Geraghty, I. Humphreys, P. McDonald, "When TCP Breaks: Delay- and Disruption-Tolerant Networking", *IEEE Internet Computing*, vol. 10, no. 4, pp. 72–78, 2006.

[2] K. L. Scott, S. Burleigh, "Bundle Protocol Specification", *RFC 5050*, IETF, 2007.

[3] S. F. Symington, S. Farrell, H. Weiss, P. Lovell, "Bundle Security Protocol Specification", *RFC 6257*, IETF, 2011.

[4] Y. Challal, H. Bettahar, A. Bouabdallah, "A Taxonomy of Multicast Data Origin Authentication: Issues and Solutions", *IEEE Comm. Surveys & Tutorials*, vol. 6, no. 3, pp. 34–57, 2004.

[5] S. Miner, J. Staddon, "Graph-Based Authentication of Digital Streams", *Proc. IEEE Symp. on Security and Privacy—S&P 2001*, pp. 232–246, 2001.

[6] C. Tartary, H. Wang, J. Pieprzyk, "A coding approach to the multicast stream authentication problem", *Int. J. of Information Security*, vol. 7, no. 4, pp. 265–283, 2008.

[7] C. Tartary, "Authentication for Multicast Communication", Thesis, 2007.

[8] Y. Zhou, X. Zhu, Y. Fang, "MABS: Multicast Authentication Based on Batch Signature", *IEEE Trans. on Mobile Computing*, vol. 9, no. 7, pp. 982–993, 2010.

[9] R. Canetti, J. Garay, G. Itkis, D. Micciancio, M. Naor, B. Pinkas, "Multicast Security: A Taxonomy and Efficient Constructions", *Proc. 18th Annual Joint Conf. of the IEEE Computer and Comm. Societies—INFOCOM '99*, vol. 2, pp. 708–716, 1999.

[10] D. Boneh, G. Durfee, M. Franklin, "Lower Bounds for Multicast Message Authentication", *Proc. Advances in Cryptology—EUROCRYPT 2001, LNCS*, vol. 2045, pp. 437–452, 2001.

[11] A. Perrig, R. Canetti, J. D. Tygar, D. Song, "Efficient Authentication and Signing of Multicast Streams over Lossy Channels", *Proc. IEEE Symp. on Security and Privacy—S&P 2000*, pp. 56–73, 2000.

[12] R. Gennaro, P. Rohatgi, "How to Sign Digital Streams", *Proc. Advances in Cryptology—CRYPTO '97, LNCS*, vol. 1294, pp. 180–197, 1997.

[13] P. Golle, N. Modadugu, "Authenticating Streamed Data in the Presence of Random Packet Loss", *Proc. Network and Distributed System Security Symp.—NDSS '01*, The Internet Society, 2001.

[14] C. K. Wong, S. S. Lam, "Digital Signatures for Flows and Multicasts", *IEEE/ACM Trans. on Netw. (TON)*, vol. 7, no. 4, pp. 502–513, 1999.

[15] J. M. Park, E. K. P. Chong, H. J. Siegel, "Efficient Multicast Packet Authentication Using Signature Amortization", *Proc. IEEE Symp. on Security and Privacy—S&P 2002*, pp. 227–240, 2002.

[16] S. Even, O. Goldreich, S. Micali, "On-line/off-line digital signatures", *Proc. Advances in Cryptology—CRYPTO '89*, pp. 263–275, 1989.

[17] A. Fiat, "Batch RSA", *Proc. Advances in Cryptology—CRYPTO '89, LNCS*, vol. 435, pp. 175–185, 1989.

[18] D. Naccache, D. M'Raïhi, S. Vaudenay, D. Raphaeli, "Can D.S.A. be Improved?", *Proc. Advances in Cryptology—EUROCRYPT '94, LNCS*, vol. 950, pp. 77–85, 1995.

[19] B. J. Matt, "Identification of Multiple Invalid Signatures in Pairing-based Batched Signatures", *Proc. Int. Conf. on Theory and Practice of Public-Key Cryptography—PKC 2009, LNCS*, vol. 5443, pp. 337–356, 2009.

[20] G. M. Zaverucha, D. R. Stinson, "Group Testing and Batch Verification", *Proc. 4th Int. Conf. on Information-Theoretic Security—ICITS '09*, pp. 140–157, 2010.

[21] https://www.ietf.org/mail-archive/web/dtn-security/current/msg00201.html, IRTF, April 2005.

[22] S. Farrell, S. F. Symington, H. Weiss, P. Lovell, "Delay-Tolerant Networking Security Overview", *draft-irtf-dtnrg-sec-overview-06* (expired), IRTF, 2009.

[23] N. Asokan, K. Kostiainen, P. Ginzboorg, J. Ott, C. Luo, "Towards Securing Disruption-Tolerant Networking", *NRC-TR-2007-007*, Nokia Research Center, 2007.

[24] W. Itani, A. Tajeddine, A. Kayssi, A. Chehab, "Slow But Certain Wins the Race: Authenticated Bundle Communication in Delay Tolerant Networks", *Proc. 6th ACM Workshop on QoS and Security for Wireless and Mobile Networks—Q2SWinet'10*, pp. 90–97, 2010.

[25] C. Partridge, "Authentication for Fragments", *Proc. 4th ACM Workshop on Hot Topics in Networks—SIGCOMM*, 2005.

Searching a Needle in (Linear) Opportunistic Networks

Esa Hyytiä
Aalto University
Finland
esa@netlab.tkk.fi

Suzan Bayhan
University of Helsinki
Finland
bayhan@hiit.fi

Jörg Ott
Aalto University
Finland
jo@netlab.tkk.fi

Jussi Kangasharju
University of Helsinki
Finland
jakangas@cs.helsinki.fi

ABSTRACT

Searching content in mobile opportunistic networks is a difficult problem due to the dynamically changing topology and intermittent connections. Moreover, due to the lack of global view of the network, it is arduous to determine whether the best response is discovered or search should be spread to other nodes. A node that has received a search query has to take two decisions: (i) whether to continue the search further or stop it at the current node (current search *depth*) and, independently of that, (ii) whether to send a response back or not. As each transmission and extra hop costs in terms of energy, bandwidth and time, a balance between the expected value of the response and the costs incurred must be sought. In order to better understand this inherent trade-off, we assume a simplified setting where both the query and response follow the same path. We formulate the problem of optimal search for the following two cases: a node holds (i) exactly matching content with some probability, and (ii) some content partially matching the query. We design *static search* in which the search depth is set at query initiation, *dynamic search* in which search depth is determined locally during query forwarding, and *learning dynamic search* which leverages the observations to estimate suitability of content for the query. Additionally, we show how unreliable response paths affect the optimal search depth and the corresponding search performance. Finally, we investigate the principal factors affecting the optimal search strategy.

Categories and Subject Descriptors

C.4 [**Performance of Systems**]: Design studies; C.2.1 [**Computer-Communication Networks**]: Network Architecture and Design —*Wireless communication*

Keywords

Mobile opportunistic networks, mobile search, mobile cloud computing, dynamic programming.

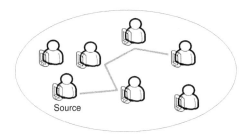

Figure 1: Search query travels from a node to another and the path forms a linear trajectory in space. The response is assumed to follow the same path backwards.

1. INTRODUCTION

Mobile opportunistic networks, also dubbed *Pocket switched networks* [6, 10], are networks in which mobile devices carried by humans can exchange information via short-range communication interfaces, e.g., Wi-Fi, Bluetooth, when they come in transmission range of each other and physically carry the content on their way. Certainly, this operation mode is vital for cases where the network infrastructure fails (e.g. after natural disasters), does not exist, or access to infrastructure services or even the Internet at large is blocked [3]. In addition, this communication involves only the peers in wireless contact, in contrast to the frequently used cloud-based third party services (e.g. Dropbox) which may take a long distance detour across the Internet and potentially half-way around the world. *Delay-tolerant networking* (DTN) [4, 5] defines such a networking paradigm facilitating communication without an infrastructure support for a variety of application scenarios including inter-planetary, vehicular, underwater, and opportunistic networks.

The wealth of data produced or downloaded by the mobile devices requires efficient search algorithms that can locate the relevant content quickly and cost-effectively rather than naïve enquiry of each node upon a contact. Searching content in mobile opportunistic networks is a difficult problem due to the dynamically changing topology and intermittent connections. A question arising in this context is what are the fundamental determinants of search in mobile opportunistic networks. In this work, we aim to provide insights on this question by designing static and dynamic search schemes. We focus on a single query that visits a node after another along some (natural) path as illustrated in Fig. 1 (i.e., the query is not replicated). The response follows the same path backwards. However, the response path is assumed to be unreliable, e.g., due to mobility during the search. More specifically, we assume that searches terminate relatively quickly (say, order of ten seconds) and a link backwards exists if the response can be transmitted shortly (but not necessarily immediately). In other words, we do not require persistent end-to-end paths.

In practice, the search path can form naturally based on some path selection criteria such as a similarity metric for nodes, which reflects positively to the probability of finding relevant information in the node. Similarly, the actual search can consist of multiple (independent) linear paths.

In this paper, we consider three types of search strategies: static, dynamic, and learning dynamic search. Regarding a node's value for the issued query, first we assume that a node either holds a relevant content or not for the query. Second, we assume that a node may hold some relevant content whose relevance has either uniform or exponential distribution. The former corresponds to the *binary response* whereas the latter is the *partial response* scenario. We start with *static strategies* where the search is extended to a predefined number of nodes n. Then we consider *dynamic strategies* that may stop the search before depth n depending on what has been found so far (and whether some response has already been sent back). Both of these assume that each node knows the distribution of information in the nodes (value of response to given search). Our final search strategy, referred to as the *learning strategy*, is more robust and estimates the value distribution dynamically as the search progresses from a node to another. Although we assume that response follows the same path as the query, we model the unreliability of the link between two nodes on the response path and analyze how it affects the optimal search. The results in this paper serve two purposes: First, they enable design of efficient distributed search algorithms. Second, they provide insight on under what circumstances searching for content in mobile opportunistic networks is feasible and present the optimal operating region (in terms of search depth) for various scenarios.

Rest of this paper is organized as follows. First, in Section 2 we briefly review the related work. Then, Section 3 introduces our model and notation. The different search strategies are analyzed in Section 4, followed by a performance evaluation in Section 5, and a discussion in Section 6. Section 7 concludes the paper.

2. RELATED WORK

In a broad context, we can consider every forwarding algorithm in a DTN as a search scheme for a specific target node. We exclude broadcast algorithms as they aim to reach each and every node. In content search, first the searched content is mapped to some node(s) that have a high likelihood of holding this particular content. Next, nodes upon encounters forward the query with the aim of reaching the specified destination(s) that matches the mapping between content and the node profile. For example, *seeker-assisted search* (SAS) [2] vaguely maps a content to the nodes of a particular community which is a group of nodes sharing common interests. Hui et al. [6], design Haggle – a content sharing scheme, by leveraging the node's self-declared interests to locate the contents that might fall in the interest of the node. In Haggle, each content and node have some attributes that are manually defined. These attributes provide the basis of mapping between a content and its target nodes.

See also the *Bubble* forwarding algorithm [7], which tries to exploit the social structures when making the forwarding decisions.

Any rational search scheme should direct the search towards the nodes that have higher likelihood of holding the searched item. This forwarding decision can exploit various characteristics of the network, e.g., the community structure, content and node relevance. For example, SAS [2] exploits the *homophily principle*, tendency to associate and interact with similar others, and directs the search towards the nodes of the same community as this content might have been searched and be readily available at a node in this community. SAS expands the search to the other parts of the network, although there is a lower probability of matching there, to avoid searching only in a particular part of the network. In Haggle, nodes exchange contents at each encounter so that contents are constantly *pushed* towards the nodes with some interests for this content rather than an explicit search. In this paper, similar to SAS, we consider a *pull-based* search scheme in which a node issues a query for finding a specific content.

Another challenge in opportunistic search is deciding when to stop the spreading of the search query. As nodes operate distributedly, the completion of search cannot be signalled immediately to the other parts of the network. Hence, each node should decide on forwarding or terminating the spread. An early termination may result in search getting no responses whereas late termination leads to over-consumption of the resources, e.g., battery. Pitkänen et al. [9] define a termination logic in which each node using the observed degree of itself estimates the number of nodes the query might have been received by and the number of possible responses generated by these nodes. The query is terminated if the estimate is above some threshold. Under transmission bandwidth and storage capacity constraints, RAPID [1] replicates the messages to the node's contact in decreasing order of message utilities such as expected delivery delay and deadline violation level. In this manner, messages yielding higher cost compared to their utilities are terminated based on the benefit and cost evaluation at each node. Setting time-to-live (TTL) for a query is another way of limiting the spread as a message is dropped after the expiry of its TTL. However, determining the optimal TTL is not straightforward as it depends on various network dynamics including the traffic load and content availability. Our solution is similar to [1] in the sense that each node evaluates the expected utility of the next hop and the increased cost due to involving it. This decision can be intricate depending on the degree of information available to the decision maker. In this work, different than the listed approaches, we find the *optimal depth* - the hop distance from the searching node - to stop the search under various settings.

Search, although having similarities with opportunistic forwarding, is more complicated due to its birectional nature, i.e., the discovered content or other responses have to be forwarded back to the searching node. What is more, treating search as a twofold process, e.g. *query forwarding* and *response forwarding*, may lead to a sub-optimal performance or even hinder the search success. For instance, search message eventually discovering some related content, might already be too far from the searching node that the response is obsolete or too difficult to route back. Therefore, the response path should also be taken into account

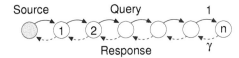

Figure 2: Linear network, where a query travels to the right and a possible response(s) to the left.

explicitly. In this work, we assume that the response messages follow the path of the query backwards. In our basic model, we assume that this path exists for the duration of the search, but numerically we also investigate what happens if the path back to the searching node becomes unreliable.

3. MODEL AND NOTATION

As already mentioned, searching content in an opportunistic wireless network is not trivial. Therefore, we resort to analyze a simplified setting to understand how much an optimal search scheme can save. In particular, we consider a search in a linear network, where the basic action at each node is to decide if the search should continue further, or if we are satisfied with the content found so far. More specifically, our model is as follows.

- We assume a linear network, where the source node is located at the origin and there are an infinite number of nodes along the positive x-axis, see Fig. 2. Please note that this linear model is a logical abstraction rather than a physical interpretation (cf. Fig. 1), however under our assumption of no replication for query messages, every query will follow such a linear path.

- A query travels on the *forward path*, where the loss probability is assumed to be zero. (A node meets another node within a reasonable time with a high probability).

- A possible response travels in the opposite direction on the *backward path* and the response can be delivered to the previous node in the chain with a fixed probability of γ (during the search). In the ideal case, $\gamma = 1$. However, in practice, depending on the connectedness of the network, there are many reasons for $\gamma < 0$, including that a node may have carried the search request away or that a previous hop may have gotten out of range.

- For each query, each node i has a response which value is described by i.i.d. random variables denoted by V_i. Note that $V_i = 0$ corresponds to "nothing useful". This value can be interpreted as the ranking or relevance of the response similar to ranked search results returned by a search engine.

- We let m denote the total number of transmissions when the search has completed, and d the highest valued response that is returned back to the source. A possibly failed transmission on the return path is also included in m.

- Each transmission costs e (say energy & time), which is assumed to be the same for both the query and response for simplicity. In practice, responses might have a higher cost if they return a lot of data (e.g., music, photos, ...)

- If a search is terminated after n hops and nothing useful has been found, there is no need to send a response back to the source, $n = m$, and the transmission costs are ne.

- As the metric we consider the net profit of a search, i.e., *the utility*, which is the value of the response minus the expenses,

$$U := d - m \cdot e. \qquad (1)$$

- Node i along the search path must choose its action from the following four options:

  1. Stop the search

  2. Stop the search and send a response back to the source

  3. Continue the search to Node $i + 1$

  4. Continue the search to Node $i + 1$ and also send a response back to the source

- The optimal search algorithm α chooses dynamically the action that maximizes the utility given by (1).

We note that our problem is related to the *optimal stopping problem* in the routing at DTNs, see, e.g., [8] and [12]. However, there is a fundamental difference because in our setting there are multiple ways to "stop": one can simply stop and give up, or stop and send a response back to the searching node (which costs more in terms of energy and time). Moreover, it is possible to send a response while still proceeding further with the search. The search forwarding algorithm must take all these different options and the earlier observations into account when making the decisions.

4. OPTIMAL SEARCH STRATEGIES

In this section, we will analyze the optimal search strategies. We consider static strategies, where the search distance is defined at the start, and dynamic strategies, where the actions may depend on what has been found so far, and if some responses have already been sent. The dynamic strategies may also learn the value distribution during the search.

4.1 Bernoulli distribution

Let us start with the binary case where a node either has the complete response to the query, or no relevant information at all. That is, the value of the response from node i obeys Bernoulli distribution $V_i \sim \text{Bernoulli}(p)$, where p denotes the probability that a node has the searched content. We refer to p as the *content availability*, and q denotes the probability of the opposite case, $q = 1 - p$. Moreover, the links on the return path can be unreliable ($\gamma < 1$), and at most one response is sent per query.

4.1.1 Static strategy

A static search strategy is defined by a fixed depth n, i.e., each search will check the first n nodes and then return the highest response found. The number of transmissions on the return path is $r_n = \sum_{i=1}^{n} i\gamma^{i-1}(1 - \gamma) + n\gamma^n$, which gives

$$r_n = \begin{cases} \dfrac{1 - \gamma^n}{1 - \gamma}, & \text{when } 0 < \gamma < 1, \\ n, & \text{when } \gamma = 1. \end{cases} \qquad (2)$$

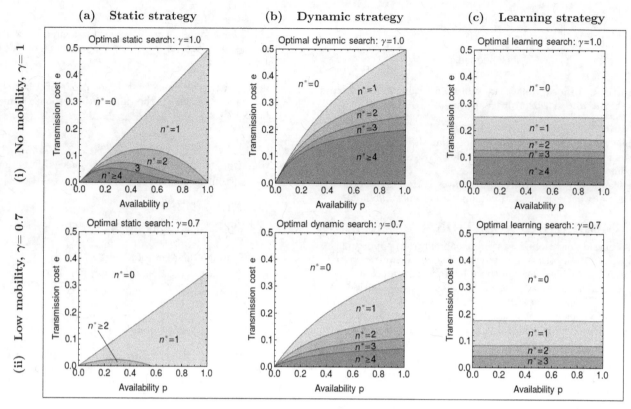

Figure 3: Optimal max. search depth n^* in Bernoulli case ($v_{max} = 1$) with (a) the static strategy, (b) dynamic strategy and (c) learning strategy (which does not know p *a priori*). The top row corresponds to the ideal case with $\gamma = 1$, whereas on the bottom row the return path is unreliable and $\gamma = 0.7$.

The total number of transmissions is $m = n + r_n$, and the response reaches the searching node with probability of γ^n. The expected search result with depth n is

$$
\begin{aligned}
R_n &= E[\max\{V_1, .., V_n\}] \cdot \gamma^n \\
&= (0 \cdot q^n + 1 \cdot (1 - q^n)) \gamma^n \\
&= (1 - q^n)\gamma^n.
\end{aligned} \tag{3}
$$

Thus, the expected utility under n hop search is

$$
U_n = R_n - (n + r_n)e.
$$

which reduces to

$$
U_n = (1 - q^n)\gamma^n - (n + r_n)e, \tag{4}
$$

and with $\gamma = 1$,

$$
U_n = 1 - q^n - 2ne. \tag{5}
$$

The optimal static policy is obtained by finding the depth n that maximizes the expected utility:

$$
n^* = \arg\max_{n \in \mathbb{N}} \quad U_n. \tag{6}
$$

We note that this is clearly a non-optimal strategy: if Node 1 already has the searched content it is useless to search any further. Nonetheless, we consider this simple strategy first and later compare how far it is from the optimal.

Case $\gamma = 1$.

Let us first assume the ideal case with $\gamma = 1$. Note that if $p < 2e$, then the optimal search depth n is zero, i.e., it is

not worth initiating a search at all. The optimal (integer-valued) search depth n is found by studying the gain from expanding the search by one step, i.e, $\Delta U(n) = U_{n+1} - U_n$:

$$
\Delta U(n) = (1 - q^{n+1} - 2(n+1)e) - (1 - q^n - 2ne) = pq^n - 2e.
$$

The gain becomes negative at the optimal search depth, giving

$$
\boxed{n^* = \left\lceil \frac{\log(2e/p)}{\log q} \right\rceil.} \qquad (p > 2e) \tag{7}
$$

The optimal search depth n^* is illustrated in Fig. 3(a.i). In the upper left "triangle", where $p < 2e$, we have $n^* = 0$, i.e., the value of the searched information is too low to justify a search. Note also that when $p \to 1$, i.e., when the content becomes highly available, the optimal search depth is $n^* = 1$ *for any fixed transmission cost $e < p/2$.* This is due to the fact that the content is always found at the first node, and still continuing the search further would just waste energy and time. Indeed, this inability to dynamically stop the search is the Achilles heel of all *static* search strategies.

Case $0 < \gamma < 1$.

Let us next consider unreliable return paths. The condition remains the same, i.e., at the optimal depth n we have $U_{n+1} - U_n \leq 0$. Unfortunately, in this case we cannot express n^* in closed form. However, we can determine the *critical transmission cost e_n^*,*

$$
e_n^* = \frac{\gamma^n(q^n + \gamma - \gamma q^{n+1} - 1)}{1 + \gamma^n}
$$

which is the smallest transmission cost for which the optimal search depth is $n^* = n$. Conversely,

$$n^* = \arg\min_n \{n \mid e_n^* < e\}.$$

Fig. 3(a.ii) depicts the optimal static search depth when the return path is unreliable and each link backward exists with the probability of $\gamma = 0.7$.

4.1.2 Dynamic strategy

Let us next consider search strategies that adjust the search depth dynamically as the search progresses. In the Bernoulli case, the obvious dynamic search strategy searches at most n nodes (the max. depth) and terminates immediately if the content is found. Hence, e.g., with the probability of p, the first node has the content and the total number of transmissions is 2 (out of which, the latter is successful with probability of γ).

Note that the expected value of the content *found* (but not necessarily successfully returned) is the same as with the static strategy, $\mathrm{E}[\max_i V_i] = 1 - q^n$. However, the search may terminate earlier, which (i) saves in the number of transmissions and also (ii) improves the probability of successfully returning a response.

Case $\gamma = 1$.

Let us again start with the ideal case with $\gamma = 1$. Then the mean number of transmissions is

$$N_n = (2p + 4qp + \ldots + 2nq^{n-1}p) + nq^n = \frac{2 - q^n(2 + np)}{p}.$$

The expected response reaching the source node is given by (3). Hence, the mean utility is

$$U_n := 1 - q^n - \frac{2 - q^n(2 + np)}{p} \cdot e$$
$$= \frac{p - 2e - (p - e(2 + np))q^n}{p}.$$

The gain from including one more hop, $U_{n+1} - U_n$, becomes negative at the optimal maximum depth n^*. Solving this gives the exact solution for the optimal maximum search depth n^*,

$$\boxed{n^* = \left\lceil \frac{1}{e} - \frac{1}{p} \right\rceil - 1.} \tag{8}$$

Solving for e gives the critical transmission cost,

$$e_n^* = \frac{p}{(n+1)p + 1}.$$

The optimal search depth with the dynamic strategy is illustrated in Fig. 3(b.i). Note that the maximum search depth (but not the mean) with the dynamic strategy is always greater than or equal to the search depth with the static strategy. Moreover, the equicontour lines are strictly increasing functions of the availability p due to the fact that this strategy is able to stop the search dynamically. In passing we note that if we are required to return also a null answer with the Bernoulli case, then the optimal search depth becomes ∞ if $p > 2e$, and otherwise it is zero.

Case $0 < \gamma < 1$.

The forward path remains identical and we can condition on the number of hops travelled before the searched content

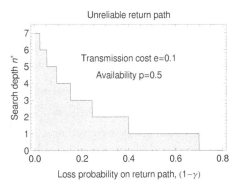

Figure 4: **The optimal dynamic search depth with fixed $e = 0.1$ and $p = 0.5$ as a function of $1 - \gamma$.**

is found. The probability that the content is found at the ith hop is $q^{i-1}p$, and thus the mean value of the response is

$$R_n = \sum_{i=1}^n q^{i-1}p \cdot \gamma^i = \frac{(1-q)(1 - (q\gamma)^n)\gamma}{1 - q\gamma}.$$

For the cost we need to determine the mean number of hops. To this end, we condition also on the number of transmissions on the return path (out of which the last one may have failed). Let i denote the number of hops the query travels, i.e., the length of the forward path, and j the number of transmissions on the return path. Then the mean number of transmissions is given by

$$N_n = \sum_{i=1}^n q^{i-1}p \cdot \left(i + \sum_{j=1}^i j\gamma^{j-1}(1-\gamma) + i\gamma^i \right) + nq^n,$$

where the last term corresponds to a search that did not find the content. Subtracting $e N_n$ from R_n gives the mean utility U_n. Subsequently, for the difference $\Delta U(n) = U_{n+1} - U_n$ we obtain

$$\Delta U(n) = \left(p\gamma^{1+n} - \left(1 + \frac{p(1 - \gamma^{n+1})}{1 - \gamma} \right) e \right) q^n.$$

Similarly as before, determining the root of $\Delta U(n)$ gives the optimal search depth. After some manipulation, we get

$$\boxed{n^* = \left\lceil \log \left(\frac{e(1 - \gamma + p)}{p(1 - \gamma + e)} \right) \middle/ \log \gamma \right\rceil - 1.}$$

Alternatively, solving for e gives the critical transmission cost,

$$e_n^* = \frac{p(1 - \gamma)\gamma^{1+n}}{p(1 - \gamma^{1+n}) + 1 - \gamma},$$

which was the minimum transmission cost at which $n^* = n$.

Fig. 3(b.ii) illustrates the optimal search depth n^* as a function of the availability p and transmission cost e for fixed $\gamma = 0.7$. The curves appear as scaled down versions of Fig. 3(b.i).

In Fig. 4, we have fixed $e = 0.1$ and $p = 0.5$, and vary $1 - \gamma$ that corresponds to the loss probability on the links of the return path. We notice that n^* decreases to 1 as the loss probability increases, i.e., when the return path becomes uncertain. As the intuition suggests, *under a high mobility, long paths become fragile and should be avoided, and only the neighboring node(s) should be involved in the search.*

4.1.3 Learning dynamic strategies

All earlier strategies, both static and dynamic, have made the crucial assumption that the value distribution (defining the value of information per node for the query) is known *a priori*. In practice this may not be the case, even though one can envision that empirical distribution have been obtained based on past encounters. In this section, we take the Bayesian approach and refine our estimate of the value distribution as the search progresses further. For simplicity of notation, we assume Bernoulli case with unknown information availability p, but note that the approach itself can be generalized to other value distributions.

A priori we assume that p is uniformly distributed on $(0,1)$. As the source node does not have an answer, we consider that initially one node has been checked and found out not to have a valid response. Suppose that in state i we have checked i nodes and none of them had a valid response. The Bayes formula gives the conditional pdf for p,

$$f(p \mid i) = \frac{P\{i \mid p\} \cdot f(p)}{\int_0^1 P\{i \mid p\} \cdot f(p)\, dp},$$

where $P\{i \mid p\} = q^i$ and[1] $f(p) = 1$, giving

$$f(p \mid i) = \frac{q^i}{\int_0^1 q^i\, dp} = (i+1)q^i.$$

Subsequently, the expected value of $p = 1 - q$ after i negative observations is

$$\hat{p}_i = \frac{1}{i+2}.$$

Case $\gamma = 1$.

Let w_i denote the expected final outcome from state i with optimal strategy, i.e., we have already checked $i+1$ nodes (including oneself) without luck. Then the search strategy bases its action on the assumption that $\hat{p}_i$ is the probability that the ith node has the searched content (i.e., on the condition that none of the previous nodes had it). Recursively this gives

$$w_i = \max \left\{ -ie, \; \frac{1}{i+3}(1 - 2e(i+1)) + \frac{i+2}{i+3} w_{i+1} \right\}, \quad (9)$$

where the first case corresponds to terminating the search after i transmissions, and the second case corresponds to continuing the search to the $(i+1)$th node. This otherwise infinite recursion can be constrained by noting that there is no use to continue if the possible gain is less than what it takes to return an answer back to the source, i.e., when

$$(i+2)e \geq 1 \quad \Rightarrow \quad i \geq \frac{1}{e} - 2.$$

That is, for states $i \geq 1/e - 2$, we have $w_i = -ie$. The learning search strategy, based on the Bayesian thinking, thus continues the search as long as the second option in (9) is greater than $-ie$.

In particular, for the maximum search depth n^* we have $w_{n^*} > w_{n^*+1} = -(n+1)e$. Consequently, letting $\Delta U(n)$ denote the gain from continuing the search exactly one step

---

[1] Note that the approach allows an arbitrary *a priori* distribution for the availability, which can be in practice based on, e.g., earlier similar queries.

further,

$$\Delta U(n) := \frac{1}{n+3}(1 - 2e(n+1)) + \frac{n+2}{n+3}(-(n+1)e) + ne$$
$$= \frac{1 - 2e(2+e)}{n+3},$$

we need to find n for which $\Delta U(n)$ becomes negative. Therefore,

$$\boxed{n^* = \left\lceil \frac{1}{2e} \right\rceil - 2.} \qquad (e < 0.25) \qquad (10)$$

Comparing (10) to (8), we note that both behave according to $\propto e^{-1}$. The knowledge of the availability of the content, p, affects the factor of e^{-1} term and the constant term. The optimal search depth with the learning strategy is illustrated in Fig. 3(c.i). Note the independence to the availability p, which this strategy does not know.

Case $0 < \gamma < 1$.

Similarly as with the two earlier cases, we can consider unreliable return path also in this case. In particular, we assume that parameter γ is stationary and has been determined when the search is triggered (γ depends on mobility, not on the content searched). Due to space constraints, here we simply give the results. The expected gain in utility from depth n to $n+1$ is

$$\Delta U(n) = \frac{\gamma^{1+n} - 2e(2+n)}{3+n}.$$

In this case, n^*, corresponding to the root of $\Delta U(n)$, cannot be expressed in closed form, but one needs to find $k = 2+n$ that satisfies (cf. Lambert W function)

$$\frac{\gamma^k}{k} = 2\gamma e.$$

However, for the critical transmission cost we have explicitly

$$e_n^* = \frac{\gamma^{1+n}}{2(2+n)},$$

which holds also for $\gamma = 1$. We note that as γ decreases, the critical transmission costs decrease by factor of γ^{n+1} for each n.

Fig. 3(c.ii) illustrates the optimal search depth n^* as a function of the transmission cost e for fixed $\gamma = 0.7$.

4.2 Partial information

Next we assume that some nodes may be able to provide partial answers to a query, i.e., responses that are good but not complete. For example, recent but not current information about football results could be considered as good but not complete answer to a query. For simplicity, in this section we assume ideal return paths with $\gamma = 1$. As example cases, we assume that value of the response from a node obeys either uniform or exponential distribution, for which we derive the optimal static strategies.

4.2.1 Uniform distribution

Suppose first that $V_i \sim U(0, v_{\max})$, i.e., nodes may have partial answers to the query measured by the *value*. Value $v_{\max}$ corresponds to a complete answer. The CDF of the maximum value among n samples is

$$P\{\max_i V_i < x\} = P\{V < x\}^n = (x/v_{\max})^n.$$

Subsequently, the expected value of the response is

$$E[\max_i V_i] = \frac{n}{n+1} v_{\max},$$

and the utility reduces to

$$U_n = \frac{n}{n+1} v_{\max} - 2ne. \tag{11}$$

Similarly as in the previous case, one can determine the optimal static search depth n^*. Let q denote the ratio of the maximum value of the response to unit transmission cost, $\beta = v_{\max}/e$. Then it follows that

$$\boxed{n^* = \left\lceil \frac{\sqrt{1+2\beta}-3}{2} \right\rceil.} \qquad (\beta > 4).$$

4.2.2 Exponential distribution

Next we assume that $V_i \sim \text{Exp}(\lambda)$. In this case, the expected value of the response from an arbitrary node is $E[V_i] = 1/\lambda$, and CDF of the maximum value is

$$P\{\max_i V_i < x\} = (1 - e^{-\lambda x})^n.$$

It follows that the expected value of the query is

$$E[\max_i V_i] = \frac{H(n)}{\lambda},$$

where $H(n)$ denotes the nth harmonic number,

$$H(n) = 1/1 + 1/2 + \ldots + 1/n.$$

Our objective is to maximize the expected utility,

$$U_n = \frac{H(n)}{\lambda} - 2ne, \tag{12}$$

Considering again the difference $U_{n+1} - U_n = \frac{1}{\lambda(n+1)} - 2e$ yields the optimal search depth,

$$\boxed{n^* = \left\lceil \frac{1}{2\lambda e} \right\rceil - 1.} \qquad (1/\lambda > 2e) \tag{13}$$

4.2.3 General case

In the previous section, we considered *static* strategies when the value of the content had a continuous distribution. In such a case, a search will never find the complete answer, but has to settle with something that is hopefully sufficiently high. The static strategy suits well to such scenario. Next we will assume a finite set of values and determine the optimal *dynamic search strategy* using dynamic programming. Thus, the decisions may depend also on what has been found so far. Moreover, we allow multiple responses which make more sense in this case, where even a better response can be found later.

We let $z = (m, n, d, b)$ denote **the state** of the search when the query reaches node n, where

- m is the number of transmissions so far
- n is the distance to the source (in hops)
- d is the highest valued response already sent towards the source (by an earlier node)
- b is the highest valued response that node n could send, $b = \max\{V_1, \ldots, V_n\}$

We can write at state $z = (m, n, d, b)$ the (expected) final utility for each action (see the model), and choose the best among them,

$$w(m, n, d, b) = \max\{a_1, a_2, a_3, a_4\},$$

where a_j denotes the (expected) final utility with action j,

$$\begin{cases} a_1 = d - m \cdot e, \\ a_2 = b - (m+n) \cdot e, \\ a_3 = E[w(m+1, n+1, d, \max\{b, V_{n+1}\})], \\ a_4 = E[w(m+n+1, n+1, b, \max\{b, V_{n+1}\})], \end{cases}$$

where

$$\begin{cases} a_1 \to & \text{stop the search,} \\ a_2 \to & \text{stop the search and send a response back,} \\ a_3 \to & \text{continue the search further,} \\ a_4 \to & \text{continue the search, but also send a response back.} \end{cases}$$

The optimal action in state z is given by $\arg\max_j\{a_j\}$. Clearly the actions 2 and 4 make no sense when $d = b$, i.e., when no better response than already delivered is available. The evaluation of the above equations directly leads to an infinite recursion as both a_3 and a_4 are defined in terms of $w(z)$. However, we can exclude both actions when n and m become too large by a simple observation. Namely, one should not forward a query if even the maximum value of the response, denoted by $v_{\max}$, from the next node is not worth the trouble of forwarding and sending back the response, i.e., if

$$v_{\max} - (m+n+2)e \leq \max\{a_1, a_2\}, \quad \text{for } a_3, \text{ and}$$
$$v_{\max} - (m+2n+2)e \leq \max\{a_1, a_2\}, \quad \text{for } a_4.$$

With these, the recursion becomes finite and the optimal actions can be determined for any state. Unfortunately, the number of states still explodes when $e \to 0$, which narrows the usability of the dynamic programming approach at this limit. On the other hand, when $e \to 0$ and V_i obey a discrete distribution, the optimal strategy can neglect the transmission costs.

5. PERFORMANCE EVALUATION

We now evaluate the performance of the developed search strategies with several numerical examples. We start with the Bernoulli case, where a node either has the complete information (e.g. a particular file) to a query or nothing, and then continue with the more complicated scenarios where also partial information exists.

5.1 Bernoulli: Search of a specific content

In our first example, we assume that a node either has the (complete) answer to a query, or nothing, i.e., the Bernoulli case. We compare the learning strategy (see Section 4.1.3) that determines the content availability p during the search to the optimal dynamic strategy that (miraculously) already knows the correct value of p. Our numerical results show that the difference in the performance is typically minimal. In other words, the learning search strategy works very well across many values of p and one only has to know the transmission cost e.

Fig. 5 (left) illustrates the maximum search depth n^* with the learning strategy (bold green line) and the optimal dynamic strategies that know the probability p of a node having the searched content, when $p = \{10\%, 20\%, 50\%\}$. Note

193

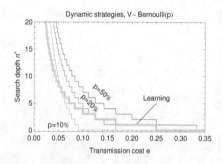 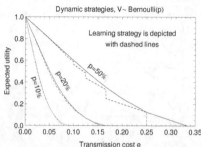 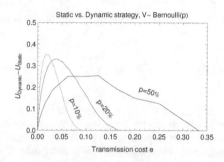

Figure 5: Left: The learning strategy unaware of p vs. dynamic strategies that know p exactly. Middle: Mean utility with the learning and dynamic strategies. Right: Decrease in utility if static strategy instead of the dynamic. ($\gamma = 1$)

that the maximum search depth with the learning strategy is independent of p (by design) and essentially depends only on the ratio of the value of the searched information (normalized to one here) to the unit transmission cost e. We see that the learning strategy is an educated compromise, as expected.

Fig. 5 (middle) illustrates the resulting performance, i.e., the mean utility of a search as a function of the transmission cost e in the three cases, $p = \{10\%, 20\%, 50\%\}$. The dashed lines correspond to the performance with the learning strategy, and the solid lines to strategy that is aware of the correct value of p. We notice that the difference is negligible as soon as $p < 50\%$, or $e < 0.25$. In particular, when p is smaller than 50%, a typical search involves several nodes before the content is found, and during this time a good estimate for p becomes available, which explains the observed good performance of the learning strategy.

Static policy, included merely for comparison, cannot be expected to perform well. Fig. 5 (right) shows the difference in the expected utility when compared to the dynamic strategy. We note that the difference is considerable when the absolute values vary from zero to one.

Next we consider the performance penalty in terms of the mean utility U_n due to an unreliable return path characterized by the parameter γ. Fig. 6 illustrates the equivalue contours of the utility in the ideal case with $\gamma = 1$ (solid lines) against the setting where $\gamma = 0.7$ (dashes lines). We can observe that the performance deteriorates when links become unreliable (e.g., due to mobility), but, at least with $\gamma = 0.7$, the performance loss is reasonable given the search algorithm takes γ into account. This suggests that a well executed search makes sense also in low to moderate mobility scenarios corresponding to $\gamma = 0.7$.

5.2 Partial information: Continuous case

Let us then consider the case where nodes can provide good but incomplete answers to a query. We study the static search strategies where the search depth is fixed to n. That is, the query is forwarded to the distance of n, and then the best response found is returned along the same path back to the source (with $\gamma = 1$). The utility of such a search was $\max\{V_1, \ldots, V_n\} - 2ne$. We consider the following two value distributions discussed already in Section 4.2:

- Uniformly distributed values, $V_i \sim U(0, 1)$

- Exponentially distributed values, $V_i \sim \text{Exp}(2)$

Note that $E[V_i] = 0.5$ in both cases.

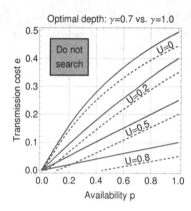

Figure 6: Equivalue curves for the utility U_{n^*} with the dynamic strategy when $\gamma = 1$ (solid lines) and $\gamma = 0.7$ (dashed lines).

Fig. 7 (left) depicts the optimal search depth n^* as the function of the unit transmission cost e. We can see that as $e \to 0$, the optimal search depth goes again to infinity, as expected. With exponential distribution, the value of the response is not limited and the optimal search depth n^* is somewhat higher than with the uniform distribution. We also note that as $e > 1/4$, i.e., when $2e > E[V_1]$, the cost of a transmission is too expensive and one should search only the "own pockets", $n^* = 0$.

Fig. 7 (right) depicts the mean utility with the optimal search strategies. We can see that with the finite valued distribution, $V_i \sim U(0, 1)$, the utility converges to 1 as the transmission cost goes to zero, $e \to 0$. In contrast, with $V_i \sim \text{Exp}(2)$ the utility is unbounded in this limit. In general, the shapes are similar to the Bernoulli cases depicted in Fig. 5.

5.3 Dynamic strategy with partial information

Finally, we assume that a response to a query may have four different values: no information (0), related (1), good response (2) and a perfect answer (3). In particular, we assume discrete values $V_i \sim U(0, 3)$, i.e., V_i obtains values $0, 1, 2, 3$ uniformly in random. As explained in Section 4.1.2, in this case we can determine the optimal dynamic search strategy (*Dynamic*). This is a sophisticated strategy that may return also with partial information. As reference strategies, we consider also the *static* strategy that searches always n nodes and returns the maximum response

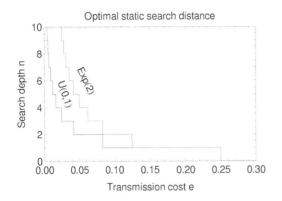

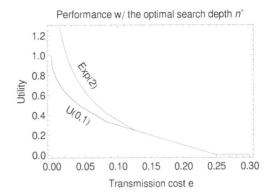

Figure 7: Optimal search depth n* with static strategies for two continuous value distributions.

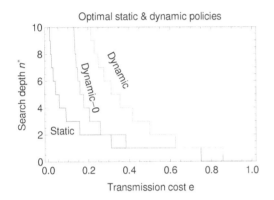

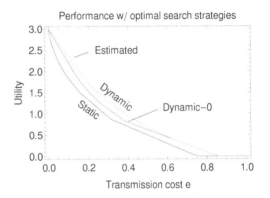

Figure 8: Optimal dynamic vs. static strategy with a discrete $V_i \sim U(0,3)$.

found (even if zero value), and the *Dynamic-0* strategy that returns immediately if the perfect answer has been found ($V_i = 3$) and does not send a response at all if nothing useful was found.

Fig. 8(left) illustrates the resulting optimal strategies. On the x-axis is the transmission cost e, and the y-axis corresponds to the maximum search depth n^*. Note that with the optimal dynamic strategy, this depth n^* is sought (at least) if all earlier $n^* - 1$ nodes had no information, i.e., if $V_i = 0$, $i = 1, \ldots, (n-1)$. We can see that the dynamic strategies cover a wider distance than the static one (when needed), as expected. Fig. 8(right) depicts the resulting performance in terms of the mean utility per search. We can observe that the dynamic search makes sense even when e is a bit higher. The absolute gain is about the same for a quite large range of unit transmission costs e. At the limit when $e \to 0$, all schemes will search until the best possible response ($V_i = 3$) is found, i.e., at the limit $e \to 0$ all curves converge to 3. As e increases, the mean performance behaves as a convex function, until at some point $n^* \to 0$.

6. DISCUSSION

In our model, we focused on the actions that a single query takes along the search path. However, in a mobile opportunistic network, rather than a single linear path, the search (with replicated queries) can be represented as a union of several paths. Search along multiple paths may implicate two points: (i) the average distance to valuable response is likely to get shorter, (ii) each decision (i.e., to forward or not, to respond or not) is based on partial information, i.e., on what has happened along its path, whereas the state of the other search path is unknown and can only be estimated. For the former, we plan to explore the average distance, i.e., the hop count, from the searching node that the search should be expanded for the most efficient search. In this work, we have provided the optimal hop count using the theoretical formalism along with several simplifications. In our future work, we would like to focus on a more relaxed scenario, e.g., realistic mobility models, and discover the optimal hop count by the help of simulations. For the latter, each node on the search path can use its observations of the network as in [9] (e.g., the number of nodes that has received the search packet and possibility of a response) to predict the state of the search, e.g., utility.

Note that a static strategy with a multiple concurrent search paths (returning a response at the end of each path) has the same cost as in the case of a single path. Thus, also in this case one needs to solve max $\{V_1, \ldots, V_{n_1+\ldots+n_k}\}$ − $2ne$. Obviously, if $P\{V_i = 0\}$ is non-negligible, declining from returning a response with a zero value improves the performance with multiple search paths more than with a single (longer) search path. The mean response time also becomes shorter due to the parallel operation. In any case, the analysis of multipath search needs further investigations.

Additionally, we plan to study models with unequal transmissions costs; e_{fwd} for query and e_{back} for the response. For longer paths, we need to consider also alternative return paths that may take "shortcuts" as the response knows which nodes *were* the closest to the origin initially.

7. CONCLUSIONS

Forwarding packets in a meaningful manner in opportunistic networks is not an easy task. The basic routing schemes such as the plain flooding and the *spray and wait* algorithm [11] try to solve the one directional problem of sending information from a source to a particular destination. In our case, the setting is significantly more challenging because (i) we do not know who has the information, and (ii) the searched content must be delivered back to the searching node. The important contribution of this paper is the analytical treatment of the "self-guiding" search process in wireless ad-hoc networks, where the query takes actions based on its *a priori* information and the observations made during the search. In many cases, we were able to characterize the optimal search strategy that maximizes the expected utility. Despite of the shortcomings of our simplified models, we believe that the similar principles as studied in this paper can be also applied in practice in a more complete setting. In our future work, we will include to the model more realism by adding the option to replicate the query, where the additional challenge comes from the distributed decision making.

Acknowledgements

This work was supported by the Academy of Finland in the PDP project (grant no. 260014).

8. REFERENCES

[1] Aruna Balasubramanian, Brian Levine, and Arun Venkataramani. DTN routing as a resource allocation problem. *ACM SIGCOMM Computer Communication Review*, 37(4):373–384, 2007.

[2] Suzan Bayhan, Esa Hyytiä, Jussi Kangasharju, and Jörg Ott. Seeker-assisted information search in mobile clouds. In *Proc. of the Second ACM SIGCOMM Workshop on Mobile Cloud Computing*, MCC '13, 2013.

[3] Alberto Dainotti, Claudio Squarcella, Emile Aben, Kimberly C Claffy, Marco Chiesa, Michele Russo, and Antonio Pescapé. Analysis of country-wide internet outages caused by censorship. In *Proc. of the ACM SIGCOMM conference on Internet measurement*, pages 1–18, 2011.

[4] K. Fall and S. Farrell. DTN: an architectural retrospective. *IEEE Journal on Selected Areas in Communications*, 26(5):828–836, June 2008.

[5] Kevin Fall. A delay-tolerant network architecture for challenged internets. In *Proc. of conference on Applications, technologies, architectures, and protocols for computer communications*, pages 27–34, 2003.

[6] Pan Hui, Augustin Chaintreau, James Scott, Richard Gass, Jon Crowcroft, and Christophe Diot. Pocket switched networks and the consequences of human mobility in conference environments. In *ACM SIGCOMM Workshop on Delay Tolerant Networking*, 2005.

[7] Pan Hui, Jon Crowcroft, and Eiko Yoneki. Bubble Rap: Social-based forwarding in delay tolerant networks. In *Proc. of ACM MobiHoc '08*, pages 241–250, 2008.

[8] Cong Liu and Jie Wu. An optimal probabilistic forwarding protocol in delay tolerant networks. In *Proc. of ACM MobiHoc '09*, pages 105–114. ACM, 2009.

[9] Mikko Pitkänen, Teemu Karkkainen, Janico Greifenberg, and Jörg Ott. Searching for content in mobile DTNs. In *Proc. of IEEE Pervasive Computing and Communications (PerCom)*, 2009.

[10] Nishanth Sastry, D Manjunath, Karen Sollins, and Jon Crowcroft. Data delivery properties of human contact networks. *IEEE Transactions on Mobile Computing*, 10(6):868–880, 2011.

[11] Thrasyvoulos Spyropoulos, Konstantinos Psounis, and Cauligi S. Raghavendra. Spray and wait: An efficient routing scheme for intermittently connected mobile networks. In *Proceedings of the 2005 ACM SIGCOMM Workshop on Delay-tolerant Networking*, pages 252–259, 2005.

[12] Ying Zhu, Bin Xu, Xinghua Shi, and Yu Wang. A survey of social-based routing in delay tolerant networks: Positive and negative social effects. *IEEE Communications Surveys Tutorials*, 15(1):387–401, First 2013.

Duty Cycling in Opportunistic Networks: the Effect on Intercontact Times

Elisabetta Biondi, Chiara Boldrini, Marco Conti, Andrea Passarella
IIT-CNR
Pisa, Italy
first.last@iit.cnr.it

ABSTRACT

In opportunistic networks, putting devices in energy saving mode is crucial to preserve their battery, and hence to increase the lifetime of the network and to foster user cooperation. However, a side effect of duty cycling is to reduce the number of usable contacts for delivering messages, thus increasing intercontact times and delays. In order to understand the effect of duty cycling in opportunistic networks, in this paper we propose a general model for deriving the pairwise intercontact times when a duty cycling policy is superimposed on the original encounter process determined only by node mobility. Then, we specialise this model when the original intercontact times are exponential (an assumption popular in the literature), and we show that, in this case, the intercontact times measured after duty cycling are, approximately, again exponential, but with a rate proportional to the inverse of the duty cycle.

Categories and Subject Descriptors

C.2.1 [**Computer-Communication Networks**]: Network Architecture and Design—*Wireless Communication*

Keywords

intercontact times; duty cycling; opportunistic networks

1. INTRODUCTION

The widespread availability of smart, handheld devices like smartphones and tablet has stimulated the discussion and research about the possibility of extending the communication opportunities between users. Particularly appealing, towards this direction, is the opportunistic networking paradigm (both as a standalone solution and in synergy with the infrastructure in mobile data offloading scenarios [12]), in which messages arrive to their final destination through consecutive pairwise exchanges between users that are in radio contact with each other. Thus, user mobility, and especially user encounters, are the key enablers of opportunistic communications. Unfortunately, ad hoc communications

tend to be very energy hungry [4] and no user will be willing to participate in an opportunistic network if they risk to see their battery drained in a few hours.

Energy issues in opportunistic networks have still to be fully addressed. In particular, there are very few contributions that study how power saving mechanisms impact on the amount of contacts that can be exploited to relay messages. With duty cycling, messages can be exchanged only when two nodes are in one-hop radio range *and* they're both in the active state of the duty cycle. So, power saving effectively reduces forwarding opportunities, because contacts are missed when at least one of the devices is in a low-energy state that does not allow it to detect the contact. Since some contacts are missed, the measured intercontact times, defined as the time interval between two consecutive *detected* encounters between the same pair of nodes, is, in general, larger and this clearly affects the delay experienced by messages. So far, this aspect (i.e., the fact that duty cycling can affect the detected pairwise contacts) has been largely ignored in the literature, despite the fact that all popular off-the-shelf wireless technologies (e.g., WiFi, Bluetooth) already implement some sort of periodic contact probing.

The goal of this work is to understand how the exploitable mobility, i.e., the amount of contacts that can be used by node pairs for communicating, is modified by the duty cycling policy. To this aim, the contribution of this paper is twofold. First, we derive an analytical model of the measured intercontact times between nodes *after* duty cycling is factored in, i.e., by taking into account that some contacts may be missed. While deriving a closed-form characterisation of the detected intercontact times is in general too complex from an analytical standpoint, this model can be used to compute numerically their first two moments. As it is well-known, this is sufficient to approximate the distribution of the detected intercontact times using hyper- or hypo- exponential distributions, using standard techniques [9]. Thus, with this model, we are able to obtain an approximated representation of intercontact times measured when a duty cycling policy is in place under virtually any distribution.

The second contribution of the paper is the solution to the above model for the case of exponential intercontact times, which is a popular assumption in the related literature [6, 7] (even if a general consensus on which is the best distribution for representing realistic intercontact times has yet to be achieved). With exponential intercontact times, the proposed model can be solved approximately in closed form and, under a specific condition that we derive, *the detected intercontact times are still exponential, but with a rate pro-*

portional to the inverse of the duty cycle. This result tells us that models (e.g., of the delay [3, 7]) that assume exponential intercontact times (which are typically tractable and thus very popular in the literature) can still be used when a duty cycling policy is in place, since the original rates are scaled proportionally to the inverse of the duty cycle[1].

2. PROBLEM STATEMENT

We use duty cycling in a general sense here, meaning any power saving mechanism that hinders the possibility of a continuous scan of the devices in the neighbourhood. We assume that nodes alternate between the ON and OFF states. In the ON state, nodes are able to detect contacts with other devices. In the OFF state (which may correspond to a low-power state or simply to a state in which devices are switched off) contacts with other devices are missed. In this work we consider a duty cycling policy in which the duration of the ON and OFF states is fixed[2] and we abstract from the specific wireless technology used for pairwise communications. We assume that the duty cycle process and the contact process are independent and, considering a tagged node pair, we denote with τ the length of the time interval in which both nodes are ON, and with T the period of the duty cycle. Thus, $T - \tau$ corresponds to the duration of the OFF interval and $\Delta = \frac{\tau}{T}$ is the actual duty cycle (i.e., the percentage of time nodes are in the ON state). We specifically assume that ON and OFF intervals are *coarsely* synchronised across nodes, such that all nodes stay active only for a portion of time equal to Δ while still having the opportunity to detect all the other nodes during ON intervals[3]. We assume that the ON interval can start anywhere within T and we denote its starting time with s_0 (for convenience of notation, we count duty cycles starting from the first one in which a contact is detected). Then, $s_1 = s_0 + \tau$ denotes the time instant at which the ON interval ends. Hence, ON intervals will be of type $[s_0 + iT, s_1 + iT]$, with $i \geq 0$ and OFF intervals of type $[s_1 + iT, s_0 + (i+1)T]$, with $i \geq 0$. Focusing on a tagged node pair, we can represent how the duty cycle function evolves with time as in Equation 1:

$$d(t) = \begin{cases} 1 & \text{if } t \bmod T \in [s_0, s_1) \\ 0 & \text{otherwise.} \end{cases} \qquad (1)$$

When $d(t) = 1$, both nodes are ON, thus their contacts, if any, are detected. The opposite holds when $d(t) = 0$. Basically, $d(t)$ operates a bandpass filtering on the contact process between a pair of nodes.

Function d determines the way contacts are discovered. In the following, to make the analysis more tractable, we

<hr>

[1]For example, in [1] we have exploited this result for investigating how to optimally configure the duty cycling process in order to meet a target performance metric.

[2]It has been shown in [11] that, under certain conditions, this strategy is optimal for minimising the probability of missing a contact. However, please note that designing an effective duty cycling scheme is out of the scope of this paper, which focuses only on the effects of duty cycling on intercontact times.

[3]Fine grained synchronisation is not necessary to this end, and time drifts due to clock inaccuracies are perfectly tolerable. For example, in the case of mobile offloading – one of the most popular recent applications of opportunistic networks [12] – this synchronisation can be controlled by the cellular infrastructure.

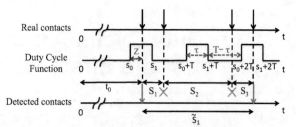

Figure 1: Contact process with duty cycling

assume that a contact event is detected only if it starts during an ON period. This assumption is reasonable when the duration of a contact is much smaller than the duration of the OFF interval. In fact, in this case the probability of the contact lasting until the next ON interval is negligible. In real contact datasets (see, e.g., [5] or those considered in Section 3.2) the contact duration is in the order of tens of seconds for the majority of samples. In [5], for example, more than 50% of contact duration samples are smaller than $48s$. Since Trifunovic et al. [10] have derived that, with Bluetooth and WiFi, scanning intervals greater that $100s$ perform significantly better energy-wise, the above assumption can be considered reasonable[4].

We now focus on the contact process. Similarly to the related literature [7, 3], we assume that, from the mobility standpoint, node pairs are independent and that the contact process of each pair can be described as a renewal process. We denote the time between the $(i-1)$-th and i-th contacts as S_i. By definition of renewal process, the intercontact times S_i between a given pair of nodes are independent and identically distributed (while they can follow different distributions for different pairs), hence $S_i \sim S$, for all i.

In order to understand how the *detected* contact process depends on the contact process described above, let us denote with $\tilde{S}_j$ the time between the $(j-1)$-th and the j-th detected contact and assume that at time t_{j-1} a contact has been detected, as shown in Figure 1 for case $j = 1$. Then, the detected intercontact time $\tilde{S}_j$ is the time from t_{j-1} until the next detected contact, which can be obtained by adding up the intercontact times S_i between t_{j-1} and the next detected contact. Denoting with N_j the random variable measuring the number of intercontact times between the $(j-1)$-th and the j-th detected contact, we obtain $\tilde{S}_j = \sum_{i=1}^{N_j} S_i$. Recalling that S_i are i.i.d. by definition, if N_j were i.i.d. for all j and independent of the inter-contact times S_i occurred before the $(j-1)$-th detected contact, then also $\tilde{S}_j$ would be i.i.d. and the detected contact process could be treated as a renewal process. Unfortunately, it is possible to prove (see [2]) that this is not true in the general case. In particular, N_j depends on $\tilde{Z}_{j-1}$, defined as the displacement of the last detected contact in its ON interval (hence it can take values in $[0, \tau)$, see Figure 1) and $\tilde{Z}_{j-1}$ depends on $\tilde{Z}_{j-2}$ (the displacement of the second last detected contact). Since $\tilde{Z}_j$ are not independent, N_j is not i.i.d. and the detected contact process is, in general, not renewal. However, for the particularly relevant case where intercontact times S_j are exponential, which we develop in detail in the paper, we

<hr>

[4]For scenarios in which this assumption does not hold, the results presented in this paper provide a lower bound for the detected intercontact times, since when contact duration is considered, the probability of detecting a contact under a fixed duty cycling policy increases.

show that $\tilde{Z}_j$ are i.i.d. and independent of the past evolution of all stochastic processes. Therefore, in this case, the detected intercontact times are a renewal process. For making the analysis tractable, we assume that the same property holds in general. This is a reasonable approximation under the assumption that ON intervals are very short compared to the average intercontact times $E[S]$, which, as discussed later in the paper, is commonly verified in practice. Therefore, in the following we express $\tilde{S}$ as a random sum of i.i.d. random variables, according to the following definition.

DEFINITION 1. *The detected intercontact time $\tilde{S}$ can be obtained as $\tilde{S} = \sum_{i=1}^{N} S_i$, where N is the random variable describing the number of contacts needed to get one detected.*

Random sums of i.i.d. variables have some useful properties, which we will exploit in Section 3.2 in order to derive the first two moments of $\tilde{S}$. Please also note that Definition 1 is general, i.e., holds for any type of continuous intercontact time distribution and for any type of duty cycling policy.

3. THE DUTY CYCLING EFFECT ON INTERCONTACT TIMES

In the next sections, building upon Definition 1, we show how the duty cycling model and the contact process can be studied together in order to uncover the features of the detected intercontact times.

3.1 Deriving the distribution of N

We start by studying the probability distribution of N, defined as the number of contacts needed, after a detected contact, in order to catch the next one. We first discuss the case in which real intercontact times feature a generic distribution with PDF $f(x)$ and CDF $F(x)$, then we solve the case of exponential intercontact times. Recall that we are assuming the detected contact process to be renewal, so we focus on the portion of this process between two detected contacts. Under the renewal assumption, we can focus, without loss of generality, on what happens between the first and second detected contact. Then, the rationale behind the derivation of N is pretty intuitive. In fact, $N = 1$ corresponds to the case where the first intercontact time after a detection ends in an ON interval. For case $N = 2$, the first intercontact ends in an OFF interval, while the following one ends in an ON interval *after* the point in time where the first intercontact time has finished. All other cases follow using the same line of reasoning (for example, Figure 1 depicts a case where N=3). Please note that in the following, ON and OFF intervals will be denoted with $\mathcal{I}^{ON}$ and $\mathcal{I}^{OFF}$, respectively.

The derivation of the PMF of N in Theorem 1 below quantifies the probability $P(N = k)$. The line of reasoning for deriving this result is as follows (see Figure 2 for a graphical representation). We denote with $\tilde{X}_0$ the time of the last detected contact and we fix $\tilde{X}_0 = t_0$. Let us thus focus on the sequence of contacts after t_0 and define random variable E_k, which is equal to one when the k-th of these contacts is in an ON interval, equal to zero otherwise. It is easy to see that the following holds true:

$$P\left(N = k | \tilde{X}_0 = t_0\right) = P\left(E_1 = 0, ..., E_{k-1} = 0, E_k = 1\right), \quad (2)$$

i.e., the k-th contact is the first contact detected after t_0 if it falls into an ON interval and all previous ones fall in an

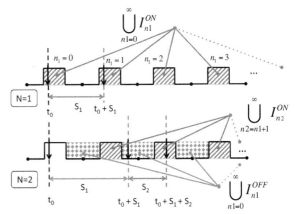

Figure 2: Example for case $N = 1$ and $N = 2$

OFF interval.. In the following we will study cases $N = 1$ and $N = 2$, then $N = k$ follows by analogy.

Let us start with $N = 1$. The above Equation 2 becomes $P(N = 1 | \tilde{X}_0 = t_0) = P(E_1 = 1)$, which is equivalent to saying that the first intercontact time has to finish in any of the ON intervals after t_0. From Figure 2, we see that this happens when $S_1 + t_0 \in \cup_{n_1=0}^{\infty} \mathcal{I}_{n_1}^{ON}$, where $\cup$ denotes the union operator and n_1 the interval in which the first contact takes place. The probability of this event is given by the sum of the probability that $S_1 + t_0 \in \mathcal{I}_{n_1}^{ON}$, for all $n_1 \geq 0$. Any ON interval after t_0 is in the form $[s_0 + n_1 T, s_1 + n_1 T)$. Therefore, recalling that $F(x)$ is the CDF of intercontact times, the probability that $S_1 + t_0 \in \mathcal{I}_{n_1}^{ON}$ for each n_1 is given by $F(s_1 + n_1 T - t_0) - F(s_0 + n_1 T - t_0)$. Then, denoting the latter as $p_{n_1}(t_0)$ and summing over all n_1 we obtain $P(N = 1 | \tilde{X}_0 = t_0) = \sum_{n_1=0}^{\infty} p_{n_1}(t_0)$.

Let us now consider the case $N = 2$. It occurs when the first contact happens during an OFF interval and the second contact during an ON interval, i.e., it occurs with probability $P(E_1 = 0, E_2 = 1)$ (Figure 2). The two events are dependent, since the second contact is constrained to start after the first one. Exploiting the knowledge on the contact process (Figure 2) and denoting with n_1 the interval in which the first contact after t_0 falls and with n_2 the interval in which the second contact happens, we can rewrite the above equation as follows:

$$P\left(S_2 + S_1 + t_0 \in \cup_{n_2=n_1+1}^{\infty} \mathcal{I}_{n_2}^{ON}, S_1 + t_0 \in \cup_{n_1=0}^{\infty} \mathcal{I}_{n_1}^{OFF}\right). \quad (3)$$

We condition on the event $\{S_1 = y_1\}$ and then apply the law of total probability, obtaining $\int_0^{\infty} P(S_1 = y_1) \cdot P(S_2 + y_1 + t_0 \in \cup_{n_2=n_1+1}^{\infty} \mathcal{I}_{n_2}^{ON}, y_1 + t_0 \in \cup_{n_1=0}^{\infty} \mathcal{I}_{n_1}^{OFF}) dy_1$. The event $\{S_2 + y_1 + t_0 \in \cup_{n_2=n_1+1}^{\infty} \mathcal{I}_{n_2}^{ON}, y_1 + t_0 \in \cup_{n_1=0}^{\infty} \mathcal{I}_{n_1}^{ON}\}$ happens with the same probability of event $\{S_2 + y_1 + t_0 \in \cup_{n_2=n_1+1}^{\infty} \mathcal{I}_{n_2}^{ON}\}$ if $y_1 + t_0$ falls in one of the OFF intervals after t_0, and with probability 0 otherwise. Therefore, after noting that OFF intervals in which the first contact takes place are of type $[s_1 + n_1 T, s_0 + (n_1 + 1)T)$, Equation 3 can be rewritten as follows:

$$\sum_{n_1=0}^{\infty} \int_{s_1+n_1 T - t_0}^{s_0+(n_1+1)T - t_0} P(S_1 = y_1) \cdot P\left(S_2 + y_1 + t_0 \in \cup_{n_2=n_1+1}^{\infty} \mathcal{I}_{n_2}^{ON}\right) dy_1. \quad (4)$$

We now characterise $P(S_2 + y_1 + t_0 \in \cup_{n_2=n_1+1}^{\infty} \mathcal{I}_{n_2}^{ON})$. The probability of the event $\{S_2 + y_1 + t_0 \in \cup_{n_2=n_1+1}^{\infty} \mathcal{I}_{n_2}^{ON}\}$ can be computed following the same line of reasoning used for deriving $P(N = 1)$. Thus, after defining $p_{n_k}(t) \triangleq F(s_1 + n_k T - t) - F(s_0 + n_k T - t)$, we can write $P(S_2 + y_1 + t_0 \in$

$\cup_{n_2=n_1+1}^{\infty} \mathcal{I}_{n_2}^{ON}$) as $\sum_{n_2=n_1+1}^{\infty} p_{n_2}(t_0 + y_1)$. Please note that this expression has the same form as the one for $N = 1$ after considering that the second contact is constrained to start after the first one (hence, n_2 starts from n_1+1 and the starting time for S_2 is $t_0 + y_1$). After simple substitutions, we obtain that $P(N = 2|\tilde{X}_0)$ is given by the following:

$$\sum_{n_1=0}^{\infty} \int_{s_1+n_1T-t_0}^{s_0+(n_1+1)T-t_0} f(y_1) \sum_{n_2=n_1+1}^{\infty} p_{n_2}(t_0 + y_1)dy_1. \quad (5)$$

Then, the derivation of the general case $N = k$ follows the same line of reasoning and it is discussed in the proof of Theorem 1 below.

Now that we have fully characterised $P(N = k|\tilde{X}_0 = t_0)$ we can obtain $P(N = k)$ by simply deconditioning, i.e., applying the law of total probability. To this aim, we can write $\tilde{X}_0 = s_0 + \tilde{Z}$, where $\tilde{Z}$, as discussed in Section 2, represents the displacement within the ON interval and it is assumed to feature the same distribution for all detected contacts. Knowing the distribution of $\tilde{Z}$, one can easily derive that of $\tilde{X}_0$. The modelling of $\tilde{Z}$ should be evaluated on a case-by-base basis, depending on the actual distribution of intercontact times. An approximation that holds in the vast majority of real scenarios is discussed in the proof of Theorem 1 below.

Now we can finally state Theorem 1, which characterises the PMF of N.

THEOREM 1 (DISTRIBUTION OF N). When $E[S] \gg T$, the probability mass function of N can be approximated by the following:

$$P(N = k) = \int_{s_0}^{s_1} f_{\tilde{X}_0}(t_0)P\{N = k|\tilde{X}_0 = t_0\}dt_0, \quad (6)$$

where $\tilde{X}_0 = s_0 + \tilde{Z}$ characterises the time instant of the last detected contact and, defining $p_{n_k}(t) \triangleq F(s_1 + n_kT - t) - F(s_0 + n_kT - t)$, the following holds:

$$P(N = 1|\tilde{X}_0 = t_0) = \sum_{n_1=0}^{\infty} p_{n_1}(t_0) \quad (7)$$

$$P(N = 2|\tilde{X}_0 = t_0) =$$
$$= \sum_{n_1=0}^{\infty} \int_{s_1+n_1T-t_0}^{s_0+(n_1+1)T-t_0} f(y_1) \sum_{n_2=n_1+1}^{\infty} p_{n_2}(t_0 + y_1)dy_1$$
$$(8)$$

$$\vdots$$

$$P(N = k|\tilde{X}_0 = t_0) = \sum_{n_1=0}^{\infty} \cdots \sum_{n_k=n_{k-1}+1}^{\infty} \int_{s_1+n_1T-t_0}^{s_0+(n_1+1)T-t_0} f(y_1) \cdot$$
$$\cdots \int_{s_1+n_{k-1}T-t_0-\sum_{i=1}^{k-2} y_i}^{s_0+(n_{k-1}+1)T-t_0-\sum_{i=1}^{k-2} y_i} f(y_{k-1}) \cdot$$
$$\cdot p_{n_k}(t_0 + \sum_{i=1}^{k-1} y_i)dy_{k-1}\ldots dy_1. \quad (9)$$

PROOF. Cases $N = 1$ and $N = 2$ have been discussed above and will not be further considered. As anticipated, the derivation for case $N = k$ with $k > 2$ follows the same line of reasoning of the previous cases. The only difference is that, for $N = k$ ($k > 2$), in order to make the analysis tractable, we need to introduce an approximation. Specifically, we neglect the case of two consecutive contacts falling in the same OFF interval. This choice is justified by a property that holds in the vast majority of real scenarios, i.e., that

the average duration of the real intercontact times is much larger than the duty cycling period (i.e., $E[S] \gg T$). The implication of this property is that the probability of having two consecutive real contacts in the same OFF interval is very low, hence negligible. When this property holds, it is possible to simplify Equation 6. Since $\tilde{X}_0 = s_0 + \tilde{Z}$, with Equation 6 we are taking into account the effect of the displacement $\tilde{Z}$ on N. However, we know that $\tilde{Z}$ varies in $[0, \tau)$, while $E[S] \gg T$ also implies $E[S] \gg \tau$. Then, consider for the sake of simplicity case $N = 1$ (the same line of reasoning applies to all other cases), which corresponds to $P(S_1 + \tilde{X}_0 \in \cup_{n_1=0}^{\infty} \mathcal{I}_{n_1}^{ON})$. We can rewrite it as $P(S_1 + s_0 + \tilde{Z} \in \cup_{n_1=0}^{\infty} \mathcal{I}_{n_1}^{ON})$. However, since $E[S_1] \gg E[\tilde{Z}]$, we can assume that $\tilde{Z}$ is negligible. Hence, $P(N = k)$ can be simply obtained from Equation 7-9 after setting t_0 equal to an arbitrary point in $[s_0, s_1)$, e.g., $t_0 = s_0$. $\square$

Theorem 1 provides an accurate approximation of the PMF of N when the probability of two undetected contacts falling in the same OFF interval is very low. In Section 3.2 we show that the condition under which this assumption is reasonable is satisfied by the most popular traces of human contacts. Despite this approximation, finding a closed form for the distribution of N in Theorem 1 might be prohibitive in the general case, and we have been able to obtain only numerical solutions. However, when intercontact times are exponential, a closed form solution for the PMF of N is available (Corollary 1 below, whose proof can be found in [2]), from which the first two moments of N can be computed using standard probability theory.

COROLLARY 1 (N IN THE EXPONENTIAL CASE). When real intercontact times S_i for a tagged node pair are exponential[5] with rate λ, the probability density of N is given by:

$$\begin{cases} P\{N = 1\} = 1 + \frac{e^{-\lambda\tau}-1}{\lambda\tau} + \frac{e^{\lambda\tau}(1-e^{-\lambda\tau})^2}{\lambda\tau(e^{\lambda T}-1)} \\ P\{N = k\} = e^{\lambda\tau} \frac{(1-e^{-\lambda\tau})^2}{\lambda\tau(1-e^{-\lambda T})} \left[\frac{\lambda(T-\tau)}{e^{\lambda T}-1}\right]^{k-1}, \quad k \geq 2 \end{cases}$$
$$(10)$$

Please note that condition $E[S] \gg T$, required by Theorem 1, in the exponential case of Corollary 1 becomes $\lambda T \ll 1$. In [2] we have verified analytically the error introduced by this approximation.

3.2 Deriving $\tilde{S}$

Exploiting the results in the previous section, here we discuss how to compute the first and second moment of the detected intercontact time $\tilde{S}$ for a generic node pair A, B. The relation between S and $\tilde{S}$ is stated by Definition 1, i.e., $\tilde{S} = \sum_{i=1}^{N} S_i$. Thus, $\tilde{S}$ is a random sum of random variables, and we can exploit well-known properties to compute its first and second moment (in [2] we also specialise this result for the exponential case).

PROPOSITION 1. The first and second moment of $\tilde{S}$ are given by $E[\tilde{S}] = E[N]E[S]$ and $E[\tilde{S}^2] = E[N^2]E[S]^2 + E[N]E[S^2] - E[N]E[S]^2$.

While the above formula holds in general, in the case of exponential intercontact times it is possible to derive an even

---

[5]For ease of notation, for λ we omit the subscript indicating the specific node pair considered. Please note, however, that the network model we are referring to is still heterogenous.

stronger result, described in Theorem 2 below. This result is the key derivation of this work, and it tells us that, under condition $\lambda T \ll 1$, exponential intercontact times are modified by duty cycling only in terms of the parameter of their distribution but they still remain exponential.

THEOREM 2. *When $\lambda T \ll 1$, the detected intercontact times $\tilde{S}$ follow approximately an exponential distribution with rate $\lambda \Delta$.*

PROOF. We can calculate the moment generating function (MGF) of $\tilde{S}$ using the expression described at the beginning of the section, i.e., $M_{\tilde{S}}(s) = M_N(M_S(s))$. First of all, we have to calculate the MGF of N, that we can obtain from Equation 10. In fact, recalling $\tau = T\Delta$, we have

$$M_N(s) = \sum_{k=0}^{\infty} s^k \cdot P\{N = k\} =$$

$$= s\left[1 - \frac{1 - e^{-\lambda T\Delta}}{\lambda T\Delta} + e^{\lambda T\Delta}\frac{(1 - e^{-\lambda T\Delta})^2}{\lambda T\Delta(e^{\lambda T} - 1)}\right] +$$

$$+ s^2\frac{e^{\lambda T\Delta}(1 - e^{-\lambda T\Delta})^2}{\Delta(e^{\lambda T} - 1)}\frac{1 - \Delta}{e^{\lambda T} - 1 - \lambda Ts(1 - \Delta)}.$$

As we are in the hypothesis $\lambda T \ll 1$, we can use the Taylor expansion to find that $M_N(s) = s\Delta + s^2\frac{\Delta(1-\Delta)}{1-s(1-\Delta)} + o(1)$. As the MGF of an exponential distribution S is given by $M_S(s) = \frac{\lambda}{\lambda - s}$, we obtain the following:

$$M_{\tilde{S}}(s) = \frac{\lambda\Delta}{\lambda - s} + \frac{\lambda^2}{(\lambda - s)^2} \cdot \frac{\Delta(1 - \Delta)}{1 - \frac{\lambda}{\lambda - s}(1 - \Delta)} + o(1) =$$

$$= \frac{\lambda\Delta}{\lambda\Delta - s} + o(1).$$

Since the above equation corresponds, approximately, to the MGF of an exponential random variable with rate $\lambda\Delta$, we conclude that $\tilde{S}$ can be approximated as an exponential random variable with rate $\lambda\Delta$. A longer version of this proof is provided in [2]. □

In order to validate the assumption $\lambda T \ll 1$, we consider four popular datasets often used in the related literature (and publicly available at http://crawdad.cs.dartmouth.edu/): Infocom05, Infocom06, RollerNet, and Reality Mining . The average contact rates estimated from these traces are, respectively, $3.2\cdot10^{-4}s^{-1}$, $1.13\cdot10^{-4}s^{-1}$, $4.07\cdot10^{-3}s^{-1}$, and $1.2\cdot10^{-6}s^{-1}$. Thus, considering T values around $100s$, identified in [10] as a good trade-off between energy efficient and accuracy in contact detection, λT remains below 1 for all these datasets.

4. RELATED WORK

In the literature, the works closest to ours are [13] [8]. Our contribution is more general than [13] as it is not bound to the RWP model but it can be applied to any well known distribution for intercontact times, if numerical solutions are sufficient, or it can be solved in closed form for the heterogenous exponential case. Moreover, despite its simplicity, our duty cycling function with ON/OFF states allows for more flexibility than the simple scanning every T seconds, as done in [13]. Qin et al. [8] perform a study that is exactly orthogonal to this work. In fact, they evaluate how link duration (or contact duration, in our terminology) is affected by the contact probing interval. We investigate the effect of duty cycling (which, as already discussed, can be easily translated into a contact probing problem) on the intercontact time rather than on the contact time. The motivation

for this choice is that intercontact times are typically much larger than contact times in real human mobility, thus the delay in opportunistic networks is mainly determined by the intercontact time. Intercontact times are larger when contacts are not detected immediately or missed and thus it is important to understand how they increase and how this affects the delay experienced by messages.

5. CONCLUSIONS

In this work we have investigated the effects of duty cycling on intercontact times, delay, and energy consumption in opportunistic networks. To the best of our knowledge, this is the first contribution that evaluates the actual effects of duty cycling on the forwarding opportunities between nodes. To this aim, we have provided a general formula for the derivation of the intercontact times under duty cycling, and we have specialised this formula obtaining a closed-form expression for the case of exponential intercontact times. Surprisingly enough, under condition $\lambda T \ll 1$ (satisfied by most popular contact datasets), the intercontact times after duty cycling can be approximated as exponentially distributed with a rate scaled by a factor $\frac{1}{\Delta}$.

6. ACKNOWLEDGMENTS

This work was partially funded by the European Commission under the EINS (FP7-FIRE 288021), MOTO (FP7 317959), and EIT ICT Labs MOSES (Business Plan 2014) projects.

7. REFERENCES

[1] E. Biondi, C. Boldrini, A. Passarella, and M. Conti. Optimal duty cycling in mobile opportunistic networks with end-to-end delay guarantees. In *European Wireless*, pages 1–6, 2014.

[2] E. Biondi, C. Boldrini, A. Passarella, and M. Conti. Duty cycling in opportunistic networks: intercontact times and energy-delay tradeoff. Technical report, IIT-CNR 2013, http://cnd.iit.cnr.it/chiara/pub/techrep/mswim14_tr.pdf.

[3] C. Boldrini, M. Conti, and A. Passarella. Performance modelling of opportunistic forwarding under heterogenous mobility. *Computer Communications*, 48:56–70, 2014.

[4] R. Friedman, A. Kogan, and Y. Krivolapov. On power and throughput tradeoffs of wifi and bluetooth in smartphones. *IEEE Trans. on Mob. Comp.*, 12(7):1363–1376, 2013.

[5] S. Gaito, E. Pagani, and G. P. Rossi. Strangers help friends to communicate in opportunistic networks. *Computer Networks*, 55(2):374–385, 2011.

[6] W. Gao and G. Cao. User-centric data dissemination in disruption tolerant networks. In *IEEE INFOCOM*, pages 3119–3127, 2011.

[7] A. Picu, T. Spyropoulos, and T. Hossmann. An analysis of the information spreading delay in heterogeneous mobility DTNs. In *IEEE WoWMoM'12*, pages 1–10. IEEE, 2012.

[8] S. Qin, G. Feng, and Y. Zhang. How the contact-probing mechanism affects the transmission capacity of delay-tolerant networks. *IEEE Trans. on Vehic.Tech.*, 60(4):1825–1834, 2011.

[9] H. Tijms and J. Wiley. *A first course in stochastic models*, volume 2. Wiley Online Library, 2003.

[10] S. Trifunovic, A. Picu, T. Hossmann, and K. A. Hummel. Slicing the battery pie: fair and efficient energy usage in device-to-device communication via role switching. In *ACM CHANTS'13*, pages 31–36, 2013.

[11] W. Wang, V. Srinivasan, and M. Motani. Adaptive contact probing mechanisms for delay tolerant applications. In *ACM MobiCom'07*, pages 230–241, 2007.

[12] J. Whitbeck, Y. Lopez, J. Leguay, V. Conan, and M. D. De Amorim. Push-and-track: Saving infrastructure bandwidth through opportunistic forwarding. *Pervasive and Mobile Computing*, 8(5):682–697, 2012.

[13] H. Zhou, H. Zheng, J. Wu, and J. Chen. Energy-efficient contact probing in opportunistic mobile networks. In *IEEE ICCCN'13*, 2013.

A Simple Method for the Deployment of Wireless Sensors to Ensure Full Coverage of an Irregular Area with Obstacles*

Ines Khoufi
Inria Rocquencourt
78153 Le Chesnay Cedex
France
ines.khoufi@inria.fr

Pascale Minet
Inria Rocquencourt
78153 Le Chesnay Cedex
France
pascale.minet@inria.fr

Anis Laouiti
TELECOM SudParis
CNRS Samovar UMR 5157
91011 Evry Cedex, France
anis.laouiti@telecom-sudparis.eu

Erwan Livolant
Inria Rocquencourt
78153 Le Chesnay Cedex
France
erwan.livolant@inria.fr

ABSTRACT

In this paper, we focus on the deployment of wireless sensor nodes in an arbitrary realistic area with an irregular shape, and with the presence of obstacles that may be opaque. Moreover, we propose a simple projection-based method that tends to minimize the number of sensor nodes needed to fully cover such an area. This method starts with the optimal uniform deployment based on the triangular tessellation encompassing the whole area. Then, it projects some external sensor nodes on the border to ensure full coverage and connectivity. We show that this method outperforms the contour-based one using various types of irregular areas.

Categories and Subject Descriptors

C.2.1 [**Computer-Communication Networks**]: Network Architecture and Design—*Wireless communication*

General Terms

Algorithms, Design, Performance

Keywords

Wireless Sensor Network; Deployment algorithm; Full coverage; Area with irregular shape; Opaque obstacle; Hidden zone

---

*This work has been partly funded by the Cluster Connexion.

1. MOTIVATION

We are witnessing the deployment of many wireless sensor networks in various application domains such as pollution detection in the environment, intruder detection at home, preventive maintenance in industrial process, monitoring of a temporary industrial worksite, damage assessment after a disaster, etc. Many of these applications require the full coverage of the area considered. With the full coverage of the area, any event occurring in this area is detected by at least one sensor node. In addition, the connectivity ensures that this event is reported to the sink in charge of analyzing the data gathered from the sensors and acting according to these data.

Depending on the application targeted, and for optimality reasons, we may require a uniform deployment to fully cover such an area with a minimum number of wireless sensors. Although optimal uniform wireless sensor network deployment is a key factor for minimizing the overall cost of a wireless sensor network, it may not be accomplished in many cases. In fact the shape of the area to cover, the possible presence of obstacles within this area as well as their properties (shape, opaque or transparent to sensing range, etc) may prevent the deployment of a uniform wireless sensor network. These constraints must be considered when designing a deployment algorithm in order to reach an acceptable deployment.

Examples of applications where wireless sensor networks have proved their efficiency include monitoring of a temporary industrial worksite, damage assessment after a disaster, precision farming, intruder detection in a warehouse, health monitoring of a building. In all these cases, 2D coverage is sufficient to meet the applications requirements. Furthermore, the area to cover has an irregular shape with many edges and is not necessarily convex and may include several obstacles.

In the literature, many studies assume that this area is rectangular and adopt the classical deployment which is based on the triangular lattice that has been proved optimal [1]. In real life, things are more complex. Moreover, few papers take obstacles into account. Those that do assume that obstacles are constituted by a juxtaposition of rectangles that seems an unrealistic assumption. In real deployments, the shape of obstacles may be irregular. Like in [2], we distinguish two types of obstacles: the transparent ones like ponds in outdoor environment, or tables in an indoor site that only prevent the location of sensor nodes inside them; whereas the opaque obstacles like walls or trees prevent the sensing by causing the existence of hidden zones behind them: such zones may remain uncovered, as illustrated in Figure 1. Authors in [3] propose a solution to provide an $(1 - \epsilon)$ coverage of an area of arbitrary shape with obstacles. This solution selects some landmarks in the area and covers them. However, the boundary and the obstacles are assumed to be transparent.

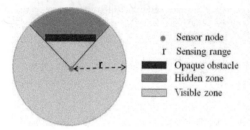

Figure 1: Hidden zone caused by an opaque obstacle.

Opaque obstacles are much more complex to handle than transparent ones and require the deployment of additional sensors to eliminate coverage holes. That is why in this paper, we focus on the deployment of wireless sensor nodes in an irregular area with obstacles that may be opaque and propose a projection-based method that tends to minimize the number of sensor nodes needed to fully cover this area. This number is smaller than the one given by the contour-based methods [4] and [5]. Our method is characterized by its simplicity. In contrast to Delaunay triangulation [6], coverage holes are intrinsically known by our method.

The method presented here computes the deployment that is given as an input to a mobile robot. This robot is in charge of placing the sensor nodes (unable to move) at the right location in the area to fully cover. The goal is to provide a deployment of a wireless sensor network assisted by a mobile robot. An additional step can be done after the deployment to collect measures on site. These measures are used as a feedback to adapt the real deployment on the given area. Notice however that in our solution all sensor nodes are needed to provide full coverage, unlike [7] where some redundant sensor nodes can be switched off.

The remaining of this paper is organized as follows. We define the problem in Section 2. In Section 3, we give a brief state of the art, recalling known results about full coverage complexity and optimal deployment. We distinguish two approaches to deal with irregular borders and obstacles: contour-based and Delaunay-Triangulation-based. We establish general bounds on the number of sensor nodes independently from the method used. We then propose our method to fully cover an area with irregular transparent borders but no obstacles in Section 5. In Section 6, we show how to take obstacles into account. In Section 7, we generalize to borders and obstacles that can be opaque. In Sections 5 to 7, we present the main principles with an illustrative example, provide a bound dependent of our method and compare the

performances of our contribution with those of a contour-based method. Finally, we conclude in Section 8.

2. PROBLEM STATEMENT

In this paper, we consider wireless sensors that must be deployed to fully cover a given 2D-area of irregular shape with the presence of several obstacles.

2.1 Goal

Our goal is to minimize the number of sensors needed to achieve the full coverage of the area given, denoted $\mathcal{A}$, while meeting the assumptions listed in Subsection 2.2. The full coverage of $\mathcal{A}$ means that any event occuring in $\mathcal{A}$ is detected by at least one sensor node. The deployment of wireless sensor nodes is computed by a single entity that takes as inputs the vertices of the polygon defining $\mathcal{A}$ the area to cover as well as for each obstacle, the vertices of its polygon.

2.2 Models

For that purpose, we adopt the following models:
• The wireless sensors are assumed to have the same sensing range denoted r and the same radio range R. The sensing model adopted is the simplest one: the disk of radius r. Similarly, the radio transmission model is also disk-based: any wireless node located in the disk of radius R centered at the sensor considered has a symmetric radio link with it. For the sake of simplicity, we also assume that the condition $R \geq \sqrt{3}r$ is met. This condition guarantees that any deployment of wireless sensor nodes ensuring full coverage also ensures full connectivity.
• $\mathcal{A}$, the area to fully cover, is considered as a polygon which may be not convex. This polygon is defined by its edges. These edges constitute the borders of the area. We distinguish two types of borders:

- Transparent border: a transparent border does not prevent the sensing of sensor nodes. The only constraint added by transparent borders is that no sensor must be outside the area to cover.

- Opaque border: an opaque border prevents the sensing of nodes located behind the border: a sensor node s can cover a point u within its sensing disk if and only if u is in the line of sight of s (see Figure 1). Hence, such a border modifies the *is covered* relation, which is of prime importance in the problem we want to solve.

• The area considered usually has obstacles. No sensor node must be located within an obstacle. Like for borders, we distinguish two types of obstacles: transparent and opaque. An obstacle is defined by the edges of its polygon that may be of irregular shape and not convex. Let $\mathcal{O}$ denote the set of obstacles.

3. STATE OF THE ART

Coverage is a basic issue in wireless sensor networks. The reader can refer to [8] for a survey on the various problems related to coverage. The pioneering work on the full coverage of an infinite 2D area was published by Kershner [1]. He proved that the triangular tessellation achieves a full coverage with an asymptotic minimum number of sensors. In this tessellation, each sensor node at the center of an hexagon has six neighbors at a distance of $r\sqrt{3}$ that occupy the vertices of this hexagon as depicted in Figure 2 and Figure 4. The rectangular area is covered by several lines of sensor nodes. We notice that the first sensor of an odd line is located at a distance $r\sqrt{3}/2$ from the left border, whereas the first sensor of an even line is located at the left border. Furthermore, the first line starts at a distance $r/2$ from the top border, and the interline is equal to $3r/2$.

This result has been applied in many network deployments: radio cellular networks as well as wireless sensor networks. It has been extended in [9] to find the optimal tessellation (e.g. rhombus, square, hexagon, triangle) for different conditions binding the radio range R and the sensing range r. Authors of [2] show how to take obstacles into account. They also show that the problem of full coverage of a 2D-area with opaque obstacles is NP-hard.

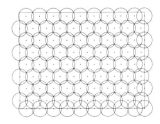

Figure 2: Optimal deployment based on a triangular tessellation.

To cope with this problem, the large majority of approaches encountered in the literature adopt the optimal deployment based on the triangular tessellation as a starting point. Then, sensors nodes located within an obstacle or outside the border of the area to fully cover are eliminated. This elimination usually causes coverage holes. The existing approaches differ in the way they heal the coverage holes. We distinguish the following two approaches:

• The contour-based approaches like [4, 5]: they deploy sensor nodes at a constant distance along the border of the area and along the border of each obstacle in order to heal coverage hole occurring on these contours. The distance between two successive sensor nodes deployed successively on a given contour is computed from the sensing range. Such approaches are simple but may require a high number of sensors in case of many irregular borders as shown in [6]. In contrast to our projection-based method, the coverage holes that are not adjacent to the area border or the obstacle border are not detected as shown in Figure 3.

• The Delaunay-triangulation-based approaches like [6]: they use the Delaunay triangulation to detect coverage holes and then place sensor nodes at some vertices of the triangles defined using a vertex coloring technique. However the complexity may be high, due to the presence of two modules: (a) the determination of coverage holes followed by (b) the computation of sensor locations that may be greedy in computation resources. In contrast to this approach, our method determines the sensor location without searching coverage holes. To reduce the number of sensors, our method eliminates redundant sensor nodes.

That is why we propose a simple solution requiring less computational complexity. We present in Sections 5, 6 and 7 three problems of increasing complexity. We solve these problems using our simple and efficient approach. Before, we

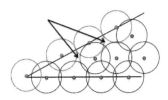

Figure 3: Coverage hole that is undetected by a contour-based method.

establish general bounds on the number of sensors required to fully cover the area.

4. GENERAL BOUNDS ON THE NUMBER OF SENSOR NODES

In this section, we establish upper and lower bounds on the number of sensor nodes required, independently from the method used to fully cover the given area. These bounds are derived from the optimal deployment based on a triangular tessellation. We will see in the next sections whether these bounds can be improved taking into account the method used to provide the full coverage of $\mathcal{A}$.

4.1 Lower bound

We first establish a lower bound on the number of sensor nodes required to fully cover the area considered. This bound is deduced from the fraction between the surface to cover and the surface covered by a sensor node. For that purpose, we focus on Figure 4 depicting the optimal deployment based on a triangular tessellation. We notice that in this optimal deployment, we can make the following approximation: any sensor node s that is not adjacent to a border can be considered as the only sensor node covering the hexagon $ABCDEF$ of edge r centered at itself and depicted in red in this figure. We can compute the surface of the triangle ABS. It is equal to $r^2\sqrt{3}/4$. The surface of the hexagon, denoted $S_\mathcal{H}$, is equal to the surface of the six triangles composing it. We have $S_\mathcal{H} = 3\sqrt{3}r^2/2$. With this result, we can give a lower bound on the number of sensor nodes needed to fully cover the area $\mathcal{A}$ without obstacles. Let Min_N be this bound. Let $S_\mathcal{O}$ be the cumulative surface of the obstacles. The surface to cover is then equal to $S_\mathcal{A} - S_\mathcal{O}$. We get $Min_N = \lceil \frac{S_\mathcal{A} - S_\mathcal{O}}{S_\mathcal{H}} \rceil$. Finally, we have:

$$Min_N = \lceil \frac{2(S_\mathcal{A} - S_\mathcal{O})}{3\sqrt{3}r^2} \rceil. \tag{1}$$

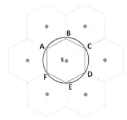

Figure 4: Hexagon covered by the sensor node s.

4.2 Upper bound

We can now establish an upper bound Max_N on the number of sensor nodes needed to fully cover $\mathcal{A}$ in the presence of transparent obstacles. This bound is based on:

- N_{In} the number of sensor nodes within $\mathcal{A}$ but outside the obstacles $\mathcal{O}$. This number can be obtained by counting the number of sensor nodes meeting this condition in the optimal deployment based on a triangular tessellation.

- N_{Add} the number of additional sensor nodes to fully cover $\mathcal{A}$ added after the elimination of sensor nodes that are either outside $\mathcal{A}$ or within an obstacle. To compute this number, we consider the contour of the area and the obstacles, segment by segment.

To fully cover a segment of length L, we use the principle of the optimal deployment in a rectangular area given in Section 3 and adapted to a segment as shown in Figure 5. Hence, we need N_b sensor nodes, with:

$$N_b = \lfloor \frac{L - \frac{r\sqrt{3}}{2}}{r\sqrt{3}} \rfloor + 1 + \delta_b \qquad (2)$$

$$with \; \delta_b = \begin{cases} 1 & if \; L - r\sqrt{3} - \lfloor \frac{L - \frac{r\sqrt{3}}{2}}{r\sqrt{3}} \rfloor r\sqrt{3} > 0 \\ 0 & otherwise \end{cases}$$

δ_b is equal to 1 if the distance between the projection of the last sensor on the border and the extremity of the border is higher than $\frac{r\sqrt{3}}{2}$.

We now apply this method to all edges of $\mathcal{A}$ and the obstacles $\mathcal{O}$. We then get $N_{Add} \leq \sum_{b \in edge(\mathcal{A} \cup \mathcal{O})} N_b$. Since $Max_N = N_{In} + N_{Add}$, we get:

$$Max_N = N_{In} + \sum_{b \in edge(\mathcal{A} \cup \mathcal{O})} N_b. \qquad (3)$$

We now show that in case of transparent borders and obstacles, this number Max_N is sufficient to eliminate all coverage holes resulting from the elimination of sensor nodes outside $\mathcal{A}$ or within an obstacle. Let us consider any edge of $\mathcal{A}$ such that a sensor node s outside the area (or inside an obstacle) at a distance $\varepsilon > 0$ from this edge has been eliminated. This elimination can create a coverage hole in the stripe of width r parallel to this edge. If now we consider the first line of the optimal deployment that starts at a distance $r/2$ from the border, we notice that this line fully covers the stripe of width r parallel to this border, as illustrated in Figure 5. Hence, we propose to deploy additional sensor nodes on a line parallel to the border, at a distance $r/2$ from the border. Notice that if such a sensor is outside $\mathcal{A}$, it is put at the first location inside $\mathcal{A}$ according to a projection along the border.

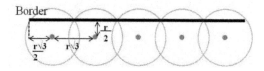

Figure 5: Optimal deployment along a border.

We can apply the same principle to the obstacles, considering the sensor nodes within the obstacles that have been eliminated.

5. OPTIMIZED DEPLOYMENT IN AN IRREGULAR AREA

In this section, we propose a deployment algorithm to cope with the irregular shape of an area.

5.1 Problem definition

In this first coverage problem, we consider any irregular 2-D area and assume that there is no obstacle and the border of the area is transparent.

5.2 Principle

Our method proceeds as follows:

1. We start with the optimal deployment in the rectangle circumscribing the given area $\mathcal{A}$: see Figure 7(a).

2. Sensor nodes that are outside $\mathcal{A}$ are eliminated, which may cause coverage holes: see Figure 7(b).

3. For each sensor node s located outside the area at a distance strictly less than r from a border, we check whether the border segment initially covered by s is still covered by other sensor nodes within $\mathcal{A}$, even if s is eliminated. Otherwise s is orthogonally projected on the border: see Figure 7(c). Due to this projection technique, illustrated in Figure 6, we can guarantee that the zone initially covered by the eliminated sensor node s, stills covered after the projection of s.

4. Finally, to optimize the number of sensor nodes needed, we check if some of them are providing redundant coverage, which can be eliminated in that case. They can be eliminated if and only if the intersection of $\mathcal{A}$ and the zone they covered is fully covered by other sensor nodes that are kept (see Figure 7(d)).

Notice that the projection of a senor node is not always on the border considered as shown in Figure 6(b). In this case, the position of the projected node is shifted in the middle of the border segment covered by this node in order to heal coverage holes.

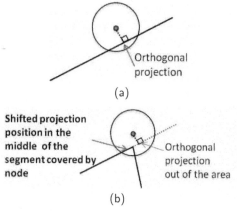

Figure 6: Projection technique.

5.3 Upper bound on the number of sensors required

We now establish $OurMax_N$, an upper bound on the number of sensors needed by our method to fully cover an

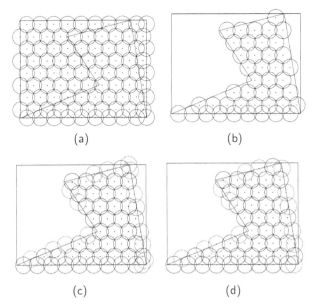

(a)   (b)

(c)   (d)

Figure 7: Principles of our method.

area with irregular shape but with transparent borders. This bound does not take into account the elimination of redundant sensor nodes done in step 4. Let $Outr$ denote the set of sensor nodes outside $\mathcal{A}$ at a distance less than r from a border and N_{Outr} denote the cardinality of $Outr$. We recall that N_{In} denotes the number of sensor nodes within $\mathcal{A}$. Since the sensor nodes that are added come from the projections of nodes in $Outr$ and these projections are done only on edges whose distance is less than r, we then have our upper bound:

$$OurMax_N = N_{In} + \sum_{P \in Outr} \sum_{e \in edge(\mathcal{A})} 1_{distance(P,e)<r} \quad (4)$$

with $1_{distance(P,e)<r} = 1$ if $distance(P,e) < r$ and 0 otherwise.

5.4 Comparative evaluation

In this subsection, we compare the performances of our method (projection-based) with the contour-based method on the boot configuration depicted in Figure 7(d). This boot configuration has a circumscribing rectangle of size $20r$ x $18r$. In Sections 5 and 7 we study more complex configurations.

The contour-based method chosen applies the method explained in Subsection 4.2 to each edge of $\mathcal{A}$. Hence, it needs N_b sensor nodes to fully cover an edge of length L (see Equation 2).

We make vary the sensing range (i.e. r, $r/2$, $r/4$), whereas the dimensions of the area are kept constant. We study the impact on the number of sensor nodes required to fully cover the area. As expected, when the sensing range decreases from r to $r/2$, the number of sensor nodes increases from 57 to 184. The lower bound Min_N suggests that this number should be multiplied by 4. We observe a multiplication by 3.23. Respectively, when the sensing range decreases from r to $r/4$, the number of sensor nodes increases from 57 to 652. Similarly, the lower bound Min_N suggests that this number should be multiplied by 16. We observe a multiplication by 11.46. This can be explained by the irregularity of the

border. The contour-based method adds 35 nodes on the border whereas our method adds only 14 nodes. Hence, the contour-based method leads to a total number of sensor nodes of 78 which is higher than this of our method (i.e. 57 nodes).

We observe that the upper bound $OurMax_N$ is very close to the number of sensor nodes needed by our method: we obtain an upper bound of 60, 188 and 656 whereas the exact number is 57, 184 and 652. Meanwhile, we notice that the gap between the real number of sensor nodes and the number given by the contour-based method drastically increases when the sensing range decreases. It reaches 21, 39 and 73 sensor nodes when the sensing range is equal to r, $r/2$ and $r/4$. This would increase the deployment cost by a factor of 36% for a sensing range r for instance.

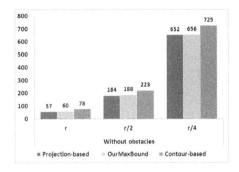

Figure 8: Impact of the sensing range on the number of sensor nodes (Boot configuration without obstacles).

6. OPTIMIZED DEPLOYMENT IN AN IRREGULAR AREA WITH OBSTACLES

Because of the presence of obstacles, sensor nodes of the optimal deployment that are located within an obstacle must be eliminated. They can cause coverage holes that must be healed.

6.1 Problem definition

In this second coverage problem, we consider any irregular 2-D area that includes obstacles and assume that both the obstacles and the border of the area are transparent.

6.2 Principle

We proceed as previously except that:

1. We start with the optimal deployment in the rectangle circumscribing the given area $\mathcal{A}$: see Figure 13(a).

2. Sensor nodes that are outside $\mathcal{A}$ or inside the obstacles $\mathcal{O}$ are eliminated, which may cause coverage holes: see Figure 13(b).

3. For each sensor node s outside the area at a distance strictly less than r from a border of the area, we check that the border segment initially covered by s is still covered by sensor nodes within $\mathcal{A}$, even if s is eliminated. Otherwise s is orthogonally projected on the border. We proceed similarly with any sensor node s inside an obstacle at a distance strictly less than r from a border of the obstacle: see Figure 13(c).

4. As a last step, redundant sensor nodes are eliminated.

6.3 Upper bound on the number of sensors required

We now extend our previous bound on the maximum number of sensor nodes needed by our method in the presence of obstacles. To deal with obstacles, our method projects nodes within an obstacle at a distance less than r from an edge of the obstacle. That is why, we add a third term to account for obstacles as follows:

$$OurMax_N = N_{In} + \sum_{P \in Outr} \sum_{e \in edge(\mathcal{A})} 1_{distance(P,e)<r} +$$

$$\sum_{P \in InObstr} \sum_{e \in edge(\mathcal{O})} 1_{distance(P,e)<r} \qquad (5)$$

where $InObstr$ denotes the set of sensor nodes within an obstacle at a distance strictly less than r from a border of an obstacle and $1_{distance(P,e)<r} = 1$ if $distance(P,e) < r$ and 0 otherwise.

6.4 Comparative evaluation

We consider different configurations to compare our method with the contour-based method described in Section 4. The configurations are various:

- The boot configuration with obstacles, (see Figure 9(a)) with the circumscribing rectangle of size $20r \times 18r$. This configuration is the simplest one we study.

- The star configuration. This configuration is representative of a complex shape of area with many salient angles. Its circumscribing rectangle is of size $24r \times 28r$. See Figure 9(b).

- The warehouse configuration, see Figure 9(c), with the circumscribing rectangle of size $28r \times 18r$. This configuration is representative of an indoor area with several rooms and many obstacles.

In the boot configuration, our method needs only 59 sensor nodes, 2 among them are used to cope with obstacles (see Figure 10). The contour-based method needs to deploy 93 sensor nodes. Among these sensor nodes, 17 are due to the presence of obstacles. The overestimation of the contour-based method contributes to increase the deployment cost by a factor of 58%. Furthermore, we notice that this overestimation increases with the number of vertices of the area to cover and the obstacles to avoid.

When we vary the sensing range from r to $r/2$ and $r/4$, the number of sensor nodes increases drastically as without obstacles. Our method outperforms the contour-based method. For instance, with $r/4$ the contour-based method requires 737 sensor nodes instead of 645 for our method. This would require the deployment of 92 sensor nodes that could be spared. In addition, the upper bound $OurMax_N$ is still very accurate, even in the presence of obstacles. It indicates 62, 197 and 652 instead of the real values 59, 191 and 645 provided by our method.

We obtain similar results with the star configuration: the benefit of our method reaches 40% as depicted in Figure 11. With the more complex configuration of the warehouse, the benefit increases up to 76% as depicted in Figure 12. This can be explained by the fact that this configuration includes several walls inside the area and many obstacles.

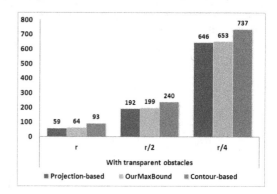

Figure 10: Impact of the sensing range on the number of sensor nodes (Boot configuration).

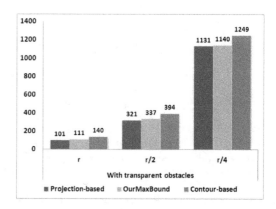

Figure 11: Impact of the sensing range on the number of sensor nodes (Star configuration).

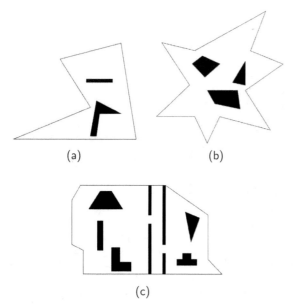

Figure 9: Configurations studied (Boot, Star, Warehouse).

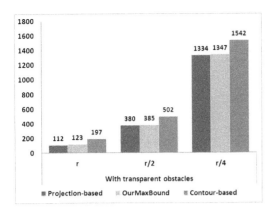

Figure 12: Impact of the sensing range on the number of sensor nodes (Warehouse Configuration).

7. HIDDEN ZONE

In this section, we propose a deployment algorithm to cope with the hidden zone due to opaque obstacles.

7.1 Problem definition

In this third coverage problem, we consider any irregular 2-D area that includes obstacles and assume that some obstacles and/or some borders of the area are opaque. This may result in hidden zones (see Figure 1). Sensor nodes must be added to cope with them.

7.2 Principle

In the presence of opaque borders or opaque obstacles, our method checks whether a hidden zone (see step 4 hereafter) exists. If so, sensor nodes are added. More precisley, the method proceeds according to the following steps:

1. We start with the optimal deployment in the rectangle circumscribing the given area $\mathcal{A}$: see Figure 13(a).

2. Sensor nodes that are outside $\mathcal{A}$ or inside the obstacles $\mathcal{O}$ are eliminated, which may cause coverage holes: see Figure 13(b).

3. For each sensor node s outside the area at a distance strictly less than r from a border of the area, we check that the border segment initially covered by s is still covered by sensor nodes within $\mathcal{A}$, even if s is eliminated. Otherwise s is orthogonally projected on the border. We proceed similarly with any sensor node s inside an obstacle at a distance strictly less than r from a border of the obstacle: see Figure 13(c).

4. For each sensor node s remaining after step 2, we check whether it is the only sensor node covering a zone in $\mathcal{A} \setminus \mathcal{O}$ that becomes hidden because of the opacity of a border or an obstacle. If so, a new sensor node is added as the projection of s in the zone it should cover (see Figure 13(d)).

5. Finally, redundant sensor nodes are eliminated.

7.3 Upper bound on the number of sensors required

We now extend our previous bound on the maximum number of sensor nodes needed by our method in the presence of

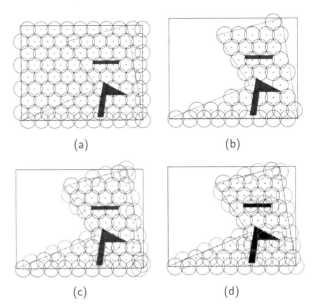

(a)   (b)

(c)   (d)

Figure 13: Principles of our method.

opaque obstacles or opaque borders. We add a fourth term to deal with opaque borders and opaque obstacles.

$$OurMax_N = N_{In} + \sum_{P \in Outr} \sum_{e \in edge(\mathcal{A})} 1_{distance(P,e)<r} +$$

$$\sum_{P \in InObstr} \sum_{e \in edge(\mathcal{O})} 1_{distance(P,e)<r} +$$

$$\sum_{P \in In} \sum_{e \in Opaque_e dge(\mathcal{A} \cup \mathcal{O})} 1_{distance(P,e)<r}, \qquad (6)$$

where In denotes the set of sensor nodes that remain after the elimination of step 2 and $1_{distance(P,e)<r} = 1$ if $distance(P,e) < r$ and 0 otherwise.

7.4 Comparative evaluation

We consider again the configurations defined in the previous section, but now the obstacles are opaque.

The contour-based method needs to deploy 93 sensor nodes in the boot configuration, 140 sensor nodes in the star configuration and 197 in the warehouse configuration. Notice that the contour-based method does not distinguish between opaque and transparent obstacles.

In the boot configuration, our method needs only 64 sensor nodes, 5 among them are used just to avoid hidden zones. These sensor nodes are depicted in blue in Figure 13(d). Our method out performs the contour-based method by 48%.

In the star configuration, our method needs only 105 sensor nodes, 4 among them are used to avoid hidden zones. Our method saves 33% of the deployment cost compared to the contour-based method.

In the warehouse configuration, our method needs 134 sensor nodes, 22 among them are added to avoid hidden zones. Our method saves 47% of the deployment cost compared to the contour-based method.

When we vary the sensing range from r to $r/2$ and $r/4$, we still observe that our method outperforms the contour-based method as depicted in Figures 14, 15 and 16. The bound

OurMax$_N$ always provides a very good approximation of the number of sensors required by our method.

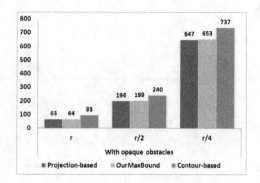

Figure 14: Impact of the sensing range on the number of sensor nodes (Boot configuration).

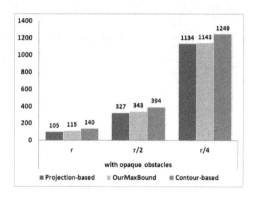

Figure 15: Impact of the sensing range on the number of sensor nodes (Star configuration).

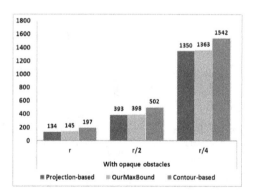

Figure 16: Impact of the sensing range on the number of sensor nodes (WarehouseConfiguration).

The comparative evaluation reported in Sections 5, 6 and 7 has the merit to quantitatively evaluate the impact of the complexity of the area (i.e. with/without obstacles, opaque/transparent borders, opaque/transparent obstacles) on the number of sensor nodes needed for a full coverage. The bound we computed *OurMax$_N$* is very accurate, whatever the configuration. Our method is always better than the contour-based method. Furthermore, we noticed the strong impact of border edges and obstacle edges whose length is

smaller than $r\sqrt{3}/2$ on the number of edges required by a contour-based method.

8. CONCLUSION

With the tremendous progress in technology miniaturization and the high reduction of costs, many monitoring applications are supported by wireless sensor networks. The quality of this monitoring strongly depends on data gathering which assumes the full coverage of the area to monitor. For cost reason, minimizing the number of sensor nodes deployed is sought. In addition, there are many constraints related to the area to monitor: an irregular shape that may be not convex, existence of transparent obstacles, existence of opaque borders and obstacles. To ensure the coverage of such an area constitutes a challenging task that we tackle in this paper. We evaluate the impact of these three factors and propose a method whose complexity gradually increases with the complexity of the coverage problem. The performances of this method are compared with the contour-based method: using our projection-based method, simulation results show that at least 30% of the deployment cost are saved. Our method is simpler than other method based on computational geometry like Delaunay triangulation. Furthermore, we establish bounds on the number of sensors required. The deployment computed by our method can be provided to a mobile robot in charge of placing the static wireless sensor nodes at their optimized location.

9. REFERENCES

[1] R. Kershner, *The number of circles covering a set*, American Journal of Mathematics, vol. 61, No. 3. pp. 665-671, Jul. 1939.

[2] M. Shyam, K. Anurag, *Obstacle constrained total area coverage in wireless sensor networks*, arxiv-web3.library.cornell.edu/pdf/1001.4753v1, January 2010.

[3] H. Tan, X. Hao, Y. Wang, F. C.M. Lau and Y. Lv *An Approximate Approach for Area Coverage in Wireless Sensor Networks*, Procedia Computer Science 19 (2013): 240-247.

[4] C.Y. Chang, C.T. Chang, Y.C. Chen, *Obstacle-resistant deplyment algorithms for wireless sensor networks*, IEEE Trans. on Vehicular Technology, Vol.58, N6, July 2009.

[5] Y.C. Wang, C.C. Hu, Y.C. Tseng, *Efficient placement and dispatch of sensors in a wireless sensor network deployment*, IEEE Trans. on Mobile Computing, Vol.7 N2, February 2008.

[6] H. Tan, Y. Wang, X. Lao, Q-S Hua, F. Lau, *Arbitrary obstacles constrained full coverage in wireless sensor networks*, WASA 2010, Beijing, China, September 2010.

[7] A. Fotouhi, and M. Razzazi *Redundancy and coverage detection in wireless sensor networks in the presence of obstacles*, MIPRO, 2011 Proceedings of the 34th International Convention. IEEE, 2011.

[8] B. Wang, *Coverage problems in sensor networks: a survey*, ACM Computing Surveys, vol43, N4, article 32, 2011.

[9] X. Bai, S. Kumar, D. Xuan, Z. Yun, T.H. Lai, *Deploying wireless sensors to achieve both coverage and connectivity*, MobiHoc 2006, Florence, Italy, 2006.

Organic Wireless Sensor Networks: A Resilient Paradigm for Ubiquitous Sensing

Sharief M. A. Oteafy
School of Computing
Queen's University
Kingston, ON, Canada
K7L 2N8
oteafy@cs.queensu.ca

Hossam S. Hassanein
School of Computing
Queen's University
Kingston, ON, Canada
K7L 2N8
hossam@cs.queensu.ca

ABSTRACT

We advocate for a novel paradigm in Wireless Sensor Networks (WSNs). As a technology, it has evolved to a scalable networking paradigm with minimalistic operational mandates. However, inherited design principles of static functionality, that are pre-determined at design stage, hinder WSN evolvement. More importantly, while we design WSNs to endure harsh environments and scale in both urban and remote settings, we neglect two major factors. The over-deployment of WSNs renders many sensing nodes redundant in functionality, and inflates the cost of running applications; not to mention the resulting medium contention. In this paper we present a novel approach to expanding the operational scale of WSNs by adapting to the environment in which it is deployed. That is, capitalizing on an organic approach in thriving on available resources in the region of interest to reduce deployment cost, and solicit incentivized interaction among communicating resources to deliver dynamic sensing. Not only does this span a new dimension of reliability, over garnered resources, but presents a novel approach to assigning sensing tasks to available resources in correlation to their abundance and serviceability. We present our performance evaluation of reduction in operational costs, and the uptake of sensing tasks by neighboring resources via extensive simulations. We aim to benchmark WSN operational versatility and present a rigorous basis for evaluating the ability of WSNs to resiliently scale to new applications as well as handle intermittent and permanent failures.

Categories and Subject Descriptors

C.2.1 [**Computer-Communication Networks**]: Network Architecture and Design – *Wireless Communication*, C.2.3 [**Computer-Communication Networks**]: Network Operations – *Network Management*

General Terms

Algorithms, Management, Design, Reliability.

MSWiM'14, September 21–26, 2014, Montreal, QC, Canada.
Copyright © 2014 ACM 978-1-4503-3030-5/14/09...$15.00.
http://dx.doi.org/10.1145/2641798.2641810

Keywords

Novel WSN paradigm; Resilience Benchmark; Resource-Reuse; Elastic Incentives; Maximal matching; Dynamic WSN operation.

1. INTRODUCTION

Wireless Sensor Networks (WSNs) have evolved over a wide spectrum of applications. Over the years we have witnessed a considerable drive to optimize the energy footprint of sensing applications, their resilience to failures and scalability; both in density (per unit area) and spread (over deployment regions).

In recent years, the mounting density of deployments has generated overwhelming underutilization of resources across multiple WSNs. Practitioners seldom consider the wirelessly accessible resources in the vicinity of a deployment region, only – at best – incorporate their RF interference and impact on link quality [1][2]. This includes the proliferation of smart devices that harness significant communication and sensing resources, in addition to static (mostly municipally owned) sensing architectures. As such, the design stage is mostly tailored to the application requirements under operational and budgetary constraints. The problem is further complicated by assuming that once nodes are deployed, they will continue to do what they were initially designed to do (static application space) and will communicate only with in-network nodes (black-boxes to all other networks).

In this work we advocate that future WSNs should not develop on a premise of black-box deployments. That is, given a set of resources in a given node, it should be able to cope with changes in application requirements, and neighboring networks with common goals should be able to solicit the utility of local resources to improve performance; for a fee. We argue that WSNs should *organically* span new application requirements, and interact with neighboring networks to evolve and sustain resilience. As such, the sustained operation would be a factor of the environment in which a WSN thrives, and how well it could interact – and potentially barter – with neighboring resources.

It is important to highlight that this paradigm stems from a debilitating underutilization of visible resources, hindering the potential for dynamic operation and post-deployment changes in WSN duties; especially resource-rich nodes that visit our region of interest. The importance of incorporating transient resources stems from their pervasiveness projected uptake in the near future.

First, we note that a resource is defined as a component with predetermined functional capabilities, and the means (e.g., wireless transceivers) to interact with the network. A rigorous definition is discussed by [3] in the static case, and [4] in the dynamic case where transient resources pass by the WSN region of interest.

This paradigm targets a dynamic facilitation of running concurrent applications over a group of connected WSNs. This is not a mere aggregation of the pre-deployment applications to which they were engineered, but more importantly to the new applications that emerge in the field of deployment, to which current resources could adapt and serve. In fact, our long term target is to establish a benchmark for WSN resilience in terms of sustaining functional requirements beyond the death of its constituting sensor nodes. Practically, we extend the definition of functional lifetime coined by Dietrich and Dressler in [5] to extend to network life that is sustained by probed resources in the field of deployment. Thus, both functional changes and maintaining operation to serve a given application set, becomes a sheer factor of re-assignment of tasks to available resources.

We thus summarize our core contributions in (1) presenting a novel Organic-WSN paradigm that adapts to resources in the deployment region to boost resilience, functional capacity and lifetime, (2) introduce a new benchmark for extending functional lifetime as a function of communicating resources that are incentivized to contribute with their resources, and (3) present a dynamic heuristic for optimizing network performance over available resources, via a maximal-matching formulation.

The remainder of this paper is organized as follows. In Section 2 we detail the pertinent background to this work, highlighting the foundational contributions in [3][4][6], in addition to current cloud-sensing paradigms that target versatile WSN operation, and related work on post-deployment modifications in WSNs. Section 3 elaborates on the O-WSN model in general, highlighting the role of transient resources. The core of this work is presented in Section 4 as we detail the incentive schemes that will entice contribution from neighboring resources for O-WSN to thrive, and the elastic pricing model that enables dynamic assignment of resources to applications as they emerge. We present our performance evaluation of O-WSN in Section 5, and conclude in Section 6 with remarks on future work.

2. BACKGROUND AND MOTIVATION

The argument for O-WSN builds upon the resource reuse (RR) WSN paradigm presented in [3] [4]. The vision of this work is that future large-scale integrations would facilitate an abundance of resources that are ubiquitously available in the vicinity of WSNs. As such, maintaining and improving operation would be a function of integration and cross-network utilization, rather than that of re-deployment and over-deployment.

2.1 The case for Resource Reuse

Intrinsically, WSNs serve a simple goal; namely to collect data from a sensed field and report back to the sink(s). In the early days of WSN applications, the cost of components and limited scope of applications deemed WSN design a mere branch of embedded-systems engineering. Simply put, designers would engineer the optimal component configuration stringent environment and cost constraints. The resulting network was designed to do that in a black-box model.

This coupling between design and application is not a requirement for WSNs, yet a mere inheritance. Today, WSNs are deployed in environments where not only could the applications change, but the operational mandates of the network could drastically impact

operation post deployment. Accordingly, Oteafy and Hassanein presented a Resource-Reuse WSN paradigm in which the design phase constitutes integrating components that would serve the current application, and future manifestations of new requirements. The idea was built on an intrinsic decoupling of WSN design from application requirements, and focusing on the accessibility of resources that are within the WSN.

To enable such a paradigm, the need for a rigorous and unified set of attributes to define what a resource is (Transceiver, memory, MCU, sensor, etc) was presented in [3]. On the other hand, an atomic functional decomposition of application requirements in terms of attributes that wold match the descriptors of resources, was also introduced. Thus, WSN design and operation was reduced to an assignment problem, to which a linear optimization approach was used an evaluated in [3] and [6].

2.2 Crowd sensing

The abundance of smart devices has enabled a new model for sensing networks, dubbed crowd/public sensing. The notion simply builds upon the aggregation of collected data from a diverse group of users who are willing to provide sensing tasks, either via active reporting or passive participation. Many services developed around this model, such as Cosm™ (previously Pachube). However, it is important to note that public sensing is not a WSN paradigm. It lends itself to some literature on data aggregation and fidelity checking, yet the core concepts of how the two paradigms operate are different.

For one, reporting is a function of when the users (whether passively or actively) report their findings. This could be based on dedicated hardware, generic smartphones with dedicated applications, or simply text (SMS) reporting. Most of public sensing research takes place under the participatory sensing paradigm. This is largely due to ensuring an acceptable level of data quality and reducing the overhead of filtering and verification.

2.3 WSNs Post-deployment

Traditionally, limited deployments in terms of size and scale, allowed practitioners to re-visit the field of deployment to perform maintenance. Moreover, most initial deployments where deterministic in their region of operation, and witnessed limited/no mobility. Thus, intervening in the field of deployment incurred few hardships (at least on field).

In a technology that is advancing on the premise of large scale deployments and self-healing operation, this is evidently short term practice. Even more, potential (and currently practiced) deployment in hazardous/inaccessible terrains deems this approach impossible. Researchers have invested significant efforts in realizing autonomous operation and maintenance of WSNs. The scale and diversity of WSN operation should not have an effect on its post-deployment maintenance; however this is the trend in current literature. This is a direct result of the application-specific design that governs SN operation.

3. O-WSN MODEL

In O-WSM, the operation of a WSN is defined over a set of distinct resources with predefined operational attributes. The typical view of sensing nodes inherently encompassed the resources it holds (such as transceivers, sensors, etc). However, in O-WSN we formally define a resource as

Definition 1: *A resource is as an active entity in the network with pre-known functional capability, and the means to communicate its capability. Each resource has the capacity to cater for r_k requests, where $r_k \geq 1$. Thus, it has r_k instances.*

3.1 Resources and Functional Requirements

We adopt a model where applications are defined in terms of a dissection of functional requirements, which are coupled with the underlying resources of nodes. A significant notion presented here is the cost for using a resource. Since we now expand to include resources that do not necessarily belong to one proprietary, the utilization of resources across different networks is intrinsically a question of cost vs. utility. That is, how much would network owner **A** charge network **B** to use a given set of **A**'s resources. We argue that cross-network resource utilization is in fact a mutually profitable architecture. That is, a resource that is owned by **A** could generate revenue while idle.

The scope of improvement we aim for stems from a unique problem. Our prime concern is not sheer scarcity of nodes or operational efficiency; but the utilization of resources currently in the field of deployment. In O-WSN, we elaborate on the utilization of in-field resources, especially transient ones, highlighting their utility, predictability and usage tradeoff that dictate the efficiency of relying on them for network operations. These attributes are detailed in Section 3.2. The core competency of a WSN in this paradigm is handling the sheer number of resources, both static and transient, that constitute its resource pool (ReP). Thus we first dissect the group of resources that would contribute to the resource pool as either static or dynamic resources, as depicted in Figure 1.

Thus, the network is an aggregation of resources polled form static nodes n^S and transient nodes n^T. The ReP is an aggregation of these resources. However, n^T have deterministic sojourn times that are coupled with spatial limitations. Hence, we introduce the notion of dissecting the WSN deployment space into regions, and assume the presence of an entity dubbed the **Arbitrator**, in each one of those regions. Thus, the locality and relationship with n^T would be dictated by their relative position to an Arbitrator. These spatial correlations are elaborated upon in Subsection 3.2.2.

3.2 Capitalizing on abundant resources

The capital gain of O-WSN is utilizing abundant resources in the field of deployment, when weighed against their incurred cost of operation. The utility function that dictates this cost is elaborated upon in Section 4, mainly depending on the scarcity and quality of the resource to be used.

In assessing the value and contribution of a resource, we take into consideration the 6 attributes presented in [3]. Namely, the functional capabilities of the resource (e.g., taking pictures, video), the levels of operation for each of them (e.g., resolution, frame size), power consumption for each level, the duty cycling scheme of the governing node, the region in which the resource operates (coverage) and finally its current location. These are shared attributes whether or not the resource is static or transient. In the latter case, more attributes are to be calibrated to evaluate the viability of considering a given transient resource in the ReP, and accordingly the cost factor of soliciting its services.

3.2.1 The abundance of transient resources

Transient resources, ones which pass by the deployment/interest region in the WSN, gain value via their pervasiveness and functional capabilities. To formally elaborate on the utility of

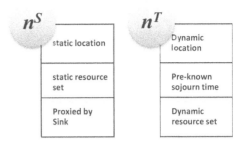

Figure 1 - Distinction between static and transient nodes in the O-WSN paradigm

transient resources, and their specific attributes, a formal definition is first presented as follows:

Definition 2: *A transient resource extends a resource (Definition 1) as one with varying spatial and temporal properties. It lingers in the vicinity of the WSN for a deterministic **sojourn time**, during which it is of potential utility to the Resource Pool (ReP). The term "transient" reflects the limit on the duration this resource could be visible/utilized by functional requests.*

We note that transient resources are quite abundant. In an urban setting, transient resources are seen in high-end vehicles, tablets and smart-phones, mobile weather stations and industrial sensors deployed by different proprietaries. Governed by their sojourn time and mobility models, we introduce the effective connectivity point/region and cost function associated with the use of its functionalities.

3.2.2 Spatial properties

Attributing a location to a transient resource is a difficult problem. Despite the extensive literature on localization for both static and moving nodes, the common issue is the overhead of multilateration required to accurately estimate a node's position. While adopting a crude metric for location would often suffice, we aim to identify a contact zone of each transient resource. That is, if we can communicate with it and identify it within a given region, then its resourcefulness would be tied to that region, until it leaves it.

In our model we assume that transient resources have a direct communication link with their local Arbitrators. That is, they are within communication range in a single hop. This facilitates a faster exchange of resources and cost functions within the short sojourn time; thus yielding higher utilization of its resources. This assumption is supported by the rapid deployment of higher end nodes which can take over the task of the Arbitrator, or present themselves as proxies to enable wider reach for the Arbitrator.

3.2.3 Temporal properties

A major property of a transient resource is the constrained time in which the network could utilize its functionalities. This is attributed to physical disappearance from the network region, or a duty cycling property that is contingent upon its own operational mandate. We highlight two important factors to calibrate the utility of a transient resources over the time dimension.

3.2.3.1 Sojourn time

Is a duration, in milliseconds, in which a resource maintains its attachment to the WSN at hand. This directly depends on the method adopted for determining location in the paradigm, yet is beyond the scope of this work. For example, if we consider the connectivity degree coupled with a hop-count as the indicator of a node's location, then *sojourn time* is defined as the span of time in which this aggregated metric of location is maintained. Thus, to ground sojourn time to an anchor, we define it as

Definition 3: *Sojourn time of a transient node n^T is the duration in which it resides in the vicinity of the current governing arbitrator.*

We further note that sojourn time of a given transient resource is solely *effective* when coupled with availability, hence we expand into the notion of resource duty cycling.

3.2.3.2 Resource duty cycling

It is important to note that transient resources belong to devices that are inherently non-WSN nodes. That is, a luminosity sensor or a transceiver on a passing smart-phone, are already engaged in the applications of the home device and might not be available for utilization by the arbitrator at all times. Thus, it is important to note that only considering the sojourn time of such resources is insufficient. We instead consider the resources' *effective time*. Accordingly, a transient resource is viable when its duty cycling schemes is known. This could be represented via a pre-identified duty cycling schedule, or simply a timer of remaining milliseconds in operation in the vicinity of the current arbitrator.

In O-WSN, a viable transient resource would declare, upon its entry into the vicinity of an Arbitrator, its sojourn time and duty cycling pattern. Moreover, its trajectory and location(s) are relayed to the Arbitrator based on the mobility model of the transient node.

4. ELASTIC INCENTIVE SCHEMES

A core premise of the O-WSN paradigm is that future deployments of WSNs would converge towards functional diversity and cooperation, lowering the cost per node and maximizing the resource pool over nodes across networks.

The premise we need to justify, however, is the exchange of benefits. That is, "why would a transient resource (of a device) offer its resources in the first place"? since offering a resource for use by another network would entail energy, coordination, communication and potentially internal request-latency, it is important to caliber the impact of offering such a resource. In short, metrics that quantify how much a SN would be impacted by carrying out a specific task.

Although this topic delves into an already established literature on incentive schemes and rewarding "socially positive" behavior by arbitrary nodes, we highlight two important factors. First, in a heterogeneous network it would be farfetched to assume collusion free and socially-favorable behavior of nodes as they contribute their resources for the network they join. Second, establishing a fixed method that stresses equated contributions would facilitate a benchmark for assessing the valuation of each resource as it is offered for the network.

We thus focus on the two most intrinsic factors that dictate the value of a resource. The first is a proportional influence by remaining energy reservoir. That is, the more energy the node can sustain for a given operation, the more likely (and inversely the less it would valuate) it would contribute its resource. This scheme is detailed in Section 4.1. The second method is a sheer relationship to resource scarcity. That is, a higher abundance of that resource would result in a lower valuation at the current round. This approach is elaborated upon in Section 4.2.

4.1 Asymptotic Sigmoidal Pricing

We employ a static scheme for assigning cost units to utilizing a resource. That is, carrying out a functional requirement $f_{j,m}$ on a given node n_i at any given round τ_k depends on the energy impact of utilizing that resource. This takes into consideration two main factors. The normalized (w.r.t. to maximal battery power of node) indicator of energy depleted at n_i at the time of its use, denoted as ϵ_i and the maximal cost (asymptotic limit) for how much a resource could valuate to, denoted as C_r^{max}. Thus, aggregating these values would determine the total cost $\mathbf{C_r}$ for a resource $\mathbf{r}$ by using the asymptotic *Gompertz* function [7]

$$C_r = C_r^{max} * e^{\varrho * e^{-s_r * \epsilon_r}} \tag{1}$$

We chose the Sigmoidal Gompertz function due to its controlled increase in pricing of a resource, based on three important factors. Namely, the cap on valuation dictated by C_r^{max}, the flexibility to set a starting valuation by varying the Y-axis intercept dictated by ϱ and finally controlling the rate of increase in resource valuation based on the slope dictated by s_r. Thus, the cost function demonstrates significant sensitivity to remaining energy reservoir as it gets depleted, yet it never reaches C_r^{max} which is set by the arbitrator. This growth and its derivative are depicted in Figure 2. The green line demonstrates the growing cost function and the grey line shows the gradient of increase; diminishing as the function approaches the asymptotic limit.

4.2 Elastic Pricing – Impact of scarcity on price

This approach accounts for scenarios where the abundance of a resource dictate its cost to the network. The dynamics of functional gain depend on the availability of resources and the costs associated with each, and the willingness of the application to pay for a resource to carry out the functional requirement. Thus, it is imperative to include a scenario for "open markets" where a resource would probe a local arbitrator to offer its resources for a monetary reward.

To capture the essence of this approach, which is resource offerings made by transient resources, we present a cost function built upon two main factors. The resource offered, and its market valuation based on abundance. We assume that each arbitrator B_α

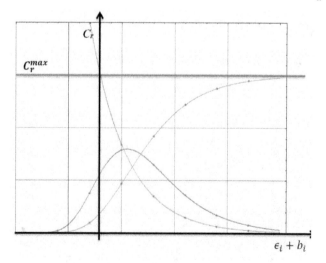

Figure 2 - Growth of the cost function in relation to depleting energy following the *Gompertz* model

214

is aware of the resources available in its vicinity, and can identify the density of each class of resource.

Accordingly, the arbitrator can dictate the valuation of a given resource as V_r

$$V_r = \frac{C_r}{|\Theta_r| * \alpha_r * \hat{C}_r} \tag{2}$$

Where $\hat{C}_r$ is the normalized network valuation of resource C_r. However, the impact of this valuation on the elastic pricing of C_r is subject to a weighted factor α_r.

It is important to account for both factors when determining a price, especially for a transient resource. If there is only a single resource that would deliver a given functionality, then a "market valuation" has to be incorporated in its price to determine the need for it. For example, a camera pointing at the door of a grocery store might not strike great value until an incident exists around the store for which its utility rises.

4.3 On maximal matching and construed equality between resource providers

The mapping problem has to cater for transient resources to utilize them in time; thus only real-time solutions are viable. Time bottlenecks, cost constraints and system resilience are presenting major obstacles. Thus, we present a model to cater for dynamic assignment of resources to functional requests, yet now catering for rapid changes in locations, sojourn times and responsiveness. The remainder of this section details the system model, built upon the O-WSN paradigm to address these issues, and how the system adopts a dynamic heuristic to find the best possible match of functional requests to ReP constituents.

4.4 System model

We adopt a novel view of scalability, coupling the definition with functional coverage, rather than the number and distribution of sensing nodes. We envision wirelessly-enabled devices that did not belong to WSNs to aid and extend "functional scalability".

We represent the WSN network as a weighted bipartite graph, with resources and functional requirements creating two mutually exclusive sets of vertices. This formulation is depicted in Figure 3. The network is partitioned into sub-networks, each centered around the Arbitrator that handles the local ReP and functional requests to be made over its physical region. This partitioning allows for a rapid assignment of resources to functional requests, and remedies the significant variance between sojourn times and localities of transient resources over the whole network region. Thus, we represent the network as a graph $G = (V, E)$, where

$$V = V^R \cup V^F \tag{3}$$

and V^R represents all polled resource instances in the current vicinity of the arbitrator, and V^F includes all the atomic functional requests of the applications to run in this vicinity. The weighted edges are defined as

$$E = \{ \forall\, e_{u,v} \mid \exists\ u \in V^F\ \wedge\ v \in V^R\ \wedge\ u.type \equiv v.type \} \tag{4}$$

where the type matching indicates that the resource identified by node v meets the functional requirements of request represented by node u. This includes both static and dynamic requirements; i.e., the 6 core attributes highlighted in Section 3.2 in addition to spatial and temporal properties induced by transient resource attributes if $v \in n^T$.

The value of an edge $e_{u,v}$ represents the cost of utilizing resource v, is computed as

$$e_{u,v} = \kappa(v) \tag{5}$$

where the cost function denoted as $\kappa(v)$ is computed according to the utility function explained in Section 4.2.

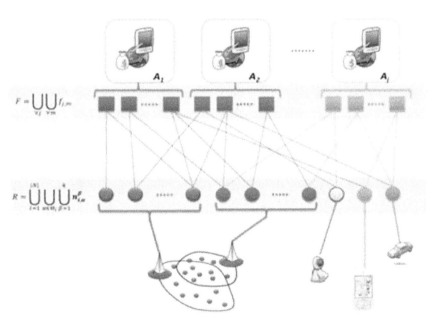

Figure 3 - Maximal bipartite matching of resources to functional requirements

215

4.6 Dynamic rounds – Capturing transient resources

The dynamic nature of transient resources dictates a fine tuned operation scheme that caters for their varying linger times. As highlighted in motivating the use of local arbitrators, the variance of spatial, temporal and mobility properties across transient resources introduce a significant impact on catering for their utilization. That is, short round times could deem many "slower" resources useless to the network, or incur significant control overhead in their discovery and utilization, and longer round times would impact the discovery rate of "faster moving" resources or ones with shorter duty cycles. Thus dynamic rounds are an intrinsic property of the O-WSN paradigm to cater for transient resources.

We define network operation in terms of rounds, τ_t. Each τ_t could vary in duration, yet constitutes three main phases. The first phase τ_t^{setup} addresses the setup phase in which the local ReP is built, and functional requests are aggregated over all applications in the arbitrators vicinity. The second phase, τ_t^{map} involves the mapping time during which minimum cost mapping of $V^F \to V^R$ takes place. The final phase in each round, $\tau_t^{operational}$ is when the network actually operates to fulfill the functional requests per the matching mandate dictated during τ_t^{map}.

At each round, the durations of τ_t^{setup} and τ_t^{map} do not change. The former has a time out period during which all functional requests have to be reported by all $a_j \in A$ and all nodes willing to participate report their aggregated resource sets R_i and cost of utilizing each, i.e., $\kappa(v)$. The latter duration τ_t^{map} is the running time of the mapping algorithm, elaborated upon in Section 4.6.

However, the duration of $\tau_t^{operational}$ would vary each round and is impacted by all $v \in n^T$. That is, we introduce the notion of resource *effective time* in the vicinity of the current arbitrator, indicating the duration for which a transient resource v would be an active member of the arbitrators current ReP. We thus denote the *effective time* of a transient node v with a duty cycle percentage of v_{DC} and sojourn time of v_{st} as v_{et}

$$v_{et} = v_{st} * v_{DC} \qquad (6)$$

There are different methods for assessing the impact of transient resources on the duration of a round. For example, the network could reassess every time a transient resource leaves the network, thus creating a void, or whenever a new one is expected to enter (according to the mobility models known a priori and the interconnection between arbitrators).

However, we note the motivation behind this work as maximizing functional gain while utilizing current resource pools. The notion of re-invoking a matching algorithm every time a transient resource is introduced contradicts the stability of network operation. Thus, we depend on a tunable duration time to utilize as many, not all, transient resources.

From a functional perspective, transient resources are of higher viability when they introduce one of two edges: (1) A scarce resource that the ReP is shy of, or (2) a cost reduction that significantly reduces the cost for meeting functional requirements of current set of A.

We hereby introduce a dynamic function that assesses the impact of transient resources on round duration $\tau_t^{operational}$ is explained in Equation (7)

$$\tau_t^{operational} \propto \sum_{v \in n^T} v_{et} \\ * \left(\omega_f * \frac{1}{|\Theta_v|} + \omega_c \right. \\ \left. * \frac{\kappa(\Theta_v) - \kappa(v)}{max\,(\kappa(\Theta_v))} \right) \qquad (7)$$

where $|\Theta_v|$ is the number of resources in the current ReP of a matching type to v and $\overline{\kappa(\Theta_v)}$ is the average cost requested by resources of type v to contrast with the maximum cost requested for resources type v denoted as $max\,(\kappa(\Theta_v))$; as a normalization factor. To cater for a fine tuned operation of O-WSN that could favor one impact over the other (depending on the design goals of the network practitioner), we introduce impact weights for functional and cost impacts, as ω_f and ω_c respectively. We highlight that $0 \leq \omega_f, \omega_c \leq 1$ and are set by the arbitrator.

4.7 Utilizing the Hungarian method

The formulation of the O-WSN model as a bipartite graph under a cost function for each resource instance, i.e., each edge with a matching as described in Equation (4), lends itself to the significant literature on maximal bipartite matching. There is a wealth of algorithms that address the issue of finding an optimal matching between V^R and V^F. We adapt the maximal bipartite matching algorithm developed by H. Kuhn commonly referred to as the Hungarian method [8]. It is a polynomial time algorithm, which is computationally tolerated in our model since it would run independently on local vicinities of Arbitrators. A more thorough discussion of the assignment problem, and the use of the Hungarian method adopted in this work, are detailed in [9].

5. PERFORMANCE EVALUATION

The performance evaluation for RR-WSN adapting to transient resources is carried out in MATLAB. We set up an experiment with variable number of nodes, both static and transient, and adopt a dynamic assignment scheme of functional requirements for each run. The locations of nodes follow a uniform random distribution over the deployment region. We run our simulation models with different energy levels for sensing nodes, to fall randomly in the range of 80% to 100% of an initial battery power set to a maximum of 3 kJ. Transient nodes also start with a random battery level in the same range, with an upper limit of 5 kJ (as dedicated for O-WSN). We assume that transient nodes hold a vastly heterogeneous pool of resources [10], and static sensing nodes have a more homogeneous pool. In our experiments we assume static sensing nodes have an arbitrary number of resources from the set of {'Temperature sensor' ; 'Light sensor' ; 'Micro controller' ; 'Memory' ; 'Transceiver' ; 'Camera' ; 'Radar' }. Transient resources could have any of these resources, in addition to a more smartphone oriented pool of resources that we abstract as {'GPS' ; 'microphone' ; 'geomagnetic'; 'barometer' }. Naturally, each node holds a transceiver, micro controller and one type of sensor as a minimum. Even indoor networks hold a significant abundance of such resources [11].

The impact of transient resources on network performance is complex. On one hand, they leverage functional requests and aid energy-deprived sensor nodes. On the other hand, they incur

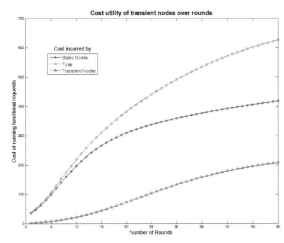

Figure 4 - Transient nodes leveraging network performance over rounds

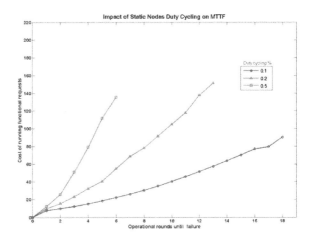

Figure 5 - Impact of Duty cycling of SNs on MTTF of network under O-WSN

significant costs to the owner of the static nodes as they charge for carrying out the tasks. We next examine the operation of O-WSN aided with transient resources, over a number of dynamic rounds. Figure 4 depicts O-WSN operation with 60 static nodes, for 50 rounds, on a typical region for an arbitrator of size 100 x 100 m. Each round has a $\tau_t^{operational}$ duration of 5000 sec in addition to a variable round time in the range of [0,5000] dependent on the impact of transient resources, as per Eq. 7. transient resources have a random effective time v_{et} in the range [500,1500], and arrive according to a Poisson process with average 1000 seconds.

The network significantly depends on static resources with lower cost incurred for functional tasks at the earlier rounds. However, due to the relative pricing of resources dictated by the Gompertz model, in Eq. 1, over later rounds, it becomes more cost effective to depend on transient resources. An interesting phenomena occurs after approximately 20 rounds, when energy reservoirs at both static and transient nodes start witnessing equal depletion, hence the uptake of resources from both classes of resources grow in a balanced pattern.

However, it is important to note the impact of another factor, which is the growth scaling factor S_r highlighted in Eq. 1 following the growth model depicted in Figure 2. In Figure 4, both static and transient nodes share an equal S_r value of -0.05, since it has the steadiest increase in resource valuation. Mean time to failure and Network resilience

Failures happen. However, the definition of a failure varies significantly across different WSN paradigms. A common metric of interest is the mean time to failure (MTTF) of nodes, and that of the network. That is, how long does it take the network, on average, to fail? We cannot generalize failure to encompass any node that has failed (ceased to operate) in the network. It is critical to understand that failure's impact on network operation; since it could very well occur without disturbing network operation. This is mostly evident in dense networks.

In RR-WSN we define network MTTF as the time (from deployment) until the first functional request could not be satisfied. Accordingly, MTTF is not affected by the failure of a resource unless it is irreplaceable in its field of operation. A resource r_i is replaceable if another resource r_j exists within the same fidelity region served by r_i and has the capacity and

attributes to serve the functional requests previously assigned to r_i as per the definitions in Section 3.2.

In O-WSN, it is important to note the impact of static resources on MTTF. While transient resources offer a dynamic ReP, there are no guarantees in terms of sustained functional matching for the duration of the network. Thus, it is important to sustain network functionality via static nodes. However, increasing static resources is a constant overhead. Moreover, increasing resource availability (via increasing duty cycling time) has an impact on cost of running the network. In Figure 5 we depict O-WSN operation under static resources only. This experiment was designed to measure the impact of duty cycling static resources to match functional requirements, until network failure. The MTTF is shown as the last point on each respective curve. Evidently, increasing duty cycling time has an impact on cost of running functional requirements, thus the differentiated increase depicted for each simulation at any given round (common until the first 6 rounds. It is important to note this experiment was run under varying nodal locations, and energy reservoirs, yet with a fixed total energy value across all static resources. The experiment was run with 50 static nodes, in a 100 x 100 m area, each node having a combination of 4 resources, two of which are a transceiver and an MCU. The experiment was setup to enforce 100 functional requirements that are static over the rounds, i.e., the functional requirements did not change in attributes.

Under this experiment, it was also shown that MTTF is negatively impacted by increasing duty cycling time, as nodes consume more energy in each round, resulting in a quicker battery depletion. Thus, network failure occurs sooner (at earlier rounds) as we increase duty cycling of static nodes. It is important to note that survivability of the network over rounds is manifested in longer network lifetime. Introducing transient resources in O-WSN operation impacts our definition of lifetime, and inherently MTTF. At any given point, even if static resources fail to meet functional requests, transient resources offer a pool of resources that aid in meeting the requests.

We also note the resilience of O-WSN in recovering from static resource failures, and the utility of transient resources when more static resources fail. This transient property makes for an alternating but sustained performance, as depicted in Figure 6. where the same experiment was repeated, yet with a varying rate of arrival for TNs. We simulate a scenario where TNs arrive according to a Poisson process, with an average arrival rate of 10 TNs per round. More TNs are utilized as they preserve higher energy reservoirs, thus increasing the network cost of carrying the same functional requirements.

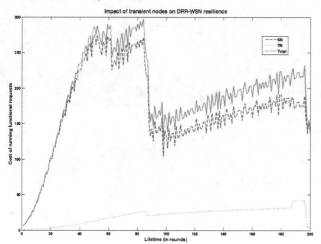

Figure 6 - The utility of transient nodes in maintaining O-WSN resilience, under a Poisson arrival process with average 10 TNs per round

6. CONCLUSIONS AND FUTURE WORK

Current practices for designing and deploying Wireless Sensor Networks (WSN) persistently yield application specific networks. Such limitation in applicability has thus far been driven by a basic tradeoff between functionality and resource availability – a tradeoff that has received great research attention over the years [12]. O-WSN parts from this traditional model and offers a new WSN approach that decouples application considerations from network architecture and protocol.

This paper introduced the O-WSN paradigm. The goal was to reduce the cost impact of running multiple functional tasks, on an ever-changing base of resources that are wirelessly accessibly [13]. Significant parameters of O-WSN were developed to cater for a varying rate of arrival of transient resources, and their volatile availability in network vicinity. Moreover, it was important to devise cost functions that resemble the willingness of both static and transient resources to cater for functional requests. Normalized operation mandated that all nodes be held to a common metric of arbitration, which is the cost in O-WSN.

We adopted the *Gompertz* model of growth, whereby an increasing exponential function would map the stringency of power at a resource to the valuation of utilizing its resource. The *Gompertz* function allowed for a flexible growth scaling via tunable parameters, and sustained an asymptotic limit (cap on possible valuation) that enables a more viable contribution of resources to the functional resource pool (ReP).

O-WSN promises a great potential for realizing a truly large-scale WSN unity that alleviates resource waste in redundancy, and delivers maximized utility for required applications. As future work, more investigations are required to determine the viability, gain and energy-efficiency of adopting a partial-allocation scheme in O-WSN. While it could be a communication waste to spend considerable overhead in partitioning a functional request to allow

for multiple assignments, yet the possibility of not finding a sufficient ReP deems this an important point to investigate.

7. ACKNOWLEDGMENTS

This research is funded by a grant from the Ontario Ministry of Economic Development and Innovation under the Ontario Research Fund-Research Excellence (ORF-RE) program.

8. REFERENCES

[1] S. Gollakota, F. Adib, D. Katabi, and S. Seshan, Clearing the RF Smog: Making 802.11N Robust to Cross-technology Interference. In Anonymous*Proceedings of the ACM SIGCOMM 2011 Conference*. ACM, New York, NY, USA, 2011, pp.170-181.

[2] Y. Hou, M. Li and S. Yu, Surviving the RF smog: Making Body Area Networks robust to cross-technology interference. In Anonymous *Sensor, Mesh and Ad Hoc Communications and Networks (SECON), 2013 10th Annual IEEE Communications Society Conference on*, 2013, 353-361.

[3] S. Oteafy and H. Hassanin, Re-Usable Resources in Wireless Sensor Networks: A Linear Optimization for a Novel Application Overlay Paradigm over Multiple Networks. In Anonymous *Global Telecommunications Conference (GLOBECOM 2011), 2011 IEEE.* , 2011, 1-5.

[4] S. Oteafy and H. Hassanein, Utilizing transient resources in dynamic wireless sensor networks, *Wireless Communications and Networking Conference (WCNC), 2012 IEEE* , pp.2124,2128, 1-4 April 2012

[5] I. Dietrich and F. Dressler, On the Lifetime of Wireless Sensor Networks. ACM Trans.Sen.Netw., Vol. 5, Iss.1 (2009), pp.1-39.

[6] S. Oteafy and H. Hassanein, Resource Re-use in Wireless Sensor Networks: Realizing a Synergetic Internet of Things. Journal of Communications, 7, 7 (2012), 484-493.

[7] A. Cárdenas, M. García-Molina, S. Sales and J. Capmany, A new model of bandwidth growth estimation based on the gompertz curve: Application to optical access networks," Journal of Lightwave Technology, vol. 22, no. 11, pp. 2460-2468, 2004.

[8] H. Kuhn, The Hungarian method for the assignment problem. Naval Research Logistics Quarterly, Vol. 2, Iss. 1, No. 2 (1955), pp. 83-97.

[9] R. Burkard, E. Rainer, M. Dell'Amico and S. Martello, *Assignment Problems, Revised Reprint*. Siam, 2009.

[10] D. Miorandi, S. Sicari, F. Pellegrini, and I. Chlamtac, Internet of things: Vision, applications and research challenges. Ad Hoc Networks, 10, 7 (2012), 1497.

[11] Y. Zhang, R. Yu, S. Xie, W. Yao, Y. Xiao and M. Guizani, Home M2M networks: Architectures, standards, and QoS improvement. Communications Magazine, IEEE, 49, 4 (2011), 44-52.

[12] R Kulkarni, A. Forster and G. K. Venayagamoorthy, Computational intelligence in wireless sensor networks: A survey, IEEE Communications Surveys & Tutorials, vol. 13, no. 1, pp. 68-96, 2011.

[13] A. Taha, H. Hassanein, and H. Mouftah, Vertical handoffs as a radio resource management tool. Comput. Commun., Vol. 31, Iss. 5 (2008), pp. 950-961.

Transmission Power Control-based Opportunistic Routing for Wireless Sensor Networks

Rodolfo W. L. Coutinho[1,2], Azzedine Boukerche[2], Luiz F. M. Vieira[1],
Antonio A. F. Loureiro[1]

[1]Federal University of Minas Gerais, Belo Horizonte, MG, Brazil
{rwlc, lfvieira, loureiro}@dcc.ufmg.br

[2]University of Ottawa, Ottawa, ON, Canada
boukerch@site.uottawa.ca

ABSTRACT

Energy efficient and reliable communication are two very important and conflicting requirements in the design of large-scale, self-organizing wireless sensor networks (WSNs). By reducing the transmission power level of the nodes, energy conservation is achieved whereas the communication reliability is degraded.

We propose a novel opportunistic routing protocol to reduce the energy consumption while keep the communication reliability in acceptable levels. Transmission power Control-based Opportunistic Routing (TCOR) saves energy by reducing the transmission power of the nodes while maintains the communication reliability by employing the opportunistic forwarding paradigm, leveraging the broadcast nature of wireless transmission medium. We propose an expected energy cost function for next-hop forwarder set selection, which considers the multiple available transmission power levels and the impact of each one on the next-hop packet reception probability.

Simulation results show the proposed TCOR routing protocol can lower the energy consumption per packet by an average of 80% as compared with two opportunistic routing related protocols using the maximal power transmission. While significantly reduces the energy cost to deliver a data packet, TCOR keeps the packet delivery ratio in acceptable levels, being only 4% less than when maximum power level is used.

Categories and Subject Descriptors

C.2.2 [**Computer-Communication Networks**]: Network Protocols

Keywords

Energy-efficiency; wireless sensor networks; power control; opportunistic routing

1. INTRODUCTION

Wireless sensor networks (WSNs) are a special kind of wireless ad hoc networks, composed by a collection of sensor nodes densely deployed over a geographic area [1, 2]. Commonly, WSNs are expected to run in inhospitable environments where the human intervention is difficult or even impractical. In WSNs, sensor nodes organize themselves autonomously in a network to collaboratively perform sensing, processing and communication functions in order to monitor and track events of interest. Also, sensor nodes are responsible to report, over wireless links in a multihop way, the gathered data to the sink node. They are characterized by having limited sensing, computing and wireless communication capabilities. Furthermore, each sensor node has a finite power source supply often consisting of a battery with a limited energy budget [3]. From the limited energy supply of sensor nodes and the difficulty recharging or replacement their batteries, energy awareness is a very important and well-known key factor in design of algorithms and protocols in these networks.

Given the communication as the most energy-consuming operation in wireless networks [4], one of the most effective way to save energy is through the determination of energy efficient network topologies. This is done by using the transmission power level, at each node, as low as possible [5, 6, 3]. The main motivation for this is that the energy required to transmit a message is, at least, quadratically proportional to the distance [7, 8]. Thus, long-range communication links are abandoned in favor of the short-range communication links. In reducing the transmission power level at the nodes, the constraint of whole network connectivity guarantee should be considered. Furthermore, other metrics might be used in designing power control–based topology control algorithms, such as throughput and delay. In addition, power control–based topology control can increases the communication capacity of ad hoc networks by confining interference, specially of WSNs which have high densities deployments.

However, low transmission power may lead to degradation of link reliability. For instance, Lin et al. [9] investigated the radio communication quality between wireless sensor nodes when different transmission powers are considered. Experiments revealed the correlation between Received Signal Strength Indicator (RSSI)/Link Quality Indicator (LQI) and link quality, which can guide the design of power control–based topology control approaches to properly select an enough transmission power guarantying a good packet reception ratio. Hackmann et al. [10], although found RSSI and LQI are not always indicators of link quality in indoor environments, also argued that increasing transmission power improves the quality of individual links.

A new way to improve reliability and network throughput is through the usage of opportunistic routing paradigm [11, 12, 13]. In opportunistic routing (OR), taking advantage of the shared transmission medium, each packet is broadcast to a forwarder set of neighbors. The packet will be retransmitted only if none of the neighbors in the set receive it. OR has advantages and disadvantages impacting on the network performance. OR reduces the number of possible retransmissions, the energy cost involved in those retransmissions, and help to decrease the amount of possible collisions. However, it leads to a high end-to-end delay since neighboring nodes should wait for the time needed to the packet reaches the furthest node in the forwarder set. However, the well-known opportunistic routing proposed for wireless mesh networks are not suitable for WSNs, due to its particular characteristics, such as high density deployments.

In this work, we propose a novel opportunistic routing protocol for wireless sensor networks that combines power control and opportunistic routing to reduce the energy consumption while maintain an acceptable link reliability. Transmission power Control-based Opportunistic Routing (TCOR) uses the expected energy cost function for next-hop forwarder set selection. This function considers the multiple available transmission power levels and the impact of each one on the next-hop packet reception probability. Simulation results show TCOR can lower the energy consumption per packet by an average of 80% and maintain the packet delivery ratio only 4% lower as compared with two opportunistic routing related protocols using the maximal power transmission.

The rest of the paper is organized as follows. In Section 2 we summarize and discuss some relevant related work. In Section 3, we provide some preliminary concepts used by the proposed routing protocol. Section 4, we present our proposed protocol, transmission power control-based opportunistic routing. In Section 5 , we evaluate performance of the proposed protocol, in comparison with two opportunistic routing protocols. Finally, we conclude with remarks on future work in Section 6.

2. RELATED WORK

Energy conservation is a well-know problem in wireless sensor networks and have been subject in several works in literature.

Lin et al. [9] proposed the ATPC protocol to perform the transmission power control adapting to external changes. The proposed protocol finds the minimum transmission power at each node that still can provide a good link quality. To do so, ATPC has a predictive model to approximate the distribution of RSSIs at different transmission power level, which is considered as an indicative of the link quality. From this model, ATCP employs a feedback-based transmission power control do dynamically maintain individual link quality over time.

Hackmann et al. [10] proposed the ART topology control protocol for indoor wireless sensor networks. In ART, each node is initially set to transmit at its maximum power. In the beginning, ART monitors all outgoing packet trans-

missions and record of whether each transmission failed or succeeded in a sliding window of size w. When the window is full, ART temporarily lowers the power by one level if the number of failures is below a threshold. If the number of failures is above the threshold, ART adjusts the transmission power to improve the link quality.

Similarly, our proposal address the problem of energy conservation by adjusting the transmission power of the nodes. However, we employ the opportunistic forwarding strategy instead of the usage of mechanisms to actively measure or predict the link quality, in order to make our power control procedure simple and efficient to cope with time and spatial link quality variations.

Other works address the problem of link quality through a new routing paradigm called of opportunistic routing. Commonly, opportunistic routing in WSNs have been proposed for the scenarios of duty cycled networks. The goal is to reduce the need of signaling to coordinate the moment in which the sender and the next-hop node should be awake, consequently, reducing the energy consumption. Moreover, some proposals leverage the broadcast transmission to seek reduce the delay. In these approaches, when a node has a packet to transmit, it selects the forwarder set and broadcast the packet. The first wake-up node, closest to the sink, that successful received the packet, continues the forwarding process.

Ghadimi et al. [14], introduces a new metric called of Estimated Duty Cycled wake-ups (EDC), for forwarder set selection in opportunistic routing. EDC minimizes the expected number of transmissions required to forward a packet by determining a forwarder set, by focusing on the radio-on time of duty cycled neighbors. An opportunistic routing protocol employing this metric was proposed in [15].

Aitsaadi et al. [16] proposed a cross-layer scheme combining three variants of geographic opportunistic routing with receiver-initiated (RI) MAC protocol for low duty-cycled WSNs. In RI-MAC protocol, whenever a node awakes and switches on its transceiver, it sends a beacon to inform its neighbors. At the routing level, the basic-opportunistic variant selects the next hop as the next active neighbor that decrease the remaining distance to the sink. In this variant, the packet waits for an unlimited period if there is no neighbor with smaller distance to the sink. The opportunistic with delay variant works as the basic-opportunistic variant, except that the packet will be discarded after a fixed limited amount of time if it is not transmitted. In the opportunistic with backtracking variant, instead the packet is discard as in opportunistic with delay, the packet is moved further away from the sink until a path to the destination is found and the node is tagged as a forbidden hop, to avoid transmissions for it in the future.

Similarly, So and Byun [17] proposed the opportunistic routing with in-network aggregation (ORIA) to further reduce energy consumption through aggregation off packets generated from multiple nodes. In ORIA, sensor node that has received a packet, holding the packet and temporarily increase its duty cycle ratio that temporarily increase duty cycle ratio to augment the chance of in-network data aggregation.

In [18] the authors proposed an energy efficient opportunistic routing (EEOR) protocol. In EEOR, the next-hop forwarder set selection and forwarder prioritization is based according with the expected energy cost to delivery the packet. In determining the next-hop forwarder set, a neighbor will be included in the forwarder set if its expected energy cost to continue forwarding the packet is less than of the current node.

Our work is similar to the EEOR [18] in the sense that we also determine the next-hop forwarder set based on the expected energy cost. However, in our expected energy cost function, we also consider the energy cost relative to the packet reception of the neighbors. It is important because, for the current technology, the energy cost to transmit and to receive a packet are within a factor of two [19]. Furthermore, we combine power control with opportunistic routing to achieve better results in energy conservation.

3. PRELIMINARIES

3.1 Network Model and Assumptions

We consider a WSN with N nodes and assume that all wireless nodes are deployed randomly over a 2-dimensional monitored area with side equal to l. We assume that each node knows its position location through GPS or some localization method [20]. We consider that there are n transmission power levels $P_t^1 < P_t^2 < \ldots < P_t^i < \ldots < P_t^n$ for each node, and its respective transmission energy consumption $E_t^1 < E_t^2 < \ldots < E_t^i < \ldots < E_t^n$. The network topology is then modeled by a communication graph $\mathcal{G} = (\mathcal{V}, \mathcal{E})$, with the following properties:

- $\mathcal{V} = \{v_1, \ldots, v_n\}$, $|\mathcal{V}| = N$, is the set of sensor nodes;

- $\mathcal{E}$ is a set of directed links between the nodes;

- $\langle i, j \rangle \in \mathcal{E}$ if and only if v_i can communicate directly with v_j, i.e., if v_j is within the communication range of v_i considering the maximum transmission power level P_t^i;

- $e(i, j, p) = [0, 1]$ is the *weight* associated with the link $\langle i, j \rangle$, that corresponds to the probability that a transmitted packet from v_i to v_j using the transmission power level P_t^p, will not be successfully.

Since the number of neighboring nodes of a node v_i will depend of its transmission power level, we define $\mathcal{N}_p(i)$ as the neighboring nodes set of v_i formed by the all nodes v_j such that v_i will can communicate directly when is using transmission power level p, that is, $\mathcal{N}_p(i) = \{v_j : e(i, k, p) < 1\}$.

Finally, we define the forwarder set $\mathcal{F}_p(i) \subseteq \mathcal{N}_p(i)$ of a node v_i using the transmission power level p, as the subset of its neighbor set, composed by the neighbors closest to the sink, such that the weight of the link is less than 1. Nodes in the forwarder set will participate forwarding packets from v_i towards to sink.

3.2 Packet Delivery Probability Estimation

We use the following channel model in order to measure the link quality between two nodes with distance d. Like in [12], we assume that the channel impairments are characterized by a shadowing propagation model. In the shadowing propagation model, the power received at a distance d, in terms of the transmitted power P_t is:

$$P_r(d)|_{dB} = 10log_{10}\left(\frac{P_t G_t G_r \lambda^2}{L(4\pi)^2 d^\beta}\right) + X_{dB}, \qquad (1)$$

where G_t and G_r are the transmission and reception antenna gain, respectively; L is the system loss; λ is the signal wavelength; β is a path loss exponent, and X_{dB} is a Gaussian random variable with zero mean and standard deviation σ_{dB}.

Packets are correctly received if the received power $P_r(d)|_{dB}$ is equal to or greater than $RXThresh$. From Equation 1, the delivery probability at a distance d is:

$$p(d_{ij}) = Q\left(\frac{1}{\sigma_{dB}} 10log_{10}\left(\frac{RXThresh \times L(4\pi)^2 d^\beta}{P_t G_t G_r \lambda^2}\right)\right), \qquad (2)$$

where $Q(z) = \frac{1}{\sqrt{2\pi}} \int_z^\infty e^{-y^2/2} dy$.

3.3 Expected Energy Cost Model

We present the expected energy cost model used in each node to determine both its forwarder set and transmission power level. The expected energy cost function is a combination of the one hop expected energy cost corresponding to the cost relative transmission of the packet from the source node to its forwarder set, at the transmission power level p and, the expected energy forwarding cost, that means the energy cost for delivery the packet from some nodes in the forwarder set to the sink.

With the proposed expected energy cost function, the idea is to capture the tradeoff between the selection of a small and a large transmission power and, consequently, the number of neighbors to act as next hop forwarder. By choosing a small transmission power, less neighbors will be selected as next-hop forwarder. The energy consumption will be reduced whereas the end-to-end delay might increases and the link reliability might decreases. Oppositely, a high transmission power might result in a large number of nodes in the next-hop forwarder set, increasing the probability of successfully delivery the packet.

Consider a node u and its neighbors set $\mathcal{N}_p(u)$ for each p-transmission power level. $\mathcal{N}_p(u)$ is increasing order according by the expected cost. In the beginning, the expected cost of the neighbors is set to infinity. In each node, we will compute the expected cost of its next-hop forwarder set at transmission level p, based on the expected cost of its neighbors of sending data to the sink node. As in [18], the goal is to select a power transmission level p and a subset of neighbor nodes $\mathcal{N}_p(u)$ as forwarder set $\mathcal{F}_p(u)$ such that the expected cost for u, using the pth transmission power level, to send a packet to the sink node is minimized.

Let $C_h^p(u)$ denote the one hop expected energy cost incurred by the transmission of the node u at the pth transmission power level to send a packet to be successful received by at least one node in the forwarder set $\mathcal{F}_p(u)$. $C_h^p(u)$ can be calculated as follows:

$$C_h^p(u) = \frac{E_h}{\rho}, \qquad (3)$$

where E_h captures the energy consumption due to transmission and reception of announcement and data packets from the node and its neighbors; and ρ is the probability that the packet sent by node u will be received by at least one node in the forwarder set given by:

$$\rho = 1 - \prod_{j=1}^{|\mathcal{F}_p(u)|} e(u, j, k). \qquad (4)$$

To determine the energy consumption relative to transmission and reception of data packets (E_h), we define the random variable $T_p(i)$ as the number of transmissions using the transmission power level p until some awake forward node receives the announcement packet from the node i. The successful reception of the data packet by a forwarder node at the r tries, requires that all the $r-1$ transmissions between i and $j \in \mathcal{F}_p(i)$ fail. Hence $T_p(i)$ follows a geometric distribution with pdf:

$$Pr\{T_p(i) = r\} = \prod_{j \in \mathcal{F}_p(i)} e(i,j,p)^{r-1} \left(1 - \prod_{j \in \mathcal{F}_p(i)} e(i,j,p)\right),$$
$$(5)$$

and mean:

$$E\{T_p(i)\} = \sum_{r=0}^{\infty} r \times Pr\{T_p(i) = r\} = \frac{1}{1 - \prod_{j \in \mathcal{F}_p(i)} e(i,j,p)}.$$
$$(6)$$

From Equation 6, the energy consumption relative to transmission and reception of data packets is

$$E_h = (\mid \mathcal{N}_p(u) \mid E_r + E_t^p) E\{T_p(u)\} \times \frac{L}{B}, \qquad (7)$$

where E_r is the energy consumption for reception, E_t^p is the energy consumption for transmitting at transmission power level p, B is bandwidth, and L is the data packet size.

Let $C_{\mathcal{F}_p(u)}$ denote the expected energy forwarding cost from $u's$ forwarder set to the sink node. Assume the forwarder set $\mathcal{F}_p(u) = \{v_1, v_2, \ldots, v_n\}$ is ordering in increasing order by the expected energy cost, where $i < j \Rightarrow C(v_i) \leq C(v_j)$. Let the probability of the node $v_i \in \mathcal{F}_p(u)$ forward the packet equal to $1 - e(u,i,p)$, and its expected energy cost $C(v_i)$. We can calculate the expected energy forwarding cost ($C_{\mathcal{F}_p(u)}$), at transmission power level p, as follows. The highest priority node in the forwarder set, $v_1 \in \mathcal{F}_p(u)$, will forward the data packet according with probability $1 - e(u, v_1, p)$ and the cost for delivery it to the sink will be $C(v_1)$. The node $v_2 \in \mathcal{F}_p(u)$ (second highest priority node) will forward the packet if the highest priority node fails and it successfully receives the packet, where the probability of this event is $e(u, v_1, p)(1 - e(u, v_2, p)$; $C(v_2)$ will be the cost incurred. Basically, the $v_i \in \mathcal{F}_p(u)$ node will forward the packet if it receives the packet and its predecessors did not. In this case, the cost will be $C(v_i)$. Thus, under the condition that at least one forwarder node receives the packet, the expected energy forwarding cost can be computed as:

$$C_{\mathcal{F}_p(u)} = \left(\left(1 - e(u, v_1, p)\right) C(v_1) + \right.$$
$$\left. \sum_{i=2}^{|\mathcal{F}_p(u)|} \left(\prod_{j=1}^{i-1} e(u, v_j, p)\right) \left(1 - e(u, v_i, p)\right) C(v_i)\right) / \rho \quad (8)$$

Finally, combining Equation 3 and Equation 8, the expected energy cost of the node u when it is using the power transmission level p is:

$$C_p(u) = C_h^p(u) + C_{\mathcal{F}_p(u)}. \qquad (9)$$

Algorithm 1 TCOR Forwarding Set Selection Algorithm

```
 1: for all  (p ∈ P)  do
 2:     C_p(u) ← ∞, F_p(u) ← ∅
 3:     for all  (v ∈ N_p(u))  do
 4:         if D(v,s) < D(n,s) then
 5:             if  (C_p(u) > C(v))  then
 6:                 F_p(u) ← F_p(u) ∪ v
 7:                 compute C_p(u) according w/ Equation 9
 8:             end if
 9:         end if
10:     end for
11: end for
```

4. ROUTING PROTOCOL DESIGN

In this section, we describes each procedure of the proposed routing protocol. In a nutshell, TCOR is composed by a *neighborhood discovery phase*, where beacons are disseminated in order to each node builds its neighbor table; the *forwarder set selection*, where each node determines its forwarder set by means of the expected energy cost described in the previous section.

4.1 Neighborhood Discovery

When nodes are deployed, they start the neighborhood discovery phase. The neighborhood discovery phase lasts for r rounds. The goal of this phase is that each node builds its neighboring table with the location and link quality information to reach each neighbor along the different power transmissions levels.

Link quality is frequently obtained by dividing the rate of packets overhead from a neighbor by the forwarding rate of the same neighbor. This manner refers to the packet reception ratio (PRR). The main drawback in the calculation of PRR arises from the fact that a long period of time is necessary [9, 15]. In [9] the authors analyzed the correlation between the RSSI and the link quality in different wireless sensor network deployment conditions. However, in [10] the authors showed that RSSI and LQI are not always indicators of link quality in indoor environments.

Herein, for the sake of simplicity, we determine the link quality between a pair of nodes by means of signal propagation model as in Equation 2. Thus, each node broadcasts beacon messages using its maximum transmission power. Each beacon message contains the unique id of the sender, and its x, y location. Whenever a node v_j receives a beacon message from v_i, it determines the link error probability $e(j, i, p)$ for each transmission power level, to reach v_i, and updates its neighbor table $\mathcal{N}_p(j)$ with the error probability and the location of the neighbor.

4.2 Forwarder Set Selection

In the forwarder set selection phase, each node determines the neighbor nodes that are allowed to received the data packet, and its respective forwarding priority. The goal is to compute the most appropriate transmission power level and the forwarder set such that the expected energy cost is minimum. We employ a mechanism similar to the used in [18]. The basic idea is including the neighbor in the forwarder set and stop the algorithm when the cost starts to increase.

After the neighborhood discovery phase, the sink node sets its expected energy cost to 0 and then broadcasts to its neighbors. Whenever a node receives a message with an updated cost, it runs the Algorithm 1 to find the transmission power level and the forwarder set. For each transmission power level, the node starts with expected energy cost equals to infinity and an empty forwarder set. Considering each neighbor node from the neighborhood set in increasing order by the expected energy cost, the node adds the neighbor in the forwarder set if: i) it leads the packet to a positive progress towards the sinks, that is, the neighbor is closest the sink; and ii) the expected energy cost of the neighbor is less than of the node considering the current forwarder set.

At the end, the node selects the transmission level and the forwarder set satisfying the following statements:

1. The probability that, at least, one node in the forwarder set must be equals or upper to σ, that is $\rho_p \geq \sigma$;

2. The cost of the forwarder set is the minimum, that is, the pth transmission power level and the corresponding forwarder set $\mathcal{F}_p$ will be considered if $\forall k \in \mathcal{P}, \mathcal{F}_p < \mathcal{F}_k$;

3. The cost is less than the previous calculated: $C_p \leq C(u)$.

In above, the first statement tries to capture the tradeoff between the energy consumption and reliability. Reducing the transmission power leads to saving energy, however, the reliability is degraded. Setting an appropriate value of σ should be done according with the most critical requirement, that is, this value can be low if the application can tolerate some failures and it is envisioned to perform for a long time. The second statement means that the transmission power level must be the one from those guarantying reliability of σ, that spent less energy cost. Finally, the node will update its transmission level and the forwarding set if the select is best than the previous one. If the difference between the cost of the new forwarder set and the previously selected is less than a threshold τ, the node broadcasts its new cost. Unless otherwise specified, the value of σ is 0.98 and τ is 10^{-3}.

After a time without update its cost, a node sets its new transmission power level and starts the environment monitoring.

4.3 Packet Forwarding

When a node goes to forward a packet generated by itself, it includes the forwarder set of the selected transmission power level, into the header of the packet, and then broadcasts it. A timer t is scheduled to retransmit the packet if no acknowledgment message of this packet is received during this time. After four tries, the packet will be discarded.

Different approach is performed when the packet is coming from a neighbor. Firstly, the node checks if the incoming packet was already forwarded. If it was not, the node determines its priority in the forwarding set contained into the header of the packet, and then schedules an acknowledgment and after the packet transmission. This procedure, besides to increase the end-to-end delay, is a common way to prioritize transmissions in opportunistic routing reducing duplicated packets in the network.

During the waiting time, if an acknowledgment or data packet with the same identifier arrives from a neighbor closest to the sink, the node cancels its waiting time and discard the packet. Otherwise, the node broadcasts the acknowledgment packet and subsequently, the data packet, towards to the sink.

Output power	Consumption
$\mathcal{P}_t^1 = 0\,\mathrm{dBm}$	17.4 mA
$\mathcal{P}_t^2 = -1\,\mathrm{dBm}$	16.5 mA
$\mathcal{P}_t^3 = -3\,\mathrm{dBm}$	15.2 mA
$\mathcal{P}_t^4 = -5\,\mathrm{dBm}$	13.9 mA
$\mathcal{P}_t^5 = -7\,\mathrm{dBm}$	12.5 mA
$\mathcal{P}_t^6 = -10\,\mathrm{dBm}$	11.2 mA
$\mathcal{P}_t^7 = -15\,\mathrm{dBm}$	9.9 mA
$\mathcal{P}_t^8 = -25\,\mathrm{dBm}$	8.5 mA

Table 1: Output power and corresponding current consumption.

Parameter	Value
Supply voltage	3.3 V
Receive mode current	19.7 mA
Receiver sensitivity	-90 dBm
Frequency	914 MHz
Bandwidth	250 kbps

Table 2: Transceiver configuration parameters

5. PERFORMANCE EVALUATION

In this section, we present the performance evaluation of our proposed routing protocol. We compare TCOR against opportunistic routing where the forwarder set selection is done according with the EDC metric [14] and Energy Efficient Opportunistic Routing (EEOR) [18]. All evaluated routing protocols have been implemented using Network Simulator 2.35. In Section 5.1, we describe the configuration of scenario and the parameters used in the simulations. In Section 5.2, we present the results. In our comparison, we have considered four main metrics: *packet delivery ratio*, which is the fraction of delivered packets; *average latency*, that is the average delay for a packet to reach the sink node; *average number of redundant packets*, which is the redundant copies received by the sink; and *energy per packet*, which is the energy consumption for delivered data packet. As in [9], we calculate the total energy spent in the transmit state of the system, that is, when the node is sending or receiving packets.

5.1 Simulation Setup

In our simulations, the number of sensor nodes ranges from 25 to 125, randomly deployed in a region of size l of 250 m x 250 m. The sink node is located at the (0,0) fixed position. At the beginning of the simulation, all other sensor nodes on the network have 25 J of energy. Once the nodes are deployed, control messages are exchanged in order to calculate the forwarder set selection function at the nodes. After, nodes start generating packets. We consider that each node generates a data packet of L = 50 bytes of payload, with probability of 50% in each interval of 5 minutes. The simulations last 3 hours.

In this study, the values were set according with the parameters of the sensor node Telos [21] that uses the Chipcon

Parameter	Value
G_t, G_r, L	1
β	2.7
σ_{dB}	6

Table 3: Propagation model parameters

CC2420 radio. The values are summarized in Table 1 and 2. Using TCOR, sensor nodes can select its transmission power level for the set of eight discrete values (please refer to Table 1). Using opportunistic routing with EDC metric and EEOR, each node transmits at the maximum power level. For the sake of simplicity, the weight $e(i, j, p)$ and link quality in EDC and EEOR of all links are determined from the Shadowing propagation model, according with parameter values showed in Table 3. Fig. 1 depicts the packet delivery probability as a function of the distance and transmission power level for the Shadowing propagation model. The results correspond with an average value of 50 runs with a 95 percent confidence interval.

5.2 Simulation Results

Fig. 2 shows the fraction of nodes that selected each transmission power level for different network density scenarios. We can note for low density scenario (Fig. 2a) most part of the sensor nodes select an intermediate transmission power level, which results approximately in communication radius ranging from 50 m to 75 m, when we observe a delivery probability of 80% (please refer Fig. 1). We can also note more than 10% of the nodes select the maximum transmission power level. As the network density increases, the nodes trend to select medium to low transmission power. For instance, for high density scenario (Fig. 2d), the results show the nodes are using low transmission power, where more than 97% of them are with communication radius varying from 25 m to 45 m. This trend is due to the fact that when the density is lower, a high communication radius is necessary in order to keep the network connectivity. As density increases, the nodes reduce their transmission power aiming to save energy, give that the network connectivity will be not degraded.

Fig. 3a depicts the packet delivery ratio. This result shows EDC and EEOR outperforms TCOR. For low density scenarios, the difference between them achieves 4%. This is due to the fact that some nodes in TCOR opt to use less transmission power, as corroborated in Fig. 2a.

Fig. 3b shows the average end-to-end delay. As expected, the delay is high in TCOR as compared with EDC and EEOR, mainly for high density scenarios. The reason for that is as the nodes lower their transmission power, data packets will be routed along more hops until their reach the destination. Besides the processing delays in each hop, the packet transmissions are delayed in order to coordinate the transmissions of the packet according with the priority of the nodes in the forwarder set.

Fig. 3d shows the energy consumption per delivered packet. In this figure, we can see that TCOR outperforms EDC and EEOR in all density scenarios studied. TCOR achieves a reduction of until 80% when compared with the other analyzed routing protocols. Moreover, we can note different trends when the network density increases. In TCOR, the energy per delivered packet decreases, whereas in EDC and EEOR increases. The reason for that is, as the network density increases, EDC and EEOR will have forwarder set with a large number of nodes. Thus, more acknowledgment packets are transmitted. Moreover, EDC and EEOR will have more nodes receiving the same packet. Meanwhile, the increment of the density leads to TCOR to reduce the transmission power level of the nodes, as showed in Figs. 2a and 2d, saving energy from transmissions, reception and packet collisions.

To summarize, the transmission power control of TCOR and the utilization of opportunistic routing cope as well in different densities scenarios and properly leads to the selection of transmission level in what the QoS is guaranteed and the energy cost is considerably reduced.

6. CONCLUSIONS AND FUTURE WORKS

In this work, we proposed and evaluated transmission a novel power control and opportunistic routing protocol for wireless sensor networks. The proposed protocol uses transmission power control to save energy, and the opportunistic routing paradigm to keep the reliability in adequate level. Simulation results showed for different network densities, the sensor nodes adequately selected an appropriated transmission power level from a discrete set of possible values, keeping the fraction of delivered data packet higher than 96% for the most difficult scenario of low density, whereas the energy cost for delivery a data packet was reduced in 80% when compared with other opportunistic routing protocols.

As future work, we plan to better investigate our proposal by comparing it against some power control proposals. Yet, we intend to analyze the power control–based topology control combined with opportunistic routing in scenarios of duty cycled wireless sensor networks, with the objective of reducing the waiting time until the sender find a wake-up next-hop node.

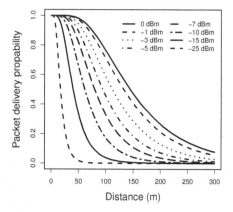

Figure 1: Probability of delivery a packet according with the transmission power level and distance between the sender and receiver.

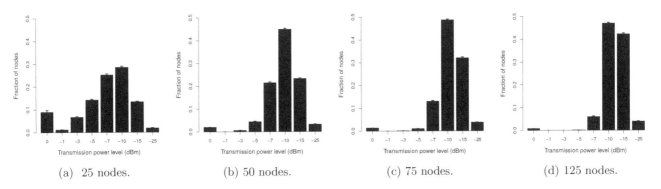

(a) 25 nodes. (b) 50 nodes. (c) 75 nodes. (d) 125 nodes.

Figure 2: Fraction of nodes *versus* transmission power levels for different network density scenarios.

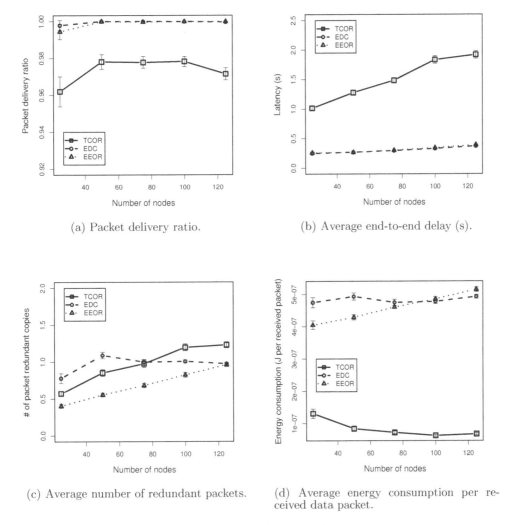

(a) Packet delivery ratio.

(b) Average end-to-end delay (s).

(c) Average number of redundant packets.

(d) Average energy consumption per received data packet.

Figure 3: Simulation results.

7. ACKNOWLEDGMENTS

This work was partially supported by the Canada Research Chairs program, NSERC Strategic Project Program and NSERC DIVA Network Research Program, and ORF/MRI Program. The authors also wish to thank CNPq and CAPES.

8. REFERENCES

[1] J. Yick, B. Mukherjee, and D. Ghosal. Wireless sensor network survey. *Computer Networks*, 52(12):2292 – 2330, 2008.

[2] A. Boukerche. *Algorithms and Protocols for Wireless Sensor Networks*, volume 62. Wiley-IEEE Press, 2008.

[3] G. Anastasi, M. Conti, M. Di Francesco, and A. Passarella. Energy conservation in wireless sensor networks: A survey. *Ad Hoc Networks*, 7(3):537 – 568, 2009.

[4] L. M. Feeney and M. Nilsson. Investigating the energy consumption of a wireless network interface in an ad hoc networking environment. In *Proceedings of The Twentieth Annual Joint Conference of the IEEE Computer and Communications Societies. INFOCOM '01*, volume 3, pages 1548–1557 vol.3, 2001.

[5] R. Wattenhofer, Li Li, P. Bahl, and Yi-Min Wang. Distributed topology control for power efficient operation in multihop wireless ad hoc networks. In *Proceedings of the Twentieth Annual Joint Conference of the IEEE Computer and Communications Societies. INFOCOM '01*, volume 3, pages 1388–1397 vol.3, 2001.

[6] L. H. A. Correia, D. F. Macedo, A. L. dos Santos, A. A.F. Loureiro, and J. M. S. Nogueira. Transmission power control techniques for wireless sensor networks. *Computer Networks*, 51(17):4765 – 4779, 2007.

[7] M. Burkhart, P. von Rickenbach, R. Wattenhofer, and A. Zollinger. Does topology control reduce interference? In *Proceedings of the 5th ACM International Symposium on Mobile Ad Hoc Networking and Computing*, MobiHoc '04, pages 9–19, 2004.

[8] P. Santi. Topology control in wireless ad hoc and sensor networks. *ACM Comput. Surv.*, 37(2):164–194, June 2005.

[9] S. Lin, J. Zhang, G. Zhou, L. Gu, J. A. Stankovic, and T. He. Atpc: Adaptive transmission power control for wireless sensor networks. In *Proceedings of the 4th International Conference on Embedded Networked Sensor Systems*, SenSys '06, pages 223–236, 2006.

[10] G. Hackmann, O. Chipara, and C. Lu. Robust topology control for indoor wireless sensor networks. In *Proceedings of the 6th ACM Conference on Embedded Network Sensor Systems*, SenSys '08, pages 57–70, 2008.

[11] S. Biswas and R. Morris. ExOR: Opportunistic multi-hop routing for wireless networks. *SIGCOMM Comput. Commun. Rev.*, 35(4):133–144, August 2005.

[12] L. Cerdà-Alabern, A. Darehshoorzadeh, and V. Pla. Optimum node placement in wireless opportunistic routing networks. *Ad Hoc Networks*, 11(8):2273 – 2287, 2013.

[13] A. Boukerche and A. Darehshoorzadeh. Opportunistic routing in wireless networks: Models, algorithms, and classifications. *ACM Comput. Surv.*, 2014.

[14] E. Ghadimi, O. Landsiedel, P. Soldati, and M. Johansson. A metric for opportunistic routing in duty cycled wireless sensor networks. In *Proceedings of the 9th Annual IEEE Communications Society Conference on Sensor, Mesh and Ad Hoc Communications and Networks*, SECON '12, pages 335–343, June 2012.

[15] O. Landsiedel, E. Ghadimi, S. Duquennoy, and M. Johansson. Low power, low delay: Opportunistic routing meets duty cycling. In *Proceedings of the 11th International Conference on Information Processing in Sensor Networks*, IPSN '12, pages 185–196, 2012.

[16] N. Aitsaadi, B. Blaszczyszyn, and P. Muhlethaler. Performance of opportunistic routing in low duty-cycle wireless sensor networks. In *IFIP Wireless Days (WD)*, pages 1–3, Nov 2012.

[17] J. So and H. Byun. Opportunistic routing with in-network aggregation for asynchronous duty-cycled wireless sensor networks. *Wireless Networks*, pages 1–14, 2013.

[18] X. Mao, S. Tang, X. Xu, X.-Y. Li, and H. Ma. Energy-efficient opportunistic routing in wireless sensor networks. *IEEE Transactions on Parallel and Distributed Systems*, 22(11):1934–1942, Nov 2011.

[19] G. Resta P. Santi D. M. Blough, M. Leoncini. Topology control with better radio models: Implications for energy and multi-hop interference. In *Proceedings of the 8th ACM/IEEE International Symposium on Modeling, Analysis and Simulation of Wireless and Mobile Systems*, MSWiM '05, pages 260–268, 2008.

[20] A. Boukerche, H. A.B. Oliveira, E. F. Nakamura, and A. A. F. Loureiro. Localization systems for wireless sensor networks. *Wireless Commun.*, 14(6):6–12, December 2007.

[21] Telos: Ultra low power ieee 802.15.4 compliant wireless sensor module. http://www.eecs.harvard.edu/~konrad/References/TinyOSDocs/telos-reva-datasheet-r.pdf, 2004. [Online; accessed April-2014].

Imputing Missing Values in Sensor Networks Using Sparse Data Representations

Liang Ze Wong, Huiling Chen,
Shaowei Lin
Institute for Infocomm Research, A*STAR
1 Fusionopolis Way, #21-01 (Connexis)
Singapore 138632
{wonglz,chenhl,lins}@i2r.a-star.edu.sg

Daniel C. Chen
Massachusetts Institute of Technology
77 Massachusetts Ave
Cambridge, MA 02139
dcchen@mit.edu

ABSTRACT

Sensor networks are increasingly being used to provide timely information about the physical, urban and human environment. Algorithms that depend on sensor data often assume that the readings are complete. However, node failures or communication breakdowns result in missing data entries, preventing the use of such algorithms. To impute these missing values, we propose a method of exploiting spatial correlations which is based on the sparse autoencoder and inspired by the conditional Restricted Boltzmann Machine that contested for the Netflix Prize. We modify the autoencoder to cope with missing data, and test it on data from a sensor testbed in Santander, Spain. We show that our algorithm extracts features from datasets with high proportions of missing data and uses these features to accurately and efficiently impute missing entries.

Categories and Subject Descriptors

H.4 [**INFORMATION SYSTEMS**]: Information systems applications—*Spatial-temporal systems: Sensor networks*; I. [**COMPUTING METHODOLOGIES**]: Machine Learning—*Machine learning approaches: Neural networks*

Keywords

Sensor Networks; Missing Data; Neural Networks

1. INTRODUCTION

Sensor networks are increasingly being deployed in a variety of settings to sense and report on properties of physical (e.g. temperature, humidity, air quality) and human (e.g. crowds, traffic) environments. Wireless Sensor Networks (WSN) are a variant of sensor networks that rely on wireless communications rather than landlines to report their readings. However, the depletion of a sensor's limited energy supplies, the unreliable nature of wireless communications and the implementation of duty-cycling protocols or sparse

deployments all result in the loss of sensor information in WSNs. This is detrimental in sensor-actuator networks and intruder detection systems. There thus is a need for fast and simple data reconstruction algorithms on sensors and gateways. This paper proposes a method of imputing missing data that is based on the Sparse Auto-Encoder (SAE) [3]. We modify the autoencoder so that it produces good encodings even in the presence of missing data. These encodings are then decoded to provide an estimate of the missing entries. The encoding and decoding phases are fast to compute and can be easily carried out on the sensor nodes and gateways themselves.

The rest of this paper is organized as follows: in the next two subsections, we present related work on existing methods for imputing missing data in wireless sensors and neural networks. Section 2 presents the missing data problem in sensor networks, and lists desired properties of potential solutions to this problem. In Section 3, we present our version of the SAE that accounts for and imputes missing data. In Section 4, we benchmark the performance of our algorithm against existing algorithms on temperature data from a deployed sensor network testbed in Santander, Spain [7]. We conclude in Section 5 by discussing our results and presenting further applications of our method in WSNs.

1.1 Related Work in Sensor networks

In [2], a compressive sensing (CS) method for reconstructing data using spatio-temporal correlations is proposed. This involves carrying out the Singular Value Decomposition (SVD) of the entire sensor data matrix, rendering it too computationally intensive for on-site imputation. Our SAE-based method splits the computations into a computationally intensive training phase, which can take place on backend servers, and a fast, simple imputation phase, which can take place on gateways and sensor nodes. In [4], the authors propose a K-Nearest Neighbors (KNN)-based algorithm for estimating missing data in sensor networks. This essentially learns the single strongest linear feature present in the sensor data, whereas our SAE-based method is capable of learning multiple non-linear features.

1.2 Related Work in Neural networks

In [9], the authors suggest training the NN on data with missing values artificially filled in. This procedure introduces bias into the system and causes the NN to learn the filled-in estimates as features. Network reduction [8] trains a separate network for each pattern of missing data. Our al-

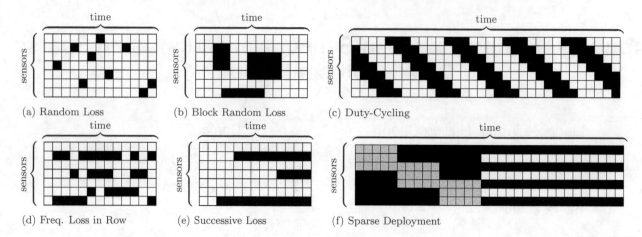

Figure 1: Missing Data Patterns. Figures (a,b,d,e) are from [2]; (c,f) show how resource-saving measures lead to missing data. Black represents missing data; in (f), grey represents the pre-deployment phase and white represents the final deployment.

gorithm can be though of as a way of fusing these separate networks and training it on data that has not be artificially filled.

The method that bears the greatest similarities with ours is the conditional RBM [6]. Our algorithm differs in both the kind of data that it receives, and the training algorithm. Further, [6] suggests that the conditional RBM can be unfolded and trained as an autoencoder, but that "overfitting becomes an issue and more careful model regularization is required". The successful derivation of the appropriate sparsity regularizer (8) is a key contribution of this paper. Two other related NN variants have been developed: DropOut [1] and DropConnect [10] which deliberately drop parts of the system in the training phase to act as a regularizer. Missing data essentially "drops" inputs to the hidden layer, while DropOut drops outputs of the hidden layer and DropConnect drops weights between layers.

2. MISSING DATA IN SENSOR NETWORKS

We have N sensors distributed in the environment, sensing over a period of T time-slots. The **environment matrix** [2], $\mathbf{X}$, is an $N \times T$ matrix, where the entry $x_{n,t} \in \mathbb{R}$ is the reading of the nth sensor node at time t. This matrix represents the ground truth, and is the data we are trying to reconstruct. The **observation matrix**, $\mathbf{\Theta}$, is a $N \times T$ binary matrix with entries

$$\theta_{n,t} = \begin{cases} 1 & \text{if } x_{n,t} \text{ is observed,} \\ 0 & \text{if } x_{n,t} \text{ is missing.} \end{cases} \quad (1)$$

The **sensing matrix** is the matrix of readings that are observed, and is defined as

$$\mathbf{X_s} := \mathbf{X} \star \mathbf{\Theta}, \quad (2)$$

where $\star$ denotes the elementwise product. Similarly, the **missing data matrix**, $\mathbf{X_m} := \mathbf{X} \star (1 - \mathbf{\Theta})$, is the matrix of readings that are misisng.

Given only $\mathbf{X_s}$ and $\mathbf{\Theta}$, the **missing data problem** is to obtain a reconstruction $\hat{\mathbf{X}}(\mathbf{X_s}, \mathbf{\Theta})$ such that the root-mean-square error (RMSE)

$$\sqrt{\frac{\|\mathbf{X_m} - \hat{\mathbf{X}_m}\|^2}{\|1 - \mathbf{\Theta}\|}} := \sqrt{\frac{\sum_{n,t}(1 - \theta_{n,t})(x_{n,t} - \hat{x}_{n,t})^2}{\sum_{n,t}(1 - \theta_{n,t})}} \quad (3)$$

is minimized. Note that we only compute the error over the missing entries (i.e. those for which $\theta_{n,t} = 0$).

2.1 Missing Data Patterns

A good characterization of missing data patterns and their causes can be found in [2]. They introduce these patterns: Random Loss, Block Random Loss, Frequent Loss in Row, and Successive Loss in Row, which are illustrated in Fig. 1. We supplement this list with patterns that arise from resource-saving measures. Duty-Cycling (Fig. 1c) involves alternately turning on and off sensors to conserve battery power. Sparse Deployment (Fig. 1f) consists of a few pre-deployments in overlapping locations, followed by a final deployment in a subset of the pre-deployment locations. Missing data reconstruction allows us to estimate the readings at pre-deployment sensor locations that do not have sensors in the final deployment.

2.2 Temporal vs. Spatial Reconstructions

From Fig. 1, it is clear that naïve time-based methods such as using the last known reading will only work for Random Loss (Fig. 1a) and occasionally, Block Random Loss (Fig. 1b) and Duty-Cycling (Fig. 1c). Such methods are completely unsuitable for situations where a sensor fails to report readings for long periods of time, such as Successive Loss in Row (Fig. 1e) and Sparse Deployments. Reconstruction methods that rely on the correlations *between* sensors are necessary to deal with such situations.

2.3 On-site, on-time algorithms

For the purposes of data fusion, data compression and actuation, it is necessary to reconstruct missing data in a timely fashion. We require algorithms that can impute a missing value $x_{n,t}$ given only some other readings from the same time-slot t. SVD-based algorithms, such as the one proposed in [2], require readings from all sensors over all time-slots and thus fail to fulfil this requirement. Further, we would like algorithms that are divided into a computationally intensive training phase, to be carried out on back-end servers, and a fast reconstruction phase, which can be carried out on gateways. The SAE is able to provide both on-site and on-time reconstruction of missing data.

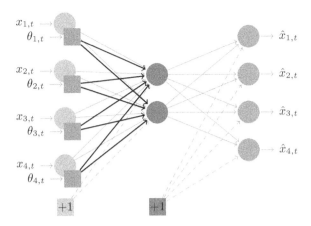

Figure 2: Modified neural network that accounts for missing data.

3. THE SAE FOR MISSING DATA

The sparse autoencoder (SAE) is a 3-layer neural network, with a complete bipartite graph between layers. Our variant is capable of handling datasets with missing data. We will follow the presentation of [3] while highlighting the areas where our variant differs from the original.

We refer to the three layers of the SAE as the input, hidden and output layers, respectively. The original SAE has N nodes in the input and output layers, and M in the hidden layer, and is specified by choosing an $M \times N$ matrix $\mathbf{W}$, an $N \times M$ matrix $\mathbf{W}'$, an M-dim. vector $\mathbf{b}$, and an N-dim. vector $\mathbf{b}'$. The vector $\mathbf{b}$ is learned under the assumption that all data is observed. When data is missing, we ideally require 2^N different $\mathbf{b}$ vectors for each pattern of missing data, but this is unfeasible for large N. Instead, we assume that these 2^N vectors are additive, and obtained by appropriate combinations of the columns of an $M \times N$ matrix $\mathbf{B}$.

3.1 Encoding and Decoding

Given a partially observed input vector $\mathbf{x_s}$ and its corresponding observation vector $\boldsymbol{\theta}$, our SAE first encodes the hidden layer

$$\mathbf{h} = \sigma(\mathbf{W}\,\mathbf{x_s} + \mathbf{B}\,\boldsymbol{\theta} + \mathbf{b}). \qquad (4)$$

where $\sigma(x) = \frac{1}{1+e^{-x}}$ is the logistic function, and $\mathbf{W}\,\mathbf{x_s}$ and $\mathbf{B}\,\boldsymbol{\theta}$ are matrix-vector multiplications. The encoding process takes into account not only the observed readings $\mathbf{x_s}$, but also $\boldsymbol{\theta}$, which indicates which readings were observed (see Fig. 2). The output is then obtained by linearly decoding the hidden layer

$$\hat{\mathbf{x}} = \mathbf{W}'\,\mathbf{h} + \mathbf{b}'. \qquad (5)$$

The intuition behind this is that with the addition of the $\mathbf{B}\,\boldsymbol{\theta}$ term, the resulting $\mathbf{h}$ is a good estimate of the hidden layer had we observed all the data. Our final estimate of the missing values $\mathbf{x_m}$ is given by $\hat{\mathbf{x}}_{\mathbf{m}}$.

3.2 Training

We would like to choose the parameters $\mathbf{W}, \mathbf{W}', \mathbf{b}, \mathbf{b}'$ and $\mathbf{B}$ such that the reconstruction $\hat{\mathbf{X}}_{\mathbf{s}}(\mathbf{W}, \mathbf{W}', \mathbf{b}, \mathbf{b}', \mathbf{B}, \mathbf{X_s})$ as defined by (5) is similar to $\mathbf{X_s}$. Since we observe only $\mathbf{X_s}$ instead of $\mathbf{X}$, we seek to minimize the average error over only the observed readings:

$$\frac{1}{\mathbf{T}} || \mathbf{X_s} - \hat{\mathbf{X}}_{\mathbf{s}} ||^2 := \sum_n \left(\frac{\sum_t \theta_{n,t}(x_{n,t} - \hat{x}_{n,t})^2}{\sum_t \theta_{n,t}} \right) \qquad (6)$$

Here, $1/\mathbf{T}$ is notational sugar to indicate that we are not simply dividing by a single scalar T.

3.2.1 Weight Decay

To prevent overfitting, it is common to introduce a weight decay term

$$|| \mathbf{W} ||^2 + || \mathbf{W}' ||^2 := \sum_{n,t} w_{n,t}^2 + \sum_{n,t} w'^2_{n,t} \qquad (7)$$

which prevents the matrices $\mathbf{W}, \mathbf{W}'$ from being too large. This term is unaffected by the presence of missing data.

3.2.2 Sparsity

To guide the autoencoder towards learning sparse representations of the data, a sparsity penalty on the hidden layer $\mathbf{H} = \sigma(\mathbf{W}\,\mathbf{X_s} + \mathbf{B}\,\boldsymbol{\theta} + \mathbf{b})$ is introduced

$$\mathrm{Sp}\big(\mathbb{E}_{\boldsymbol{\Theta}}[\mathbf{H}]\|\rho\big) := \frac{1}{N} \sum_{m,n} \mathrm{KL}\left(\frac{1}{\mathbf{T}} \sum_t \theta_{n,t} h_{m,t} \middle\| \rho \right)$$
$$= \frac{1}{N} \sum_{m,n} \mathrm{KL}\left(\frac{\sum_t \theta_{n,t} h_{m,t}}{\sum_t \theta_{n,t}} \middle\| \rho \right). \qquad (8)$$

Here $0 < \rho < 1$, and KL is the Kullback-Leibler divergence

$$\mathrm{KL}(\rho'\|\rho) = \rho' \log \frac{\rho'}{\rho} + (1 - \rho') \log \frac{1 - \rho'}{1 - \rho} \qquad (9)$$

which attains it's unique minimum of zero when $\rho' = \rho$, the desired sparsity. Minimizing this term encourages the learning of sparse representations. This sparsity penalty is more involved than in the original SAE, as each entry of $\mathbf{W}, \mathbf{b}$ contributes differently to each hidden node, depending on whether a data entry is missing. The term $\frac{1}{\mathbf{T}} \sum_t \theta_{n,t} h_{m,t}$ represents the average value of the mth hidden node *only when the reading from sensor node n was observed*. This is crucial in making the SAE work on missing data.

Combining these three factors, we get the final objective:

$$\underset{\mathbf{W}, \mathbf{W}', \mathbf{b}, \mathbf{b}', \mathbf{B}}{\arg\min} \quad \frac{1}{\mathbf{T}} || \mathbf{X_s} - \hat{\mathbf{X}}_{\mathbf{s}} ||^2 + \beta \, \mathrm{Sp}\big(\mathbb{E}_{\boldsymbol{\Theta}}[\mathbf{H}]\|\rho\big)$$
$$+ \lambda \left(|| \mathbf{W} ||^2 + || \mathbf{W}' ||^2 \right) \qquad (10)$$

$$\text{subject to} \quad \mathbf{H} = \sigma(\mathbf{W}\,\mathbf{X_s} + \mathbf{B}\,\boldsymbol{\Theta} + \mathbf{b}) \text{ and}$$
$$\hat{\mathbf{X}} = \mathbf{W}'\,\mathbf{H} + \mathbf{b}'.$$

The hyperparameters β and λ reflect the relative importance of each factor. The optimization problem can be solved using backpropagation [3,5], which is an efficient way of carrying out gradient descent on layered neural networks.

Note that if all data is observed, then $\boldsymbol{\Theta} = \mathbb{1}$, a matrix with all ones. We will have $\mathbf{X_s} = \mathbf{X}$ and $\sum_t \theta_{n,t} = T$, and $\mathbf{B}\,\mathbb{1} + \mathbf{b}$ can be combined into a single vector, which is the case in the original SAE. Our modified SAE is thus a generalization of the original SAE, which reduces to the original SAE when there is no missing data.

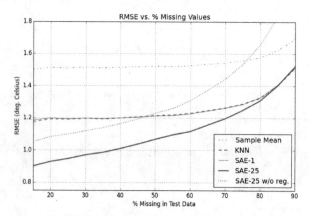

Figure 3: Comparison of algorithms trained on 10,000 samples with 25% of the entries missing, and tested on a dataset of 1,500 time-slots with varying percentages of entries missing.

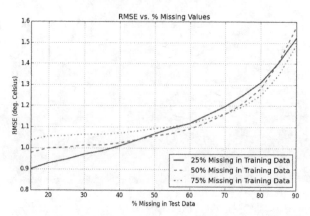

Figure 4: RMSE against percentage of missing entries in the test data. SAE-25 was trained on a 3 datasets with varying percentages of missing data: 25%, 50% and 75%.

4. EXPERIMENTAL RESULTS

We illustrate the capabilities of our algorithm missing data estimation on a dataset containing temperature readings of 49 sensors distributed around the city of Santander, Spain [7]. The training data is drawn from 10,000 time-slots with 25% entries missing. The test data is drawn from 1,500 time-slots, with 15% to 90% of the data entries artificially masked out. For Fig. 3, we trained our modified SAE with 25 hidden nodes (SAE-25) on the training dataset and used it to reconstruct the test data with varying percentages of missing data. We benchmarked our algorithm against the KNN-based method [4], and against filling in missing values with the mean of each time-slot. We also trained an SAE with 1 hidden node (SAE-1), as well as an SAE with 25 hidden nodes but without sparsity or decay weight penalties (SAE-25 w/o reg.). SAE-25 achieves the lowest RMSE (3), over almost all percentages of missing data. SAE-25 w/o reg. does not do as well, confirming the need for decay and sparsity penalties. KNN's performance is better than using sample means, but is indistinguishable from SAE-1! This suggest that KNN learns the strongest feature in the data, while SAE-N is capable of learning the N strongest features. For Fig. 4, we varied the percentage of missing *training* data. As we increase the percentage of missing *test* data, the SAE with the lowest RMSE changes from that trained on 25% missing data to 50% and finally, 75%. Thus, for the best performance, we should train the SAE on data with a similar proportion of missing data to that of the dataset we wish to reconstruct.

5. CONCLUSIONS AND FUTURE WORK

Our experiments show that our SAE variant can be used to reliably estimate missing data. The experiments also suggest that our method generalizes the KNN-based method proposed in [4], which is equivalent to our SAE with a single hidden node. Future work will incorporate temporal (intra-sensor) correlations as sensor data tends to be highly temporally correlated. The observation matrix Θ can also be allowed to take values between 0 and 1. This will be useful in WSNs with different sensors having different levels of accuracy. Our method can then be interpreted as fusion of data coming from sources of varying reliability, with missing data as a special case.

Acknowledgments

This work was partly supported by the A*STAR SERC Grant PG/20130430/005.

6. REFERENCES

[1] G. E. Hinton, N. Srivastava, A. Krizhevsky, I. Sutskever, and R. R. Salakhutdinov. Improving neural networks by preventing co-adaptation of feature detectors. *arXiv preprint arXiv:1207.0580*, 2012.

[2] L. Kong, M. Xia, X.-Y. Liu, M.-Y. Wu, and X. Liu. Data loss and reconstruction in sensor networks. In *INFOCOM, 2013 Proceedings IEEE*, pages 1654–1662. IEEE, 2013.

[3] A. Ng. Sparse autoencoder. *CS294A Lecture notes*, page 72, 2011.

[4] L. Pan and J. Li. K-nearest neighbor based missing data estimation algorithm in wireless sensor networks. *Wireless Sensor Network*, 2(2), 2010.

[5] D. E. Rumelhart, G. E. Hinton, and R. J. Williams. Learning internal representations by error propagation. Technical report, DTIC Document, 1985.

[6] R. Salakhutdinov, A. Mnih, and G. Hinton. Restricted Boltzmann machines for collaborative filtering. In *Proceedings of the 24th international conference on Machine learning*, pages 791–798. ACM, 2007.

[7] L. Sanchez, J. A. Galache, V. Gutierrez, J. Hernandez, J. Bernat, A. Gluhak, and T. Garcia. SmartSantander: The meeting point between future internet research and experimentation and the smart cities. In *Future Network & Mobile Summit (FutureNetw), 2011*, pages 1–8. IEEE, 2011.

[8] P. K. Sharpe and R. Solly. Dealing with missing values in neural network-based diagnostic systems. *Neural Computing & Applications*, 3(2):73–77, 1995.

[9] P. Vamplew and A. Adams. Missing values in a backpropagation neural net. In *Proceedings of the 3rd. Australian Conference on Neural Networks (ACNN), I*, pages 64–66, 1992.

[10] L. Wan, M. Zeiler, S. Zhang, Y. L. Cun, and R. Fergus. Regularization of neural networks using DropConnect. In *Proceedings of the 30th International Conference on Machine Learning (ICML-13)*, pages 1058–1066, 2013.

On Control of Inter-session Network Coding in Delay-Tolerant Mobile Social Networks

Neetya Shrestha and Lucile Sassatelli
Université Nice Sophia Antipolis, Laboratory I3S, CNRS UMR 7271
06903 Sophia Antipolis, France
Email: {shrestha,sassatelli}@i3s.unice.fr

ABSTRACT

Delay (or disruption) Tolerant Networks (DTNs) are networks made of wireless nodes with intermittent connections. In such networks, various opportunistic routing algorithms have been devised so as to cope with the lack of contemporaneous end-to-end route between a source and a destination. We consider DTNs made of mobile nodes clustered into social communities, with unicast sessions. Network coding is a generalization of routing that has been shown to bring a number of advantages in various communication settings. In particular, inter-session network coding (IS-NC) is known as a difficult optimization problem in general. In this article, we introduce a parameterized pairwise IS-NC control policy for heterogeneous DTNs, that encompasses both routing and coding controls with an energy constraint. We derive its performance modeling thanks to a mean-field approximation leading to a fluid model of the dissemination process, and validate the model with numerical experiments. We discuss the optimization problem of IS-NC control in social DTNs. By showing numerical gains, we illustrate the relevance of our approach that consists in designing IS-NC control policies not reasoning on specific nodes but instead on the coarse-grained underlying community structure of the social network.

Categories and Subject Descriptors

C.2.1 [**Computer-Communication Networks**]: Network Architecture and Design—*Store and forward networks*

General Terms

Algorithms, Measurement, Performance

Keywords

Delay Tolerant Networks; Mobile Opportunistic Networks; Routing Algorithms; Network coding; Control policy

1. INTRODUCTION

Delay (or disruption) Tolerant Networks (DTN) are sparse Mobile Ad-hoc NETworks (MANETs) that can rely neither on any infrastructure to support communication nor on the guarantee that a path exists between a source and a destination at any instant of time. Sparsity arises owing to short radio range, obstruction or intermittent sleeping mode.

In order to achieve end-to-end communication in the absence of a contemporaneous path between the source and the destination at the time of the transmission, the nodes rely on the store-carry-and-forward paradigm, taking advantage of the transmission opportunities between relays. The packet delay can be lowered by spreading multiple copies of the same packet. The possible ways to spread multiple copies have been investigated in several proposals [34, 31]. In particular, Spray-and-Wait (SaW) [31] has been proposed to achieve a trade-off between network resource (memory and energy) consumption and performance.

In this paper we focus on mobile social DTN, that are Pocket Switched Networks (PSN) formed by people carrying portable devices [14, 9]. Target applications include vehicular ad hoc networks [26], Publish-Subscribe [5] and content-centric systems for DTNs [36]. Human mobility exhibits heterogeneous patterns where node clustering into communities arises owing to social relationships [13]. A characteristic of DTNs is the distribution of the node inter-contact durations. In this article, a DTN with identically (resp. non-identically) distributed inter-contact times across the nodes is referred to as "homogeneous" (resp. "heterogeneous") DTN. Social DTNs are hence heterogeneous DTNs.

To improve the benefit of disseminating redundant packets, coded redundant packets can be generated by the relays instead of or additionally to replicated copies, that is performing Network Coding (NC) in DTN. NC is a networking paradigm that is a generalization of routing [1, 18]. Specifically, random NC [12] has attracted an increasing interest for DTNs [35, 22]. The benefits are increase in throughput, as well as adaptability to network topology changes. There are two types of NC: in intra-session NC, only the packets belonging to the same session are coded together (i.e., combined), while in inter-session NC (IS-NC) packets pertaining to different sessions can be combined. IS-NC is necessary to achieve optimal throughput in general (see [8] and references therein) but represents a difficult optimization problem, in particular for DTNs, as detailed in Section 2.

Contributions:

- We design a parameterized pairwise IS-NC control policy for heterogeneous DTNs, that encompasses both routing and coding controls with an energy constraint. We present the resulting dissemination protocol.

- We derive its performance modeling thanks to a mean-field approximation leading to a fluid model of the dissemination process. We validate the model by numerical experiments.

- We discuss the optimization of IS-NC control policy benefits in social DTNs, and show that the fluid model can be used to devise such optimal policy that jointly exploits the nodes' social acquaintances and the IS-NC. By showing numerical gains, we illustrate the relevance of our IS-NC control policy that is based on the coarse-grained community structure rather on individual nodes.

This paper does not aim at presenting a self-contained decentralized IS-NC protocol that can be confronted with existing routing policies in DTN. It aims at devising, modeling and proving the benefit of a centralized social-aware (community-based) pairwise IS-NC policy. Hence, the next step after this work is to study numerically the optimization problem in order to extract heuristics to devise a decentralized IS-NC policy for social DTNs.

This article is organized as follows. Section II presents related works. Section III presents the network model and the IS-NC protocol. In Section IV, we derive the performance modeling, and we discuss the optimization problem in Section V, then illustrate the relevance of controlling IS-NC based on communities to obtain some gains. Section VI concludes the paper discussing limitations and future works.

2. RELATED WORK

For homogeneous DTN, several works have considered intra-session NC which is now well understood in this case. Lin et al. in [22] investigated the use of intra-session NC using the SaW algorithm and analyzed the performance in terms of the bandwidth of contacts, the energy constraint and the buffer size. However, neither background traffic nor other running session are assumed beside the unicast session of interest. In [28], we have lifted this assumption and modeled information dissemination of several concurrent unicast sessions in homogeneous DTNs, when IS-NC and SaW routing are employed. In the present article, we extend this work not only to heterogeneous DTNs to predict the performance of contending unicast sessions, either inter-session network coded or not, but also model the control of IS-NC decisions based on the social features of the DTNs.

On the other hand, a number of routing policies have been proposed for heterogeneous DTNs to improve the trade-off between performance and resource consumption. Their principle is not to spend the allowed number of transmissions with the first met nodes, contrary to SaW [31], but instead to smartly choose the relays to give the copies to, in terms of the network social features. We can cite BubbleRap [15] and SimBet [6], where some global and local ranks are used for each node to orientate and control the spreading. In [32], Spyropoulos et al. introduced the mobility model we consider, and also used a fluid model to prove that one of the utility-based replication policies they consider achieves lower delivery delay than greedy. The optimality of such forwarding policies based on such a model is investigated in [29].

In [2], NC is considered at some intermediate hub nodes, but only across packets destined to the same destination node. In [37], Zhang et al. consider both intra- and inter-session NC in homogeneous DTNs. For unicast sessions with different sources and destinations, uncontrolled IS-NC is shown not to perform better than intra-session. In this paper we tackle the more general problem of control of pairwise IS-NC for unicast sessions with different destinations. When considering several unicast sessions, IS-NC can bring throughput and fairness gains [33, 17] both on lossless and lossy links. However, the optimization problem of IS-NC for multiple unicast sessions has been proven NP-hard [18], in particular because of the joint problems of subgraph selection and cod-

ing decisions, that can be solved independently for a single multicast session [23]. Therefore, all the works addressing the problem of IS-NC target suboptimal, yet continually improved, methods [16, 33, 8, 17]. These approaches are not directly applicable to DTNs as they assume fixed topologies and may incur heavy signaling. In particular, in [8], Eryilmaz and Lun introduced a routing-scheduling-coding strategy using back-pressure techniques. Modeling the coded flows as "poisoned" [33], the queue-length exchange is meant to determine the location of the encoding, decoding, and remedy generating nodes. The control policy of IS-NC and its modeling we introduce here, allow to account simultaneously for coding and remedy packets, that is the fact that a node may send to a destination packets not destined to it so as to help decoding mixed packets. Furthermore, all these works considered directed networks. However, there is a priori no reason for considering that two nodes can exchange packets in a single direction in DTNs. Li and Li in [20] have shown theoretically what can be the maximum throughput improvement with intra-session NC in undirected networks, compared with what can be obtained with integral, half-integer and fractional routing. In particular, for the multicast problem, the throughput increase ratio is upper-bounded by two between NC and half-integer routing, or even less with fractional routing [20, 24]. However, the shared resources (buffer, contact bandwidth) in DTNs make IS-NC attractive as in wireless mesh networks [16], though these networks are undirected. Hence, we are tackling the open problem of IS-NC design in social DTN, and want to study, thanks to the tunable pairwise IS-NC control policy and its performance model introduced in the present paper, what improvement can be brought by IS-NC, and how.

3. NETWORK MODEL

We consider the heterogeneous mobility model introduced in [32, 4]: the network is made of N mobile nodes divided into C communities such that $N = \sum_{i=1}^{C} N_i$ where N_i is the number of nodes in community i, and we assume that a node pertains to only one community. Table 1 gathers the main parameters' notation used throughout the paper. In this model, the time between two consecutive contacts is exponentially distributed with a certain mean. The accuracy of this model has been discussed in [11] and shown for a number of mobility models (Random Walker, Random Direction, Random Waypoint). The inter-meeting intensity β_{ij} is defined as the inverse of this mean and represents the mean number of contacts per time unit between a given node of community i and another given node of community j. We assume that $\beta_{ii} > \beta_{ij}$, for $i \neq j$, for all $i, j \in \{1, \ldots, C\}$. The matrix β storing the $\{\beta_{ij}\}_{i,j=1}^{C}$ defines the inter-meeting intensity of any pair of nodes.

Two sources S_1 and S_2 of communities s_1 and s_2, respectively, want to send a file each to their respective destinations D_1 and D_2 in communities d_1 and d_2, respectively. We assume that the file to be transferred needs to be split into K packets: this occurs owing to the finite duration of contacts among mobile nodes or when the file is large with respect to the buffering capabilities of the nodes. The message is considered to be well received if and only if all the K packets of the source are recovered at the destination. We do not assume any feedback.

We assume that the bandwidth, defined as in [22] as the number of packets that can be exchanged during a contact in each direction (thereby accounting both for the rate and the contact duration), is stochastic and follows any known distribution of mean Bw. The buffer size is assumed to be any known integer, denoted by B, equal for all the nodes in the network. Note that these assumptions are not necessary for the dissemination protocol presented in Algo. 1-2 to work.

3.1 Inter-session NC

Let us now describe simply how a node having two packets of two different sessions, performs IS-NC to forge a new coded packet to be sent out. The process described hereafter is depicted in Fig. 1. All nodes can identify the session number of each packet. Consider that packets P_1 and P_2, belonging to sessions S_1 and S_2, are Random Linear Combinations (RLC) of the K_1 and K_2 original information packets, respectively. The header coefficients of P_1 and P_2 are hence K_1-long and K_2-long, while payloads are L_1 and L_2-long, where L_1 and L_2 are the maximum size of packets of S_1 and S_2, respectively. The packet resulting from an RLC of P_1 and P_2 has header coefficients $(K_1 + K_2)$-long, and payload $\max(L_1, L_2)$-long. The original K_1 packets of session 1 can be recovered if and only if the matrix made of the coding coefficients can undergo a Gauss-Jordan elimination resulting in only elements of the K_1-size identity matrix over the K_1 columns assigned to session 1 and for the corresponding rows, all the other columns are zero. Thereafter, the number of received Degree of Freedom (DoF) of session 1 is the number of identity elements over these K_1 columns.

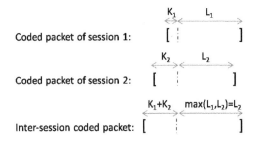

Figure 1: Generation of an inter-session network coded packet

3.2 The parameterized pairwise IS-NC control policy

We build on the buffer structure for intra-session NC framework employed with SaW [21], that we modify to account for IS-NC of two sessions. Note that binary SaW is considered for implementation, but any other spraying with a token mechanism allowing to control the dissemination, such as that of [37], can be considered for implementation and modeling. At a relay node buffer, a packet is associated with 3 fields: index, spray-counter, payload. Both sources S_1 and S_2 spread $K_1' \geq K_1$ (resp. $K_2' \geq K_2$) RLCs over the K_1 (resp. K_2) information packets. Each RLC sent out by S_1 (resp. S_2) is associated with an index in $S_{11} = \{1, \dots, K_1'\}$ (resp. $S_{22} = \{K_1' + 1, \dots, K_1' + K_2'\}$) and with a counter M (resp. Q). A node is said to be a $(c, \mathbf{l})$-node, if it belongs to community c and has in its buffer $\mathbf{l} = (l_{11}, l_{22}, l_{31}, l_{32})$ indices of S_{11}, S_{22}, S_{31} and S_{32}, respectively. Also, we take $l = \sum_i l_i$. In order to control the IS-NC decisions, we introduce the policy $\mathbf{u}_{ab}(t) = (u_{ab}^{11}(t), u_{ab}^{31}(t), u_{ab}^{22}(t), u_{ab}^{32}(t))$, for all a and b in $\{1, \dots, C\}$. It corresponds to the probability to draw, at each transmission opportunity, an index of each kind for sending it from a node of community a to a node of community b. As aforementioned, the number of transmission opportunities at each contact has an arbitrary distribution with mean Bw. The components of $\mathbf{u}_{ab}$ are defined in Table 1. We constrain $\sum_i u_{ab}^i \leq 1$ to allow for a node not to spread as many packets as possible if it is better to keep some transmissions for later meetings. Algo. 1-2 describes the dissemination protocol we consider with IS-NC. The cases where the sources or destinations are met can be found in Algo. 1.

Symbol	Meaning
Network settings	
N	total number of nodes excluding the sources and the destinations
C	number of node communities
N_i	number of nodes in community i
β_{ij}	inter-meeting intensity of a node in community i with a node in community j
Bw	bandwidth: mean number of packets that can be exchanged during a contact in each direction
Communication settings	
S_1, S_2	source node of session 1, 2
D_1, D_2	destination node of session 1, 2
K_1, K_2	number of information packets of session 1, 2
K_1', K_2'	maximum number of packets that can be released by S_1, S_2
M, Q	maximum number of copies of an index released by S_1, S_2
S_{11}, S_{22}	set of indices associated to pure payloads sent out by source S_1, S_2
S_{31}, S_{32}	set of indices emitted by S_1 (resp. S_2) associated to a mixed payload, that a combination from pure payloads of S_1 and S_2
X_{ic}, Y_{ic}	number of nodes in community c that carry i indices in S_{11} (resp. S_{22})
Z_{ic}^1, Z_{ic}^2	number of nodes in community c that carry i indices in S_{31} (resp. S_{32})
$\tilde{X}_{Ic}, \tilde{Y}_{Ic}$	number of nodes in community c that carry index I of S_{11} (resp. S_{22})
$\tilde{Z}_{Ic}^1, \tilde{Z}_{Ic}^2$	number of nodes in community c that carry index I of S_{31} (resp. S_{32})
$u_{ce}^{11}(t),$ $u_{ce}^{22}(t)$	probability that a node of community c gives a packet with an index in S_{11} (resp. S_{22}) to a node of community e upon meeting at time t, provided that it is possible to copy such an index (it exists at the sending node and its spray-counter is below M (resp. Q))
$u_{ce}^{31}(t),$ $u_{ce}^{32}(t)$	probability that a node of community c gives a packet with an index in S_{31} (resp. S_{32}) to a node of community e upon meeting at time t, provided that it is possible to copy such an index (it exists at the sending node and its spray-counter is below M (resp. Q))
l	$l = \sum_{i=11,22,31,32} l_i$ for a $(c, \mathbf{l})$-node

Table 1: Main notation used throughout the paper

DEFINITION 3.1. *An index I is said to be part of S_{11} or S_{31} (resp. S_{22} or S_{32}) if either I or $I - (K_1' + K_2')$ are in $[1, K_1']$ (resp. I or $I - (K_1' + K_2')$ are in $[K_1' + 1, K_1' + K_2']$).*

For this protocol, we consider that no packet exchange is possible once the buffer of the receiving node is full, but note that it is straightforward to adapt the framework to any kind of buffer management policy (including possible exchange when the buffers are full). As well, D_1 (resp. D_2) is allowed to make a meeting relay drop only packets of S_{11} (resp. S_{22}) it already got. It is worth noting also that the binary split of the counter in between the replicated packet and that remaining in the sending node is not a constraint of the framework, and can be changed for any other counter sharing, such as that based on some utility and presented in [6].

4. MODELING DISSEMINATION

The goal is to predict the evolution over time of the different numbers of nodes describing the dissemination process and defined in Table 1. To do so, we resort to a mean-field approximation that allows to predict the mean behavior of a system, modeled as a Markov chain, made of a growing number of interacting objects. Owing to the lack of space, we do not provide a formal proof that such a mean-field approximation hold in the present case, but rather only a sketch of the proof, and assess numerically the accuracy of the model in Section 4.3. By Theorem 3.1 of [19], the quantities $X_{ic}, Y_{ic}, Z_{ic}^1, Z_{ic}^2, \tilde{X}_{Ic}, \tilde{Y}_{Ic}, \tilde{Z}_{Ic}^1, \tilde{Z}_{Ic}^2$ defined in Table 1, that are random processes depending on the random mobility process, can be approximated by deterministic processes that are the solutions of certain coupled Ordinary Differential Equations (ODEs). These ODEs stem from the limit of the system dynamics (the "drift") for large N and are called the fluid model. Let us now present the ODEs of the fluid model.

Below we present the main components of the model and in particular we highlight how the control of IS-NC over the time and the communities is taken into account. As in the protocol description above, the notation in what remains corresponds to considering a node A that may send packets to a node B that is it meeting.

4.1 Evolution of the buffer occupancy distribution

The ODEs for X_{ic} and Z_{ic}^1 write as:

$$dX_{ic}(t) = \beta_{s_1 c} N_c \sum_{\mathbf{1}^B} P_j(c, \mathbf{1}^B) P_{gs11}(i - l_{11}^B, \mathbf{1}^B, \mathbf{u}_{s_1 c}) \dots$$

$$+ \beta_{cd_1} N_c \sum_{\mathbf{1}^B} P_j(c, \mathbf{1}^B) P_{ls11}(l_{11}^B - i, \mathbf{1}^B, \mathbf{1}^{D_1}, \mathbf{u}_{cd_1}) \dots$$

$$+ N_c \sum_{e=1}^{C} \sum_{\mathbf{1}^A, \mathbf{1}^B} \beta_{ec} N_e P_j(c, \mathbf{1}^A) P_j(c, \mathbf{1}^B) \dots$$

$$P_{grs11}(i - l_{11}^B, \mathbf{1}^A, \mathbf{1}^B, \mathbf{u}_{ec}) \dots$$

$$- \beta_{cs_1} N_c \sum_{\mathbf{1}^B : l_{11}^B = i, p_{11} > 0} P_j(c, \mathbf{1}^B) P_{gs11}(p_{11}, \mathbf{1}^B, \mathbf{u}_{s_1 c}) \dots$$

$$- \beta_{cd_1} N_c \sum_{\mathbf{1}^B : l_{11}^B = i, p_{11} > 0} P_j(c, \mathbf{1}^B) P_{ls11}(p_{11}, \mathbf{1}^B, \mathbf{1}^{D_1}, \mathbf{u}_{cd_1}) \dots$$

$$- N_c \sum_{e=1}^{C} \sum_{\substack{p_{11} \mathbf{1}^A, \\ \mathbf{1}^B : l_{11}^B = i}} \beta_{ec} N_e P_j(c, \mathbf{1}^A) P_j(c, \mathbf{1}^B) \dots$$

Algorithm 1: Protocol with IS-NC - Part 1

Data: a $(a, \mathbf{1}^A)$-node A (i.e., in community a with $\mathbf{1}^A$), and a node $(b, \mathbf{1}^B)$-node B, $\mathbf{u}_{ab} = (u_{ab}^{11}, u_{ab}^{22}, u_{ab}^{31}, u_{ab}^{32})$, the number of packet transmission opportunities w

Result: How many and what packets generated by A to be stored at B

Let $Hd(\mathbf{u})$ be the distribution of a discrete random variable Y with 4 values, value i being taken with probability u_{ab}^i.

if $A == S_1$ *and* $B \neq D_1$ *and* $B \neq D_2$ **then**

 Draw q_{11} from a binomial distribution (w, u_{ab}^{11}).

 if *Num_of_RLCs_sent_by_S_1* $< K_1'$ **then**

  Send $x = \min(q_{11}, K_1' - Num\_of\_sent\_RLCs\_by\_A, B - l^B)$ RLCs with indices from *Num_of_sent_RLCs_by_S_1* $+ 1$ up to *Num_of_sent_RLCs_by_S_1* $+ x$

else if $A == S_2$ *and* $B \neq D_1$ *and* $B \neq D_2$ **then**

 Draw q_{22} from a binomial distribution (w, u_{ab}^{22}).

 if *Num_of_RLCs_sent_by_S_2* $< K_2'$ **then**

  Send $x = \min(q_{22}, K_2' - Num\_of\_sent\_RLCs\_by\_A, B - l^B)$ RLCs with indices from *Num_of_sent_RLCs_by_S_2* $+ 1$ up to *Num_of_sent_RLCs_by_S_2* $+ x$

else if $B == D_1$ **then**

 Drop the packets with indices of S_{11} already present at D_1. Update l_{11}^A accordingly.

 $x = 0$;

 while $x \leq w$ **do**

  Draw y from $Hd(\mathbf{u})$.

  if $y == 11$ **then**

   Send 1 packet whose index is in S_{11} to D_1 and drop it from A.

  if $y == 22$ **then**

   Send 1 packet whose index is in S_{22} to D_1.

  if $y == 31$ **then**

   Send 1 packet whose index is in S_{31} to D_1. The payload is an RLC of all the packets of A.

  if $y == 32$ **then**

   Send 1 packet whose index is in S_{32} to D_1. The payload is an RLC of all the packets of A.

  $x = x + 1$;

 end

else if $B == D_2$ **then**

 The same as above, replacing D_1 by D_2 and 11 by 22.

$$P_{grs11}(p_{11}, \mathbf{1}^A, \mathbf{1}^B, \mathbf{u}_{ec}) \,.$$

$$dZ_{ic}^1(t) = N_c \sum_{e=1}^{C} \sum_{\mathbf{1}^A, \mathbf{1}^B} \beta_{ec} N_e P_{grs31}(i - l_{31}^B, \mathbf{1}^A, \mathbf{1}^B, \mathbf{u}_{ec}) \ldots$$

$$- N_c \sum_{e=1}^{C} \sum_{\substack{p_{31}>0, \mathbf{1}^A, \\ \mathbf{1}^B : l_{31}^B = i}} \beta_{ec} N_e P_{grs31}(p_{31}, \mathbf{1}^A, \mathbf{1}^B, \mathbf{u}_{ec}) \,.$$

The ODEs for Y_{ic} and Z_{ic}^2 can be deduced from those of X_{ic} and Z_{ic}^1, replacing 1 by 2 everywhere. The components of the above equations are defined as follows:

- $P_j(c, \mathbf{l})$: fraction of relay nodes that are $(c, \mathbf{l})$-nodes. $P_j(c, \mathbf{l})$ is computed such that the following constraints are satisfied: $P_j(c, \mathbf{l}) = 0$ for $l^B > B$, $\sum_{\mathbf{l}} P_j(c, \mathbf{l}) = 1$, $\sum_{\mathbf{l}:l_{11}=i} P_j(c, \mathbf{l}) = \frac{X_{ic}}{N_c}$, $\sum_{\mathbf{l}:l_{22}=i} P_j(c, \mathbf{l}) = \frac{Y_{ic}}{N_c}$, $\sum_{\mathbf{l}:l_{31}=i} P_j(c, \mathbf{l}) = \frac{Z_{ic}^1}{N_c}$ and $\sum_{\mathbf{l}:l_{32}=i} P_j(c, \mathbf{l}) = \frac{Z_{ic}^2}{N_c}$.

- Let $K_{S_1}(t)$ be the number of indices released by S_1 up to time t and P_{sc} be the average number of indices that S_1 gives around time t to community c. Then, $\frac{dK_{S_1}(t)}{dt} = \sum_{c=1}^{C} \beta_{s_1 c} N_c P_{sc}$ where, $P_{sc} = \sum_{p_{11}} \sum_{\mathbf{1}^B} p_{11} P_{gs11}(p_{11}, \mathbf{1}^B, \mathbf{u}_{s_1 c}) P_j(c, \mathbf{1}^B)$. The number of indices of S_{11} that D_1 has received until time t is denoted by $R_{11}(t)$; $\frac{dR_{11}(t)}{dt}$ can be expressed from $P_{ls11}(.)$ in the same way as $K_{S_1}(t)$.

- $P_{nic,e,c}(n_{11}, \mathbf{1}^A, \mathbf{1}^B, K_{S_1}(t), \mathbf{v}(t))$: probability that for a $(e, \mathbf{1}^A)$-node and a $(c, \mathbf{1}^B)$-node, there are n_{11} indices of S_{11} at node A not in common with $S_{11} \bigcup S_{31}$ at node B and whose corresponding spray-counters are still below M, when S_1 has already spread out $K_{S_1}(t)$ indices. The vector $\mathbf{v}_{11}(c, t)$ stores the occurrence probability of each index of S_{11} at time t in community c: $\mathbf{v}_{11}(c, t) = \left(\frac{\tilde{X}_{1c}}{\tilde{X}_c}, \ldots, \frac{\tilde{X}_{K_{S_1}(t)c}}{\tilde{X}_c} \right)$ with $\tilde{X}_c = \sum_{I \in S_{11}} \tilde{X}_{Ic}$. Similarly, we define $\mathbf{v}_{31}(c, t)$ from the $\tilde{Z}_{Ic}^1$ and we take $\mathbf{v}(t) = \frac{l_{11}^A}{s} \mathbf{v}_{11}(c, t) + \frac{l_{31}^A}{s} \mathbf{v}_{31}(c, t) + \frac{j}{s} \mathbf{v}_{11}(c, t)$, $s = l_{11}^B + l_{31}^B + j$ and $p_s = \frac{\sum_{I \in E} \tilde{X}_{Ie}(t)}{\sum_{I \in T_c} \tilde{X}_{Ie}(t)}$, with $T_e = \{I \in S_{11} : \tilde{X}_{Ie} > 0\}$ and E be the set of indices of S_{11} that can still spread: $E = \{I \in S_{11} : 0 < \sum_{c=0}^{C} (\tilde{X}_{Ic} + \tilde{Z}_{Ic}^1) < M\}$. Then $P_{nic,e,c}(n_{11}, \mathbf{1}^A, \mathbf{1}^B, K_{S_1}(t), \mathbf{v}(t))$ and $P_{nicD,e,d_1}(n_{11}, \mathbf{1}^A, \mathbf{1}^{D_1}, K_{S_1}(t), \mathbf{v}(t))$ (the probability that there are n_{11} indices of S_{11} at node B, not in common with S_{11} at D_1) are given by a combination of the above quantities with the function $S_z(.)$ defined hereafter. If S_e is a set of pairwise different elements from T_e whose cardinality is $|S_e|$, the probability to have exactly z different elements occurring among a set of $K_{S_1}(t)$ elements, the ith elements having an occurrence probability $\mathbf{v}_i(t)$, is $S_z(K_{S_1}(t), z, \mathbf{v}(t)) = \sum_{S_e \subset T_e : |S_e| = z} \prod_{i \in S_e} v_i(t) \prod_{i \in T_e \setminus S_e} (1 - v_i(t))$. Further details of these derivations are given in the extended version of the paper [30].

In what follows, q_{11} (Q_{11} for the random variable (r.v.)) denotes the number of draws of S_{11} out of the bandwidth realization, n_{11} (N_{11} for the r.v.) denotes the number of indices of S_{11} that are in node A but not in B, p_{11} denotes the number of indices of S_{11} given by A to B, and s (ζ for the r.v.) denotes the bandwidth realization. Hence we have:

$$Pr(Q_{11} = q_{11}) = \sum_{r \ge q_{11}} Pr(\zeta = r) \binom{s}{q_{11}} (u_{s_1 c}^{11})^{q_{11}} (1 - u_{s_1 c}^{11})^{r - q_{11}} \,,$$

Algorithm 2: Protocol with IS-NC - Part 2

/∗ Else $A \ne S_1$ and $A \ne S_2$ and $B \ne D_1$ and $B \ne D_2$ ∗/

else

$x = 0$;

while $x \le w$ **do**

Draw y from $Hd(\mathbf{u})$.

if $y == 11$ **then**

(1) Let $\mathbf{n}^{11}$ be the list of indices in S_{11} at A that are neither in S_{11} nor in S_{31} at B (according to def. 3.1) and whose counter is strictly greater than 1.

Let $\mathbf{p}$ be the set of packets at A corresponding to these indices.

if $\mathbf{n}^{11}$ *not empty and* $B - l^B \ge 1$ **then**

Send a packet q to B with:

$q.index = p_1.index = n_1^{11}$

$q.counter = \lfloor \frac{p_1.counter}{2} \rfloor$

$q.payload = p_1.payload$

Update

$l_{11}^B = l_{11}^B + 1$

$p_1.counter = \lceil \frac{p_1.counter}{2} \rceil$

Remove n_1^{11} from $\mathbf{n}^{11}$

if $y == 22$ **then**

Same steps from (1) as above, replacing 11 by 22 and M by Q.

if $y == 31$ **then**

(2) Let $\mathbf{n}^{31} = [v, \mathbf{n}^{11}]$, where $\mathbf{n}^{11}$ stems from step (1) and v is the list of indices in S_{31} at A that are neither in S_{11} nor in S_{31} at B (according to def. 3.1) and whose counter is strictly greater than 1.

Let $\mathbf{p}$ be the set of packets at A corresponding to these indices.

if $\mathbf{n}^{31}$ *not empty and* $B - l^B \ge 1$ **then**

Send a packet q to B with:

$q.index = p_1.index = n_1^{31}$

$q.counter = \lfloor \frac{p_1.counter}{2} \rfloor$

$q.payload = \text{RLC(all packets at } A)$

Update

$l_{31}^B = l_{31}^B + 1$

$p_1.counter = \lceil \frac{p_1.counter}{2} \rceil$

if $y == 32$ **then**

Same steps from (2) as above, replacing $11, 31$ and M by $22, 32$ and Q.

$x = x + 1$;

end

Go to the beginning of Algo. 2, exchange A and B and perform again all the steps.

$$Pr(N_{11}=n_{11})=\begin{cases} P_{nicD,c,d_1}(n_{11},\mathbf{1}^B,\mathbf{1}^{D_1},K_{S_1}(t),\mathbf{v}(t))\,, \\ \quad \text{if } B=D_1 \\ P_{nic,e,c}(n_{11},\mathbf{1}^A,\mathbf{1}^B,K_{S_1}(t),\mathbf{v}(t))\,, \\ \quad \text{otherwise} \end{cases}$$

$Pr(\zeta=r)$ is given by the network configuration and can be any (taken as Poisson in the numerical examples below). Similar quantities are defined for S_{22}, S_{31} and S_{32}.

- $P_{gs11}(p_{11},\mathbf{1}^B,\mathbf{u}_{s_1c})$: probability that S_1 gives p_{11} indices (of S_{11}) to node B.
- $P_{ls11}(p_{11},\mathbf{1}^B,\mathbf{1}^{D_1},\mathbf{u}_{cd_1})$: probability that node B, upon meeting with D_1, drops p_{11} indices of S_{11} that D_1 already has or that B hands over to D_1. The derivations of both quantities above are quite straightforward and detailed in [30].
- $P_{grs31}(p_{31},\mathbf{1}^A,\mathbf{1}^B,\mathbf{u}_{ec})$: probability that node B receives p_{31} indices of S_{31} from node A.

$$P_{grs31}(p_{31},\mathbf{1}^A,\mathbf{1}^B,\mathbf{u}_{ec})=(p_{31}\leq B-l^B)\sum_{\substack{s,\\n_{11},n_{31}}}F(p_{31})\ldots$$

$$Pr(S=s)Pr(N_{11}=n_{11})Pr(N_{31}=n_{31})\ldots$$

$$\left(l_{31}^A>0 \text{ or } \left(l_{31}^A=0, l_{11}^A>0 \text{ and } (l_{22}^A \text{ or } l_{32}^A)>0\right)\right)\,,$$

that represents the condition for generating a IS-NC packet (out of mixed S_{31} or unmixed packets in S_{11} and S_{22}). The r.v. S stands for the number of draws that elect a S_{11} or S_{31} index to be sent out, hence $Pr(S=s)=\sum_{r\geq s}Pr(\zeta=r)\binom{r}{s}(u_1)^s(1-u_1)^{r-s}$ with $u_1=u_{s_1c}^{11}+u_{s_1c}^{31}$. Let $v_1=u_{s_1c}^{11}/u_1$ and $v_3=u_{s_1c}^{31}/u_1$. Specifically, $F(p_{31})$ captures the coding decision: when a contact occurs, at each transmission opportunity (below denoted by "a draw", the mean number of these being Bw), one of the four types of indices is drawn. If S_{31} is drawn, such an index is either directly one of the S_{31} indices at node A, or is one of the S_{11} if no S_{31} are yet available (the payload being forged by combining S_{11} and S_{22} or S_{32}). Hence, it leaves less S_{11} indices available for the subsequent draws of S_{11}. We have
$F(p_{31})=Pr(p_{31} \text{ packets of } S_{31}\text{received in } s \text{ draws})=(p_{31}\leq n_{31})f(p_{31},s)+(p_{31}>n_{31})$
$Pr\left(n_{31} \text{ of } S_{31} \text{ sent then } p_{31}-n_{31} \text{ sent from the } S_{11} \text{ until } s\right)$ with $f(p_{31},s)=\binom{s}{p_{31}}v_3^{p_{31}}v_1^{s-p_{31}}$, and

$$Pr\left(n_{31} \text{ of } S_{31} \text{ sent then } p_{31}-n_{31} \text{ sent from the } S_{11} \text{ until } s\right)=$$

$$\sum_{a=n_{31}}^{s}Pr\left(\text{all } n_{31} \text{ of } S_{31} \text{ exhausted at draw } a\right)\ldots$$

$$\sum_{b=a+p_{31}-n_{31}+1}^{\min(s,n_{31}+n_{11})}Pr\left(\text{last packet in } S_{31} \text{ received at draw } b\right)\ldots \qquad (1)$$

$$Pr\left(p_{31}-n_{31}\text{drawn in } b-a \text{ draws}\right)\,,$$

$$Pr\left(\text{all } n_{31} \text{ of } S_{31} \text{ exhausted at draw } a\right)=\binom{a}{n_{31}}v_3^{n_{31}}v_1^{a-n_{31}}\,,$$

$Pr\left(\text{last packet in } S_{31} \text{ received at draw } b\right)=v_1^{s-b}+(b-n_{31}==n_{11})-(b-n_{31}==n_{11})v_1^{s-b}$, and $Pr\left(p_{31}-n_{31}\text{drawn in } b-a \text{ draws}\right)=\binom{b-a}{p_{31}-n_{31}}v_3^{p_{31}-n_{31}}v_1^{b-a-(p_{31}-n_{31})}$.

- $P_{grs11}(p_{11},\mathbf{1}^A,\mathbf{1}^B,\mathbf{u}_{ec})$: probability that node B gains p_{11} indices of S_{11} from node A.

$$P_{grs11}(p_{11},\mathbf{1}^A,\mathbf{1}^B,\mathbf{u}_{ec})=(p_{31}\leq B-l^B)\ldots$$

$$\begin{cases} \sum_{n_{11},q_{11}}Pr(Q_{11}=q_{11})Pr(N_{11}=n_{11})\ldots \\ (p_{11}==\min(n_{11},q_{11}))\,, \text{if } l_{31}^A=0 \text{ and } l_{22}^A=0 \\ \sum_{s,n_{11},n_{31}}Pr(S=s)Pr(N_{11}=n_{11})Pr(N_{31}=n_{31})\ldots \\ G(p_{11}), \text{otherwise} \end{cases}$$

with $G(p_{11})=Pr(p_{11} \text{ packets of } S_{11}\text{received in } s \text{ draws})=$

$$\sum_{p_{31}}^{n_{31}+n_{11}-p_{11}}(p_{31}\leq n_{31})A+(p_{31}>n_{31})B$$

with $A=Pr\left(p_{31} \text{ of } S_{31} \text{ drawn until } s \text{ and } p_{11} \text{ of } S_{11} \text{ sent}\right)=\binom{s}{p_{31}}v_3^{p_{31}}v_1^{s-p_{31}}\left((s-p_{31}>n_{31})(p_{31}==n_{31})+(p_{31}\leq n_{31})(s-p_{31}==n_{31})\right)$ and $B=Pr\left(n_{31} \text{ of the } n_{31} \text{ sent and then } p_{31}-n_{31} \text{ sent from the } S_{11} \text{ and } p_{11} \text{ of } S_{11} \text{ sent until } s\right)$ is given by eq. 1 with $Pr(\text{last packet in } S_{31} \text{ received at draw } b)$ changed to:

$Pr(\text{last packet in } S_{31} \text{ received at draw } b \text{ and } p_{11} \text{ sent in } s)=(a-n_{31}+b-a-(p_{31}-n_{31})==n_{31})\,Pr(\text{all } S_{11} \text{ exhausted in } b \text{ draws})+Pr(\text{no } S_{31} \text{ drawn in } s-b)\,Pr(\text{exactly } p_{11}-b+p_{31} \text{ sent between draws } b \text{ and } s)$ the latter being obtained in a similar manner as for P_{grs31}.

4.2 Evolution of the index dissemination distribution

The ODEs for $\tilde{X}_{Ic}$ and $\tilde{Z}_{Ic}^1$ can be written as:

$$\frac{d\tilde{X}_{Ic}}{dt}=\sum_{e=1}^{C}\beta_{ce}N_eN_cA_{R11,e,c}+\beta_{s1c}N_cA_{S11,c}-\beta_{cd_1}\tilde{X}_{Ic}A_{D11,c}\,.$$

$$\frac{d\tilde{Z}_{Ic}^1}{dt}=\sum_{e=1}^{C}\beta_{ec}N_eN_cA_{R31,e,c}\,.$$

The ODEs for $\tilde{Y}_{Ic}$ and $\tilde{Z}_{Ic}^2$ can be deduced from those of $\tilde{X}_{Ic}$ and $\tilde{Z}_{Ic}^1$, replacing 1 by 2 everywhere. We have the following components:

- $A_{D11,c}$: fraction of nodes in community c that have I of S_{11} in their buffer and that drop it upon meeting with D_1.
- $A_{S11,c}$: fraction of nodes in community c that are infected by S_{11}. The derivations of both quantities above are quite straightforward and detailed in [30].
- $pnth_{11,c}(I,\mathbf{1}^B)$: probability for node B not to have I of S_{11} in its buffer.

$$pnth_{11,c}(I,\mathbf{1}^B)=\frac{\sum_{j=l_{11}^B}^B S_{z,c}(K_{S_1}(t)-1,j,\mathbf{v}_{T_c-\{I\}}(t))}{\sum_{j=l_{11}^B}^B S_{z,c}(K_{S_1}(t),j,\mathbf{v}(t))}\,,$$

where $\mathbf{v}(t)=\mathbf{v}_{11}(c,t)$. We define $pnth_{31,c}(I,\mathbf{1}^B)$ similarly, replacing $\mathbf{v}_{11}(c,t)$ by $\mathbf{v}_{31}(c,t)$.

- $A_{R11,e,c}$: fraction of nodes in community c without index I of S_{11} that obtain I from a relay in community e.
$A_{R11,e,c}=$

$$\begin{cases} 0 \quad , \text{if } \sum_{e=1}^{C}\left(\tilde{X}_{Ie}+\tilde{Z}_{Ie}^1\right)\geq M \\ \sum_{\mathbf{1}^A,\mathbf{1}^B}P_j(e,\mathbf{1}^A)P_j(c,\mathbf{1}^B)pnth_{11,c}(I,\mathbf{1}^B)pnth_{31,c}(I,\mathbf{1}^B)\ldots \\ \left(1-pnth_{11,e}(I,\mathbf{1}^A)\right)\sum_{s,n_{11},n_{31}}Pr(S=s)Pr(N_{11}=n_{11})\ldots \\ Pr(N_{31}=n_{31})\frac{p_{11}}{n_{11}}G(p_{11}), \text{otherwise} \end{cases}$$

with $G(p_{11})$ is given in the above section. The term $\frac{p_{11}}{n_{11}}G(p_{11})$ is the probability that I is chosen to get forwarded given these conditions.

- $A_{R31,e,c}$: fraction of nodes in community c without index I of S_{31} that obtain I from another relay in community e. $A_{R31,e,c} =$

$$
\begin{cases}
0 & \text{, if } \sum_{e=1}^{C} \left(\tilde{X}_{Ie} + \tilde{Z}_{Ie}^{1} \right) \geq M \\[2mm]
\sum_{1^A, 1^B} P_j(e, 1^A) P_j(c, 1^B) pnth_{11,c}(I, 1^B) pnth_{31,c}(I, 1^B) \ldots \\[2mm]
\left((l_{31}^A > 0) A_R^{Case1} + \left((l_{31}^A = 0)(l_{11}^A > 0) \ldots \right. \right. \\[2mm]
\left. \left. (l_{22}^A \text{ or } l_{32}^A) > 0) \right) A_R^{Case2} \right) \text{, otherwise .}
\end{cases}
$$

$$
A_R^{Case1} = \left(1 - pnth_{31,e}(I, 1^A) \right) pnth_{11,e}(I, 1^A) \sum_{\substack{p31 \leq B - l^B, \\ s, n31, n11}} (p31 \leq
$$

$$
n31) \frac{p31}{n31} H + pnth_{31,e}(I, 1^A) \left(1 - pnth_{11,e}(I, 1^A) \right) \sum_{\substack{p31 \leq B - l^B, \\ s, n31, n11}} (p31 >
$$

$$
n31) \frac{(p31 - n31)}{n11} L ,
$$

$$
A_R^{Case2} = \left(1 - pnth_{11}(I, 1^A) \right) \sum_{\substack{p31 \leq B - l^B, \\ q31, n11}} \frac{p31}{n11} M .
$$

The expressions of H, L and M are easily derived from the decomposition of P_{grs31} in the above section.

- $P_I^{11}(t)$: probability that D_1 has received index I of S_{11} by time t.

$$
\frac{dP_I^{11}(t)}{dt} = \sum_{c=1}^{C} \beta_{cd_1} N_c \left(1 - P_I^{11}(t) \right) A'_{D11,c} ,
$$

where $A'_{D11,c}$ is the fraction of nodes in community c that hold I of S_{11} and that hand I over to D_1 provided that D_1 does not have I. We refer to the extended version [30] for the detailed derivation of $A'_{D11,c}$.

Decoding Criterion: Let $P_{S_1}(\tau)$ be the success probability at time τ. To account for the possible benefit brought by coding while keeping a simple criterion, we consider that D_1 can recover the K_1 packets sent by S_1 if (i) it receives at least K_1 indices of S_{11}, or (ii) if it receives non-coded and coded packets so that all the K_1 and K_2 packets are received. Note that case (ii) is pessimistic as the coding matrix can be inverted even though it is not met, but it is so in order to keep a tractable decoding criterion. Yet, it allows to account for a coding benefit. Hence we have: $P_{S_1}(\tau) = P_{S_1}^{(i)}(\tau) + P_{S_1}^{(ii)}(\tau)$. The derivations of $P_{S_1}^{(i)}(\tau)$ and $P_{S_1}^{(ii)}(\tau)$ are given in [30].

4.3 Numerical validation

In this section, we assess the accuracy of the fluid model above, that captures the effect of the joint control of routing and IS-NC on various quantities. We consider a synthetic contact trace on which we run the IS-NC protocol described in Algo. 1-2 thanks to a discrete event simulator written in Matlab. The simulation results are averaged over 30 runs and the 5% confidence intervals are plotted. The trace is made of $N = 1000$ nodes, $C = 1$ for the sake of clarity of the curves and $\beta = 5.10^{-4}$. The buffer size is set to $B = 2$ packets. The bandwidth is Poisson distributed with mean $Bw = 3$ packets. The communication settings of the two sessions are: $K_1 = K_2 = 3$, $K_1' = K_2' = 5$ and $M = Q = 200$. We set the control policy $\mathbf{u}$ to $u_{11} = u_{22} = 0.3$, $u_{31} = 0.4$ and $u_{32} = 0$. Fig. 2 depicts the number of indices of each type packets, namely $\sum_{i=1}^{B} X_i$, $\sum_{i=1}^{B} Y_i$, $\sum_{i=1}^{B} Z_i^1$ and $\sum_{i=1}^{B} Z_i^2$. We observe the relative good fit between analysis and simulation for both non-coded and coded type packets. Fig. 3 represents the evolution of the normalized (i.e., divided by K_1 or K_2) number of DoFs of S_1 (resp.

S_2) received by D_1. These numbers of DoFs are determined by a Gauss-Jordan elimination of the coding matrix in the simulation, and by the sum of the pairwise different received indices of S_{11} and S_{31} (resp. S_{22} and S_{32}) in the analytical model. We observe a good fit between the simulation results and the analytical prediction.

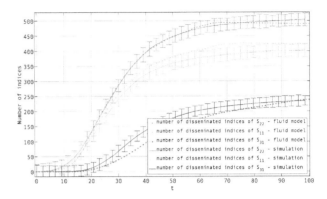

Figure 2: Evolution along time of the number of infected nodes with packets of different types.

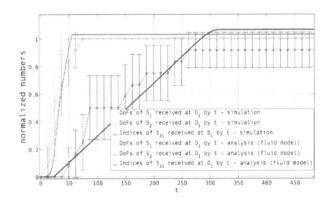

Figure 3: Evolution along time of the number of DoF of each source received by D_1.

5. THE IS-NC CONTROL PROBLEM

The problem we want to address thanks to (i) the introduced control policy of routing and IS-NC and (ii) the fluid model that predicts the delivery probability, is that of control policy optimization under some energy or memory constraint.

5.1 Discussion on the optimization problem

Let $U(.)$ be any classical utility function, such as $\log(1 + x)$ if x is a probability, and $P_1(\tau)$ (resp. $P_2(\tau)$) the probability that D_1 (resp. D_2) has obtained its K_1 information packets by τ. The problem of finding the optimal policy $\mathbf{u}$ which jointly controls routing and pairwise IS-NC decisions under some energy constraint can be formulated as:

$$
\max_{\{\mathbf{u}_{ec}\}_{e,c=1}^{C}} obj(\tau) = U(P_1(\tau)) + U(P_2(\tau))
$$

subject to $\mathbf{u}$ satisfying the energy constraint.

Note that other objectives, such as the mean completion delay for each session, can be considered. Optimizing IS-NC decisions is a difficult problem in general, as discussed in Section 2, and in the social DTN scenario considered, this problem corresponds to a Markov decision process where at each time step, a central controller chooses an action so as to maximize the expected reward over a finite time horizon. It has been shown in [10] that when the system is made of N interacting objects and the occupancy measure is a Markov process (that has been discussed in Section 4), the optimal reward converges to the optimal reward of the mean field approximation of the system, which is given by the solution of an Hamilton-Jacobi-Bellman (HJB) equation.

Thanks to the ODEs presented in Section 4, that allow to get the fluid limits $P_{S_1}(\tau)$ and $P_{S_2}(\tau)$ of $P_1(\tau)$ and $P_2(\tau)$, the optimal IS-NC policy for a finite N can hence be approximated by the asymptotically optimal policy built by solving the HJB equation for the associated mean field limit. However, owing to the intricacy of our model made of coupled ODEs, the HJB equation cannot be solved in a closed-form. We would hence need to resort to a numerical solver, but the dimension of the involved vectors prevents from using this kind of solvers (see, e.g., [25]). A feasible implementation of the optimization procedure is to use heuristic optimization methods, such as Differential Evolution [27]. Besides, let us specify that in DTNs, a simple way of accounting for the energy consumption incurred by a routing policy is for example with the number of transmissions. This number can be easily extracted from the quantities modeled in Section 4, allowing to implement the energy constraint in the optimization process.

Investigating this optimization problem in social DTN thanks to the above fluid model is the subject of future work. In particular, in order to design a decentralized IS-NC policy, the model will be adapted to powerful existing decentralized routing policies (such as SimBet [6]) in order to devise relevant local IS-NC decisions.

5.2 Numerical example

We now provide a numerical example that shows the relevance of the approach trying to get benefit from IS-NC in social DTNs. We consider the topology depicted in Fig. 4 where the communities 1 and 3 are connected through another community 2. Community 1 (resp. 3) is that of the source node of session 1 (resp. 2) and of the destination node of session 2 (resp. 1) (these are 4 different nodes). This topology refers to the toy-example of two Wifi stations willing to exchange packets through an access point (AP) [16]. In this case, transmissions and hence time and throughput are saved if the AP combines the packets of the two stations. Whether this kind of IS-NC advantage can exist in DTNs is an open question, in particular with a policy taking decisions based on the community structure rather than on individual nodes, that is when the source and destination nodes of both sessions are not exchanged but represent four different nodes. On the simple topology of Fig. 4, we illustrate in Fig. 5, by simulations on a synthetic trace, that (community-based) IS-NC can be indeed beneficial with respect to intra-session NC. The intra-session NC policy we compare to is the best dissemination policy we found amongst those with varying values of $\mathbf{u}_{11}$ and $\mathbf{u}_{22}$ controlling spreading in community 1 and 3. Zhang et al. have shown empirically in [37] that uncontrolled IS-NC of different source-destination pairs is not beneficial in general in homogeneous DTNs. We illustrate in Fig. 5 that it can be beneficial in heterogeneous DTNs. Specifically, it turns out that that the highest benefit is obtained when session mixing is performed at the side communities, and not at the relay community, as the direct analogy with connected networks would suggest. Further study is needed, allowed by the presented protocol and its analytical model, to investigate on what social graph topologies (amongst which undirected like in Fig. 4) and under what conditions IS-NC can be beneficial.

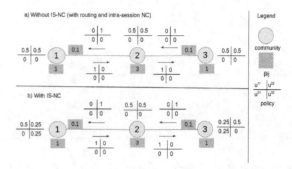

Figure 4: The community topology considered. Each community is made of 333 nodes and the inter-meeting intensities are in green. For both policies: $K_1 = K_2 = 7$, $K_1' = K_2' = 7$, $M = Q = 200$. **(a) The non IS-NC policy (that is, a policy where only intra-session NC is used). (b) The IS-NC policy.**

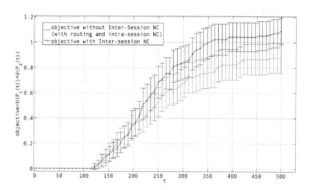

Figure 5: The obtained objective values for the above social DTN topology and policies.

5.3 Relevance to real-world traces

Finally, let us briefly show that even the simple topology of Fig. 4 can arise in real-world social DTNs. We consider as an example the MIT Reality Mining contact trace [7], corresponding to Bluetooth contacts collected with 100 smartphones distributed to students and staff at MIT over a period of 9 months. The people come into contact owing to the mobility and these contact patterns can reflect the social features such as the clustering of nodes into different communities, as analyzed in several studies such as [13]. We aggregated the contact trace into a weighted contact graph whose weights represent the tie strength (combining contact frequency and duration) between the nodes. We then applied Louvain community detection algorithm [3] to detect the communities in the contact graph and computed the β matrix describing the community structure. The following β matrix has been obtained with 7 communities detected: $\beta_{MIT} =$

$$
\begin{bmatrix}
2.12 & 0.09 & 0.03 & 0.00 & 0.01 & 0.05 & 0.01 \\
0.09 & 5.89 & 0.52 & 0.17 & 0.73 & 0.33 & 0.12 \\
0.03 & 0.52 & 1.71 & 0.14 & 0.47 & 0.27 & 0.09 \\
0.00 & 0.17 & 0.14 & 1.97 & 0.19 & 0.13 & 0.07 \\
0.01 & 0.73 & 0.47 & 0.19 & 12.00 & 0.64 & 0.21 \\
0.05 & 0.33 & 0.27 & 0.13 & 0.64 & 10.87 & 0.17 \\
0.01 & 0.12 & 0.09 & 0.07 & 0.21 & 0.17 & 6.48
\end{bmatrix} .
$$

A similar topology as in Fig. 4 arises when, for example, a node of community 1 and another node in community 4 want to exchange packets. In this case, a good route is to go through community 6, and the involved β_{ij} are then: $\beta_{11} = 2.1$, $\beta_{66} = 10.8$, $\beta_{44} = 1.9$, $\beta_{16} = 0.05$, $\beta_{64} = 0.13$.

6. CONCLUDING REMARKS

We have devised a parameterized pairwise IS-NC control policy and expressed the control optimization problem thanks to a performance model. The scheme is at the same time a routing and a coding policy that allows to optimize for a utility function defined over the two sessions, under some energy constraint. Our policy decides which nodes can mix the sessions based on their communities rather than on their individual properties, making the devised policy scalable with the number of nodes if the number of communities keeps limited. We have shown that numerical gains of IS-NC over intra-session NC can indeed be obtained.

This paper does not aim at presenting a self-contained decentralized IS-NC protocol that can be confronted with existing routing policies in DTN. It aims at devising, modeling and proving the benefit of a centralized social-aware (community-based) pairwise IS-NC policy. Specifically, the problem of grouping sessions by two is not investigated here. Detecting and selecting what pairs of sessions to be mixed is part of the decentralization problem. Moreover, further study is needed, allowed by the presented protocol and its analytical model, to investigate on what social graph topologies (amongst which undirected like in Fig. 4) and under what conditions (e.g., sizes K_1 and K_2 of the sessions and energy budget) IS-NC can be beneficial. The next step after this work is to study numerically the optimization problem in order to extract heuristics to devise a decentralized IS-NC policy for social DTNs. In particular, the model will be adapted to powerful existing decentralized routing policies (such as SimBet [6]) in order to devise relevant local IS-NC decisions.

7. ACKNOWLEDGEMENTS

This work has been funded by the French Research Agency under contract ANR-10-JCJC-0301.

8. REFERENCES

[1] R. Ahlswede, N. Cai, S. R. Li, and R. W. Yeung. Network information flow. *IEEE Trans. on Inf. Th.*, 46(4), Jul. 2000.

[2] S. Ahmed and S. S. Kanhere. Hubcode: hub-based forwarding using network coding in delay tolerant networks. *Wireless Comm. and Mob. Comp.*, 13(9):828–846, May 2011.

[3] V. D. Blonde, J.-L. Guillaume, R. Lambiotte, and E. Lefebvre. Fast unfolding of communities in large networks. *J. Stat. Mech.*, Jul. 2008.

[4] E. Bulut, W. Zijian, and B. Szymanski. Impact of social networks in delay tolerant routing. In *IEEE Globecom*, Honolulu, HI, Dec. 2009.

[5] P. Costa, C. Mascolo, M. Musolesi, and G. Picco. Socially-aware routing for publish-subscribe in delay-tolerant mobile ad hoc networks. *IEEE JSAC*, 26(5), mar 2008.

[6] E. Daly and M. Haahr. Social network analysis for information flow in disconnected delay-tolerant MANET. *IEEE Trans. on Mob. Comp.*, 8(5):606 – 621, May 2009.

[7] N. Eagle and A. Pentland. Reality mining: sensing complex social systems. *Pers. and Ubi. Comp.*, 10(4):255–268, Mar. 2006.

[8] A. Eryilmaz and D. Lun. Control for inter-session network coding. In *Inf. Theory and Appl. workshop (ITA)*, San Diego, CA, Jan. 2007.

[9] J. Fan, Y. Du, W. Gao, J. Chen, and Y. Sun. Geography-aware active data dissemination in mobile social networks. In *IEEE MASS*, pages 109–118, Nov. 2010.

[10] N. Gast, B. Gaujal, and J.-Y. Le Boudec. Mean field for markov decision processes: From discrete to continuous optimization. *IEEE Trans. on Automatic Control*, 57(9):2266–2280, Sep. 2012.

[11] R. Groenevelt and P. Nain. Message delay in MANETs. In *ACM SIGMETRICS*, pages 412–413, Banff, Canada, Jun. 2005.

[12] T. Ho, R. Koetter, M. Médard, D. R. Karger, and M. Effros. The benefits of coding over routing in a randomized setting. In *IEEE Int. Symp. on Info. Theory (ISIT)*, page 442, Yokohama, Japan, Jul. 2003.

[13] T. Hossmann, T. Spyropoulos, and F. Legendre. A complex network analysis of human mobility. In *IEEE NetSciCom 11 (co-located with IEEE INFOCOM 2011)*, Shanghai, China, 2011.

[14] P. Hui, A. Chaintreau, J. Scott, R. Gass, J. Crowcroft, and C. Diot. Pocket switched networks and human mobility in conference environments. In *ACM SIGCOMM workshop on DTN*, pages 244–251, Aug. 2005.

[15] P. Hui, J. Crowcroft, and E. Yoneki. Bubble rap: Social-based forwarding in delay tolerant networks. *IEEE Trans. on Mob. Comp.*, 10(11):1576 – 1589, Nov. 2011.

[16] S. Katti, H. Rahul, W. Hu, D. Katabi, M. Medard, and J. Crowcroft. XORs in the air: Practical wireless network coding. *IEEE/ACM Trans. on Netw.*, 6(3):497 – 510, 2008.

[17] A. Khreishah, W. Chih-Chun, and N. Shroff. Rate control with pairwise intersession network coding. *IEEE/ACM Trans. on Netw.*, 18(3):816–829, Jun. 2010.

[18] R. Koetter and M. Medard. An algebraic approach to network coding. *IEEE/ACM Trans. on Netw.*, 11(5):782–795, 2003.

[19] T. G. Kurtz. Solutions of ordinary differential equations as limits of pure jump markov processes. *J. of Appl. Prob.*, 7(1), Apr. 1970.

[20] Z. Li and B. Li. Network coding in undirected networks. In *Annu. Conf. Inf. Sciences and Systems (CISS)*, Princeton, NJ, Mar. 2004.

[21] Y. Lin, B. Li, and B. Liang. Efficient network coded data transmissions in disruption tolerant networks. In *IEEE INFOCOM*, pages 1508–1516, Phoenix, USA, Apr. 2008.

[22] Y. Lin, B. Li, and B. Liang. Stochastic analysis of network coding in epidemic routing. *IEEE JSAC*, 26(5), Jun. 2008.

[23] D. S. Lun, M. Medard, T. Ho, and R. Koetter. Network coding with a cost criterion. In *Int. Symp. on Info. Theory and its Appl. (ISITA)*, pages 1232–1237, 2004.

[24] S. Maheshwar, Z. Li, and B. Li. Bounding the coding advantage of combination network coding in undirected networks. *IEEE Trans. Inf. Theory*, 58(2):570– 584, 2012.

[25] I. M. Mitchell. A toolbox of level set methods, 2012.

[26] G. Neglia, X. Zhang, J. Kurose, D. Towsley, and H. Wang. On optimal packet routing in deterministic dtns. In *IEEE VTC*, Jun. 2013.

[27] K. Price and R. Storn. Differential Evolution (DE) for continuous function optimization.

[28] L. Sassatelli and M. Medard. Inter-session network coding in delay-tolerant networks under spray-and-wait routing. In *IEEE WiOpt*, pages 103–110, Paderborn, Germany, May 2012.

[29] N. Shrestha and L. Sassatelli. On optimality of routing policies in delay-tolerant mobile social networks. In *IEEE VTC*, Jun. 2013.

[30] N. Shrestha and L. Sassatelli. Extended version - http://www.i3s.unice.fr/tildesassatelli/MSextended2014.pdf, 2014.

[31] T. Spyropoulos, K. Psounis, and C. Raghavendra. Efficient routing in intermittently connected mobile networks: the multi-copy case. *IEEE/ACM Trans. Netw.*, 16(1):77–90, Feb. 2008.

[32] T. Spyropoulos, T. Turletti, and K. Obraczka. Routing in delay-tolerant networks comprising heterogeneous node populations. *IEEE Trans. on Mob. Comp.*, 8(8):1132 – 1147, Aug. 2009.

[33] D. Traskov, N. Ratnakar, D. Lun, R. Koetter, and M. Medard. Network coding for multiple unicasts: An approach based on linear optimization. In *IEEE Int. Symp. on Info. Theory (ISIT)*, pages 1758–1762, 2006.

[34] A. Vahdat and D. Becker. Epidemic routing for partially-connected ad hoc networks. In *Tech. Rep. CS-200006*, Duke University, 2000.

[35] J. Widmer and J.-Y. Le Boudec. Network coding for efficient communication in extreme networks. In *ACM SIGCOMM workshop on DTN*, pages 284–291, Philadelphia, USA, 2005.

[36] P. Yang and M. Chuah. Performance evaluations of data-centric information retrieval schemes for dtns. *ACM Comput. Netw.*, 53(4):541–555, mar 2009.

[37] X. Zhang, G. Neglia, J. Kurose, and D. Towsley. Benefits of network coding for unicast applications in disruption-tolerant networks. *IEEE/ACM Trans. on Netw.*, 21(5):1407–1420, Oct. 2013.

Space-Time Efficient Wireless Network Coding

Yan Yan
Research Center of Ubiquitous Sensor Networks, University of Chinese Academy of Sciences,
Beijing 100049, China
+861088256565
yany@ucas.ac.cn

Baoxian Zhang
Research Center of Ubiquitous Sensor Networks, University of Chinese Academy of Sciences,
Beijing 100049, China
+861088256565
bxzhang@ucas.ac.cn

Zheng Yao
Research Center of Ubiquitous Sensor Networks, University of Chinese Academy of Sciences,
Beijing 100049, China
+861088256565
yaozheng@ucas.ac.cn

ABSTRACT

Network coding has been as a new coding paradigm that can significantly improve the throughput performance of a wireless multi-hop network. However, most previous studies either assume a fixed transmission power or do not take the impact of transmission power/rate to the network coding into consideration. Since in many scenarios, the selection of the transmission power/rate has big impact on network coding gains due to the fact the reception and overhearing probability, spatial reuse are both rely on transmission power/rate. Therefore, how to achieve high network throughput by appropriate selection of transmit power level and its corresponding packet transmit rate, network coding gain (if any) via localized network operations has been a critical issue in distributed multihop wireless networks, or alternatively, what is the best trade-off between the space-time resource (level of spatial reuse and transmission time) and the network coding gain? In this paper, our goal is to achieve the best trade-off between transmission power/rate and coding gains. Aiming at this, we propose a decentralized network coding aware power and rate control mechanism to enable each node to adjust its transmit power and data rate such that the network coding gains and the network throughput is maximized. Simulation results show that the proposed mechanism yields higher performance in network throughput as compared with existing work.

Keywords

Network coding; Spatial reuse; Power control.

1. INTRODUCTION

Network coding has recently emerged as a new coding paradigm that has demonstrated a wide range of applications for improving the network performance of a wireless multihop network. Network coding allows the packets received from multiple links to be mixed at an intermediate relay node, which may significantly improve the network performance in terms of throughput. Fig. 1 gives a typical example illustrating how network coding reduces the total number of transmissions in a network. In this example, nodes *A* and *B* want to send packets p_1 and p_2 to nodes *C* and *D*, respectively, via a common relay node R. After R receives both p_1 and p_2, it will generate a new packet by performing "p_1 XOR p_2" and then broadcast it to the air. Upon receipt of the new packet, both *C* and *D* can decode their interested packets by using the information that they directly overheard from nodes *A* and *B*, respectively. In this way, the number of transmissions is reduced from four to three.

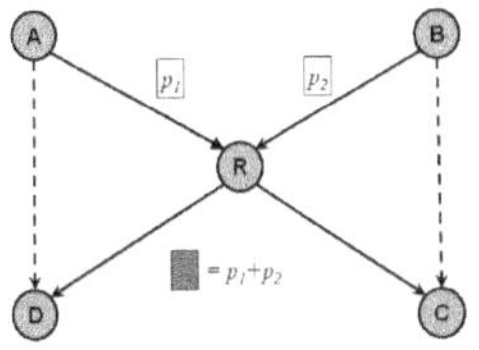

Figure 1. A typical example illustrating how network coding improves the throughput of wireless networks.

Although network coding could improve the capacity of a wireless network, achieving network capacity also depends on the achievable channel capacity and the level of spatial reuse – The total number of allowable concurrent transmissions in the network. In a traditional wireless network, increasing spatial reuse by allowing more concurrent transmissions always helps with the network throughput[1], which means traditional transmission power control schemes always try to find minimal transmission powers (if existing) for them so that receivers SINR(signal to interference and noise ratio) requirements were all satisfied.

However, in a network coding enabled wireless network, there might be a counter effect to arbitrarily increasing the level of spatial reuse. That is because that network coding requires nodes to overhear native packets and to ensure the successful reception for all recipients of a coded packet, which both depends on the transmission range (proportional to the transmission power with fixed carrier sense threshold) or channel quality between nodes. When the level of spatial reuse is high, more concurrent transmissions can be accommodated, which lead to small transmission range or low channel quality, and consequently, potentially low coding gains. Besides, given a transmission power level, the transmission rate of relay node should meet the SINR requirement of all recipients of coded packet to achieve the coding gain.

On the other hand, a low transmission power could lead to low transmission data rate. For given carrier sense threshold and transmit rate, there exists a lowest SINR requirement for each node. The higher the transmit rate is, the higher the required lowest SINR will be. If the SINR requirement is given, we can

MSWiM'14, September 21–26, 2014, Montreal, QC, Canada.

ACM 978-1-4503-3030-5/14/09…$15.00.
http://dx.doi.org/10.1145/2641798.2641806

only choose the maximal data rate that still satisfies the SINR requirement to guarantee the packet reception. As the transmit power decreases or the carrier sense threshold increases, the SINR and consequently the maximal data rate will be decreased as a result. If the SINR at the receiver is below the threshold, then the transmission is not successful. Thus, the transmission data rate accordingly has a big impact on the network throughput. Low transmission data rate, which means long transmission time, can obviously have negative effect on the network throughput.

Therefore, in conclusion, the broadcast nature of wireless channel leads to inherent tension between high spatial reuse and providing coding opportunities. These facts lead to the following question. What is the tradeoff between the proper power/rate selection and the network coding enabled network throughput? In this paper, we are aiming at archiving the optimal trade-off between network coding gain and power/rate selection. Specifically, unlike previous work, we intend to enhance the network throughput of wireless multihop networks by using Coding Aware transmission Power/rate Adjustment mechanism, referred to as CAPA. The contributions in the paper are as follows. First, we propose a framework for power /rate control, which facilitates the selection of the power and rate for each packet transmission by considering the space-time efficiency of wireless inter-flow network coding, in order to find the optimal trade-off between spatial reuse and network coding gain. Second, the problem of maximizing the network throughput of a wireless multihop network is known to be NP-hard [1]. Therefore, based on the designed framework, we propose a distributed heuristic mechanism CAPA to increase the network throughput as much as possible. The decision on power/rate control at each node is made in a localized manner. Simulation results demonstrate that our mechanism can greatly improve the performance of wireless multihop networks with multiple concurrent flows as compared with existing work.

The rest of this paper is organized as follows. In Section 2, we briefly review related work. In Sections 3 and 4, we present the detailed design description of the proposed mechanism. In Section 5, we conduct detailed simulations to evaluate the performance of our mechanism by comparing it with existing work. In Section 6, we conclude this paper.

2. RELATED WORK
2.1 Network Coding
Network coding was first proposed by Ahlswede et al. [2] and it was originally targeted at tackling the multicast issue in traditional loss-free wireline networks [3-6]. It has been shown that network coding can provide throughput gain in wireless networks for both multicast [7] and unicast [8] applications. COPE [8] is the first practical network coding mechanism for supporting efficient unicast communications in a wireless multihop network. It employs opportunistic listening for each node to learn local state information and encoded packet broadcasting to improve the network throughput. However, neither COPE nor its variants consider the space-time trade off in packet delivery and the dynamic availability of network coding opportunities at a network node due to different power values. This largely limits their capabilities for improving network throughput.

2.2 Power/Rate Control
Some transmission power control (TPC) schemes [9-11] for increasing the throughputs of wireless networks have been proposed. In [9], MRPC-MAC (multi-rate power controlled MAC) was proposed to use multiple transmission rates. The used transmission rate was selected by rate adaptation algorithm. In [10], MRPC (multi-rate power control) was proposed to improve the network throughput by tuning the transmission power and transmission rate. The issue of jointly tuning the transmit power and the data rate has been also addressed in [11], which extends the auto rate fallback scheme to power auto rate fall back (PARF) and power estimated rate fallback (PERF). The basic idea is to increase the power level after failing to send frames with the minimum data rate. However, none of the above schemes takes network coding into consideration.

2.3 Coding Related Power/Rate Control
Recently, some coding aware power control mechanisms have been proposed. In [12][13], the authors investigated the trade-off between spatial reuse and network coding gain. Although they provided theoretical performance limits of coding aware power control, the centralized nature makes them hard to be used in practice In [14][15], distributed coding aware rate control mechanisms were proposed. However, the lack of power control function limits their performance. Different from these existing mechanisms, our mechanism in this paper focuses on improving the network throughput by selecting both appropriated power level and data rate for each transmission in a localized manner.

3. MECHANISM OVERVIEW
In this section, we first provide several simple observations and motivations. We then present the basic idea of our coding aware power control mechanism

3.1 Design Consideration
Let us consider the example in Fig. 1. Node R is a relay node that relays packets from nodes A to C and also from nodes C to D. In traditional networks without power/rate control, each node sends packets using the maximum power. We assume that D could overhear A's transmission and C is able to overhear B's transmission. Relay node R transmits the XORed packets received from A and B. Nodes C and D could decode their interested packets by using their overheard packets.

3.1.1 Power Control for Native Packets
Now assume that we apply a traditional power control mechanism [1], in which each node tries to set the transmit power as low as possible while meets the SINR requirement of its nexthop reception. With this consideration, node A adjusts the transmit power to P_A to guarantee the correct reception at its nexthop R. However, in a network coding enabled network, the transmission range of node A should also cover node D, which means A should guarantee the SINR requirement for node D to overhear its transmission, to be able to decode coded packets from relay node R. If A decreases its transmission power to P_A, the use of power P_A might lead to poor channel quality between A and D and inadequate for D to (correctly) overhear A's transmission. If D fails to overhear the transmission from A, there would be no coding opportunity at relay node R. Therefore, relay node R cannot perform XOR-based network coding due to the failure of transmission overhearing at D. The same situation applies to nodes B and C. Thus, although power control could increase the level of spatial reuse, it might degrade the network coding gain in the network.

3.1.2 Power Control for Coded Packets

Now assume relay node R can perform XOR coding. In traditional wireless networks, due to the broadcast nature of wireless channel, the transmission power/rate chose by node R (with fixed carrier sensing threshold) must meet the SINR requirement of both recipients C and D of a coded packet. If we decrease the transmission power or increase the data rate of the relay node R, the network coding opportunities might be lost if either of the links R-C or R-D has poor quality, which might reduce the network throughput. Therefore node R must use a transmit power large enough to preserve the coding gain but reduce spatial reuse. Therefore, the power/rate control for transmissions of XORed packets also has dual impact on the throughput of wireless networks. Large transmission power could increase the potential coding gains by covering more neighboring nodes while reducing the level of spatial reuse. Large data rate could decrease the transmission time of a packet but could also lead to bad channel quality and reduced network throughput.

3.1.3 Space-Time Efficiency

In wireless networks, each transmission consumes two kinds of limited resources: space and time. The "space" refers to the affected area of the transmission while the "time" refers to the total time consumed by the transmission. To improve the network throughput, efficient design of a transmission scheme should lead to efficient utilization of the space-time resource. We would like to reduce the space and time consumed by each transmission, meaning that Space-Time efficient transmissions are preferred.

To begin, in traditional networks, power control has dual impacts on the space-time efficiency. To reduce the space occupation, we need to reduce the transmit power. To decrease the time span, we need to use higher data rate, which requires larger transmission power for fixed carrier sensing threshold. [1]

In network coding enabled networks, achieving the space-time optimal transmission is quite complicated. First, increased transmission power means increased transmission range to cover more nodes, which can possibly achieve more coding gains. However, transmission with higher power will also consume more space resource. Second, by increasing power to be able to encode more native packets, we can decrease the time resource by sending more native packets in one transmission. Finally, larger transmit power could lead to higher data rate, which could also reduce the time spent by each transmission.

Therefore, choosing the optimal power level and data rate can increase the space-time efficiency of each transmission. The throughput of the network will be increased as a result. This motivates us to study how to effectively integrate space-time efficient power/rate control with wireless network coding to increase the throughput of lossy wireless networks.

3.2 Basic Idea

In this paper, we aim at improving the network throughput by coding aware Space-Time efficient power/rate control for wireless multihop networks wherein multiple concurrent unicast flows exist. The basic idea is based on a coding aware and efficient utilization of the limited space-time resource, which can improve the network throughput.

We illustrate the idea by an example. Figure 2 illustrates the idea regarding how to achieve space-time efficiency, where each transmission is represented by a cylinder. Figure 2 shows several different concurrent transmissions. The volume of a cylinder can

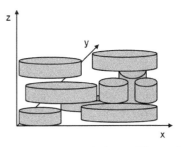

Figure 2. Representation of Space-Time efficiency as cylinders.

be regarded as a space-time product, where the height of a cylinder represents the time taken by the transmission and the space is the area of a cylinder in the x-y plane. We assume that each transmission's affected range forms a circle. Thus, the space represents the affected range of the corresponding transmission. Two transmissions can be sent simultaneously, if their affect ranges do not interfere with each other, which mean they are well separated from each other to ensure an acceptable SINR at their respective target recipients.

From Figure 2, it is obvious that in order to have a higher throughput, we expect to have as more cylinders as possible during a given time length. In order to have a great number of cylinders, the volume of each cylinder should be maintained as small as possible. Thus, based on the above discussions, the basic idea behind our proposed mechanism is to reduce the volume of each cylinder in a way such that the space-time efficiency of each transmission is maximized.

The volume of a cylinder is influenced by the coding gains, transmission power, and transmission rate, which are correlated. First, the space is influenced by power and data rate. On the one hand, the highest achievable transmission rate depends on the transmission power used. On the other hand, the minimal transmission power required depends on the SINR requirement, which is related with the transmission rate used. Second, the time is influenced by coding gain and transmission rate. Both larger coding gain and higher data rate could lead to shorter transmission time. However, at the same time, the network coding gain is also implicitly related to transmission power and data rate as we discussed before.

In summary, unlike traditional power/rate control scheme, in this paper, we take the wireless network coding gain into consideration. The power level and data rate of each transmission is chosen in a way so as to deliver more information (by getting more coding gains) with shorter time (by getting more coding gains and higher data rate) and smaller transmission range (by setting smaller transmission power).

4. PROPOSED MECHANISM

The problem of maximizing the throughput of a wireless ad hoc network is known to be NP-hard, even if only one single transmission power/rate is supported [1]. Therefore, we resort to heuristic approach to increasing the network throughput. In this section, we first give an analysis framework regarding how to compute the Space-Time efficiency associated with each transmission. We use this analysis framework to subsequently present the detailed design of our distributed coding aware power/rate control mechanism.

4.1 Preliminaries

4.1.1 Network Model

In this paper, we study a multi-hop wireless network that can be modeled as a graph $G = (N, E)$, where N and E represent the set of nodes and links in the network, respectively. A node in the network is denoted by n_i ($1 \leq i \leq |N|$), where $|N|$ represents the number of nodes in the network. Let e_{ij} represent the link connecting node n_i and node n_j.

There are M discrete transmission power levels, denoted by p_1, p_2, ..., p_m and Z data rates, denoted by $r_1, r_2, ..., r_Z$, respectively, in an increasing order. For example, IEEE 802.11b could support four transmission rates: 1, 2, 5.5, and 11 Mbps.

4.1.2 Radio Propagation Model

We assume that nodes are distributed uniformly and independently in an area with reasonably high node density. We use the radio propagation mode given below to characterize the power loss, which is referred to as simple path loss model [16].

$$P_{rx} = \frac{P_{tx}}{d^{\alpha}} \tag{1}$$

Where P_{tx} and P_{rx} are, respectively, the transmit powers at the transmitter and the received signal strength at the receiver, d is the distance between the transmitter and the receiver, and α is the path loss exponent, ranging from 2 (Line-of-Sight path) to 4 (indoor) [17].

4.1.3 Affected area

The affected area of a transmission in wireless multihop network is not a new concept. That is, for each packet transmission, there is a ceased area, in which all nodes but the transmitter should keep silent, in order to render the transmission successful. If a node initiates a transmission, it will create a carrier sensing range area (CSR area) in which no other node could transmit packets at the same time. With a fixed carrier sensing threshold, the stronger the transmission power, the larger the CSR area is. On the other hand, besides CSR area, there is an interference area (IR area) near the receiving node. Transmission in the IR area could cause collisions at the receiving node. The IR area is associated with received signal strength. The stronger the signal is, the smaller the IR area is. The ceased area is the union of both the CSR area and IR area. The optimal ceased area of Ad Hoc network has been studied and calculated [18]

However, in coding enabled network, the IR area is hard to calculate due to dynamic nature of the recipients of different coded packets. Thus, we only consider the CSR area as the affected area of an outgoing transmission for simplicity. If there are simultaneous transmissions in the IR area, which cause the receiving node's failure to recognize packets, we treat it as a normal packet loss.

Therefore, by setting the minimum P_{rx} satisfying the SINR requirement of the receiving node, the corresponding transmission affected range S can be calculated directly from (1), which is given by

$$S = \pi d^2 \tag{2}$$

4.1.4 The power/rate control

It has been proved that the network capacity is the function of transmit power and carrier sense threshold. It further shows that tuning the transmit power is sufficient if there is a sufficient number of power levels available [19]. Although our framework is based on the coding enabled network. The transmission of coded packet has no difference with normal native packet. Therefore, we calculate and fix the carrier sense threshold value as in normal wireless network [19] and only tune the power/rate to maximize the network capacity.

The power/rate trade off is as follows: We consider the case that there are fixed number Z of available data rates $r_1, r_2, ..., r_Z$. Let $SINR(i)$ represent the SINR threshold required to support data rate r_i, which means $SINR(i)$ to $SINR(i+1)$ is the range for data rate r_i. SINR must exceed certain threshold in order to support the corresponding data rate [19].

When initiating a transmission, the sending node tries to find the maximal SINR level at the receiving node when using power level p_i. We denote it as $SINR_{rx}^{max}(i)$. The $SINR_{rx}^{max}(i)$ can be obtained by having each receiver piggyback its perceived SINR to the transmitter. Then the transmission rate is selected as follows: If the transmitter uses power level p_i and the corresponding SINR at the receiver is $SINR_{rx}^{max}(i)$, then the data rate can be chosen as r_z if:

$$SINR_z \leq SINR_{rx}^{max}(i) < SINR_{z+1}, \ 1 \leq z \leq Z-1 \tag{3}$$

The sending node then uses data rate r_z for transmission at power level p_i. The receiving node can sustain the SINR level. For the coded transmission, the data rate r_z should be chosen to meet the SINR requirement of all target recipient nodes, which means r_z should be the minimal data rate of all the recipient nodes of the coded transmission.

4.2 Space-Time Efficiency

In this section, we provide an analysis framework for space-time efficiency. Suppose that the transmissions in Figure 2 occur during the time period from 0 to t. We would like to have as many independent concurrent transmissions as possible during a given time period. In order to have a large number of concurrent transmissions, the volume of each cylinder should be maintained as small as possible. The above observation motivates us to define a metric for evaluating the Space-Time efficiency for each transmission.

Consider an ongoing transmission with transmission power p_i and corresponding data rate r_z for receiver's SINR level. Let S_i denote the size of the transmission range induced by it, and T_i denote the transmission time it requires. L_i denotes the expected number of bits carried by this transmission, which is determined by the coding gains. We define per-bit space-time efficiency as follows.

Definition 1: space-time per bit

$$\frac{S_i T_i}{L_i} \tag{4}$$

The per-bit space-time efficiency gives the space-time resource consumed during per bit transmission. Since $S_i T_i$ is the volume of the corresponding cylinder, smaller per-bit space-time efficiency implies a smaller cylinder volume, which leads to higher throughput.

To increase the total throughput of the network, we would like to minimize each transmission's range S_i to accommodate more concurrent transmissions, and we would like to maximize L_i/T_i for each transmission. In conclusion, we should maximize the $L_i/T_i S_i$ for each transmission in order to increase the network throughput.

Therefore, if there are multiple choices for power level p_i, the selection of p_i that results in the minimum space-time per bit is preferred to maximize the network throughput. Next, we will show how to obtain the optimal power level and consequently the power/rate control mechanism.

4.3 Framework Design

Next, we describe the framework used to achieve optimal space-time efficiency for each transmission. The proposed framework consists of two parts:

4.3.1 Power/Rate Selection for Native Packets:

The first part is to select the power/rate for sending native packets. Let us return to the example in Figure 1, wherein node A can identify the set of its neighboring nodes that are also neighboring nodes of its relay node R. These common neighbors are the potential recipients of coded packets sent by R. Then, node A should select the power level p_m that maximizes the expected throughput both to itself and node R, while at the same time, the probability of successful overhearing at these common neighboring nodes is larger than a predefined threshold P_h.

We need to give how to determine the threshold P_h. The encoding algorithm needs to consider the probability at which each intended receiver of the coded packet could decode its interested native packet. We use the same guessing mechanism as in COPE to compute the decodability probability P_D. The P_D for each receiver must be greater than a predetermined threshold G. We set $G = 0.8$ like in COPE.

Suppose relay node R could encode n native packets. We denote the senders of these native packets by s_i. Then the probability that another node n_j overhears a sender s_i's transmission to R with power level $p_m(s_i)$ is denoted by $P_{heard}(n_j, s_i, R, p_m(s_i))$, which is given by:

$$P_{heard}(n_j, s_i, R, p_m(s_i)) = \sum_{k=1}^{\infty} \{(1 - P_{pdr}(s_i, R, p_m(s_i))P_{ACK}(R, s_i))^{k-1} \cdot P_{pdr}(s_i, R, p_m(s_i))P_{ACK}(R, s_i) \cdot \sum_{l=1}^{k}(1 - P_{pdr}(s_i, n_j, p_m(s_i)))^{l-1}P_{pdr}(s_i, n_j, p_m(s_i))\} \qquad (5)$$

Where $P_{pdr}(s_i, R, p_m(s_i))$ is the delivery probability of $e_{s_i,R}$ at selected data rate $r_z(s_i)$ of power $p_m(s_i)$ as in (3). $P_{ACK}(R, s_i)$ is the delivery probability of ACK packet of e_{R, s_i} at the lowest data rate. $\sum_{l=1}^{k}(1 - P_{pdr}(s_i, n_j, p_m(s_i)))^{l-1}P_{pdr}(s_i, n_j, p_m(s_i))$ is the probability that n_j successfully overhears the transmission from s_i in exactly k transmissions. Equation (5) says that the successful overhear probability $P_{heard}(n_j, s_i, R, p_m(s_i))$ at neighboring node n_j is the probability that the node n_j overhears packets sent by s_i to its nexthop R before the packet is ACKed by R.

If node n_j wants to decode the coded packet successfully, it should overhear the transmissions of all $n-1$ senders s_i ($\forall i, i \neq j$). Therefore, decodable probability P_D for node n_j is:

$$P_D(n_j) = \prod_{1 \leq i \leq n, i \neq j} P_{heard}(n_j, s_i, R, p_m(s_i)) \qquad (6)$$

Then, our goal is to select a transmission power level for each native packet that the decoding probability $P_D(n_j)$ at each recipient n_j of the coded packet is larger than the predetermined threshold G. Since the overhear probability $P_{heard}(n_j, s_i, R, p_m(s_i))$ is independent of different s_i. We can require that each overhear

probability $P_{heard}(n_j, s_i, R, p_m(s_i))$ is larger than the predefined threshold $P_h = G^{-(n-1)}$. Hence, for successful decoding, we must have:

$$P_D(n_j) = \prod_{1 \leq i \leq n, i \neq j} P_{heard}(n_j, s_i, R, p_m) \geq P_h^{n-1} \quad G \qquad (7)$$

Then we can ensure the decoding probability $P_D(n_j)$ is larger than the predetermined threshold G.

Next, we need to determine the expected transmission time $T_m(s_i)$ of transmission from s_i with power level $p_m(s_i)$. The expected number of transmissions of a packet sent by node s_i to the receiver relay node R is given by

$$N(s_i, R) = \frac{1}{P_{pdr}(s_i, R, p_m(s_i))P_{ACK}(R, s_i)} \qquad (8)$$

Thus, the expected transmission duration $T_m(s_i)$ is given by:

$$T_m(s_i) = N(s_i, R)\frac{l_{pkt}(s_i)}{r_z(s_i)} \qquad (9)$$

Where $l_{pkt}(s_i)$ is the length of the packet sent by s_i. The data rate $r_z(s_i)$ should be chosen according to (3).

Then, each sender s_i tries to select the power level from M discrete transmission power levels, which minimizes the Space-Time per bit on the link to the relay node R. This translates to the following optimization problem:

$$\min_{1 \leq m \leq M} \frac{S_m(s_i)T_m(s_i)}{L_m(s_i)} \qquad (10)$$

Subject to:

$$S_m(s_i) = \pi d_m^2(s_i) \qquad (11)$$

$$P_{heard}(n_j, s_i, R, p_m(s_i)) \geq P_h, \quad 1 \leq j \leq n, i \neq j \qquad (12)$$

$$L_m(s_i) = l_{pkt}(s_i) \qquad (13)$$

$$T_m(s_i) = N(s_i, R)\frac{l_{pkt}(s_i)}{r_z(s_i)} \qquad (14)$$

4.3.2 The Power/Rate Selection of Coded Packets

Once a relay node R received enough native packets from its neighbors, it chooses appropriate power level, encodes the packets (as necessary) and forwards the coded packet further using pseudo-broadcast, which requires the relay node R to choose a primary receiver. The primary receiver will send ACK to the coded packet, if correctly received. The native packets coded in this transmission will be retransmitted if the ACK is not received in time.

This transmission power selection problem for coded transmission can also be translated into the following optimization problem:

$$\min_{1 \leq m \leq M} \frac{S_m(R)T_m(R)}{L_m(R)} \qquad (15)$$

Here we need to determine the expected number of bits $L_m(R)$ and time $T_m(R)$ for power $p_m(R)$. Suppose that for this transmission power $p_m(R)$ and affected range $S_m(R)$, relay node R has packets that could be coded together to send to several neighboring nodes, denoted by set $Nbr_{coded}(p_m(R))$. Given this, for power level $p_m(R)$,

```
Input:      Packet p for next transmission
Output:     p_result /* selected power level */
begin
1. if p is a native packet then
2.     Get the common set of neighbors N between s and its next hop
3.        for m = 1 to M do            //loop for transmit power levels
4.            if P_heard(s, n_j, p_m)≥P_h, ∀ n_j∈N then
5.                if E_tmp>S_mT_m/L_m then  // calculated according to (10)
6.                    E_tmp = S_mT_m/L_m
7.                    p_result = p_m
8.                endif
9.            endif
10.       endfor
11. else
12.    for m = 1 to M do
13.       Find the recipients set Nbr_coded(p_m) of the coded packet
14.          for r=1 to Nbr_coded(p_m) do
15.              if E_tmp>S_mT_m/L_m then   //Calculated according to (21)
16.                  E_tmp = S_mT_m/L_m
17.                  p_result = p_m
18.              endif
19.          endfor
20.       endfor
21. endif
22. return p_result
end
```

Figure 3. Procedures for CAPA executed when a node s chooses to forward a packet p.

the expected number of bits $L_m(R)$ and transmission time $T_m(R)$ is determined by the set of these neighboring nodes $Nbr_{coded}(p_m(R))$. We let $n = |Nbr_{coded}(p_m(R))|$.

In a coded transmission, the selection of the primary receiver determines the expected transmission time $T_m(R)$. The primary receiver should be chosen in a way such that the transmission duration $T_m(R)$ is minimized. We denote the primary receiver chosen to ACK the coded packet as n_r. Thus, the transmission duration $T_m(R)$ with the primary receiver n_r is given by:

$$T_m(R) = N(R, n_r)\frac{l_{coded}(R)}{r_z(R)}, \ n_r \in Nbr_{coded}(p_m(R)) \tag{16}$$

Where $l_{coded}(R)$ is the packet length of the coded packet, which is the longest $l_{pkt}(s_i)$ in this coded packet. The data rate $r_z(R)$ of coded transmission should be chosen in a way such that it can satisfy the SINR requirement of all recipient nodes.

Next, we need to determine the total expected delivered number of bits to all recipient nodes with network coding. The total delivered bits $L_m(R)$ is composed of two parts: The bits received by ACK node n_r, denoted by $L_{AckerRvd}(n_r)$, and the bits received by another recipient n_k, denoted by $L_{Rvd}(n_k)$.

$$L_{AckerRvd}(n_r) = l_{pkt}(n_r) \cdot P_{AckerRvd}(R, n_r)$$
$$\cdot \prod_{1\le l\le n, l\ne r} P_{heard}(n_r, s_l, R, p_m(s_l)) \tag{17}$$

$$L_{Rvd}(n_k) = l_{pkt}(n_k)$$
$$\cdot P_{heard}(n_k, R, n_r, p_m(R))$$
$$\cdot \prod_{1\le l\le n, l\ne k} P_{heard}(n_k, s_l, R, p_m(s_l)) \tag{18}$$

Where $l_{pkt}(n_i)$ is the length of the packet sent to node n_i. The $P_{AckerRvd}(R, n_r)$ is the probability that the coded packet sent from R is successfully received and ACKed by node n_r, which is given by:

$$P_{AckerRvd}(R, n_r) = \sum_{k=1}^{\infty} \{(1 - P_{pdr}(R, n_r, p_m(R))P_{ACK}(d_r, R))^{k-1}$$
$$\cdot P_{pdr}(R, n_r, p_m(R))P_{ACK}(n_r, R)\} \tag{19}$$

Eq. (17) means if primary receiver n_r wants to decode its packet, it should successfully receive and acknowledge the transmission from R, and overhear the transmission from all other nodes in $Nbr_{coded}(p_m(R))$ to meet the coding requirement.

Eq. (18) means if another recipient node n_k wants to decode its packet, it should have overheard and decoded the packet sent via pseudo-broadcast from the relay node R to the primary receiver n_r, and overheard transmissions from all other nodes in $Nbr_{coded}(p_m(R))$ to meet the coding requirement.

The expected number of bits $L_m(R)$ delivered by coded transmission to $Nbr_{coded}(p_m(R))$ recipient nodes is then given by:

$$L_m(R) = L_{AckerRvd}(n_r) + \sum_{k=1, k\ne r}^{n} L_{Rvd}(n_k) \tag{20}$$

Finally, based on the above discussion, the transmission power selection problem is given by:

$$\min_{1\le m\le M} \frac{S_m(R)T_m(R)}{L_m(R)} \tag{21}$$

Subject to:

$$S_m(R) = \pi d_m^{2}(R) \tag{22}$$

$$L_m(R) = L_{AckerRvd}(n_r) + \sum_{k=1, k\ne r}^{n} L_{Rvd}(n_k) \tag{23}$$

$$T_m(R) = N(R, n_r)\frac{l_{coded}(R)}{r_z(R)}, \ n_r \in Nbr_{coded}(p_m(R)) \tag{24}$$

Each relay node will try to find the solution of (21). The total throughput of the network can then be increased as a result. Therefore, with the above proposed analysis framework, the space-time efficiency of each transmission will be maximized and the throughput will be increased consequently.

4.4 Distributed Mechanism

Our objective is to maximize the network throughput by applying power/rate control. However, it has been known that maximizing the network throughput of a wireless multihop network is NP-hard [1]. Therefore, we resort to a heuristic based distributed mechanism to increasing the network throughput.

Based on the above analysis framework, we propose a distributed Coding Aware Power/rate Adjustment mechanism (CAPA). CAPA is localized and requires only local information. The proposed mechanism adopts inter-flow network coding like done in COPE. Specifically, we adopt the pseudo-broadcast, hop-by-

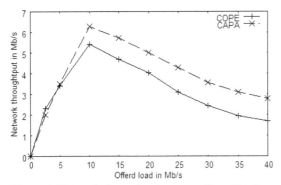

Figure 4. Network throughput versus offered load.

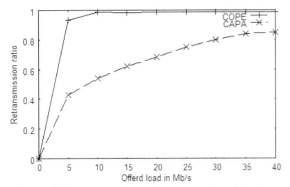

Figure 6. Retransmission ratio versus offered load.

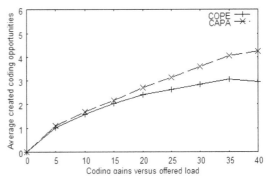

Figure 5. Coding gains versus offered load.

hop asynchronous ACKs, and periodic reception report broadcasting procedures in COPE.

In CAPA, each node will collect local state information such as packet delivery ratio, SINR requirement, and overheard packets at its neighbors. Nodes exchange information periodically to its neighbor nodes via piggybacking or reception reports. Each node will use such information to calculate the space-time efficiency according to above analysis framework. The detailed design of CAPA is given in Fig. 3. The procedures will be executed whenever a node tries to perform a transmission (either native or coded).

4.4.1 Complexity analysis
The available power level number M is in general quite limited. For example, M is 4 for 802.11a, and 12 for 802.11g. Therefore, the solution space is also small. For the transmission power/rate selection of native packets, we only need to go through the M available power levels. Thus, the complexity is $O(M)$. For the transmission power/rate selection of coded packets, for each power level, we need to check n neighbor nodes in $Nbr_{coded}(p_m(R))$, thus, the overall computational complexity is $O(Mn)$

5. SIMULATION RESULTS
In this section, we evaluate the performance of CAPA through simulations using *ns*-2. We compared CAPA with COPE. In the experiments, we used 802.11a, which has eight data rate levels (6, 9, 12, 18, 24, 36, 48 and 54Mbps), as the underlying MAC-layer protocol for all the mechanisms. The signal attenuation is modeled by the 2-ray ground propagation model. We set maximal power level P_{max} to -10dbm, minimal power level P_{min} to -15dbm and use 20 discrete power levels. The COPE protocol uses a fixed transmission power/rate throughout in all simulations. The

transmission power of COPE is set to $(P_{max}+P_{min})/2$, which corresponds to the transmission rage of 30-50 meters. The exchange of RTS/CTS packets is disabled as in the implementation of COPE. Both protocols use the fixed carrier sense threshold that is fixed to -72dbm as in [19].

We considered 200 static nodes that were deployed in a $500{\times}500m^2$ square fields. We randomly generated UDP flows and varied the offered load by adjusting the number of flows. Each flow has a packet arrival rate ranging from 200 Kbps to 2 Mbps with a random duration. The packet size ranges from 32bytes to 1500bytes. The source and destination of each flow were randomly chosen. The routing path of each flow is chosen by the DSR routing protocol [20]. We used the overall end-to-end throughput of all flows in the network as the performance metric, and only data packets are counted. For each setting, five random network topologies were considered. Each simulation lasts for 900 seconds. The network nodes work in a promiscuous mode to enable promiscuous listening.

Throughput gains: In this test, we evaluated the impact of coding aware power/rate control on the overall throughput. Only data packets were considered in the computation of throughput. In this test, we varied the offered load in the network to test the throughput. Fig. 4 shows the network throughput due to different mechanisms versus offered load. It is seen that CAPA can improve the network throughput substantially as compared with COPE. On average, CAPA provides 30 percent throughput gain over COPE, and with a maximum ratio of 69 percent. When the offered load is small, COPE performs better than CAPA because the requirement for spatial reuse is low. Therefore, COPE can create more coding opportunities by using maximal transmission power. As the offered load grows, the gap between COPE and CAPA continues to increase because it is hard to meet the requirement of spatial reuse due to heavy concurrent transmission. However, CAPA provides greater throughput gains across a wide range of offered load, especially when the offered load is high, due to the fact that it can achieve good trade-off between coding opportunities and concurrent transmissions.

Coding gains: Fig. 5 plots the average total number of coding opportunities in each transmission versus traffic load. This total number is calculated as follows: The figure shows that the coding opportunities of both mechanisms vary with traffic demands. It is also observed that, the performance difference between CAPA and COPE is small. As the offered load increases, the coding gains of CAPA exceed the coding gains of the COPE. The coding gain is maintained at high levels with our coding aware power/rate control mechanism. That is because collision induced by the heavy load can be alleviated by the power/rate control in CAPA.

Our mechanism enables nodes to encode more native packets into every new encoded packet. The performance of COPE, however, is decreased due to the lack of sufficient spatial reuse. The results again demonstrate the effectiveness of the coding-aware power/rate control that our proposed protocol outperforms COPE.

Retransmission ratio: Next, to evaluate the performance of power/rate control, we evaluated the retransmission ratio with varying offered loads. The retransmission ratio is defined as the total number of re-transmissions by each mechanism divided by the total number of retransmissions of regular 802.11a. A lower retransmission ratio is preferred because it indicates less collision of concurrent transmissions, thus better spatial reuse. Fig. 6 gives the results of different mechanisms. It is seen that the retransmission ratio of CAPA is much lower than that by COPE. That is because the localized power/rate control used in CAPA can greatly increase the spatial reuse level and reduce the collision of concurrent transmissions.

6. CONCLUSION

In this paper, we propose a Space-Time efficient transmission power/rate adjustment mechanism for achieving optimal trade-off between spatial reuse and wireless network coding. With our mechanism, power/rate control is carried out with the awareness of local coding opportunities. Our mechanism does not require synchronization (either global or local) among nodes. Simulation results demonstrate that our mechanism achieves high performance in increasing the network throughput. The proposed mechanism is simple, efficient, and easy to implement in dynamic wireless multihop networks.

7. ACKNOWLEDGMENTS

This work was supported in part by National Natural Science Foundation of China under Grant Nos. 61173158, 61101133.

8. REFERENCES

[1] K. Jain, J. Padhye, V. N. Padmanabhan, and L. Qiu, "Impact of interference on multi-hop wireless network performance," *Wireless Networks*, vol. 11, no. 4, pp. 471-487, July 2005.

[2] R. Ahlswede, N. Cai, S.-Y. R. Li, and R. W. Yeung, "Network information flow," *IEEE Trans. on Information Theory*, vol. 46, no. 4, pp. 1204-1216, July 2000.

[3] S.-Y. R. Li, R.W. Yeung, and N. Cai, "Linear network coding," *IEEE Trans. on Information Theory*, vol. 49, no. 2, pp. 371-381, Feb. 2003.

[4] R. Koetter and M. Médard, "An algebraic approach to network coding," *IEEE/ACM Trans. on Netw.*, vol. 11, no. 5, pp. 782-795, Oct. 2003.

[5] T. Ho, M. Médard, J. Shi, M. Effros, and D. Karger, "On Randomized Network Coding," in *Proc. Allerton'03*, Oct. 2003.

[6] P. A. Chou, Y. Wu, and K. Jain, "Practical network coding", in *Proc. Allerton'03*, Oct. 2003.

[7] D. S. Lun, N. Ratnakar, R. Koetter, M. Mdard, et al., "Achieving minimum cost multicast: A decentralized approach based on network coding", in *Proc. IEEE INFOCOM'05*, pp. 1607-1617, Mar. 2005.

[8] S. Katti, H. Rahul, W. Hu, D. Katabi, M. Medard, and J. Crowcroft, "XORs in the air: practical wireless network coding", in *Proc. ACM SIGCOMM'06*, pp. 243-254, Sept. 2006.

[9] P. Li, Q. Shen, Y. Fang, and H. Zhang, "Power controlled network protocols for multi-rate ad hoc networks," *IEEE Trans. on Wireless Communications*, vol. 8, no. 4, pp. 2142-2149, Apr. 2009.

[10] K. P. Shih, C. C. Chang, and Y. D. Chen, "MRPC: a multi-rate supported power control MAC protocol for wireless ad hoc networks," in *Proc. IEEE WCNC'09*, pp. 1-6, Apr. 2009.

[11] A. Akella, G. Judd, P. Steenkiste, and S. Seshan, "Self Management in Chaotic Wireless Deployments," In *Proc. ACM MobiCom'05*, pp. 185-199, Aug.-Sept. 2005.

[12] J. El-Najjar, H.M.K. AlAzemi, C. Assi, "On the Interplay Between Spatial Reuse and Network Coding in Wireless Networks," *IEEE Trans. on Wireless Communications*, vol. 10, no. 2, pp. 560-569, Feb. 2011.

[13] J. Hwang and S.-L. Kim, "Cross-Layer Optimization and Network Coding in CSMA/CA-Based Wireless Multihop Networks," *IEEE/ACM Trans. on Networking*, vol. 19, no. 4, pp. 1028- 1042, Aug. 2011.

[14] T.-S. Kim, S. Vural, S. Broustis, D. Syrivelis, S.V. Krishnamurthy, "A Framework for Joint Network Coding and Transmission Rate Control in Wireless Networks," in *Proc. IEEE INFOCOM'10*, pp. 1-9, Mar. 2010.

[15] R. Kumar, S. Tati, F. de Mello, S.V. Krishnamurthy, and T. La Porta, "Network Coding aware Rate Selection in multi-rate IEEE 802.11," in *Proc. IEEE ICNP'10*, pp. 92-102, Oct. 2010.

[16] T. Rappaport, Wireless Communications: Principles and Practices, *Prentice Hall*, 1996.

[17] J. Kivinen, X. Zhao, and P. Vainikainen, "Empirical characterization of wideband indoor radio channel at 5.3 GHz," *IEEE Trans. on Antenna and Propagation*, vol. 49, no. 8, pp. 1192–1203, Aug. 2001.

[18] Luo, Han-Chiuan, EH-K. Wu, and Gen-Huey Chen. "Minimizing ceased areas with power control for spatial reuse in IEEE 802.11 ad hoc networks." In *Parallel and Distributed Systems (ICPADS)*, 2011 IEEE 17th International Conference on, pp. 449-457. IEEE, 2011.

[19] Kim, Tae-Suk, Hyuk Lim, and Jennifer C. Hou. "Understanding and improving the spatial reuse in multihop wireless networks." *IEEE Transactions on Mobile Computing*, vol. 7, no. 10 (2008): 1200-1212.

[20] Johnson, David B., and David A. Maltz. "Dynamic source routing in ad hoc wireless networks." In *Mobile computing*, pp. 153-181. Springer US, 1996.

Community-Based Forwarding for Low-Capacity Pocket Switched Networks

Khadija Rasul, Shaiful Alam Chowdhury, Dwight Makaroff and Kevin Stanley
Department of Computer Science, University of Saskatchewan
Saskatoon, SK, CANADA, S7N 5C9
{khr667, sbc882}@mail.usask.ca, {makaroff, kstanley} @cs.usask.ca

ABSTRACT

Sensor devices and the emergent networks that they enable are capable of transmitting information between data sources. Since these devices have low-power and intermittent connectivity, latency of delivery for certain classes of data may be tolerated in an effort to save energy. The BUBBLE routing algorithm, proposed by Hui *et al.*, provides consistent routing, employing a model which considers the popularity of individual nodes within communities and only passes messages to nodes with higher probability of delivery. We have developed an improvement to BUBBLE, called Community-Based-Forwarding (CBF) that considers the interactions between communities as an additional factor in message forwarding. By using community information, CBF is able to exploit intermediate connections between clusters to route messages with more balanced node participation and higher levels of reliability and efficiency.

Categories and Subject Descriptors

C.2.2 [**Network Protocols**]: Routing protocols; C.2.1 [**Network Architecture and Design**]: Network Topology

Keywords

delay-tolerant networks; pocket-switched networks; social-based routing; resource-constrained devices; clustering

1. INTRODUCTION

The number and variety of mobile computing/sensing devices is steadily increasing from smartphones, to personal medical monitors to smart badges. These devices vary in capabilities, but all desire to minimize energy consumption. We consider the least powerful class of devices with a single radio only capable of short-range transmissions on an opportunistic basis when other devices are detected.

Device sensing methodology and parameters as well as associated software may need to adapt in ways impossible to

capture in an *a priori* manner. As well, delay-tolerant message generation paradigms can be anticipated. In particular, the recording of sensor values from many sensors to a single node for long-term trend analysis can be tolerant of delays on the order of days where message flooding is impractical due to energy concerns [25]. Individual nodes may communicate (one-to-one) when an implicit overlay of social connectivity exists that is unrelated to physical connectivity [16].

Pocket switched networks (PSNs) are a special case of delay tolerant networks (DTNs) where packets are routed from person to person in an ad-hoc manner, based on historical data regarding dynamic, non-uniform contact patterns [1, 13, 15]. Significant differences in contact patterns have been observed in environments for which datasets are available [3, 10, 11]. These dynamics suggest that routing based on inter-community contacts may aid routing performance.

Ideally, multi-hop routing tables would keep track of each PSN node's dynamic path length to all other nodes. This overhead rapidly outstrips the storage or power capacity of each node [20]; instead, researchers have leveraged the community structures that naturally arise from human interaction patterns [15], eliminating routing tables. Naive/greedy utilization of the network structure can favour nodes with high centrality measures. Where resources are limited, these "popular" nodes can experience packet loss due to buffer overflow and cause network failure through power depletion.

We develop and evaluate a Community-based Forwarding algorithm (CBF) that explicitly uses community structure as well as individual node-based connections of previous social-based approaches. Leveraging community linkages can exploit lower-centrality "bridging nodes" [6] to reduce buffer and power strain on the popular nodes. We compare CBF to a well known social-based algorithm (BUBBLE) [15], and both to a set of oracles to compare with optimal measures.

The contributions of this paper are threefold: 1) an approach identifying structures within the dynamic contact networks that can be leveraged for routing, 2) a new routing algorithm that provides superior performance in resource constrained environments, and 3) quantitative comparison of the impact of limiting key node resources on routing performance/efficiency of the algorithms considered.

2. RELATED WORK

The potential benefits and tradeoffs of DTN routing policies were first examined using a combination of simple routing strategies and oracle algorithms [16]. The simplest is Epidemic routing (ER) [30] where all nodes attempt to deliver all packets. While ER with unlimited resources provides optimal reliability and delay, it is wasteful of bandwidth and buffers, forwarding packets to nodes with a low probability of being on the shortest path. Other researchers have tried to constrain the growth of multiple copies through adaptive limitations on packet time-to-live (TTL) [8] or by only passing additional packets through privileged nodes [2, 9]. While these approaches tend to improve both delivery ratio and latency, it is unclear whether these tradeoffs are worthwhile, given the delay tolerant properties of the data.

Many resource-conserving strategies consider the single copy case [28] which exhibits high latency and potentially poor delivery ratio, particularly when packet TTL indicates delay tolerance, but not delay immunity. Lindgren *et al.* proposed PRoPHET [20], which models nodes' future contacts directly from contact history. Context-Aware Adaptive Routing (CAR) [22] forwards packets to nodes with the highest probability of seeing the destination. Plankton [7] predicts the probability of future contacts and duration by classifying links based on the quantity/burstiness of previous contacts combined with a replica quota system controlling the number of copies allowed in the network. Node-level bookkeeping and communication overhead required can be prohibitively expensive for large networks or multi-hop routing.

Some researchers have attempted to model the overall behaviour of the dynamic graph by segmenting the graph into cliques, which we call communities in the rest of this paper. SimBet [6] employs betweenness and similarity metrics to route packets. Hui *et al.* [15] developed BUBBLE, which uses time-variant rankings based on recent history to route packets. A node is a member of at least one community and nodes are locally ranked, based on the number of contacts with other members of that community. Likewise, a global ranking is assigned to a node based on its global contacts.

Higher contact-rate, lower contact-duration nodes have been shown to play a major role in efficiently forwarding data [24]. In Lobby-Influence [18], the influence of the community structure derived from the dynamic network dominated the routing protocol employed.

The work presented in this paper extends work in PSNs by identifying the importance of intermediate bridging links for clusters of nodes, and by proposing a new heuristic-based routing algorithm which can capitalize on these links.

3. BACKGROUND

The stochastic processes that underlie human contact patterns have a non-uniform structure when aggregated over time. The contact probability network formed by summing time in contact between pairs of nodes in the graph tends to have small world properties [12]. This structure has been used in attempts to increase routing efficiency in PSNs [9, 15, 27] admitting that aggregate representation fails to capture instantaneous contact pattern dynamics. Periodicity of contact patterns has also been shown to influence the performance of DTN routing algorithms [23]. In particular, small world networks with highly connected clusters, containing short paths connecting every pair of nodes provide a promising means of improving routing [15]. Determining routing heuristics can then be reduced to solving two separate performance problems: 1) choosing the graph cluster structure, and 2) choosing nodes for inter-cluster communications.

Our approach is based on two observations of human contact network properties: 1) strong paths within communities due to small-world properties should provide fast intra-

community routes, and 2) bridging nodes can be exploited to transfer packets closer to destination communities.

To use bridging nodes, some understanding of the cluster-level connectivity is required. For example, consider routing a packet from community A to community C. A does not contain any nodes that have strong connections to C, therefore its community-connection to C is low. However, if community B has nodes with strong connections to both A and C, then it could serve as an intermediate community.

Most PSN performance research uses simulation to compare algorithms fairly using the same contact patterns, which are typically generated in three ways: 1) directly from contact pattern traces [11, 12] datasets; 2) inferred from higher-level mobility data such as class [29] or bus [2] schedules; or 3) from synthetic contacts generated directly from theoretically grounded mobility patterns [19]. Our datasets are representative of university environments, and are among the longest datasets available. Synthetic and mobility datasets are likely to have different characteristics.

4. ALGORITHMS

4.1 Assumptions

We designed our algorithm subject to the following limiting assumptions: 1) PSN devices are **Resource Limited** in memory and computational power; energy usage is critical [16]; 2) packets possess a **Delay Tolerant** property encoded in TTL such that packet delivery is successful if delivered prior to TTL expiry [14]; 3) the contact durations have no effect on the ability to exchange buffer content metadata and messages themselves [5], simplifying the analysis; 4) the system represents a PSN that has non-degenerate **Human Mobility** patterns [20]; and 5) nodes are sufficiently **Socially Connected** to form quasi-stable cliques [27] with medium-term dynamics in which contact patterns change over time, but can be considered stable for an empirically determined particular amount of time (epoch).

Assuming delay tolerance and resource limitation permits us to emphasize delivery ratio and resource usage under resource constrained profiles. Energy savings and increased delivery ratio at the cost of latency is a beneficial because packet delivery prior to TTL is the primary metric.

4.2 Forwarding Algorithm

We employ communities to eliminate the routing table; community affiliations determine whether a message is to be forwarded or retained. CBF uses BUBBLE's *local popularity* (Eq. (1)) for intra-community delivery. For 'inter-community' routing, BUBBLE's *global popularity* (Eq. (2)) is replaced by *community betweenness count* (CBC) and *nodal contribution factor* (NCF) (Eqs. (3) and (4)). CBC is the number of contacts between two communities; NCF(n,C) is a node's contacts with every other community. In all equations, $g(x,y,k) = 1$ if an encounter between nodes x and y occurs in the kth measurement interval, and 0 otherwise, C is a node's community, k is a particular aggregation interval within the epoch and K is the epoch duration. Epoch e's data is used in forwarding decisions in epoch $e + 1$.

Local Popularity:

$$\forall(x) \quad LP_x = \sum_{y \in C_x} \sum_{k=0}^{K} g(x,y,k) \qquad (1)$$

Global Popularity:

$$\forall(x) \quad GP_x = \sum_{y \notin C_x} \sum_{k=0}^{K} g(x,y,k) \qquad (2)$$

Community Betweenness Count:

$$\forall(C_x, C')_{s.t.(C_x \neq C')} \quad CBC_{C_x,C'} = \sum_{x \in C_x} \sum_{y \in C'} \sum_{k=0}^{K} g(x,y,k)$$
$$(3)$$

Nodal Contribution Factor:

$$\forall(x)\forall(C')_{s.t.(x \notin C')} \quad NCF_{x,C'} = \sum_{y \in C'} \sum_{k=0}^{K} g(x,y,k) \qquad (4)$$

A formal algorithm representation of CBF is shown in Algorithm 1. In each timestep, a node encounters a (possibly empty, but normally small) set of other nodes and potentially transfers messages to these nodes. A node may also receive messages as the encountered nodes simultaneously execute CBF.

Algorithm 1 CBF (Node me, Node dest, Node metNode[], int numEncountered, msgType Msg)

Node $maxCBC$= me; Node $maxNCF$=me;
Node $maxLP$ = NULL;
for $(i = 1$ to $numEncountered)$ **do**
    if $(metNode[i] == dest)$ **then** // Destination
        $dest.addMessageToBuf(Msg)$; **return;**
    end if
    if $(C(metNode[i]) == C(dest))$ **then**
        $maxLP = maximumLP(metNode[i], maxLP)$;
    else if $(C(metNode[i]) \neq C(me))$ **then**
        $maxCBC = maximumCBC(metNode[i], maxCBC)$;
    else $maxNCF = maximumNCF(metNode[i], maxNCF)$;
    end if
end for
if $((maxLP \neq$ NULL$)$ & $(C(me) \neq C(dest)))$ **then** //
entering dest. comm.
    $maxLP.addMessageToBuf(Msg)$
else if $((maxLP \neq$ NULL$)$ & $(LP_{maxLP} > LP_{me}))$ **then**
    $maxLP.addMessageToBuf(Msg)$ // in dest. comm.
else if $(maxCBC \neq me)$ **then**
    $maxCBC.addMessageToBuf(Msg)$ // new comm.
else if $(maxNCF \neq me)$ **then**
    $maxNCF.addMessageToBuf(Msg)$ // same comm.
end if

Packet forwarding is accomplished through a set of heuristics. We never forward outside the community when the carrier is in the destination community, and and choose the node with the greatest LP value as the next carrier. When the carrier encounters a node that neither belongs to its own community nor to that of the destination, CBC values with the destination community are used, selecting the encountered node with the maximum CBC. Finally, when the encountered node and carrier are in the same non-destination community, NCF with the destination community is used.

No routing loops are possible during an epoch, as only nodes with higher delivery metrics are chosen. It is possible that a carrier node will change communities between epochs. A message may return to a previous community, as a type of backtracking. With TTL less than the epoch, at most one backtracking operation per message is possible for messages in-transit at epoch end.

4.3 Comparator Algorithms

We compare CBF with BUBBLE as an implementation of a context-aware forwarding approach and Epidemic Routing (ER) [30], a commonly considered performance benchmark algorithm ([15, 20, 21, 22]). Additionally, we are interested in determining how both algorithms perform in comparison to oracles that are optimal with respect to two of our main metrics: delivery latency and number of message transmissions.

We use two oracles: the *Minimum Cost Oracle* and the *Fastest Oracle*. For the minimum cost oracle we take the shortest of all ER paths that successfully delivered a packet to the destination. The minimum cost oracle should approach one hop for a fully connected graph as time goes to infinity. Values greater than 1 indicate both the small world nature of the graph and the time horizon on simulation forced by the duration of the datasets considered. The fastest oracle records the first arrival at the destination using ER with unlimited resources.

4.4 Clustering Algorithm

The K-Cliques algorithm has been used for detecting communities in different kinds of networks and was used in BUB-BLE [15]. It requires the minimum size of communities to be specified prior to forming the communities. Outlier nodes are placed in communities by K-cliques, but should be left isolated to avoid poor intracommunity routing decisions.

Inspired by this concern and Pietiläinen and Diot's methods [24], we used the Louvain algorithm [4] to find communities characterized by frequent, sustained contacts. Louvain clustering is fast, simple to implement and does not require a predefined minimum community size. Extensive evaluation on a variety of datasets shows superior performance in terms of modularity/centrality than comparable techniques, though the communities obtained are not always identical. We believe the small number of nodes and similar contact properties make this an appropriate clustering algorithm and that Louvain clustering will cause CBF to ignore isolated individuals. Future work will compare routing performance with different clustering algorithms.

The Louvain algorithm works in multiple iterations, each consisting of two phases. During the first phase, each node is considered as a separate community. In each iteration, every node is selected and potentially merged with each of its neighbouring communities to see if the merger improves network *modularity*. If no potential merges improve the modularity, the algorithm stops. During the second phase, new community formed in phase 1 is converted to a single node, represented by some centroid value. The phases are repeated until a locally near optimal point or a proscribed number of iterations is reached. The algorithm is guaranteed to converge, but may not be optimal, as the greedy approach is a heuristic solution to this NP-hard problem.

Since the graph is dynamic, and evolves over time, communities should be refreshed periodically.[1] Community formation based on a very short period or number of contacts may not reflect the actual graph structure (e.g., when only day 1's contacts are used, 33 communities are generated for SHED1 as few contacts occurred on that day).

[1]refresh interval depends on stability of contact patterns

5. EXPERIMENTAL DETAILS

Our first dataset, Flunet [11], contains contacts information for 36 computer science graduate students at the University of Saskatchewan, as well as staff and undergraduate students associated with those labs, collected over a period of 3 months. Approximately 70,000 contact records were collected from wireless sensor motes (MicaZ). Our second data set is St. Andrews (Sassy) [3] measuring the contacts of 22 undergraduate students, three postgraduate students and two staff members of the University of St. Andrews for 79 days (similar to Flunet) with 113,000 contacts. Our last data set - the Saskatchewan Human Ethology Dataset 1 (SHED1) [10] - covers 5 weeks of Bluetooth contact records of 39 participants who were primarily CS graduate students and staff (22721 distinct contacts).

A custom simulator was developed for our experiments as the integration of clustering and routing was simpler and could be more focussed than existing simulators such as ONE [17] and OMNET++.[2] Source and destination were chosen randomly from different communities to focus on the impact on inter-community message passing. Twenty experimental runs were performed for each parameter combination.

The values assigned to each input parameter are described in Table 1. In all experiments, a single parameter was varied. For all datasets, in the limited resource experiments, 10% of the number of messages generated was used as the fixed buffer capacity; trial and error showed that increased buffer did not provide a proportionate increment in delivery ratio for either algorithm. Similarly, maximum TTL values were set to 15 days for Flunet/Sassy and 7 days for SHED1. Unless otherwise specified, 100K, 80K and 48K messages were generated for Flunet, Sassy, and SHED1, respectively.

Table 1: Experimental Factor Input Ranges

Input	Limited Resource		
	Flunet	Sassy	SHED1
TTL(hours)	1-336	1-336	1-168
Buffer Capacity	10% msgs	10% msgs	10% msgs
Messages	10-80000	10-100000	10-480000
	Unlimited Resource		
	Flunet	Sassy	SHED1
TTL(hours)	1-4320	1-4320	1-2160
Buffer Capacity	10-200000	10-200000	2-100000
Messages	10-80000	10-100000	5-48000

We first investigated algorithm performance without resource constraints to establish best case performance baselines where one parameter was varied and the others set to inexhaustible values. The limited resource cases constrained parameters within a limited range. A cool-down period is not used; no algorithm delivers messages generated late in the simulation. The first epoch's data is used as a training session; packets are forwarded starting in the second epoch. More details can be found in Rasul [26].

6. PERFORMANCE EVALUATION

6.1 Community Determination

Our data sets ranged from extremely clustered to more isolated. Further examination of the datasets shows that

[2]www.omnetpp.org

between 62% and 79% of the encounters are local encounters (intra-community) and 21% to 38% are inter-community (i.e. global encounters). Intra-community message passing is expected to have short/fast paths for all heuristics, as nodes are placed communities by contact frequency. This intuition to optimize inter-community delivery is additionally inspired by the work done by Sastry et al. [27] where routing performance has a crucial dependence on the less frequent contacts. In all our datasets, global encounters can be treated as the somewhat 'rare' or 'novel' contacts.

Figure 1 shows the total number of membership changes for different community formation periods for all 3 datasets. The number of changes decreases with increasing time period. Membership changes are frequent for very short peri-

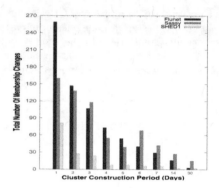

Figure 1: Membership Changes

ods. We also measured the average number of communities for different community formation periods. The number of communities stabilizes for SHED1 and Flunet after 4 and 7 days, respectively. In Sassy, the number of communities varies slightly, regardless of the measurement period. We choose 7 days as the epoch duration, since it fits two of the three datasets well. A notable consequence of an epoch duration of 7 days and a maximum TTL of 15 days (as in the limited resource experiments) is that messages exist in at most 3 epochs before expiring, for a maximum of 2 community changes for message undelivered during re-clustering.

6.2 Dataset Characteristics

We investigated the overall internal network structure for each dataset by sending 5000 inter-community messages. Figure 2 provides an overall idea of the delivery behaviour of each of the algorithms, visualized in communities formed over all contacts. For all detailed forwarding experiments, weekly community membership is used and will not exactly match the aggregated membership visualized here.[3]

In particular, we see the underlying network structure, the contact patterns and the message forwarding behaviour. Since the same community determination and same contact patterns are used for both BUBBLE and CBF, network connectivity remains unchanged. Encounters are represented as edges in the graph where edge thickness is proportional to the number of encounters between nodes; node size is proportional to the number of packets forwarded. BUBBLE has nodes that transmit many messages, while load is spread

[3]e.g. weekly data for Sassy produces 5 communities in each week, whereas contacts aggregated over the entire dataset produce only 2 communities.

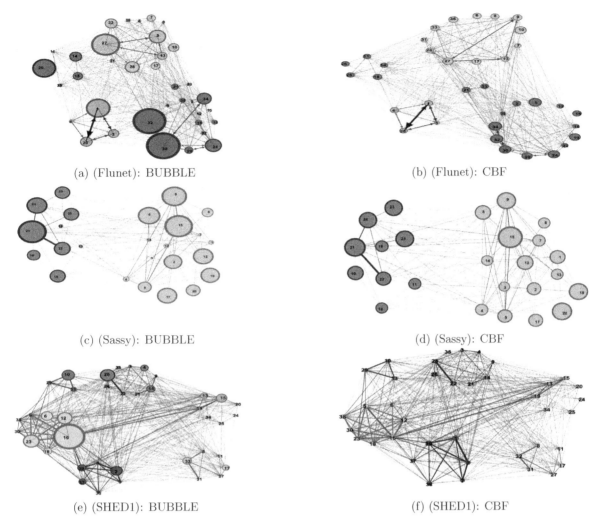

(a) (Flunet): BUBBLE

(b) (Flunet): CBF

(c) (Sassy): BUBBLE

(d) (Sassy): CBF

(e) (SHED1): BUBBLE

(f) (SHED1): CBF

Figure 2: Internal Network Structure

more evenly in CBF. Further analysis showed that the median number of messages forwarded per node was similar, but some nodes transmitted disproportionately many messages using BUBBLE, especially in Flunet/ SHED1, implying high energy usage and potential buffer overflow at the over-utilized nodes. In particular, 25% of the nodes transmit over 45,000/22000 messages, using BUBBLE. CBF has no node send over 30000/15000 messages.

6.3 Forwarding Results

Delivery Ratio. In the first set of experiments we varied buffer size, but TTL was unlimited and the number of messages was generated as in Table 1. Figure 3 shows the mean (bar) and the standard deviation (whiskers) for the delivery ratio. The differences between the algorithms were not significant for unlimited buffer sizes (80%) for Flunet and SHED1. With large buffer (over 100 KB), ER performed the best (90%). For Sassy, delivery ratios were worse overall, because of the instability of the network, but CBF had about 5% higher delivery ratio than BUBBLE for buffer sizes above 2.5 KB. ER with unlimited buffer and TTL delivers the maximum number packets.

We expect that CBF will deliver more messages than BUBBLE by having fewer packet deletions due to buffer

overflow. Therefore, we examined the impact of varying buffer size keeping TTL and number of messages constant. Figure 4 shows delivery ratio as a function of buffer space. At moderate buffer space (500 to 1000 msgs), CBF increases delivery ratio by between 30% and 40% for Flunet/SHED1. For Sassy, delivery ratio is improved by 16%. At larger buffer sizes, there was still an almost 20% improvement for Flunet/SHED1. In the limited environments, ER quickly saturates all node buffers and its delivery ratio plummets.[4]

Next, TTL was varied, constraining the buffer and number of messages as specified above. Increasing TTL in ER decreases delivery ratio, likely since fewer packets expire, causing potentially deliverable packets to be dropped. For BUBBLE and CBF, delivery ratio increases similarly to increasing buffer size as TTL is varied between 24, 72, 168, and 336 hours. Due to space considerations, the graph is not shown. The instability of the community associations in Sassy causes slightly poorer performance for both BUBBLE and CBF under constrained resources, as the fundamental assumptions about network structure are violated.

---

[4]The remaining graphs omit ER, because messages transmitted and dropped packets are substantially higher.

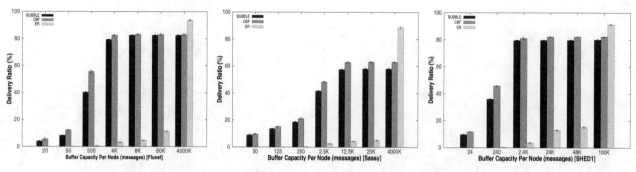

Figure 3: Delivery Ratio: Unlimited Resource Environment

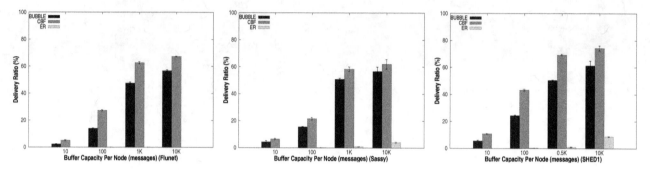

Figure 4: Delivery Ratio: Limited Buffer Capacity

Latency. Each subgraph of Figure 5 shows the results for a sample run at a particular level of load. All runs had a similar latency profile. As the number of messages increases, the oracle delivers more messages closer to TTL expiry, increasing the latency profile. For BUBBLE and CBF, however, the concentration of simultaneous live messages increases; more messages are delivered to their respective destinations faster, decreasing average delay.

For the majority of messages successfully delivered, CBF has a lower delay. In particular, for the sample run of 500 messages with SHED1, 310 out of the fastest 390 messages had a lower latency for CBF (by between 10 and 15 hours). Other datasets show a similar trend: CBF slightly outperforms BUBBLE for a majority of the low-latency messages, and then suffers high latency for the hard-to-deliver messages. In these cases, a high contribution to total delay is provided by that relatively small proportion of such messages, plus those that BUBBLE could not deliver, but that CBF did deliver, albeit slowly.

Over all experimental runs, the CBF median delay is between 73% and 97% of BUBBLE's (500 messages), between 66% and 90% (5000 messages) and between 61% and 89% (40,000 messages). For lower loads, SHED1 has the smallest relative median delay and Sassy the largest. With 40,000 messages, SHED1 actually had the largest relative median delay, but the median for BUBBLE was substantially lower than with 5000 messages (reduced from 53 to 37 hours).

When we consider the average delay of the *same number of messages* delivered by BUBBLE and CBF, there is very little difference between the algorithms (some runs produce at most 7% difference for the 500 message case). For SHED1, CBF delay is 7.5% to 12% lower than BUBBLE. For smaller numbers of messages, BUBBLE outperformed CBF for Sassy and Flunet by as much as 6%, but with the 40000 message case, Flunet's CBF delay was only 83% of

BUBBLE's. When the additional messages that only CBF could deliver are included, the mean delay increases. For 5000 messages and 40000 messages, we see a similar trend, but the delay measurements are even closer between CBF and BUBBLE. Sometimes CBF even surpasses BUBBLE. In particular, for the SHED1 dataset, the average delay is 1.8 hours less under CBF than BUBBLE with 5000 messages. The worst performance for CBF was a 21% increase in delay for Flunet (500 messages), though there was only a 6% increase for the fastest 390 messages delivered.

For CBF with Flunet, messages were continued to be delivered until TTL expiry, but not with BUBBLE, whose longest successful delivery was 230 hours. Similar results are shown for SHED1. Even more dramatic are the results for Sassy, where there were no messages delivered close to the TTL expiry time in either forwarding scheme, the longest successful latency being 294 hours for CBF. Extending the TTL does not necessarily allow more messages to be delivered, even with unlimited buffer space. In the samples, only Flunet using CBF has a substantial percentage of messages delivered after 7 days.

Message Transmissions. We next compare the efficiency of BUBBLE and CBF with the *Minimum Cost Oracle*, measuring the total number of transmissions required to deliver the same set of messages unconstrained. Table 2 shows that CBF uses 2 more hops on average than the oracle in SHED1, whereas BUBBLE uses 3 more hops. The differences between CBF and BUBBLE are less for the other 2 datasets.

After comparing with the oracle, we compared the forwarding cost between the algorithms in a realistic, resource-constrained environment. Figure 6 shows transmissions as a function of buffer space, indicating absolute differences of transmissions between CBF and BUBBLE for larger buffer sizes. In this scenario, CBF also had a higher delivery ratio (see Figure 4), so the transmission is more efficient.

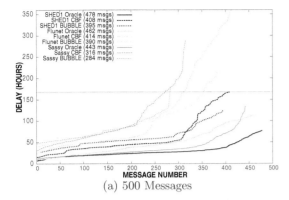

(a) 500 Messages

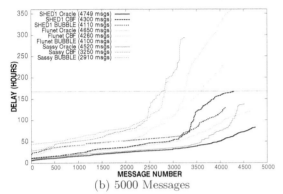

(b) 5000 Messages

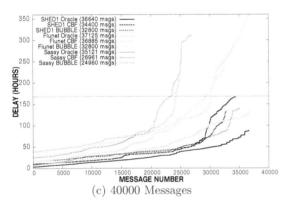

(c) 40000 Messages

Figure 5: Message Latency (Sample Runs)

By increasing TTL, the lifespans of messages were increased, allowing them undergo more exchanges before getting dropped, shown in Figure 7. Increasing the TTL has a diminishing effect on the *difference* between number of messages sent by each algorithm. For both algorithms, SHED1 has no noticeable increase in transmissions with a TTL longer than 7 days, and doubling the TTL (from 168 to 336 hours) for the other 2 datasets has the effect of increasing the average number of transmissions by only 25-28% in CBF and only 12-18% in BUBBLE. Doubling it again had less than a 10% effect in any of the algorithms. The fact that SHED1 has a stable number of transmissions indicates that all messages were delivered before the original TTL, were victims of buffer overflow, or found no suitable carriers.

For all datasets, CBF outperforms BUBBLE by transferring more messages with fewer transmissions. Results using the SHED1 dataset shows the maximum difference, whereas the least difference is seen in Sassy.

Table 2: Hop Count

Msgs	Algorithm	Flunet	Sassy	SHED1
50	Oracle	2	1.6	2
	BUBBLE	4.8	4.6	5
	CBF	4.6	4	4
500	Oracle	1.2	1.4	2
	BUBBLE	4.4	4.3	5.1
	CBF	4	4.2	3.5
5000	Oracle	1.1	1.33	2
	BUBBLE	4.33	4.2	5.06
	CBF	4	4.13	3.67
40000	Oracle	1.06	1	2
	BUBBLE	3.83	5	5
	CBF	3	4	4

Packets Dropped. As suggested by Figure 2, CBF spreads traffic more evenly, reducing buffer congestion. Table 3 shows the average and standard deviation of packet drops when TTL is varied and buffer space is limited. Social nodes in BUBBLE experience more packet drops. The standard deviation in packet drops is comparable, but is usually lower with CBF. Both algorithms have nodes drop older packets to make space for newer messages. As TTL is increased, more long-lived packets must be dropped due to congestion. With short TTL, CBF has close to an order of magnitude fewer drops for all datasets. This difference drops to less than twice for the longest TTL. At the default TTL (168 hours), the differences range from 33% (Flunet) to 60% (Sassy).

Table 3: Packet Drops

TTL (hrs)	Alg.	Flunet		Sassy		SHED1	
		Mean	SD	Mean	SD	Mean	SD
24	BUBBLE	341	9	208	31	3693	20
	CBF	64	18	20	5	267	21
72	BUBBLE	2135	38	1831	68	11163	92
	CBF	491	24	785	14	6754	87
168	BUBBLE	12486	52	14080	133	17418	507
	CBF	4150	71	8232	102	9171	332
336	BUBBLE	20666	230	26436	784	17658	3650
	CBF	12212	191	17384	483	9210	3811

In SHED1, where the top four social nodes belong to the same community, there is higher packet drop. For all three datasets, Pearson's correlation coefficient was calculated to determine the impact of node GP on the number of packets dropped. Packets dropped by nodes using BUBBLE have a high positive correlation with global popularity, whereas with CBF packet drop has a low positive correlation with global popularity. In Sassy, nodes using BUBBLE have a high correlation of +0.85, but using CBF have a low correlation of +0.41. These values are +0.90/+0.70 and +0.26/0.30 in SHED1/Flunet, respectively. In a realistic limited resource environment, the dependency of BUBBLE on the most social nodes becomes its major drawback rather than its strength.

Analysis of Forwarding Dynamics. To illustrate the underlying mechanics which lead to the trends observed, we consider a final experimental scenario. A fixed number of messages, TTL and and 10% buffer capacity was employed as in Section 5. With lower packet transmission for CBF than BUBBLE (Figures 6 and 7), a higher proportion of passes (12.34% - Flunet, 5.87% - Sassy, 17.91% - SHED1) were made based on inter-community factors in CBF than in BUBBLE, indicating that CBF prefers an appropriate node along a likely path rather than a globally popular node.

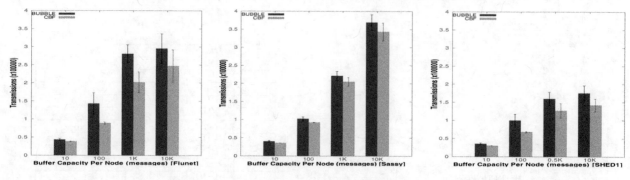

Figure 6: Transmissions: Limited Buffer Capacity

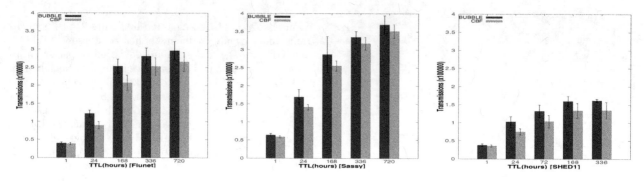

Figure 7: Transmissions: Limited TTL

7. DISCUSSION

Contributions. Our primary contribution is the CBF algorithm which uses more nuanced information about social network structures arising from human mobility patterns in forwarding decisions. We also analyzed the role of network versus personal interconnectivity in PSNs. Well-connected nodes may span communities, but nodes close to the destination bridging relevant communities are important in reducing packet drops in resource constrained systems and asymmetric resource utilization on globally popular nodes compared to BUBBLE [15] or PRoPHET [20].

By employing datasets with varying degrees of community stability, we established that even under varying community membership, CBF can provide superior performance to BUBBLE. Obviously, there are limits to the extent to which our assumptions apply to degenerate systems: for example contact networks at immigration points where few people will ever see each other again, will require different routing systems. Finally, by comparing the limited and unlimited cases, we quantified the degree to which resource constraints impact the performance of PSN algorithms. Severe performance degradation for greedier schemes was noted, as expected. CBF increases the delivery ratio by up to 40% as the number of messages and TTL were varied in the limited resource situation. When buffer capacity was varied, delivery ratio and transmissions were consistently better for CBF than BUBBLE; packet loss was lower with CBF as well.

Limitations and Future Work. While constituting a significant contribution to the study of PSN routing, there are several short-comings to be addressed in future work. Our datasets are strongly biased toward University lifestyles and relationships. Replicating these results with datasets from other populations or on synthetic data [12] could shed fur-

ther light on design tradeoffs. We also neglected channel noise, a common assumption in DTN work, as packet drops are to some extent implicitly encoded in the datasets. Modelling communication channel noise and investigating the role of packet size would substantially extend our work. Message source and destination were generated at random from different communities. More realistic message generation scenarios would help quantify the applicability of the results. In particular, the many-to-one scenario should show different packet drop profiles. Finally, we only investigated a single community generation technique. Additional community formation techniques and even self-identification may enhance CBF generalizability.

8. CONCLUSIONS

Social networks often exhibit small world network traits. For efficient routing in social contexts, forwarding algorithms can use routing heuristics that encompass small world network properties. Moreover, in a resource constrained PSN system, the routing algorithm must use available resources appropriately. Our algorithm balances the use of resources with the likelihood of delivery, by employing decision making metrics that can evaluate arising social structure of a network, in turn enabling CBF to preferentially choose nodes with a greater probability of being in the target community. When compared to BUBBLE, CBF's transmission performance reaches closer to that of the shortest route oracle and in all cases CBF transmits fewer messages, making it more energy-efficient. Quantitative analysis shows that more stable networks reap the benefits of CBF's enhancements to a greater degree. The delivery ratio of CBF is bounded below by BUBBLE and we experience acceptable additional delay for a DTN, due to the additional messages delivered.

9. REFERENCES

[1] L. Amaral, A. Scala, M. Barthelemy, and H. E. Stanley. Classes of Small-world Networks. *Proceedings of the National Academy of Science USA*, 97:11149–11152, 2000.

[2] N. Banerjee, M. D. Corner, D. Towsley, and B. N. Levine. Relays, base stations, and meshes: enhancing mobile networks with infrastructure. In *ACM Mobicom*, pages 81–91, San Francisco, CA, Sept. 2008.

[3] G. Bigwood, D. Rehunathan, M. Bateman, T. Henderson, and S. Bhatti. Exploiting Self-Reported Social Networks for Routing in ubiquitous Computing Environments. In *WIMOB*, pages 484–489, Avignon, France, Oct. 2008.

[4] V. D. Blondel, J. Guillaume, R. Lambiotte, and E. Lefebvre. Fast Unfolding of Communities in Large Networks. *Journal of Statistical Mechanics: Theory and Experiment*, 2008(10):P10008, 2008.

[5] A. Chaintreau, A. Mtibaa, L. Massoulie, and C. Diot. The Diameter of Opportunistic Mobile Networks. In *CoNEXT*, pages 12:1–12:12, Copenhagen, Denmark, Dec. 2007.

[6] E. M. Daly and M. Haahr. Social network analysis for routing in disconnected delay-tolerant MANETs. In *ACM Mobihoc*, pages 32–40, Montreal, Canada, Sept. 2007.

[7] X. F. Guo and M. C. Chan. Plankton: An efficient DTN routing algorithm. In *IEEE SECON*, pages 550–558, New Orleans, LA, June 2013.

[8] Z. J. Haas and T. Small. A new networking model for biological applications of ad hoc sensor networks. *IEEE/ACM Transactions on Networking*, 14(1):27–40, Feb. 2006.

[9] M. Hashemian and K. G. Stanley. Effective utilization of place as a resource in pocket switched networks. In *Local Computer Networks*, pages 247–250, Bonn, Germany, Oct. 2011.

[10] M. S. Hashemian, K. G. Stanley, D. L. Knowles, J. Calver, and N. Osgood. Human network data collection in the wild: the epidemiological utility of micro-contact and location data. In *ACM SIGHIT International Health Informatics Symposium*, pages 255–264, Miami, FL, Jan. 2012.

[11] M. S. Hashemian, K. G. Stanley, and N. Osgood. Flunet: Automated tracking of contacts during flu season. In *WiOpt*, pages 348–353, Avignon, France, May 2010.

[12] T. Hossmann, T. T. Spyropoulos, and F. Legendre. Putting contacts into context: mobility modeling beyond inter-contact times. In *ACM Mobihoc*, pages 18:1–18:11, Paris, France, May 2011.

[13] P. Hui, A. Chaintreau, J. Scott, R. Gass, J. Crowcroft, and C. Diot. Pocket switched networks and human mobility in conference environments. In *ACM SIGCOMM Workshop on Delay-tolerant Networking*, pages 244–251, Philadelphia, PA, Aug. 2005.

[14] P. Hui and J. Crowcroft. How Small Labels Create Big Improvements. In *PERCOM Workshops*, pages 65–70, White Plains, NY, Mar. 2007.

[15] P. Hui, J. Crowcroft, and E. Yoneki. Bubble rap: social-based forwarding in delay tolerant networks. In *ACM Mobihoc*, pages 241–250, Hong Kong, China, May 2008.

[16] S. Jain, K. Fall, and R. Patra. Routing in a delay tolerant network. In *ACM SIGCOMM*, pages 145–158, Portland, OR, Sept. 2004.

[17] A. Keränen, J. Ott, and T. Kärkkäinen. The one simulator for dtn protocol evaluation. In *Simutools '09*, pages 55:1–55:10, Rome, Italy, 2009.

[18] S. Khan, R. Mondragon, and L. Tokarchuk. Lobby Influence: Opportunistic forwarding algorithm based on human social relationship patterns. In *IEEE PERCOM Workshops*, pages 211–216, Lugano, Switzerland, Mar. 2012.

[19] K. Lee, S. Hong, S. Kim, I. Rhee, and S. Chong. SLAW: self-similar least-action human walk. *IEEE/ACM Transactions on Networking*, 20(2):515–529, Apr. 2012.

[20] A. Lindgren, A. Doria, and O. Schelen. Probabilistic Routing in Intermittently Connected Networks. *SIGMOBILE Mobile Computing and Communication Review*, 7(3):19–20, 2004.

[21] A. Mtibaa, M. May., C. Diot, and M. Ammar. Peoplerank: Social opportunistic forwarding. In *IEEE INFOCOM*, pages 1–5, San Diego, CA, Mar. 2010.

[22] M. Musolesi and C. Mascolo. CAR: Context-Aware Adaptive Routing for Delay-Tolerant Mobile Networks. *IEEE Transactions on Mobile Computing*, 8(2):246–260, 2009.

[23] A. Nguyen, P. Senac, and M. Diaz. How Disorder Impacts Routing in Human-centric Disruption Tolerant Networks. In *Workshop on Future Human-centric Multimedia Networking*, pages 47–52, Hong Kong, China, Sept. 2013.

[24] A. Pietilänen and C. Diot. Dissemination in opportunistic social networks: the role of temporal communities. In *ACM MobiHoc*, pages 165–174, Hilton Head, SC, June 2012.

[25] V. Pulimi, T. Paul, K. Stanley, and D. Eager. Near-optimal Routing for Contour Detection in Wireless Sensor Networks. In *Local Computer Networks*, pages 462–469, Clearwater, FL, Oct. 2012.

[26] K. Rasul. Community-based forwarding for low-capacity pocket switched networks. Master's thesis, University of Saskatchewan, 2013.

[27] N. Sastry, K. Sollins, and J. Crowcroft. Delivery properties of human social networks. In *IEEE INFOCOM Miniconference*, pages 2586–2590, Rio de Janiero, Brazil, Apr. 2009.

[28] T. Spyropoulos, K. Psounis, and C. Raghavendra. Efficient routing in intermittently connected mobile networks: The single-copy case. *IEEE/ACM Transactions on Networking*, 16(1):63–76, Feb. 2008.

[29] V. Srinivasan, M. Motani, and W. T. Ooi. Analysis and implications of student contact patterns derived from campus schedules. In *ACM Mobicom*, pages 86–97, Los Angeles, CA, Sept. 2006.

[30] A. Vahdat and D. Becker. Epidemic Routing for Partially-connected Ad Hoc Networks. Technical Report CS-2000-06, Duke University, Apr. 2000.

Lane Detection and Tracking System Based on the MSER Algorithm, Hough Transform and Kalman Filter

Abdelhamid Mammeri   Azzedine Boukerche   Guangqian Lu

DIVA Strategic Research Network
University of Ottawa, Ottawa
Canada
amammeri@uottawa.ca; boukerch@site.uottawa.ca; lguan077@uottawa.ca

ABSTRACT

We present a novel lane detection and tracking system using a fusion of Maximally Stable Extremal Regions (MSER) and Progressive Probabilistic Hough Transform (PPHT). First, MSER is applied to obtain a set of blobs including noisy pixels (e.g., trees, cars and traffic signs) and the candidate lane markings. A scanning refinement algorithm is then introduced to enhance the results of MSER and filter out noisy data. After that, to achieve the requirements of real-time systems, the PPHT is applied. Compared to Hough transform which returns the parameters ρ and θ, PPHT returns two end-points of the detected line-markings. To track lane markings, two kalman trackers are used to track both end-points. Several experiments are conducted in Ottawa roads to test the performance of our framework. The detection rate of the proposed system averages 92.7% and exceeds 84.9% in poor conditions.

Categories and Subject Descriptors

I.4.8 [**Computing Methodologies**]: Scene Analysis

Keywords

Intelligent transportation system; lane detection and tracking; MSER; Hough Transform.

1. INTRODUCTION

Lane detection and tracking is an important component of the Advanced Driver Assistance System (ADAS). As a fundamental part of ADAS, lane detection and tracking system plays the role of a mechanism designed for localizing and tracking lane boundaries in road images. Lane detection and tracking systems have attracted an extensive amount of interest from both academia and automobile industry. Many architectures and commercial systems have been proposed in the literature, for example [1], [2] and [3].

In this paper we introduce a Real-time lane detection and tracking system. To the best of our knowledge, this is the first system that combines Maximally Stable Extremal Region (MSER) with Hough transform. Our architecture not only takes advantage of the MSER features of road images, but also refines MSER blobs, so that MSER fits better with Hough transform. Our system consists of the following stages: preprocessing (Refined MSER Segmentation), detection (Hough Transform) and tracking (Kalman Filter). This framework is distinguished from our predecessor's by the following: 1) The detection stage is carried out using texture information, which is generated by MSER. Different from traditional edge segmentation methods (e.g., Canny or Sobel), MSER feeds more effective and stable lane marking information to Hough transform by only recognizing Stable Extremal Region. A scanning refinement algorithm is then introduced to enhance the results of MSER and filter out noisy data. 2) To achieve the requirements of real-time systems, the Progressive Probabilistic Hough Transform (PPHT) is used in the detection stage. Compared to Hough transform which returns the parameters ρ and θ, PPHT returns two end-points of the detected line-markings. 3) In the tracking stage, Kalman filter is used to track both ends of each detected line-marking instead of tracking the parameters (ρ, θ) of Hough transform as performed in many research papers, e.g., [4].

The rest of this paper is organized as follows. We start this paper by reviewing the main research works in Section 2. The segmentation method used in this paper is described in Section 3. Then, in Section 4, we introduce the main idea used for lane detection. Next, in Section 5, Kalman operator is used as a tracking method. Several experiments are conducted in Section 6, and we conclude our paper and present our future work in Section 7.

2. RELATED WORKS

The detection stage extracts the lane markings from the region of interest using feature extraction methods such as edge-based methods and colour-based methods. An example of edge-based methods is the well-known Hough transform which is used in many papers (as in [3], [5], [6] and [2]). However, Hough transform has some drawbacks which are the high false positive rate and the computational complexity. Steerable filter is an edge-based method which is efficiently used to detect lane markings in many papers (as in [7], [8] and [9]). This method has good effects when road markings are clearly painted and consistently smooth. Color-based methods are quite efficient for rural roads without clear lane boundaries. However, unlike edge-based methods, color-based methods are not widely used by researchers. Color information has its own drawbacks as it is influenced by lightning. For example, the authors in [10] use a color-based method in the HIS color space by computing the cylindrical distribution of color features. For further refinement of the detection result, many techniques such as B-Spline fitting and RANAC are used, as shown in [5, 9, 11–13]. Road modeling is also used in detection-refinement in many research papers, e.g., [13], [11], [14], and [9]. Such methods improve, not only the efficiency, but the robustness of the whole system. However, road modeling is a challenging task when a road has very complex shapes or rapidly changing curvatures.

To enable the tracking of lane markings over time, a tracking operator is usually incorporated. The most common trackers used in tracking systems are Kalman and Particle filters. Previous work has been done on tracking the parameters of Hough transform by using variants of Kalman Filter or Extended Kalman Filter. Despite the advantages of Kalman filter in terms of real-time performance, it is unable to reject all outliers that cause failure of tracking, which consequently decreases the accuracy of detection. To alleviate these problems, an extended Kalman filter for road tracking was introduced in [15] and [4]. Apart from those, the authors in [16] and [17] have used Particle Filter for lane tracking stage.

In this paper we propose a real-time framework for lane detection which combines MSER (Maximum Stable Estimation Region) with Hough transform to detect lane boundaries. It is composed of the following modules: Pre-processing, Lane Detection and Lane Tracking (Figure 1). Particularly to be mentioned, we use MSER-based Segmentation and Progressive Probabilistic Hough Transform (PPHT) as the core method of Pre-processing and Detection, respectively.

3. SEGMENTATION

In this paper, Hough transform is used as the main detection method. As an effective and concise method for line detection, Hough transform has drawn massive attention of researchers. By only accepting binarized pictures, Hough transform brings a very important question to users: how to generate a binarized picture, which contains desired line-information while effectively reduces noisy information?

To the best of our knowledge, the most commonly used method to solve the above problem is segmentation based on edge and area information. The key to select suitable segmentation methods for lane detection is to balance between keeping lane marking pixels and weakening noisy pixels. Most researchers deploy edge information by convolving different masks (e.g., Canny, Sobel or Prewitt) with gray images ; while only a few of them use blob-extraction-based methods (e.g., MSER) to extract desired pixels.

3.1 Edge-based Segmentation

Edge-based segmentation is usually performed on the Region of Interest (ROI) in gray scale to enhance edges and to obtain pixels that belong to the desired lane markings.

Region of Interest is always mandatory for Edge-based Segmentation. Different methods have been used to extract the ROI from the target frame as in [3] and [18]. In fact, input images contain lane markings and some unwanted objects

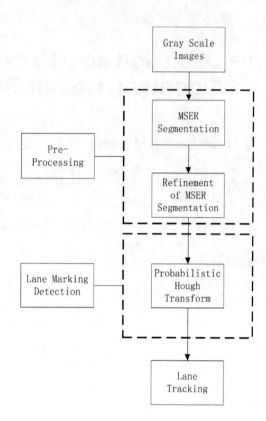

Figure 1: The general architecture of the proposed system

such as electrical poles, pedestrians, trees and cars. In order to reduce undesirable objects which might affect the LDT results, detection area should be focused only on road surface.

After getting ROI, some classical segmentation methods, for example Sobel, Prewitt, Robert or Canny filters can be used to detect edge information. It is well-known that Canny's operator outperforms other operators such as Sobel in the general edge detection problem. However, the authors in [19] have revealed that, for the purpose of lane detection, Canny filter is very sensitive to irrelevant objects as well as lane markings, which rapidly increases the number of false positives. Furthermore, the Canny operator is computationally expensive compared to other edge detection algorithms. Conversely, the Sobel operator is less sensitive to noise and less complex than Canny, and it is able to detect the main markings.

3.2 MSER-based Segmentation

One effective area-based segmentation method is Maximally Stable Extremal Region (MSER), which was proposed in [20]. This algorithm has rarely been used in lane detection. In [21], Hao Sun proposed a method of describing MSER patches using SIFT-based descriptors, followed by a graphical model to localize lane markings.

Different from [21], which involves unsupervised learning algorithm and off-line training, our system directly takes advantage of MSER blobs to extract the features of lane markings. Besides, the proposed method uses MSER results as the ROI of detection stage, which also differentiates from [21] and allows the improvement of MSER and Hough transform results, and the increasing of the detection rate of lane markings. The following stages are used to correctly detect lane markings: 1) Segmentation of gray images based on MSER; 2) Results refinement; and 3) Lane-markings detection using PPHT.

3.2.1 Background on MSER

For a gray image I which can be described as a mapping: $(X, Y) \in Z^2 \to L$, where Z^2 represents a set of pixel points (with the coordinate of (x, y)), and L represents a set of luminance of pixel points ranges between $[0; 255]$. The term **region** we used here represents a contiguous subset S of the space Z^2 (specifically for 4-neighbourhoods) which satisfied: $\forall\ p, q \in S;\ p, q \neq \emptyset;\ \exists$ series $\{p, a_1, a_2, a_3, ..., a_{i-1}, a_i, q\}$, where $a_1, a_2, a_3, ..., a_{i-1}, a_i \in S$, $s.t. |p - a_1| = 1$, $|a_i - q| = 1$, $\sum_{j=2}^{i} |a_j - a_{j-1}| = i - 1$. A region S is called an **extremal region** when an arbitrary element in the region satisfies the mapping rule $S \to m \leq l$; where $m, l \in L$, m represents the mapped value in L of an arbitrary element in S, and l is a pre-defined threshold which ranges in $[0; 255]$. A **stable extremal region** is an extremal region S that does not change a lot while varies. Let:

$$R(S_l) = \{S_l, S_{l+1}, S_{l+2}, ..., S_{l+\Delta-1}, S_{l+\Delta}\} \quad (1)$$

which is a branch of tree rooted in S_l satisfied $S_l \subset S_{l+1} \subset S_{l+2} \subset ... \subset S_{l+\Delta-1} \subset S_{l+\Delta}$. In order to measure the stability of different extremal region, we use the following equation (as proposed in [20]):

$$q(l) = \frac{card(S_{l+\Delta} - S_l)}{card(S_l)} \quad (2)$$

where $card(S_l)$ represents the cardinality of a set S (one extremal region). An extremal region S_l can be chosen as a stable extremal region only in case that $q(l)$ of S_l is in the lower level among the entire extremal regions. For certain $\Delta \in L$, **Maximally Stable Extremal Region** can be obtained by choosing the stable extremal region with the smallest $q(l)$ of all stable extremal regions.

3.2.2 Application of MSER

As stated above, researchers have tried many methods to extract the edge information of ROI, which is a very important step of the pre-processing stage. Additionally, they tend to use smooth methods (Gaussian Filter, Median Filters, etc.) before edge detection to remove noise, blur the difference inside the region and keep regions with stable luminance. But it also causes missing in details, especially in the edge of region where luminance changes rapidly. To balance between keeping desired details and noise removal, we use MSER for pre-processing stage.

Compared to edge-based segmentation, the biggest advantage of MSER is that it recognizes only the stable extremal region (e.g., lane markings, traffic signs or dark parts of cars), which successfully ignores unpredicted noisy region (e.g., potholes and obstacles on the road). Unfortunately, a fact which should be noticed is that MSER is more computationally expensive than edge-based detectors. Moreover, sometimes, MSER-blobs contain noisy details as well as desired pixels (as shown in Figure 3 and 2). This makes it necessary to refine the results of MSER. In order to improve the time-efficiency of the entire system, we propose a new scanning method to reduce the pixel points in binarized MSER blobs, so that we can reduce the input pixels

of Hough transform. This will be discussed in the following section.

3.3 MSER Refinement

Experimentally, we find that MSER-blobs contain considerable noisy details as well as desired pixels (as shown in Figure 2). This makes it necessary to refine the results of MSER segmentation stage. Based on the fact that objects (cars, pedestrians, etc.) located between left and right lane markings are much less than objects outside lane (as shown in Figure 2), it is reasonable to say that lane marking blobs are located near the middle column (as the red dash line in Figure 2) compared to other blobs located outside lane boundaries. As a usual fact, areas between lane markings are mainly road surface, which has very weak luminance comparing with other objects in gray scale images. Since MSER only extracts stable extremal region, noisy points within left and right lane markings can be eliminated from MSER-blobs. This is different from edge detection that extracts features of both stable extremal regions and noisy regions.

Algorithm 1: Scanning Refinement of MSER

---

1 **Input:** Binarized images with MSER blobs
2 **Output:** Refined contours of MSER blobs
3 x and y: coordinates of a pixel point (x, y) in the binarized image
4 *width* and *height*: the width and height of binarized image
5 $P(x, y)$: pixel value of the point (x, y)

6 **if** *Scanning for left area* **then**
7   **for** $y = 0$ *to height* **do**
8   **for** $x = \frac{width}{2}$ *to* 0 **do**
9   **if** $P(x, y)! = 0$ **then**
10          $x - -$;
11   continue;
12   **else**
13          $y + +$;
14   break;

15 **else**
16   **for** $y = 0$ *to height* **do**
17   **for** $x = \frac{width}{2} + 1$ *to width* **do**
18   **if** $P(x, y)! = 0$ **then**
19          $x + +$;
20   continue;
21   **else**
22          $y + +$;
23   break;

Hence we propose a scanning method for the binarized picture as described in Algorithm 1. Starting from the middle pixel of each row, scanning is performed in left and right directions, respectively. MSER blobs are drawn white, while the non-MSER area is kept black. The scanning of each image row stops when we find the first white pixel in left and right area respectively.

The output of the proposed scanning method is MSER blobs shrunken into pieces of lines, which are actually partial con-

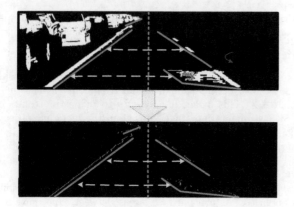

Figure 2: The scanning method. Red dash line in (Top) and (Bottom) in the middle indicates the "middle column" of the ROI, while dash arrows in (Top) indicate the scanning direction of left and right areas divided by middle column. For every row of each area, the scanning process stops when the first white pixel is reached by the arrow. Red solid lines depicts the entire contour after refinement.

tours of MSER blobs (as shown as Figure 2). More importantly, because the scanning process starts from the middle column, these contours only belong to blobs that are near to middle column in left and right areas. To the most extent, this method actually depicts the contours of lane-marking-blobs which are near to middle column. Moreover, the proposed scanning rule makes the selected contours to be one-pixel width, which weakens noisy blobs and makes long lines easier to be recognized by Hough transform.

However, the proposed scanning method has two drawbacks.

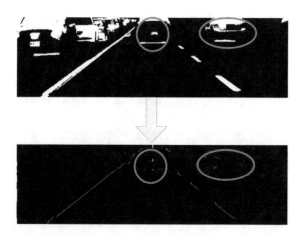

Figure 3: Drawbacks of the proposed scanning rule: blobs between lane markings and outside the current lane

First, even though noisy points within areas between left and right lane markings can hardly form MSER-blobs, real scenarios occasionally have MSER-blobs located between left and right lane markings (coming from cars or some erosion area on the road, as shown as red circular area in Figure 3). Our proposed scanning method might inevitably take

the contour of those noisy blobs as lane marking candidates, and then feed those pixels together with real lane marking pixels to Hough transform.

To eliminate noisy blobs, as shown in Figure 2, we proceed as follows. We know that the scanning method only selects at most two pixels in a row (one pixel per area), which makes the selected line candidates have only one-pixel width. This dramatically weakens the contour of noisy blobs between lane markings, and makes the continuous contours of lane marking blobs more prominent. On the other hand, Hough transform can further remove contours of MSER-blobs by thresholding length and angle of detected line segments (see Section 4).

The second drawback of the proposed scanning method is that, for dashed lines, blobs outside lane boundaries (as described as red ellipse area in Figure 3) have white pixels in rows between dashes. This might bring noisy contours for those rows. Similar to the first drawback, experimentally we find that Hough transform can handle the above issues by thresholding the length and angles of line candidates, which is discussed in the next section. By an appropriate thresholding, lines located in irrelevant regions can hardly be selected as lane markings.

4. PPHT

After segmentation, there may be some spatial deviations between the real marking and the noisy points generated by the proposed scanning method. Hence, we use the Progressive Probabilistic Hough Transform (PPHT) to group edge features into an appropriate set of segments. PPHT is a lightweight version of Hough transform which returns the end-points of the detected segment $Pt_0(x_0, y_0)$ and $Pt_1(x_1, y_1)$, instead of the parameters λ and θ generated by the Hough transform from the Equation: $\lambda = x cos(\theta) + y sin(\theta)$, where λ is the length between the origin and the pedal of detected line, and θ the angle of its perpendicular line. With the sampled end-points $Pt_0(x_0, y_0)$ and $Pt_1(x_1, y_1)$, PPHT thresholds the length of segments in order to remove weak segment candidates. For segments with the same angle, PPHT links them when the gap (between them) is smaller than a given threshold.

In this paper, we preferred to use PPHT instead of Hough transform for the following reasons. First, it is known that Hough transform is too sensitive to straight lines and, thus, generates undesired marking candidates. Moreover, Hough transform is computationally expensive. Experimentally, we find that PPHT outperforms Hough transform on lane detection. To remove noisy pixels which cause the two drawbacks mentioned in Section 3.3, the results obtained from PPHT are used. It is easy to threshold the length of detected lines, which helps to remove short lines. Besides, we can remove lines with noisy angles by applying the following constraints:

$$T_1 \leq \left| \frac{y_1 - y_0}{x_1 - x_0} \right| \leq T_2 \qquad (3)$$

where T_1 and T_2 are the pre-defined threshold set by users to define the angle values, and (x_0, y_0) and (x_1, y_1) are the coordinates of end-points Pt_0 and Pt_1, respectively.

5. TRACKING OF LANE MARKINGS

It is well known that the addition of a lane tracking stage after lane detection increases the probability of detecting lane markings, especially in harsh conditions (e.g., rough and rural roads or rainy weather). The most common lane trackers used in the literature are Kalman and Particle filters. Actually, Kalman is used predicts the post state based on the previous state and current measurements by updating their covariance matrix. This process is then looped by feeding the corrected state to the next instance. In fact, Kalman Filter has been used to track (λ, θ) of Hough transform [29]. In this paper, Kalman filter is used to track both ends of each lane markings, because as we have used PPHT in detection. We construct two Kalman trackers for right and left lane markings. For the end-points Pt_0 and Pt_1 of a given segment, the state vector X_k is:

$$X_k = AX_{k-1} + BU_k \quad (4)$$

where A is the state updating matrix and B is the input control matrix. In this case, we define the state

$$X = [X_{Pt_0} Y_{Pt_0} X_{Pt_1} Y_{Pt_1} X'_{Pt_0} Y'_{Pt_0} X'_{Pt_1} Y'_{Pt_1}]^T \quad (5)$$

where X' and Y' are the first derivatives of X and Y, respectively. Experimentally, with the best tracking performance for our testing video, we define the state updating matrix as following:

$$A = \begin{pmatrix} 1 & 0 & 0 & 0 & 0.5 & 0 & 0 & 0 \\ 0 & 1 & 0 & 0 & 0 & 0.5 & 0 & 0 \\ 0 & 0 & 1 & 0 & 0 & 0 & 0.5 & 0 \\ 0 & 0 & 0 & 1 & 0 & 0 & 0 & 0.5 \\ 0 & 0 & 0 & 0 & 1 & 0 & 0 & 0 \\ 0 & 0 & 0 & 0 & 0 & 1 & 0 & 0 \\ 0 & 0 & 0 & 0 & 0 & 0 & 1 & 0 \\ 0 & 0 & 0 & 0 & 0 & 0 & 0 & 1 \end{pmatrix}$$

$$U_k = 0 \quad (6)$$

We take the detected coordinates of Pt_0 and Pt_1 as measurement Z_k for every frame, where Z is given by:

$$Z = [X_{Pt_0} Y_{Pt_0} X_{Pt_1} Y_{Pt_1}]^T \quad (7)$$

6. EXPERIMENT

To test the real-time performance of our proposed lane detection system, several videos were taken from Ottawa roads, using a $FL3 - U3 - 13S2C - CS$ camera mounted in the front of an experimental car and fixed at a height of 1.3 m above the ground. The specifications of the camera and the lens used in our experimentations are listed in Tables 1 and 2. The program was implemented in C++ under Windows using the OpenCV library, with the hardware environment of Intel core i3 CPU having 2.30GHz and 4G RAM. Particularly to be mentioned, before using MSER, for the purpose of time efficiency, we resized the original images (with original resolution of 640×480) into 640×240. This resizing does not influence the final experimental results.

The videos we used include real scenarios of highways and urban roads in Ottawa. These videos represent some common situations with different lightening conditions (sunny, cloudy and night), traffic (heavy, medium and light), and road surface (rough and smooth), which people might encounter in real life. Some of the videos were listed in detail, see examples in Table 3.

We perform several experiments to evaluate the efficiency and accuracy of our system. The evaluation of each method

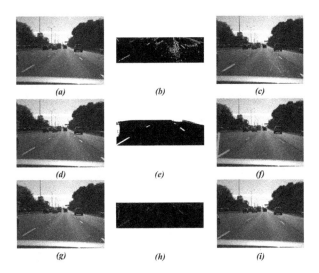

Figure 4: Detection performance of Edge-based, MSER-based and the proposed refined MSER-based segmentation methods. Images (a), (d) and (g) represent the same frame taken from Clip #1. Images (b), (e) and (h) are the segmentation results of edge-based, MSER-based and refined MSER-based methods, respectively. Images (c), (f) and (i) are the results of the application of PPHT after edge-based, MSER-based and refined MSER-based methods, respectively.

Table 1: Camera Parameters.

Camera attribute	Camera parameters
Company	Point Grey
Model No.	FL3-U3-13S2C-CS
Image Sensor	Sony IMX035 CMOS
Image Sensor Size	Diagonal 1/3", $4.8mm \times 3.6mm (H \times V)$
Unit Size	$3.63 \mu m$
Maximum Resolution	1328×1048 at 120fps
Interface	USB 3.0

is performed using some performance metrics, as explained in Section 6.1. Figure 5 shows some frames with correct detection of lane markings. These pictures show that our proposed detection method performs acceptably well in different conditions. It is also clear to see from Figure 4, that the refined MSER Segmentation (Figure 4(i)) keeps desired details (lane marking areas) and removes some noisy details (e.g., cars, trees and curbs), when comparing with edge segmentation (Figure 4(c)) and MSER segmentation without refinement (Figure 4(f)).

6.1 Lane Detection and Tracking Results

For the purpose of performance evaluation, two metrics are used: False Positive Rate (FPR) and False Negative Rate (FNR). False Positive (FP) and False Negative (FN) considers the presence or absence of lane markings. FPR refers to the probability of falsely selecting a given object or contours such as vehicles, curbs of road, trees or electric poles, as a lane marking. On the other hand, FNR refers to the situation when a lane marking is falsely rejected by the detection method.

Three methods are considered and implemented for comparative evaluation, method (a), method (b) and our method

Table 3: Video clips for experiment. (D: Dashed; W: White; S: Solid; Y: Yellow)

	Clip #1	Clip #2	Clip #3	Clip #4	Clip #5	Clip #6
Lightening	Cloudy	Sunny	Sunny	Cloudy	Night	Night
Location	Highway	Urban	Highway	Urban	Urban	Urban
Traffic condition	heavy	light	medium	light to heavy	heavy	medium
Road Surface	Rough	Flatly Smooth	Flatly Smooth	Smooth to Rough	Smooth	Rough
Frame NO.	912	864	1080	960	1200	1043
Frame speed	24fps	24fps	24fps	24fps	24fps	24fps
Lane markings/frame	2	1	2	2	2	2 or 1
Line type	DW	SY	DW-SW	DW-SY	DW	DW-SY
NO. frames with departure	48	28	68	72	63	57

(a)   *(b)*   *(c)*   *(d)*

(e)   *(f)*   *(g)*   *(h)*

Figure 5: Correct detection in different scenarios: (a) urban area: curvy lane marking occluded with cars; (b) urban area: single lane marking; (c) urban area: heavy traffic with strong lightening; (d) urban area: medium traffic; (e) urban area: medium traffic, sunny, rough and shadowy road; (f) urban area: rough road with heavy traffic, cloudy; (g) highway: slope and curvy lane; (h) highway: different road colour, heavy traffic.

Table 2: Lens Parameters.

Lens Attribute	Lens Parameters
Company	Edmund Optics
Model No.	#55-256
Focal Length (Mm)	5.0 – 50.0
Maximum Camera Sensor Format	1/3"
Aperture (F/#)	F1.3 – 16C
FOV, For 1/3" Sensor	51.8 – 5.6
Working Distance (Mm)	800 –

There are 600 lane markings to be detected for these 300 frames. Experimental results are presented in Table 4.

Table 4: Edge Segmentation for Lane Detection

	Process-time	No. Markings	TPR	FPR
Robert	26 ms	582	66%	31%
Canny	94.5 ms	788	87%	44%
Prewitt	48.3 ms	812	90%	45%
Sobel	32.3 ms	609	92%	9.5%

Table 4 proves that Canny is not suitable for lane detection, with a False Positive Rate (FPR) of 44% and consumes much more time than other methods (94.5*ms*). On the other hand, Sobel performs the best comprehensively of all four methods. This makes it reasonable to use Sobel as a representation of edge segmentation in comparison with MSER segmentation and our proposed method (as explained in Section 6.1.2)

called (*c*). The method (*a*) uses edge-segmentation method based on Sobel filter, followed by PPHT to detect lane markings. Whereas the method (*b*) uses MSER segmentation without refinement, followed by PPHT. The reason behind this choice is to show the accuracy and efficiency of our method (*c*) (which refines method (*b*)) against edge-based methods, and MSER-based segmentation without refinement.

6.1.1 Comparison between edge detectors

Experimentally, we compared the Sobel operator with other filters such as Canny, Prewitt and Robert, as shown in Table 4. Different edge segmentation methods are applied on 300 frames. After segmentation, we only use PPHT to detect lane markings, without tracking and other refinement stages.

6.1.2 Comparative performance evaluation

Conventionally, for experiments on lane detection, ground truth is either hand-annotated on each frame or determined by visual inspection, as performed in [5], [9] and [3]. Researchers usually qualitatively judge if the result fits well with ground truth for each frame or not. Different experi-

Figure 6: Examples of False Positive and False Negative results in different scenarios: (b) and (e) show the False Positive detection as well as correct detection; (a) and (f) show the False Negative detection for one lane marking while the other one correctly detected; (c), (d), (g) and (h) show the False Negative detection for both left and right lane markings as well as some False Positive detection.

Table 6: Comparative Performance Evaluation for lane detection in daytime

	Clip #1			Clip #2			Clip #3			Clip #4		
	DR	FPR	FNR	DR	FPR	FNR	DR	FPR	FNR	DR	FPR	FNR
(a)	72.7%	18.7%	27.3%	84.3%	0	15.7%	80.1%	7.7%	19.9%	77%	10.7%	23%
(b)	69.6%	14.2%	30.4%	89.2%	5.1%	10.8%	84.3%	5.5%	15.7%	95.8%	9.8%	4.2%
(c)	75.3%	7.4%	24.7%	97.9%	4.2%	2.1%	94.9%	0	5.1%	100%	3.6%	0

Table 5: Comparative Performance Evaluation for lane detection at night

	Clip #5			Clip #6		
	DR	FPR	FNR	DR	FPR	FNR
(a)	57.8%	1%	42.2%	64.1%	0	35.9%
(b)	74%	14.8%	26%	80.6%	9.7%	19.4%
(c)	77.6%	7.1%	22.4	83.3%	4.5%	16.7%

mental results are presented in Tables 5 and 6 for night and day time, respectively.

It is shown in Table 5 that, in spite of highest FNR and lowest DR, edge-based segmentation (method (a)) has much lower FPR than other two methods (only 1% and 0%). This is mainly because weak lightening at night makes the noisy edges less visible. Besides FPR, MSER segmentation performs significantly better than edge segmentation during night time, and method (c) refines the results of MSER segmentation.

From Table 6 we can see that MSER-based segmentation (b) performs mostly better than edge-based segmentation (a), especially for Clip #4, which represents very common situations in urban area. In Clip #4, method (b) increases the detection rate from 77% of method (a) to 95.8%, with dramatically reducing the FNR from 23% to 4.2%. However, method (b) presents some instability when it comes to other clips (having a FPR of 30.4% and FNR of 5.1%). In response to the instability of MSER segmentation, method (c) effectively refined the results of method (b). Method (c) increases the detection rate by almost 10% for Clip #2 and Clip #3, comparing with method (b). Moreover, method (c) decreases FPR and FNR for all four video clips.

It has to be noticed that, because of poor sunlight in night time and unpredictable lightening interference of cars, lane detection system may perform much worse than daytime, which is reflected in our experimental results in Table 5. We find out that the successfulness of lane detection during night time is mostly affected by the traffic density and sometimes by lightening system on the road.

7. CONCLUSION

In this paper, we presented a real-time lane detection and tracking system, which uses the MSER and PPHT methods as a segmentation and detection stages, respectively. The MSER was mainly used to obtain the lane marking blobs. However, a set of noisy blobs were usually generated by MSER. For that reason, we developed a scanning refinement algorithm to enhance the results of MSER and filter out noisy data. Lane detection was carried out using a lightweight version of Hough transform called PPHT. To track lane markings, a Kalman-based tracking method was developed based on the results of PPHT. Through an extensive set of experiments, we have shown the efficiency of MSER to improve the quality of detecting lane markings.

Acknowledgement

This work was partially supported by Canada Research Chair Programs, DIVA Strategic Research Network, Natural Sciences and Engineering Research Council of Canada (NSERC), and Fonds de Recherche du Quebec, Nature et Technologie (FRQNT).

References

[1] Xiangjing An, Erke Shang, Jinze Song, Jian Li, and Hangen He. Real-time lane departure warning system based on a single fpga. *EURASIP Journal on Image and Video Processing*, 2013(1):1–18, 2013.

[2] David Hanwell and Majid Mirmehdi. Detection of lane departure on high-speed roads. In *ICPRAM (2)*, pages 529–536, 2012.

[3] DO Cualain, C Hughes, M Glavin, and E Jones. Automotive standards-grade lane departure warning system. *IET Intelligent Transport Systems*, 6(1):44–57, 2012.

[4] Vincent Voisin, Manuel Avila, Bruno Emile, Stephane Begot, and Jean-Christophe Bardet. Road markings detection and tracking using hough transform and kalman filter. In *Advanced Concepts for Intelligent Vision Systems*, pages 76–83. Springer, 2005.

[5] Amol Borkar, Monson Hayes, and Mark T Smith. Robust lane detection and tracking with ransac and kalman filter. In *Image Processing (ICIP), 2009 16th IEEE International Conference on*, pages 3261–3264. IEEE, 2009.

[6] D. Schreiber, B. Alefs, and M. Clabian. Single camera lane detection and tracking. In *Intelligent Transportation Systems, 2005. Proceedings. 2005 IEEE*, pages 302–307, Sept 2005.

[7] Joel C McCall and Mohan M Trivedi. Video-based lane estimation and tracking for driver assistance: survey, system, and evaluation. *Intelligent Transportation Systems, IEEE Transactions on*, 7(1):20–37, 2006.

[8] Jung-Ming Wang, Yun-Chung Chung, Shyang-Lih Chang, and Sei-Wang Chen. Lane marks detection using steerable filters. In *Proc. of 16th IPPR Conf. on Computer Vision, Graphics and Image Processing*, pages 858–865, 2003.

[9] S. Sivaraman and M.M. Trivedi. Integrated lane and vehicle detection, localization, and tracking: A synergistic approach. *IEEE Transactions on Intelligent Transportation Systems*, 14(2):906–917, June 2013.

[10] Miguel Angel Sotelo, Francisco Javier Rodriguez, Luis Magdalena, Luis Miguel Bergasa, and Luciano Boquete. A color vision-based lane tracking system for autonomous driving on unmarked roads. *Autonomous Robots*, 16(1):95–116, 2004.

[11] Yue Wang, Eam Khwang Teoh, and Dinggang Shen. Lane detection and tracking using b-snake. *Image and Vision computing*, 22(4):269–280, 2004.

[12] Mohamed Aly. Real time detection of lane markers in urban streets. In *Intelligent Vehicles Symposium, 2008 IEEE*, pages 7–12. IEEE, 2008.

[13] Hong Wang and Qiang Chen. Real-time lane detection in various conditions and night cases. In *Intelligent Transportation Systems Conference, 2006. ITSC'06. IEEE*, pages 1226–1231. IEEE, 2006.

[14] Yifei Wang, Naim Dahnoun, and Alin Achim. A novel system for robust lane detection and tracking. *Signal Processing*, 92(2):319–334, 2012.

[15] Min Tian, Fuqiang Liu, and Zhencheng Hu. Single camera 3d lane detection and tracking based on ekf for urban intelligent vehicle. In *Vehicular Electronics and Safety, 2006. ICVES 2006. IEEE International Conference on*, pages 413–418, Dec 2006.

[16] Zu Kim. Realtime lane tracking of curved local road. In *Intelligent Transportation Systems Conference, 2006. ITSC'06. IEEE*, pages 1149–1155. IEEE, 2006.

[17] Nicholas Apostoloff and Alexander Zelinsky. Vision in and out of vehicles: Integrated driver and road scene monitoring. *The International Journal of Robotics Research*, 23(4-5):513–538, 2004.

[18] B. Fardi, U. Scheunert, H. Cramer, and G. Wanielik. A new approach for lane departure identification. In *Intelligent Vehicles Symposium, 2003. Proceedings. IEEE*, pages 100–105, June 2003.

[19] W. Phueakjeen, N. Jindapetch, L. Kuburat, and N. Suvanvorn. A study of the edge detection for road lane. In *Electrical Engineering/Electronics, Computer, Telecommunications and Information Technology (ECTI-CON), 2011 8th International Conference on*, pages 995–998, May 2011.

[20] Jiri Matas, Ondrej Chum, Martin Urban, and Tomás Pajdla. Robust wide-baseline stereo from maximally stable extremal regions. *Image and vision computing*, 22(10):761–767, 2004.

[21] Hao Sun, Cheng Wang, and N. El-Sheimy. Automatic traffic lane detection for mobile mapping systems. In *Multi-Platform/Multi-Sensor Remote Sensing and Mapping (M2RSM), 2011 International Workshop on*, pages 1–5, Jan 2011.

Incorporating User Motion Information for Indoor Smartphone Positioning in Sparse Wi-Fi Environments

Wasiq Waqar
Department of Computer
Science
Memorial University of
Newfoundland
St. John's, Canada
wasiq.waqar@mun.ca

Yuanzhu Chen
Department of Computer
Science
Memorial University of
Newfoundland
St. John's, Canada
yzchen@mun.ca

Andrew Vardy
Department of Computer
Science and Department of
Electrical & Computer
Engineering
Memorial University of
Newfoundland
St. John's, Canada
av@mun.ca

ABSTRACT

Indoor localization using mobile devices such as smartphones remains a challenging problem as GPS (Global Positioning System) does not work inside buildings and the accuracy of other localization techniques typically comes at the expense of additional infrastructure or cumbersome war-driving. For such environments, we propose a localization scheme which uses motion information from the smartphone's accelerometer, magnetometer, and gyroscope sensors to detect steps and estimate direction changes. At the same time, we use a Wi-Fi based fingerprinting technique for independent position estimation. These measurements along with an internal representation of the environment are combined using a Bayesian filter. This system will allow us to reduce the amount of training required and work in sparse Wi-Fi environments. We test our approach in two real-world environments to show the benefits of incorporating user motion for indoor localization.

1. INTRODUCTION

In the past, most of the attention was given to Location Based Services (LBS) in outdoor environments as GPS played the dominant role in localization. Recently, we are seeing a paradigm shift in the mobile applications market, where indoor LBS is being considered the new frontier. Due to the increasing number of mega size multi-level constructions like airports, shopping malls, universities and other facilities, people tend to spend more time indoors. Research shows people only spend 10-20% of their time outdoors [1] and more than 70% calls originate from indoors which indicates great potential fot indoor LBS.

The proliferation of smartphones is motivating researchers to look at other ways for more reliable and energy efficient indoor positioning of users which have a reasonable tradeoff

between accuracy, reliability, cost, and scalability. To minimize deployment and infrastructure costs, different techniques and technologies are being explored. Indoor positioning is challenging as GPS does not work inside buildings so most common solutions take advantage of existing RF (Radio Frequency) infrastructures like Wi-Fi and cellular. There are several ways in which RF signals can be used for positioning. It is not easy to model the radio propagation in indoor environments because of diffraction, scattering, shading, severe multipath, low probability for availability of line-of-sight (LOS) path, and specific site parameters such as floor layout, moving objects, and numerous reflecting surfaces. There is no single good model for an indoor radio multipath characteristic so far. Different techniques have different advantages and disadvantages. Hence, using more than one type of positioning algorithm at the same time could yield better performance. There are different triangulation, proximity or fingerprinting based algorithms available which deal with the indoor positioning problem in various ways.

On the other hand in robotics, inertial sensors, laser rangefinders, and computer vision are used to provide accurate localization without the requirement of fixed infrastructure. Mobile devices, such as smartphones and music players, have recently begun to incorporate a powerful yet diverse set of sensors. These sensors include GPS receivers, microphones, cameras, proximity sensors, magnetometers, temperature sensors, accelerometers, and gyroscopes. In the future, other sensors like altimeters, barometers, etc., may be incorporated into these devices. Inertial measurement units (IMUs) like accelerometers and gyroscopes are being embedded in most of the latest smartphones. Accelerometers measure 3D linear accelerations of the device whereas gyroscopes give angular velocities. Most modern smartphones also include a magnetometer for raw magnetic readings and heading information. Using these sensors one can estimate the user's motion and characterize their activity as, for example, walking, standing, jumping, running etc. User motion can then also be used to keep track of position via dead reckoning.

Problems arise when using RF based positioning schemes in environments where RF signals are sporadic or sparsely deployed. Due to the placement of APs (Access Points) and cell towers, there might be areas where RF signals are not available. Similarly there may be disruption in the RF signals due to limits on radio range, energy resources, and other sources of noise. In such environments it is better to incorporate additional information from IMUs for localization with opportunistic RF based position correction.

Our main contributions to address the above challenges can be summarized as follows:

- **We identify an opportunity to use sensor-based dead-reckoning and opportunistic Wi-Fi positioning for localization using smartphones in areas where there is sparse Wi-Fi coverage.** Our approach does not require the installation of additional infrastructure.

- **We developed and used an iOS app on the Apple iPhone 4 to evaluate our technique. This app was tested in the tunnels of Memorial University of Newfoundland which have very limited Wi-Fi coverage.**

The subsequent sections expand on each of these contributions, beginning with a short related research overview followed by our proposed idea, evaluation, and conclusion.

2. RELATED WORK

Smartphone accelerometers have been used in some mobile localization schemes in an assistive or collaborative manner. In Surroundsense [9], they are used as one of the parameters for the fingerprint, whereas CompAcc [2] uses them to count the number of steps taken to estimate the distance travelled by a pedestrian.

In [11] the authors gave a novel particle filtering based scheme for indoor positioning which does not rely on any infrastruction and uses only the sensors from the smartphones. But their system is not stand alone as their design requires a centralized system. In [6] the authors dont rely on any Wi-Fi but depend on a more accurate step counter and turn detections for position accuraccy. We feel that in buildings where multiple floors have the same layout, this scheme might fail and some kind of auto correction measure has to be taken. In other work [10][3][12][5], researchers have used accelerometer data to detect human activities such as walking, standing, climbing stairs, jogging, etc. A short overview of related work is covered in [14].

3. SYSTEM ARCHITECTURE

In probabilistic robotics, a *belief* is the internal knowledge of the robot or a system about the state of the world. In our case state means the location of the subject in our environment. States cannot be measured directly, but we can represent and estimate the probability that the system lies in each possible state. We use the term *belief* to refer to the conditional probability distribution over all possible states. This distribution assigns a probability to each possible hypothesis with regards to the true state. State x_t is generated stochastically from state x_{t-1} meaning that the belief at time t is calculated from its past belief at time $t-1$. The most general algorithm for calculating beliefs is given by the *Bayes filter* algorithm. Algorithm 1 depicts Bayes Filter which is a recursive Bayesian state estimation technique utilized in mobile robotics and other applications [13].

This algorithm is recursively applied at every iteration when belief $bel(x_t)$ needs to be calculated from $bel(x_{t-1})$.

Algorithm 1: *The general algorithm for Bayes filtering*

Input: $u_t, z_t, bel(x_{t-1})$

1: **for all** x_t **do**
2: $\quad \overline{bel}(x_t) = \int p(x_t|u_t, x_{t-1})bel(x_{t-1})dx_{t-1}$
3: $\quad bel(x_t) = \eta p(z_t|x_t)\overline{bel}(x_t)$
4: **end for**

Output: $bel(x_t)$

Bayes filter possesses two essential steps. In Line 2, it processes the control u_t. It does so by calculating a belief over the state x_t based on the prior belief over state x_t and the control u_t. u_t in our case is the motion captured from the motion model. This step of the algorithm is also called *prediction* [13].

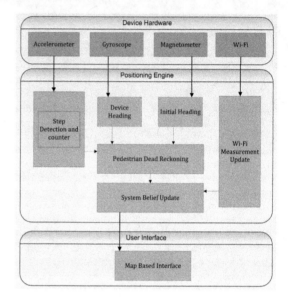

Figure 1: Block diagram of the proposed system

The second step of Bayes filter is called the measurement update. In line 3, the Bayes filter algorithm multiplies the belief $\overline{bel}(x_t)$ by the probability that measurement z_t may have been observed. It does so for each hypothetical posterior state x_t. To compute the posterior belief recursively, the algorithm requires an initial belief $bel(x_0)$ at time $t = 0$. If we are ignorant about the initial condition we can initialize using the uniform distribution.

3.1 Design Overview

Figure 1 shows the block diagram of our proposed system. In our localization scheme we divided our map into a grid. The center of these grid cells are referred to as anchor points which have known physical coordinates (x, y). The grid space between two anchor positions determines the resolution or granularity of the positioning system. The system state variable x_t indicates the anchor point that is closest to the current position. The initial belief of the system is assumed to be uniform as the system will not know where the user is positioned. The on-board magnetometer is noisier compared to gyroscope when giving heading estimation [15]. Therefore, we only use the magnetometer to initialize the orientation of the user and calibrate the gyroscope. This is one of the assumptions of our system that we ask the user to face one of the corridors (potential path where the user can walk). After this initialization/calibration process we keep track of the heading using the gyroscope. We use the step counter [15] to estimate the distance travelled and the gyroscope to estimate the direction in which this distance is travelled. As shown in the figure 1, accelerometers are used to detect the steps taken.

3.2 Motion Model

Using a step counter and gyroscope one can estimate the user's recent trajectory and then predict $\overline{bel}(x_t)$. Step detection is the automatic determination of the moments in time at which footsteps occur. If one wants to use accelerometer data to detect just the instant motion of the device, one needs to be able to isolate sudden changes in the movement from the constant effect of gravity.

Peak detection is a method which calculates the steps from the 3-axis accelerometer readings. A threshold value can be used to detect a peak. If changes in acceleration are too small, the step counter will discard them. The step counter can work well using this algorithm, but sometimes it can be overly sensitive. The algorithm that we chose for our step counter is inspired by an analog pedometer [17]. The algorithm used for our step counter using mobile phone accelerometer is available in [15]. There are several other algorithms available for step counters but most of them are primarily for accelerometers attached to the foot, hip or other body part.

The iPhone 4 has a 3-axis gyroscope which can measure angular velocities about the axes. The Core Motion Framework of the Apple iOS SDK also provide us access to built in functions which manage and keep track of the device's attitude after the application starts. Rotation around the z-axis is called yaw and at the start of the application it is calibrated with the initial stable magnetic heading. The comparison and performance of estimating direction with gyroscope compared with magnetomenter is discussed in [15].

3.2.1 Belief Update Strategies

To study our motion model, we divided our map into grid spaces. The centers of these grid spaces are the anchor points which have known physical coordinates (x, y). A set of anchor points is maintained and the probability distribution over this set is represented by $bel(x_t)$. Figures 11 and 12 show the test environments and the positions of all anchor points.

In the time interval $[t-1, t]$ the user advances from position x_{t-1} to position x_t. The step counter and gyroscope report back the relative change in position (x_{rel}, y_{rel}). As we know the initial heading and current heading of the user, we can determine the user's direction of travel. So from the last position and the new position we can determine x_{rel} and y_{rel} which are distances travelled in the x-direction and the $y-$direction with respect to our map.

$$x_{rel} = \alpha \cos(\theta + \beta) \quad (1)$$

$$y_{rel} = \alpha \sin(\theta + \beta) \quad (2)$$

where θ is the initial orientation of the device during initialization, β is the yaw of the device and α is the step length.

The corresponding relative motion parameters (x^*, y^*) for the given poses x_{t-1} and x_t are calculated in lines 1 and 2.

These basically come from the known positions in the map. The function $norm(a, b)$ implements an error distribution over a with zero mean and standard deviation of b which was empirically chosen as 4m. The motion model is used as step 2 in our Bayes filter implementation.

3.3 Wi-Fi Fingerprinting

In classic fingerprinting algorithms, vectors of Received Signal Strength (RSS) measured in online phase and offline phase are directly compared to each other. The nearest neighbour method simply calculates the euclidean distance in signal space between the live RSS reading and the fingerprint. A major drawback of using this technique is that different devices, becasue of their hardware and software (sometimes devices of the same make and model), report different RSS values which may differ from the RSS stored in the database. This will degrade the performance of the positioning system. In contrast, rank based localization [8] uses only ranks of the RSS values because the rank information is less sensitive to any bias and scale.

Figure 2 shows the block diagram of the rank based fingerprinting algorithm. In this algorithm, first the RSS values measured in the online phase from different APs are first sorted from strongest to weakest. Ranks $(1, 2, 3, ...)$ are assigned to APs based on the position in the sorted vector. Rank 1 is given to the strongest AP, meaning with the highest RSS value. Rank vectors are created from the fingerprints stored in the database. Ranks are assigned based on the MAC address and rank of AP in the online phase. Then this vector is also sorted strongest to weakest keeping the rank assigned to them. In ideal cases, the sorted ranked vector from online phase and sorted ranked vector fron offline phase will be identical hence showing perfect similarity.

In case an AP which was in the online phase was not found in the database, the rank vector created from the database is padded with 0, to achieve the same length as the rank vector from the online. Other techniques, including via Gaussian kernel [4] which calculates the likelihood of an anchor point using the RSS value similarity between two vectors, also face the dimension mismatch problem. In real indoor environments the dimension of the fingerprints of different anchor points vary considerably. If simple likelihood calculation mechanism (e.g., Euclidean distance or cosine similarity) is used, mismatching could lead to large positioning errors.

Spearman's footrule distance measures total elementwise displacement between two vectors. It is similar to the Manhattan distance for quantitative variables. According to [7] Spearman's footrule perform the best amongst other similarity measures. Assuming u_k is the rank of the k-th element in vector U, v_k is the rank of the k-th element in vector V and n is the number of elements in vectors U and V, Spearman's footrule distance can be computed as follows:

$$D_s = \sum_{k=1}^{n} |u_k - v_k|.$$

The similarity measure above return the scores for every anchor point. The anchor point with the lowest score is considered the best match. Ideally using k smallest reference points to calculate the estimated position yields a better result. In [7] the author solves a p-center problem to estimate the final position estimate. In the rank based technique the

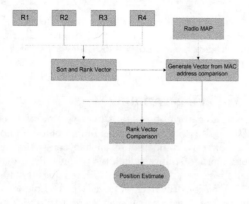

Figure 2: **Block Diagram of the Wi-Fi Rank based fingerprinting**

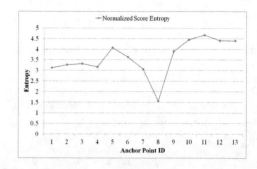

Figure 4: **After normalizing the scores, entropy is calculated.**

distribution of scores will differ because of several reasons. The number of APs visible in the querying scan and position where the scan was done affects the distribution of the scores. For instance if the scan is done at a corner where 20 APs are visible compared to another location where only 5 APs are visible, the distribution of scores will differ a lot. The random test on 13 anchor points in the Engineering Building was done. It was noted that the accuracy of the position estimate was independent from the score distribution. Figure 3 shows the maximum and minimum score distribution and Figure 4 shows the normalized entropy of the score distribution. As the user initiates the application, the belief is uniformly distributed. Entropy is a measure of the uncertainty associated with a random variable and is also referred to as the expected value of the information contained in a message, which in our case is the belief. At position 5 to 9 the accuracy was under 8m whereas 1-4 and 10-13 the error was greater then 8m. The best match at position 6 and 8 were estimated the correct position but both the entropy and min-max distribution does not infer a trend. The distribution of scores tells us that our certainty of our position estimate is not dependent on the score distribution. Hence we used a different approach to use Wi-Fi for position correction. We assign weights $w1, w2$, and $w3$ to the best 3 matched anchor points only if they are all within 2 hop neighbors to each other. Otherwise we ignore the Wi-Fi scan. It means that when the Wi-Fi localization module estimates the best 3 matches, the weights are assigned only if each anchor point is at least 2-anchor point distance to any of the other two. For our experiments we assign 0.4, 0.3 and 0.2 weight to the three best matched positions.

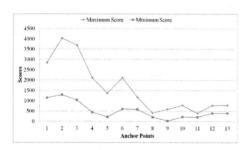

Figure 3: **The minimum and maximum scores at different anchor points.**

4. PERFORMANCE EVALUATION

We will explain our experiment methodology, settings, scenarios, and results in this section. Our main experimental goal is to measure the benefit of using motion information from the user to track and position in an indoor environment.

4.1 Methodology

The system evaluation contains multiple phases. The first phase is to test the performance of our step counter which is a foundation of our motion model. After checking the accuracy we can determine if it is good enough to be used in our motion model. The accuracy and precision of our motion model is then tested in two different indoor environments.

The second phase is the evaluation of our measurement model. By analyzing the performance metrics, we can determine if it can be used for opportunistic measurement update. Furthermore, it is important to test our system in an environment with sporadic Wi-Fi signal. Next, we explore the benefit of using motion for localization and tracking and analyze the advantages of using rank based Wi-Fi in sparsely distributed Wi-Fi environment. We measure the benefit in the following aspects:

- *System Performance:*

  Hypothesis 1: *The system accuracy and precision is comparable to other Wi-Fi only localization system while using less training*

- *Cost:*

  Hypothesis 2: *The system training and maintenance cost can be reduced.*

- *Scalibility*

  Hypothesis 3:: *The system can work in different indoor environment.*

4.2 Experimental settings

Experiments and evaluations of our motion model, measurement model and hybrid localization scheme were carried out at two contrasting environments at Memorial University. The first area was part of the 2nd floor of Engineering Building. The space was divided into a grid using a $3 \times 3m$ cell size. 33 positions were selected within the hallways for the anchor points. Each anchor point is surveyed for Wi-Fi data and a fingerprint is created for each survey point. The anchor points are possible locations that the user can be in the environment. The distance between two anchor points is nearly 6 steps. The belief is chosen to be updated after every 6 steps in this environment. Figure 5 shows the map of the Engineering Building field test environment.

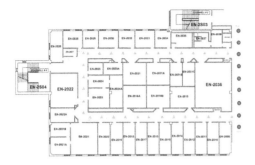

Figure 5: Map of the Engineering Building. Green triangles are the anchor points where data has been collected and the system has fingerprints for those locations. Red circles are untrained areas.

The second environment is the Unversity Tunnel system which connects different buildings of the university. There is no Wi-Fi coverage provided for the tunnels. Figure 6 shows the map of the tunnel system. The only Wi-Fi signals available are at entrance positions to the tunnel. Hence the areas of Wi-Fi AP visibility is very limited and also sporadic in nature. This place is a good testbed for our system. Both the environments are different. The Engineering Building has more sharp turns, whereas the the tunnel has smaller turns. The distance between two anchor points here is 5.5m. Therefore the belief update happens after 9 steps.

The major assumptions for our experiments are as follows

- The user is always located in the areas for which the anchor points are defined in the system.

- The device is always pointing in the direction of the user motion.

- The user walks close to the corridor's center.

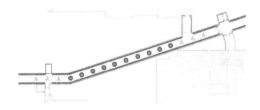

Figure 6: Map of part of the university tunnel. Green triangles are the points where Wi-Fi is sporadically available and red discs are positions where no Wi-Fi is available. Fingerprints for locations with green triangles are available.

4.3 Motion Model Evaluation

In an experiment the user was asked to walk in the corridor with our localization app in the trained areas of Engineering Building. Figure 7 shows the heat map of the probability distribution over time. The x-axis describe the ith update of belief. The position IDs are listed on y-axis where the

color intensity shows the probability of being at each location. The belief at x36, x64 and x88 are examples where the position correction happens due to turning. Overall it can be seen that the position is tracked pretty well along the path of the user. From belief update x112 to x128 the user changed his direction of walking after a few steps a couple of times creating a to-and-from user trail. It can be observed in the heat map that the uncertainty starts to increase as the probability distribution spreads out. So a malicious behavior by the user in terms of walking in circles and moving to and fro in the corridor over short distance might confuse the belief system.

Figure 8 shows the entropy of the same heat map. At x5 the entropy falls greatly due to a turn. Initially as the probability was uniform so the entropy was maximum but as soon the user turned the belief became more certain due to the recognition of a corner. Every time the user turns the corner, the uncertainty decreases and we can see a drop in entropy. After x112 the entropy increases a little bit showing the confusion caused by user motion.

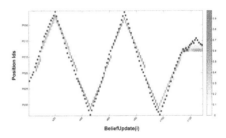

Figure 7: Motion model heat map at Engineering Building with dense Wi-Fi coverage. Black annotations describing actual user position.

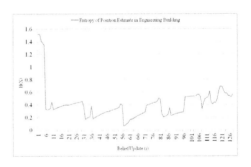

Figure 8: Entropy in the Engineering Building

4.4 Rank Based Wi-Fi Measurement Model Evaluation

Our Wi-Fi localization scheme returns similarity scores between the current measurement and every anchor point which has been surveyed for stored Wi-Fi data. The lowest score is considered the best match. To test the rank based fingerprinting technique we assumed that the best match anchor point is the estimated position. We tested this in our Engineering Building where we tested it at each anchor point. The error was recorded by logging the distance between the ground truth and the estimated output position. Figure 9 shows the cumulative error distribution. The mean error was about 4.1m. We compared our system with the Wi-Fi based localization scheme by Yan et al [7] which uses a completely different approach for localization.

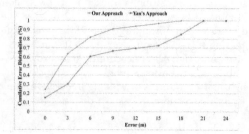

Figure 9: Cumulative error distribution of the Rank Based fingerprinting in Engineering Building

4.5 Performance in Sparse Wi-Fi Environment

To test our system in an environment which has sporadic Wi-Fi signals we chose the university tunnel system which has no Wi-Fi available but sporadic signals are available at the different entrances of the tunnels from different buildings. Figure 6 shows the map of one such section of the tunnel. This figure shows 16 anchor points from one entrance to another. All anchor points are equally distant from each other. It is assumed that initially the system does not know the user's true position. Initializing with a Wi-Fi scan can initialize user position if the user is in one of the entrance areas.

Figure 10 shows the heat map of the user's walk in the tunnel. On x-axis we have the belief updates and on y-axis we have the 16 anchor points. We annotated the map with approximate actual position of the user to compare the belief distribution with the movement of the user. From x0 to x12 we can see that the belief is randomly distributed but it converges towards one direction. From x12 to x45 the probability distribution is not that scattered and position estimates are more confident. From x45 to x60 the probability distribution becomes less reliable as the user changes his direction more frequently similar to the test done in Engineering Building. At x60 the Wi-Fi measurement update is triggered. At this point it detects P001 as the most likely position. The probability distribution shifts heavily towards that position as we give higher weight to the anchor points with higher Wi-Fi similarity. In the tunnels the Wi-Fi is sporadically available in only P001-P004 and then P015-P016 as described before. No Wi-Fi is detected in any anchor points between them. Hence when the Wi-Fi update step is triggered, due to the diversity of visible AP's between these two regions, the position correction has smaller error.

Figure 11 shows the entropy of the belief in the tunnel. If we compare the entropy graphs of Engineering and tunnel it can be observed that the entropy in the tunnel does not drop as much as compared to the entropy in the Engineering. This is because the tunnel lacks sharp turns as compared to the Engineering Building. Although the accuracy from the most probable position estimate is comparable in both locations the certainty is less because of the absence of sharp turns. At x51 to x59 it can be observed that due to the frequent turning around in the same corridor the entropy increases. It sharply decreases again at x60 when Wi-Fi measurement update is triggered.

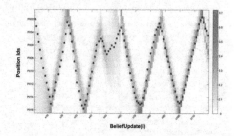

Figure 10: Heat map of motion model in the tunnel with sparse Wi-Fi

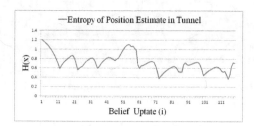

Figure 11: Entropy in the Tunnel

5. CONCLUSION

This paper explores the idea to incorporate user motion for indoor localization for sparse Wi-Fi environments, where other Wi-Fi only systems would not perform accurately. We discuss our results in relation to the three hypotheses mentioned earlier.

- *System Performance*

  Hypothesis 1: *The system accuracy and precision is comparable to other Wi-Fi only localization system.* As it can see from the heat maps of both environments that the system tracks the user. For our experiments the accuracy at Engineering Building was under 4m whereas in the tunnels it was around 6m on average. It is marginally worse than the 0.7m to 4m average positioning error yielded by the best-performing but intensively trained Horus system (using 100 Wi-Fi scans and much smaller grid space (1.52 m and 2.13 m)) [16]. But generally for our system a single accuracy figure can not be given as it depends upon the shape and size of the environment. Sharp turns help reduce positioning error estimates and long corridors accumulate errors. The second factor is the amount of Wi-Fi landmarks available for position correction.

- *Cost*

  Hypothesis 2: *The system training and maintenance cost can be reduced.* We tested our system in two different environment. One which had very dense Wi-Fi and had training data available for all the anchor points. On the other hand in the tunnel environment the Wi-Fi was sporadically available at only 6 locations. There was no survey done for those anchor points. As different areas in such environment have distinct Wi-Fi visibility, so it can be exploited to our advantage to correct the position only and rely more on human motion for positioning. Due to less reliance on Wi-Fi, minor changes in Wi-Fi infrastructure would not affect the system.

- *Scalability*

  Hypothesis 3: *The system can work in different indoor environment.* We tested our system in two completely contrasting environments. One had sharper turns with denser Wi-Fi coverage and the other having few turns but sparse Wi-Fi coverage. The grid size in both the environment was also different. This system is more scalable than other indoor positioning systems as it would require less training and would even work in sporadic Wi-Fi environment where Wi-Fi only systems would fail.

6. FUTURE WORK

We believe that this system can be further improved in a lot of ways. For example in the step counter we are detecting the number of steps taken but using the height of the user as a parameter to determine the stride length. Perhaps more adaptive approach can be used here which uses information from accelerometer to also calculate the stride length. Artificial intelligence techniques can be employed in the initialization phase for the system to learn the human walking pattern and determine the style of the user to more accurately determine the number if steps.

Similarly for Wi-Fi based localization, preprocessing the APs after observing the environment for fluctuations can be done which might improve the localization error.

Another interesting aspect in which the system can be improved is to integrate human-centric collaborative feedback. Positioning accuracy and precision can be improved by collecting both positive and negative feedback from users in terms of orientation.

Developing a magnetic map is also one idea which can be explored. In that case we have to observe how stable is the magnetic environment over time. In indoor environments there may be areas due to electronic equipment or wiring, where the magnetic field perturbations are distinctive. They can be used as landmarks similar to how we use Wi-Fi.

We believe that some organizations or companies will devise specifications for indoor positioning system in the near future. With the potential rapid growth of location-aware services for public indoor environments such as airports, subway systems, museums, university campuses, shopping centers, etc there will always be areas where Wi-Fi infrastructure will not be available and hence some alternative technology would be needed which is reliable and scalable at the same time. At this time we believe human motion based localization schemes have great potential and look to be very promising in reducing the cost both in the sense of maintenance and energy consumption. We also believe that more and more researchers will be attracted to exploit the various sensors now available in smartphones for indoor localization.

7. REFERENCES

[1] Indoor LBS And Hyper - Local Content Is the Next Gold Rush for Mobile Commerce. http://www.indoorlbs.com/2010/06/indoor-lbs-and-hyper-local-content-is.html, October 2010.

[2] Ionut Constandache, Xuan Bao, Martin Azizyan, and Romit Roy Choudhury. Towards Mobile Phone Localization without War-driving. In *Proceedings of the 29th Conference on Information Communications (Infocom)*, pages 2321–2329, 2010.

[3] Adil Mehmood Khan, Young-Koo Lee, Sungyoung Lee, and Tae-Seoung Kim. Human Activity Recognition via an Accelerometer-Enabled-Smartphone Using Kernel Discriminant Analysis. In *Proceedings of the 5th International Conference on Future Information Technology*, 5 2010.

[4] Azadeh Kushki, Konstantinos N. Plataniotis, and Anastasios N. Venetsanopoulos. Kernel-based positioning in wireless local area networks. *IEEE Transactions on Mobile Computing*, 6(6):689 –705, 6 2007.

[5] Jennifer R. Kwapisz and Gary M. Weissand Samuel A. Moor. Activity Recognition using Cell Phone Accelerometers. In *Proceedings of the Fourth International Workshop on Knowledge Discovery from Sensor Data*, 2010.

[6] Fan Li, Chunshui Zhao, Guanzhong Ding, Jian Gong, Chenxing Liu, and Feng Zhao. A reliable and accurate indoor localization method using phone inertial sensors. In *Proceedings of the 2012 ACM Conference on Ubiquitous Computing*, UbiComp '12, pages 421–430, New York, NY, USA, 2012. ACM.

[7] Yan Luo, Y.P. Chen, and O. Hoeber. Wi-fi-based indoor positioning using human-centric collaborative feedback. In *Communications (ICC), 2011 IEEE International Conference on*, 6 2011.

[8] J. Machaj, P. Brida, and R. Piche. Rank based fingerprinting algorithm for indoor positioning. In *Indoor Positioning and Indoor Navigation (IPIN)*, sept. 2011.

[9] Azizyan Martin, Constandache Ionut, and Roy Choudhury Romit. SurroundSense: Mobile Phone Localization via Ambience Fingerprinting. In *Proceedings of the 15th Annual International Conference on Mobile Computing and Networking (MobiCom)*, pages 261–272, 2009.

[10] Andrew Offstad, Emmett Nicholas, Rick Szcodronski, and Romit Roy Choudhury. AAMPL: Accelerometer Augmented Mobile Phone Localization. In *Proceedings of the 1st ACM international workshop on mobile entity localization and tracking in GPS-less environments*, pages 13–18, New York, NY, USA, 2008. ACM.

[11] Anshul Rai, Krishna Kant Chintalapudi, Venkata N. Padmanabhan, and Rijurekha Sen. Zee: Zero-Effort Crowdsourcing for Indoor Localization. In *Proceedings of the 18th annual international conference on Mobile computing and networking*, Mobicom '12, pages 293–304, New York, NY, USA, 2012. ACM.

[12] Nishkam Ravi, Nikhil Dandekar, Prreetham Mysore, and Michael L. Littman. Activity recognition from accelerometer data. 2005.

[13] Sebastian Thrun. Probabilistic Robotics. *Communications of the ACM*, 45(3):52–57, March 2002.

[14] Wasiq Waqar, Yuanzhu Chen, and Andrew Vardy. Exploiting smartphone sensors for indoor positioning: A survey. In *Proceedings of the Newfoundland Conference on Electrical and Computer Engineering*, 2011.

[15] Wasiq Waqar, Andrew Vardy, and Yuanzhu Chen. Motion Modelling using Smartphones for Indoor Mobilephone Positioning. In *Proceedings of the Newfoundland Conference on Electrical and Computer Engineering*, 2011.

[16] Moustafa Youssef and Ashok Agrawala. The Horus WLAN location determination system. In *Proceedings of the 3rd International Conference on Mobile Systems, Applications, and Services*, pages 205–218, 2005.

[17] Neil Zhao. Full-Featured Pedometer Design Realized with 3-Axis Digital Accelerometer. http://www.analog.com/library/analogdialogue/archives/44-06/pedometer.html, 10 2011.

Extending Wireless Algorithm Design to Arbitrary Environments via Metricity[*]

Helga Gudmundsdottir
School of Computer Science,
CRESS
Reykjavik University, Iceland
helgag10@ru.is

Eyjólfur I. Ásgeirsson
School of Science and
Engineering, ICE-TCS
Reykjavik University, Iceland
eyjo@ru.is

Marijke H. L. Bodlaender
School of Computer Science,
ICE-TCS
Reykjavik University, Iceland
marijke12@ru.is

Joseph T. Foley
School of Science and
Engineering
Reykjavik University, Iceland
foley@ru.is

Magnús M. Halldórsson
School of Computer Science,
ICE-TCS
Reykjavik University, Iceland
mmh@ru.is

Ymir Vigfusson
School of Computer Science,
ICE-TCS, CRESS
Reykjavik University, Iceland
ymir@ru.is

ABSTRACT

Efficient spectrum use in wireless sensor networks through spatial reuse requires effective models of packet reception at the physical layer in the presence of interference. Despite recent progress in analytic and simulations research into worst-case behavior from interference effects, these efforts generally assume geometric path loss and isotropic transmission, assumptions which have not been borne out in experiments.

Our paper aims to provide a methodology for grounding theoretical results into wireless interference in experimental reality. We develop a new framework for wireless algorithms in which distance-based path loss is replaced by an arbitrary gain matrix, typically obtained by measurements of received signal strength (RSS). We experimentally evaluate the framework in two indoors testbeds with 20 and 60 motes, and confirm superior predictive performance in packet reception rate for a gain matrix model over a geometric distance-based model.

At the heart of our approach is a new parameter ζ called *metricity* which indicates how close the gain matrix is to a distance metric, effectively measuring the complexity of the environment. A powerful theoretical feature of this parameter is that *all* known SINR scheduling algorithms that work in general metric spaces carry over to arbitrary gain matrices and achieve equivalent performance guarantees in terms of ζ as previously obtained in terms of the path loss constant. Our experiments confirm the sensitivity of ζ to the nature of the environment. Finally, we show analytically and empirically how multiple channels can be leveraged to improve metricity and thereby performance. We believe our contributions will facilitate experimental validation for recent advances in algorithms for physical wireless interference models.

[*]Supported by grant-of-excellence no. 120032011 from the Icelandic Research Fund.

Categories and Subject Descriptors

C.2.1 [**Network Architecture and Design**]: Wireless Communication

Keywords

Wireless Ad-hoc Networks; Wireless Interference Models; SINR model; Wireless Algorithm Design; Experiments

1. INTRODUCTION

There is mounting demand for tomorrow's wireless networks to provide higher performance while lowering costs. A central challenge in meeting this demand is to improve the utilization of the wireless spectrum to enable simultaneous communications at the same radio frequency. To accommodate research into efficient use of wireless channels, for instance through spatial reuse, we require practical models of signal propagation behavior and reception at the physical layer in the presence of wireless interference.

Early models of worst-case wireless communication under interference were graph-based, most commonly based on distances. In comparison, physical models, or *SINR* (signal to interference and noise ratio) models, capture two important features of reality: signal strength decays as it travels (rather than being a binary property) and interference accumulates (rather than being a pairwise relation).

Analytic work on SINR – introduced by Gupta and Kumar [14] in an average-case setting and Moscibroda and Wattenhofer [26] in worst-case – has generally assumed *geometric path loss*, referred to here as the GEO-SINR model: signals decay as a fixed polynomial of the distance traveled.

While free space exhibits geometric decay, the reality for *real-world* wireless environments is more complex. When located above an empty plane, a signal bounces off the ground, resulting in complicated patterns of superpositions known as *multi-path fading*. Most real scenarios are more complex, with walls and obstructions. In particular, cityscape and indoor environments are notoriously hard to model. Moreover, the simple range-based models often make further assumptions into geometric path loss that do not concord with experiments, such as smooth and isotropic polynomial decrease in the signal strength. In fact, quoting recent meta-analysis [3], "link quality is not correlated with distance."

Various stochastic extensions of geometric path loss have been proposed to address the observed variability in signal propagation. The most common are *log-normal shadowing* and *Rayleigh fading* for addressing long- and short-distance variability, respectively. Both modify the signal strength multiplicatively by an exponentially distributed random variable. These models are highly useful both for generating input for signal propagation simulations and for average-case analysis of wireless interference algorithms.

A complementary view to stochastic studies, with deep roots in computer science theory, is to allow for worst-case behavior and obtain guarantees that hold for *all* instances to the problem at hand. To avoid such results becoming too pessimistic, proper characterizations or parameterizations are often essential. Our goal is to contribute to such "any-case" analysis that avoids making assumptions about the environment that may not be reflected in actual real-world scenarios.

Our contributions. We propose moving theoretical algorithm design away from assuming geometric path loss models to an abstract SINR formulation with a matrix representing the fading (or signal decay) between pairs of nodes in an arbitrary environment. The matrix would typically be generated from direct measurements of *received signal strength* (RSS) provided by motes, as proposed by experimentalists [34, 32, 24]. The RSS matrix could also be generated by other means, such as by inference, history, stochastic models or by accurate environmental models.

Following this approach, worst-case algorithmic analysis is heavily contingent on the contents of the RSS matrix, with unconstrained settings causing computational intractability. We introduce a new measure that reflects the attenuation complexity of the environment described by the RSS matrix. Dubbed *metricity* and denoted ζ, this parameter intuitively represents how close the RSS matrix is to a distance metric. From a theoretical standpoint, the definition of metricity has extensive implications: **All** SINR algorithms that work in arbitrary metric spaces work seamlessly in the abstract model, with performance ratio in terms of metricity that is equivalent to the original dependence on the path loss constant.

In an experimental evaluation on two testbeds of 20 and 60 nodes, our measurements indicate that the metricity parameter corresponds to the complexity of the environment. The experiments also suggest that the SINR model – without the geometric assumption – is of high fidelity, capturing signal propagation and reception well, even in environments with obstacles and lack of line-of-sight.

We further address the effect of multi-path fading by giving transmitters the choice of several channels/frequencies. Empirically, we find that in an environment with extensive multi-path propagation (but otherwise simple), the choice improves the metricity parameter significantly. Analytically, we show that a known algorithm for capacity maximization can be extended to handle multiple channels without loss in performance.

Roadmap. In the following section, we formally define our concepts, describe and calibrate our experimental setup in and validate the basic premises of our framework. We analyze the metricity parameter ζ in Section 3 and present experimental results. By leveraging the metricity concept in our framework, we introduce an approach for tackling multi-path fading using multiple frequencies in Section 4 and present experimental and theoretical results. We survey related work in Section 5 and conclude in Section 6.

2. MODEL VALIDATION

Our first order of action is to verify that the SINR model, without the geometric assumption, is faithful to reality. We assess the predictability of packet reception rate (PRR) under interference, and the assumption of the additivity of interference, by comparing our abstract model to the original GEO-SINR through experiments. The experiments are conducted in two testbeds (Fig 1): one in the middle of a large open classroom (TB-20) and another in a challenging basement corridor (TB-60).

2.1 The Physical Model

The SINR model is based on two key principles: **(i)** a signal decays as it travels from a sender to a receiver, and **(ii)** interference – signals from other sources than the intended transmitter – accumulates. A transmission is successfully received if and only if the strength of the received signal relative to interference is above a given threshold.

Formally, a *link* $\ell_v = (s_v, r_v)$ is given by a pair of nodes, sender s_v and a receiver r_v. The channel *gain* G_{uv} denotes the reciprocal of the signal decay of ℓ_u as received at r_v. If a set S of links transmits simultaneously, then the SINR at ℓ_v is

$$\text{SINR}_v := \frac{P_v G_{vv}}{N + \sum_{u \in S} P_v G_{uv}} , \qquad (1)$$

where P_v is the power used by the sender s_v of ℓ_v, and N is the ambient noise. In the *thresholded* SINR model, the transmission of ℓ_v is *successful* iff $\text{SINR}_v \geq \beta$, where β is a hardware-dependent constant.

The common assumption of *geometric path loss* in SINR models states that the gain is inversely proportional to a fixed polynomial of the distance traveled, *i.e.*, $G_{uv} = d(s_u, r_v)^{-\alpha}$, where the range of the *path loss constant* α is normally between 1 and 6. The geometric path loss assumption is valid in free space; we have $\alpha = 2$ in perfect vacuum.

The MB-SINR model refers to the SINR formula (1) applied to a general *gain matrix* G obtained through pairwise RSS measurements.

2.2 Experimental Setup

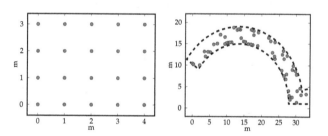

Figure 1: *Topologies of our 20-node testbed* (TB-20) *(left) and 60-node curved corridor testbed* (TB-60) *(right).*

Wireless hardware. Since a motivating goal of our study is to understand raw interference between wireless transceivers, we elected to operate at the physical-layer of a wireless device. We needed a mote with granular control over MAC-level capabilities, such as power and frequency control, over one tailored to specific protocol stacks, such as the 802.11 suite. For example, we require the ability to disable low-level features such as clear channel assessment (CCA).

We chose the Pololu Wixel, a development board for the TI CC2511F32 [35], as our mote hardware platform. The CC2511F32 is an 8051 micro controller SystemOnChip with integrated 2.4 GHz FM-transceiver stage (CC2500). In addition to meeting our functional requirements, the Wixels are inexpensive (14–20 USD), enabling larger scale deployments.

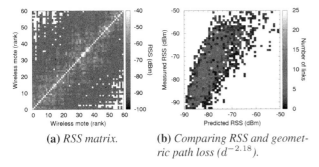

(a) *RSS matrix.*　　　**(b)** *Comparing RSS and geometric path loss* $(d^{-2.18})$*.*

Figure 2: *(a) RSS matrix. Gain between directed pairs of nodes in* TB-60, *measured by RSS and averaged over 1000 packets. (b) Comparing measured and predicted RSS. Correlation between RSS as predicted by distance with geometric path loss (α = 2.18) and measured in* TB-60 *testbed.*

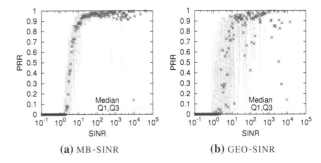

(a) MB-SINR　　　　　**(b)** GEO-SINR

Figure 3: *Packet reception rate for (a)* MB-SINR *(b)* GEO-SINR. *Fraction of packets correctly decoded by receivers in* TB-60 *as the SINR is varied by evaluating different pairs, possibly invoking multiple senders. The plots show a transition from 0 to about 100% PRR as the SINR grows.*

Configuration. In our experiments, every sender node in each trial transmits a burst of 1000 packets with 4 ms delay between consecutive packets to facilitate successful delivery to the receiver. The length of each packet is 22 bytes, including a 16-bit CRC. Only packets that pass a CRC check are considered successful transmissions, with all error correction capabilities on the mote disabled. The radio is configured to use data whitening and Minimum Shift Keying (MSK) modulation format. During experiments, the wireless motes report details about packets sent or received to an auxiliary log via USB which also provides control signals and power for the experiments. Packet details include the received signal strength (RSS) as an integer in dBm.

TB-20 testbed. In the first testbed, we arranged 20 wireless motes on an 4×5 grid with 1 m spacing in an empty classroom. The motes in the grid were mounted on wooden poles 1 m from the ground in order to minimize reflection and attenuation from the ground; see Fig. 1 for the topology. The testbed was deployed temporarily for a focused set of tests.

TB-60 testbed. In the second testbed, we suspended 60 wireless motes about 0.3 m from metal wire trays and 2.5 m from the concrete floor in a curved basement corridor; see Fig. 1 for the topology. The corridor provides a challenging environment: limited line of sight between motes, obstacles such as water pipes and thick electric cables, and reinforced concrete walls. Approximately 94% of the directed links are in range for communication. The length of the corridor is 40.1 m, the longest distance (direct line) between any two motes is 21.8 m while the shortest distance is 0.4 m. The TB-60 testbed is a more permanent setup, with the experiments conducted over the span of several weeks.

2.3 Model calibration

We ran several experiments on the testbeds to gather calibration data for the MB-SINR and GEO-SINR models. The figures with error bars show the median, and upper and lower quartiles of the distribution of experimental trials.

Ambient noise parameter N. We evaluated N by sampling the noise level registered by each mote, over several hours in both early morning and during nighttime. All of our experiments use the 2.44 GHz frequency unless otherwise stated. We found the average ambient noise in TB-60 to be around -99.1 dBm, but considerably higher in TB-20 at around -94.4 dBm, in part due to external interference from 802.11 infrastructure.

Power setting P. We configured the wireless mote's transmission power to 1 mW in all of our experiments.

RSS matrix. We measured the RSS for all directed node pairs (s_v, r_v) in both testbeds. In each time slot, a chosen node transmits 1000 packets in a sequence, while other nodes act as receivers. The procedure was repeated for each pair of directed nodes. For temporal robustness, including day and night variations, the experiments were repeated at different times of the day.

Fig. 2a illustrates the RSS_{vv} for all node pairs (s_v, r_v) in testbed TB-60. The motes on both axes are ordered by the angle of their polar coordinates due to the arced positioning of the corridor, thus making neighboring motes in the testbed likely to be adjacent in Fig. 2a. The figure further demonstrates that every mote can hear some other mote in the testbed, that some mote pairs cannot communicate, and that transmissions are not fully symmetric.

Path loss constant α. Assuming geometric signal decay, the best linear least-squares fit for the path loss constant α given link lengths and the RSS values from Fig. 2a was $\alpha = 2.18 \pm 0.07$. By using geometric path loss $d(s_v, r_v)^{-2.18}$ to predict RSS values, we plot the correlation between the predicted RSS and measured RSS values in Fig. 2b. If the prediction were perfect, the points would fall on the $y = x$ diagonal line. Instead, the results in Fig. 2b confirm that geometric path loss is not a reliable predictor for RSS.

2.4　Comparison of GEO-SINR and MB-SINR

We next evaluate the predictive power of the two models in experiments with varying interference.

Controlling wireless interference in practice. One of the challenges with hardware experiments is the synchronization of the wireless motes. Our focus on measuring interference requires us to ensure that interfering motes are transmitting at the same time as the sender. Although we investigate sets of links that are transmitting at the same time, our analysis is focused on the performance of individual links. We therefore circumvent the problem of synchronizing the motes by running our experiments for each individual link in the link set. To analyze how a single link ℓ_v would perform in the presence of the other sender-receiver pairs in a set S, the links in $S \setminus \{\ell_v\}$ transmit continuously while we measure the transmission of ℓ_v. This continuous transmission ensures that the receiver in link ℓ_v experiences interference from other links.

Experimental design. With the synchronization issues in mind, we devised an experiment to compare the predictive power of the two models. We repeatedly select a random pair of nodes to act as sender and receiver, and a subset of 1–10 other nodes to cause interference. During the trial, the interfering nodes continuously transmit packets on the same frequency. We deploy low-level packet

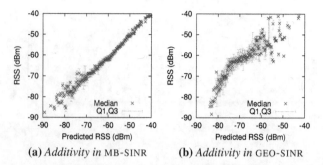

(a) *Additivity in* MB-SINR **(b)** *Additivity in* GEO-SINR

Figure 4: *Additivity in (a)* MB-SINR *and (b)* GEO-SINR. *Correlation between predicted and measured (RSS) in* TB-60.

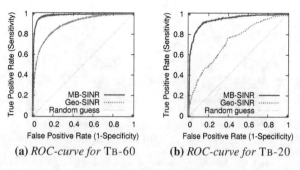

(a) *ROC-curve for* TB-60 **(b)** *ROC-curve for* TB-20

Figure 5: *ROC-curves for (a)* TB-60 *and (b)* TB-20. *Comparison of* MB-SINR *and* GEO-SINR *as estimators for successful transmission of packets as the acceptance threshold β is varied. Each trial consists of 1000 packets exchanged in* TB-60. *A positive trial outcome has PRR $\geq$ 80% whereas a negative one has PRR $\leq$ 20%.*

filtering at the receiver to minimize processing overhead due to interfering packets.

Packet reception rate by model. For every possible link in each testbed, we generated over 15,000 packet transmission trials over the link and measured the packet reception rate as a function of the SINR as calculated by the two models. Fig. 3a shows the PRR as a function of the SINR in MB-SINR, calculated using the RSS matrix shown in Fig. 2a. Corresponding results for GEO-SINR where the SINR is based on distances between nodes are shown in Fig. 3b.

The MB-SINR behaves as expected: generally the PRR and SINR values are either both small or both large. There is a swift transition from low to high PRR as the SINR value increases. We note that occasional trials produce a small PRR value despite SINR being large, as indicated by the two large error bars where SINR $\approx 10^3$. These outliers stem from occasionally no packets being received even for a large SINR, likely due to details of the testbed topology, such as destructive interference caused by signal reflection. Contrary to the GEO-SINR model, the MB-SINR model has a discernible threshold for successful transmissions.

Additivity of interference. Among the assumptions made by the SINR model is that interference is additive. In other words, if multiple senders transmit simultaneously, the RSS at the receiver can be estimated as the sum of the individual signals. Fig. 4a and 4b show the actual RSS as a function of the predicted RSS as given by MB-SINR (Fig. 4a) and GEO-SINR (Fig. 4b). We note that the variability evident in the measured RSS arises due to sparsity of data in those regions. If the additivity assumption is true, we would expect the values in the figures to fall on the diagonal line $y = x$.

The GEO-SINR appears more closely described by a pair of line segments with different slopes than a linear fit. Using linear regression, the coefficient of variation between the axes is low ($r^2 \simeq 0.031$), implying a low goodness-of-fit. Conversely, the MB-SINR model has a strong linear trend, with linear regression to the diagonal line incurring only 3.2% error and producing a large coefficient of variation ($r^2 \simeq 0.968$) between the predicted and measured RSS. The MB-SINR therefore more closely captures the additivity of interference than the canonical GEO-SINR model.

Sensitivity and specificity analysis. The GEO-SINR and MB-SINR models can be viewed as binary classifiers that compare the SINR to a threshold (β) to determine whether or not a transmission will be successful. We say that a transmission is experimentally successful if PRR $\geq T_{high}$ and declare it to be a failure if PRR $\leq T_{low}$. We focus on those links that were clearly either feasible or infeasible in our experiments, and set $T_{high} = 0.8$ and $T_{low} = 0.2$. Roughly 6% of the tested links fall within the $0.2 - 0.8$ range and are thus not considered. A single instance in an SINR binary classifier can have four outcomes:

- True positive (TP): SINR $\geq \beta$, PRR $\geq T_{high}$
- False positive (FP): SINR $< \beta$, PRR $\geq T_{high}$
- True negative (TN): SINR $< \beta$, PRR $< T_{low}$
- False negative (FN): SINR $\geq \beta$, PRR $< T_{low}$

A binary classifier incurs an inherent trade-off between true positive rate (sensitivity), defined as $\frac{TP}{TP+FN}$, and false positive rate (1-specificity), defined as $1 - \frac{TN}{FP+TN} = \frac{FP}{FP+TN}$. The trade-off balance can normally be tuned by a threshold parameter of the classifier, in this case β. By varying β, the trade-off can be graphically depicted on a ROC-curve (Receiver Operating Characteristic) that shows true and false positive rates on two axes. If $\beta = 0$, the classifier predicts that all transmissions will be successful, and if β is large, the classifier predicts that all transmissions will fail. A naïve classifier making uniformly random guesses would fall on the diagonal line from $(0, 0)$ to $(1, 1)$, whereas the $(0, 1)$ point denotes perfect classification.

Fig. 5a and 5b show the ROC-curves for the TB-60 and TB-20 testbeds, respectively. MB-SINR provides significantly better classification than GEO-SINR. In TB-60, the best trade-off between true and false positive rates occurs when $\beta = 2.15$, with a true positive rate of 94.8% and false positive rate of 5.2%.

In contrast, the predictions made by the canonical GEO-SINR on the same testbed plateaus at true positive rates of 81.4% and false positive rates of 18.6%. Both models give less accurate predictions for TB-20 compared to TB-60. The topology for TB-20 is more compact than TB-60. However, the larger and more variable ambient noise in TB-20 makes it more difficult to accurately predict the outcome of a transmission than in the TB-60 testbed.

As expected, MB-SINR provides significantly superior predictive power for PRR than GEO-SINR on both testbeds. Our results are robust against modifying the thresholds to $T_{high}, T_{low} = 0.5$. Note that RSS measurements used to compute SINR in MB-SINR were performed weeks in advance of these experiments. This suggest that the RSS matrix is resilient to temporal factors, with MB-SINR correctly predicting nearly 95% of all instances.

3. METRICITY

A plethora of important wireless interference algorithms rely on the GEO-SINR model, many of which have no obvious generalization to arbitrary metrics. Moreover, several problems in the domain, such as finding the maximum set of links that can simultaneously transmit (the LINK CAPACITY problem), have been proved to be computationally hard in an unconstrained SINR model [11].

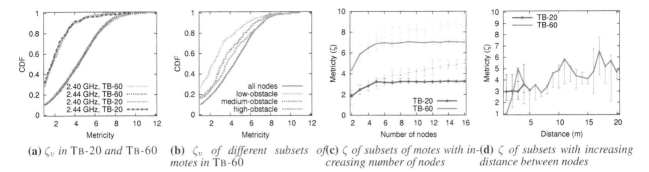

(a) ζ_v *in* TB-20 *and* TB-60   **(b)** ζ_v *of different subsets of* **(c)** ζ *of subsets of motes with in-* **(d)** ζ *of subsets with increasing*   *motes in* TB-60   *creasing number of nodes*   *distance between nodes*

Figure 6: *(a) Metricity (ζ_v). CDF comparison of computed ζ_v values for RSS matrices on both testbeds. The lines show ζ_v values for two different frequencies, which are representative of other frequencies in the respective testbeds. (b) Environmental factors. CDF comparison of computed ζ_v values on three different subsets of nodes. low-obstacle has the fewest environmental obstacles; high-obstacle has the most. (c) Impact of scale on ζ. Metricity compared to the number of nodes calculated as the average metricity of 200 randomly generated subsets of nodes of size at most 16, calculated for both testbeds. The thick lines represent the average of the 95th percentile ζ of subsets of the same size, whereas the thin lines represent the average maximum ζ of the subsets of the same size. The error bars represent the inter-quartile range. (d) Influence of pairwise distances on ζ. Metricity calculated on subsets of nodes with similar distances on both testbeds. The lines represent the 95th percentile of the ζ value of each set. The error bars represent the interval between the highest value of ζ and the median.*

To facilitate algorithmic analysis under the more realistic MB-SINR model, we introduce a *metricity* parameter ζ that reflects how well signal decay resembles a metric space.

In what follows, we assume arbitrary path loss with gain $G_{uv} = 1/f(s_u, r_v)$ for some function f of pairs of points. Note that the RSS between sender s_u to receiver r_v is $P_u G_{uv}$.

Definition. The *metricity* $\zeta(x, y)$ of a given node pair (x, y) in gain matrix G is defined to be the smallest number satisfying for any mote z with links also in G,

$$f(x,y)^{1/\zeta(x,y)} \leq f(x,z)^{1/\zeta(x,y)} + f(z,y)^{1/\zeta(x,y)} . \quad (2)$$

For notational simplicity we use $\zeta_v = \zeta(s_v, r_v)$.

Definition. We define ζ as the maximum value over all ζ_v in G unless specified otherwise. ζ is well defined, namely, consider $\zeta = \zeta_0 := \log_2(f_{max}/f_{min})$, where $f_{max} = \max_{x,y} f(x, y)$ and $f_{min} = \min_{x,y} f(x, y)$. Then, we can see that the LHS of (2) is at most $f_{max}^{1/\zeta_0} = 2f_{min}^{1/\zeta_0}$, while the RHS is at least that value. In the case of geometric path loss, $\zeta \leq \alpha$, since $f(x, y) = d(x, y)^\alpha$ and the distance function $d(x, y)$ satisfies the ordinary triangle inequality.

Theoretical implications. The ζ parameter has the advantage that theoretical results in the GEO-SINR can be imported *without significant changes* to the MB-SINR. Specifically, the following is true.

> All results that hold for general metrics in the GEO-SINR carry over to the MB-SINR with trivial modifications, giving practically identical performance ratios in terms of ζ as the original result had in terms of α.

Results that were proven for general metric spaces therefore do not depend on the particular value of the path loss constant α or that the value holds homogeneously. The results rely upon the triangle inequality, for which Eqn. 2 applies equally well in arbitrary gain matrices.

Taking the LINK CAPACITY problem as an example, approximation results carry over for numerous cases: fixed power [16]; arbitrary power control [20, 21]; distributed setting based on regret minimization [2] and under jamming [7]; and the weighted version with linear power [17].

In a sibling paper [5], we have examined in detail how exactly the current body of analytic results carries over to the MB-SINR. With only few exceptions, results that have been derived specifically for the Euclidean plane also hold in the MB-SINR model, making only an elementary assumption about the convergence of interference: that the collective interference of uniformly distributed nodes does not tend to infinity.

A consequence of these translations between models is that previous theoretical work in the GEO-SINR model is in fact highly robust to spatial signal variability.

3.1 Experimental evaluation

Method and evaluation. Using values obtained for the RSS matrices in both testbeds, shown for TB-60 in Fig. 2a, we evaluate the minimal value of ζ_v, (as defined in Eqn. 2) for every directed node pair within communication range. The cumulative distribution function (CDF) of the resulting ζ_v values is shown for two frequencies (2.40 GHz and 2.44 GHz) in Fig. 6a. In both testbeds the values for ζ_v range up to 12. However, note that the metricity values in TB-60 are generally a bit larger than in TB-20. The discrepancy is to be expected, since the challenging TB-60 environment both contains longer links with more variable signal strength as well as more variable signal attenuation due to obstacles.

In both testbeds, we find that a small fraction of the links have comparatively higher values of ζ_v, as seen by the long tapering at the top in Fig. 6a, which in turn drives the value for ζ to a relatively high number. To quantify, we find that the 95th and 99th percentile of the ζ_v value of links are significantly smaller than the global maximum ζ. In TB-60 some of the weakest links are only able to communicate at particular frequencies. These links correspond to pairs that have weak signals, and limited or no line-of-sight. In TB-20, while all pairs have line-of-sight and can communicate with one another, the large ζ value is an artifact of relatively high ζ_v values for only a handful of links. We investigate the effect further in Section 4.

Factors affecting ζ. One of the drivers behind the definition of ζ is to measure the "complexity" of the environment. To be more precise, we investigated the impact of obstacles in the environment, the number of nodes of a network and the distances between nodes in order to better pinpoint what features most influence the ζ value.

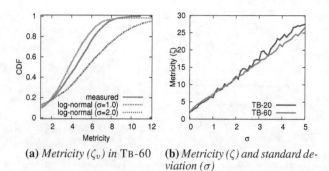

(a) *Metricity (ζ_v) in* TB-60   **(b)** *Metricity (ζ) and standard deviation (σ)*

Figure 7: *(a) Metricity (ζ_v) with log-normal shadowing in* **TB-60***. CDF of comparison on the metricity ζ_v using log-normal shadowing on distances in* TB-60 *averaged over 10 instances compared to actual measurements.* **(b) Metricity (ζ) with log-normal shadowing vs. standard deviation.** *Metricity ζ (as the 95th percentile on ζ_v) using log-normal shadowing on distances in both testbeds with growing standard deviation σ.*

To examine the impact of different environmental characteristics, we divide the nodes in TB-60 into three subsets of 20 nodes in Fig. 6b. The set of motes with the lowest values of ζ_v has the fewest number of obstacles (*low-obstacle*), whereas the set with the higher ζ_v values (*high-obstacle*) has a variety of barriers, such as electric cables suspended in the ceiling and greater distances between nodes. The *medium-obstacle* group has an average number of barriers while also having the most condensed topology. We calculated the values for ζ_v on the different links in the induced gain matrix for each set to obtain Fig. 6b. The figure suggests that the complexity of the environment, in the form of physical obstacles, might have a significant impact on the value of ζ.

We further examine the impact of the size of the set of motes on ζ. Using the RSS matrices for TB-60 and TB-20, we calculate ζ for randomly generated subsets of different sizes. Fig. 6c shows metricity as a function of set size. The thick lines represent ζ as the average 95th percentile of the values for ζ_v, which is relatively stable with increased sizes for sets of five or more nodes. The corresponding thin lines, which represent the average ζ as the highest value for ζ_v in each testbed, demonstrate that the global maximum ζ continues to grow with the set size. The increase is to be expected, as larger sets are more likely to include the links with the highest ζ_v values.

We also looked into the relationship between node distances and the ζ value of a set. We took different subsets of nodes that have roughly the same distances to one another, as shown in Fig. 6d. The figure suggests that the distances between nodes are poorly correlated with the value of ζ.

3.2 Log-normal shadowing and metricity

One of the most commonly used stochastic extensions of geometric path loss to address observed variability in signal propagation is log-normal shadowing. According to this model, signal decay follows the geometric model d^α, but with a multiplicative exponentially distributed factor:

$$f(s_u, r_v) = d(s_u, r_v)^\alpha \cdot e^X,$$

where X is a normally distributed random variable with zero mean.

We note that log-normal shadowing is an approach to introduce non-geometric properties into gain matrices. Since metricity is a

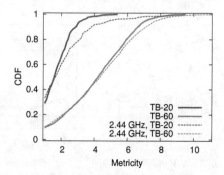

Figure 8: *Metricity (ζ_v) in* **TB-20** *and* **TB-60***. CDF comparison of computed ζ_v values for RSS matrices on both testbeds. The thick lines represent values computed for the $\widehat{RSS}$ matrices. The dashed lines show ζ values for the 2.44 GHz frequency, which is representative of other frequencies in the respective testbeds.*

measure of such discrepancy, it might be instructive to calculate metricity on instances generated with log-normal shadowing.

We used the topology of the TB-60 testbed and generated log-normal distributions with standard deviations $\sigma = 1.0$ and 2.0, and computed the CDF of the metricity of the resulting gain matrices. Averages over 10 instances are shown in Fig. 7a, interposed with the actual ζ_v measurements. We note a similarity between the measured values and the log-normal values with $\sigma = 1.0$, although the tail is measurably heavier in the latter.

We also examined how global metricity ζ grows with the standard deviation σ in the generated log-normal distributed instances in both testbeds. We show the results on Fig. 7b, where we display the 95th percentile of the distribution of ζ_v values. The plot exhibits a linear relationship, as shown in Fig. 7b, or roughly $\zeta = 2.5 + 4.9\sigma$. The agreement accords with the expected signal variations produced by a multiple of an exponentially distributed random variable.

4. FINESSING MULTI-PATH FADING WITH MULTIPLE CHANNELS

In our experiments, high metricity values were primarily caused by a handful of links. In particular, experiments in the simple environment of the TB-20 testbed exhibited a higher value of ζ than we suspected. One potential source of the complexity may be due to adverse signal reflection.

When signals travel along different paths, the superposition of the different signals produces patterns of signal cancellation and amplification known as multi-path fading ([10, Sec. 2]). This effect is particularly pronounced and systematic in simpler settings. The interference pattern will necessarily shift with frequency. Hence, the influence of multi-path fading on signal reception between a pair of points is likely to vary greatly with the chosen channel.

We propose to tackle the problem of signal cancellation and destructive interference by supplying algorithms with multiple channels (frequencies) from which to choose. First, we propose a variation of the metricity parameter ζ and evaluate the difference from the experimental data from our testbeds. As a case study, we then formulate a multi-channel version of the link LINK CAPACITY problem and obtain worst-case approximation results.

4.1 Experimental Evaluation

We performed additional experiments to obtain RSS matrices RSS^f for 8 different frequencies f ranging from 2.40 GHz to

2.48 GHz or wavelengths between 7 and 7.15 cm. These frequencies mean that multi-path alignment can shift from fully destructive to fully constructive interference when the difference in the path lengths is at least 1.4 m.

We calculated ζ_v values separately for each RSS^f. Although they can vary significantly on a per link basis, we found the differences in the overall distributions to be insignificant. Fig. 8 shows $f = 2.40$ GHz — other frequencies had similar distributions.

To factor out frequency-dependent fading, we computed for each node pair (s_v, r_v) the median $\widehat{RSS}_v$ of the eight RSS_v^f values ranging over the different frequencies. We observe that ζ_v values of the matrix $\widehat{RSS}$ are significantly lower, as the thick lines in Fig. 8 indicate.

The frequency dependency is more apparent in TB-20, which suggests that signal reflection plays a relatively large role in that environment. The increased reliance on a particular frequency can be explained by the regular grid structure and condensed setting of TB-20 (Fig. 1), which makes the testbed a good candidate to observe (frequency dependent) multi-path fading phenomena. However, the links in TB-60 are on average longer and thus reflection plays a smaller role in signal attenuation. Furthermore, the greater number of obstacles in TB-60 may also explain the decreased dependency on frequency.

The observation that the channels have different fading properties brought us to introduce a new version of the LINK CAPACITY problem to incorporate different frequencies.

4.2 Link capacity with multiple frequencies

The empirical indications – that having a choice of channels use results in smaller values of ζ_v, and thus better approximation factors – motivate us to generalize the LINK CAPACITY problem. Namely, in MULTI-CHANNEL LINK CAPACITY, we assign links to a set of frequencies, but each link is only *eligible* to use a subset of the frequencies. As before, we want to assign as many links as possible with the constraint that those assigned to a given frequency form a feasible set.

This formulation considers links that experience significant frequency-dependent fading as not usable in that frequency. It does not take into consideration the possible decrease in *interference* due to such fading. One reason is that such fading is too unpredictable to expect any algorithm to utilize that to obtain better solutions than otherwise, and thus it is also not fair to compare with such a strong adversary. The other reason is that with arbitrary fading patterns, we are back in the *abstract SINR* model, for which very strong inapproximability results hold [11].

The classic LINK CAPACITY problem is to find a maximum subset $S \subseteq L$ of a given set L of links that can successfully transmit simultaneously. We modify the LINK CAPACITY problem to fit our observations on the use of multiple frequencies:

MULTI-CHANNEL LINK CAPACITY
Given: A set L of n links, and k subsets $L_1, L_2, \ldots, L_k \subseteq L$.
Find: Sets $S_1, S_2, \ldots, S_k$ with $S_i \subseteq L_i$ and S_i feasible, for $i = 1, 2, \ldots, k$.
Maximize: $|S_1 \cup S_2 \cup \ldots \cup S_k|$.
Here L_i represents the links that are eligible for frequency i and S_i those scheduled for that frequency.

Additional definitions. To simplify notation we write $f_{uv} = f(s_u, r_v)$ and $f_v = f_{vv}$. We assume a total order $\prec$ on the links, where $\ell_v \prec \ell_w$ implies that $f_v \leq f_w$. We use the shorthand notation $\ell_v \prec L$ to denote that $\ell_v \prec \ell_u$ for all links ℓ_u in L. A power assignment P is *decay monotone* if $P_v \leq P_w$ whenever $\ell_v \prec \ell_w$, *reception monotone* if $\frac{P_w}{f_w} \leq \frac{P_v}{f_v}$ whenever $\ell_v \prec \ell_w$, and simply

monotone if both properties hold.[1] This captures the main power strategies, including uniform and linear power.

We modify the notion of *affectance* [11, 22]: The affectance $a_w^{\mathcal{P}}(v)$ of link ℓ_w on link ℓ_v under power assignment $\mathcal{P}$ is the interference of ℓ_w on ℓ_v normalized to the signal strength (power received) of ℓ_v, or

$$a_w(v) = \min\left(1, c_v \frac{P_w G_{wv}}{P_v G_{vv}}\right) = \min\left(1, \frac{P_w}{P_v} \frac{f_v}{f_{wv}}\right), \quad (3)$$

where $c_v = \frac{\beta}{1 - \beta N/(P_v G_{vv})} > \beta$ is a constant depending only on universal constants and the signal strength G_{vv} of ℓ_v, indicating the extent to which the ambient noise affects the transmission. We drop $\mathcal{P}$ when clear from context. Furthermore let $a_v(v) = 0$. For a set S of links and link ℓ_v, let $a_v(S) = \sum_{\ell_w \in S} a_v(w)$ and $a_S(v) = \sum_{\ell_w \in S} a_w(v)$. Assuming S contains more than two links we can rewrite Eqn. 1 as $a_S(v) \leq 1$ and this is the form we will use. Observe that affectance is additive and thus $a_S(v) = a_{S_1}(v) + a_{S_2}(v)$ for any partition (S_1, S_2) of S.

We define a weight function $W_+(v, w) = a_v(w) + a_w(v)$, when $\ell_v \prec \ell_w$ and $W_+(v, w) = 0$, otherwise. The plus sign is to remind us that weights are from smaller to larger decay links. Also, $W_+(X, v) = \sum_{\ell_w \in X} W_+(w, v)$, representing the sum of the in- and out-affectances (as in Eqn. 3) of a link v to and from those links in set X that have smaller decay.

A set S of links is *anti-feasible* if $a_v(S) \leq 2$ for every link $\ell_v \in S$ and *bi-feasible* if both feasible and anti-feasible [15]. More generally, for $K \geq 1$, S is *K-feasible* (*K-anti-feasible*) if $a_S(v) \leq 1/K$ ($a_v(S) \leq 2/K$), and *K-bi-feasible* if both.

Approximation of MULTI-CHANNEL LINK CAPACITY. We extend a greedy algorithm for LINK CAPACITY [16] and show that it gives equally good approximation algorithm for MULTI-CHANNEL LINK CAPACITY, even in MB-SINR. We assume that the links are assigned monotone power.

Algorithm 1 MULTI-CHANNEL LINK CAPACITY in MB-SINR

Let L be a set of links using monotone power $\mathcal{P}$ and $L_1, L_2, \ldots, L_k \subseteq L$ be subsets.
Set $X_1, X_2, \ldots X_k \leftarrow \emptyset$
for $\ell_v \in L$ in order of increasing f_v values **do**
    for $i \leftarrow 1 \ldots k$ **do**
        if $W_+(X_i, v) \leq 1/2$ **then**
            $X_i \leftarrow X_i \cup \{\ell_v\}$
            break
for each X_i **do**
    $S_i \leftarrow \{\ell_v \in X_i | a_{X_i}(v) \leq 1\}$
    return $(S_1, S_2, \ldots, S_k)$

Note that the sets returned by Algorithm 1 are feasible by construction.

We turn to proving a performance guarantee for the algorithm. The following key result bounds the affectance of a feasible set to a (shorter) link outside the set to a constant. A similar but weaker bound was first introduced by Kesselheim and Vöcking [22].

LEMMA 1. *Let L be a $3^\zeta/\beta$-bi-feasible set with monotone power assignment $\mathcal{P}$ and let ℓ_v be a link (not necessarily in L) with $\ell_v \prec L$. Then, $W_+(v, L) = O(1)$.*

We prove Lemma 1 by splitting it into two lemmas bounding in-affectance for links in a feasible set and similarly bounding out-affectance for links in an anti-feasible set.

---

[1] This corresponds to *length monotone* and *sublinear* power assignments in GEO-SINR [22].

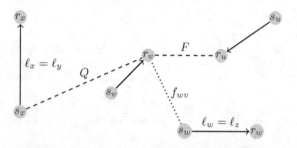

Figure 9: *We show that for each link ℓ_x it holds that $Q \geq \frac{F}{2^\varsigma}$.*

LEMMA 2. *Let L be a $3^\varsigma/\beta$-feasible set with monotone power assignment $\mathcal{P}$ and let ℓ_v be a link with $\ell_v \prec L$. Then, $a_L^{\mathcal{P}}(v) = O(1)$.*

PROOF. The basic idea is to identify a "proxy" for ℓ_v within the set L. Namely, we bound the affectance of L on ℓ_v in terms of the affectance on the "nearest" link ℓ_u in L, which is small since L is feasible and contains ℓ_u.

Formally, consider the link $\ell_u = (s_u, r_u) \in L$ such that $F := f(r_v, r_u)$ is minimum and link $\ell_w = (s_w, r_w) \in S$ such that $f_{wv} = f(s_w, r_v)$ is minimum (possibly $\ell_u = \ell_w$). Let ℓ_x be an arbitrary link in L and define $Q = f_{xv}$. See Fig. 9.

We first show that

$$F \leq 2^\varsigma Q . \tag{4}$$

Let ℓ_y, ℓ_z be renamings of the links ℓ_x, ℓ_w such that $f_y = \max(f_x, f_w)$ and $f_z = \min(f_x, f_w)$.

By definition of ℓ_u and ℓ_w, it holds that $\max(f_{yv}, f_{zv}) \leq Q$. Thus, using the weak triangular inequality,

$$f(s_y, s_z)^{1/\varsigma} \leq f_{yv}^{1/\varsigma} + f_{zv}^{1/\varsigma} \leq 2Q^{1/\varsigma} . \tag{5}$$

Using Eqn. 5 and that $f_z \leq f_y$, it holds that

$$f_{yz}^{1/\varsigma} \leq f_z^{1/\varsigma} + f(s_y, s_z)^{1/\varsigma} \leq f_y^{1/\varsigma} + 2Q^{1/\varsigma} . \tag{6}$$

By the feasibility condition on L, $a_y(z) \leq \beta/3^\varsigma$, while by definition of affectance and reception monotonicity (i.e., $P_y/f_y \leq P_z/f_z$),

$$a_y(z) = c_z \frac{P_y}{P_z} \frac{f_z}{f_{yz}} \geq \beta \frac{f_y}{f_{yz}} .$$

Combining the two bounds on $a_y(z)$, we get that $3^\varsigma \cdot f_y \leq f_{yz}$. That, combined with Eqn. 6 and canceling a f_y factor, gives that $3^\varsigma \leq \left(1 + 2(Q/f_y)^{1/\varsigma}\right)^\varsigma$, which implies that $f_y \leq Q$ and further that $f_w \leq f_y \leq Q$. Then, by the definitions of F, ℓ_w and Q,

$$F^{1/\varsigma} = f(r_v, r_w)^{1/\varsigma} \leq f_{wv}^{1/\varsigma} + f_w^{1/\varsigma} \leq 2 \cdot Q^{1/\varsigma} , \tag{7}$$

implying Eqn. 4, as desired.

Now, using the weak triangular inequality, the definition of F, and Eqn. 7, we get that

$$f_{xu}^{1/\varsigma} \leq f_{xv}^{1/\varsigma} + f(r_v, r_u)^{1/\varsigma} \leq Q^{1/\varsigma} + F^{1/\varsigma} \leq Q^{1/\varsigma} + 2Q^{1/\varsigma} .$$

Thus,

$$f_{xu} = 3^\varsigma Q = 3^\varsigma f_{xv} . \tag{8}$$

Observe that since $f_v \leq f_u$ and power is monotone, it holds that $c_v \leq c_u$. Then, using Eqn. 8 and the definition of affectance,

$$a_x(v) = c_v \frac{P_x}{f_{xv}} \frac{f_v}{P_v} \leq c_u \frac{3^\varsigma P_x}{f_{xu}} \frac{f_u}{P_u} = 3^\varsigma a_x(u) .$$

Finally, letting $L_w = L \setminus \{\ell_w\}$, we sum over all links in L,

$$a_L(v) = a_w(v) + a_{L_w}(v) \leq 1 + 3^\varsigma a_{L_w}(u) \leq 1 + 3^\varsigma \cdot \frac{\beta}{3^\varsigma} = O(1) ,$$

using the feasibility assumption for the last inequality. $\square$

For anti-feasible sets a similar result holds with a nearly identical proof, swapping the roles of senders and receivers of the links.

LEMMA 3. *Let L be a $3^\varsigma/\beta$-anti-feasible set with monotone power assignment $\mathcal{P}$ and let ℓ_v be a link with $\ell_v \prec L$. Then, $a_v^{\mathcal{P}}(L) = O(1)$.*

PROOF. Form the dual links L^*, which has a link $l_v^* = (s_v^*, r_v^*)$ for each link $l_v = (s_v, r_v) \in L$ such that $s_v^* = r_v$ and $r_v^* = s_v$. Clearly the lengths of l_v^* and l_v are the same so $f_{v^*v^*} = f_{vv}$. Also, $f_{v^*u^*} = f_{uv}$. Observe that the anti-feasibility assumption on L implies that L^* is $3^\varsigma/\beta$-feasible. Then, we can follow the proof of Lemma 2, applied to the set L^*, to get that

$$f_{ux} = f_{x^*u^*} \leq 3^\varsigma f_{x^*v^*} = 3^\varsigma f_{vx} .$$

This implies, using the monotonicity of power, that

$$a_v(x) = c_x \frac{P_v}{f_{vx}} \frac{f_x}{P_x} \leq c_x \frac{3^\varsigma P_u}{f_{ux}} \frac{f_x}{P_x} = 3^\varsigma a_u(x) .$$

The rest of the proof is identical. $\square$

Combining Lemma 2 and 3 implies Lemma 1.

Finally, to analyze the performance ratio of Algorithm 1, we will use an adaptation of the following signal-strengthening lemma from [8, Prop. 8] and a lemma generalizing a popular argument used to show that the size of a subset of links of another set of links is large.

LEMMA 4 ([8]). *Let L be a feasible set and $K \geq 1$ be a value. Then, there exists a K-bi-feasible subset of L of size $\Omega(|L|/K)$.*

The approximation that we can prove for MULTI-CHANNEL LINK CAPACITY has actually better dependence on ζ than what follows for LINK CAPACITY from [16]. A lower bound of $\Omega(2^{\varsigma - o(1)})$ on the approximability of LINK CAPACITY [16, 5] implies that the bound is close to best possible.

THEOREM 5. *Algorithm 1 yields a $O(3^\varsigma)$-approximation for MULTI-CHANNEL LINK CAPACITY.*

PROOF. Let L be a set of links and let $L_1, L_2, \ldots, L_k \subseteq L$ be subsets of L where L_i contains the links that are eligible in frequency i. Let $OPT = OPT_1 \cup OPT_2 \cup \ldots \cup OPT_k$ be an optimum solution to MULTI-CHANNEL LINK CAPACITY on L. Let $K = 3^\varsigma/\beta$. By Lemma 4, there is a K-bi-feasible subset OPT_i' in OPT_i of size $\Omega(|OPT_i|/K)$, for each $i \in \{1, \ldots, k\}$. Let $OPT' = OPT_1' \cup OPT_2' \cup \ldots \cup OPT_k'$.

Let $S = S_1 \cup S_2 \cup \ldots S_k$ and $X = X_1 \cup X_2 \cup \ldots X_k$ be the sets computed by Algorithm 1 on input L. We first bound $|S|$ in terms of $|X|$ and then $|X|$ in terms of $|OPT'|$. To bound $|S|$ to $|X|$ we bound $|S_i|$ to $|X_i|$ for every $i \in \{1 \ldots k\}$. Note that by the construction of X_i, $a_{X_i}(X_i) = W_+(X_i, X_i) \leq |X_i|/2$, and thus the average in-affectance of links in X_i is at most $1/2$. Since each S_i consists of the links in X_i of affectance at most $1/2$, by Markov's inequality, $|S_i| \geq |X_i|/2$.

By the definition of the algorithm, $W_+(X_i, \ell_w) > 1/2, \forall \ell_w \in OPT' \setminus X, X_i \in X$. Summing over all links ℓ_w in $OPT' \setminus X$, we get that $W_+(X_i, OPT' \setminus X) > |OPT' \setminus X|/2$. Furthermore,

282

since OPT' contains k K-feasible sets, it follows by Lemma 1 that $W_+(\ell_v, OPT') = O(k)$, for each $\ell_v \in X$. Summing over all links in X_i, we get that $W_+(X_i, OPT) = O(k|X_i|)$. Combining yields that for any set X_i we have $|OPT' \setminus X|/2 < W_+(X_i, OPT' \setminus X_i) \in O(k|X_i|)$, giving that $|X_i| = \Omega(|OPT' \setminus X|/k)$.

Summing over i then gives $|X| = \sum_i |X_i| = \Omega(|OPT' \setminus X|)$. Thus, the solution output by the algorithm satisfies $|S| \geq |X|/2 = \Omega(|OPT'|) = \Omega(|OPT|/K) = \Omega(|OPT|/3^\zeta)$. $\square$

In summary, the metricity definition implies that a large range of algorithmic results from GEO-SINR carries over without change. Thus, MB-SINR has both the desired generality and amenability to algorithmic analysis. We also extend known results on LINK CAPACITY to handle frequency-sensitive links, and improve the dependence of the approximation on ζ along the way.

5. RELATED WORK

Numerous experimental results have indicated that simplistic range-based models of wireless reception are insufficient [9, 37, 23, 1, 29, 38, 36]. Besides directionality and asymmetry, signal strength is not well predicted by distance. Interference patterns are also insufficiently explained by pairwise relationships, suggesting the need for additive interference models, both experimentally [23, 27, 24] and analytically [27, 26, 19].

The weakness of the known prescriptive models for interference and packet reception has led experimentalists to form models based on measurements. Son, Krishnamachari and Heidemann [34] showed that the SINR formula, using separately measured RSS values, is the main factor in predicting PRR. They found PRR to be dependent on the number of interferers, which was not supported in later studies [24, 6] and attributed to hardware variability or the quality of the CC1000 radios used. Reis et al. [32] independently proposed a similar approach on a 802.11 platform. They found substantial variability across nodes, and that similarity across time was sufficient over moderate time scales of minutes to hours, but that prediction accuracy degrades over longer periods.

Maheshwari, Jain and Das [24] compared different models of interference using two testbeds with variations in hardware, power level, and indoor/outdoor. They concluded that the physical model gives best accuracy, albeit less than perfect. In their followup workshop paper [25], they focus on the relationship of *joint interference* (SINR with multiple interferers) to PRR. They gave strong evidence that the basic formula works, and verify the *additivity* of the SINR model.

Chen and Terzis [6] proposed a method for calibrating RSSI readings to combine interference measurements from different motes. They found that Tmote Sky motes consistently report RSSI values inaccurately, even reporting non-injective relationships. By aligning measurements from different motes, they obtained much better SINR vs. PRR relationship, reducing the width of the intermediate range significantly. They suggested that this may explain much of the imperfect relationship observed in [24].

Measurement-based approaches have also been proposed in the context of 802.11 [13, 31, 33], where carrier sense and control packets complicate the picture. Recent efforts have focused on reducing the required measurements by deducing interference using, e.g., linear algebra [30] or regression [18]. Boano et al. [4] also studied the impact of external interference on sensor-network MAC protocols, and identified mechanisms to improve their robustness.

The engineering literature has introduced various extensions in order to capture reality more faithfully. In the *two-ray* model [10], which captures reflection off the ground, signal decays in the near-term as a certain polynomial, but as a higher degree polynomial

further away. More generally, the *multi-ray* model has the signal (in dBm, log scale) decaying via a piecewise linear model with segments of increasing slopes. The function is typically empirically determined. We note that these models can be captured by MB-SINR, with ζ as the steepest slope.

There are also *empirical models* [10], such as the *Okumura* and *Hata* models, that take the environment into account. These could also be used to generate a gain matrix. Also, accurate estimates can be obtained via general *ray tracing* when highly detailed information is available.

Some studies have allowed signal strength to fluctuate from the geometric path loss by up to a constant factor [28, 11]. This is of limited help in general, however, since even minor fluctuations of the value of α can cause arbitrarily large changes in signal strength [12].

Various probabilistic models also exist. On one hand, they are means to prescribe non-geometric components to signal reception, which is useful for simulation studies (which MB-SINR cannot provide), but which could be captured more accurately by actual measurements. On the other hand, these can also model aspects that are necessarily random, in which case they could complement the deterministic MB-SINR.

6. CONCLUSION

Effective use of the wireless spectrum requires an understanding of interference from theoretical and experimental vantage points. A growing body of algorithmic work on worst-case wireless interference under the SINR threshold model assumes that signals decay geometrically with distance, the GEO-SINR model.

We outlined an approach for incorporating realism into the interference model while seamlessly generalizing previous theoretical results. By leveraging a matrix of pairwise RSS between wireless motes instead of geometric path loss, the MB-SINR model predicted PRR performance significantly better in our experiments on two indoors testbeds. The RSS matrix also appears resilient to temporal factors, with prediction accuracy of 95% when using an RSS matrix created weeks in advance.

We defined the notion of metricity, which quantifies the proximity of the RSS matrix to a distance metric. Through experiments, we showed how the concept effectively measures the complexity of the underlying environment. With metricity as a harness, worst-case theoretical results that hold under general metrics in the GEO-SINR model can now be translated with trivial modifications to the more realistic MB-SINR model. Moreover, the translation retains almost identical performance ratios for all such algorithms, with the metricity parameter ζ replacing the path loss constant α in the GEO-SINR model.

As a case study of the metricity concept, we addressed multi-path fading by allowing transmitters to choose between several frequencies. We found that environments with extensive multi-path effects exhibited better metricity values. By fusing empirical measurements into an analytical model commonly used for worst-case theoretical analysis, our approach suggests a methodology for harmonizing algorithmic theory of wireless interference with real-world observations.

Acknowledgments

This research is supported by grant-of excellence no 120032011 from the Icelandic Research Fund. We thank Henning Ulfarsson and members of RU Syslab for their valuable contributions and assistance with experiments, and the anonymous reviewers for their constructive feedback.

7. REFERENCES

[1] D. Aguayo, J. Bicket, S. Biswas, G. Judd, and R. Morris. Link-level measurements from an 802.11b mesh network. *ACM SIGCOMM Computer Communication Review*, 34(4):121–132, 2004.

[2] E. I. Ásgeirsson and P. Mitra. On a game theoretic approach to capacity maximization in wireless networks. In *INFOCOM*, 2011.

[3] N. Baccour, A. Koubaa, L. Mottola, M. A. Zuniga, H. Youssef, C. A. Boano, and M. Alves. Radio link quality estimation in wireless sensor networks: a survey. *ACM Trans. Sensor Networks (TOSN)*, 8(4):34, 2012.

[4] C. A. Boano, T. Voigt, N. Tsiftes, L. Mottola, K. Römer, and M. A. Zúniga. Making sensornet MAC protocols robust against interference. In *Wireless Sensor Networks*, pages 272–288. Springer, 2010.

[5] M. H. Bodlaender and M. M. Halldórsson. Beyond geometry: Towards fully realistic wireless models. In *PODC*, 2014. arXiv:1402.5003.

[6] Y. Chen and A. Terzis. On the mechanisms and effects of calibrating RSSI measurements for 802.15.4 radios. In *Wireless Sensor Networks*, pages 256–271. Springer, 2010.

[7] J. Dams, M. Hoefer, and T. Kesselheim. Jamming-resistant learning in wireless networks. In *ICALP*, 2014. arXiv:1307.5290.

[8] A. Fanghänel, T. Kesselheim, H. Räcke, and B. Vöcking. Oblivious interference scheduling. In *PODC*, pages 220–229, August 2009.

[9] D. Ganesan, B. Krishnamachari, A. Woo, D. Culler, D. Estrin, and S. Wicker. Complex behavior at scale: An experimental study of low-power wireless sensor networks. Technical report, UCLA/CSD-TR 02, 2002.

[10] A. Goldsmith. *Wireless Communications*. Cambridge Univ. Press, 2005.

[11] O. Goussevskaia, M. M. Halldórsson, and R. Wattenhofer. Algorithms for wireless capacity. *IEEE/ACM Trans. Netw.*, 22(3):745–755, 2014.

[12] Z. Gu, G. Wang, and Y. Wang. Path-loss fluctuations towards robust scheduling algorithms in the SINR model. In *MASS*, pages 416–424. IEEE, 2012.

[13] R. Gummadi, D. Wetherall, B. Greenstein, and S. Seshan. Understanding and mitigating the impact of RF interference on 802.11 networks. In *SIGCOMM*, pages 385–396. ACM, 2007.

[14] P. Gupta and P. R. Kumar. The Capacity of Wireless Networks. *IEEE Trans. Information Theory*, 46(2):388–404, 2000.

[15] M. M. Halldórsson and P. Mitra. Nearly optimal bounds for distributed wireless scheduling in the SINR model. In *ICALP*, 2011.

[16] M. M. Halldórsson and P. Mitra. Wireless Capacity with Oblivious Power in General Metrics. In *SODA*, 2011.

[17] M. M. Halldórsson and P. Mitra. Wireless capacity and admission control in cognitive radio. In *INFOCOM*, pages 855–863, 2012.

[18] J. Huang, S. Liu, G. Xing, H. Zhang, J. Wang, and L. Huang. Accuracy-aware interference modeling and measurement in wireless sensor networks. In *ICDCS*, pages 172–181, 2011.

[19] A. Iyer, C. Rosenberg, and A. Karnik. What is the right model for wireless channel interference? *IEEE Transactions on Wireless Communications*, 8(5):2662–2671, 2009.

[20] T. Kesselheim. A Constant-Factor Approximation for Wireless Capacity Maximization with Power Control in the SINR Model. In *SODA*, 2011.

[21] T. Kesselheim. Approximation algorithms for wireless link scheduling with flexible data rates. In *ESA*, pages 659–670, 2012.

[22] T. Kesselheim and B. Vöcking. Distributed contention resolution in wireless networks. In *DISC*, pages 163–178, August 2010.

[23] D. Kotz, C. Newport, R. S. Gray, J. Liu, Y. Yuan, and C. Elliott. Experimental evaluation of wireless simulation assumptions. In *MSWiM*, pages 78–82. ACM, 2004.

[24] R. Maheshwari, S. Jain, and S. R. Das. A measurement study of interference modeling and scheduling in low-power wireless networks. In *SenSys*, pages 141–154, 2008.

[25] R. Maheshwari, S. Jain, and S. R. Das. On estimating joint interference for concurrent packet transmissions in low power wireless networks. In *WinTech*, pages 89–94. ACM, 2008.

[26] T. Moscibroda and R. Wattenhofer. The Complexity of Connectivity in Wireless Networks. In *INFOCOM*, 2006.

[27] T. Moscibroda, R. Wattenhofer, and Y. Weber. Protocol Design Beyond Graph-Based Models. In *Hotnets*, 2006.

[28] T. Moscibroda, R. Wattenhofer, and A. Zollinger. Topology control meets SINR: The scheduling complexity of arbitrary topologies. In *MOBIHOC*, pages 310–321, 2006.

[29] J. Padhye, S. Agarwal, V. N. Padmanabhan, L. Qiu, A. Rao, and B. Zill. Estimation of link interference in static multi-hop wireless networks. In *IMC*, 2005.

[30] X. Qi, Y. Wang, Y. Wang, L. Xu, and C. Hu. EIM: Efficient online interference measurement in wireless sensor networks. In *WiOpt*, pages 548–555. IEEE, 2013.

[31] L. Qiu, Y. Zhang, F. Wang, M. K. Han, and R. Mahajan. A general model of wireless interference. In *MobiCom*, pages 171–182, 2007.

[32] C. Reis, R. Mahajan, M. Rodrig, D. Wetherall, and J. Zahorjan. Measurement-based models of delivery and interference in static wireless networks. In *SIGCOMM*, pages 51–62, 2006.

[33] V. Sevani and B. Raman. SIR based interference modeling for wireless mesh networks: A detailed measurement study. In *COMSNETS*, pages 1–10. IEEE, 2012.

[34] D. Son, B. Krishnamachari, and J. Heidemann. Experimental study of concurrent transmission in wireless sensor networks. In *SenSys*, pages 237–250. ACM, 2006.

[35] TI Corporation. CC2510Fx/CC2511Fx: Low-power SoC (system-on-chip) with MCU, memory, 2.4 GHz RF transceiver, and USB controller. http://www.ti.com/product/cc2511f32. [Online; accessed 27-Nov-2013].

[36] M. Z. Zamalloa and B. Krishnamachari. An analysis of unreliability and asymmetry in low-power wireless links. *ACM Trans. Sensor Networks (TOSN)*, 3(2):7, 2007.

[37] J. Zhao and R. Govindan. Understanding packet delivery performance in dense wireless sensor networks. In *SenSys*, pages 1–13. ACM, 2003.

[38] G. Zhou, T. He, S. Krishnamurthy, and J. A. Stankovic. Models and solutions for radio irregularity in wireless sensor networks. *ACM Transactions on Sensor Networks (TOSN)*, 2(2):221–262, 2006.

Understanding the Interactions of Handover-Related Self-Organization Schemes

Kais Elmurtadi Suleiman
University of Waterloo
Electrical and Computer
Engineering
Waterloo, Ontario, Canada
kelmurta@uwaterloo.ca

Abd-Elhamid M. Taha
Alfaisal University
Electrical Engineering
Riyadh, KSA
ataha@alfaisal.edu

Hossam S. Hassanein
Queen's University
School of Computing
Kingston, Ontario, Canada
hossam@cs.queensu.ca

ABSTRACT

A Self Organizing Network (SON) scheme monitors certain Key Performance Indicators (KPIs) and responds by adjusting system control parameters. Multiple SON schemes may have related KPIs or use the same control parameters. This leads these schemes and their use cases to interact either constructively or destructively. In this paper, we study these interactions between three SON use cases all aiming at improving the overall handover procedure in LTE femtocell networks. These use cases are namely: handover self optimization, call admission control self optimization and load balancing self optimization. This work is motivated by the lack of interaction studies conducted so far between these three self optimization use cases. First, we have surveyed related individual scheme proposals in order to identify schemes which represent these three use cases in our interaction study. Then, several interaction experiments are conducted in realistic scenarios using our in-house built and LTE-compliant simulation environment. We conclude by drawing guidelines that we believe can help designers realize better coordination policies between these three handover-related SON use cases.

Categories and Subject Descriptors

C.2.1 [**Computer-communication Networks**]: Network Architecture and Design–*wireless communication, distributed networks*; C.4 [**Performance of Systems**]: *performance attributes*.

Keywords

Femtocell; LTE; Self Organizing Network; Optimization; Handover; Call Admission Control; Load Balancing; Interaction; Coordination; Simulation.

MSWiM'14, September 21–26, 2014, Montreal, QC, Canada.
Copyright 2014 ACM 978-1-4503-3030-5/14/09 ...$15.00.
http://dx.doi.org/10.1145/2641798.2641830.

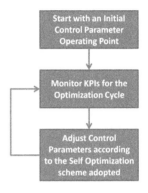

Figure 1: **Self Optimization Scheme Cycle**

1. INTRODUCTION

It is expected that 28 million femtocell units are to be deployed by 2017 [1]. Such high scale ad hoc deployments will face the major challenge of frequent system control parameter adjustments. This challenge is addressed by adopting SON use cases. Self optimization use cases, a subclass of SON use cases, are all based on implementing a scheme that monitors KPIs and adjusting system control parameters in response. An initial operating point is defined by the initial control parameter values. These control parameters can be either standardized or scheme-specific. Figure 1 illustrates this self optimization scheme cycle.

However, interactions could occur when several SON use cases, with related KPIs and/or common control parameters, are simultaneously operating in the same network. These interactions could either be positive or negative. In this work, we address three interacting SON use cases all aiming at enhancing the overall handover process in LTE femtocell networks. They are namely: handover self optimization, call admission control self optimization and load balancing self optimization.

This paper is organized as follows: in Section 2, we briefly review the overall LTE handover procedure. The definitions of the three handover-related self optimization use cases in light of some of the most commonly used KPIs are also defined in this section. This background section helps in identifying possible interaction scenarios between the handover-related self optimization use cases of interest. In Section 3, we first survey previous interaction studies to show the need for an interaction study that gathers the chosen handover-related self optimization use cases. After that, proposed individual schemes are surveyed and representative schemes are chosen. Section 4 first presents the individual scheme experiments and then the mutual scheme interaction experiments. Individual experiments are conducted first to verify that each representative scheme meets its use case objective. In order to have realistic scenarios and due to the lack of such environments, all of these experiments are conducted in our in-house LTE compliant simulation environment [2]. Section 5 discusses experiment results and gives some guidelines which we believe should be followed when coordinating the handover-related self optimization use cases covered in this work. Finally, Section 6 concludes our findings and outlines future work.

2. BACKGROUND

2.1 Handover Procedure

There are three main phases in the overall LTE handover procedure: preparation, execution and completion. The handover preparation phase is when handover decisions are made at the source cell and admission decisions are made at the target cell. Therefore, it is the phase at which the three handover-related SON use cases take place.

In the Radio Resource Control (RRC) IDLE state, the UE always seeks to identify a suitable cell with the highest signal strength to "camp on". In fact, RRC IDLE state handovers are UE controlled. When transitioning from the RRC IDLE state to the RRC CONNECTED state, the UE begins by selecting the neighbouring target cell with the highest signal strength. If this cell selection request is rejected, then a barring timer will be triggered and the UE returns back to the RRC IDLE state [3]. Until this timer is expired, choosing the same target cell by the same UE is barred. However, if the UE manages to access another target cell, the timer will reset and an RRC connection will be established (RRC CONNECTED state). In this state, the UE starts the handover procedure by sending measurements to the current source cell which is responsible of making any future handover decisions. Therefore, RRC CONNECTED state handovers are network controlled but still UE assisted.

During the RRC CONNECTED state, the cell with the highest signal strength is chosen for handover if the following condition is met for a duration of at least TReselection and after at least 1 second of dwelling time at the current source cell [4]:

$$Q_{meas,n} > Q_{meas,s} + Qoffset_{s,n} + QHyst_s$$

where:

$Q_{meas,n}$	is the RSRP measurement of the neighbouring cell in dBm.
$Q_{meas,s}$	is the RSRP measurement of the serving cell in dBm.
$Qoffset_{s,n}$	is the cell individual offset of the neighbouring cell as stored in the serving cell in dB.
$QHyst_s$	is the handover hysteresis margin of the serving cell in dB.

Both $QHyst$ and TReselection are system control parameters which can affect handovers globally. Whereas,

$Qoffset$ is a cell-pair specific system control parameter which can affect handovers only between the corresponding serving-neighbouring (source-target) pair of cells.

If the target cell denies the source cell handover request, then we will have a **Handover Failure**. Successive handover failures could eventually lead to a **Radio Link Failure**. However, if the handover request is granted, the handover execution phase is initiated followed by the handover completion phase. If the user spends less than 5 seconds in the target cell(s) before returning back to the same source cell, the handover is considered a **Ping Pong Handover**.

2.2 Handover-related Self Optimization

This process starts with the adjustment of the femtocell's coverage footprint by self optimizing its handover-related control parameters (e.g. QHyst, TReselection,Qoffset or the conventional admission control guard channel policy threshold). Before introducing the three handover-related self optimization use cases, we define some of the most commonly used KPIs as follows:

- Handover Failure Ratio (**HOFR**): the ratio between the the Number of Handover Failures and the total summation of the Number of Handover Failures and the Number of Successful Handovers.
- Ping Pong Handover Ratio (**PPHOR**): the ratio between the Number of Ping Pong Handovers and the total summation of the Number of Handover Failures and the Number of Successful Handovers.
- Call Dropping Probability (**CDP**): the ratio between the Number of Radio Link Failures and the Number of Accepted Calls into the cell.
- Call Blocking Probability (**CBP**): the ratio between the Number of Call Blocks and the total summation of the Number of Call Blocks and the Number of New Calls.

The three handover-related self optimization use cases can now be introduced as follows:

- **Handover Self Optimization:** the effect of this use case takes place at the source cell. The main task is to reduce HOFR and PPHOR.
- **Call Admission Control Self Optimization:** the effect of this use case takes place at the target cell. The main task is to admit as many calls as possible while maintaining an acceptable level of service for the ongoing calls. This usually leads to decreasing HOFR and CDP.
- **Load Balancing Self Optimization:** the effect of this use case takes place at the source cell. The main task is to balance the load across the network cells in order to decrease both HOFR and CBP. This comes at the cost of increasing PPHOR.

As it can be seen, these use cases might monitor some related KPIs which might lead to interactions. **Negative interactions** occur when one of the interacting schemes contradicts or limits the benefits of the others, whereas **Positive interactions** occur when the interacting schemes help each other improve the overall network performance. This judgment should be made in light of the different KPIs while considering that interactions might be negative for one use case but positive for the other.

3. RELATED WORK

3.1 Interaction Studies

The authors in [5] study the interaction between a handover self optimization scheme and a load balancing self optimization scheme. The handover self optimization scheme is based on adjusting QHyst and TReselection while being triggered by a high HOFR, a high CDP or a high PPHOR. The load balancing self optimization scheme is based on adjusting Qoffset while being triggered by the load differences between neighbouring cells. In both [6] and [7], the work done in [5] is enhanced by prohibiting the handover self optimization scheme from causing backward handovers.

The authors in [8] study the interaction between a handover self optimization scheme and a call admission control self optimization scheme. The handover self optimization scheme is based on periodically monitoring the trend followed by a weighted summation of HOFR, CDP and PPHOR. Depending on this trend, new QHyst and TReselection values are chosen. For the call admission control self optimization scheme, the conventional guard channel policy is adopted with a dynamic threshold. The monitored KPIs are HOFR, the ratio of calls with a low throughput and CBP. Both schemes are interacting constructively in terms of achieving a lower HOFR and a lower CDP, while no effect is taking place between them in terms of PPHOR. The call admission control self optimization scheme is benefiting from this interaction by blocking less calls.

To the best of our knowledge, no further interaction studies have been conducted to date between the SON use cases of interest here. This has led us to conduct the following survey in order to identify the representative schemes to be used in this study.

3.2 Handover Self Optimization (HO-SO)

3.2.1 Overview of Schemes

In reference [9], the authors propose an empirical formula that uses the current cell load and type in order to modify the UE RSRP measurement received and therefore affect future handover decisions. Other schemes adjust standardized control parameters. In reference [10], either QHyst or TReselection is adjusted in reaction to three handover defect types which are: Too Early Handovers, Too Late Handovers and Handovers To Wrong Cells. The scheme differentiates between these three handover defect types by measuring their HOFR, PPHOR and CDP. Based on this, a decision is made on how different control parameter adjustments should be made.

Contrary to [10], the authors in [11] claim that adjusting Qoffset gives more flexibility. They also exploit the fact that different handover defect types dominate depending on the user mobility status and therefore different Qoffset adjustments should be made.

A multi-control parameter adjusting scheme is proposed in [12]. The scheme starts by exchanging with neighbouring cells the number of radio link failure events, the number of too early handover events and the number of handover to wrong cell events. If their weighted summation exceeds a threshold value, then the scheme starts checking whether a global optimization or a local

optimization is necessary. QHyst and TReselection are adjusted in global optimization attempts and the relevant Qoffsets are adjusted in local optimization attempts.

Three multi-control parameter adjusting schemes are proposed in the European Union (EU) project of Self Optimization and self ConfiguRATion in wirelEss networkS (SOCRATES) [5]. These schemes are: the Simplified Trend-based scheme, the Trend-based scheme and the Handover Performance Indicator Sum-based scheme. The Simplified Trend-based scheme periodically monitors HOFR, CDP and PPHOR. The trend followed by each KPI is determined by comparing its current value against its predefined threshold. Based on the trend detected, both the standardized QHyst and TReselection control parameters are adjusted.

The Trend-based scheme still monitors the same KPIs adopted by the Simplified Trend-based scheme but does not run periodically. In fact, it starts by verifying that the network is experiencing a tangible and lasting trend and then changes the handover operating point, as defined by QHyst and TReselection, according to an empirical criteria [13].

The Handover Performance Indicator Sum-based scheme works periodically like the Simplified Trend-based scheme. It monitors a weighted summation of HOFR, CDP and PPHOR and then compares this summation value to its most recent value. If a performance improvement is detected, then the same optimization direction is followed, otherwise the optimization direction is reversed. The same empirical criteria mentioned in [13] is adopted. However, the drawback here is that any slight handover performance indicator change may cause a change in the optimization direction needlessly. Therefore, authors in [14] propose a strategy that would prevent the optimization direction from switching back unless the handover performance indicator change percentage is higher than a threshold called the "Performance Degradation Percentage" (PDP). A very high PDP can result in tolerating an excessive handover degradation before reacting and changing the optimization direction. As a result, a T-test is proposed by authors in [15] to be implemented just before the PDP strategy which yields the Enhanced Handover Performance Indicator Sum-based scheme.

3.2.2 Representative Scheme

We choose the Simplified Trend-based scheme proposed by [5] as the handover self optimization representative scheme. Algorithm 1 shows the pseudocode. This scheme is chosen for the following reasons:

- It is a multi-control parameter adjusting scheme, which gives more flexibility in altering handover decisions,
- Both QHyst and TReselection are commonly used standardized control parameters,
- It is generic and does not rely on any empirical formula,
- Lastly, it is based on monitoring locally processed KPI measurements with no signalling needed.

This scheme starts by initializing the operator KPI thresholds. Then, it periodically measures the local HOFR, CDP and PPHOR in order to evaluate how QHyst and TReselection should be changed. Most importantly, this scheme trades off HOFR and PPHOR with CDP.

Algorithm 1 HO-SO Representative Scheme
```
 1. Initialize HOFR_TH, CDP_TH and PPHOR_TH
 2. while Cell is ON do
 3.     if an optimization interval has passed then
 4.         Compute optimization interval HOFR, CDP and PPHOR
 5.         if HOFR<HOFR_TH and PPHOR<PPHOR_TH then
 6.             if CDP>CDP_TH then
 7.                 Decrease QHyst;
 8.                 Decrease TReselection;
 9.             else
10.                 Decrease HOFR_TH;
11.                 Decrease CDP_TH;
12.                 Decrease PPHOR_TH;
13.             end if
14.         else
15.             if CDP≤CDP_TH then
16.                 Increase QHyst;
17.                 Increase TReselection;
18.             else
19.                 Increase HOFR_TH;
20.                 Increase CDP_TH;
21.                 Increase PPHOR_TH;
22.             end if
23.         end if
24.     end if
25. end while
```

3.3 Call Admission Control Self Optimization (CAC-SO)

3.3.1 Overview of Schemes

All of the schemes surveyed in this category are based on bandwidth reservations. To begin with, the authors in [16] claim that reserving resources for real-time calls would not automatically prevent these delay intolerant services from being dropped, whereas reserving resources for non-real-time calls would at least result in reducing congestions. Therefore, a scheme that reserves resources for non-real-time calls is proposed. The reservation threshold is adjusted periodically based on the packet drop rate.

The authors in [17] and [18] propose schemes which prioritize handover calls over new calls by adopting the conventional guard channel policy with a dynamic threshold. In reference [17], the dynamic threshold is adjusted in response to HOFR and the number of successful handover attempts; authors claim that reacting to low HOFR after a number of successful handover attempts prevents the system from oscillating. In reference [18], the scheme monitors HOFR, CDP and the fraction of calls with a throughput lower than the minimum throughput required by the packet scheduler. This scheme tends to increase the dynamic guard channel threshold faster than decreasing it which gives handovers a higher priority over new calls.

The authors in [19] derive users handover probabilities based on their predictable mobility habits. Admission decisions are based on these probabilities and a dynamic threshold. Handovers are prioritized over new calls by not subjecting them to this threshold. The monitored KPI is HOFR.

The work in reference [20] is the only scheme that prioritizes handovers over new calls while still differentiating between real-time and non-real-time calls. Real-time new calls are admitted only if the desired amount of bandwidth is available at the target cell and its neighbours, whereas real-time handovers are given a higher priority by being satisfied even with the minimum bandwidth at the target cell and its neighbours. However, non-real-time handovers and new calls consider only the target cell when making such admission decisions. This gives them a higher priority over real-time calls. In all cases, a reserved bandwidth pool is increased if HOFR is higher than a predetermined threshold value and vice versa.

3.3.2 Representative Scheme

We choose the scheme proposed by [17] as our call admission control self optimization representative scheme. Algorithm 2 shows the pseudocode. However, we have modified the scheme slightly in order to account for the mobile operator's call blocking probability threshold, and to make the mobile operator thresholds adjustable if they were initially set to extremely low or high values. These modifications are shown on lines 6 through 10 and 15 through 22. This scheme is chosen for two reasons:

- It is based on the most commonly used dynamic guard channel policy which prioritizes handover calls over new calls,
- It monitors the locally processed HOFR and therefore no signalling is needed.

This scheme starts by initializing the operator KPI thresholds. Then, it periodically measures the local HOFR and CBP in order to evaluate how the guard channel policy's dynamic threshold (CAC_TH) should be adjusted. The two parameters (α_1 and α_2) are used to prevent oscillations, where $\alpha_1 > \alpha_2$ and both $\alpha_1 \& \alpha_2 < 1$. Responses to high HOFR are accelerated by including the Number of Handover Failures (NHOF), whereas responses to low HOFR are slowed down by including the Number of Successful Handovers (NSHO). This gives handovers a higher priority over new calls. Most importantly, this scheme trades off HOFR with CBP.

3.4 Load Balancing Self Optimization (LB-SO)

3.4.1 Overview of Schemes

All of the schemes surveyed in this category are based on adjusting the cell coverage area either actually, by adjusting the transmission power or virtually, by adjusting Qoffset. An exchange of cell load information is always needed.

In reference [21], a scheme is proposed that is based on adjusting the transmission power in response to the current cell load. It starts by exchanging neighbouring cells load information and then compares current cell load with the neighbouring cells average load. If this average load is lower than the current cell load, then the current cell power is decreased and vice versa. The scheme also controls the current cell's minimum power level in order to avoid gaps and overlaps. Gaps are detected whenever a high CDP is encountered whereas the opposite applies for overlaps.

The authors in [22] claim that trying to balance the load using power adjustments can still result in gaps and overlaps.

Algorithm 2 CAC-SO Representative Scheme
```
1.  Initialize HOFR_TH and CBP_TH
2.  while Cell is ON do
3.      if an optimization interval has passed then
4.          Compute optimization interval HOFR and CBP
5.          if HOFR≥α₁×HOFR_TH and NHOF>0 then
6.              if CBP≤CBP_TH then
7.                  Decrease CAC_TH;
8.              else
9.                  CAC_TH=CAC_TH;
10.             end if
11.         end if
12.         if HOFR≤α₂×HOFR_TH and NSHO≥NSHO_TH then
13.             Increase CAC_TH;
14.         end if
15.         if HOFR<HOFR_TH and CBP<CBP_TH then
16.             Decrease HOFR_TH;
17.             Decrease CBP_TH;
18.         end if
19.         if HOFR>HOFR_TH and CBP>CBP_TH then
20.             Increase HOFR_TH;
21.             Increase CBP_TH;
22.         end if
23.     end if
24. end while
```

Algorithm 3 LB-SO Representative Scheme
```
1.  Initialize Load_Diff_TH
2.  while Cell is ON do
3.      if an optimization interval has passed then
4.          for all neighbouring cells do
5.              Collect last optimization interval CLₙ
6.          end for
7.          for all neighbouring cells do
8.              if CLₙ − CLₛ >Load_Diff_TH then
9.                  Increase Qoffsetₛ,ₙ;
10.             end if
11.             if CLₙ − CLₛ <Load_Diff_TH then
12.                 Decrease Qoffsetₛ,ₙ;
13.             end if
14.             if abs(CLₙ − CLₛ) ≤Load_Diff_TH then
15.                 Qoffsetₛ,ₙ = Qoffsetₛ,ₙ;
16.             end if
17.         end for
18.     end if
19. end while
```

Therefore, a scheme that is based on monitoring cell loads and adjusting Qoffsets is proposed.

Several other schemes are based on adjusting Qoffsets. In reference [23], the authors propose that Qoffsets should be adjusted in response to the CBP difference between cells. This difference along with the current Qoffset values are used as inputs to a fuzzy logic algorithm in order to make Qoffset adjustments. The authors in [24] propose a Qoffset-adjusting scheme based on an Autonomic Flowing Water Balancing Method (AFWBM) inspired by the connected vessels theory in physics.

The work in [25] is the only scheme that is based on adjusting both the transmission power and Qoffsets. Similar to [23], both of these adjustments are made using a fuzzy logic controller. For the Qoffset adjustments, the fuzzy inputs are the current Qoffset values and the difference in the load ratios between the two cells targeted by the load balancing, whereas the outputs will be the adjusted Qoffsets. For the power adjustments, the fuzzy inputs are the difference in the load ratios, the difference between the current cell transmission power level and its default level, and another input called the ping pong parameter. With a low ping pong parameter, the power adjustment process would be stopped to avoid causing gaps and overlaps. The outputs of this power adjustment process are the required transmission power levels.

3.4.2 *Representative Scheme*

We choose the scheme proposed by [22] as our load balancing self optimization representative scheme. Algorithm 3 shows the pseudocode. This scheme is chosen for the following two reasons:

- It avoids causing coverage gaps and overlaps by not adjusting the cell transmission power levels,
- It adjusts the commonly used standardized Qoffset control parameters.

This scheme starts by initializing the operator load difference threshold (Load_Diff_TH). Then, it periodically measures the serving cell load (CL_s) and the neighbouring cell loads (CL_n) in order to evaluate whether Qoffset should be decreased, increased or stay the same. All of these adjustments are processed locally after gathering load information from the neighbouring cells. Most importantly, this scheme trades off PPHOR with CBP and HOFR.

4. EXPERIMENTS

4.1 Scenario

The network topology is shown in Figure 2. Each apartment has one randomly dropped femtocell. This apartment block is located at the intersection area of three macrocell sectors where the macrocellular tier coverage is expected to be limited. Surrounding these three macrocell sectors are two rings of 3-sector macrocells to account for the macrocell tier interference affect. The resulting weak macrocell coverage, reaching our topology area, leads the user handsets to never choose the macrocellular tier for their new call and handover requests. In fact, we have found that adopting this scenario has successfully led the network performance to capture exclusively the effect of the self optimization schemes being studied and implemented only in the femtocellular tier. Reader should refer to our thesis work in [2] for experiments confirming these findings.

We adopt the measurement based method [26] to set the femtocells downlink transmission power levels. However, thermal noise, shadow fading, all interfering macrocell and femtocell signals are all considered. Indoor users walk randomly while bouncing back at each apartment walls. Five vehicles, with one user in each vehicle, are mobilizing in the streets periodically in a predetermined path with a fixed velocity. The same standardized cell barring technique, as discussed in Subsection 2.1, is assumed for handovers.

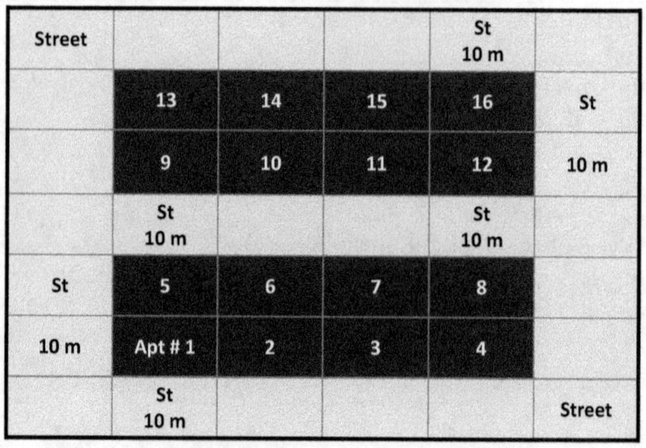

Figure 2: **An illustration of network topology**

The traffic mix of 30% VoIP, 20% Interactive Gaming, 20% Near Real Time Video Streaming, 20% HTTP and 10% FTP is adopted. For VoIP, Interactive Gaming and Near Real-Time Video Streaming services, the active and the idle call durations are drawn from exponential distributions. Whereas, both HTTP and FTP services are assumed to continuously download webpages and files each time reading finishes. The reading times are drawn also from exponential distributions. Table 1 summarize the most important simulation scenario assumptions. Our thesis work in [2] gives further details about the simulation environment including SINR computations and the representative scheme assumptions made.

Table 1: **Parameters used in simulation scenario**

Item	Assumption
Center Carrier Frequency	2 GHz
Downlink System Bandwidth	3 MHz
Number of PRBs	15
Number of Macrocells	36
Macrocell Intersite Distance	1732 metres
Number of femtocells	16
Macrocell Antenna	3-Sector antennas
Femtocell Antenna	Omnidirectional
Macrocell DL TX Power Level	Fixed: 43 dBm
Femtocell DL TX Power Level	Varied: 2-20 dBm
Outdoor User Vehicle Speed	30 km/h
Initial barring Timer value	15 seconds
UE Number of Receiver Antennas	1 (SISO)
UE Class's Peak Data Rate	10 Mbps
Minimum acceptable SINR level	-10 dB
UE Receiver Sensitivity	-110 dBm

The following set of abbreviations are adopted in all of our upcoming mutual interaction experiment figures:

- **Static:** represents the Static control parameters or simply the fact that no self optimization scheme is implemented.
- **HOCAC-SO:** represents the interaction between the representative HO-SO scheme and the representative CAC-SO scheme.

- **HOLB-SO:** represents the interaction between the representative HO-SO scheme and the representative LB-SO scheme.
- **CACLB-SO:** represents the interaction between the representative CAC-SO scheme and the representative LB-SO scheme.

For the three handover-related self optimization schemes when operating simultaneously, we notice that no additional three-scheme interactions are observed. Reader should refer to our thesis work in [2] for further details.

4.2 Individual Experiments

Figure 3 shows the representative schemes performance in terms of HOFR, CDP, CBP and PPHOR. We notice that in femtocell environments, PPHOR is high which leads the HO-SO scheme to aggressively increase its QHyst and TReselection parameters while decreasing the number of outbound handovers, PPHOR and HOFR. However, this leads these outbound handovers to be locked to a femtocell that has a signal strength that is lower than its neighbours which will eventually lead to call drops, an increased CDP, a less utilization and therefore a less CBP.

We also notice that CAC-SO scheme prioritizes handovers over new calls which leads to more new call blocks, less handover failures and therefore less call drops. Less call drops are due to the fact that users are getting their handover requests granted. However, this scheme does not clearly differentiate between normal and ping pong handovers, which means no clear effect on PPHOR.

Finally, LB-SO scheme always tries to balance the load as soon as it discovers a tangible load difference. This balancing enhances the chances for new calls and handovers of finding bandwidth which decreases both HOFR and CBP while increasing PPHOR. However, and since the main cell selection/reselection criterion is based on choosing the cell with the highest signal strength, most of the overutilized cells would be the cells with the highest downlink transmission power levels and vice versa. Therefore, this load balancing technique forces users to leave the higher power overutilized cells to the lower power underutilized cells which means a higher interference for these users and as a result an increased CDP.

4.3 Interaction Experiments

4.3.1 HOCAC-SO schemes interaction

Figure 4 shows this performance interaction in terms of HOFR, CDP, CBP and PPHOR. We find that the CAC-SO scheme at the target femtocell guards some resources to the handover requests initiated by the HO-SO scheme at the source femtocell. This makes the CAC-SO scheme share the burden of decreasing HOFR with the HO-SO scheme and overall we have an even less HOFR. The HO-SO scheme is now using a bit smaller QHyst and TReselection parameters and therefore we have a slight CDP decrease but a slight PPHOR increase. In addition, the CAC-SO scheme now neither needs to reserve as many resources for handovers nor block as many new calls. Therefore, the system experiences a slight CBP decrease.

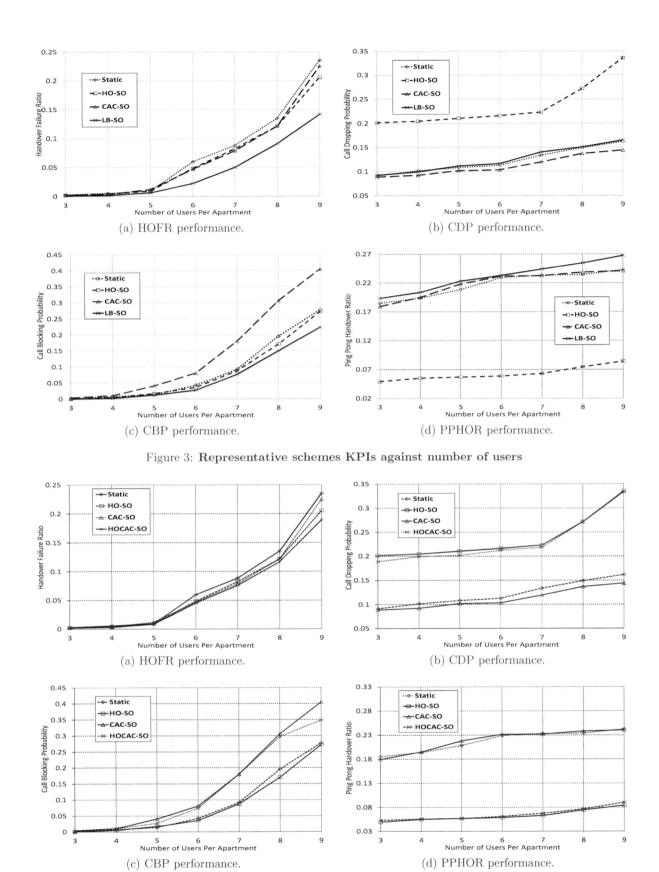

(a) HOFR performance.

(b) CDP performance.

(c) CBP performance.

(d) PPHOR performance.

Figure 3: **Representative schemes KPIs against number of users**

(a) HOFR performance.

(b) CDP performance.

(c) CBP performance.

(d) PPHOR performance.

Figure 4: **HOCAC-SO interaction KPIs against number of users**

4.3.2 HOLB-SO schemes interaction

Figure 5 shows this performance interaction in terms of HOFR, CDP, CBP and PPHOR. The HO-SO scheme attempts to limit the number of outbound handovers in order to decrease HOFR. This strategy contradicts the LB-SO scheme strategy and therefore leads the LB-SO to perform sub-optimally in terms of decreasing HOFR and CBP. However, the HO-SO scheme is now observing less HOFR, with the help of the LB-SO scheme, which leads to smaller HO-SO control parameters. This causes a slight CDP decrease and a slight PPHOR increase. In fact, PPHOR is still much lower than what it used to be when the LB-SO scheme was operating separately due to the HO-SO scheme effect.

4.3.3 CACLB-SO schemes interaction

Figure 6 shows this performance interaction in terms of HOFR, CDP, CBP and PPHOR. The LB-SO scheme has found channels for its outbound handover decisions reserved by the CAC-SO scheme at the target cells, which results in further decreasing HOFR. This in fact has spoiled the LB-SO scheme by allowing it to initiate even more handovers from the overutilized high power cells towards the underutilized low power cells, and therefore causing more call drops. However, the CAC-SO scheme is no longer blocking as many new calls as it used to do before. But since the CAC-SO scheme is still taking part in the process of decreasing HOFR, the CAC-SO scheme is still causing a high CBP. For the PPHOR, the LB-SO scheme still causes a high PPHOR. However, no clear interaction effect is observed in terms of PPHOR.

4.4 Discussion

In Table 2, we give the different performances a ranking. Positive numbers indicate a KPI increase in comparison to the static setting, whereas negative numbers indicate the opposite. The ranking indicates the relative performance of a certain KPI against its counterparts from the other schemes and interactions. A "zero" means that there is no clear effect demonstrated. The large bold numbers indicate when the KPI value is the lowest or the most desired.

Table 2: **Comparing the Schemes and their Interactions**

KPI	HOFR	CDP	CBP	PPHOR
HO-SO	-1	+5	-1	**-3**
CAC-SO	-1	**-1**	+3	0
LB-SO	-4	+1	**-3**	+1
HOCAC-SO	-2	+4	+2	-2
HOLB-SO	-3	+3	-2	-1
CACLB-SO	**-5**	+2	+1	+1

From this comparison, we deduce that if we are merely interested in achieving the lowest value for each KPI *independent* from its accompanying values of the other KPIs, then the following guidelines can be recommended:

- To decrease HOFR, the CAC-SO scheme and the LB-SO scheme only should be enabled. This is due to the fact that, even though all of the three handover-related self optimization schemes cause HOFR to decrease when separate, enabling both of

the HO-SO scheme and the LB-SO scheme limits the LB-SO scheme's potential in terms of decreasing HOFR. This limitation or restriction negates the slight advantage introduced by the HO-SO scheme when it interacts with the CAC-SO scheme. Therefore, the best plan would be having the CAC-SO scheme and the LB-SO scheme only cooperating in terms of decreasing HOFR.

- To decrease CDP, the CAC-SO scheme only should be enabled, since it is the only scheme that decreases CDP.

- To decrease CBP, the LB-SO scheme only should be enabled. The HO-SO scheme is disabled to avoid restricting the LB-SO scheme from giving its full potential in terms of decreasing CBP. For the CBP decrease introduced by the HO-SO scheme, this decrease is in fact a side effect of the CDP increase introduced by the HO-SO scheme which should always be avoided at all costs.

- To decrease PPHOR, the HO-SO scheme only should be enabled. This is because the LB-SO scheme increases PPHOR, while the CAC-SO scheme causes the HO-SO scheme to use even lower control parameter values which triggers more ping pong handovers.

5. CONCLUSION AND FUTURE WORK

With the large number of femtocells expected to be deployed, several SON use cases have been proposed. Some of them might be monitoring related KPIs or adjusting the same control parameters. This can lead to either positive or negative interactions. In this work, we address interactions occurring between three self optimization use cases all aiming at optimizing the overall handover procedure in LTE femtocell networks. These use cases are: handover self optimization, call admission control self optimization and load balancing self optimization. Three representative schemes are elected after conducting a survey.

Using our in-house LTE-compliant simulation environment, representative schemes are verified first to meet their individual objectives. After that, mutual interaction experiments are conducted. Based on these simulation results, some guidelines are recommended which we believe can help in designing better coordination policies especially in LTE femtocell environments.

For our future work, we would consider other handover-related self optimization use cases (e.g. neighbour cell list self optimization use case). After studying the resulting interactions, we plan to develop coordination policies to fit scenarios even beyond what has been considered so far.

6. ACKNOWLEDGMENTS

K. Suleiman would like to acknowledge the support of the Libyan Ministry of Higher Education and Scientific Research. The authors would also like to acknowledge the support and funding of the National Science and Engineering Research Council of Canada (NSERC).

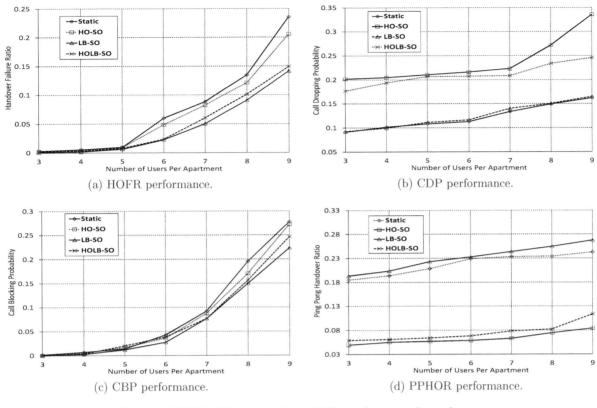

(a) HOFR performance.

(b) CDP performance.

(c) CBP performance.

(d) PPHOR performance.

Figure 5: **HOLB-SO interaction KPIs against number of users**

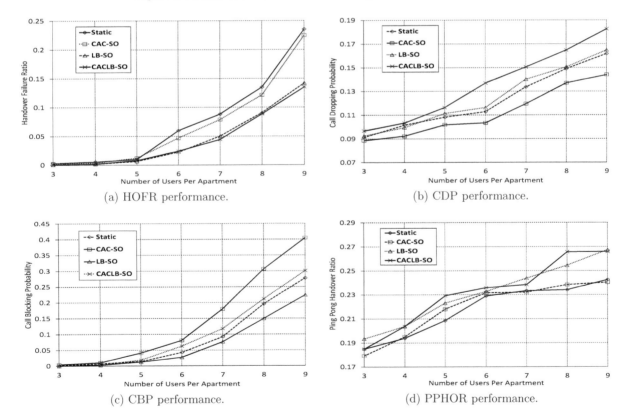

(a) HOFR performance.

(b) CDP performance.

(c) CBP performance.

(d) PPHOR performance.

Figure 6: **CACLB-SO interaction KPIs against number of users**

293

7. REFERENCES

[1] ABI Research. "High Inventory and Low Burn Rate Stalls Femtocell Market in 2012." Internet: http://www.abiresearch.com/press, Jul. 5, 2012 [Nov. 13, 2012].

[2] K. Suleiman, "Interactions Study of Self Optimizing Schemes in LTE Femtocell Networks." M.A.Sc. thesis, Queen's University, Canada, 2012.

[3] 3GPP. "Technical Specification Group Radio Access Network; Evolved Universal Terrestrial Radio Access (E-UTRA); Radio Resource Control (RRC); Protocol specification (Release 10)." TS 36.331, 3rd Generation Partnership Project (3GPP), Jun. 2011.

[4] 3GPP. "Technical Specification Group Radio Access Network; User Equipment (UE) procedures in idle mode and procedures for cell reselection in connected mode (Release 10)." TS 25.304, 3rd Generation Partnership Project (3GPP), Jun. 2012.

[5] T. Kürner, M. Amirijoo, I. Balan, H. Berg, A. Eisenblätter, T. Jansen, L. Jorguseski, R. Litjens, O. Linnell, A. Lobinger, M. Neuland, F. Phillipson, L. C. Schmelz, B. Sas, N. Scully, K. Spaey, S. Stefanski, J. Turk, U. Türke and K. Zetterberg. "Final Report on Self-Organisation and its Implications in Wireless Access Networks." Deliverable 5.9, *SOCRATES, EU Project*, Jan. 2010.

[6] L. C. Schmelz, M. Amirijoo, A. Eisenblaetter, R. Litjens, M. Neuland and J. Turk. "A coordination framework for self-organisation in LTE networks," in *IFIP/IEEE International Symposium on Integrated Network Management (IM)*, 2011, pp. 193-200.

[7] A. Lobinger, S. Stefanski, T. Jansen and I. Balan. "Coordinating Handover Parameter Optimization and Load Balancing in LTE Self-Optimizing Networks," in *IEEE 73rd Vehicular Technology Conference (VTC)*, 2011, pp. 1-5.

[8] B. Sas, K. Spaey, I. Balan, K. Zetterberg and R. Litjens. "Self-Optimisation of Admission Control and Handover Parameters in LTE," in *IEEE 73rd Vehicular Technology Conference (VTC)*, 2011, pp. 1-6.

[9] H. Zhang, X. Wen, B. Wang, W. Zheng and Y. Sun. "A Novel Handover Mechanism Between Femtocell and Macrocell for LTE Based Networks," in *Second International Conference on Communication Software and Networks (ICCSN)*, 2010, pp. 228-231.

[10] C. Feng, X. Ji and M. Peng. "Handover parameter optimization in self-organizing network," in *IET International Conference on Communication Technology and Application (ICCTA)*, 2011, pp. 500-504.

[11] K. Kitagawa, T. Komine, T. Yamamoto and S. Konishi. "A handover optimization algorithm with mobility robustness for LTE systems," in *IEEE 22nd International Symposium on Personal Indoor and Mobile Radio Communications (PIMRC)*, 2011, pp. 1647-1651.

[12] L. Ewe and H. Bakker. "Base station distributed handover optimization in LTE self-organizing networks," in *IEEE 22nd International Symposium on Personal Indoor and Mobile Radio Communications (PIMRC)*, 2011, pp. 243-247.

[13] T. Jansen, I. Balan, J. Turk, I. Moerman and T. Kürner. "Handover Parameter Optimization in LTE Self-Organizing Networks," in *IEEE 72nd Vehicular Technology Conference (VTC)*, 2010, pp. 1-5.

[14] I. Balan, T. Jansen, B. Sas, I. Moerman and T. Kurner. "Enhanced weighted performance based handover optimization in LTE," in *Future Network and Mobile Summit*, 2011, pp. 1-8.

[15] I. M. Balan, I. Moerman, B. Sas and P. Demeester. "Signalling minimizing handover parameter optimization algorithm for LTE networks." *Wireless Networks Journal*, vol. 18, no. 3, pp. 295-306, Apr. 2012.

[16] S. S. Jeong, J. A. Han and W. S. Jeon. "Adaptive connection admission control scheme for high data rate mobile networks," in *IEEE 62nd Vehicular Technology Conference (VTC)*, 2005, pp. 2607-2611.

[17] Y. Zhang and D. Liu. "An adaptive algorithm for call admission control in wireless networks," in *IEEE Global Telecommunications Conference (GLOBECOM)*, 2001, pp. 3628-3632.

[18] K. Spaey, B. Sas and C. Blondia. "Self-optimising call admission control for LTE downlink," presented at the Joint Workshop of COST 2100 SWG 3.1 & FP7-ICT-SOCRATES, Athens, Greece, 2010.

[19] F. Yu and V. C. M. Leung. "Mobility-based predictive call admission control and bandwidth reservation in wireless cellular networks," in *Proceedings of IEEE INFOCOM, 20th Annual Joint Conference of the Computer and Communications Societies*, 2001, pp. 518-526.

[20] C. Oliveira, J. B. Kim and T. Suda. "An adaptive bandwidth reservation scheme for high-speed multimedia wireless networks." *IEEE Journal on Selected Areas in Communications*, vol. 16, no. 6, pp. 858-874, Aug. 1998.

[21] I. Ashraf, H. Claussen and L. T. W. Ho. "Distributed Radio Coverage Optimization in Enterprise Femtocell Networks," in *IEEE International Conference on Communications (ICC)*, 2010, pp. 1-6.

[22] R. Kwan, R. Arnott, R. Paterson, R. Trivisonno and M. Kubota. "On Mobility Load Balancing for LTE Systems," in *IEEE 72nd Vehicular Technology Conference (VTC)*, 2010, pp. 1-5.

[23] P. Muñoz, R. Barco, I. De la Bandera, M. Toril and S. Luna-Ramirez. "Optimization of a Fuzzy Logic Controller for Handover-Based Load Balancing," in *IEEE 73rd Vehicular Technology Conference (VTC)*, 2011, pp. 1-5.

[24] H. Zhang, X. Qiu, L. Meng and X. Zhang. "Design of Distributed and Autonomic Load Balancing for Self-Organization LTE," in *IEEE 72nd Vehicular Technology Conference (VTC)*, 2010, pp. 1-5.

[25] J. M. R. Aviles, S. Luna-Ramirez, M. Toril, F. Ruiz, I. De la Bandera-Cascales and P. Munoz-Luengo. "Analysis of load sharing techniques in enterprise LTE femtocells," in *IEEE Wireless Advanced (WiAd)*, 2011, pp. 195-200.

[26] H. Claussen, L. T. W. Ho and L. G. Samuel. "Self-optimization of coverage for femtocell deployments," in *Wireless Telecommunications Symposium (WTS)*, 2008, pp. 278-285.

FGPC: Fine-Grained Popularity-based Caching Design for Content Centric Networking

Dung Ong Mau, Min Chen
School of Computer Science and Technology
Huazhong University of Science and Technology, China
omdung@gmail.com, minchen2012@hust.edu.cn

Tarik Taleb
NEC Europe Labs, Germany
talebtarik@ieee.org

Xiaofei Wang, Victor C. M. Leung
Dept. of Electrical and Computer Engineering
The University of British Columbia, Canada
{xfwang, vleung}@ece.ubc.ca

ABSTRACT

Content Centric Networking (CCN) is a content name-oriented approach to disseminate content to edge gateways/routers. In CCN, a content is cached at routers for a certain time. When the associated deadline is reached, the content is removed to cope with the limited size of content storage. If the content is popular, the previously queried content can be reused for multiple times to save bandwidth capacity. It is, therefore, critical to design an efficient replacement policy to keep popular content as long as possible. Recently, a novel caching strategy, named Most Popular Content (MPC), was proposed for CCN. It considers the high skewness of content popularity and outperforms existing default caching approaches in CCN such as Least Recently Used (LRU) and Least Frequency Used (LFU). However, MPC has some undesirable features, such as slow convergence of hitting rate and unstable hitting rate performance for various cache sizes. In this paper, a new caching policy, dubbed Fine-Grained Popularity-based Caching (FGPC), is proposed to overcome the above-mentioned weak points. Compared to MPC, FGPC always caches coming content when storage is available. Otherwise, it keeps only most popular content. FGPC achieves higher hitting rate and faster convergence speed than MPC. Based on FGPC, we further propose a Dynamic-FGPC (D-FGPC) approach that regularly adjusts the content popularity threshold. D-FGPC exhibits more stability in the hitting rate performance in comparison to FGPC and that is for various cache sizes and content sizes. The performance of both FGPC and D-FGPC caching policies are evaluated using OPNET Modeler. The obtained simulation results show that FGPC and D-FGPC outperform LRU, LFU, and MPC.

Categories and Subject Descriptors

H.4 [**Information Systems Applications**]: Miscellaneous; D.2.8 [**Software Engineering**]: Metrics—*complexity measures, performance measures*

Keywords

NDN;Future Internet;CCN;Caching Policy

1. INTRODUCTION

With the convergence of cloud computing, social media, and mobile communications, the types of data traffic are becoming more diverse and the community of Internet users is exponentially growing. Millions of multimedia files (e.g., pictures, voices and videos) are generated and shared by producers and consumers. This trend has posed high requirements on network bandwidth and data storage, congesting networks and overloading servers.

In order to alleviate the problem of bandwidth scarcity, Content Centric Networking (CCN) has been proposed to effectively distribute popular content to a potential number of users [1] [2]. To maximize the probability of content sharing while ensuring minimal upstream bandwidth demand and lowest downstream latency, routers/gateways should cache exchanged content as long as possible. Caching decision and replacement policies play a crucial role in CCN's overall performance. The Least Recently Used (LRU) and Least Frequently Used (LFU) replacement policies were originally proposed for CCN. However, LRU and LFU suffer from low efficiency and that is due to the following reason: LRU and LFU make replacement decision based on only existing content located on the cache, i.e., LRU uses a time stamp of the content while LFU counts delivery frequency of the content. It should be noted that the name of content in CCN has the same form with the Uniform Resource Locator (URL), e.g., ccnx://root/prefix1/prefix2/../. In both schemes, content popularity is overlooked, which causes inaccuracy in identifying the popular level of a newly arriving content. Thus, inadequate content replacement may happen: old popular content may be replaced by new unpopular one.

In order to address the above limitation and improve the precision of content replacement decision, a novel caching strategy, named Most Popular Content (MPC), was proposed in [3]. In MPC, every router/gateway counts the local number of requests for each content name, and stores the pair (content name; popularity count) into a content popularity table. Once the popularity of a content object reaches a predetermined threshold in a caching node, it is tagged as a popular content and is stored in the cache. By storing only popular content, MPC caches less content, saves resources and reduces the number of cache operations, which makes it achieve a higher hitting ratio in comparison to LRU and LFU.

Although some memory space is saved in MPC, the utilization of the cache is typically not high. Based on our observation, higher hitting rates can be achieved by intelligently utilizing vacant cache memory to contribute to a certain amount of hitting ratio. For example, when there is room in available memory, unpopular content can be stored. When the cache becomes full, unpopular content are removed, yielding space for popular ones. Furthermore, such strategy of caching less content, adopted by MPC, results in a slow convergence of MPC in terms of hitting rate performance.

As a remedy to the above limitations, we propose a novel replacement policy, dubbed Fine-Grained Popularity-based Caching (FGPC). Similar in spirit to MPC, FGPC maintains a large table to generate three kinds of statistic information, namely i) content names, ii) popularity levels of content by counting the frequency of appearances of a content name, and iii) time stamp of used content located in a cache. In order to quickly achieve high hitting rate, the cache always stores new coming content when it has available memory. To avoid inadequate replacement decision, once the cache is overflowed, FGPC checks the counting value of new content names. If the counter reaches a predetermined popularity threshold value, the new content will be stored using the LRU replacement policy; otherwise the new content is simply deleted.

Compared with the existing LRU/LFU or MPC solutions, the FGPC scheme has the following unique features:

- In FGPC, we carefully investigate the characteristics of CCN where content name includes prefixes. Thus, the high skewness of content popularity is the main reason to make MPC/FGPC ourperform LRU. We add a content popularity table to handle content name, content counter, and time stamp.

- The way Internet users request content is fine tuned with *Pareto* principle; that is 20% popular content are requested by 80% number of users.

- Popular content always appear with a high probability and vice versa. These common characteristics also indicate that the FGPC algorithm is feasible, practical, and compliant with the current Internet object access behavior.

Moreover, an enhanced version of FGPC, dubbed Dynamic FGPC (D-FGPC), is proposed. Because the number of content can be stored in a cache and the number of arrival requests to a

Table 1: Notation

Symbol	Definition
F	File size by default
F^P	Practical file size
$\alpha = \frac{F^P}{F}$	The variety factor of F
$\|F\|$	File number
$\|F\|F$	Catalog size
C_{size}	Cache size
$C_{size}^R = \frac{C_{size}}{\|F\|F} * 100\%$	Relative cache size

gateway/router is changing dynamically over time, the popularity threshold value should be adaptively adjusted on-the-fly over time, too. For this reason, the enhanced version of FGPC is called D-FGPC.

From the background of CCN [2], we import CCN strategy to all network elements on top of IP layer in the OPNET simulator [4] [5]. The existing LRU, MPC and our proposed FGPC and D-FGPC policies are successfully constructed in CCN nodes. Our simulation results prove that CCN is a good solution to existing challenges of traditional IP networks. The results indicate that FGPC and D-FGPC outperform LRU and MPC with highly effective caching.

For the sake of better readability, Table I lists up the notations used in this paper. The remainder of this paper is organized as follows. Section II provides some related research work. Section III introduces the two proposed content replacement algorithms, FGPC and D-FGPC. Section IV portrays the simulation setup and discusses the simulation results. Finally, Section V concludes this paper.

2. RELATED WORK

Recently, CCN has become a hot research area, and several projects and prototypes have applied CCN [6]- [11]. CCN is a network architecture, built on the Internet Protocol (IP) engineering principle, but treats content as a primitive. Further details on the CCN architecture can be found in [2].

Along with the overwhelming library of applications and services, millions of content exist on the Internet nowadays; an important portion of it being "User Generated Content" (UGC) [12]. To understand the nature and impact of UGC systems, the work conducted in [12] analyzes YouTube and Daum, the world's largest UGC Video on Demand (VoD) systems. The results show 10% of the top YouTube popular videos account for nearly 80% of views, while the rest 90% of the YouTube videos account for small number of requests. Daum data also reveals a similar behavior. In fact, the skewness in content popularity had been considered for a long time ago [13] [14] [15]. At this moment, the robustness of data traffic becomes critical and researches in ICT need to find out optimal solutions such as in-network caching to offload data traffic [16] [17].

Similarly, data traces are collected from two UGC sites in China, namely Youku and 6CN in [19]. The results indicate that top 5% videos contribute to over 80% views, which demonstrate higher skewness in video popularity in comparison to YouTube or Daum. An interesting implication of this skewed distribution is that, by storing only 5% to 10% of long-term popular videos, a cache can serve 80% of requests [18].

Edge caching is of vital importance for CCN. CCN becomes highly efficient with intelligent caching at edge routers/gateways. This efficiency degrades as caching occurs far from end-users [20]. However, global CCN caching, supported with Self-Organized Networking (SON) functions among caches can offer benefits well beyond only edge caching in sub-networks [21]. A variety of cache sizes and popularity skewness are often considered to have a positive effect on the performance of different replacement policies. In [22] and [23], the simulation results show that the overall network performance improves in case of large cache sizes or high skewness factors.

3. FGPC ALGORITHM

In MPC, the drawback of LRU is identified: the CCN default caching (as known as LRU/LFU) strategy always stores content at all nodes on the delivery path. This approach could replace popular content by unpopular ones. MPC is proposed with a caching less approach to solve the limitations of LRU/LFU. In the MPC, they key idea is to cache only the most popular content and that is in order to achieve high performance and save resources. However, on the other hand, caching less strategy causes two other problems. First, despite the fact that the probability appearance of unpopular content is small, they still help to contribute to a certain amount of hitting ratio. Moreover, in CCN standards, it is specified that to maximize the content-sharing probability with minimal upstream bandwidth demand and lower downstream latency, Content Stores (CS) should keep arriving data packages (DataPks) as long as possible. Second, with cashing less strategy, hitting rate slowly converges to a steady state. Hereunder, we introduce FGPC highlighting how it copes with the issues of LRU, LFU and MPC. A new variant of FGPC is portrayed afterwards.

3.1 FGPC strategy

In FGPC, each CCN node maintains a table containing statistics about the popularity of a content name and that is in the form of a content counter, along with a time stamp. Indeed, FGPC keeps track of popular content by locally counting the frequency of appearances of each content name. As shown in Fig. 1, there are three main operations conducted by FGPC:

- FGPC constantly updates three kinds of statistic information in the popularity table, i.e., content name, content counter and time stamp when receiving a content from upstream or delivering a content downstream.

- FGPC always stores newly arriving content (regardless their popularity) when CS has available space.

- When a CS is about to get full and a new content arrives, FGPC compares the popularity level of the new content (P_X) to a predefined popularity threshold value (P_{th}).If Px exceeds P_{th}, FGPC adopts the LRU policy to store the new content into CS. Otherwise, FGPC ignores the content and does not cache it.

In FGPC, CCN nodes achieve effective caching when they recognize the popularity levels of all content and keep popular content for longer times than other less popular content items. The

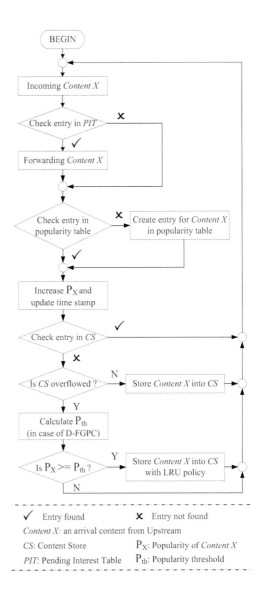

Figure 1: FGPC and D-FGPC flowchart.

trade-offs between performance and space availability as well as with computational complexity should be taken into account. In order to significantly reduce the overhead of the popularity table, algorithms such as the message-digest (MD5) Hash algorithm or mapping content names to digital numbers could be effective. For instance, to keep one million content names, and given the fact that a MD5 Hash value uses $16Bytes$ (i.e., $1B$ for counter and $3B$ for time stamp [3]), a CCN node would need an additional memory of merely $20 * 10^6 B$ or $19.0735MB$ for the popularity table. Nowadays, there is a clear technical trend that network devices are provided powerful packet processing and large memory. This makes no extra cost impact to the provider or to the users for in-network caching with FGPC approach.

3.2 D-FGPC strategy

In the basic FGPC scheme, the popularity threshold (P_{th}) is fixed for filtering popular content. Admittedly, this is not realistic as in real-life implementations, the popularity of a content changes with time. In addition, the number of arriving interest packages ($n_{interest}$), the practical file sizes (F^P) as well as available cache sizes (C_{size}) of different routers/gateways dynamically change. In this section, we define D-FGPC, as a new variant of FGPC with dynamic P_{th} adjustment. For the sake of better illustration, Fig.1 shows the main operations of both the FGPC and D-FGPC schemes. Hereunder, we discuss the relationship between the parameters P_{th}, $n_{interest}$, F^P and C_{size} as follows:

- Given a fixed F^P, when C_{size} increases, available memory of CS increases too. Then, P_{th} must decrease to relax the popularity-based content filtering and help fill up the available memory of CS as soon as possible. For this reason, D-FGPC fully utilizes the cache and converges faster than FGPC in case of large C_{size}.

- Given a fixed C_{size}, when F^P increases, the number of practical files stored on CS decreases. Then, P_{th} must increase to improve the popular content filtering. It should be noted that content in the memory are constructed by a lot of chunk files, and users normally request for completed content which include a group of chunk files together.

- Given a fixed C_{size}, when $n_{interest}$ increases, the number of newly coming content will also increase. In order to efficiently use the limited cache size and to accommodate the largest number of content requests, P_{th} must set up to higher values to enhance the popular content filtering.

Similarly, we have reverse situations and operations when C_{size}, F^P and $n_{interest}$ decrease, respectively. As above discussion about the relationship between the parameters P_{th}, $n_{interest}$, F^P and C_{size}, a dynamic setting of the popularity threshold can be achieved using Eq.1, whereby β is a constant that reflects the content filtering factor.

$$P_{th} = \beta * \frac{n_{interest} * F^P}{C_{size}} \qquad (1)$$

In the MPC and FGPC schemes, P_{th} is fixed at five [3]. In case of D-FGPC scheme, β should make the threshold value around five for a fair comparison with the MPC/FGPC performance. For example, when we set F^P and C_{size} to constant default values, e.g., the middle values in the range, $n_{interest}$ can be estimated every minutes, then β is determined when P_{th} is set at five. With the calculated β, when either F^P or C_{size} varies, P_{th} will vary around five too.

4. SIMULATION AND RESULTS

4.1 Network architecture

To evaluate the performance of FGPC and D-FGPC, we implemented CCN and conducted simulations using the OPNET Modeler 16.0 [4] [5]. In the simulations, CCN is overlayed over the IP layer. Indeed, we integrated the CCN processing modules into all network elements, such as routers, PCs, servers and IP Cloud. Fig.2 shows the envisioned OPNET model for CCN node processor which is integrated into routers.

With every intention to consider a typical Internet network topology, we envision the network topology as shown in Fig.3. Almost

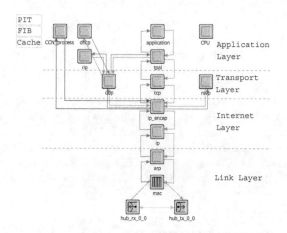

Figure 2: Procesor model of a simulated CCN node.

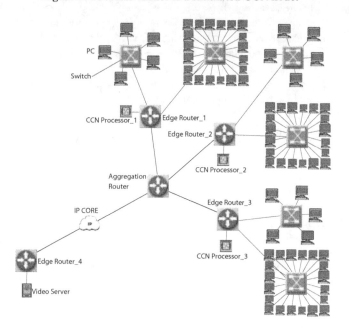

Figure 3: Envisioned network architecture.

all networks are built with three layers, i.e. *i)* the core layer provides optimal transport between core routers and distribution sites, *ii)* the distribution layer provides policy-based connectivity, peer reduction and aggregation, and *iii)* the access layer provides common group access to the internetworking environment. The simulated network includes three clusters of end users, distributed over a wide area network (WAN). Each cluster has an edge router, a CCN processor node, a switch and 25 PCs. All PCs request video content from a video server following a *Pareto* distribution: 20 PCs (80% traffic) request popular video content while the remaining five PCs (20% traffic) request unpopular video items. Videos are streamed from the video server through an IP core and then via aggregation routers, edge routers and finally received by CCN processors. After executing underlying video caching/replacement policies, CCN processors supply requesting PCs with requested video content when available at CCN nodes. In this paper, we apply FGPC and D-FGPC to edge routers to achieve the benefits of CCN [20] [21].

Table 2: Simulation parameters.

Element	Attribute	Value
WAN	Link between routers	OC-24 data rate
	Link for server	1000 BaseX
	Link for PCs	100 BaseT
Server	CCN root	ccnx://hust.edu.cn/epic/video/
	Publish root's name interval	100 seconds
	Number of video files ($|F|$)	500000 files
	A video size by default (F)	1 MB
	Practical video size (F^P)	0.5/ 1/ 1.5/ 2/ 2.5/ 3 MB
	The variety factor of F (α)	0.5/ 1/ 1.5/ 2/ 2.5/ 3
	Packet size	1024 bits
PCs	CCN directory	root/prefix1/.../prefix5
	File based popularity	*Pareto* principle
	Start time	100 + random(10) seconds
	Stop time	20000 seconds
	IntPk inter-arrival time	5 + random(2) seconds
	DataPk time-out	2 seconds
CCN node	Relative cache size (C_{size}^{R})	0.05/ 0.1/ 0.15/ 0.2/ 0.25/ 0.3%
	Replacement policy	LRU/ MPC/ FGPC/ D-FGPC
	The popularity threshold (P_{th})	5 (in case of MPC/FGPC)
	Hitting rate results sampling rate	0.1 Hz

The performance evaluation is conducted considering the impact of two metrics on the hitting rate; they are namely the relative cache size (C_{size}^{R}) and the factor of default file size (α) [22] [23]. The hitting rate for the three simulated edge routers is calculated as the ratio of the number of Interest packages (*IntPks*) satisfied at edge routers to the total number of *IntPks* from all PCs. Table II lists the values of important parameters considered in the simulations. These values were selected to reflect real-world implementations of in-network caching and that is considering prior research work [3] [22] [24] [25]. The simulations were run multiple times and the presented results are an average of these runs.

4.2 Simulation results

We first evaluate the performance of the different content caching/replacement policies for different cache sizes. The simulation duration is set to 20000 seconds. In the simulations, all PCs start sending *IntPks* from the 100th second. In Fig.4, the hitting rate results are obtained for each 1000 seconds.

In Fig.4, the relative cache size (C_{size}^{R}) at CCN node is increased by 0.05%, 0.1%, 0.15%, 0.2%, 0.25% and 0.3%. It should be noted that in the simulations, the catalog size is large (500000 files) while the cache size is small (equal to or less than 1500 files). For this reason, the relative cache size is equal to or less than 0.3%. In Fig.4, the obtained simulation results show that high hitting rates can be achieved for high cache sizes and that is for all simulated policies. From the figure, it becomes apparent that this increase in the hitting rate is not linear to increase in the cache volume. The figure also indicates that when the relative cache size is equal to 0.25%, the cache can handle most requests for popular content. However, increasing the relative cache size to 0.3% degrades the performance gain. There is thus a tradeoff between cache volume

(cost) and performance and there is consequently need to retrieve a suitable cache size.

Fig.4 also shows that in case of LRU, the hitting rate quickly increases when the cache becomes full. When the cache becomes overflowed, drawbacks of LRU happen and the hitting rate decreases gradually. This performance is mainly attributable to the intrinsic nature of LRU whereby caches store every new content. In contrast to LRU, MPC caches less and requires time to collect information about the popularity of content. Thus, we notice a slow increase of the hitting rate in case of MPC till it reaches a steady state. Incorporating the nice features of both LRU and MPC, the proposed FGPC scheme always stores new content when CCN nodes have available space. This explains the quick increase of FGPC's hitting rate. When the cache becomes overflowed, FGPC behaves similar to MPC and requires time to collect enough information about the popularity level of content. This feature results in a temporal decrease of the hitting rate (for a short time) before it continues increasing to the final state. Given the dynamic setting of the popularity threshold in D-FGPC, its hitting rate tends to be more stable, in comparison to FGPC, and that is during the entire simulation time as well as for several relative cache sizes.

Fig.5 compares among the performances of the four schemes when the relative cache size is set to 0.1%. The figure shows that D-FGPC outperforms all the other schemes, followed by FGPC, MPC and LRU, respectively. The figure also shows that LRU reaches higher cache hit ratio than others in the beginning of the simulations (i.e., until 6400s). The performance of LRU then degrades while other schemes achieve higher hitting rates. This is mainly due to the fact that D-FGPC, FGPC and MPC need time to assess the popularity of content before they start caching popular content.

Fig.6 further compares among the four schemes for different relative cache sizes. D-FGPC and FGPC exhibit always higher hitting

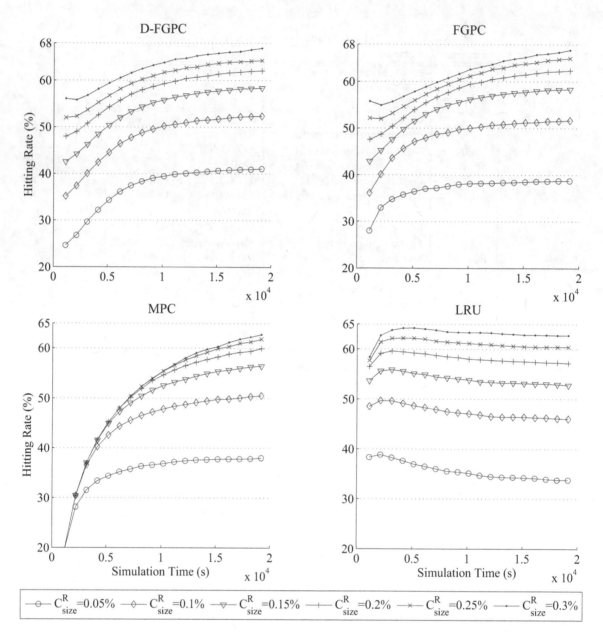

Figure 4: Performance of D-FGPC, FGPC, MPC and LRU for varying relative cache sizes.

rates in comparison to the conventional MPC and LRU schemes and that is in all situations. Furthermore, the figure reveals two important observations. First, when the relative cache size reaches 0.3%, the MPC performance quickly degrades and its hitting rate is just slightly higher than LRU. Second, with a dynamic threshold popularity value, the performance of D-FGPC is independent from the cache sizes. For example, when the relative cache size is small (e.g., 0.05%), the value of the popularity threshold is not optimal, making FGPC perform poorly in comparison to MPC. On the other hand, D-FGPC maintains always the highest hitting rate.

Fig.7 illustrates the effect of the factor of the default file size (α) on the hitting rate of the four simulated schemes and that is for a fixed relative cache size (0.15%). In this scheme, F^P is set to 0.5/1/1.5/2/2.5/3 MB in turn at the beginning of the simulation. It should be noted that despite the fact F^P may vary in real-life,

we do not capture this in the envisioned simulations and that is for the sake of simplicity. D-FGPC exhibits the best performance, followed by FGPC, MPC and LRU, respectively. From the figure, it becomes clear that for a small file size (e.g., $\alpha = 0.5$), the cache stores higher numbers of content. This trivially yields higher hitting rates. Furthermore, another reason is related to the number of arriving *IntPks* from all PCs. Indeed, in case of a stable data transmission rate, CCN nodes may take shorter times to satisfy requests for small-size files than in case of requests for large files.

5. CONCLUSION

In this paper, we introduced two variants of a new cache decision and replacement policy for CCN that takes into account content popularity. The performance of the proposed policy was eval-

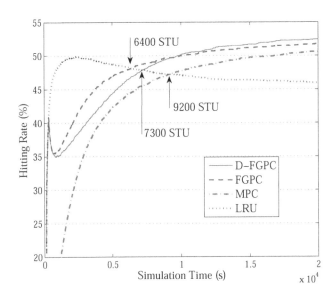

Figure 5: Multiple replacement policies with relative cache size (C_{size}^R) 0.1%.

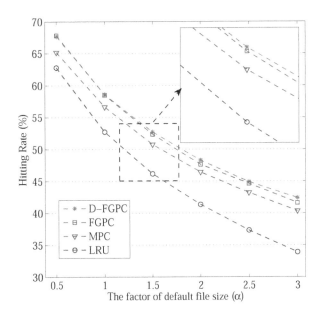

Figure 7: Final state of multiple replacement policies for varying values of α.

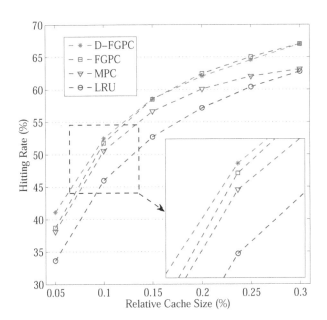

Figure 6: Final state of multiple replacement policies for varying C_{size}^R.

uated using computer simulations. The obtained results demonstrated the good performance of the proposed policy in achieving higher hitting rates and that is under different working conditions (e.g., cache size and file size). The performance of the proposed policy is expected to be largely improved with an efficient cooperation/contextual information (e.g., content popularity) sharing among neighboring CCN nodes to achieve self-organized networking of the CCN nodes and their caching. This defines one of the authors' future research directions with regard to CCN.

6. REFERENCES

[1] V. Jacobson, D. Smetters, J. Thornton, M. Plass, N. Briggs, and R. Braynard, "Networking named content", *Communication of the ACM*, Vol. 55, No. 1, pp. 117-124, Jan. 2012.

[2] CCNx protocol. Available: http://www.ccnx.org

[3] C. Bernardini, T. Silverston, and O. Festor, "MPC: Popularity-based Caching Strategy for Content Centric Networks", *IEEE International Conference on Comminication (ICC2013)*, pp. 2212-2216, Budapest, Hungary, Jun. 2013.

[4] OPNET Modeler. Available: www.opnet.com

[5] M. Chen, "OPNET Network Simulation", Press of Tsinghua University, ISBN 7-302-08232-4, 2004.

[6] Named Data Networking. Available: http://www.nameddata.net

[7] NS-3 based Named Data Networking (NDN) simulator. Available: http://ndnsim.net/index.html

[8] B. Han, X. Wang, T. Kwon, Y. Choi, and N. Choi, "AMVS-NDN : Adaptive Mobile Video Streaming with Offloading and Sharing in Wireless Named Data Networking", *IEEE INFOCOM, NOMEN Workshop*, Turin, Italy, April, 2013.

[9] X. N. Nguyen, D. Saucez, and T. Turletti, "Efficient caching in Content-Centric Networks using OpenFlow", *INFOCOM 2013 Workshop Proceedings (2013)*, pp. 1-2, Feb. 2013.

[10] M. Xie, I. Widjaja, and H. Wang, "Enhancing Cache Robustness for Content-Centric Networking", *INFOCOM 2013 Workshop Proceedings (2012)*, pp. 2426-2434, Mar. 2012.

[11] Y. Li ,H. Xie, Y. Wen, and Z. Zhang, "Coordinating In-Network Caching in Content-Centric Networks: Model

and Analysis", *Distributed Computing Systems (ICDCS) 2013*, pp. 62-72, Jul. 2013.

[12] M. Cha, H. Kwak, P. Rodriguez, Y. Ahn, and S.Moon, "Analyzing the Video Popularity Characteristics of Large-Scale User Generated Content Systems", *IEEE/ACM Transaction on Networking*, Vol. 17, No. 5, pp. 1357-1370, Oct. 2009.

[13] N. Eisley, L. Peh, and L. Shang, "In-Network Cache Coherence", *Proceedings of the 39th Annual IEEE/ACM International Symposium on Microarchitecture*, pp. 321-332, Dec. 2006.

[14] I. Psaras, W. K. Chai, and George Pavlou, "Probabilistic In-Network Caching for Information-Centric Networks", *ICN '12 Proceedings of the second edition of the ICN workshop on Information-centric networking*, pp. 55-60, Aug. 2012.

[15] T. Taleb, N. Kato, and Y. Nemoto, "Neighbors-Buffering Based Video-on-Demand Architecture", *in Signal Processing: Image Communication J.*, Vol. 18, No. 7, Aug. 2003, pp. 515-526.

[16] T. Taleb, Y. Hadjadj-Aoul, and K. Samdanis, "Efficient Solutions for Data Traffic Management in 3GPP Networks", *in IEEE Systems J.* (to appear)

[17] K. Samdanis, T. Taleb, and S. Schmid, "Traffic Offload Enhancements for eUTRAN", *in IEEE Communications Surveys & Tutorials J.*, Vol. 14, No. 3, Third Quarter 2012. pp. 884-896.

[18] X. Wang, M. Chen, T. Taleb, A. Ksentini, and V.C.M. Leung, "Cache in the air: exploiting content caching and delivery techniques for 5G systems", *in IEEE Communications Magazine*, Vol. 52, No. 2, Feb. 2014. pp.131-139

[19] G. Li, M. Wang, J. Feng, L. Xu, B. Ramamurthy, W. Li, and X. Guan, "Understanding User Generated Content Characteristics: A Hot-Event Perspective", *IEEE Communications Conference (IEEE ICC2011)*, pp. 1-5, Kyoto, Japan, Jun. 2011.

[20] G. Tyson, S. Kauney, S. Miles, Y. El-khatibz, A. Mauthez and A. Taweel, "A Trace-Driven Analysis of Caching in Content-Centric Networks", *IEEE Conference on Computer Communications and Networks (ICCCN)*, Munich, Germani, 2012.

[21] A. Ghodsi, T. Koponen, B. Raghavan, S. Shenker, A. Singla and J. Wilcox, " Information-Centric Networking: Seeing the Forest for the Trees", *Procedure of 10th ACM Workshop Hot Topics in Networks*, Nov. 2011.

[22] J. Li, H. Wu, B. Liu, J. Lu, Y. Wang, X. Wang, Y. Zhang, and L. Dong, "Popularity-driven Coordinated Caching in Named Data Networking", *ACM/IEEE symposium on Architectures for networking and communications systems (ANCS)*, pp. 15-26, Oct. 2012.

[23] Z. Ming, M. Xu, and D. Wangy, "Age-based Cooperative Caching in Information-Centric Networks", *IEEE Conference on Computer Communication Workshops (INFOCOM)*, pp. 268-273, Mar. 2012.

[24] D. Rossi, G. Rossini, "Caching performance of content centric networks under multi-path routing (and more)", Telecom ParisTech, Technical report, Paris, France, 2011.

[25] D. Rossi, G. Rossini, "A dive into the caching performance of Content Centric Networking", *Computer Aided Modeling and Design of Communication Links and Networks (CAMAD), 2012 IEEE 17th International Workshop on*, pp. 105-109, Sept. 2012.

Application Caching for Cloud-Sensor Systems

Yi Xu
CISE Department
University of Florida
Gainesville, FL32611, USA
yixu@cise.ufl.edu

Sumi Helal
CISE Department
University of Florida
Gainesville, FL32611, USA
helal@cise.ufl.edu

ABSTRACT

Driven by critical and pressing smart city applications, accessing massive numbers of sensors by cloud-hosted services is becoming an emerging and inevitable situation. Naïvely connecting massive numbers of sensors to the cloud raises major scalability and energy challenges. An architecture embodying distributed optimization is needed to manage the scale and to allow limited energy sensors to last longer in such a dynamic and high-velocity big data system. We developed a multi-tier architecture which we call Cloud, Edge and Beneath (CEB). Based on CEB, we propose an Application Fragment Caching Algorithm (AFCA) which selectively caches application fragments from the cloud to lower layers of CEB to improve cloud scalability. Through experiments, we show and measure the effect of AFCA on cloud scalability.

Categories and Subject Descriptors

C.2.1 [**Network Architecture and Design**]: Network Communications

Keywords

Cloud-sensor systems; Cloud computing; Application caching.

1. INTRODUCTION

Considering the emerging smart city developments and the massive number of sensors, devices and applications to be integrated into the cloud – the expected platform of choice, we argue that any proposed architecture for an efficient, scalable cloud-sensor operation must address the following challenges.

Cloud Scalability: Extensive interactions between cloud services and sensors could pose huge challenges to the cloud scalability. Connecting millions of sensors directly to the cloud is extremely demanding on cloud resources. It results in expensive cloud "attention", not only per sensor, but per each sensor duty cycle. For example, if sensors push data once every minute, millions of sensors will produce billions of sensor-cloud interactions, daily. As a result, the cloud economies of scale per sensor will not stand.

Sensor Energy Constraint: Unlike cloud resources with elastic supply, sensor devices cannot be provided on demand, and many of them are extremely vulnerable to power drainage. In smart city scenarios, a sensor may be queried by hundreds of applications each of which requires constant sensor readings. Without optimization, sensors' energy could be depleted rapidly, failing services and making them unreliable and unavailable.

Thus, a structural basis for optimizing the cloud's use of sensor hardware is needed or cloud-sensor systems will not be

dependable. To achieve this, we adopt a three-tier architecture that enables cross-layer optimizations [1]. Based on this architecture, we present a bi-directional waterfall optimization framework under which several optimizations can be carried out to achieve greater cloud scalability and energy-efficiency of sensors. We focus on one optimization in this paper – application caching and presents experiments and analysis of the algorithm.

2. CEB ARCHITECTURE OVERVIEW

In [1], we proposed a three-tier Cloud, Edge and Beneath (CEB) architecture whose layers are depicted in Figure 1. CEB is built on top of Atlas [2] that implements the service-oriented device architecture (SODA) model [3] and automates the process of sensor integration through a sensor platform and middleware which are integrated into the cloud availed for use by cloud applications. Because of the scope of this paper (cloud-to-edge application caching), we only explain the cloud and edge layers.

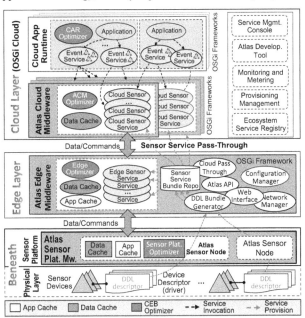

Figure 1. Overview of the CEB architecture

The edge runs one prong of the Atlas middleware which uses OSGi [4] as its basis to provide service discovery and configuration. The middleware includes a bundle generator, which when contacted by an initializing Atlas sensor platform, creates a pair software bundles for each sensor: 1) *edge sensor service* to be hosted at the Atlas edge middleware, 2) *cloud sensor service* to be uploaded to the Atlas cloud middleware. The pair of services communicate with each other enabling interlayer data passing.

The Cloud layer is built on OSGi Cloud [5] in which application is composed by loosely-coupled modules as OSGi services hosted at a distribution of cloud nodes (host OSGi framework) via cloud-wide discovery, configuration mechanisms. To help elaborate our work in this paper, we explain two specific components in the cloud layer most relevant to application caching.

Atlas Cloud Middleware (ACM): For every edge, there exists a corresponding ACM at the cloud. It hosts the cloud sensor service (passed from the edge) to be subscribed to by other cloud services. ACM acts as the cloud gateway to the lower layers, and meanwhile, it hosts the most basic "clouding" of sensors based on which sensor-based cloud applications can be built.

Cloud Application Runtime (CAR): The container where application-specific services are deployed and managed. Applications make invocation to the sensor services at the ACM to acquire raw sensor readings from the physical deployment.

CEB supports different application models that program smart space sensors into different levels of abstractions (e.g., events, activities, and phenomena). In this paper, we choose a specific application model E-SODA that abstracts sensor data into events.

2.1 E-SODA Application Model

E-SODA presents a particular service type *Event Service* which subscribes to and invokes the sensor services at the ACM to implement event-level abstractions of sensor data. An event service listens to the occurrence of a particular event which is a logical expression over sensor values (event composite grammars are shown in Equation 1) by processing its *event representation tree* (ERT) (Figure 2 illustrates an example).

$$
\begin{aligned}
E &= sensor\,(value)\mid sensor\,[a,b] &\text{(atomic event)}\\
&=\mid \sim E &\text{(negation)}\\
&=\mid E \vee E\mid E \wedge E &\text{(or/and)}\\
&=\mid E\,?\,E:E &\text{(condition operation)}\\
&=\mid E*time*E &\text{(sequence)}\\
&=\mid \{E\} &\text{(scope block)}
\end{aligned}
\tag{1}
$$

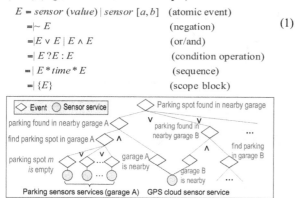

Figure 2. An example event representation tree (ERT)

We also introduce an application-specific relaxation operator, the time/frequency modifier (TFM), which is specified as follows:

$$
\begin{aligned}
TFM &=<W, I_e>\\
W &= nil\mid date/time - date/time\mid time - time\\
I_e &= Interval\ (\#\ of\ seconds)\ between\ two\ successive\ evaluations
\end{aligned}
\tag{2}
$$

W is a time window in which the affected event is evaluated with interval I_e. TFM allows programmers to relax event evaluations based on user specific demands or sensor semantics. It also enables aggregate query (piggyback) to be performed on multiple sensors connected to the same edge and applied to the same TFM.

3. BI-DIRECTIONAL WATERFALL OPTIMIZATION FRAMEWORK

In plain cloud-sensor systems, applications reside in the cloud which request and process data originating from the physical layer. We extend the plain model and propose a *bi-directional waterfall optimization framework* [7] which allows not only data to move upward but also allow application (fragment) to move downward and get cached at lower layers. In E-SODA, the cacheable application fragments are *events*. A cached event is evaluated at the layer it is cached to and its event value is pushed

back to its upper layer only when it changes (i.e., *selective push*). With application caching, the workload on the cloud can be dispersed or diffused across a group of edges or even sensor platforms. Therefore, *cloud scalability* as one challenge of cloud-sensor systems can be addressed effectively. Metaphorically, the bi-directional waterfall approach allows for most interesting data to flow up and for most curious applications to propagate down. Consequently, a local view of both data and applications and hence their interactions and interplays can be monitored and analyzed at any layers of the CEB, and therefore a number of optimization strategies can be implemented to optimize the energy consumption of the sensors. In this paper, we focus on one of the algorithms – Cloud-to-Edge Application Fragment Caching Algorithm (AFCA-1) which aims to improve the cloud scalability.

4. CLOUD-TO-EDGE APPLICATION FRAGMENT CACHING ALGORITHM

Caching application from the cloud to the edge layer reduces the workload of processing events on the cloud servers. Given the elasticity of the cloud, such workload reduction will shrink or slow down the growth of the cloud dimension in terms of the number of reserved cloud instances. Consequently, cloud scalability is improved. Meanwhile, caching events to the edge layer consumes resources in edge servers. Unlike the cloud, edge servers have limited resources and cannot unlimitedly cache applications from the cloud. In this sense, we propose the AFCA-1 algorithm to select the application fragments (i.e., events) from the cloud to cache down at the edge layer with the the Objective: *to minimize the cloud dimension (i.e., number of cloud instances)*, under the Constraint: *to stay within the resource limitations in edge servers*.

4.1 Implementation of Application Caching

Figure 3 depicts our implementation of caching applications from the cloud to the edge layer. In E-SODA, *event services* make for an ideal application fragments to cache. The machine instances in the cloud and edge layer all install the same OSGi environment, and after an event service is cached at the edge layer, it can automatically re-bind to the edge-level sensor services (peers of the cloud-level sensor services it subscribes to) via the *soft service binding* implemented by CEB [1] with minimum overhead. In addition, for any event (e.g., E_2 in Figure 3) cached to the edge layer, a "shadow service" of the cached event is correspondingly created in the ACM acting as a proxy of the cached event (e.g., E_2) to its consumers (e.g., E_1).

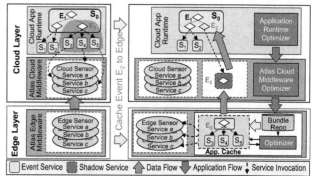

Figure 3. Implementation of application (event) caching

4.2 Understanding the Effect of App Caching

In our design, all cloud instances install the same AMI instantiated on a standard machine type *m1.medium* whose resource capacity is shown in Table I. For all instances, we adopt a common maximum memory and CPU utilization denoted as γ_1 and γ_2. Of all the components in the cloud layer, caching applications to the edge primarily affects the cloud resource usage in two components: CAR and ACM. In [6], we found that for both ACM and CAR, the dominant resources that determine the cloud dimension can be either *processing* or *memory*. For ACM, when processing resource becomes dominant, caching events to the edge reduces communication between CAR and ACM and between ACM and edge servers for evaluating the cached event. Thus, processing resource in ACM is saved due to reduced data transmission. On the other hand, event caching causes the addition of a shadow service to the ACM which introduces additional processing cost due to sending and receiving the value of the shadow event. When memory becomes dominant, caching event to the edge increases the memory cost because of the additional shadow service. For CAR, when processing becomes dominant, caching event to the edge reduces the processing resource consumed by the cached services. When memory becomes dominant, event caching releases the memory resource allocated for the cached service. The above cause-effect analysis between dominant resource usage at the ACM and CAR directly influences and guides the AFCA-1 algorithm.

Table I. Cloud instance resource capacity [6]

ECU	Memory	Storage	Bandwidth
2	3.75 GB	160 GB	–

4.3 Algorithm Description

AFCA-1 selects a set of events in the cloud applications to cache at the edge to maximize the reduction of the overall dominant resource usages in all affected cloud components. We describe the AFCA-1 (run at the cloud side) as follows. For each event in a cloud application, it calculates the overall *Benefit* of caching that event to the edge layer, and based on the calculation a group of events is selected to send to the edges for final caching decisions.

AFCA-1 (run at the Cloud App Runtime)
---
1. **for** each *Event* in an application construct its *ERT* as *T*
2. Partition *T* into areas (*sensors of an area connect to the same edge*);
3. **for** each *area*
4.   **for** each event *E* calculate its *Benefit(E)*; **endfor**
5.   ***selectedEvents = EventSelect**(area)*;
6.   Send *selectedEvents* to edge and wait for the response;
7.   Receive response (the events approved to cache) from edge;
8.   ***endfor***
9. ***endfor***

EventSelect method is to achieve the maximal total *Benefit* for the selected events while ensuring that at most one event is chosen at any branch in the *ERT*. *EventSelect* returns a *selectedEvents* which is a list of vectors for all selected events <*eventId, Benefit, C_{edge}*> ordered by *Benefit* (decreasing order). *Benefit(E)* is calculated as $(S_{AR}+S_{ACM})/C_{edge}$, where S_{AR} (Equation 3) and S_{ACM} (Equation 4) denote respectively the saving of resource usage for CAR and ACM after caching event *E* to the edge, and C_{edge} (Equation 5) denotes the extra resource usage added to edge.

$$S_{AR} = \begin{cases} 1/\gamma_1 \times \dfrac{\sum_{es \in ES} mem(es)}{M_c} & \text{(memory critical)} \\ 1/\gamma_2 \times \dfrac{\sum_{es \in ES} cpu\_time(es)}{elapsed\ time} & \text{(processing critical)} \end{cases} \quad (3)$$

ES denotes the event services that compose event *E*. In Figure 3, the *ES* for E_2 is $\{S_3, S_4, S_5\}$. *cpu_time(es)* denotes the observed amount of time spent for processing service *es* while the *elapsed time* is the total time of observation. *mem(es)* denotes the memory footprint of *es* while M_c is the total memory of the cloud instance.

$$S_{ACM} = \begin{cases} -\dfrac{1}{\gamma_1} \cdot \dfrac{mem_{shadow}}{M_c} & \text{(memory critical)} \quad (4) \\ \dfrac{1}{\gamma_2} \dfrac{(cc_s + cc_r)(\sum_{es \in ES} K \cdot f_e(es) - R_c)}{CR_c} & \binom{processing}{critical, K=1,2} \end{cases}$$

mem_{shadow} denotes the memory footprint of a shadow event service (constant). CR_c is the CPU clock rate of the cloud instance. cc_s and cc_r indicate the number of CPU cycles per packet send and receive respectively. $f_e(es)$ is the event evaluation frequency of *es* (*TFM*) which is also the rate at which *es* sends aggregate queries to the ACM before event caching (will be eliminated after caching). R_c denotes the change rate of the value of event E which is also the rate at which the cloud receives the event value from the edge after event caching. *K* is 1 if *es* only subscribes to public sensors, or 2 otherwise (invoke at least one dedicated sensor).

$$C_{edge} = \begin{cases} \dfrac{1}{\gamma'_1} \times \dfrac{\sum_{es \in ES} mem(es)}{M_e} & \text{(memory critical)} \quad (5) \\ \dfrac{1}{\gamma'_2} \times (C_{eval} + C_{trans}) & \text{(processing critical)} \end{cases}$$

γ_1' and γ_2' denote respectively the maximum memory and CPU utilization allocated for the edge. M_e is the total memory of the edge. C_{eval} and C_{trans} calculate the addition of CPU usage caused by evaluating event *E* (Equation 6) and by the change of data transmission rate between edge and cloud (Equation 7) respectively.

$$C_{eval} = \frac{\sum_{es \in ES} cpu\_time(es)}{elapsed\ time} \cdot \frac{CR_c}{CR_e} - \frac{\sum_{es \in ES} f_e(es) \cdot (cc_s + cc_r)}{CR_e} \quad (6)$$

$$C_{trans} = \frac{R_c \times cc'_s - req \times (cc'_s + cc'_r)}{CR_e} \quad (7)$$

CR_e is the CPU clock rate of the edge server. cc_s' and cc_r' are the number of CPU cycles per packet send and receive by the edge server. *req* denotes the frequency at which the cloud sends request to the edge to evaluate *E* before caching *E* to the edge.

When an edge makes decisions for event caching, events with higher *Benefit* always have higher priority to cache. To do so, for all the cached events the edge maintains a list of vectors <*eventId, Benefit, C_{edge}*> a.k.a. *EBC* whose elements are ordered by *Benefit* in the increasing order. When a new request (i.e., *selectedEvents*) arrives, the edge determines whether to cache or reject the events or replace with existing events based on the *EBC* and its resource availability. The edge-side AFCA-1 is described as follows.

AFCA-1 (run at the Edges)
---
1. Receive *selectedEvents* from the cloud;
2. **for** each <*eventId, Benefit, C_{edge}*> in *selectedEvents*
3.   **if** edge is not saturated *CL.add(eventId)*; // approve caching
4.   **else**
5.   *tSave, tCost, i = 0*;
6.   **while** *i < EBC.size* **and** *tCost < C_{edge}*
7.   <*e, b, c*>*=EBC.get(i)*; // (i+1)th smallest *Benefit* in *EBC*
8.   *tSave += b*c; tCost += c; i++*;
9.   **if** *i < EBC.size* **and** *Benefit > tSave/tCost*
10.   *CL.add(eventId)*; // replace existing events in *EBC*
11.   **endif**
12.   **endelse**
13. **endfor**
14. Cache events in *CL*, send *CL* to the cloud and update *EBC*
---

5. Validation of AFCA-1 Algorithm

To validate AFCA-1, we set up a prototype of CEB [1] as experimental testbed on which smart home apps are deployed. We synthesized a benchmark for both sensor data and applications

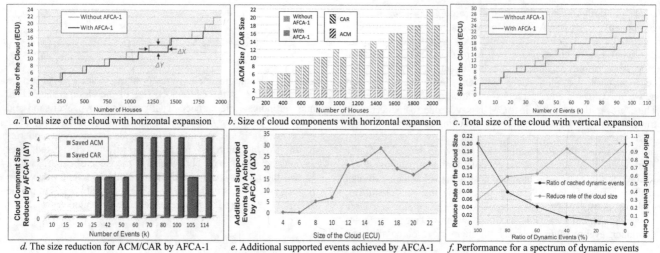

a. Total size of the cloud with horizontal expansion   *b.* Size of cloud components with horizontal expansion   *c.* Total size of the cloud with vertical expansion

d. The size reduction for ACM/CAR by AFCA-1   *e.* Additional supported events achieved by AFCA-1   *f.* Performance for a spectrum of dynamic events

Figure 4. Experiment Results of AFCA-1 Validation

and also classified two types of cloud-sensor system expansion: "*Horizontal*" in which applications are built on dedicated or exclusive sensors (deploying a new application requires installing its associated sensors), and "*Vertical*" where applications are built on pre-existing, sharable sensors which are not bounded to any individual application (adding new services does not require installing additional sensors).

For *horizontal expansion*, Figure 4.*a* shows the growth of the entire cloud and Figure *b* shows the growth of individual CAR and ACM. We observed two offsets: ΔY, the reduction of the cloud size achieved by AFCA-1 to support a particular number of houses, and ΔX, the number of additional houses that can be supported in the cloud by AFCA-1. From the results, both ΔX and the average of ΔY increase as more houses joining the system. However drop for both offsets occurs when the house number reaches ~1500 and then go back to increase again. This can be explained by Figure *b*, in which AFCA-1 reduces the size of CAR, but increases the size of ACM. This is because, with horizontal expansion, the sensor sampling rate is relatively low (applications rarely share sensors) which makes memory become the dominant resource for ACM. The caching of applications adds to the memory cost to the ACM, so more cloud instances are required to accommodate the increased memory demand.

Under *vertical expansion*, the number of events increases with constant number of sensors. Figure 4.*c* shows the growth of the size of the entire cloud. Figure *d* presents the reduction of the size for each of ACM and CAR achieved by AFCA-1 (ΔY), while Figure *e* shows the additional events that can be held by the cloud achieved by the AFCA-1 (ΔX). From Figure *c* and *d*, AFCA-1 does not show any effects until the number of events reaches ~25k. This is because the sensor sampling rate is relatively low when there are few events sampling the sensors which makes the memory become the dominant resource for the ACM, and AFCA-1 thinks the cost of application caching to ACM outweighs the saving to CAR. From Figure *d* and *e*, both the ΔX and ΔY offsets increase as the system expands, and stop after the scale reaches a certain level (event number: ~60k, cloud size: 16). This is because most of the edge servers are saturated and event replacement is used in applications caching.

We also validated the reaction of AFCA-1 to event dynamics. We first classified the events into *dynamic event* and *static event*

in terms of the rate of event value change. We changed the ratio of the dynamic events in the event set and kept all edge servers in saturate mode, and recorded the results in Figure 4.*f*. From the results, we can see that as the number of the dynamic events decreases, AFCA-1 performance improves from ~6% to ~20%, and the proportion of the dynamic events among all cached events decreases but in a non-liner manner. This result validates that the AFCA-1 performs better when there are more static events in the applications.

6. CONCLUSION

We presented an application caching algorithm (AFCA-1) whose objective is to improve cloud scalability in large-scale cloud-sensor systems anticipated to implement emerging smart urban spaces and smart cities. We also briefly presented the overarching architecture for AFCA-1 - the CEB architecture which embodies a bi-directional data/application caching optimization framework. We presented an extensive evaluation study based on analysis and experimental validation of target performance metrics.

7. REFERENCES

[1] Xu, Y. and Helal, A. 2014. Scalable Cloud-Sensor Architecture for the Internet of Things, Submitted for pub. UF Mobile and Pervasive Computing Lab Technical Report: http://www.icta.ufl.edu/projects/publications/ceb.pdf

[2] King, J., Bose, R., Yang, H., Pickles, S., and Helal, A. 2006. Atlas - A Service-Oriented Sensor Platform: Hardware and Middleware to Enable Programmable Pervasive Spaces. In *Proceedings of the first IEEE International Workshop on Practical Issues in Building Sensor Network Applications*. Tampa, Florida, November 2006, 630-638.

[3] Deugd, S., Carroll, R., Kelly, K.E., Millett, B., and Ricker. J. 2006. SODA: Service Oriented Device Architecture. *IEEE Pervasive Computing*, Volume 5 Issue 3, July 2006.

[4] OSGi 4.2. http://www.osgi.org/Download/Release4V42

[5] OSGi Cloud Computing. https://www.osgi.org/bugzilla/show_bug.cgi?id=114.

[6] Amazon EC2. http://aws.amazon.com

[7] Xu, Y. and Helal, A. 2014. An Optimization Framework for Cloud-Sensor Systems. To be submitted. http://www.icta.ufl.edu/projects/publications/waterfall.pdf

Efficient Data Compression with Error Bound Guarantee in Wireless Sensor Networks

Mohammad Abu Alsheikh
Nanyang Technological
University
Singapore 639798
mohammad027@e.ntu.edu.sg

Puay Kai Poh
National University of
Singapore
Singapore 119077
puaykai@nus.edu.sg

Shaowei Lin
Institute for Infocomm
Research
Singapore 138632
lins@i2r.a-star.edu.sg

Hwee-Pink Tan
Institute for Infocomm
Research
Singapore 138632
hptan@i2r.a-star.edu.sg

Dusit Niyato
Nanyang Technological
University
Singapore 639798
dniyato@ntu.edu.sg

ABSTRACT

We present a data compression and dimensionality reduction scheme for data fusion and aggregation applications to prevent data congestion and reduce energy consumption at network connecting points such as cluster heads and gateways. Our in-network approach can be easily tuned to analyze the data temporal or spatial correlation using an unsupervised neural network scheme, namely the autoencoders. In particular, our algorithm extracts intrinsic data features from previously collected historical samples to transform the raw data into a low dimensional representation. Moreover, the proposed framework provides an error bound guarantee mechanism. We evaluate the proposed solution using real-world data sets and compare it with traditional methods for temporal and spatial data compression. The experimental validation reveals that our approach outperforms several existing wireless sensor network's data compression methods in terms of compression efficiency and signal reconstruction.

Categories and Subject Descriptors

C.2.1 [**Network Architecture and Design**]: Wireless Communication; E.4 [**Coding and Information Theory**]: Data Compaction and Compression

Keywords

Lossy data compression; error guarantee; wireless sensor networks; neural network

1. INTRODUCTION

Many wireless sensor networks today play an important role in collecting big amounts of real-time sensing data over

large areas. A gateway, for instance, may gather data from the sensor network before sending it over long distances to a base station. The sensor network might also have cluster heads that aggregate the data from its corresponding nodes for transport to other cluster heads. Data compression and dimensionality reduction in wireless sensor networks (WSNs) refer to the problem of encoding the data collected from sensor nodes using fewer bits. Compression at cluster heads, gateways, or even within a sensor node with multiple sensing units, is one key ingredient in prolonging network lifetime [2]. Moreover, archiving the collected data for several years requires a tremendous capacity of storage that ranges from terabytes to petabytes [3]. However, traditional data compression schemes from information and coding theory cannot be directly applied to a resource limited framework like WSNs as they are designed to optimize storage rather than energy consumption [8].

Lossy compression methods in WSNs are preferable over the lossless ones as they provide better compression ratio at lower computational cost [8]. However, most traditional lossy data compression algorithms in WSNs lack an error guarantee mechanism due to the high computational demand of data decompression and reconstruction [8]. Therefore, many existing lossy methods rely on statistical analysis to examine the probability of data loss or assume the data loss is due to noise effects such that the loss can be ignored [13]. Moreover, the complexity of the decompression routine becomes critical when the data destination is another node in the network. Thus, the computational complexity of data decompression is still an important concern.

The above discussion motivates the need for one solution that collectively supports the aforementioned design essentials. Briefly, our main contributions are as follows.

- We propose a low-cost (both compression and decompression) lossy compression technique with error bound guarantee. The routines for compression and decompression are implemented using only linear and sigmoidal operations.

- Unlike many traditional methods, our method is easily customized for both temporal and spatial compression. This allows the design of a uniform sensing framework that does not require many dedicated compression solutions, one for each application.

- Experiments over real world data sets show that the algorithm outperforms several well-known and traditional methods for data compression in WSNs.

2. RELATED WORKS

In this section, we identify a variety of coding schemes in the literature [8, 13, 16], and discuss some important considerations for signal compression in WSNs.

The lightweight temporal compression (LTC) algorithm [12] is an efficient method that finds a piece-wise linear representation for time series in sensor data. Unfortunately, it performs poorly if the sensor readings fluctuate frequently, even when the fluctuations follow some fixed patterns over time. Moreover, as its name implies, it can only be used for temporal data compression. Principal component analysis (PCA) has been widely used to extract dominant linear features in sensor readings [9]. Another large class of lossy data compression techniques involves the transformation of the raw data into other data domains. Examples of these methods are based on discrete Fourier transforms (DFT) and fast Fourier transforms (FFT) [16] and the different types of discrete cosine transforms (DCT) [7]. However, such algorithms suffer from poor performance when used to compress data spatially or when noise is present in the collected readings.

If a sparse representation for the given signals is known, compressive sensing (CS) is another framework for transforming the signal into an efficient compressed form, which will be used later to recover an approximation of the original signal, e.g., [14]. However, the assumption of sparsity in the input signal can be highly restrictive, as the sensor data may not be sparse in the time domain, the frequency domain, or even in some other traditional domains. Moreover, introducing a few noisy readings may corrupt the sparse data representation, and the complexity of CS's data decoding hinders the development of an error bound for such lossy methods. For dictionary-based lossless data compression in WSNs, the Sensor Lempel-Ziv-Welch (S-LZW) algorithm [10] is a typical approach. However, S-LZW does not consider the temporal and spatial characteristics of collected data which, if used, can significantly enhance the compression performance.

3. NEURAL AUTOENCODERS

An autoencoder (or auto-associative neural network encoder) is a three-layer neural network that maps an input vector $\vec{x} \in \mathbb{R}^N$ to a hidden representation $\vec{y} \in \mathbb{R}^K$ and finally to an output vector $\vec{z} \in \mathbb{R}^N$ that approximates the input $\vec{x}$, as shown in Figure 1. The vectors satisfy

$$\vec{y} = F\left(\mathbf{W}_{enc}\vec{x} + \vec{\mathbf{b}}_{enc}\right) \tag{1a}$$

$$\vec{z}_{\boldsymbol{\theta}}(\vec{x}) = F\left(\mathbf{W}_{dec}\vec{y} + \vec{\mathbf{b}}_{dec}\right) \tag{1b}$$

$$F(v) = \frac{1}{1 + \exp(-v)} \tag{1c}$$

where $\boldsymbol{\theta} := [\mathbf{W}_{enc}, \vec{\mathbf{b}}_{enc}, \mathbf{W}_{dec}, \vec{\mathbf{b}}_{dec}]$ are real-valued parameters that must be learned by a suitable training algorithm,

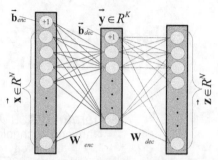

Figure 1: Using AE to project the data to a lower dimensional representation ($K \ll N$).

and $F(\cdot)$ is the sigmoidal logistic function (other nonlinear function such as the hyperbolic tangent can also be used). The parameters $\mathbf{W}_{enc}$ and $\vec{\mathbf{b}}_{enc}$ are the encoding weight matrix and bias respectively, while $\mathbf{W}_{dec}$ and $\vec{\mathbf{b}}_{dec}$ are the decoding weight matrix and bias. The entries of $\vec{y}$ and $\vec{z}$ are sometimes called activations.

To learn optimal neural weights $\boldsymbol{\theta}$ using training data $\mathbf{D}$, we define the cost function of the basic autoencoder (AE):

$$\Gamma_{\text{AE}}(\boldsymbol{\theta}, \mathbf{D}) = \frac{1}{|\mathbf{D}|} \sum_{\vec{x} \in \mathbf{D}} \frac{1}{2} \|\vec{x} - \vec{z}_{\boldsymbol{\theta}}(\vec{x})\|^2. \tag{2}$$

This function penalizes the difference between each input data vector $\vec{x}$ and its reconstruction $\vec{z}_{\boldsymbol{\theta}}(\vec{x})$. Consequently, the optimal neural weights may be computed using standard optimization algorithms such as the limited memory Broyden–Fletcher–Goldfarb–Shanno (L-BFGS) algorithm.

Different variants of the basic AE have been introduced in the literature to discourage the neural network from overfitting the training data. Generally speaking, these regularization methods penalize the neural weight characteristics or the hidden layer sparsity characteristics.

Weight decaying autoencoder (WAE): In this variant, the cost function is defined with an extra weight decay term:

$$\Gamma_{\text{WAE}}(\boldsymbol{\theta}, \mathbf{D}) = \Gamma_{\text{AE}}(\boldsymbol{\theta}, \mathbf{D}) + \frac{\beta}{2}\left(\|\mathbf{W}_{enc}\|^2 + \|\mathbf{W}_{dec}\|^2\right) \tag{3}$$

where $\|\mathbf{W}\|^2$ represents the sum of the squares of the entries of a matrix $\mathbf{W}$, and β is a hyperparameter[1] that controls the contribution from the weight decay term.

Sparse autoencoder (SAE): This version extracts a sparse data representation at the hidden layer, i.e. we want most of the entries of $\vec{y}$ to be close to zero. Sparsity is encouraged by adding the Kullback–Leibler (KL) divergence function [6]:

$$\Gamma_{\text{SAE}}(\boldsymbol{\theta}, \mathbf{D}) = \Gamma_{\text{WAE}}(\boldsymbol{\theta}, \mathbf{D}) + \eta \sum_{k=1}^{K} \text{KL}(\rho \| \hat{\rho}_k) \tag{4a}$$

$$\text{KL}(\rho \| \hat{\rho}_k) = \rho \log_e \frac{\rho}{\hat{\rho}_k} + (1 - \rho) \log_e \left(\frac{1 - \rho}{1 - \hat{\rho}_k}\right) \tag{4b}$$

where η is a hyperparameter that controls the sparsity weight, ρ is the sparsity parameter (target activation) that is chosen

---

[1]A hyperparameter is a variable that is selected a priori. This differentiates it from a model parameter, e.g., the encoding weight, which is adjusted during the learning process.

to be close to zero, and $\hat{\rho}_k$ is the average activation of the k-th node in the hidden layer.

4. LOSSY COMPRESSION WITH ERROR BOUND GUARANTEE

We propose to apply the autoencoder to the data compression and dimensionality reduction problem in WSNs to represent the captured data using fewer bits as demonstrated in Figure 2. This is motivated by reasons related to WSN characteristics, as well as the ability of AEs to automatically extract features in the data. Firstly, similar to other lossy data compression algorithms, it is important to realize that AEs are used to extract a suitable, low-dimensional, code representation that retains most of the information content of the original data. This process of automatic feature extraction is not, by any means, intended to randomly discard data items, but instead to find better data representation domains. Secondly, sensor networks are used to collect data in a variety of distinct situations each with its network structure and data patterns. Therefore, the designer must be familiar with a collection of temporal and spatial compression algorithms to support each case. In contrast, the proposed algorithm has the flexibility of supporting many scenarios using one technique. Thirdly, AEs are commonly used to extract intrinsic features that can be used by several data analysis, manipulations, storage, communications, and visualization algorithms [4]. Further, AEs with nonlinear activation transfer functions, such as the logistic regression, can learn more representative features than the well-known PCA algorithm [5]. Fourthly, the distributed data compression alleviates the need for data archiving and storage solutions (for such lossy data archiving solution on database systems, please see [3]). Indeed, the centralized solutions focus on data compression and archiving into the database systems, without considering the bandwidth and the energy limitations during the data funneling and aggregation. Finally, after learning the AE's parameters, the process of data encoding and decoding can be simply programmed with a few lines of code. On the one hand, the simplicity of the encoding process is important as the nodes are resource limited devices. On the other hand, the decoder complexity is crucial when sending data between the sensors or when dealing with thousands of sensor nodes sending their compressed data continually to a central base station, i.e., as the base station will be required to decompress big data set.

4.1 Error bound mechanism

In some applications, it is important to provide a guarantee that the reconstructed signal is close to the original (source). The error bound ϵ_{bound} is defined as the maximum acceptable difference between each collected reading by the sensor and the recovered one by the receiver after receiving the compressed representation. Basically, the error bound is tuned by considering several factors such as the application requirements and the used sensors' precision. For example, the RM Young/05103 wind monitor sensor [15] measures the wind speed and direction with accuracy of 0.3 m/s and 5°C, respectively. Thus, setting the error bound to be equal to the sensor accuracy may be an acceptable design basis.

Our method first computes the residual $\vec{r} = \vec{p} - \vec{q}$ between the source $\vec{p}$ and the recovered data $\vec{q}$, as shown in Figure 3. Any entry of the residual vector exceeding the bound ϵ_{bound}

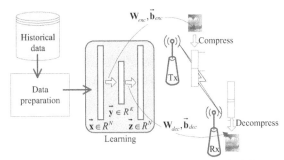

Figure 2: AE adoption for data compression and dimensionality reduction in wireless sensor networks. Initially, the network's parameters $\mathbf{W}_{enc}, \vec{\mathbf{b}}_{enc}, \mathbf{W}_{dec}$, and $\vec{\mathbf{b}}_{dec}$ are adjusted during the learning stage (offline mode). Subsequently, the encoding part will be executed in the transmitter side (Tx) to achieve a compressed representation of the data. Then the receiver (Rx) will deploy the decoding part to recover a proper approximation of the original signal.

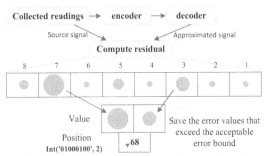

Figure 3: The error bound mechanism performed by the transmitting node.

will be transmitted, using the residual code

$$\vec{\varepsilon} = \text{residualCode}(\vec{r}, \epsilon_{bound}) = \left(\mathbb{1}_I, (r_i)_{i \in I}\right) \quad (5)$$

where $I \subset \{1, \ldots, N\}$ is the set of indices i where $r_i > \epsilon_{bound}$ and $\mathbb{1}_I$ is the indicator vector for the subset I, i.e. $(\mathbb{1}_I)_i = 1$ if $i \in I$ and $(\mathbb{1}_I)_i = 0$ if $i \notin I$. Conversely, given the code $\vec{\varepsilon}$, it is easy to compute an estimate of the original residual by constructing a vector whose zeros are determined by $\mathbb{1}_I$ and whose non-zero entries are given by $(r_i)_{i \in I}$. We denote this vector as residual($\vec{\varepsilon}$).

4.2 Data sphering

The entries of the output vector $\vec{z}$ of the AE come from the sigmoid function, so they are all between 0 and 1. Because the AE attempts to reconstruct the input vector $\vec{x} \in \mathbb{R}^N$, we need to normalize our input data so that the entries are also between 0 and 1. Moreover, for the AE to work, the input data vectors must be distributed somewhat uniformly near the unit sphere in $\mathbb{R}^N$. This process is called data sphering [6]. One simple method involves truncating readings that lie outside three standard deviations from the vector mean, and rescaling the remaining readings so that they lie between 0.1 and 0.9. In particular, the formula is

$$\begin{aligned} \vec{x} &= \text{normalize}(\vec{p}, \sigma) \\ &= 0.5 + \frac{0.4}{3\sigma} \max\left(\min\left(\vec{p} - \text{mean}(\vec{p}), 3\sigma\right), -3\sigma\right) \end{aligned} \quad (6)$$

where $\vec{p}$ is the data vector and σ is the standard deviation of the entries of $\vec{p} - \text{mean}(\vec{p})$ over all $\vec{p}$ in the training data set. Furthermore, assuming the data is normally distributed, the probability that a reading is located within three standard deviations from the mean is 99.7%. Conversely, given the mean m, the original data vector $\vec{p}$ may be reconstructed (up to truncated outliers) using the formula:

$$\text{denormalize}(\vec{x}, m, \sigma) = \frac{3\sigma}{0.4}(\vec{x} - 0.5) + m. \qquad (7)$$

4.3 Training, encoding and decoding

After describing different components of our algorithms, we are now ready to put them together. We assume that all the data mentioned in this section have been aligned and that missing values have been filled in. For the training data $\mathbf{D}$, we also ensure that outliers were removed and that readings were normalized. Let σ denote the standard deviation used in the normalization of the data.

We first learn optimal weights $\boldsymbol{\theta}$ for the autoencoder by minimizing the cost function $\Gamma_{\text{WAE}}(\boldsymbol{\theta}, \mathbf{D})$ using the L-BFGS algorithm. This computationally-intensive process only occurs once at the start of our network deployment, and the parameters $\boldsymbol{\theta}, \sigma$ are distributed to the transmitters and receivers.

The algorithms for compressing and decompressing the sensor readings are outlined in Algorithms 1 and 2 respectively. For our experiments, we send the compressed signal $(\vec{y}, \vec{\varepsilon}, m)$ using floating point representation for the real numbers and binary string for the indicator vector $\mathbb{1}_I$ in $\vec{\varepsilon}$. Note that all the steps have low computational complexity. Here, we also see why decoder complexity in algorithms like compressed sensing impedes the provision of error bound guarantees.

Algorithm 1: The online data compression

Input: readings $\vec{p}$; parameters
$\qquad \sigma, \mathbf{W}_{enc}, \vec{\mathbf{b}}_{enc}, \mathbf{W}_{dec}, \vec{\mathbf{b}}_{dec}$
Output: signal $\vec{y}, \vec{\varepsilon}, m$
begin
$\qquad m \leftarrow \text{mean}(\vec{p})$
$\qquad \vec{x} \leftarrow \text{normalize}(\vec{p}, \sigma)$
$\qquad \vec{y} \leftarrow F(\mathbf{W}_{enc}\vec{x} + \vec{\mathbf{b}}_{enc})$
$\qquad \vec{z} \leftarrow F(\mathbf{W}_{dec}\vec{y} + \vec{\mathbf{b}}_{dec})$
$\qquad \vec{q} \leftarrow \text{denormalize}(\vec{z}, m, \sigma)$
$\qquad \vec{\varepsilon} \leftarrow \text{residualCode}(\vec{p} - \vec{q}, \epsilon_{bound})$

Algorithm 2: The online data decompression

Input: signal $\vec{y}, \vec{\varepsilon}, m$; parameters $\sigma, \mathbf{W}_{dec}, \vec{\mathbf{b}}_{dec}$
Output: reconstruction $\vec{p}$
begin
$\qquad \vec{z} \leftarrow F(\mathbf{W}_{dec}\vec{y} + \vec{\mathbf{b}}_{dec})$
$\qquad \vec{q} \leftarrow \text{denormalize}(\vec{z}, m, \sigma)$
$\qquad \vec{r} \leftarrow \text{residual}(\vec{\varepsilon})$
$\qquad \vec{p} \leftarrow \vec{q} + \vec{r}$

---

5. EXPERIMENTAL RESULTS

We evaluate the performance of the proposed algorithm using data from actual sensor test beds. Our data set is divided into 10 random folds for training and testing. In each experiment, the system is trained using 9 folds and tested using the last fold. Due to randomness in initializing the neural weights, we conduct each experiment 20 times to ensure consistency in the test results. Therefore, the system performance presented is the average obtained from 200 experiments. Our implementation adopts the L-BFGS algorithm [1] to tune the AE's weights during the learning stage. We define the following error metrics:

$$\text{Mean absolute error} = \epsilon_{abs} = \frac{1}{N}\sum_{i=1}^{N}|p_i - q_i| \qquad (8a)$$

$$\text{Relative error} = \epsilon_{rel} = \frac{\sum_{i=1}^{N}|p_i - q_i|^2}{\sum_{i=1}^{N}p_i^2} \times 100 \qquad (8b)$$

where p_i is the i-th entry of the input vector $\vec{p} \in \mathbb{R}^N$ and q_i is the reconstructed value for p_i. To measure the extent that the data is being compressed, we use the following metric:

$$\text{Compression ratio} = CR = \left(1 - \frac{B(\vec{y}) + B(\vec{\varepsilon})}{B(\vec{p})}\right) \times 100 \qquad (9)$$

where $B(\vec{y})$, $B(\vec{\varepsilon})$, and $B(\vec{p})$ are the number of bits used to represent the compressed, the residual, and the original data, respectively. We evaluate our solution using meteorological data set from the Grand-St-Bernard deployment [11]. We use data from 23 sensors that collect surface temperature readings between Switzerland and Italy at an elevation of 2.3km. This data set contains readings ranging from $-32°C$ to $48°C$, though observations suggest that the maximum and minimum values are most likely from a malfunctioning sensor node.

5.1 Overall performance

As shown in Figure 4, our algorithm demonstrates better performance on real world data sets when compared to traditional methods for data compression in WSNs. The data compression is considered as a challenging task due to the non-uniform data distribution through different sensor nodes. Comparatively, using basic AE or WAE provides the best performance over the other AE's variants (Figure 4a). Moreover, WAE outperforms other traditional compression methods such as PCA, DCT and FFT (Figure 4b).

LZW is commonly used as a basis for comparison against other data compression algorithms. In our modified method, we first convert the base-10 floating point readings into the base-2 representation, e.g., 10.51 is represented as 00001010.1 under 0.1 error bound. As a result, the truncated LZW algorithm can be realized as a lossy data compression scheme with a compression ratio that significantly outperforms the traditional LZW method. Moreover, we chose LTC algorithm for bench-marking as several comparative studies, e.g., [16], discussed the efficiency of the LTC algorithm over other methods. Even though the used high resolution data set is very suitable for the LTC method as the data changes slowly between subsequent samples, the compression efficiency of the proposed algorithm is still superior (Figure 4c). We note that LTC performs as well as AE for large error bounds, but is unable to keep up when the error bound is small. On the other hand, the truncated LZW does well for small error

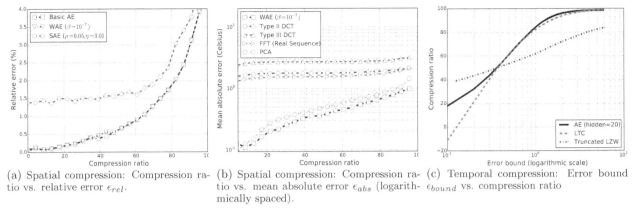

(a) Spatial compression: Compression ratio vs. relative error ϵ_{rel}.

(b) Spatial compression: Compression ratio vs. mean absolute error ϵ_{abs} (logarithmically spaced).

(c) Temporal compression: Error bound ϵ_{bound} vs. compression ratio

Figure 4: Experimental results and validation of the spatial and temporal compression techniques.

bounds since it is suited for lossless compression, but fails to handle large error bounds. Moreover, the truncated LZW is more computationally- and memory-intensive than AE, making it unsuitable for simple sensor nodes.

6. CONCLUSION

Instead of using computationally expensive transformations on raw data or introducing strong assumptions on data statistical models, we proposed an adaptive data compression with feature extraction technique using AEs. Our solution exploits spatial-temporal correlations in the training data to generate a low dimensional representation of the raw data, thus significantly prolonging the lifespan of data aggregation and funneling systems. Moreover, the algorithm can optionally be adjusted to support error bound guarantee.

7. REFERENCES

[1] R. H. Byrd, P. Lu, J. Nocedal, and C. Zhu. A limited memory algorithm for bound constrained optimization. *SIAM Journal on Scientific Computing*, 16(5):1190–1208, 1995.

[2] E. Fasolo, M. Rossi, J. Widmer, and M. Zorzi. In-network aggregation techniques for wireless sensor networks: A survey. *IEEE Wireless Communications*, 14(2):70–87, 2007.

[3] S. Gandhi, S. Nath, S. Suri, and J. Liu. GAMPS: Compressing multi sensor data by grouping and amplitude scaling. In *Proceedings of the International Conference on Management of Data*, pages 771–784. ACM, 2009.

[4] G. E. Hinton and R. R. Salakhutdinov. Reducing the dimensionality of data with neural networks. *Science*, 313(5786):504–507, 2006.

[5] N. Japkowicz, S. J. Hanson, and M. A. Gluck. Nonlinear autoassociation is not equivalent to PCA. *Neural computation*, 12(3):531–545, 2000.

[6] A. Ng. Sparse autoencoder. *CS294A Lecture notes*, page 72, 2011.

[7] G. Quer, R. Masiero, D. Munaretto, M. Rossi, J. Widmer, and M. Zorzi. On the interplay between routing and signal representation for compressive sensing in wireless sensor networks. In *Information Theory and Applications Workshop*, pages 206–215. IEEE, 2009.

[8] M. Razzaque, C. Bleakley, and S. Dobson. Compression in wireless sensor networks: A survey and comparative evaluation. *ACM Transactions on Sensor Networks*, 10(1):5, 2013.

[9] A. Rooshenas, H. R. Rabiee, A. Movaghar, and M. Y. Naderi. Reducing the data transmission in wireless sensor networks using the principal component analysis. In *Proceedings of the 6th International Conference on Intelligent Sensors, Sensor Networks and Information Processing*, pages 133–138. IEEE, 2010.

[10] C. M. Sadler and M. Martonosi. Data compression algorithms for energy-constrained devices in delay tolerant networks. In *Proceedings of the 4th International Conference on Embedded Networked Sensor Systems*, pages 265–278. ACM, 2006.

[11] T. Schmid, H. Dubois-Ferriere, and M. Vetterli. Sensorscope: Experiences with a wireless building monitoring sensor network. In *Workshop on Real-world Wireless Sensor Networks*, pages 13–17. Citeseer, 2005.

[12] T. Schoellhammer, E. Osterweil, B. Greenstein, M. Wimbrow, and D. Estrin. Lightweight temporal compression of microclimate datasets. In *Proceedings of the 29th Annual IEEE International Conference on Local Computer Networks*, pages 516–524. IEEE, 2004.

[13] T. Srisooksai, K. Keamarungsi, P. Lamsrichan, and K. Araki. Practical data compression in wireless sensor networks: A survey. *Journal of Network and Computer Applications*, 35(1):37–59, 2012.

[14] L. Xiang, J. Luo, and A. Vasilakos. Compressed data aggregation for energy efficient wireless sensor networks. In *Proceedings of the 8th Annual IEEE Communications Society Conference on Sensor, Mesh and Ad Hoc Communications and Networks*, pages 46–54, 2011.

[15] R. M. Young. *Model 05103 wind monitor manual*. R. M. Young Company.

[16] D. Zordan, B. Martinez, I. Vilajosana, and M. Rossi. To compress or not to compress: Processing vs transmission tradeoffs for energy constrained sensor networking. *arXiv preprint arXiv:1206.2129*, 2012.

Deterministic Distributed Rendezvous Algorithms for Multi-Radio Cognitive Radio Networks

Guyue Li
Tsinghua University
Beijing, P.R. China
liguyue12@gmail.com

Zhaoquan Gu
Tsinghua University
Beijing, P.R. China
demin456@gmail.com

Xiao Lin
Tsinghua University
Beijing, P.R. China
jackielinxiao@gmail.com

Haosen Pu
Tsinghua University
Beijing, P.R. China
phs199205@gmail.com

Qiang-Sheng Hua
Tsinghua University
Beijing, P.R. China
qshua@mail.tsinghua.edu.cn

ABSTRACT

Rendezvous is a fundamental process in constructing Cognitive Radio Networks (CRNs), through which the user can communicate with its neighbors by establishing a link on some licensed frequency band (channel). Most of the existing elegant rendezvous algorithms assume each user is equipped with a single radio. Nowadays the multi-radio cognitive radio architecture, where each user can access $k \geq 2$ channels at the same time, has become a reality. In this paper, we study the rendezvous problem in multi-radio CRN to see whether and to what extent the multi-radio capability can improve the rendezvous performance. To begin with, we propose a family of deterministic distributed algorithms for two special situations when $k = 2$ and $k = O(\sqrt{n})$, where n is the number of all channels. These algorithms show that the maximum time to rendezvous ($MTTR$) can be reduced (largely) in multi-radio CRN. Then we derive a lower bound of $MTTR$ as $\Omega(\frac{|V_i||V_j|}{k^2})$ for arbitrary k (V_i, V_j represents two users' available channel sets) and present a distributed algorithm to guarantee rendezvous in $O(\frac{|V_i||V_j|}{k^2})$ time slots, which meets the lower bound. Extensive simulations are conducted to corroborate our theoretical analyses.

Categories and Subject Descriptors

C.2.1 [**Network Architecture and Design**]: Wireless communication

Keywords

Multi-Radio; Cognitive Radio Network; Rendezvous

1. INTRODUCTION

Due to the rapid growth of wireless devices and the increasing demand for wireless services, the wireless spectrum

MSWiM'14, September 21–26, 2014, Montreal, QC, Canada.
Copyright 2014 ACM 978-1-4503-3030-5/14/09 ...$15.00.
http://dx.doi.org/10.1145/2641798.2641827.

has become very scarce. The unlicensed spectrum has been overcrowded such as the Industrial Scientific and Medical (ISM) band [11], while the utilization of some licensed spectrum is pretty low. Cognitive Radio Network (CRN) is such a promising paradigm to tackle the spectrum scarcity problem [2], where primary users (PUs) who own the licensed spectrum coexist with secondary users (SUs) that can opportunistically exploit and access the unused licensed spectrum. For convenience, "user" mentioned hereafter in the paper refers to SU.

Rendezvous is a fundamental process in constructing a CRN, through which two neighboring users can establish a link on some common frequency band (channel) for communication. Being a key role, rendezvous is the cornerstone of many interesting problems, such as message broadcasting [15, 24], routing [14], and data collection [6]. Generally speaking, the licensed spectrum is assumed to be divided into n non-overlapping channels (frequency bands) and the users are equipped with cognitive radios that can sense the usage of these channels. After the spectrum sensing stage, the users can find out the unused channels by the PUs, which we called *available channels* and they can access these channels for rendezvous at any time. Once two users access the same channel at the same time, rendezvous is achieved and they can communicate with each other. *Time to rendezvous(TTR)* is used to measure the time cost before rendezvous and denote *maximum time to rendezvous($MTTR$)* as the worst situation of the rendezvous algorithm, considering two users may have different sets of available channels when the spectrum usage of the PUs varies temporally and geographically.

The state-of-the-art rendezvous algorithms can be mainly divided into two categories: global sequence (GS) based algorithms [13, 19, 23] and local sequence (LS) based ones [7, 12]. GS algorithms design channel access strategies on the basis of all licensed channels, regardless of whether they are available. The best result [13] guarantees rendezvous for any two users in $O(n^2)$ time slots if their available channels sets intersect. LS algorithms make use of each user's available channels and they can reduce the TTR largely when the portion of available channels counts for a small fraction. Specifically, for two users with available channel sets V_i, V_j, [12] guarantees rendezvous in $O(|V_i|^2)$ (suppose $|V_i| \geq |V_j|$) time slots when each user has a distinct identifier and [7] guarantees rendezvous in $O(|V_i||V_j|\log\log n)$ time slots. However, all these works are proposed for single-radio CRN setting, which means each user can only access 1 channel in each time slot. In this paper, we focus on designing distributed rendezvous algorithms for multi-radio CRN, where each user can access $k \geq 2$ channels at the same time.

In recent years, multi-radio architecture has been widely used in wireless mesh networks [10,22]. Due to the hardware limitations, most works use the single-radio architecture for cognitive radio network, which implies only 1 channel can be accessed at the same time. However, [16] has implemented a multi-radio cognitive radio network at UCLA where each node is equipped with multiple radios to sense and access channels. [1] also proposed robust channel assignment for multi-radio cognitive radio network. To the best of our knowledge, only two papers considered the rendezvous process for multi-radio CRN, which should play an important role in constructing the CRN. [20] proposed a multi-interface rendezvous in self-organizing CRN. And [25] investigated multiple radios for effective rendezvous in CRN. However, these two works either did not give the theoretic $MTTR$ bound regarding the benefits of using multi-radios [20] or did not show how far their rendezvous performance is away from the optimal [25]. In our paper, we aim to answer one question: to what extent could multi-radio improve the $MTTR$ compared to single-radio CRN.

In order to solve the rendezvous problem in multi-radio CRN, we first design different algorithms for two special situations. When $k = 2$, which means the user can access two channels in the same time slot, we design both GS and LS algorithms, where the GS algorithm guarantees rendezvous in $O(n^2)$ time slots (only constant factor lower than single-radio CRN [13]) and the LS one guarantees rendezvous in $O(|V_i||V_j|)$ time slots (log log n factor lower than [7]). For the other case $k = O(\sqrt{n})$, rendezvous is guaranteed in $O(n)$ time slots based on the quorum system method. Second, we derive the lower bound as $\Omega(\frac{|V_i||V_j|}{k^2})$ when the user can access arbitrary k channels at the same time, and we present how to meet the bound based on the LS algorithm. Finally, we conduct extensive simulations and these results corroborate our theoretical analyses.

The rest of the paper is organized as follows. The next section introduces some related works. Model and problem formulation are provided in Section 3. We show the algorithms for two special situations in Section 4. The lower bound is derived in Section 5 and a general construction for rendezvous to meet this lower bound is presented in Section 6. Simulation results are depicted in Section 7 and we conclude the paper in Section 8.

2. RELATED WORK

Rendezvous algorithms can be divided into two categories: centralized and decentralized algorithm. Assuming a central controller or a dedicated Common Control Channel (CCC) exists [17,21], centralized algorithm can be realized by communicating through the central controller or the CCC, but it's vulnerable to adversary attacks and easily overcrowded when the number of users increases.

The main part of decentralized algorithms is *blind rendezvous algorithm*, where no centralization or CCC exists. The common technique used in blind rendezvous algorithms is Channel Hopping (CH), which means each user can gener-

Table 1: MTTR for Single-Radio Rendezvous

Algorithms	$MTTR$
GOS [9]	$n(n+1) = O(n^2)$
Jump-Stay [19]	$3nP^2 + 3P = O(n^3)$
CRSEQ [23]	$P(3P - 1) = O(n^2)$
DRDS [13]	$3P^2 = O(n^2)$
AHW [8]	$3P^2 \log M = O(n^2 \log M)$
MLS [12]	$O(|V_i|^2) = o(n^2)$
Result [7]	$O(|V_i||V_j| \log\log n) = O(n^2 \log\log n)$

Remarks: 1)P is the smallest prime number $P \geq n$, $n \leq P < 2n$; 2)M is the maximum value of the users' identifiers; 3) V_i, V_j represents two users' available channels sets and supposing $|V_i| \geq |V_j|$;

Table 2: MTTR for Multi-Radio Rendezvous

Algorithms	MTTR
RPS [25]	$O(\lceil \frac{P}{max\{m,n\}} \rceil \times (Q - G))$
EAR [20]	No explicit MTTR bound but simulations

Remarks: 1)Q is the number of total channels, P is the smallest prime number larger than Q, m, n are the number of radios each user is equipped with; 2) G is the number of common channels.

ate a specific sequence and hop among the available channels according to it. The state-of-the-art distributed rendezvous algorithms for single-radio CRN are summarized in Table 2. Generally speaking, there are two types of sequences used in extant works: *global sequence* (GS) is constructed based on all channels' information, and *local sequence* (LS) is generated on the basis of the user's available channels. Thus different users generate the same global sequence, but they could have different local sequences.

Generated Orthogonal Sequence (GOS) [9] is a pioneering work which generates a GS of length $n(n+1)$ based on a random permutation of $\{1, 2, \cdots, n\}$. However, this algorithm is limited to the situation that all these channels are available. Quorum-based Channel Hopping (QCH) [4,5] works efficiently for synchronous users (i.e. the users start the rendezvous algorithm at the same time), which generates the GS based on the quorum system. Asynchronous QCH [3] is modified for asynchronous users (i.e. the users' start time is different), but only applicable to two available channels.

Channel Rendezvous Sequence (CRSEQ) [23] is the first one guaranteeing rendezvous in bounded time. It firstly computes the smallest prime $P > n$ and constructs the GS with P periods. For each period, $3P - 1$ elements are then generated based on the triangle number and modular operation. Jump-Stay (JS) [19] generates the GS of P periods and each period contains two *jump* frames and one *stay* frame, where each frame contains P numbers. CRSEQ guarantees rendezvous in $O(n^2)$ time slots for any two users and it works badly for symmetric users (i.e. the users have the same available channels). JS guarantees rendezvous for symmetric users in $O(n)$ time slots but in $O(n^3)$ time slots for two asymmetric users (i.e. the users may have different available channels). This result is later improved in [18]. Disjoint Relaxed Difference Set (DRDS) [13] is the first algorithm guaranteeing quick rendezvous for both symmetric and asymmetric users. It reveals the equivalence between DRDS and GS. By constructing an appropriate DRDS and transforming it into a GS, rendezvous can be guaranteed in

$O(n^2)$ time slots for asymmetric users and in $O(n)$ time slots for symmetric users.

There are mainly three LS based algorithms. Alternate Hop-and-Wait (AHW) [8] generates different sequences when each user has a distinct identifier that can be represented as a unique binary string. However, it also uses the information of all channels to construct the sequence. [12] generates different sequences on the basis of each user's identifier and the available channels. For two sets V_i, V_j (suppose $|V_i| \geq |V_j|$), it guarantees rendezvous in $O(l_i |V_i|^2)$ time slots (l_i is a constant for most situations), which doesn't rely on the n channels. [7] constructs different sequences based on edge coloring without the user's identifer and it guarantees rendezvous in $O(|V_i||V_j| \log \log n)$ time slots.

For multi-radio rendezvous algorithm, [25] first studies how to generalize the existing algorithms to use multiple radios to achieve rendezvous. It used two strategies: (1)applying an existing algorithm to each radio independently; (2) first applying an existing algorithm to generate a CH sequence, then in each time slot the user accesses m consecutive channels of the sequence, where m is the number of user's radios. In this way, the $MTTR$ is reduced to $\frac{1}{m}$ of an existing single-radio algorithm. Then [25] proposed a new algorithm. The key idea is dividing the radios into 1 dedicated radio and $m-1$ general radios. Users stay in a specific channel in the dedicated radio for a duration while hop on consecutive $m-1$ channels in the general radios. From table 2 we can see the $MTTR$ is also about $\frac{1}{m}$ of an existing single-radio algorithm. Besides, [20] also proposed a multi-interface rendezvous algorithm based on Jump-and-Stay algorithm [19], where each user is equipped with 3 radios. The main idea is sorting the available channels by the channel quality. Channel sequence is composed of jump sequence and stay sequence. Compared to JS algorithm in [19], the difference is user hops on better channels more often. And the available channel sets are divided among 3 radios. This paper only gives a performance simulation that shows the TTR is reduced compared to JS algorithm. From the above, we can see both of the algorithms didn't study whether their rendezvous performance is optimal or not.

3. MODEL AND PROBLEM DEFINITION

We consider the blind rendezvous problem where the users try to discover each other without a dedicated common control channel and the knowledge of each other. Assume the licensed spectrum is divided into a set of n non-overlapping channels as $U=\{1,2,...,n\}$, where the indices are known to all the users. Supposing time is divided into slots of equal length $2t$ where t is the sufficient time to establish a link if two users access the same channel at the same time. Each user i is equipped with multiple cognitive radios to sense the licensed spectrum and it results in an available channel set $V_i \subseteq U$. Two users i and j can discover each other if they have overlapping channels, i.e., $V_i \cap V_j \neq \emptyset$. Different from extant works, assuming each user is equipped with $k(k \geq 2)$ cognitive radios, which implies the user can access k channels simultaneously in a single time slot, rather than 1 channel in previous works.

We mainly discuss whether the rendezvous time can be improved under the k-radio scenario and to what extent it could help. Different users may not have the same available channel sets as they are distributed in different positions and may have different interferences, which we call it asymmetric

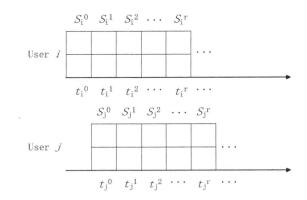

Figure 1: Channel hopping sequence and time slots with $k = 2$ in asynchronous model. User i can access 2 channels simultaneously each time slot, it hops to channel set S_i^r at t_i^r.

case. As all the users are independent, they may "wake up" at different time, then their channel-hopping sequences may have a shift. In order to be more close to reality, we focus on asymmetric and asynchronous scenarios.

As the most rendezvous algorithms do, we also adopt channel hopping sequences. In each time slot, each user i hops on k channels in V_i to attempt rendezvous with their neighbors. For example, user i obtains its own channel hopping sequence $S_i = [S_i^0, S_i^1, \cdots, S_i^x, \cdots]$, where set $S_i^x \subseteq V_i$ and $|S_i^x| = k$. When user i wakes up, it hops to channel set S_i^0 at time slot t_i^0, then hops to channel set S_i^1 at t_i^1, and so on. Now we give an example of $k = 2$, as shown in Fig. 1.

Definition 1. Given a pair of users i and j, $V_i \cap V_j \neq \emptyset$, the users i and j **rendezvous** if $S_i^x \cap S_j^y \neq \emptyset$ for some finite integers x, y, considering the different "wake-up" time.

Time to rendezvous(TTR) is an important metric to evaluate the rendezvous algorithms. In this paper, we mainly focus on asynchronous case, so our goal is to minimize the *Maximum Time to rendezvous($MTTR$)* for two users. When $MTTR$ is bounded, rendezvous is guaranteed.

4. SPECIAL CASES FOR MULTI-RADIO RENDEZVOUS

In this section, we present different distributed rendezvous algorithms for two special cases $k = 2$ and $k = O(\sqrt{n})$.

4.1 Special Case 1: $k = 2$

When each user can access 2 channels at each time slot, we extend previous single radio rendezvous algorithm to this problem and compare their performances. Firstly, we consider the global sequence (GS) based rendezvous algorithm [13]. Before presenting the algorithm, we give the definition of Disjoint Relaxed Difference Set(DRDS).

Definition 2. A set $D = \{a_1, a_2, ..., a_k\} \subseteq Z_n (Z_n = [0, n-1])$ is called a Relaxed Difference Set(RDS) if for every $d \neq 0$ (mod n), there exists at least one ordered pair (a_i, a_j) such that $a_i - a_j \equiv d \pmod{n}$, where $a_i, a_j \in D$.

LEMMA 1. *If D is an RDS under Z_n, then $D_k = \{(a_i+k) \mod n | a_i \in D\}$ is also an RDS under Z_n.*

Definition 3. A set $S = \{D_1, D_2, \cdots, D_h\}$ is called a Disjoint Relaxed Difference Set(DRDS) under Z_n if $\forall D_i \in S$, D_i is an RDS under Z_n and $\forall D_i, D_j \in S, i \neq j, D_i \cap D_j = \emptyset$.

[13] reveals the equivalence of DRDS and GS that can be used in rendezvous scheme. We present the asynchronous rendezvous algorithm based on the DRDS construction [13]. The set of all licensed channels is $U = \{1, 2, \cdots, n\}$. Find the smallest prime P such that $P \geq \frac{n}{2}$.

Algorithm 1 Global sequence based rendezvous algorithm

1: Divide the total channel set $U = \{1, 2, ..., n\}$ into two parts $U_1 = \{1, 2, ..., \frac{n}{2}\}$ and $U_2 = \{\frac{n+1}{2}, ..., n\}$;
2: Construct DRDS of Z_m where $m = 3P^2$;
3: For each user i, apply the DRDS based Rendezvous Algorithm in [13] to channel set U_1 and U_2 simultaneously, and denote the outputs to be $CH_1 = \{c_1^0, c_1^1, ..., c_1^t, ...\}$, $CH_2 = \{c_2^0, c_2^2, ..., c_2^t, ...\}$;
4: For any t, pick two channels from CH_1 and CH_2 respectively to form $S_i^t = \{c_1^t, c_2^t\}$;

THEOREM 1. *For two users i and j with available channel sets $V_i, V_j \subseteq U$, whenever they start Alg. 1, they can achieve rendezvous in $O(n^2)$ time slots if $V_i \cap V_j \neq \emptyset$.*

PROOF. In Alg. 1, we divide the channels U into two parts U_1 and U_2. Then we construct a DRDS DR_1 of Z_m where $m = 3P^2, P \geq \frac{n}{2}$. Based on DR_1 we can get a global channel hopping sequence CH_1 for channel set U_1. According to Lemma 1, we can get a similar DRDS DR_2 used for channel set U_2, then get CH_2. At each time slot, the user can access two channels from CH_1 and CH_2 respectively, and from the rendezvous guarantee in [13], we can get the $MTTR = 3P^2 = O(n^2)$. □

It's easy to verify that $\frac{n}{2} \leq P < n$, and thus the $MTTR \in [\frac{3n^2}{4}, 3n^2)$, which is nearly 4 times lower than single-radio CRN as Table 2. Moreover, when the number of available channels is not large, we can use the following local sequence (LS) based rendezvous algorithm to achieve a better result.

Algorithm 2 Local sequence based rendezvous algorithm

1: For each user i, the available channel set $V_i = \{a_1, ..., a_{|V_i|}\}$, time slot $t_i^0, t_i^1, \cdots, t_i^r, \cdots$, channel hopping sequence $S_i = [S_i^0, S_i^1, \cdots, S_i^r, \cdots]$
2: Choose primes p, p' from $[|V_i|, 3|V_i|], p \neq p'$
3: For each time slot t_i^r(stage r), $f = r \mod p$, $g = r \mod p'$
4: **if** either f or g is not in $[1, |V_i|]$ **then**
5:     choose a_f or a_g randomly from channel set V_i
6: **end if**
7: $S_i^r = \{a_f, a_g\}$

THEOREM 2. *For arbitrary two users i, j, $V_i \cap V_j \neq \emptyset$, if they execute Alg.2 asynchronously, they can achieve rendezvous in $O(|V_i| \cdot |V_j|)$ time slots.*

PROOF. Consider two users i, j, available channel sets $V_i = \{a_1, ..., a_{|V_i|}\}, V_j = \{b_1, ..., b_{|V_j|}\}$. For user j, suppose the primes are q, q'.

Suppose $V_i \cap V_j = a_x = b_y$. In synchronous model, in order to guarantee rendezvous, we need to find a time slot r such that $r \equiv x \mod p$ and $r \equiv y \mod q$, where $p \neq q$. According to Chinese Remainder Theorem, we can find a solution of r in no more than pq steps. As for S_i^r, S_j^r, we can judge whether they rendezvous in single time slot, so we need no more than $pq = O(|V_i| \cdot |V_j|)$ time slots to guarantee rendezvous.

In asynchronous model, we can double each stage r in the above construction, that is, we should execute $S_i^r = \{a_f, a_g\}$ for 2 time slots. Assume user i and j "wake up" in t_i^0 and t_j^0 respectively, $t_i^0 < t_j^0$, then we can find r such that the rth stage of user i and the $\{r - \frac{t_j^0 - t_i^0}{2}\}^{th}$ stage of user j overlap for at least 1 time slot. Like the proof above, we can guarantee rendezvous between S_i^r and $S_j^{r - \frac{t_j^0 - t_i^0}{2}}$ in pq steps. Therefore, we need no more than $2pq = O(|V_i||V_j|)$ time slots to guarantee rendezvous. □

After applying both GS and LS rendezvous algorithms to 2-channel scenario, we compare their performance as follows. Given two users i, j with available channel sets V_i, V_j, if they can access 2 channels in each time slot, for GS based rendezvous Alg. 1, MTTR is $O(3P^2)$, where P is the smallest prime larger than $\frac{n}{2}$, which is improved 4 times compared to the scenario of accessing 1 channel each time slot. For LS based rendezvous Alg. 2, MTTR is $O(|V_i| \cdot |V_j|)$, while accessing 1 channel is $O(|V_i||V_j|\log\log n)$ [7], which implies the performance has been improved with $\log \log n$ factor. Generally speaking, when each user can access 2 channels at each time slot, the performance is improved and the LS based algorithm improves more than GS ones when n is larger, for example $n > 16$.

4.2 Special Case 2: $k = O(\sqrt{n})$

When the number of channels the user can access at the same time is much larger, such as $k = O(\sqrt{n})$, we show that the rendezvous can be guaranteed much more quickly. The main technique used is quorum system, which has intersection property and the size of each quorum is $O(\sqrt{n})$, we can utilize this property to provide rendezvous between two channel hopping sequences. A quorum system can be defined as follows:

Definition 4. Given a set $S = \{s_1, s_2...s_n\}(n \geq 1)$, a set system **QS** is a quorum system over S, if and only if

$$\forall Q_1, Q_2 \in \mathbf{QS} : Q_1 \cap Q_2 \neq \emptyset.$$

Denote the total channel set $U = \{1, 2, ..., n\}$, arrange the channels in U in a square matrix $A_{\sqrt{n} \times \sqrt{n}}$, $a_{p,q}$ = channel $(p-1) * \sqrt{n} + q$ is a element in row p and column q. Now we consider the case when $k = 2\sqrt{n} - 1$.

THEOREM 3. *The distributed rendezvous algorithm based on quorum system can guarantee rendezvous asynchronously in $O(n)$ time slots.*

PROOF. Consider two users i and j with $V_i \cap V_j = a_{p,q}$. According to the construction above, the channel hopping sequences we obtained are periodic with period $\sqrt{n} \times \sqrt{n} = n$, and denote them as $S_i = \{Q_{p,q}\}$, $S_j = \{Q'_{p,q}\}$. Consider a period, let $Q_p = \{Q_{p,1}, \cdots, Q_{p,\sqrt{n}}\}$, the same for $Q'_p(1 \leq p \leq \sqrt{n})$. And the channel hopping sequence $S_i = \{Q_1, Q_2, \cdots, Q_{\sqrt{n}}\} = \{Q_{1,1}, \cdots, Q_{1,\sqrt{n}}, Q_{2,1}, \cdots, Q_{2,\sqrt{n}}, \cdots,$

Algorithm 3 Quorum system based rendezvous algorithm

1: For user i, denote time slot $t_i^0, t_i^1, \cdots, t_i^r, \cdots$, $S_i = [S_i^0, S_i^1, \cdots, t_i^r, \cdots]$, $k = 2\sqrt{n} - 1$
2: Construct a quorum system $\mathbf{QS} = \{Q_{p,q}, 1 \le p, q \le \sqrt{n}\}$ as follows: $Q_{p,q}$ contains all elements in row p and column q of square matrix $A_{\sqrt{n} \times \sqrt{n}}$. Then $\mathbf{QS}$ contains $\sqrt{n} \times \sqrt{n}$ quorums, each quorum has $2\sqrt{n} - 1$ elements
3: **if** there exist some channels in $Q_{p,q}$ that are not in V_i **then**
4:      Replace them by channels randomly selected from V_i
5: **end if**
6: At time slot t_i^r, hopping sequence $S_i^r = Q_{y+1,z+1}$, where $r = x \cdot n + y \cdot \sqrt{n} + z$, x, y, z are integers

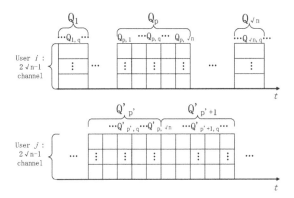

Figure 2: A period of Channel hopping sequence with $k = 2\sqrt{n} - 1$, for user i, $a_{p,q}$ appears in every element of Q_p; for user j, $a_{p,q}$ appears in $Q'_{p',q}, Q'_{p'+1,q}$.

$Q_{\sqrt{n},1}, \cdots, Q_{\sqrt{n},\sqrt{n}}\}$. In synchronous model, it is obvious that two users rendezvous in a period of $O(n)$ time slots. In asynchronous model, suppose user i wakes up earlier than user j, as shown in Fig. 2. For user i, the common channel $a_{p,q}$ will appear in consecutive $\sqrt{n}$ time slots, which correspond to channel hopping set sequence Q_p.

For user j, in the above consecutive $\sqrt{n}$ time slots, if there exist two quorum sets $Q'_{p'}$ and $Q'_{p'+1}$ that intersect with Q_p, as shown in Fig. 2. As $a_{p,q}$ appears in $Q'_{p',q} \subseteq Q'_{p'}$ and $Q'_{p'+1,q} \subseteq Q'_{p'+1}$, either $Q'_{p',q}$ or $Q'_{p'+1,q}$ intersects with Q_p, then rendezvous can be achieved. Else if there exists only one quorum set, it's obvious. So it can guarantee rendezvous asynchronously in $O(n)$ time slots. $\square$

When $k = O(\sqrt{n})$, the $MTTR$ can be reduced largely ($O(n)$ factor compared with the best result) and we try to figure out to what extent multi-radio improves in the next section.

5. LOWER BOUND

After we consider the capability of k-radio to speed up rendezvous, we mainly focus on the limit of accelerated degree when the k value is given, actually similar to [7], we can get the following lower bound.

THEOREM 4. *Any deterministic rendezvous algorithms which can access at most k channels in the single time slot require at least $\frac{|V_i||V_j|}{k^2}$ steps to guarantee rendezvous in asynchronous setting when $|V_i| + |V_j| \le n + 1$.*

PROOF. Denote $a = |V_i|$ and $b = |V_j|$. Firstly select V_i uniformly at random from all subsets with a elements of $U = \{1, 2, \ldots, n\}$, then pick an element uniformly from V_i and denote it as e, and select V'_j uniformly at random from all subsets with $b - 1$ elements of $U \setminus V_i$. Let $V_j = V'_j \bigcup \{e\}$.

Let S be the deterministic rendezvous algorithm that we use, $S_i(t)$ be the channel S accesses in time slot t for user i and $S_i(x, t)$ be the number of occurrence of the element x in first t time slots, then for any t we have

$$
\begin{aligned}
E_x(S_i(x,t)) &= E(\sum_{y \in V_i} Pr(x = y) S_i(y, t)) \\
&= E(\frac{1}{a} \sum_{y \in V_i} S_i(y, T)) \\
&= E(\frac{1}{a} tk) = \frac{tk}{a}
\end{aligned}
\tag{1}
$$

A similar result can be got for user j, denote $T_m = MTTR$ as the minimized rendezvous time and choose $T \gg T_m$. Because of the property of expectation, there exists an element x such that $a\frac{S_i(x,T)}{T} + b\frac{S_j(x,T_m)}{T_m} \le 2k$ which means $a\frac{S_i(x,T)}{T} \times b\frac{S_j(x,T_m)}{T_m} \le k^2$, thus

$$
S_i(x, T) \times S_j(x, T_m) \le \frac{k^2}{ab}
\tag{2}
$$

Finally we deal with the case that user i starts at time 0, and user j starts at time $t_j \in [0, T)$. Considering the set $Q = \{(t_1, t_2) \in [0, T) \times [0, T_m) | S_i(t_1) = S_j(t_2) = x\}$. It's quite obvious that

$$
\begin{aligned}
|Q| &\le T \cdot T_m \cdot S_i(x, T) S_j(x, T_m) \\
&\le T \cdot T_m \frac{k^2}{ab}
\end{aligned}
\tag{3}
$$

However since the algorithm guarantees rendezvous in time T_m, for any $t_j \in [0, T - T_m)$ there must be a corresponding point in Q which implies that

$$
|Q| \ge T - T_m
\tag{4}
$$

Combining the two inequalities we get (using the fact that $T \gg T_m$, let T goes to infinity)

$$
\begin{aligned}
T \cdot T_m \frac{k^2}{ab} &\ge T - T_m \\
T_m &\ge \frac{ab}{k^2}
\end{aligned}
\tag{5}
$$

Thus the theorem holds. $\square$

6. GENERAL CONSTRUCTION FOR RENDEZVOUS

In order to meet the bound, we present a general construction for distributed rendezvous process.

The main idea of Alg. 4 is to generate k channels based on special case $k = 2$ in Section 4. In the first place, the available channel set V_i is divided into $\frac{k}{2}$ subsets with size $\frac{2|V_i|}{k}$ (these subsets may not be exactly the same size, we omit the details to tackle this), and then apply Alg. 2 on each subset to generate the corresponding sequences as $S_{i,j} = \{S_{i,j}^0, S_{i,j}^1, \ldots, S_{i,j}^t, \ldots\}$. It's obvious that each element $S_{i,j}^t$ has 2 channels and all these $\frac{k}{2}$ subsets can produce k channels to access, as Line 4. We can conclude that:

Algorithm 4 General Construction for Rendezvous

1: For user i, denote the available channel set as V_i;
2: Divide V_i into $k/2$ subsets as $V_{i,1}, V_{i,2}, \ldots, V_{i,\frac{k}{2}}$, where $|V_{i,j}| = \frac{2|V_i|}{k}$;
3: For each $V_{i,j}$, use Alg. 2 to generate sequence as $S_{i,j} = \{S_{i,j}^0, S_{i,j}^1, \ldots, S_{i,j}^t, \ldots\}$;
4: For any time slot t, construct $S_i^t = \bigcup_{1 \leq j \leq k/2} S_{i,j}^t$ and access the channels in S_i^t;

THEOREM 5. *For any two users i, j with available channel sets $V_i \bigcap V_j \neq \emptyset$, Alg. 4 guarantees rendezvous in $MTTR = O(\frac{|V_i||V_j|}{k^2})$ time slots.*

PROOF. Since $V_i \bigcap V_j \neq \emptyset$, there exist $1 \leq k_1, k_2 \leq \frac{k}{2}$ such that $V_{i,k_1} \bigcap V_{j,k_2} \neq \emptyset$. When they apply Alg. 2 to each subset, we can check that: for the corresponding sequences S_{i,k_1} and S_{j,k_2}, there exist corresponding x, y such that $S_{i,k_1}^x \bigcap S_{j,k_2}^y \neq \emptyset$ and they are actually in the same time slot for different wake-up time, then rendezvous can be guaranteed in $O(|V_{i,k_1}||V_{j,k_2}|) = O(\frac{|V_i||V_j|}{k^2})$ time slots according to Theorem 2. □

Theorem 5 shows that we can guarantee rendezvous for any two users in $O(\frac{|V_i||V_j|}{k^2})$ time slots, which meets the lower bound in Theorem 4. Compared with the special cases in Section 4, when $k = 2$, the LS algorithm guarantees rendezvous in $O(|V_i||V_j|)$ time slots, which corroborate the analysis, and while $k = O(\sqrt{n})$, the quorum based algorithm guarantees rendezvous in $O(n)$ time slots, which meets the lower bound when both $|V_i|, |V_j| = \Omega(n)$.

7. SIMULATION

In this section, we evaluate the performance of our proposed distributed algorithms under multi-radio CRN circumstance and compare the results with the state-of-the-art single-radio rendezvous algorithms. (The algorithms we select is DRDS [13], which is a GS based rendezvous algorithm.) Since it is difficult to synchronize timers in practice, we focus on asynchronous environment.

For a multi-radio CRN, denote the total channel set $U = [1, 2, \cdots, n]$ and k to be the number of cognitive radios each user is equipped with. For two users i and j, denote the available channel sets as $V_i \subseteq U$ and $V_j \subseteq U$, where $V_i \cap V_j \neq \emptyset$. Define $\theta_i = \frac{|V_i|}{n}$, $\theta_j = \frac{|V_j|}{n}$. In each simulation, V_i and V_j are generated randomly from U satisfying some given conditions, and the wake-up time of each user is also randomly selected. MTTR is counted as the maximum time slots that it takes to achieve rendezvous since the second wake-up user begins its hopping sequence. The simulation results in the following figures are the maximal MTTR value of 10000 runs.

Since we have presented two different distributed rendezvous algorithms for the special case $k = 2$, we first evaluate the performance of GS based rendezvous algorithm and compare it with single-radio scenario (i.e. $k = 1$). Since the number of available channels for each user is an important factor, we consider the situations $|V_i|, |V_j|$ have small and large differences respectively. Fig. 3 shows the situation $\theta_i = \theta_j = 0.8$, while we set $\theta_i = 0.2$, $\theta_j = 0.8$ in Fig. 4. When n increases from 10 to 100, the $MTTR$ values both increase as shown in Fig. 3 and Fig. 4. Compared

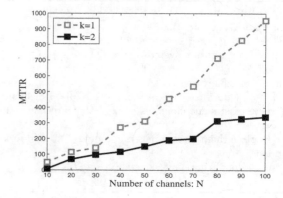

Figure 3: GS based rendezvous algorithm, $\theta_i = \theta_j = 0.8$, MTTR as n increases

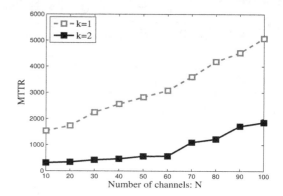

Figure 4: GS based rendezvous algorithm, $\theta_i = 0.2, \theta_j = 0.8$, MTTR as n increases

with single-radio CRN, our 2-radio CRN has better performance, which is in accordance with our theoretical analysis. As depicted, our algorithm is nearly 4 times quicker than the single-radio CRN, which verifies the analysis of Alg. 1. When θ_i and θ_j have a great difference in Fig. 4, the $MTTR$ value increase enormously compared with $\theta_i = \theta_j = 0.8$ (Fig. 3), as the number of common channels decreases.

Although the GS based rendezvous algorithm has a good performance, the LS based rendezvous algorithm (Alg. 2) achieves a better result. Like GS algorithm, we also consider the two cases of $|V_i|$ and $|V_j|$. Fig. 5 shows the situation $\theta_i = \theta_j = 0.8$, while Fig. 6 shows the result when $\theta_i = 0.2$, $\theta_j = 0.8$. Similar with Alg. 1, both Fig. 5 and Fig. 6 show that the $MTTR$ values increase as n increases from 10 to 100. However, as shown in Fig. 5, the LS based rendezvous algorithm reduces the $MTTR$ largely compared with Fig. 3 (for example, when $n = 100$, Alg. 1 shows the $MTTR$ value is about 350 time slots, while Alg. 2 has shorter $MTTR$ about 270 time slots.) This implies that Alg. 2 can improve the performance of rendezvous in 2-radio CRN when n is large. This is also verified from Fig. 6 when $|V_i|, |V_j|$ have great difference. All these results corroborate the analysis and the comparison we make in Section 4.

Considering another special case $k = O(\sqrt{n})$. Since Alg. 3 works efficiently when $k = 2\sqrt{n} - 1$, we verify the performance of the result when $\sqrt{n}$ increases from 10 to 20 as

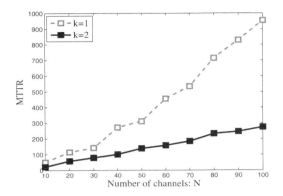

Figure 5: LS based rendezvous algorithm, $\theta_i = \theta_j = 0.8$, MTTR as n increases

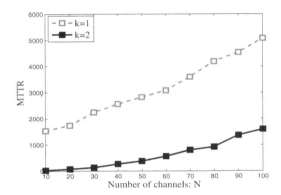

Figure 6: LS based rendezvous algorithm, $\theta_i = 0.2, \theta_j = 0.8$, MTTR as n increases

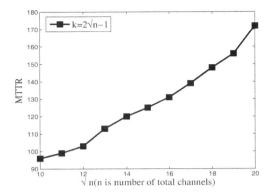

Figure 7: quorum based rendezvous algorithm, MTTR as n increases

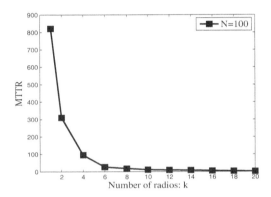

Figure 8: $n = 100$, $\theta_i = \theta_j = 0.8$, MTTR as k increases

Fig. 7. For this situation, we don't compare this algorithm with single-radio ones, since the $MTTR$ value is about $O(n^2)$, which is very large. (For example, when $n = 100$, the $MTTR$ value for the multi-radio CRN can achieve rendezvous in 100 time slots, while the previous result for single-radio CRN has the smallest $MTTR$ value about 1000 time slots.) As shown in Fig. 7, the $MTTR$ values increases when $\sqrt{n}$ increases and it's almost bounded as $O(n)$ time slots as analyzed in Theorem 3.

Moreover, we evaluate the general construction in Alg. 4 for any arbitrary k. For this simulation, we fix $n = 100$ and $\theta_i = \theta_j = 0.8$. As shown in Fig. 8, the $MTTR$ value decreases when k increases from 1 to 20. When $k = 1$, which is the previous single-radio CRN, the result shows that the $MTTR$ value is very large and it decreases largely when k is large. This result corroborates the analysis of Theorem 5 where two users can rendezvous in $O(\frac{|V_i||V_j|}{k^2})$ time slots.

In a word, our simulation results show that rendezvous can be improved in multi-radio CRN. For $k = 2$, both GS and LS based algorithms can improve the state-of-the-art result. For $k = O(\sqrt{n})$, the quorum system method (Alg. 3) reduces the $MTTR$ value largely. For more general cases, our proposed algorithm guarantees rendezvous in bounded time with good performance and the $MTTR$ value decreases when the number of cognitive radio k increases.

8. CONCLUSIONS

In this paper, we study the rendezvous problem in multi-radio Cognitive Radio Networks (CRNs), which is a fundamental process in constructing a CRN. First of all, we show the improvement of $MTTR$ in k-radio scenario by considering two special cases, where $k \geq 2$ and $k = O(\sqrt{n})$. When $k = 2$, we design both global sequence (GS) and local sequence (LS) based distributed rendezvous algorithms, where GS algorithm improves the time to rendezvous only by a constant factor, whereas the LS algorithm improves by $\log \log n$ factor, where n is the number of all channels. For another special case $k = O(\sqrt{n})$, the $MTTR$ value can be reduced largely when the quorum system method is used to guarantee rendezvous. In order to figure out the limit of the improvement, we show a lower bound of $MTTR$ as $\Omega(\frac{|V_i||V_j|}{k^2})$, where V_i, V_j represents two users' available channel sets. Moreover, we present the method for general construction to rendezvous based on the LS algorithm, which meets the lower bound. From these aspects, the rendezvous time for CRN could be improved by using multiple radios for each user, and the improvement can also be bounded. Besides, compared to the existing multi-radio rendezvous algorithm, our rendezvous algorithm improves time to rendezvous by $O(k)$ factor and is optimal. Finally, we conduct extensive simulations to compare these algorithms and the results corroborate our theoretical analyses.

9. ACKNOWLEDGMENTS

This work was supported in part by the National Basic Research Program of China Grant 2011CBA00300, 2011CBA00301, the National Natural Science Foundation of China Grant 61103186, 61033001, 61361136003.

10. REFERENCES

[1] M. Ahmadi, Y. Zhuang, and J. Pan. Distributed robust channel assignment for multi-radio cognitive radio networks. In *Vehicular Technology Conference (VTC Fall), 2012 IEEE*, pages 1–5. IEEE, 2012.

[2] I. F. Akyildiz, W.-Y. Lee, M. C. Vuran, and S. Mohanty. Next generation/dynamic spectrum access/cognitive radio wireless networks: a survey. *Computer Networks*, 50(13):2127–2159, 2006.

[3] K. Bian and J.-M. Park. Maximizing rendezvous diversity in rendezvous protocols for decentralized cognitive radio networks. *Mobile Computing, IEEE Transactions on*, 12(7):1294–1307, 2013.

[4] K. Bian, J.-M. Park, and R. Chen. A quorum-based framework for establishing control channels in dynamic spectrum access networks. In *Proceedings of the 15th annual international conference on Mobile computing and networking*, pages 25–36. ACM, 2009.

[5] K. Bian, J.-M. Park, and R. Chen. Control channel establishment in cognitive radio networks using channel hopping. *Selected Areas in Communications, IEEE Journal on*, 29(4):689–703, 2011.

[6] Z. Cai, S. Ji, J. He, and A. G. Bourgeois. Optimal distributed data collection for asynchronous cognitive radio networks. In *Distributed Computing Systems (ICDCS)*, pages 245–254. IEEE, 2012.

[7] S. Chen, A. Russell, A. Samanta, and R. Sundaram. Deterministic blind rendezvous in cognitive radio networks. *arXiv preprint arXiv:1401.7313*, 2014.

[8] I. Chuang, H.-Y. Wu, K.-R. Lee, and Y.-H. Kuo. Alternate hop-and-wait channel rendezvous method for cognitive radio networks. In *INFOCOM, 2013 Proceedings IEEE*, pages 746–754. IEEE, 2013.

[9] L. A. DaSilva and I. Guerreiro. Sequence-based rendezvous for dynamic spectrum access. In *New Frontiers in Dynamic Spectrum Access Networks. 3rd IEEE Symposium on*, pages 1–7. IEEE, 2008.

[10] R. Draves, J. Padhye, and B. Zill. Routing in multi-radio, multi-hop wireless mesh networks. In *Proceedings of the 10th annual international conference on Mobile computing and networking*, pages 114–128. ACM, 2004.

[11] A. G. Fragkiadakis, E. Z. Tragos, and I. G. Askoxylakis. A survey on security threats and detection techniques in cognitive radio networks. *Communications Surveys & Tutorials, IEEE*, 15(1):428–445, 2013.

[12] Z. Gu, Q.-S. Hua, and W. Dai. Local sequence based rendezvous algorithms for cognitive radio networks. In *Sensor, Mesh and Ad Hoc Communications and Networks (SECON)*, pages 371–379. IEEE, 2014.

[13] Z. Gu, Q.-S. Hua, Y. Wang, and F. Lau. Nearly optimal asynchronous blind rendezvous algorithm for cognitive radio networks. In *Sensor, Mesh and Ad Hoc Communications and Networks (SECON)*, pages 371–379. IEEE, 2013.

[14] X. Huang, D. Lu, P. Li, and Y. Fang. Coolest path: spectrum mobility aware routing metrics in cognitive ad hoc networks. In *Distributed Computing Systems (ICDCS), 2011 31st International Conference on*, pages 182–191. IEEE, 2011.

[15] S. Ji, R. Beyah, and Z. Cai. Minimum-latency broadcast scheduling for cognitive radio networks. In *Sensor, Mesh and Ad Hoc Communications and Networks (SECON)*, pages 389–397. IEEE, 2013.

[16] W. Kim, A. J. Kassler, M. Di Felice, and M. Gerla. Urban-x: towards distributed channel assignment in cognitive multi-radio mesh networks. In *Wireless Days (WD), 2010 IFIP*, pages 1–5. IEEE, 2010.

[17] Y. R. Kondareddy, P. Agrawal, and K. Sivalingam. Cognitive radio network setup without a common control channel. In *Military Communications Conference, 2008. MILCOM 2008. IEEE*, pages 1–6. IEEE, 2008.

[18] Z. Lin, H. Liu, X. Chu, and Y. Leung. Enhanced jump-stay rendezvous algorithm for cognitive radio networks. 2013.

[19] H. Liu, Z. Lin, X. Chu, and Y.-W. Leung. Jump-stay rendezvous algorithm for cognitive radio networks. *Parallel and Distributed Systems, IEEE Transactions on*, 23(10):1867–1881, 2012.

[20] R. Paul, Y. Z. Jembre, and Y.-J. Choi. Multi-interface rendezvous in self-organizing cognitive radio networks. In *Dynamic Spectrum Access Networks (DYSPAN), 2014 IEEE International Symposium on*, pages 531–540. IEEE, 2014.

[21] J. Pérez-Romero, O. Salient, R. Agustí, and L. Giupponi. A novel on-demand cognitive pilot channel enabling dynamic spectrum allocation. In *New Frontiers in Dynamic Spectrum Access Networks. 2nd IEEE International Symposium on*, pages 46–54. IEEE, 2007.

[22] K. Ramachandran, I. Sheriff, E. M. Belding, and K. C. Almeroth. A multi-radio 802.11 mesh network architecture. *Mobile Networks and Applications*, 13(1-2):132–146, 2008.

[23] J. Shin, D. Yang, and C. Kim. A channel rendezvous scheme for cognitive radio networks. *Communications Letters, IEEE*, 14(10):954–956, 2010.

[24] Y. Song, J. Xie, and X. Wang. A novel unified analytical model for broadcast protocols in multi-hop cognitive radio ad hoc networks. 2013.

[25] L. Yu, H. Liu, Y.-W. Leung, X. Chu, and Z. Lin. Multiple radios for effective rendezvous in cognitive radio networks. In *Communications (ICC), 2013 IEEE International Conference on*, pages 2857–2862. IEEE, 2013.

A Semi-Persistent Scheduling Scheme for Videotelephony Traffics in the Uplink of LTE Networks

Jean Thierry Stephen Avocanh
L2TI - Laboratoire de Traitement et de Transport de l'Information
Université Paris 13, Sorbonne Paris cité, France
jean.avocanh@univ-paris13.fr

Marwen Abdennebi
L2TI - Laboratoire de Traitement et de Transport de l'Information
Université Paris 13, Sorbonne Paris cité, France
marwen.abdennebi@univ-paris13.fr

Jalel Ben-Othman
L2TI - Laboratoire de Traitement et de Transport de l'Information
Université Paris 13, Sorbonne Paris cité, France
jalel.ben-othman@univ-paris13.fr

Giuseppe Piro
DEI, Politecnico di Bari
via Orabona 4, Bari, Italy
giuseppe.piro@poliba.it

ABSTRACT

Recent studies have shown that in LTE Uplink, the handshake procedure consisting of a scheduling request message from the User Equipment and a scheduling grant from the eNB required twice a communication over the air interface and caused notable delay. It could be harmful for loss and latency-sensitive applications such as Videotelephony traffics. So, we propose in this paper a new scheme which improves resource allocation for Videotelephony traffics and reduce the delay caused by Dynamic scheduling. The key idea is to schedule Videotelephony traffics using a Semi-Persistent strategy with Provisioning. The performance of our proposed algorithm have been evaluated in real LTE environments with LTE-Sim and simulations results demonstrated its effectiveness by showing that it optimized Videotelephony traffics performance and provided the best QoS support compared to the Dynamic Scheduling.

Categories and Subject Descriptors

C.2.1 [**Network Architecture and Design**]: Wireless communication

Keywords

LTE; Uplink; Scheduling; Quality of Service; Videotelephony

1. INTRODUCTION

Recently, we have seen an important increase of mobile data usage and particularly a growing demand of video ap-

plications [12] . To face this exponential growth, LTE has been proposed by the 3GPP [1] and provides ubiquitous and significant broadband access. Today with LTE it is possible for the mobile users to make natively one-to-one or one-to-many video calls, switch to video at any point during a call and drop video at any point to continue with just voice. This kind of video called Videotelephony or Conversational video is becoming more and more used and help to increase the face-to-face collaboration and allow real-time communication to take place at any location of the network.

To bring strong QoS support with fast connectivity, high mobility and security to these services, LTE introduced new features in the Radio Access network such as OFDMA (Orthogonal Frequency Division Multiple Access) in the downlink, SC-FDMA (Single Carrier Frequency Division Multiple Access) in the uplink, the use of MIMO (Multiple-Input Multiple-Output) antenna schemes and a set of advanced Medium Access Control (MAC) and physical functions. However, recent studies [6] have shown that in LTE Uplink, the handshake procedure consisting of a scheduling request message from the User Equipment and a scheduling grant from the eNB required twice a communication over the air interface and caused notable delay. It was demonstrated that the Radio Access Network One Way Delay (RAN OWD) in LTE Uplink was significantly higher compared to the previous HSPA mobile network. This could be harmful for loss and latency-sensitive applications such as Videotelephony traffics. For this purpose, we propose in this paper a new scheme which improves resource allocation for Videotelephony traffics and reduce the delay caused by Dynamic Scheduling. The key idea consists in scheduling such traffic using a Semi-Persistent strategy with Provisioning. The amount of resources to preallocate is estimated using an accurate traffic model. As consequence, we strongly reduce the latency in the uplink, but also signalization overheads used for grants (which lead to increase downlink throughput). We evaluated our strategy in real LTE environments with LTE-Sim and simulations results demonstrated its effectiveness by showing that it optimized

Videotelephony traffics performance and provided the best QoS support (reduced the packet loss ratio and provided the lowest value for the packet delays) compared to FME, which is one of powerful and recently proposed scheduling approach for the uplink.

The rest of the paper is organized as follow. Section II describes the uplink system model and shows in particularly how the transmission of Videotelephony traffics flows is handled. Section III presents a state-of-art about uplink scheduling schemes in LTE and in section IV, our proposed strategy is detailed. The performance evaluation is presented in section V and the last section, section VI concludes the paper.

2. UPLINK SYSTEM MODEL

The LTE uplink transmission scheme is based on SC-FDMA which have better Peak Average Power Ratio (PAPR) properties compared to OFDMA. Scheduling of uplink resources is done by the eNB which allocates RBs to the UEs every TTI (Transmission Time Interval) of 1 ms in the time and frequency domain. Unlike downlink, resource allocation in uplink system needs to be done per users, even though each user may have several flows [4]. Besides, Resource Blocks (RBs) to be assigned to the same User Equipment (UE) must be contiguous. UEs ask for resources depending on their queue status. In the downlink, the eNB is obviously aware of the amount of data to allocate to the terminals but in the uplink it is different. The UEs have to inform the eNB about the amount of buffered data to be transmitted and their priority. For that purpose, they send their Buffer Status Report (BSR). User data is carried on the Physical Uplink Shared Channel (PUSCH) and UEs derive the uplink resource allocation after a handshake procedure consisting of a Scheduling Request (SR) message from the UE and a scheduling grant from the eNB. This process can cause notable delay and be harmful for latency-sensitive applications such as Videotelephony.

Indeed due to the latency caused by this handshake procedure, the transmission of the first video frame can take a long while. Also we notice that it is not the entire amount of data of the first frame which will be sent at the first occasion because the first grant is minimal and is given primarily to send the BSR. So in the best case (resources are always available for UE after sending BSR and UE has a very good channel quality), at least two transmissions on PUSCH will be used for sending the entire amount of the first frame. But in reality with dynamic scheduling, resources are not always guaranteed for an UE and it can take more PUSCH (more time) for sending the first frame. It depends principally on the scheduling strategy implemented in the eNB and the channel quality (the number of bits that can be transmitted within each resource bock). As consequence, the next frames, after being available in the UE buffer, could wait for a while and be delayed. This could increase the user plane latency and cause at the same time significant End-to-End delay. The proposed strategy detailed in this paper will help to improve resource allocation for Videotelephony traffics and reduce the delay caused by dynamic scheduling.

3. RELATED WORK

Scheduling strategies play a major role in LTE systems because a great performance gain can be achieved by properly allocating resources among users. This allocation has to take into account various aspects such as meeting the expected QoS, assuring fairness and maximizing the total network throughput. Several researches have been done in recent years in order to overcome these challenges [9]. However, most of these works focused on the downlink. Nethertheless, researches have started to design scheduling schemes in the uplink. In the litterature the proposed schemes can be classified into three different groups which are opportunistic, delay-based and multiclass-based [4]. One of the powerful and recently proposed schemes is the First Maximum Expansion (FME) algorithm [11]. It is a scheduling scheme with a Proportional Fair-based utility function which allocates resources starting from the highest metric value and expanding the allocation on both sides. The allocation for a UE is stopped whenever another user with a higher metric is found. This scheme has been tested and showed good performance.

Although the good performance of this promised scheduling scheme, managing Videotelephony traffics in the uplink is still difficult taking into account the constraints imposed by the uplink direction (SR messages from the UE and scheduling grants from the eNB) and the variations of the channel conditions as well as delay and packet loss sensitive services characteristics. Indeed, although the fact that an accurate scheduling method can be used in order to provide strong QoS support, this one could become ineffective if a notable delay already occured. A solution would be to reduce this delay caused by the handshake procedure between the UE and the eNB by designing a new scheduling protocol. To the best of our knowledge, no previous work has been done for the Videotelephony traffics. So we propose a new scheduling protocol which focuses on them.

4. PROPOSED SCHEDULING STRATEGY

In what follows, we will explain our scheduling protocol strategy by firstly detailing the functioning of the protocol and after presenting the prediction model for the Videotelephony traffics. The last part will consist in highlighting the scheduling algorithm aspects.

4.1 Protocol

Our goal by designing this strategy is to improve the Videotelephony traffics resources allocation by reducing the delay caused by the dynamic scheduling in LTE uplink. For that purpose, our scheme focuses mainly on the video frames which come after the first frame and aims at reducing considerably their waiting time in the buffer. All the process is presented in Figure 1.

4.1.1 Preliminary step

Due to the fact that Variable Bit Rate Videotelephony traffics in the network are characterized by variable sized packets with constant inter-arrival time, we choose a semi-persistent mode with provisioning to allocate resources to the frames which come after the first frame. With this mode, the UE will not request RBs for these frames to come and the provisioning mode will permit to define the amount of resources to reserve for each next frame using an accurate traffic prediction model. So we define a new scheduling mode called Semi-Persistent Scheduling with Provisioning (SPS-P). This mode has to be configured by the eNB (RRC connection setup message) once a Videotelephony user is

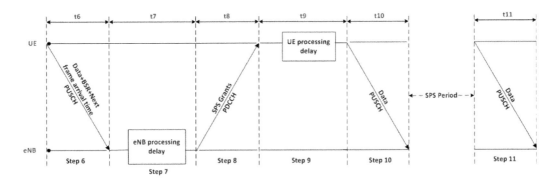

Figure 1: Semi-Persistent Scheduling With Provisioning

connected to the network and activated when required (See steps below). As mentioned early, the strategy focuses on the frames coming after the first frame. So it will take effect from the second frame. Due to few opportunities for the UE, the eNB will be in charge of forecasting the amount of resources to reserve. However, the success of this forecast has two principal constraints which are time and data. Time because the eNB has to finish the forecasting and send the grants before the arrival of the second frame. Data acquisition will help to use the prediction model to compute the bandwidth requirement of the next frames. This is why the UE will assist the eNB for the success of this task.

4.1.2 Process

After decoding the grants sent over the PDCCH and encoding the data to transmit, UE must also estimate the waiting time of the first frame. Indeed, the UE knows how long the first frame is waiting in its buffer. In **step 6**, the UE transmits the BSR, the estimation of the waiting time of the first frame and a part of data waiting in the buffer to the eNB over the PUSCH. **Step 7** is the milestone in the success of our scheme. Moreover we note that as the same time as this step is performed, eNB keeps sending dynamic scheduling grants until the entire transmission of the rest of data of the first frame. To achieve Step 7, the eNB has to predict the amount of resources to reserve for the next frames. In order to predict this amount of resources, the eNB uses a traffic prediction model to compute the bandwidth requirement of the next frames. It was shown in previous works that GBAR (Gamma-Beta Auto Regressive) process was more specialized for modeling accurately the short term fluctuation of Videotelephony traffics [5]. But the eNB cannot compute bandwidth requirements indefinitely. In other words, the number of next frames which will have preallocated resources is limited by the time available for the forecasting computations. The eNB can estimate this time using information given by the UE in step 6. If we assume T_f the information given by UE in step 6 (Waiting time of the first frame), T_c the time available for computations, T_g the time used for generating the grants and F_t the frames inter-arrival time:

$$T_c \leq F_t - T_f - T_g - t6 - t8 \qquad (1)$$

After deducing this time, the eNB knows how long at most it could take for the next frames resources prediction. Based on this interval of time and using also the traffic prediciton model, it computes the amount of resource to reserve for the

next frames. If we assume P_t the time used for predicting the amount of resource to allocate to one frame, N_f the prediction window (number of next frames which will have preallocated resources) derives from the formula:

$$N_f \in \mathbb{N}, N_f \leq \frac{T_c}{P_t} \qquad (2)$$

Once the resources prediction of the next frames is done, the eNB is ready for activating SPS-P. It generates the grants associated and then sends them to the UE over the PDCCH in **step 8**. UE will use these recurred resources in accordance with the indications of the SPS-P parameters. The main parameters are the transmission period and the number of transmission that UE is allowed to perform. The SPS-P transmission period corresponds obviously to the frames inter-arrival time and the number of transmission is limited by N_f. It means that resources will be reserved for the N_f next frames after the first frames. Two other parameters are defined to control the data transmission, namely the threshold S_t for characterizing an inaccurate transmission and the number N_i of consecutive inaccurate transmissions which is not allowed. They are used to prevent the waste of resources. Indeed, the UE releases the resource when a certain number of consecutive inaccurate transmissions is carried out. An inaccurate transmission is a transmission where the ratio R_i between the amount of data to send and the amount of preallocated resources is lower than the threshold allowed. So, a transmission will be considered as inaccurate if $R_i < S_t$ and the SPS-P mode will stop when reaching N_i consecutive inaccurate transmissions. To avoid pending data when the amount of preallocated resources is lower than the amount of data to send, the UE keeps sending BSR along with the PUSCH to help the eNB to dynamically schedule their transmission.

4.2 Prediction model

The proposed scheduling protocol requires that the eNB forecasts the amount of resources to reserve for the next frames. It can be done using models that characterize the statistical behavior of the videotelephony sources. Videotelephony traffics consists of scenes in which people are talking with moderate motion in general and almost unchanged backgrounds [3]. Also, the scene changes are not brusque and occur with panning and zooming. Several models have been proposed in the literature but it was demonstrated in [2] that the GBAR(1) is more specialized for modeling accurately the short-term fluctuations of single Videotelephony sources and authors in [5] used the model as forecasting method in their enhanced explicit-rate mechanism. The model relies on the observation that Videotelephony traffics have gamma-marginal distributions, very high lag-1 correlation coefficient ($\rho(1) = 0.98$) and exponnetially decaying autocorelations up to lags of about 100 frames. The model is based on the fact that the sum of independent $Ga(s, \lambda)$ and $Ga(q, \lambda)$ random variables is a $Ga(s + q, \lambda)$ and the product of independent $Be(t, s - t)$ and $Ga(s, \lambda)$ random variables is a $Ga(t, \lambda)$ random variable. The forecasting rule for the model is given by:

$$X_n = A_n X_{n-1} + B_n \qquad (3)$$

Since for Videotelephony traffics, we want the distribution of X_n and X_{n-1} to be $Ga(s, \lambda)$, we pick A_n to be a $Be(t, s-t)$ random variable and B_n to be a $Ga(s - t, \lambda)$ random variable. We can see that when A_n, B_n and X_{n-1} are mutually independent, X_n is distributed as desired. The lag-1 autocorrelation function is given by $\rho(1) = \dfrac{t}{s}$. Using this we determine t since we know $\rho(1)$ and s(from the mean and variance of the data). The forcasting is done in this way: Given X_{n-1} multiply it by B_n a sample from an independent beta-distributed random variable, and then add A_n drawn from a gamma distribution. The two distributions have parameters which need to be computed only once from the mean, variance, and lag-1 correlation of the Videotelephony sequence of interest.

4.3 Scheduling algorithm

Knowing the amount of data to preallocate, the number of Physical Resource Blocks (PRBs) required to transmit this preallocated data is also important to determine and depends both on the Modulation and Coding Schemes (MCS) which are chosen every TTI by link adaptation and this amount of data. The eNB is in charge of determining and selecting the PRBs in which each Videotelephony source will transmit its predicted frames. For the TTIs where the SPS-P grants occur, the Videotelephony flows have the highest priority and are scheduled first. The FME algorithm is used to assign the PRBs. Once the selected PRBs cover the amount of data to preallocate to a frame of a given Videotelephony user, this user is not anymore taken into account for the rest of the RBs within the SPS-P TTI. The process continues until all the Videotelephony users having SPS-P grants on the considered TTI are scheduled. In case of PRBs required to fulfill the amount of data to preallocate to a frame of a Videotelephony user is smaller than PRBs available in the SPS-P TTI, a non-segmentation based Semi-Persistent strategy is adopted [7]. In this strategy, available PRBs are allocated for a part of the preallocated data and the 'leftovers' are transmitted in subsequent TTIs with dynamic scheduling. For the radio resources left free in the SPS-P TTIs, they are allocated to the other users using dynamic scheduling.

It is very interesting to design a new method that solves problems but it is better to study its effectiveness in realistic scenarios. This will be done in the next section.

5. PERFORMANCE EVALUATION

We use LTE-Sim [10] to evaluate the performance of our method. It is a simulator that provides several aspects of LTE networks, including both the LTE radio access network and the evolved packet core. It enables single and multi-cell

environment, QoS management, mobility of users, handover procedures and frequency reuse techniques. The simulations results aim to compare our novel scheduling protocol SPS-P using a FME allocation scheme to the Dynamic Scheduling using the same allocation scheme. These results help to demonstrate the ability of our proposed strategy to reduce the user plane latency and provide thus, very sharp delay bounds and guarantee very low packet loss ratio with respect to Videotelephony traffics. So, we carry out simulations with different parameters which are shown in Table 1. The scenario consists in using a number of users of different configurations in the range [10 60] that moved along in a single cell. 40% of the users handle Videotelephony flows, 40% VoIP flows and the remaining 20% transmit Best Effort flows. The Cumulative Distribution Function (CDF) of the packet delays of the Videotelephony flows and their Packet Loss Ratio (PLR) are taken as key performance indicators. We consider these parameters because the Videotelephony users have no advantages in transmitting packets after their deadline expiration. This will be a waste of resource blocks.

Table 1: Simulation parameters

Parameters	Value
Simulation duration	50 s
Bandwidth	10MHz
MIMO	off
Frame structure	FDD
Cell number	1
Cell Radius	1 km
Users Range	from 10 up to 60
Users Speed	30km/h
Mobility model	Random direction
Max delay	0.1 s
Multipath	Jakes model
Prediction window N_f	20 frames

5.1 Traffic model

Trace-based applications are used as Videotelephony flows. They send packets based on realistic Videotelephony trace files (H.264) which are available on [13]. VoIP flows are G.729 flows and they are modeled with an ON/OFF Markov chain, where the ON period is exponentially distributed with a mean value of 3 s and the OFF period has a truncated exponential probability density function with an upper limit of 6.9 s and an average value of 3 s. During the ON period, the source sends 20 bytes sized packets every 20 ms (the source data rate is 8.4 kbps), while during the OFF period the rate is zero because the presence of a Voice Activity Detector is assumed. Best effort flows are created by an infinite buffer application which is modeled like an ideal greedy source that always has packets to send [8]. The part below will present the simulation results and our analyses.

5.2 Results and analysis

As shown in Figure 2 and 3, our method outperforms the other strategy by always reaching the lowest value for the PLR and by giving the best performance for the CDF of the packet delays of Videotelephony flows. The difference between the two methods is more obvious in the case of high traffic load. For instance when 60 users are in the cell, 90% of the packets scheduled with our algorithm, has a delay lower than 50 ms, which is the highest rate compared to the other strategy (See Figure 3). This is due to the fact that with our strategy, Videotelephony users do not have to wait before transmitting packets. Indeed, once the video frames belonging to the prediction window are available in the buffer, they are directly transmitted without any procedure because resources have been already preallocated for them. For the dynamic scheduling, it is different because resources are not guaranteed. So, the Videotelephony users can have significative user plane latency and thus, a great number of expired packets in their queues.

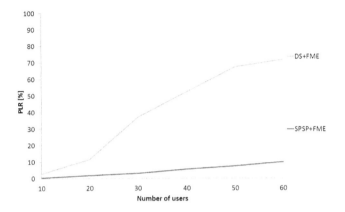

Figure 2: PLR of Videotelephony users

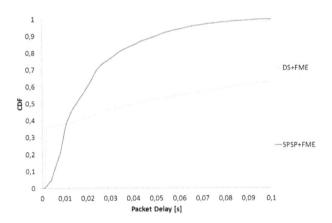

Figure 3: CDF of Video packet delays with 60 users

6. CONCLUSION

We presented in this paper an efficient scheduling protocol SPS-P for Videotelephony traffics in the uplink of LTE networks. The use of this strategy improves resource allocation for videotelephony traffics and reduce the delay caused by dynamic scheduling. It consists in scheduling Videotelephony flows in a Semi-Persistent manner with Provisioning. The amount of resources to preallocate for the transmission of the video frames is estimated using the GBAR(1) model. The proposed method has been evaluated and simulations results demonstrated its effectiveness by showing that it optimized Videotelephony traffics performance and provided the best QoS support compared to the dynamic scheduling. Netherthless the strategy could be improved since the prediction of the frames size is not perfect and contains sometimes errors. An enhancement of the method could consist in reducing the prediction errors and optimize the model. Future works will consider this issue and also help to carry out additional simulations of our protocol using advanced uplink allocation schemes.

7. REFERENCES

[1] 3GPP. http://www.3gpp.org.

[2] D. Heyman. The gbar source model for vbr videoconferences. *IEEE/ACM Transactions on Networking*, 5(4):554–560, Aug 1997.

[3] D. Heyman, A. Tabatabai, and T. V. Lakshman. Statistical analysis and simulation study of video teleconference traffic in atm networks. *IEEE Transactions on Circuits and Systems for Video Technology*, 2(1):49–59, Mar 1992.

[4] M. Iturralde, S. Martin, and T. Ali Yahiya. Resource allocation by pondering parameters for uplink system in lte networks. In *IEEE 38th Conference on Local Computer Networks (LCN)*, pages 747–750, Oct 2013.

[5] T. V. Lakshman, P. Mishra, and K. Ramakrishnan. Transporting compressed video over atm networks with explicit-rate feedback control. *IEEE/ACM Transactions on Networking*, 7(5):710–723, Oct 1999.

[6] M. Laner, P. Svoboda, P. Romirer-Maierhofer, N. Nikaein, F. Ricciato, and M. Rupp. A comparison between one-way delays in operating hspa and lte networks. In *10th International Symposium on Modeling and Optimization in Mobile, Ad Hoc and Wireless Networks (WiOpt)*, pages 286–292, May 2012.

[7] A. Patra, V. Pauli, and L. Yu. Packet scheduling for real-time communication over lte systems. In *2013 IFIP Wireless Days (WD)*, pages 1–6. IEEE, 2013.

[8] G. Piro, L. Grieco, G. Boggia, R. Fortuna, and P. Camarda. Two-level downlink scheduling for real-time multimedia services in lte networks. *Multimedia, IEEE Transactions on*, 13(5):1052–1065, Oct 2011.

[9] G. Piro, L. A. Grieco, G. Boggia, and P. Camarda. A two-level scheduling algorithm for qos support in the downlink of lte cellular networks. In *European Wireless Conference (EW)*, pages 246–253, 2010.

[10] G. Piro, L. A. Grieco, G. Boggia, F. Capozzi, and P. Camarda. Simulating lte cellular systems: an open-source framework. *IEEE Transactions on Vehicular Technology*, 60(2):498–513, 2011.

[11] H. Safa and K. Tohme. Lte uplink scheduling algorithms: Performance and challenges. In *19th International Conference on Telecommunications (ICT)*, pages 1–6, April 2012.

[12] S. Tanwir and H. Perros. A survey of vbr video traffic models. *Communications Surveys and Tutorials, IEEE (Volume:15 , Issue: 4)*, January 2013.

[13] video trace library. http://trace.eas.asu.edu/.

Channel Capacity Optimization for an Integrated Wi-Fi and Free-space Optic Communication System (WiFiFO)

Qiwei Wang
Kelley Engineering Center
Oregon State University
Corvallis, Oregon 97330, USA
wangqi@onid.orst.edu

Thinh Nguyen
Kelley Engineering Center
Oregon State University
Corvallis, Oregon 97330, USA
thinhq@eecs.oregonstate.edu

Alan X. Wang
Kelley Engineering Center
Oregon State University
Corvallis, Oregon 97330, USA
wang@eecs.oregonstate.edu

ABSTRACT

Recent advances in free-space optical technology promise a complementary approach to increasing wireless capacity with minimal changes to the existing wireless technologies. This paper puts forth the hypothesis that it is possible to simultaneously achieve high capacity and high mobility by developing a communication system called WiFiFO (WiFi Free space Optic) that seamlessly integrates the recent free-space optics technologies and the current WiFi technologies. We briefly describe the WiFIFO architecture then discuss the main contribution of this paper that is optimizing the capacity of the proposed WiFiFO system. Specifically, we consider the problem of power allocation for multiple FSO and WiFi transmitters in order to achieve maximum system capacity for given budget power. A mathematical model of the combined capacity of FSO and WiFi channel is derived. We show that the power allocation problem for WiFiFO can be approximated well as a convex optimization problem. To that end, an algorithm based on gradient decent method is developed. Simulation results indicate that the proposed algorithm, together with system architecture can provide an order-of-magnitude increase in capacity over the existing WiFi systems.

Categories and Subject Descriptors

C.2.1 [**Computer communication networks**]: Network architecture and design; C.2.5 [**Computer communication networks**]: Local and wide-area networks

Keywords

Free space optics; WiFi; Hybrid network; Capacity; Power allocation; Optimization

1. INTRODUCTION

Recent advances in free-space optical technology promise a complementary approach to increasing wireless capacity

MSWiM'14, September 21–26, 2014, Montreal, QC, Canada.
Copyright 2014 ACM 978-1-4503-3030-5/14/09 ...$15.00.
http://dx.doi.org/10.1145/2641798.2641823 .

with minimal changes to the existing wireless technologies [1], [2].

Specifically, the solid state lighting technology such as Lighting Emission Diode (LEDs) is now sufficiently mature that it is possible to transmit data at high bit rates reliably. Importantly, the free-space optical technology would not interfere with the typical RF transmissions such as WiFi devices, thus will enhance wireless capacity. However, such high data rates are currently achievable only with spot-light and short distance transmissions. This drawback severely limits the mobility of free-space optic wireless devices. This paper puts forth the hypothesis that it is possible to simultaneously achieve high capacity and high mobility by developing a communication system called WiFiFO (WiFi Free space Optic) that seamlessly integrates the recent free-space optics technologies and the current WiFi technologies. We briefly describe the proposed WiFiFO system in order to provide sufficient context for the main contribution of the paper. Specifically, this paper is focused on the problem of determining the power allocation for multiple FSO and WiFi transmitters in such a way to maximize the system capacity subject to a given power budget.

We note that there have been several studies on FSO/RF hybrid systems. The majority of these studies, however are in the context of outdoor point-to-point FSO transmission, using a powerful modulated laser beam[3], [4]. For more literature on this topic, please see [5], [6].

2. OVERVIEW OF WIFIFO

Consider the mostly widely deployed WiFi system 802.11g with a theoretically maximum rate of 54 Mbps. Typical WiFi networks operate at only a fraction of the maximum capacity, e.g., 5-15 Mbps. This rate reduction is due to a number of factors including the MAC protocol overhead and the distances between wireless devices and the access point (AP). Similarly, the 802.11n standard with its MIMO (Multiple Input Multiple Output) technology can increase the theoretical capacity, but the actual capacity is significantly less, e.g., less than 100 Mbps, depending on the operating scenarios. A simple calculation shows that such limited wireless capacities fail to provide adequate bandwidth for many scenarios.

The proposed WiFiFO system aims to overcome the WiFi overload problem by enhancing wireless capacity using complement FSO technology which does not interfere with the WiFi transmission bands. When leveraged with the existing high-speed (Gigabit) Ethernet infrastructure, the pro-

[0]The work is supported in part by NSF grant: CNS-0845476.

posed WiFiFO based just on the current FSO technology can provide a typical bandwidth of *50 Mbps per user* via *local transmissions*; Fig. 1 illustrates a typical setting for the proposed WiFiFO system. In this setting, the focus will be on the common downlink scenario where most of users will download contents from the Internet via an AP. Although users can move around, they are often stationary, e.g., sitting on terminal benches at airports or lounges in hotel lobbies. As such, a network of FSO transmitters LEDs, with the high-speed Ethernet infrastructure can be deployed directly above the appropriate spots to provide local high-rate FSO transmissions most of the time, in addition to the WiFi transmission. For the height of a typical room, the beam cone of a LED covers a small area, approximately less than one meter square directly below. Thus a laptop or a PC located in this area equipped with a silicon photodiode (PDs), i.e., the receivers, can receive data via local FSO transmissions with rates depending on the distances to the center of the projected cone. To enable wireless devices to seamlessly and optimally operate simultaneously in both FSO and WiFi channels, the WiFiFO architecture implements a number of salient features. First, the WiFiFO implements a logical layer that monitors and manages the connections based on the FSO and WiFi channel conditions. That said, the movement patterns and locations of a user relative to the transmission-cone of the LEDs dynamically determine the amount of additional FSO bandwidth for the user. As such, the feedback on both WiFi and FSO are critical to allow optimal rate allocation between the two channels . However, at the present, the feedback capability via the FSO channel is not yet practical due to the cost/power of modulating an LED in a user device. To solve this problem, the WiFiFO system uses the WiFi channel to continuously monitor and provide feedback from a receiver to the AP when the devices move around from one FSO transmission cone to others.

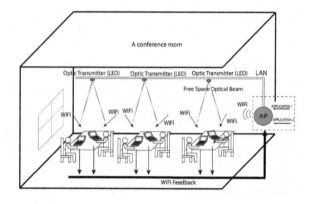

Figure 1: A realistic scenario for WiFiFO systems

The aim of the WiFiFO system is to overcome a number of practical challenges in today's WiFi networks, specifically the WiFi overload problem. The WiFiFO system will provide the high mobility of the current WiFi technology at the same time significantly increase the overall wireless capacity through local Free Space Optic (FSO) transmissions. While providing additional bandwidth through Free Space Optic technology is an obvious solution, there are several key challenges, including the design of a software and hardware architecture that optimally integrates the FSO and WiFi technologies, developing optimal packet transmission

policies and coding techniques based on heterogenous requirements from various applications and devices operating simultaneously on both FSO and WiFi channels, and the implementation of modulation techniques that dynamically adjust the transmission rates based on the varying channel characteristics of FSO and WiFi channels as well as application and device requirements. This paper will focus on a specific challenge of the proposed WiFiFO system. Specifically, *the paper will focus on how to allocate power for FSO transmitters and WiFi in order to maximize the capacity. We present this problem as convex optimization and describe an projected gradient algorithm for finding the optimal power allocation scheme.*

3. CHANNEL MODELS

To describe the mathematical models for FSO and WiFi channels, we use the notations shown in Table 1.

B_{FSO}, B_{RF}	Optical and WiFi channel bandwidths, resp.
p_{Ot}, p_{Or}	Transmitted and received optical power, resp.
$p_{Ot,max}$	Max. optical transmission power
p_{RFt}, p_{RFr}	Transmitted and received WiFi power, resp.
$p_{RFt,max}$	Maximum WiFi transmission power
p_{total}	Total transmission power for WiFi and FSO
p_{noise}	Noise power of a WiFi receiver
r	Distance from optical receiver to cone center
d	Distance between WiFi receiver and AP
N	Total number of receiver
P	Theoretical FSO channel bit error rate

Table 1: Notations

3.1 FSO Channel Model

The light comes out of an LED is assumed to be Gaussian beam. The intensity (power per unit area) $I(r,z)$ received at the receiver can be computed as [7]:

$$I(r,z) = I_0 \left(\frac{w_0}{w(z)} \right)^2 \exp\left(\frac{-2r^2}{w^2(z)} \right), \qquad (1)$$

where z is the distance to the transmitter, r is the distance to the center axis. $w(z)$ is the beam width that the intensity drop to $1/e^2$ of its center axis value. $w(z)$ is calculated by assuming the beam is a right circular cone with aperture $2\theta = 30°$. Given the transmission power p_{Ot}, the intensity at distance z and radius r is:

$$I(r,z) = p_{Ot} \left(\frac{2}{\pi w_0^2} \right) \exp\left(\frac{-2r^2}{w^2(z)} \right). \qquad (2)$$

At the receiver, a photo-sensitive diode is used to generate a current when light hits its surface area. If the receiving surface of the photo-sensitive diode S is sufficiently small, then the intensity is approximately constant. Thus, the received power is

$$p_{Or} = I(r,z)S. \qquad (3)$$

Assuming the optical signal is modulated using binary on-off keying, then the FSO channel capacity can be shown to be approximated by a well-known binary symmetric channel where the error probabilities $P(1|0)$ and $P(0|1)$ are equal. The noise is assumed to be Gaussian. Denote the mean and variance when i is transmitted as μ_i and σ_i, respectively ($i = 0, 1$), then

$$\mu_0 = 0 \qquad \mu_1 = I_{out} \qquad (4)$$

$$\sigma_1 = \sqrt{I_d{}^2 + I_s{}^2 + I_{nep}{}^2} \qquad \sigma_0 = \sqrt{I_d{}^2 + I_{nep}{}^2}. \qquad (5)$$

I_d denotes the dark current, I_s denotes the shot noise introduced by the received power, and I_{nep} denotes the noise calculated from the noise equivalent power (NEP) of the receiving device, including the thermal noise and the shot noise resulted from the dark current. I_{out} denotes the output current of the receiver due to the received optic power given the responsivity of the receiver, R_D:

$$I_{out} = p_{Or} R_D. \qquad (6)$$

In practice, $I_d >> I_s$ and $I_d >> I_{nep}$. Thus, $\sigma_1 \approx \sigma_0$. Since the bit error rate is only a function of σ, $P(1|0) \approx P(0|1)$. Approximately, this is a binary symmetric channel (BSC) with error probability P, and thus the channel capacity is:

$$C = 1 - H(P) \qquad P = \frac{1}{2} erfc\left(\frac{Q}{\sqrt{2}}\right) \qquad Q = \frac{\mu_1}{\sigma_1 + \sigma_0}. \qquad (7)$$

Given B_{FSO}, the maximum modulated frequency of an LED, the FSO channel capacity is:

$$C_{FSO} = B_{FSO}(1 - H(P)). \qquad (8)$$

3.2 RF Channel Model

The RF channel is assumed to be Gaussian with the capacity calculated as:

$$C_{RF} = B_{RF} \log_2(1 + \frac{p_{RFr}}{p_{noise}}) \; bit/s, \qquad (9)$$

where p_{RFr} denotes the received RF signal power. With IEEE 802.11b/g, the bandwidth B_{RF} for a single band around $2.4GHz$ is $22MHz$. The relationship between p_{RFr} and the transmitted power p_{RFt} is described by the Friis formula:

$$\eta = \frac{p_{RFt}}{p_{RFr}} = G_0 G_1 \left(\frac{\lambda}{4\pi d}\right)^n, \qquad (10)$$

where G_0 and G_1 denote the gains of transmit and receive antennas, respectively. λ denotes the transmitted wave length, d denotes the distance between the transmitter and receiver. n is set to 2 for indoor environments.

4. POWER ALLOCATION OPTIMIZATION

We formulate the problem of allocating power to each LED transmitter (FSO channel) and the AP (WiFi channel) to maximize the channel capacity subject to a fixed power budget. We show that the optimal solution to the power allocation optimization problem can be approximated well using convex optimization techniques. The reason for using convex optimization framework is that there exist many efficient algorithmic solutions for convex problem. We start with a scenario of single receiver that receives data from both FSO and WiFi channel simultaneously. Let us consider a single user with access to both FSO and WiFi channel. The total channel capacity is:

$$C_{total} = C_{FSO} + C_{RF}. \qquad (11)$$

Note that C_{FSO} and C_{RF} are functions of p_{Ot} and p_{RFt}, the transmitting power levels for FSO and WiFi channels, respectively. Our optimization problem is therefore:

$$\text{maximize:} \quad f(p_{Ot}, p_{RFt}) = C_{FSO} + C_{RF} \qquad (12)$$
$$\text{subject to:} \quad p_{Ot} + p_{RFt} \leq p_{total}$$
$$0 \leq p_{Ot} \leq p_{Ot,max}$$
$$0 \leq p_{RFt} \leq p_{RFt,max},$$

where $p_{Ot,max}$, $p_{RFt,max}$ and p_{total} denotes the maximum transmission power of the LED, the AP, and the total power budget, respectively.

We have the following proposition regarding the convexity of $f(p_{Ot}, p_{RFt})$ [8].

PROPOSITION 1. 1) $C_{RF}(p_{RFt})$ is concave; 2) There exists a small positive constant p_0 such that $C_{FSO}(p_{Ot})$ is concave for $p_{Ot} > p_0$; 3) Consequently, since $f(p_{Ot}, p_{RFt}) = C_{FSO} + C_{RF}$ is the sum of two separable functions, $f(p_{Ot}, p_{RFt})$ is concave in both p_{RFt} and p_{Ot} provided that $p_{Ot} > p_{Or,0}$ for some small constant $p_{Or,0} \geq 0$.

Based on the Proposition 1, the objective function $f(p_{Ot}, p_{RFt})$ can be approximated by a concave function. Specifically, we replace $C_{FSO}(p_{Ot})$ with $C'_{FSO}(p_{Ot})$ such that:

$$C'_{FSO}(p_{Ot}) = \begin{cases} ap_{Ot} + b, 0 \leq p_{Ot} < p_0 \\ C_{FSO}(p_{Ot}), p_0 \leq p_{Ot} \leq p_{Ot,max} \end{cases} \qquad (13)$$

The constant a, b and p_0 can be determined $C'_{FSO}(0) = 0$ and $\frac{d}{dp_{Ot}} C'_{FSO}(p_0) = a$. With the replacement of C'_{FSO}, we approximate the original problem with the following convex problem:

$$\text{maximize} \quad C'_{FSO}(p_{Ot}) + C_{RF}(p_{RFt}) \qquad (14)$$
$$\text{subject to:} \quad 0 \leq p_{Ot} \leq p_{Ot,max}$$
$$0 \leq p_{RFt} \leq p_{RFt,max}$$
$$p_{Ot} + p_{RFt} \leq p_{total}.$$

Now let us consider multi-user scenario. Let $\boldsymbol{p_{Ot}} \in \boldsymbol{R}^N$ and $\boldsymbol{p_{RFt}} \in \boldsymbol{R}^N$ denote the transmitted power vectors for FSO and RF channel. $p_{Ot,i}$ and $p_{RFt,i}$, the ith elements of $\boldsymbol{p_{Ot}}$ and $\boldsymbol{p_{RFt}}$ denote transmitted powers on FSO and RF channels for user i, respectively. The multi user optimization problem is to find the FSO and WiFi power allocation for each users in order to maximize the total capacity of all the users subject to a given power budget. It can be formulated as:

$$\text{maximize:} \quad \phi(\boldsymbol{p_{Ot}}, \boldsymbol{p_{RFt}}) = \sum_{i=1}^{N} \left(C'_{FSO,i} + C_{RF,i}\right) \quad (15)$$
$$\text{subject to:} \quad \sum_{i=1}^{N}(p_{Ot,i} + p_{RFt,i}) \leq p_{total}$$
$$0 \leq p_{Ot,i} \leq p_{Ot,max}, i = 1, 2, ..., N$$
$$0 \leq p_{RFt,i} \leq p_{RFt,max}, i = 1, 2, ..., N,$$

where N denotes the total number of users.

Convexity: Because $\phi(\boldsymbol{p_{Ot}}, \boldsymbol{p_{RFt}})$ is a sum of concave functions, it is concave. So the approximate problem is a convex problem with linear constraints.

Algorithm. Given the analytical expression above, we can compute the gradient, and use a standard projected gradient to solve the constrained convex problem above [8].

5. SIMULATION RESULTS

We show the simulation results for the WiFiFO system under typical settings. All receivers are placed $5m$ below their FSO transmitters. The radius of the optical cone is set to be 1.5m, i.e., $0 \leq r \leq 1.5$. The optoelectronic devices used for transmitter and receiver are the LED (LED815L), LED driver (MAX3967A), photodiodes (FDS-100) and transimpedance amplifier (MAX3665). Next, all transmitters are placed within the range of $20m$ to the RF transmitter. $B_{RF} = 22Mhz$, $p_{RFt,max} = 100mW$. We assume that all the FSO transmitters are connected to a 100 Gbits Ethernet. As a result, the WiFiFO network can theoretically support up to 200 users with 50 Mbps for each user using only FSO transmissions. Effectively, the total bandwidth for FSO is very large, however, the capacity is limited by the power consumption of the LEDs.

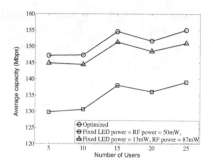

Figure 2: Capacity vs. number of users

Figure 2 shows the average capacity per receiver vs. the number of receivers. The number of receivers are 5, 10, 15, 20, and 25. The average capacity is calculated as

$$C_{ave} = \frac{1}{N} \sum_{i=1}^{N} [C_{FSO}(\hat{p}_{Ot,i}) + C_{RF}(\hat{p}_{RFt,i})] \qquad (16)$$

The result of optimization is compared with two other uniform power allocations: 1) Each LED transmitter is allocated 13 mW, which is a typical value for the LED transmitter; b) The power for each transmitter is equally allocated, i.e., all LED and RF transmitters get 50mW. As seen in Figure 2, the power allocation resulted from the proposed algorithm outperforms those of other two power allocation schemes for all 5 cases.

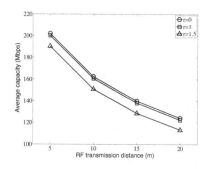

Figure 3: Capacity for different values of r;

Next, to simulate the effect of changing the RF and FSO transmission distances on the capacity, we perform the following simulations. In this setup, all ten receivers are located at a fixed distance ($r = 0, 1, 1.5$ meters) to the center

of the beam. In addition, for each r, we vary the RF transmission distances to receivers from 5 to 20 meters with 5 meter spacing. Figure 3 shows the achievable maximum capacity with different values of r and the RF transmission distances. As expected, as the RF transmission distance increases, the average capacity per receiver decreases. Also, a larger r results in smaller average capacity as expected. We note that the simulation results indicate that the ideal throughput *per user* can range from 120 Mbps to 200 Mbps. This is an order-of magnitude increase in capacity compared to the existing WiFi networks. The primary reason for this significant increase is due to additional bandwidth provided by FSO transmissions under the assumption that these LED transmitters are connected to a 100 Gbps LANs. If the LED is connected to a 10 Gbps, then the capacity gain is less due to the bottleneck of the LAN. However, we should expect a significant capacity gain over the existing WiFi networks.

6. CONCLUSION

This paper presented a mathematical model and an algorithm for maximizing the joint capacity of the proposed indoor WiFi/FSO system (WiFiFO). A multi-user channel capacity optimization problem respect to the transmitted power is studied. Simulation results show significant increase in the capacity over the existing WiFi networks.

References

[1] M. Yahya, M. Salleh, N. Akib, S. Jamalullail, and Z. Awang, "Link performance analysis of experimental led based free space optics," in *TENCON 2011 - 2011 IEEE Region 10 Conference*, pp. 1298–1302, Nov 2011.

[2] J. Vitasek, P. Siska, J. Latal, S. Hejduk, A. Liner, and V. Vasinek, "The transmitter for indoor free space optic networks," in *Telecommunications and Signal Processing (TSP), 2013 36th International Conference on*, pp. 290–293, July 2013.

[3] H. Wu, B. Hamzeh, and M. Kavehrad, "Achieving carrier class availability of fso link via a complementary rf link," in *Signals, Systems and Computers, 2004. Conference Record of the Thirty-Eighth Asilomar Conference on*, vol. 2, pp. 1483–1487 Vol.2, Nov 2004.

[4] S. Bloom and W. Hartley, *The last-mile solution: hybrid FSO radio*. AirFiber Inc., May 2002.

[5] A. Eslami, S. Vangala, and H. Pishro-Nik, "Hybrid channel codes for efficient fso/rf communication systems," *Communications, IEEE Transactions on*, vol. 58, pp. 2926–2938, October 2010.

[6] N. Letzepis, K. Nguyen, A. Guillen i Fabregas, and W. Cowley, "Outage analysis of the hybrid free-space optical and radio-frequency channel," *Selected Areas in Communications, IEEE Journal on*, vol. 27, pp. 1709–1719, December 2009.

[7] G. Einarsson, *Principles of Lightwave Communications*. John Wiley and Sons, 1996.

[8] Q. Wang and T. Nguyen, "Power allocation optimization of a wifi/fso hybrid network," tech. rep., School of EECS, Oregon State University, July 2014.

Mobility in a Large-scale WiFi Network: From Syslog Events to Mobile User Sessions

Jennie Steshenko, Vasanta G. Chaganti, James Kurose
University of Massachusetts, Amherst
140 Governors Dr., Amherst, MA, 01003
{jenstesh,vchaganti,kurose}@cs.umass.edu

ABSTRACT

Network management logs from a campus 802.11 network of nearly 4,500 ARUBA access points at the University of Massachusetts Amherst are presented. The processing steps to transform the logs from a series of individual network events, into user session trajectories are described and preliminary results are shown based on the user mobility characteristics. We plan to release a differentially private set of user trajectories for use by the research community which we hope can provide valuable insights into user mobility characterization.

Categories and Subject Descriptors

C.2.1 [**Network Architecture and Design**]: Wireless Communication; C.2.3 [**Network Operations**]: Network monitoring

Keywords

User Mobility; 802.11 WiFi Networks; Measurements; Syslog; ARUBA

1. INTRODUCTION

We live in a time where our phones, computers, and other devices leave a digital footprint behind us, that includes our network and physical locations. This data can be useful to the research community for many purposes, including the evaluation of mobility architectures and protocols in "real-world" scenarios [4, 5, 7, 10, 11][1].

This paper describes an ongoing project that uses network management logs from a campus 802.11 wireless network of nearly 4,500 ARUBA access points at the University of Massachusetts Amherst (UMass), to characterize the mobility of tens of thousands of network users. Our own particular

---

[1]For example, [11] notes "Wireless network researchers are seriously starved for data about how real users, applications, and devices use real networks under real network conditions."

use of these traces are to investigate *(i)* the use of differential privacy in publishing anonymized mobility traces, *(ii)* the level of complexity of queuing networks needed to accurately model network and user-level performance in mobile networks, and *(iii)* the performance of new mobility architectures and protocols such as those in MobilityFirst [1] using trace-based, measured mobility in real networks.

We present the processing steps that transform a log of individual network events (primarily AP (dis)association and (de)authentication events) into user session trajectories among APs around the UMass campus, with user transitions among physical locations inferred from these events.

We describe challenges involved in transforming these individual events into mobile user sessions and we overview user mobility characteristics evidenced in these traces. We have shared these traces with several research groups both inside and outside of UMass.

2. NETWORK EVENT DATA

The UMass network consists of approximately $4,500$ APs, and is typically used by approximately 35,000 students and staff. The APs are managed by 10 to 12 controllers, each of which controls up to 512 APs. The controllers log network management and user (dis)association from/to AP events (SNMP) and network (de)authentication events (DHCP) [2] to a centralized log file. The (dis)association and (de)authentication events are logged separately per event, per user. Each log file covers one calendar day from midnight to the following midnight. The clocks are synchronized by the ARUBA controllers using a Network Time Protocol (NTP) that provides synchronization to within 1ms interval, providing sufficient granularity for our purposes. Currently, we have access to 90 log files, each containing between 2 GB and 4 GB of data.

We extract raw event data from these logs and transform them into per-user movement trajectories among APs. For detailed information about the structure of ARUBA syslog messages, refer to [13]. A typical message consist of the following parts (each part is enclosed within question marks):

```
?Mon? ?mday? ?hh:mm:ss? ?controller_name?
?process_name[process_id]?:  ?<message_subtype>?
?<controller_name>?message_body?
```

In the sample message below, a disassociation message - `<501102>`, has been logged by the station (user) with MAC address `9c:e6:35:f8:c3:cb`. The message body indicates that the user has disassociated and has left the AP with name `GRGH-309-1` and BSSID `00:24:6c:bf:78:a1:`

```
Jan 20 20:00:01 lgrc-wac-106-4 stm[2014]:
<501102>  <NOTI>  <lgrc-wac-106-4 128.119.3.25>
Disassoc from  sta: 9c:e6:35:f8:c3:cb:
AP 172.22.101.44- 00:24:6c:bf:78:a1-GRGH-309-1
Reason STA has left and is disassociated.
```

3. DATA PROCESSING

The individual syslog events are transformed into movement trajectories with these high level steps: *(i)* processing the syslog data into (start, end time) presences associated with access points; and *(ii)* agglomerating presences into sessions. In the future we plan to investigate ping-pong effects, and the thresholds for removing ping-pongs from the data.

In our processing, Python is used to implement regular expressions parsing over the syslog files to identify message types, as well as the 802.11 finite state machine (FSM) [3, Section 10.3] to extract presences at each AP; MongoDB is used to store the data through the intermediate steps, and to store the final user trajectories. Both Python and MongoDB offer easy out-of-the-box parallelizable packages, improving performance with such large datasets.

The steps to process the raw syslog data files are given in Procedure 1. First we scan through the log files, parsing message parts using regular expressions. If the `message_subtype` describes user (dis)associations and (de)authentications (to/from the network), the `message_body` is parsed with an additional set of regular expressions (an example is not given as each subtype has a different structure, and we process a list of subtypes). The extracted tuples are aggregated per MAC address and ordered by the time stamp. This collection is saved to MongoDB.

The aggregated collection is then passed to the FSM to obtain a sequence of "presences" at APs. A presence corresponds to state 4 of the FSM (the user is associated and authenticated): each user first establishes an association with an AP followed by an authentication via the four-way handshake. When a user either deauthenticates or disassociates, the presence at that AP ends. The presences are ordered by the starting time and saved as a new collection in MongoDB. For a given MAC address, each entry contains the start time and end times of the presence at an AP, the name of the AP, and the BSSID.

For the sample message above, assuming the MAC had a previous association message with the timestamp `Jan 20 19:00:01`, the following is a possible entry in a trajectory:

```
[9c:e6:35:f8:c3:cb]:
(Jan 20 19:00:01, Jan 20 20:00:01,GRGH-309-1,
00:24:6c:bf:78:a1)
```

As the final processing step, we break a MAC's sequence of presences into user sessions. We define a session as an ordered sequence of presences separated by a gap of time, for which no events are recorded, less than gap length, G. To select the the gap length G between two sessions, we follow [9], and plot the number of sessions as a function of increasing gap length, as shown in Fig. 1. As the gap length increases, there is greater aggregation and the number of sessions decrease. We observe a 'knee' of the curve at the 15 minute interval, and thus choose a gap length of 15 minutes to indicate that a session has ended.

The mean session length vs. the gap length G, is also shown in Fig. 2. As in Fig. 1, as the gap length increases,

---

Procedure 1 Processing Steps to transform syslog messages to presences.

```
 1: while Scan raw text file do
 2:     Parse syslog message → regular expression
 3:     if message subtype ∈ {(de)auth,(dis)assoc} then
 4:         Parse message body → regular expression
 5:         Extract Tuple:  (timestamp, message subtype,
        user (MAC, IP), AP (name, BSSID))
 6:             Aggregate tuples by user MAC: ordered by timestamp
 7:     end if
 8: end while
 9: for all user MACs do
10:     Parse {message subtype} → 802.11 FSM
11:     Determine association and authentication per AP
12:     Define presence: (start time, end time, AP name, BSSID)
13:     Aggregate presences by user MAC: ordered by timestamp
14: end for
```

---

the mean session length increases and we observe a 'knee' of the curve at the 15 minute interval.

During processing of one week of log files, we were able to successfully process $\approx 95\%$ of the logged events with the FSM. Among, the 5% of events that we could not process using the FSM, we found user (dis)associations with missing (de)authentication messages. On an Intel i5 dual-core processor each day of data takes approximately a half hour to process.

4. USER MOBILITY CHARACTERISTICS

For each day of activity, we have identified on average $40,000$ unique MAC addresses. Fig. 3 shows the cumulative number of unique MAC addresses and usernames seen over a five-day period. Each MAC address observed in the syslog data corresponds to a (dis)association or a (de)authentication event. The usernames are logged when a user authenticates to the wireless network. From the figure, the number of MAC addresses is seen to be nearly three times the number of usernames, showing that on average, each user accesses the network using three different devices. These devices could be either UMass devices located in computer labs, libraries, etc. or personal devices (e.g., a mobile phone, tablet and laptop).

The holding time distribution $H(t)$ at an AP is shown in Fig. 4. The distribution shows a peak for hold times $H(t) \leq 1$ minute. A large fraction of hold times, $H(t) \leq 1$ minute, are due to multiple (dis)association events to the same AP, or neighboring APs (ping-pong effects). A second peak observed at $H(t) \approx 15$ minutes corresponds to the idle-timeout of a user, if the device does not respond to an ARP (Address Resolution Protocol) request which is set by default within ARUBA. The subsequent peaks observed with $H(\Delta t) \approx 15$ minutes, occur when the user's device responds to the ARP request just before the idle time out. The mean hold time at an AP was observed to be 12 minutes.

Each session of a user's trajectory consists of a sequence of presences at several APs. Within each session, however, we also observe consecutive presences to the same AP. If the gap length between two consecutive presences to the same AP is less than an aggregation gap length G_{agg}; we aggregate the presences. The results of aggregating successive presences at the same AP are shown in Fig. 5. The figure shows the mean hop count for user trajectories as a function of the aggregation gap. As G_{agg} increases, there is a decrease in the mean number of hops per session. From the figure, we aggregate two consecutive presences at the same AP if $G_{agg} \leq 10$ minutes.

Similar to previous trace studies, we observe ping-pong phenomenon among access points [6,8,12]. We plan to work on removing ping-pong effects in future work.

5. RELATED WORK

In [6] and [8] authors present WLAN traces over two large campus environments at Dartmouth and University of California, San Diego. The UMass syslog traces provide one of the largest traces across any university campus. The (4500) access points cover the entire campus, and we observe a very large flow of students (25,000) and staff (8,000). Our observation period started in November, 2013, and the traces are continuously updated in real time.

With the changing usage of wireless access from laptops to mobile phones and tablets, the data collected also presents a different perspective on mobility from those seen in [6] and [8]. In the Dartmouth traces [6], the authors identify VoIP phones and pocket PCs in total contribute to 1.09% of the users. Since then, the number of smartphones and tablets has increased dramatically, and represent a very different usage pattern today. We plan to release a differentially private data set for use by the research community which we hope can provide valuable insights into user mobility characterization.

6. ACKNOWLEGEMENT

This research was supported in part by the US National Science Foundation awards CNS-1040781.

7. REFERENCES

[1] A. Venkataramani, J. Kurose, D. Raychaudhuri, K. Nagaraja, M. Mao and S. Banerjee MobilityFirst: A Mobility-centric and Trustworthy Internet Architecture, to appear in ACM computer communication review. *ACM SIGCOMM Computer Communication Review*, June, 2014.

[2] ARUBA. *ArubaOS 7.3 Syslog Messages Reference Guide*. ARUBA Networks, Inc., 1344, Crossman Avenue, Sunnyvale California, 94089, November 2013.

[3] IEEE Standards Association, "IEEE standard for local and metropolitan area networks - Part 11: Wireless LAN Medium Access Control," IEEE Standard 802.11, March 2012.

[4] N. Aschenbruck, A. Munjal, and T. Camp. Trace-based mobility modeling for multi-hop wireless networks. *Comput. Commun.*, 34(6):704–714, May 2011.

[5] M. Conti, S. Chong, S. Fdida, W. Jia, H. Karl, Y.-D. Lin, P. Mähönen, M. Maier, R. Molva, S. Uhlig, and M. Zukerman. Research challenges towards the future internet. *Comput. Commun.*, 34(18):2115–2134, Dec. 2011.

[6] T. Henderson, D. Kotz, and I. Abyzov. The changing usage of a mature campus-wide wireless network. *Computer Networks*, 52(14):2690–2712, 2008.

[7] U. Kumar and A. Helmy. Human behavior and challenges of anonymizing wlan traces. In *Proceedings of the 28th IEEE Conference on Global Telecommunications*, GLOBECOM'09, pages 3733–3738, Piscataway, NJ, USA, 2009. IEEE Press.

[8] M. McNett and G. M. Voelker. Access and mobility of wireless PDA users. *ACM SIGMOBILE Mobile Computing and Communications Review*, 9(2):40–55, 2005.

[9] J. Padhye and J. F. Kurose. Continuous-media courseware server: A study of client interactions. pages 65–73, 1999.

[10] The Link.1 The STMS OPUS card is unsafe and unsound. NSF Workshop on Pervasive Computing at Scale, PeCS, January 2011.

[11] J. Yeo, D. Kotz, and T. Henderson. CRAWDAD: A community resource for archiving wireless data at dartmouth. *SIGCOMM Comput. Commun. Rev.*, 36(2):21–22, Apr. 2006.

[12] J. Yoon, B. D. Noble, M. Liu, and M. Kim. Building realistic mobility models from coarse-grained traces. In *Proceedings of the 4th international conference on Mobile systems, applications and services*, pages 177–190. ACM, 2006.

[13] J. Steshenko. Common Structure of ARUBA Syslog Messages. *Technical Report, University of Massachusetts, Amherst.* 2014.

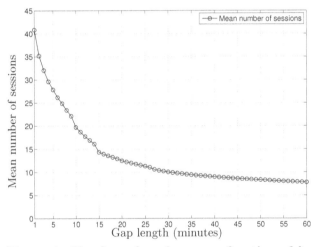

Figure 1: Number of sessions as a function of increasing gap length G.

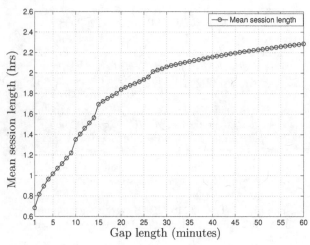

Figure 2: Mean session length versus the gap length G.

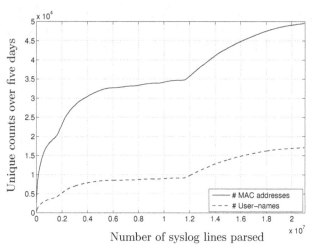

Figure 3: Number of unique MAC addresses and usernames observed over a five day period.

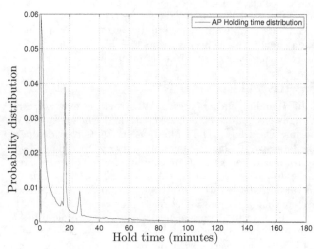

Figure 4: Holding time distribution $H(t)$ at an AP (ping-pong effects not mitigated).

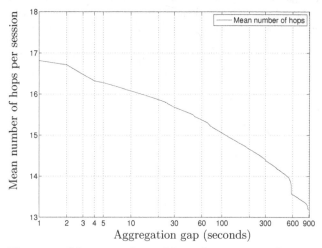

Figure 5: Mean number of hops in a user trajectory as a function of the aggregation gap length over a one-week period (ping-pong effects not mitigated).

Demo Abstract: Realistic Evaluation of Kernel Protocols and Software Defined Wireless Networks with DCE/ns-3

Emilio P. Mancini, Hardik Soni
Thierry Turletti, Walid Dabbous
INRIA, FRANCE
{emilio.mancini, hardik.soni,
thierry.turletti, walid.dabbous}@inria.fr

Hajime Tazaki
University of Tokyo
Japan
tazaki@wide.ad.jp

ABSTRACT

We propose to demonstrate Direct Code Execution (DCE), a framework that enables to execute nearly unmodified applications and Linux Kernel code jointly with the ns-3 simulator. DCE allows therefore fully deterministic reproducibility of network experiments. DCE also supports larger scale scenarios than real-time emulators by using simulation time dilatation. In this demonstration, we will showcase two main scenarios: (1) a basic example describing how to integrate in DCE the Data Center TCP (DCTCP) Linux kernel patch, and then how to customize this protocol and run it on different scenarios; (2) a more advanced use case demonstrating how to benefit from DCE to build a rich and realistic evaluation environment for Software Defined Wireless Networks based on Open vSwitch and the NOX SDN controller.

Categories and Subject Descriptors

I.1.6.7 [**Simulation and Modeling**]: Simulation Support Systems

Keywords

Direct Code Execution; Emulation; Linux; Network Stack; Simulation

1. INTRODUCTION

The need for reproducible realistic and large scale network experiments has been highlighted for several years by the networking community. Reproducibility is essential for researchers and developers in order to give them the opportunity to verify and possibly enhance proposals made by other researchers but also, it helps debugging the code. Today, two complementary approaches are widely used to evaluate the performance of networking protocols: simulators and emulators. Recently, Direct Code Execution (DCE) [1,6,11] has been proposed. This framework benefits from the pros of both simulation and emulation, while limiting the main

drawbacks of the two approaches. To the best of our knowledge, DCE is the only free open source framework that enables to evaluate real implementations of network systems in a scalable and reproducible manner, while allowing easy debugging within a deterministic and reproducible environment. In particular, DCE can run unmodified network systems written in C/C++ on top of the ns-3 networking simulator. DCE uses the ns-3 simulated time clock which makes it more scalable than most of emulators such as Mininet [8] by relaxing the real time execution constraint. In this way, CPU-greedy scenarios will take longer than they would in real time, but the results obtained will be accurate.

Basically, DCE is structured around three layers, as shown in Figure 1. DCE dynamically links the applications with the POSIX layer. It is built upon the core and kernel layers to re-implement the standard socket APIs used by emulated applications. Not the entire set of POSIX API is currently supported, so new applications may require to extend this layer to add possible missing system calls. The kernel layer takes advantage of the core services to provide an execution environment to the Linux network stack within the single-processed network simulator. The services of kernel such as the Linux bottom halves, scheduler, and timer API are presented as a new architecture based on the asm-generic implementation to minimize the modifications of the original kernel code. The core layer, at the lowest-level, handles the virtualization of stacks, heaps, and global memory. It uses a single-process model that executes every simulated process within the same host process and isolates the namespace of each simulated process. Further information on DCE is available in [6,11].

At the last MSWiM'13 conference in Barcelona, we successfully demonstrated DCE with two use cases: 1) seamless handover involving a Linux MPTCP implementation and 2) information-centric networking over ad-hoc networks based on the CCNx stack from PARC [10]. The feedback we obtained was very fruitful, stressing the benefits of demonstrating DCE with scenarios of different complexity levels, and studying its scalability. In this new demo we will showcase two new scenarios now made possible with DCE: a use case showing how to integrate the Data Center TCP (DCTCP) protocol [5] to a real kernel stack, and a more advanced use case demonstrating a wireless mesh scenario that involves the NOX [7] Software Defined Networking (SDN) controller and Open vSwitches [9]. The former use case is a simple example that will allow to demonstrate how easy it is to customize a network protocol. In particular, we will explain how to use a patched Linux kernel to analyze the behavior of

DCTCP with a real application in a simulated network. The latter scenario will explain how to conduct routing experiments in a realistic wireless environment and how to control them through the NOX SDN controller.

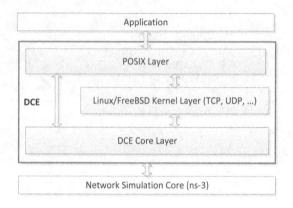

Figure 1: DCE architecture.

2. DEMONSTRATION DETAIL

2.1 Kernel protocols and scalability

This first use case is a simple example based on DCTCP [5], an enhancement of the TCP congestion control algorithm for environments specific to data centers, i.e., involving very high bandwidth links, low round-trip times, and small buffer switches. DCTCP is provided as a Linux kernel patch to Linux 2.6.38.3.

In this experiment, we will demonstrate how to use a kernel patch to study its behavior in a simulated network with full reproducibility. Moreover, we will study the scalability of DCE and will show the advantages of using the ns-3 simulation clock instead of the wall clock. The experiment will be run with different number of senders and a single receiver running the well-known *iperf* application, as shown in Figure 2.

Figure 3 shows a snapshot of the simulation animation using the NetAnim [2] tool that will be used during the demo, where we see packets flowing from twenty senders to the queue monitor.

Figure 4 plots the wall clock time required to simulate 5 seconds of TCP data transmission in function of the number of nodes. By using the ns-3 simulation clock, DCE is able to run CPU-greedy simulations scenarios that can not be run in real time on the machine due to its limited capacities.

2.2 Simulating Software Defined Wireless Networks with DCE

Testing, evaluating applications or carrying out research experiments involving a software defined wireless networking architecture requires a simulation tool, capable of generating network performance metrics and results for any required scenario, in a repeatable way. Keeping these requirements in mind, in this second use case, we plan to demonstrate the execution of the OpenFlow controller NOX [7] and Open vSwitch [3] on DCE/ns-3 to simulate a software defined wire-

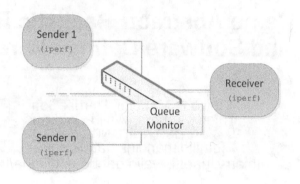

Figure 2: Schema of the DCTCP experiment.

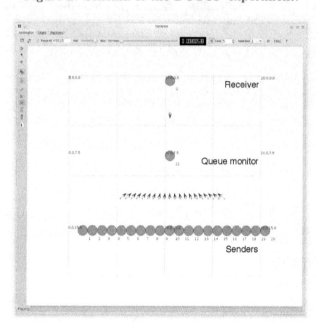

Figure 3: Snapshot of the animation showing the evolution of the simulation using the NetAnim tool.

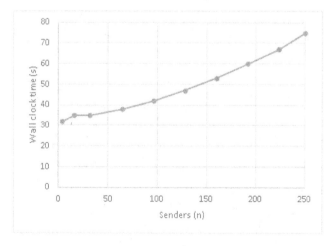

Figure 4: Wall clock time to simulate a 5s transmission for different numbers of nodes.

less network. Note that such a wireless environment is not possible to be emulated in a realistic way using Mininet [8] because the latter can only emulate point-to-point physical links using virtual ethernet pairs (e.g., MAC layer is ignored), and it does not provide mobility models for wireless nodes. Meanwhile, DCE can take advantage of different mobility models available in ns-3 along with various MAC layer protocols. In this demo, we will demonstrate the simulation capabilities available for research on SDN in a wireless context.

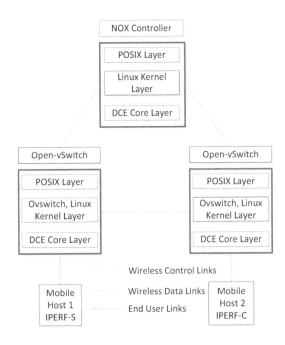

Figure 5: Simulation of a software defined wireless network

Figure 5 shows an architectural view of our proposed simulation environment. The Control Plane (CP) of the SDN architecture can be simulated using a different physical channel than the Data Plane (DP) as shown in the figure in red and green colour links, respectively. NOX code is executed on a simulated ns-3 node using DCE to simulate a SDN controller. OpenFlow-enabled wireless routers are simulated using the Open vSwitch distribution. Note that Open vSwitch can be used with or without kernel support. Purely user-space based configuration is considered experimental and not thoroughly tested as mentioned in [4]. We use Open vSwitch with data-path kernel module support as it is widely used. DCE provides a mechanism to incorporate such a kernel module based application execution, in the same way it is done for the kernel-space linux implementation of MPTCP demonstrated in [10].

The proposed simulation environment is scalable enough to model a large number of wireless end users and routers, as it operates using the ns-3 simulation clock. It can reproduce experiment results without careful resource provisioning of the host machine as required in [8]. We plan to present the demo of Open vSwitch working as basic forwarding wireless

router programmed by NOX and to test the connectivity using iperf running on two simulated hosts.

3. ACKNOWLEDGMENTS

This research is partially supported by INRIA and Japanese Society for the Promotion of Science (JSPS) Joint Research Projects in the context of the Simulbed/Designet *associated team*.

4. REFERENCES

[1] Direct Code Execution. www.nsnam.org/docs/dce/manual/html. [Accessed 6/20/2014].

[2] NetAnim. www.nsnam.org/wiki/NetAnim. [Accessed 6/20/2014].

[3] Open vSwitch. www.openvswitch.org/. [Accessed 6/20/2014].

[4] Open vSwitch Support. http://openvswitch.org/support/. [Accessed 6/20/2014].

[5] M. Alizadeh, A. Greenberg, D. A. Maltz, J. Padhye, P. Patel, B. Prabhakar, S. Sengupta, and M. Sridharan. Data center TCP (DCTCP). *SIGCOMM Comput. Comm. Rev.*, 41(4), 2010.

[6] D. Camara, H. Tazaki, E. Mancini, M. Lacage, T. Turletti, and W. Dabbous. DCE: Test the real code of your protocols and applications over simulated networks. *IEEE Comm. Mag.*, 52(3):104–110, March 2014.

[7] N. Gude, T. Koponen, J. Pettit, B. Pfaff, M. Casado, N. McKeown, and S. Shenker. Nox: Towards an operating system for networks. *SIGCOMM Comput. Commun. Rev.*, 38(3):105–110, July 2008.

[8] N. Handigol, B. Heller, V. Jeyakumar, B. Lantz, and N. McKeown. Reproducible network experiments using container-based emulation. In *Proc. of CoNEXT*, pages 253–264, New York, NY, USA, 2012. ACM.

[9] J. Pettit, J. Gross, B. Pfaff, M. Casado, and S. Crosby. Virtual switching in an era of advanced edges, 2010. 2nd Workshop on Data Center. Converged and Virtual Ethernet Switching (DC-CAVES).

[10] H. Tazaki, E. Mancini, D. Camara, T. Turletti, and W. Dabbous. DCE: Increase Simulation Realism Using Unmodified Real Implementations. In *Proc. of MSWiM (demo abstract)*, pages 29–32, NY, USA, 2013.

[11] H. Tazaki, F. Urbani, E. Mancini, M. Lacage, D. Camara, T. Turletti, and W. Dabbous. Direct Code Execution: Revisiting library OS architecture for reproducible network experiments. In *Proc. of CoNEXT*, pages 217–228, NY, USA, 2013. ACM.

Author Index

Author Index

www.ingramcontent.com/pod-product-compliance
Lightning Source LLC
LaVergne TN
LVHW060135070326
832902LV00018B/2801